Lecture Notes in Computer Science   11583

Commenced Publication in 1973
Founding and Former Series Editors:
Gerhard Goos, Juris Hartmanis, and Jan van Leeuwen

Editorial Board Members

More information about this series at http://www.springer.com/series/7409

Aaron Marcus · Wentao Wang (Eds.)

Design, User Experience, and Usability

Design Philosophy and Theory

8th International Conference, DUXU 2019
Held as Part of the 21st HCI International Conference, HCII 2019
Orlando, FL, USA, July 26–31, 2019
Proceedings, Part I

 Springer

Editors
Aaron Marcus
Aaron Marcus and Associates
Berkeley, CA, USA

Wentao Wang
Zuoyebang, K12 education
Beijing, China

ISSN 0302-9743   ISSN 1611-3349   (electronic)
Lecture Notes in Computer Science
ISBN 978-3-030-23569-7   ISBN 978-3-030-23570-3   (eBook)
https://doi.org/10.1007/978-3-030-23570-3

LNCS Sublibrary: SL3 – Information Systems and Applications, incl. Internet/Web, and HCI

This Springer imprint is published by the registered company Springer Nature Switzerland AG
The registered company address is: Gewerbestrasse 11, 6330 Cham, Switzerland

Foreword

The 21st International Conference on Human-Computer Interaction, HCI International 2019, was held in Orlando, FL, USA, during July 26–31, 2019. The event incorporated the 18 thematic areas and affiliated conferences listed on the following page.

A total of 5,029 individuals from academia, research institutes, industry, and governmental agencies from 73 countries submitted contributions, and 1,274 papers and 209 posters were included in the pre-conference proceedings. These contributions address the latest research and development efforts and highlight the human aspects of design and use of computing systems. The contributions thoroughly cover the entire field of human-computer interaction, addressing major advances in knowledge and effective use of computers in a variety of application areas. The volumes constituting the full set of the pre-conference proceedings are listed in the following pages.

This year the HCI International (HCII) conference introduced the new option of "late-breaking work." This applies both for papers and posters and the corresponding volume(s) of the proceedings will be published just after the conference. Full papers will be included in the *HCII 2019 Late-Breaking Work Papers Proceedings* volume of the proceedings to be published in the Springer LNCS series, while poster extended abstracts will be included as short papers in the HCII 2019 *Late-Breaking Work Poster Extended Abstracts* volume to be published in the Springer CCIS series.

I would like to thank the program board chairs and the members of the program boards of all thematic areas and affiliated conferences for their contribution to the highest scientific quality and the overall success of the HCI International 2019 conference.

This conference would not have been possible without the continuous and unwavering support and advice of the founder, Conference General Chair Emeritus and Conference Scientific Advisor Prof. Gavriel Salvendy. For his outstanding efforts, I would like to express my appreciation to the communications chair and editor of *HCI International News,* Dr. Abbas Moallem.

July 2019   Constantine Stephanidis

HCI International 2019 Thematic Areas and Affiliated Conferences

Thematic areas:

- HCI 2019: Human-Computer Interaction
- HIMI 2019: Human Interface and the Management of Information

Affiliated conferences:

- EPCE 2019: 16th International Conference on Engineering Psychology and Cognitive Ergonomics
- UAHCI 2019: 13th International Conference on Universal Access in Human-Computer Interaction
- VAMR 2019: 11th International Conference on Virtual, Augmented and Mixed Reality
- CCD 2019: 11th International Conference on Cross-Cultural Design
- SCSM 2019: 11th International Conference on Social Computing and Social Media
- AC 2019: 13th International Conference on Augmented Cognition
- DHM 2019: 10th International Conference on Digital Human Modeling and Applications in Health, Safety, Ergonomics and Risk Management
- DUXU 2019: 8th International Conference on Design, User Experience, and Usability
- DAPI 2019: 7th International Conference on Distributed, Ambient and Pervasive Interactions
- HCIBGO 2019: 6th International Conference on HCI in Business, Government and Organizations
- LCT 2019: 6th International Conference on Learning and Collaboration Technologies
- ITAP 2019: 5th International Conference on Human Aspects of IT for the Aged Population
- HCI-CPT 2019: First International Conference on HCI for Cybersecurity, Privacy and Trust
- HCI-Games 2019: First International Conference on HCI in Games
- MobiTAS 2019: First International Conference on HCI in Mobility, Transport, and Automotive Systems
- AIS 2019: First International Conference on Adaptive Instructional Systems

Pre-conference Proceedings Volumes Full List

1. LNCS 11566, Human-Computer Interaction: Perspectives on Design (Part I), edited by Masaaki Kurosu
2. LNCS 11567, Human-Computer Interaction: Recognition and Interaction Technologies (Part II), edited by Masaaki Kurosu
3. LNCS 11568, Human-Computer Interaction: Design Practice in Contemporary Societies (Part III), edited by Masaaki Kurosu
4. LNCS 11569, Human Interface and the Management of Information: Visual Information and Knowledge Management (Part I), edited by Sakae Yamamoto and Hirohiko Mori
5. LNCS 11570, Human Interface and the Management of Information: Information in Intelligent Systems (Part II), edited by Sakae Yamamoto and Hirohiko Mori
6. LNAI 11571, Engineering Psychology and Cognitive Ergonomics, edited by Don Harris
7. LNCS 11572, Universal Access in Human-Computer Interaction: Theory, Methods and Tools (Part I), edited by Margherita Antona and Constantine Stephanidis
8. LNCS 11573, Universal Access in Human-Computer Interaction: Multimodality and Assistive Environments (Part II), edited by Margherita Antona and Constantine Stephanidis
9. LNCS 11574, Virtual, Augmented and Mixed Reality: Multimodal Interaction (Part I), edited by Jessie Y. C. Chen and Gino Fragomeni
10. LNCS 11575, Virtual, Augmented and Mixed Reality: Applications and Case Studies (Part II), edited by Jessie Y. C. Chen and Gino Fragomeni
11. LNCS 11576, Cross-Cultural Design: Methods, Tools and User Experience (Part I), edited by P. L. Patrick Rau
12. LNCS 11577, Cross-Cultural Design: Culture and Society (Part II), edited by P. L. Patrick Rau
13. LNCS 11578, Social Computing and Social Media: Design, Human Behavior and Analytics (Part I), edited by Gabriele Meiselwitz
14. LNCS 11579, Social Computing and Social Media: Communication and Social Communities (Part II), edited by Gabriele Meiselwitz
15. LNAI 11580, Augmented Cognition, edited by Dylan D. Schmorrow and Cali M. Fidopiastis
16. LNCS 11581, Digital Human Modeling and Applications in Health, Safety, Ergonomics and Risk Management: Human Body and Motion (Part I), edited by Vincent G. Duffy

17. LNCS 11582, Digital Human Modeling and Applications in Health, Safety, Ergonomics and Risk Management: Healthcare Applications (Part II), edited by Vincent G. Duffy
18. LNCS 11583, Design, User Experience, and Usability: Design Philosophy and Theory (Part I), edited by Aaron Marcus and Wentao Wang
19. LNCS 11584, Design, User Experience, and Usability: User Experience in Advanced Technological Environments (Part II), edited by Aaron Marcus and Wentao Wang
20. LNCS 11585, Design, User Experience, and Usability: Application Domains (Part III), edited by Aaron Marcus and Wentao Wang
21. LNCS 11586, Design, User Experience, and Usability: Practice and Case Studies (Part IV), edited by Aaron Marcus and Wentao Wang
22. LNCS 11587, Distributed, Ambient and Pervasive Interactions, edited by Norbert Streitz and Shin'ichi Konomi
23. LNCS 11588, HCI in Business, Government and Organizations: eCommerce and Consumer Behavior (Part I), edited by Fiona Fui-Hoon Nah and Keng Siau
24. LNCS 11589, HCI in Business, Government and Organizations: Information Systems and Analytics (Part II), edited by Fiona Fui-Hoon Nah and Keng Siau
25. LNCS 11590, Learning and Collaboration Technologies: Designing Learning Experiences (Part I), edited by Panayiotis Zaphiris and Andri Ioannou
26. LNCS 11591, Learning and Collaboration Technologies: Ubiquitous and Virtual Environments for Learning and Collaboration (Part II), edited by Panayiotis Zaphiris and Andri Ioannou
27. LNCS 11592, Human Aspects of IT for the Aged Population: Design for the Elderly and Technology Acceptance (Part I), edited by Jia Zhou and Gavriel Salvendy
28. LNCS 11593, Human Aspects of IT for the Aged Population: Social Media, Games and Assistive Environments (Part II), edited by Jia Zhou and Gavriel Salvendy
29. LNCS 11594, HCI for Cybersecurity, Privacy and Trust, edited by Abbas Moallem
30. LNCS 11595, HCI in Games, edited by Xiaowen Fang
31. LNCS 11596, HCI in Mobility, Transport, and Automotive Systems, edited by Heidi Krömker
32. LNCS 11597, Adaptive Instructional Systems, edited by Robert Sottilare and Jessica Schwarz
33. CCIS 1032, HCI International 2019 - Posters (Part I), edited by Constantine Stephanidis

34. CCIS 1033, HCI International 2019 - Posters (Part II), edited by Constantine Stephanidis
35. CCIS 1034, HCI International 2019 - Posters (Part III), edited by Constantine Stephanidis

http://2019.hci.international/proceedings

8th International Conference on Design, User Experience, and Usability (DUXU 2019)

Program Board Chair(s): **Aaron Marcus**, *USA*, and **Wentao Wang**, *P.R. China*

- Sisira Adikari, Australia
- Claire Ancient, UK
- Jan Brejcha, Czech Republic
- Silvia De los Rios, Spain
- Marc Fabri, UK
- Josh Halstead, USA
- Wei Liu, P.R. China
- Yang Meng, P.R. China
- Judith Moldenhauer, USA
- Jingyan Qin, P.R. China
- Francisco Rebelo, Portugal
- Christine Riedmann-Streitz, Germany
- Elizabeth Rosenzweig, USA
- Patricia Search, USA
- Marcelo Soares, P.R. China
- Carla G. Spinillo, Brazil

The full list with the Program Board Chairs and the members of the Program Boards of all thematic areas and affiliated conferences is available online at:

http://www.hci.international/board-members-2019.php

HCI International 2020

The 22nd International Conference on Human-Computer Interaction, HCI International 2020, will be held jointly with the affiliated conferences in Copenhagen, Denmark, at the Bella Center Copenhagen, July 19–24, 2020. It will cover a broad spectrum of themes related to HCI, including theoretical issues, methods, tools, processes, and case studies in HCI design, as well as novel interaction techniques, interfaces, and applications. The proceedings will be published by Springer. More information will be available on the conference website: http://2020.hci.international/.

General Chair
Prof. Constantine Stephanidis
University of Crete and ICS-FORTH
Heraklion, Crete, Greece
E-mail: general_chair@hcii2020.org

http://2020.hci.international/

Contents – Part I

Design Theories, Methods and Tools

User Requirements, Preferences Emotions and Personality

Design Philosophy

Point of View When Designing Around Behavior

Julieta Aguilera[(✉)]

1129 Ferdinand Ave., Forest Park, IL 60130, USA
julieta.aguilera@plymouth.ac.uk

Abstract. What does it mean to be a creature in space, able to displace oneself? After decades of passive screens in every house and almost in every room, some video games, virtual reality, and other tracking based media have been developed with the dynamic ability to move through virtual spaces with agency. This paper will articulate the philosophical, aesthetic and design implications of this shift that are permeating though the transition to embodied technologies. First the philosophical implications of what a point of view is in terms of subjectivity will be illustrated with examples of daily individual and social experiences. Then the paper will go over the aesthetic implications of different media according to the direct or implied approaches the media may contain regarding subjectivity, and how these implications carry metaphorical assumptions we use to socialize with each other in today's public discourse. Lastly, the paper will consider notions of virtuality (Noë), simulation (Barret), and participatory sense making (De Jaegher & Di Paolo) that question the notion of subjectivity as a scalable experience which expands from individual to social situations.

Shifting from personal to collective behavior in the designed point of view is not trivial. When Nagel described disembodiment (or experience without point of view) as "a view from nowhere" perhaps there was not yet a notion of the absurdity of holding nobody's experience. To a great extent humankind already shares the common subjective experience of living on planet Earth looking out into space from the Earth's point of view, and from the umwelt of the human body. We bring that experience to everything we interact with. So the question becomes, what really is subjectivity if not the notion of a point of view in a specific place in time and space? How does that notion alone project itself into the assumptions we make of the world, of each other and of our representations? Because these assumptions become languages and cultures, perhaps we are at a crucial time to traverse these levels of meaning, liberating others from fixed and static assumptions of being, and finally from the individual subjective impositions, disguised as objectivity, we make on others and on the environments we experience.

Keywords: Virtual Reality · Umwelt · Point of view · Perception · Design

1   Introduction

A point of view in the world is more than a place in space or a way of thinking but also how the place in space is, in a way, an integral part of thinking itself. Capabilities afforded by current tools emphasize the need to better understand the situation of the

© Springer Nature Switzerland AG 2019
A. Marcus and W. Wang (Eds.): HCII 2019, LNCS 11583, pp. 3–13, 2019.
https://doi.org/10.1007/978-3-030-23570-3_1

body in space and the spatialized mind where "the debate must be moved to the concrete realm of seeing exactly how the animate body in its world is a mind" [1]. From this approach I will look at point of view as a situated mind, encompassing body and environment in the anchoring of subjectivity, and with it defining the scale or realm where a thought exists and the parameters that articulate it. This is an important aspect that needs to be integrated in the design process because it involves the body as a measure for experiences that are virtual in nature and need to be understood from the inside. In this regard, designing from the outside at different scales, as was commonly done when drawing, working in front of a screen or building small scale models to preview what a large sculpture or architectural construction would feel like, may have skipped elements that are just now coming into play for objects of representation such as those involving elements of Virtual and Augmented Reality.

When architect Juhani Pallasmaa expresses that "experiencing loneliness is one of the basic feelings given by architecture" [2], I see this as signaling the boundary of the body, a visualization of the scale of the point of view from the body of the person, expanding the body to space, and when you do that, it is indeed a lonely experience. There is no dynamic feedback, but the loneliness of the lack thereof. But then this is the situation of a dynamic body in a static architectural context where the body controls its location in relation to the environment, and the focus is on the mapping of the body into that space. On the other hand, the affect we develop over the span of segments of our individual lives comes from interacting with each other and with the environments of each other including our internal constructions when sharing our experiences. We are not fortresses: we act within networks and assemble collective points of view on top of each of our individual ones. I propose points of view are not scalable, and that this is an important consideration in designing immersive experiences and representations in general today. To this end, I will consider the common element across scales that is the point of view.

In this paper I will first mention relevant embodied technologies that have been developed in the spaces we inhabit today, and what current capabilities like tracking mean for the articulation of the point of view and representation. I will then discuss the notions of subjectivity and objectivity, and what a view from nowhere would mean for interaction design. Finally I will go over the design of point of view dependent on dynamics, materiality and abstract reasoning.

2 Embodiment

2.1 About Embodied Technologies

We construct our points of view from the body and through our senses to understand where we are in space and how we relate to what shares space with us because we make meaning from what we experience in context [3]. In this sense the knowledge of our senses comes together to help us create a model that can help us act and navigate [4]. Even when someone organizes their senses in an atypical manner, we do not walk or see the same way, we can compare our individual models of space with each other which are built from the available and specialized senses each of our bodies have. Such is the case of the blind man who uses tongue clicks as a sonar to "see" [5] or a person who measures space without walking but using a wheelchair instead. Even with these corporal reconfigurations we can confirm with each other as to what is the structure, the materiality and the significant forms that can be perceived in a shared location, all while maintaining our separate points of view and unique life experiences.

Existing in a city, on the other hand, could be described as moving through a series of constructed points of view to be navigated for a desired functionality, open spaces bounded by walls, mediated by windows and open through doors and passages. Architect Pallasmaa sees phenomenology as the observing of conscious phenomena, that is, looking at architecture from within the consciousness that experiences it: "the relationship between architectural form and how architecture is experienced" where "form only affects our feelings through what it represents" (as artistic dimension) [6]. He also observes that when there is no coupling resolution between the body and the representational form, it does not stand as form anymore. Cities are in a way action driven and pieced together devices that choreograph our points of view even as we retain agency within the established constraints that invite certain kinds of body affective states. Cities in themselves are, from this approach, a kind of media, as they mediate actions in an environment.

Because immersive environments such as Virtual Reality experiences can also constrain and choreograph actions and affective states directly and dynamically (even in abstract or extended situations such as in those of scientific visualizations at microscopic and macroscopic scales), we must consider what a point of view represents when handling objects and embodying being in those and other inaccessible or impossible environments. What are the capabilities one can have in spaces that are beyond human scale or are purely mathematical or based on data? What does it mean to navigate molecular or cosmic visualizations as if one was swimming in a calm sea? What does a point of view in those environments mean for our senses and our concepts? What aspects of reality inform the point of view one holds that grounds both our concepts and metaphors?

For example, I had this idea over a decade ago when I started working in Virtual Reality, imagining what it would take to create a perceptually real and embodied virtual experience of looking at the Earth's surface from above (as opposed to standing in a room with a hand-held controller pressing a button to move over the planet). In a way, airplanes today work as sensory chambers that replicate the atmosphere at the ground level, and aside from some discomfort, passengers forget they are flying because the air temperature and pressure are stable. At the time I envisioned a transparent swimming pool in the belly of an airplane that would indicate to the body the kind of affordances available from the familiar setting of being held by an element that would approximate the suspended feeling of flying, yet with a point of view extended by an airplane in high altitude. This experience is not that different from that of living in a house in a city where shelter, sustenance and mobility are all potentially mediated, but have become so ubiquitous that we forget how this has happened. Living in the Midwest where freezing winters are followed by scorching summers, I could not help but feel naked when inhabiting a house in Hawai'i where I would sleep with opened windows year round, listening to the ocean, the trees, the birds and the frogs which connected me closely to the weather and the state of the ocean waves. When reviewing ways in which our experiences are mediated within architectural constructions that afford navigation and orient attention, or through interactive devices that accommodate and reflect or reconfigure the body, I have turned to consider these aspects as four distinct areas, which can modulate one's point of view within virtual experiences [7]:

(1) What establishes place in space in relation to the environment? This includes depth cues predominantly through stereography, motion parallax and differential size, which form a spatial hierarchy from one's location in relation to the distance that separates said location from other points in space.
(2) What one can afford in terms of visual field, reach and dexterity? This forms the scope of one's actions that bound a focus of attention on a kind of actionable task or tasks.
(3) What one can do and what one can infer about oneself from interacting in the environment? This gives an understanding of the role one can play in the environment.
(4) How does the environment signal that one is present in a space? Can one's shadow be seen? Do the objects in the environment respond to the amount of force exerted on them? Do ripples or waves appear or objects move when one is in proximity or acting upon them? This is the feedback of the environment that gives a sense of agency to one's motion.

I have purposefully explained these four aspects in very broad terms because there are many ways in which they can be addressed. These aspects set the spatial relationships, the sensorimotor constraints, the role driven identity and the sense of agency of a point of view of embodied technologies.

2.2   The Tracking Shift

Experiencing "requires the recognition that perception is a way of encountering not only how things are, but how things are in relation to the perceiver" [8]. Philosopher Alva Noë further states that experiences in the real world are themselves virtual because we build models of the world in our minds as we navigate space. In three dimensions we see three-dimensional things over time when we move around and through forms in space. We do not see all sides of these forms at once but instead retain an understanding of them as we navigate and look at forms over time. In this regard the point of view is always moving and at the same time held by the reconstruction of form that is dynamically built in our minds when the body surveys the moving focus of attention.

When considering point of view, it is important to look at the different levels of awareness that access perception. Consciousness is but the top layer which in itself utilizes only the part of the experience that is deemed relevant in a kind of "cinemalike editing choices that our pervasive system of biological value has promoted" [9] over what is happening at a given time. In this regard, film is not a restricted or collaged view of an environment, but perhaps a kind of pre-edited borrowed point of view.

Tracked media involving shifts in the visual field attached to body motion presents a contrast to older media that is not tracked, where the point of view in a painting or a photograph is fixed, or where a point of view in a film does not rely on the movement of the body of the viewer. Tracked media does however rely on the attentional capabilities one has regarding number and complexity of forms and the speed at which forms are displayed in the visual field afforded by the tracked device being utilized.

The design implications of tracked media expand static imagery and film to use notions of architecture or constructed landscapes where body motion is paired to visual change. In this exchange the body brings in its whole world experiential library and echoes the motion internally: "Just as your brain predicts the sights, smells, sounds, touches, and tastes from the world in relation to the movements of your head and limbs, it also predicts the sensory consequences of movements inside your body" [10]. Architectural visual change entails spaces that reveal aspects of the environment as one moves inside a building or a garden via body motion such as steps. Tracked media also expands on how an environment can respond to said body motion, thus reinforcing the tracked movements as points of sensation and then articulating the body as a structure of those connected sensorimotor points. In this manner, the points of tracked motion can strengthen the role of the body as a simulation of the space around us.

3 Subjectivity and Point of View

3.1 Subjectivity

Humans directly inhabit space in many ways, both for internal and external spaces and within different scopes of spatial and temporal realms. We also can live in many distinct places simultaneously through real time video and data. Because of this, we live at many scales simultaneously just so we can handle how our point of view moves around these different mediated and non-mediated spaces and manage time, oriented to various actions. We check the geographical weather forecast to decide on certain activities, choose based on planetary seasons to travel, evaluate travel times to decide on how to get places around town, perhaps organize our calendars distributing segments of our lives for work, friends and family or personal projects when privileged to do so, thus organizing our lives' timelines on different spaces at various scales, and around certain activities that involve a world that humanity has constructed to different extents. And in all those spaces and activities we hold a point of view tailored to the environment and focused on the action which informs our individual subjective experience. One of these realms is the grand scale of the cosmos which involves abstractions of space and time that afford us to consider spatial and temporal relationships that we cannot directly experience from the spatial and temporal bounds of the human body and human civilization.

Just as the body is grounded on the floor on which one steps, so is the subjective character each of us projects grounded in one's experience. But when that experience expands to encompass a realm where many bodies are present, which overlaps the point of view of those bodies, the point of view becomes physically collective. A physically collective point of view can be that of a static or dynamic point of view such as being at the top of a mountain, or traveling on a car, a boat, a spacecraft. Understanding how planetary motion occurs gives access to understanding that one is traveling around the sun on planet Earth. When utilizing immersive scientific visualizations to understand such dynamics, the point of view becomes a wider collective experience where human mobility is much more abstracted. In that sense, cosmic spatial simulations can detach us from planet Earth to fly between planets and galaxies within scientific visualizations, while in reality we are attached to our planet, and not able to go outside our planet's atmosphere without machines that replicate our environment in order to keep our human bodies alive, and even then, we cannot go very far.

As someone working with points of view at various scales in immersive media and scientific visualization, I have devoted several years to thinking about what a physical point of view is and how it relates to subjectivity, a subjective point of view that is today extended to the microscopic and macroscopic. In extending subjectivity, "the body is best conceived as the rock on which the protoself is built, while the protoself is the pivot around which the conscious mind turns" [11]. Even in building civilization, aspects of direct experience have constrained the sensorimotor capabilities of the human body to streamline representation to the limits of the available media capabilities, therefore simplifying and modulating a sense of embodied subjectivity that is then flattened to variables which may loose the grounding of the specific point of view that anchors the relation to the scale of said subjectivity. For example, in architectural space, the scale of a room signals what affordances the room may have – whether one can only rest, or whether there is enough room to dance or play a sport, alone or with other people, and the reach that those affordances may have – how far can the environment or the actions of other people be perceived and evaluated. Being in a kind of foggy forest is very different than being in a vast desert or at the top of a mountain. When the sense of scale and reach is lost as an anchoring element in an experience, I would argue that the sense of space is lost in the representation.

Qualifying the point of view at the different scales we use to understand our place in the Universe is also very important because we adopt different characteristics at the various assumed scales. Direct experience affords the body with its sensorimotor potential and spatial navigation. For example, trees seem static in comparison to us humans, because they are attached to the soil, but at a planetary spatiotemporal scale, we are attached to the Earth's atmosphere for the most part and we share a point of view of space from our corner of the solar system [7]. Conversely, as already stated, we do not share the point of view of another person on the surface of the planet. That is to say, the scale of the geographical location is part of the point of view as much as the point in space itself, and without it, subjectivity is impossible to communicate, as abstracted as it may be. Shifting characteristics across scales that are paramount to the subjective experience in a point of view is problematic for this reason. Not knowing what one's scale is, is equivalent to not knowing where anything is.

"Without consciousness—that is, a mind endowed with subjectivity—you would have no way of knowing that you exist, let alone know who you are and what you think" [12]. Damasio further connects creativity and evolution to subjectivity. Looking inwards, a point of view of situated presence is the axis of our thoughts. Because of the understanding of media, artists know where they are because of the perceptual anchoring of thought.

3.2   Nobody's Experience

Our own points of view are often so invisible to ourselves that we may think that everybody can see what we see. This leads to not only the generalizing of one's perception but also one's experiences, emotions and conclusions about aspects of the world altogether. It can also lead to miscategorizations, such as when assuming one's subjective view is an objective one, or when a middle ground is declared simply by moving one's subjective view there.

When Thomas Nagel addresses the excessive objectification of the world, in what he calls "a view from nowhere" [13] he touches on why acknowledging one's point of view is important. Barret points out that when affect, that is, the general feeling one has in space over time, is experienced without knowing what caused it, it is more likely treated "as information about the world, rather than your experience of the world" [14]. I think it is paramount to consider that acknowledging and understanding the structure and the grounds of our own subjective experience is not only an act of self reflection but it underlies the ability we have to connect with others because we have the sufficient understanding of why we think the way we do and see our individual experiences as rooted in the unique point of view of each of us. It is that understanding that allows us to communicate with each other and compare notes, so to speak, experience together areas of overlap, and transfer aspects of non overlapping life experiences with each other. The physical point of view is a carrier of affect and as Barret states, based on interoceptive sensations where "interoception in the moment is more influential to perception, and how you act, than the outside world is [15] and further expands: "every thought, memory, perception, or emotion that you construct includes something about the state of your body: a little piece of interoception [16].

Interactive experiences such as those of Virtual or Augmented Reality afford us to play with points of view in a more fluid manner than with other media, and even share a human sized point of view in different virtual realms. These are the media of the point of view, tracked and with agency that show and bring to the forefront the simple fact that different points of view do exist and that there are boundaries to perception and the attention handled by it. It is in the simulation of this point of view being transferred to the devices we handle, to the vehicles we drive, and to the digital simulations we create that have the same root of the body. It goes without saying that each of us inhabits a unique point in time and space, with unique experiences that have informed us to that point. Yet the resulting complexities of both commonalities and exceptionalities in the human experience are not easy to reconcile among people. More so, it can be overwhelming just to accept that the same experience can be understood in a slightly different manner by different people. Even extrapolating from the physical commonalities of the body and the planetary environment, the point of view of direct experience is always different.

Perhaps it is this new ability to navigate virtual experiences in sensory rich environments that makes us feel we can navigate everybody's experiences, as if we could force others into our shoes at will, assuming they experience what we experience and do so in the same way. Such a miscalculation may also be enabled by the assumption that these environments are like a common language that, like spoken language, has the modularity of words which hold fixed meaning which can be confirmed in a dictionary.

How the meanings are agreed on when experiences are becoming so natural and synchronized to the kind of body we hold as a species can be confusing. A problem with point of view replacement can be the over-engagement with emotions, the mislabeling of emotions, and the overriding of one's own experience with these assumptions. Part of media education is the constant grounding of what is communicated on one's own experience rather than the mere comparison of experiences to declare a winner. This is where ideas such as participatory sense making [1] can be useful in articulating the physical grounding of a physical point of view in social behavior.

3.3   Objectivity as Simulation

Objectivity itself is shaken from its pedestal as we become better at defining what we hold in common with others and what we don't. The process of collectively thinking about reality by joining points of view has then increased in resolution and it can be made more precise, and less of an imposition of one point of view over another. This results in deeper exploration among points of view in the development of a general common view of reality or conceptual model of reality or the experience of reality where individual experiences are not dissolved but aggregated.

How much of what we treat as objective reality, an overarching point of view that applies to many people, is actually objective as opposed to the imposition of a subjective view? How much is actually a common point of view that addresses shared aspects of reality, a transferrable simulation of realities or an extended reality not reachable by direct means but via devices? In the case of extended reality, we share a point of view when we share a space, being that of a vehicle or a large place as in a mountain. But we also own internal models of larger scales of reality as in sharing the same planet that orbits the sun and follows the sun through the galaxy. These larger models or points of views at larger scales are constructed from technologies developed to capture spatial and temporal scales of data that are then resized to the human point of view in time and space. But are these models of point of view objective per se? Or is just that the notion of model needs to be better understood as a working and fluid collective construction with a validity span at a historic scale? [7].

While objectivity can be understood as joined present reality, the concept of biogeography [17] may be useful in envisioning potential mutual modulations of the body within a virtual space. Biogeography studies the distribution of species in geographic space and over geological time. At large timescales it is the evolution of bodies interacting with changing ecosystems which may seem static to human perception. The concept of biogeography in a way allows us to understand the dynamics of physical space in modulating life forms including the human body. It can also help consider how life has changed place and branched out as a result. This concept affords us to understand how aspects of the world we know have diverged from a point in time, therefore giving us a point of view that allows us to scale our umwelt and see through time.

Thich Naht Hanh further invites people to look at the continuum of materiality from which we emerge as a species, from mineral to plant to animal and then human [18]. He uses the word discrimination in setting apart and differentiating, as the opposite of observing the continuity between beings. Observing continuity entails a moving point of view that imagines what is being observed as a point of view looking back at us. It is a simulation exercise of spatial empathy that in action, not only allows us to see what is in front of us, but understand how we are related, and consider what it shows us about who we are.

4 The Designed Point of View

As I have argued before [19] design practice should not and formally doesn't address individual senses because we are multisensory beings. This is a misunderstanding stemming perhaps from non professional opinions and a misleading notion perhaps stemming from a recent history of excessive media focus that could be understood as the mapping of a single human sense to a specific media as if that sense could have an isolated section of the human brain. This is why it is necessary to move the understanding of designing to perception of space itself, even shared space, anchored by the point of view, better understood as point of perception, since vision arguably carries the farthest spatial range.

Designing a point of view is a kind of map making. Damasio notes that "map-making brains have the power of literally introducing the body as content into the mind process [20]. There is something very architectural and representationally visualizing about this. Attention thus attaches itself to an ongoing simulation effort to put the pieces we know into new constructions of understanding of what we are yet to grasp from the common materiality and dynamics we share with the world, where we ourselves are part of the construction. Point of view is also a social construct. The constructed aspect of it is somewhat more apparent when social network mobility is not average, for example, when there is a handicapped child in the family. In such a case, there is a boundary realignment in the family where there is a perception of less adaptability to physical and social environments and a smaller but more dense friendship network [21].

Observing and understanding is not an experience of mere mirroring. "Natural cognitive systems are simply not in the business of accessing their world in order to build accurate pictures of it. They actively participate in the generation of meaning in what matters to them; they enact a world" [22]. That is to say, we do not replicate what we experience, but create meaning from our experiences. Lisa Barret talks about experiential blindness when we see something for the first time [3]. This is when we have never connected to it. This observation says something about points of view as inhabited spaces, where lack of familiarity renders what is there invisible. Knitting a web of familiarity around a new experience may start by dissecting strangeness into aspects that appear familiar, comparing and constructing the unknown from the known. There is something about this dissecting and constructive activity that makes us build and even carefully design our own point of view that can then be transformed and utilized to look at the world around us and join views with others. This is also an event of "mutual modulation" [1] in doing so. In participatory sense making among points of view there is an "emergent autonomous organization in the domain of relational dynamics, (that emerges) without destroying in the process the autonomy of the agents involved" [23] where autonomy is the point of view itself.

5 Conclusion

The interaction of society with new means of representation and exploration of meaning such as VR and AR have resulted in renewed valuation of understanding one's own point of view. Current media capabilities also open up spaces to reflect on our personal behavior and the articulation of social interactions as well as the coupling of behaviors into collective points of view. Ongoing new knowledge correspondingly results in confirmed collective experiences of a societal point of view that assess our experience as a species.

The design process for interfaces and for environments has changed dramatically over the last decades. In the past, signage and eventually screen based content was designed for the front view exclusively. Environments used to be designed via floor plans and small scale models that provide an outside view. The ability to design from the inside out, that is, from the point of view, grant us the opportunity to review how visual hierarchy can be now updated to spatial hierarchy with an embedded perceiving and acting body as measure. Furthermore, point of view significantly changes roles and affordances as it is scaled from the human body. This is something we must learn not only to articulate in design, but educate in reading and understanding, so it is correctly mapped back to the body.

Several interfaces in virtual environments appear today in proximity to the body of the user like screens in virtual space receding to the outside view of representation. In the best case they appear attached to body limbs requiring certain arm motions to receive input, while in real life consumer devices are relatively recently beginning to accept body gestures instead of button pressing commands. I believe this is a transitional period that expands the solely visual experience to a more integrated and multisensory one. I expect more work to be done under a likewise integrated design paradigm of perceptual hierarchy, closer to an understanding of perceptual space and a scalable notion of point of view as an axis of agency both individual and collective.

The same way we consider physical context and experience in order to understand each other better, we need to have an understanding of what scale and scope we are at in virtual representations of non human scales in order to understand how the representations relate to us and each other. To that end we must design with an awareness of the connections that our bodies have to the real environment. Point of view-centered design requires an understanding of scale and scope, and how interfaces may stem therefrom.

References

1. De Jaegher, H., Di Paolo, E.: Participatory sense-making. Phenomenol. Cogn. Sci. **6**(4), 485–507 (2007)
2. Pallasmaa, J.: The geometry of feeling: a look at the phenomenology of architecture. In: Theorizing a New Agenda for Architecture: An Anthology of Architectural Theory 1995, p. 452 (1965)
3. Barrett, L.F.: How Emotions are Made: The Secret Life of the Brain. Houghton Mifflin Harcourt, Boston (2017)

4. Massumi, B.: Parables for the Virtual. Duke University Press, Durham (2002)
5. Thaler, L., et al.: Mouth-clicks used by blind expert human echolocators—signal description and model based signal synthesis. PLoS Comput. Biol. **13**(8), e1005670 (2017)
6. Pallasmaa, J. The geometry of feeling: a look at the phenomenology of architecture. In: Theorizing a New Agenda for Architecture: An Anthology of Architectural Theory 1995, p. 449 (1965)
7. Aguilera, J.: Mindfulness and Embodiment in the Design of a Synthetic Experience. Ph.D. dissertation, Planetary Collegium, University of Plymouth, 21 January 2019 (unpublished)
8. Noë, A.: Action in Perception, p. 169. MIT Press, Cambridge (2004)
9. Damasio, A.: Self Comes to Mind: Constructing the Conscious Brain. Pantheon, New York (2010). 1194
10. Barrett, L.F.: How Emotions are Made: The Secret Life of the Brain, p. 66. Houghton Mifflin Harcourt, Boston (2017)
11. Damasio, A.: Self Comes to Mind: Constructing the Conscious Brain. Pantheon, New York (2010). 427
12. Damasio, A.: Self Comes to Mind: Constructing the Conscious Brain. Pantheon, New York (2010). 146
13. Nagel, T.: The View from Nowhere. Oxford University Press, Oxford (1989)
14. Barrett, L.F.: How Emotions are Made: The Secret Life of the Brain, p. 75. Houghton Mifflin Harcourt, Boston (2017)
15. Barrett, L.F.: How Emotions are Made: The Secret Life of the Brain, p. 79. Houghton Mifflin Harcourt, Boston (2017)
16. Barrett, L.F.: How Emotions are Made: The Secret Life of the Brain, p. 82. Houghton Mifflin Harcourt, Boston (2017)
17. Wilson, E.O., MacArthur, R.H.: The Theory of Island Biogeography. Princeton University Press, Princeton (1967)
18. Hanh, T.N.: Thich Nhat Hanh: Essential Writings. Orbis Books, Ossining (2001)
19. Aguilera-Rodríguez, J.: To Embody the N-Body: Spatial Perception Utilized in Large-Scale Visualizations. In: Stephanidis, C., Antona, M. (eds.) UAHCI 2013. LNCS, vol. 8010, pp. 537–546. Springer, Heidelberg (2013). https://doi.org/10.1007/978-3-642-39191-0_58
20. Damasio, A.: Self Comes to Mind: Constructing the Conscious Brain. Pantheon, New York (2010). 1465
21. Kazak, A.E., Marvin, R.S.: Differences, difficulties and adaptation: stress and social networks in families with a handicapped child. Fam. Relat. **33**, 67–77 (1984)
22. De Jaegher, H., Di Paolo, E.: Participatory sense-making. Phenomenol. Cogn. Sci. **6**(4), 488 (2007)
23. De Jaegher, H., Di Paolo, E.: Participatory sense-making. Phenomenol. Cogn. Sci. **6**(4), 493 (2007)

Gameotics: A Game Analysis Method Based on Semiotics

Daniel Paz de Araujo[1](✉) and Hermes Renato Hildebrand[2]

[1] PUC-Campinas – CEATEC, Rod. Dom Pedro I, Km 136,
Campinas, SP, Brazil
daniel.araujo@puc-campinas.edu.br
[2] PUC-SP - TIDD, R. Monte Alegre, 984 - Perdizes, São Paulo, SP, Brazil

Abstract. The applied research in Games employs numerous instruments to carry out its investigations. The search for scientifically based analysis demands strategies that are in line with expectations regarding the efficiency and effectiveness of their studies. The intrinsic heterogeneity of games also requires that the mode of research be opportunely flexible and straightforward, to cover a greater diversity of elements. Such convergence in diversity can occur through the standard set of playful impulses of language, ritual, and myth; and its relations with the natural signal aspects of the games: interface, mechanics and narrative. Considering these specific characteristics of the games focusing on their experiences provided through the signs created, specific experimental research procedures can be applied as a possibility of research methodology. In this sense, Semiotics, as a study on systems and phenomena of signification, has the appropriate attributes to be used in the scientific research of games endowed with the mentioned aspects. Several kinds of research on Games have already been made through Semiotics, but there is no description of procedures for its application, allowing Semiotics to be adopted in a schematic way of studying these contexts. For this reason, it is proposed a fundamental methodology that enables the use of Semiotics as research structured in Games considering its intrinsic characteristics of signification and experimentation. The definition of the method is based on the correlation between the categories Primeity, Secundity and Terceity of Semiotics articulated with the interface, mechanics, and narrative of the research object, that is, the Game. In support of the theoretical rationale of the proposal, a summary methodology guide will support researchers in their application. Associating Semiotics with Games in a structured model allows for the logical cohesion of study and analysis activities, generating uniform results, but respecting the specificities of signs and experiences of each Game. To confirm the proposal, it will be applied in Study Cases with analog and digital games, demonstrating its organization, application, and flexibility of adoption.

Keywords: Game design · Semiotics · Game analysis

1 Introduction

The games have been experienced by man since antiquity, being understood by practically any individual. According to the professor and historian Huizinga [1], "(…) every thinking being can understand at first glance that the game has an autonomous

© Springer Nature Switzerland AG 2019
A. Marcus and W. Wang (Eds.): HCII 2019, LNCS 11583, pp. 14–22, 2019.
https://doi.org/10.1007/978-3-030-23570-3_2

reality (…)". The popularity of games has been driven by digital platforms, especially those based on screen devices, as they allow for collaborative and competitive gaming to be experienced almost anywhere, with diverse interaction designs. Also, such technologies promote the discovery of new games by players and extend the possibilities of creation by game designers. As games have been applied in different contexts, from pure fun to serious games that seek to train their players to perform critical activities in the real world. The scope and multiplicity of its interaction applications lead several researchers to try to understand how the elements of the games are related and how they create their meanings to produce the appropriate experiences during their use.

However, there are no specific game analysis methods that are effectively admitted by the scientific community that could be practiced by researchers. The applied investigation in games operates numerous instruments to carry out its investigations. The search for scientifically interactive audio-visual analysis also demands strategies that are in line with expectations regarding the efficiency and effectiveness of their subjects. The intrinsic heterogeneity of games also requires a mode of research to be opportunely flexible and straightforward, to cover a greater diversity of elements. Such convergence in diversity can occur through the standard set of playful impulses of language, ceremony, and story; and its relations with the natural sign aspects of the games: audio-visual interactive interface, mechanics, and narrative. Considering these specific characteristics of the games focusing on their experiences provided through the created signs, specific experimental research procedures shall be applied as a powerful investigation methodology. In this sense, Semiotics, as a study on systems and phenomena of signification, has the appropriate attributes to be used in the scientific research of games endowed with the mentioned aspects. Several types of research on games have already been made through Semiotics, but there is no description of procedures for its application. By creating these procedures, Semiotics could be allowed to be adopted in a schematic way of studying audio-visual interaction components in games.

For this reason, we propose a simple methodology that enables the use of Semiotics as structured research in games considering its intrinsic characteristics of signification and experimentation. The definition of the approach is based on the correlation between the categories firstness, secondness, and thirdness of Peirce's Semiotics [4], combined with the interface, mechanics, and narrative dimensions of the game defined by Schell [6]. In this sense, the objective of this work is to present a methodological proposal based on Semiotics concerning game design as a mechanism to assist researchers in the scientific production and publication of their studies. For this, three similar pillars are considered as theoretical bases, and these are the play impulses defined by Huizinga [1]: language, myth, and ritual; the design dimensions of games organized by Rogers [3] and Shell [6]: interface, mechanics and story; and the categories of the Peirce's Semiotics as demonstrated by Nöth [2], and Santaella [4]: firstness, secondness, and thirdness. In support of the theoretical basis of the proposal, a brief guide will support researchers for the practical application. Associating Semiotics with games design in a structured model provides a logical cohesion of study and analysis activities, generating uniform results, but respecting the specificities of signs and experiences of each game. To confirm the proposal, it will be applied in Case-Study with analog and digital games, demonstrating its organization, application, and flexibility of adoption. The proposal is structured in a simple and flexible way, to be adopted in researches of analogical and digital games with a scientific basis. Thus, it will be possible for researchers and interested in the game studies area to develop analyzes with adequate foundation, increasing acceptance by the scientific and community.

2 Games

The parallel world of the game allows the player to interact outside their reality and offers possibilities and restrictions that do not apply in the real world. McGonigal [7] argues that "the real world simply does not offer the carefully crafted pleasures, the exciting challenges, and the powerful social bond gained in virtual environments so easily." This concept is what Huizinga [1] defines as a magic circle: "within the circle of the game, the laws and customs of daily life lose validity. We are different and do different things." McGonigal [7] further argues that "it is possible to see how (games) can represent an intentional, active, powerful, and, most importantly, extremely useful escape."

There are several theories that seek to elucidate and describe the nature and meaning of the game. According to Huizinga [1], the theories range from approaching the game like energy discharge or a need for relaxation to preparing young people for future responsibilities to exercising collaboration or competition. However, there is a similarity between these perspectives, since "(they) start from the assumption that the game is connected to something other than the game itself" [1]. There are other definitions of what qualifies as a game and the action of playing, such as SUITS [3] which states that "playing a game is a voluntary effort to overcome obstacles". Rogers [3] complements the concept of gaming is an activity that requires at least one player, has rules and has a winning condition.

Victory or defeat is related to the goal of the game, which "focuses attention and continuously guides the player's participation throughout the game" [7]. For Schell [6], the game is defined as a problem-solving activity that is playfully viewed. Voluntary participation requires that the play consciously and willingly accept the goal, rules, and feedback of the game [7].

The games have been applied in different contexts, from simple fun to serious games that seek to train their players to perform critical activities in the real world. The scope and multiplicity of its applications lead various researchers to seek to understand how the elements of the games are related and how they create their meanings to produce the appropriate experiences during their use. Shell [6] explains that "the game enables the experience, but it is not the experience". The player experience is defined as (…) a set of sensations that the game provides during its use, which involves the performance of activities, and the memories that remain after use [8].

In this sense, the designer's concern is focused on the experience he wants to create with the game. To recreate an experience in a digital game, Shell [6], the game designer must discover the essential elements that define the actual experience and how the game can capture this essence. As defined by Zimmerman [9], the goal of game design is to create meaningful play interaction. In other words, Martinho [8] explains that experience is an interpretation, made by the player, of the activity of playing the game.

Mechanics is the natural feature of the game, where it is found in its most functional form. Mechanics are the rules of the game and make the interactions and relationships between aesthetics, technology, and game narrative exist [6]. Rogers [3] defines game mechanics as what creates the dynamics of the game when there is player interaction. The interaction with mechanics occurs through playful interaction in the aesthetic meaning that the game offers.

There are several other significant elements in digital games that should be highlighted because their characteristics are important for the application of this research. The space of the game concerns spatial dimensions and limits; objects are anything that can be seen or manipulated; actions are what the player can do; the rules define the space, objects, actions and their consequences, as well as restrictions on actions; skills transfer focus from play to player; the probability is the uncertainties or surprises of the game [6]. Among the elements contained in the game design process, the skills can be highlighted in the research, since this involves physical, mental and social issues, obtained through experiences in the game. According to McGonigal [7], "(...) the emotional and social rewards we really seek require active, enthusiastic and self-motivated participation."

Another significant element is the game interface. According to Schell [6], the goal of the game interface is to make players feel they have control over their experiences. The player usually has two types of interfaces in digital games: one physical and one virtual. The physical interface is what the player sees, hears, and touches the game world, while the virtual interface provides information that prevents disturbing the player's interactions [6]. Other important features of the interface relate to how the player fulfills his wishes (if it is suitable to be used without difficulty), and how feedback occurs to the player to let him or her know about the game and affect them to create sensations from their experiences [6].

Due to the subjectivity of the gaming experience, mainly caused by the significance of its elements, specific testing activities need to be performed to ensure a proper design process. Subjectivity occurs because of the difference in players' profiles and the different ways in which they play and perceive the game [6]. Of the different types of tests that can be performed in games, the most relevant for this research is the gameplay test, which "serve to test the gaming experience and not to find programming problems" [8] (Fig. 1).

Games are built based on four different elements, defined by Schell [6] as:

- **Mechanics**: these are the procedures and rules of the game. The mechanics describe the purpose of the game, how players can or can not reach it and what happens when they try.
- **Narrative**: This is the sequence of events that unfold in your game. It can be linear and predetermined (closed) or branched and emergent (open).
- **Aesthetics**: this has to do with the appearance, sounds, smells, tastes and sensations of the game. Aesthetics is an extremely important aspect of game design as it has the most direct relationship to a player's experience.
- **Technology**: We are not referring exclusively to "sophisticated" technology here, but to any materials and interactions that make the game, such as paper and pencil, plastic parts or high power lasers possible.

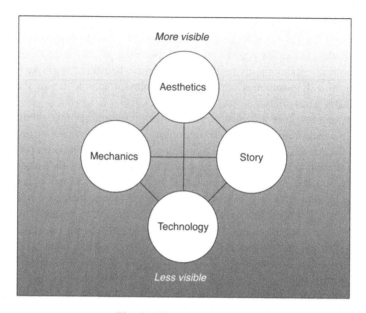

Fig. 1. Elements of games.

For Gameotics proposal, all elements above will be used, except Technology, as it is the base for building other ones in the games.

3 Semiotics

The Gameotics structure identified and conceptualized was based on the Normative Sciences of Charles S. Pierce, and later deployed in dichotomous actions. The Normative Sciences of Peirce defines:

- **Aesthetics**: what constitutes the admirability of an ideal (…), what would be sought under any circumstances.
- **Ethics**: The logic of how we should think must be an application of the doctrine of what we deliberately choose to do.
- **Semiotics**: deals with the inferences and arguments we are prepared to approve [4].

Drawing on the logical or semiotic philosophy of Charles Sanders Peirce, Santaella [5] seeks answers to the challenges posed by reality, believes that there are specific logical and cognitive roots that determine the construction of verbal, visual, sonic and all the variety of signs processes that they generate, reinforcing that such roots are much deeper and latent than the surface of channels and messages can lead us to perceive. Such matrices remain as the basis of language and human interaction from the earliest times with its materialization in stones and papyri up to the present day traveling global digital media in the most diverse devices imaginable.

Semiotics can be defined as "a general, formal and abstract theory of research methods used in the most varied sciences" [4]. The most current formulation of semiotics refers to science concerned with investigating and understanding signs, signification, and communication. This science is based on phenomenology, that is, on the investigation of "the ways in which we apprehend anything that appears to our mind" [4]. This same basis is shared by aesthetics, ethics, and logic. Peirce's main concern was with the basis of scientific thought and truth. Because he understands that no reasoning can be constructed in a purely symbolic way, without signs, he deepened his researches by creating a general theory of signification. This general theory is divided into three branches:

- **Speculative grammar**: "study of all types of signs and forms of thought they represent" [4].
- **Critical logic**: based on species of a sign, studies the types of reasoning that each supports or structure (abduction, induction, deduction).
- **Speculative rhetoric** (or methodology): from the forms of critical logic, studies methods based on different types of reasoning.

Our focus will be on the first of these branches, the speculative grammar, which can be understood as the in-depth study of signs. What is a sign? "(…) the sign is anything of any kind (a word, a book, a library, etc.) that represents something else, called the object of the sign, and which produces an interpretive effect on a mind real or potential, which is called the interpretant of the sign" [4]. Pierce categorized the signs and thinking in three main categories:

- **Firstness/First/Quality/Icon**: it maintains a relation of sensorial or emotional proximity between the sign, the representation of the object and the dynamic object itself.
- **Secondness/Secundity/Reaction/Index**: it has the physical connection with its object, as, for example, a footprint is a "clue" of who passed.
- **Thirdness/Representation/Symbol**: it is a law; in relation to its object and sign, is a symbol, a social convention.

4 Gameotics Proposal

Considering the three elements of games described at item 2 about Games and the three main categories described at item 3 about Semiotics, Gameotics proposes a view crossing these six components, as shown below:

1. **Aesthetics:** Icons, Indexes, Symbols.
2. **Mechanics:** Icons, Indexes, Symbols.
3. **Story:** Icons, Indexes, Symbols.

These dimensions can still be restructured allowing another perspective of the relations, being it necessary for the researcher to identify the organization most suitable for its purposes, as follows:

1. **Icons**: Aesthetics, Mechanics, Story.
2. **Indexes**: Aesthetics, Mechanics, Story.
3. **Symbols**: Aesthetics, Mechanics, Story.

The cross-analysis of these elements allows the different semiotic characteristics to be differentiated in their dimensions. Through the vision of the various aspects and their relations, both the player and the researcher of the game will be able to identify the intrinsic or emergent siginifcações by their relations.

5   Case Studies

To verify and validate the Gameotics proposal, the analysis will be applied in two different games as case studies, being one analog (Chess) and another digital (SimCity 2000). To exemplify the different proposed structures the first game will start from the elements of the game to the semiotics, while the second will start from semiotics to the elements of the game.

5.1   Analogic Gameotics Case Study: Chess

1. **Aesthetics**
   1.1. **Icons**: the pieces have similarity with the object that they represent, like Tower, Horse, Queen, and King.
   1.2. **Indexes**: the board has a physical connection with a war terrain, as the pieces fight for territory during the play.
   1.3. **Symbols**: the pieces format and sizes, as the board size, are based on world conventions.
2. **Mechanics**
   2.1. **Icons**: the pieces move in a similar way to what they represent, like the Horse who can jump pieces or the linear movement of the Tower.
   2.2. **Indexes**: when a piece is captured, it leaves the board representing that it is dead or out of the "war" (game) for a while.
   2.3. **Symbols**: the pieces moves and the win/loss criteria are based on world conventions.
3. **Story**
   3.1. **Icons**: the game represents two armies battling, using different types of fighters.
   3.2. **Indexes**: check situations oblige opponent to review their strategy.
   3.3. **Symbols**: the game story can be told by the conventional numbered board positions and pieces movements (Fig. 2).

5.2   Digital Gameotics Case Study: SimCity 2000

1. **Icons**
   1.1. **Aesthetics**: all the buildings, terrains and other constructions have similarity with the objects that they represent.
   1.2. **Mechanics**: the game is an city simulation, recreating situations that occur in real life.
   1.3. **Story**: real-life city stories can be part of the learning process to play the game effectively.

Fig. 2. Chess board game and pieces.

2. Indexes

2.1. **Aesthetics**: sub terrain game objects are represented to allow the gamer note and interact with.

2.2. **Mechanics**: the game user interface shows important city data to the gamer.

2.3. **Story**: gamers can create their own story by playing the game.

3. Symbols

3.1. **Aesthetics**: visual information in the interface follows interaction design conventions, like icons, pointers, windows, and menus.

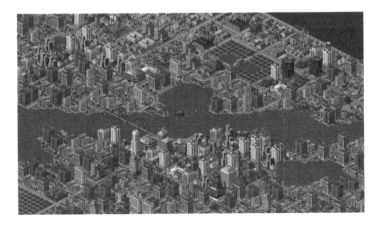

Fig. 3. SimCity 2000. EA games

3.2. **Mechanics**: the interface action buttons allow direct interaction in the game mechanics.

3.3. **Story**: SimCity 2000 gamers and non-gamers can understand the story created as the simulation follows social conventions (Fig. 3).

6 Conclusions

This paper presents an overview of two different disciplines that integrate in an articulated way creating the Gameotics concept. Initially, it was presented the definition of games, its relation with the player, culture and society. We have described the main elements of the games (aesthetics, mechanics and story), and how they relate to form a complex and meaningful interactive system. It was also presented the concept of Semiotics and its significant triad, starting from the points in common with represented objects, passing through clues of the representation and finally arriving at the meanings defined by conventions.

The objective of articulating such disciplines is to offer game researchers a perspective of double-dimensional analysis. For this, the dimensions of the games were considered in relation to the levels of signification offered by Semiotics. In this sense, two perspectives were presented. One starting from the dimensions of the game to its meanings and another starting from the meanings to the dimensions of the game. It will be up to the researcher to evaluate the perspective most appropriate for the purpose that seeks to achieve the meanings of the game.

Two Case Studies were used to represent the different perspectives of analysis, one using an analog game and another a digital game. Thus it was possible to verify that the semiotic analysis of a game is independent of the technology used since it is focused on the meaning of game design. In this way, it was possible to demonstrate the applicability of the proposed method, in a flexible and simple adoption. Detailed analyses of the significance of the games can be made while maintaining the proposed Gameotics structures articulating elements of game design with levels of significance of semiotics.

References

1. Huizinga, J.: Homo Ludens. Taylor & Francis, London (2003)
2. Nöth, W.: Handbook of Semiotics. Indiana University Press, Bloomington (1995)
3. Rogers, S.: Level Up! The Guide to Great Video Game Design. Wiley, Hoboken (2014)
4. Santaella, L.: Matrizes da linguagem e pensamento: sonora, visual, verbal: aplicações na hipermídia. Editora Iluminuras Ltda, São Paulo (2001)
5. Santaella, L., Feitoza, M.: Mapa do Jogo. Cengage CTP, São Paulo (2008)
6. Schell, J.: The Art of Game Design: A Book of Lenses, 2nd edn. CRC Press, Boca Raton (2015)
7. McGonigal, J.: Reality is Broken. MIT Press, Cambridge (2012)
8. Martinho, C., et al.: Design e Desenvolvimento de Jogos. FCA, London (2014)
9. Zimmerman, E.: Rules of Play. MIT Press, Cambridge (2003)

Art as a Living Interface

Peter Beyls[(⊠)]

The School of Arts, University College Ghent,
Jozef Kluyskensstraat, 2, 9000 Ghent, Belgium
peter.beyls@hogent.be

Abstract. Serving a concise characterization of interactive systems in the context of aesthetics-motivated interaction, we suggest a chart containing relevant keywords. We consider the nature of responsive systems providing predictable reactive responses vs. truly interactive systems offering unpredictable but coherent life-like behavior, underpinned by the notion of *a living interface*. A wider context is developed to appreciate various styles of interaction in contemporary art. Two case studies describe the implementation of the author's ideas. Initially, the pioneering work of Pask and Ihnatowicz is disclosed as exemplary and utterly significant for today's practice.

Keywords: Interactive systems · Aesthetics of interaction ·
Symbiotic interaction · Data-driven interaction

1 Introduction

This paper first aims to identify a number of keywords towards a clear understanding of the notion of 'interaction' in the global context of contemporary art. A categorization of interactive systems follows based on the type of emergent relationships afforded by specific orientations. A reference chart is developed showing features of interactive systems; from instrumental responsive systems to systems displaying unpredictable yet coherent life-like behavior. Finally, two of the author's audiovisual installations document the connection between artistic vision and effective material instantiation. However, first of all, we address the innovative work of two groundbreaking artists; Edward Ihnatowicz and Gordon Pask – the notion of a 'learning system' is implicit to the approach of both.

2 Two Pioneers

Ihnatowicz is best known for designing *The Senster* (early 1970's), a large computer driven robotic structure, probably the first one designed with behavioral rather than cosmetic objectives in mind. The machine had a repertoire of responsive behaviors in relation to what it was sensing in the environment i.e. capturing sounds and detecting people's movement. Ihnatowicz pioneered the notion of grounded cognition insisting the process of perception being informed by mechanical manipulation, the physical processes articulating the body being explicit to the emergence of meaning. In a 1977

© Springer Nature Switzerland AG 2019
A. Marcus and W. Wang (Eds.): HCII 2019, LNCS 11583, pp. 23–33, 2019.
https://doi.org/10.1007/978-3-030-23570-3_3

paper, pondering the challenge to design complex artificial systems, Ihnatowicz turns to nature suggesting: "it may help to treat the whole problem as an exercise in the simulation of evolution and try to design a system, although simple to begin with, could learn from experience…" (Ihnatowics 1977, p. 6) – however, the artist was ahead of his time, the scientific discipline of evolutionary computing would emerge about a decade later.

Gordon Pask pioneered a hybrid art integrating advanced engineering, early notions of artificial intelligence and human-machine interaction. For example, his 1968 piece *A Colloquy of Mobiles* consists of suspended electro-mechanical 'creatures' mutually communicating sound patterns and flashing lights outlining a socially oriented reactive and adaptive environment (Pask 1971). Human participants may interfere with the mobiles, complex behavior issues as the system includes adaptive sensing, memory, variable delays and various feedback loops – in other words "the machine is designed to entrain the performer and to couple him into the system" (Pask 1971, p. 80). Interestingly, mobiles were characterized as 'male' and 'female' and designed to be partially incompatible, required to communicate in order to co-operate while focusing on a common goal and finally, the biology-inspired notion of autonomous low-level action; mobiles are decoupled while still maintaining their individual integrity.

Both examples provide fascinating and compelling experiences since they establish an intimate link between artefact and viewer/participant through interfacing mechanical and bodily behavior. One projects a form of 'life' in the object – a strong affective experience follows from the appreciation of essentially simple machine activity – people project intelligence and life-like properties in inorganic artifacts. As a matter of fact, both Pask and Ihnatowicz implemented forms of adaptation and learning in their respective systems. For example, The Senster maintained a kind of dynamic sound-map documenting acoustic activity in space informing subsequent audio and spatial sensing.

3 Features of Interactive Systems

As artists, we take continuous inspiration from examples of fascinating (1) morphology and (2) behavior in natural, biological and social environments. What if we could identify the structural components leading to the complexity observed? It is quickly understood that interesting non-linear behavior issues from local interaction of minute building blocks leading to either global functionality or evolution towards a point attractor signaling global dysfunctionality: from blood cells in the immune system, to massive neuronal firing in the brain underpinning the notion of consciousness, to self-organization in ant societies, to a sudden revolution ending centralized decision-making and many other biological, social, and economic systems (Resnick 1997).

When considering the power of reciprocal interactions between distinct living species, symbiotic interaction becomes a vital force, quite often even the key to survival. Just one example: intimate symbiotic interactions develops between the sea anemone and the clown fish – the fish needs to hide and find protection from predators, it also eats algae while the anemone needs protection from competition with algae. Both entities mutually coexist in a functional relationship.

From this perspective, and in the light of implementing some observed aspects of interaction in natural/biological workspaces, let's frame a number of observations and opinions towards the accomplishment of truly interactive systems.

(1) Interaction is about exploring a particular space of options, including physical spaces explored through bodily engagement as well as conceptual spaces (often considered of infinite dimension) explored through speculative approaches. Exploration of unknown options is contrasted with viewing interaction as problem solving.

(2) Interaction implies the simultaneous activity of partners engaging in mutual action, coexisting in a common biotope, be it physical, biological, cultural, social or any playground offering common resources, preferences or opportunities.

(3) In social workspaces, interaction is often about sharing speculative initiative in mutual understanding. Individual agents interact by contributing to a pool of options in continuous flux, the environment is modulated by the very act of sharing and participation. All participating actors (human or synthetic) are at equal levels of authority.

(4) Interaction is concerned with the discovery of initially hidden relationships in high-dimensional spaces. For example, affinities between the components of an interactive audiovisual installation (logic, sensors, mapping...) might be obscure at first and inform the act of anticipation. Then, balancing perception and prediction becomes a dynamic process highly impacting the nature and depth of the aesthetic experience.

(5) In biological – including human-centered – workspaces, the concept of motivation plays a crucial role in driving complex interaction processes. Therefore, it makes sense to develop intrinsically motivation driven interactive systems. Such systems are prime examples of a methodology referred to as *speculative computing*. For example, a program develops sounds or images and tracks the complexity of the user's response aiming to figure out whether the user agrees or disagrees with the system's suggestion. An experimental platform for interactive composing integrating artificial motivations and machine learning is documented in Beyls (2017).

(6) Interactive systems should accommodate unpredictable input (on purpose or accidental) and offer non-linear behavior. In addition, while facing extreme conditions (in terms of internal logic or external conditions) the system should not break down but support graceful degradation in performance.

(7) Interactive systems should not merely offer procedural performance but dynamic behavior. Such systems are driven by positive feedback, change entails additional change, potentially steering the system into complex chaotic behavior – the human (inter)actor again engages in a predictive process balancing cause, effect and fluctuating levels of complexity.

(8) Finally, the development of interactive/generative systems offering rich and compelling modes of experience and participation is an act of aesthetic introspection – some idea is implemented, and the system talks back to the programmer exposing unanticipated forms of behavior. The exploration-based method is indeed equally paramount in the development of new work. Therefore, in creating new work let's start from scratch and without prejudice – exceedingly

difficult given the conditioning complexity of the digital medium itself. Then, intuition, rather than logic, is a more unselfish adviser informing aesthetics-driven software development.

Observing the above considerations, we conclude interaction to issue from the discovery and management of *speculative relationships* in high-dimensional spaces.

A deep and outstanding form of interaction subsists when contact leads to permanent modification of the cognitive or material qualities of interacting entities. The 1991 work entitled "Untitled. Portrait if Ross in LA" by Felix Gonzales-Torres is a prime example (Mulder 2007). It consists of a pile of candies on a gallery floor, it weighs 175 lbs, the actual weight of Torres' lover before losing weight as a consequence of AIDS. A visitor is invited to eat a candy – an enduring and irrevocable trace is left in his/her metabolism. The work of art becomes a grounded experience; the memory of Ross lives on in the body of a participant. In this case, interaction is a one-to-one exchange, where interaction itself entails transformations in the work of art as well as the participant. Human and artefact develop a bond, a sort of relationship extending in multiple dimensions; spreading from the purely materialistic to the cognitive to the purely subconscious. The notion of *relationship* is key to the categorization and understanding of different types of human/machine interaction. Interactive art can be understood according to the affordance of relationships based on (1) the formation of intimacy, i.e. a person submits to manipulation by an object, or (2) the object embodies the person – a relationship of instrumental control (Fels 2000).

A communication-theoretical definition of interactivity equally considers the notion of relationship: "Part and parcel of a system is the notion of 'relationship'. Interactional systems then, shall be two or more communicants in the process of, or at the level of, defining the nature of their relationship (Littlejohn 1989). This definition stresses a form of reciprocal, mutual engagement informing action.

Gonzales-Torres' work clearly implies a relationship of the former type. However, a conversational interaction between object and human – consider a person writing and debugging a computer program – is understood as contemplation driven while the object equally embodies the person. Aesthetic experiences follow from (intermediate) results obtained, a process of flow (Csikszentmihalyi 2009) issues from variable, dynamic associations between human input and continuous machine feedback.

Now think of someone playing the piano, not just open ended – to get the picture, consider Cecil Taylor in concert. A perception of deep connectivity between instrument and musician becomes readily apparent; Taylor embodies the instrument. An intimate relationship develops, and the aesthetic and emotional experience follows from controlling the piano. So, in contrast to contemplation, we share the excitement by imagining of engaging in physical action echoing the musician at work, especially considering the role of expression to convey a musical message.

What happens if we interact with static objects? Consider Rothko Chapel in Houston, TX. Rothko was convinced that paintings had the potential to provoke profound spiritual experiences (Rothko 2006). He claimed, "I paint big to be intimate", stressing the relationship between two forces: the emotional impact and corporal engagement of the viewer's body in relation to the canvas. The power of the aesthetic experience surely emerges as a complex dynamical process in both of these dimensions; the viewer continuously adapts through conceptual as well as physical adjustment. Again, aesthetic functionality follows from action rather than static observation. Engaging with a painting is a one-way interaction, the viewer absorbs signals from the object, however the object itself remains unchanged.

Another type of interaction happens in games; for example, people interacting collectively conditioned and constrained by a system of rules defining the game (Salen and Zimmerman 2004). Ironically, emotion and general excitement follows from submission to the objective options implicit to the game or even the constraints characteristic to the interface. Simple game strategies equally perform in exchanges between people; consider Japanese sumo wrestling, both players contribute momentum and energy until someone steps outside the circle – a complex dynamic process with mutual push-pull interaction terminating in a point attractor. An onlooker develops excitement by tracking performance over time (the expression of a relationship informed by competition) and through the active prediction of an imagined winner.

Finally, we may think of a human-machine *relationship* as the actual specification of information drift between both parties and their interpretation strategies. A computational architecture supporting unbiased human-machine interaction in the context of non-idiomatic musical improvisation implements relationships and autonomous machine motivations as actual computational components (Beyls 2018). In short, relationship objects are non-linear maps linking various momentary features of human musical input. Motivation objects are binary vectors specifying dynamic associations between relationship outputs and two competing motivations: (1) integration: connect to musical material suggested by the human performer) or (2) expression: perform in isolation from the context. An algorithm tracks melodic distance between consecutive statements by man and machine, thereby evaluating the efficiency of currently dominating motivation – effectively implementing a form of reinforcement learning. However, further technical details are beyond the scope of this paper.

4   Towards a Living Interface

We designed a map targeting the identification of a wide-ranging collection of keywords supporting a comparative study of interactive systems. Our map basically situates responsive systems on the left-hand side and systems offering life-like behavior on the right-hand side. Various features (appearing as labels on the map) are spread out in between, their horizontal position being proportional to their conceptual distance to both extremes (Fig. 1). In essence, while reading from left to right, the notion of 'interface' gradually changes meaning: from supporting explicit control to accommodating implicit behavior.

Let's consider systems complexity while browsing the map from left to right. The notion of predictability of system response is crucial in evaluating the functionality of interactive systems. For instance, a musician might expect total instrumental control and a tight relationship between instrumental gesture and sounding result. Responsive systems provide reactive behavior, they react by triggering a response usually selected from a palette of hardwired responsive options. The net result is a type of designed

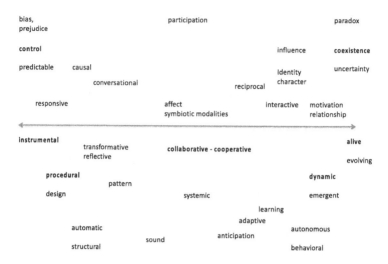

Fig. 1. From responsive to life-like interactive systems

procedural automation, responses are typically both highly constrained and fit a predictable, premeditated behavioral niche.

Conversational systems follow a linguistic paradigm, interactive composing (Bresson and Chadabe 2017) offers many examples; human and machine intermittently contribute musical arguments to a common, evolving social musical fabric, echoing musical fragments, however without exact repetition. This is conceptually close to the notion of 'reflective systems' where one conceives of the computer as a kind of qualitative mirror imitating, transforming and reflecting user actions in an augmented audiovisual language. Instrumental control still persists since perception of a clear causal link between action and reaction remains apparent. In other words: "The interactive artist must strike a balance between the interactor's sense of control, which enforces identification, and the richness of the responsive system's behaviour, which keep the system from becoming closed." (Rockeby 1996).

Playing an acoustic instrument entails interaction with a sounding body. A painting evolves from physical interaction with the mechanical properties of paint, canvas and brush. Once again, an intimate physical relationship between artist and medium totally defines the creative process. Richard Feynman explains the phenomenon to historian Charles Weiner:

> Weiner once remarked casually that [a batch of notes and sketches] represented "a record of [Feynman's] day-to-day work," and Feynman reacted sharply. "I actually did the work on the paper," he said. "Well," Weiner said, "the work was done in your head, but the record of it is still here." [Feynman's reply:] "No, it's not a record, not really, it's working. You have to work on paper and this is the paper. Okay?" (Clark 2013 p. 258).

Digital instruments offer sophisticated control structures for mapping physical activity to sounding algorithms, the performer embodies the instrument, actions inform sound and sound informs actions, man and machine coalesce into a dynamic superstructure. An excellent example is "The Hands" conceived by the late Dutch composer/performer Waisvisz (1985). Expressive instrumental abilities relate to the notion of affective interaction, the expression of emotion-driven intentions to create complex sounds in a wish to share the excitement with a receptive audience. The process is double: (1) a musician interactively navigates the expressive palette of the instrument (effectively a hybrid of hardware and software) and (2) the audience's listening process is dynamic: continuously balancing sonic expectations with perceived instrumental gestures.

The notion of expectation is equally central to the creative engagement model (Bilda et al. 2008) suggesting a strong relationship between the practice of interactive art and experience design in the research discipline of Human Computer Interaction (HCI). Engagement relates to human values in interaction such as pleasure, frustration, challenge and anger. A connection is suggested between the kind of interaction (intended vs. unintended actions) and the nature of the system's reaction i.e. causal, predictable feedback vs. uncertain, unexpected responses. Bilda's model identifies the psychological layers at play in the perception of interactive art – from adaptation and anticipation to deeper understanding of the dynamics of the work's internal relationships and receptiveness to external influence.

Then, from a more global perspective, we suggest the level of engagement, and therefore the strength of the aesthetic experience, to relate strongly to the dynamics of the anticipation process. Cognitive impact of a work of art follows from evaluating an immeasurable number of competing anticipations – typically, all potentially either implicitly or explicitly available in a complex interactive work of art. However, more universally, any artwork addresses the viewer's motivated engagement – it reveals itself through the complexity of anticipation, the flow between meaning and mystery. We conclude art to exist as a "qualitative oscillator".

5 Case Studies

Much of my work involves humans interacting with virtual creatures organized as self-organizing distributed agencies. One recent audiovisual installation, entitled *Crickets*, suggests a form of symbiotic interaction where humans and creatures coexist in a common biotope. Creatures appreciate the complexity of human input (seen through a camera and computer vision), the quantity (how much external energy is perceived) and quality (the complexity) of gestural activity. In other words, Crickets acts as a dynamic boundary – a living interface – creating a hybrid of organic and synthetic life. Aesthetic survival of both components is interdependent; artificial creatures anticipate delivery of human energy and humans expect complex and interesting behavior in return – human and machine engage in a non-trivial relationship. From the science of complex dynamical systems, we know positive feedback potentially pushes global behavior into a chaotic attractor leading to unexpected, momentarily peaking complexity (Fig. 2).

Crickets implements a simple particle system. Particles within a range of social proximity coalesce into spatiotemporal superstructures envisioned as dynamic creatures. Particles dissipate energy while moving in 2D space and engage in awake/sleep cycles according to energy level. A nascent connection between any two particles is

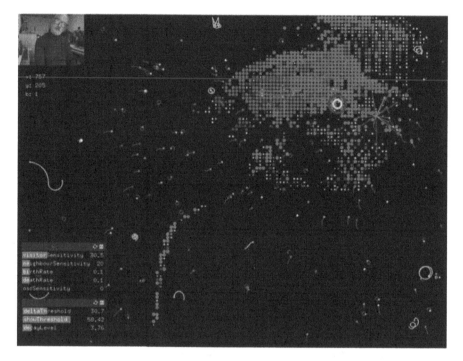

Fig. 2. Crickets (Color figure online)

reflected in a sound. A computer vision component creates an abstraction of the camera image: a low-resolution grid captures changes in pixel brightness to update grid cell values, incrementing or decrementing conditioned by a given parametric inertia. The grid acts as a slowly fading image memory, it is visualized by mapping the brightness value to a HSB color scale. An algorithm continuously computes the centroid of change of camera image – when sufficiently apparent, particles are attracted and move towards the centroid. The particle world features a specific non-binary gender system (5 options); when within the centroid zone, particles reproduce as a function of their energy and conditioned by a reproduction table – a 5 by 5 matrix enumerating reproduction probabilities. As a result, the particle population remains dynamic since positively influenced by human activity and limited by a given maximum capacity. The interplay of countless distributed internal forces and unconditioned external input affords a compelling audiovisual experience. A particular, non-inclusive cognitive link between action and reaction becomes apparent, however, the perception of fractional unidentified activity remains since particle world behavior is dynamic rather than merely procedural.

A second example is *Dusk*, a real-time web-driven audiovisual installation. Dusk extracts data from changes in external real-world events detected by online web cameras; this signal is normalized and used to condition social interaction in a particle world. Consequently, live data in a physical universe is relayed to condition interaction in a virtual abstract world. The subject of Dusk is the cyclic activity (the rhythm of timed trajectories of boats, the cycle of night and day...) in the harbor of Amsterdam.

A global brightness interval 256-element vector is computed from the signed values (−255 to 255) of the difference of very pixel in two consecutive camera images. Thus, for every potential brightness value (0 ∼ 255), the sum of all occurrences of that value in both images is collected and subtracted − a single signed value results and is added to the vector. Note the grey-scale visualization of the interval image for both cameras in Fig. 3. Finally, the vector is reorganized as a 16 by 16 two-dimensional array, the array is visualized in red (positive values) and green (negative values). The array is updated as soon as a webcam provides a fresh live image.

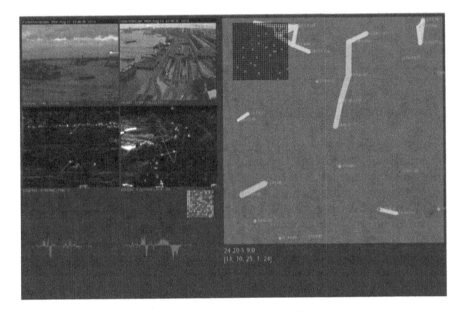

Fig. 3. Dusk (Color figure online)

Now, the array specifies how any two particles interact in their 2D world; when within a given (parametric) sensitivity range, a particle temporarily links to its neighbor (visualized by a green line segment) and addresses a single cell in the array using both particles' ID as an index pointer. Formally, particle interaction is specified as follows:

$$Particle\ system = \{M, R, A\}$$
$$A = S = array_{(12,12)}$$
$$M = \{m_1 \ldots m_8\}$$
$$a_m \in \{0 \ldots 11\}$$
$$D_{(m_1, m_2)} < S_{(am_1, am_2)} \Rightarrow (a_m \leftarrow R_{(am_1, am_2)}, a_{m_2} \leftarrow R_{(am_2, am_1)})$$

Algorithm A is equivalent to S, a sensitivity matrix; it holds numerical values expressing a threshold for interaction between any two types of particles to take place.

The system contains 16 particles stated by M with particles moving in a direction defined by their momentary angle. The state space of angles is discrete with a resolution of 30°, therefore relative angles range between 0 and 11 to cover full circle. Note that angle resolution has a strong impact on the scope of temporal complexity of the system as a whole; higher resolution will expand the state space exponentially.

Interaction rules R are described explicitly as regular 12 by 12 element arrays. The angles of interacting particles receive specific interpretation. Both angles are interpreted as to index locations in the array – to retrieve the new values of both respective angles. The array is a simple and compact way to represent and condition how particles potentially interact. Global state space of all possible matrix rules is huge[1] and thus considered virtually infinite. The effect of the rule array is qualitative control over collisions. Both particles update their respective angle when interaction becomes effective, i.e. when their physical distance is less than their mutual interaction threshold defined by array S.

6 Discussion and Conclusion

This paper suggests a feature map to study and evaluate various approaches to interactive art, starting from two poles: responsive and life-like systems. Relevant qualities are organized and labeled in between. Some artists expect a totally deterministic mapping scheme between user actions and systems' response, for example, while playing a computer-based musical instrument. Others prefer to participate, to express influence over an otherwise autonomous self-organizing system. From our experience, when initially confronted with a complex system like Crickets, many museum goers spontaneously engage in a responsive interaction format i.e. creating bodily gestures in a wish to activate the system and hope for immediate substantial audiovisual feedback. While the actual system demonstrates complex evolving audiovisual output, many people do not initially develop a spontaneous cognitive link in a wish to interrelate with unpredictable yet coherent life-like systems' behavior. However, while gradually adapting and developing an understanding of systems' generative logic and perception modalities, users shift from an instrumental/reactive format into a more participation-oriented format.

Interactive art systems provide a playground for experimental evaluation of how individuals develop sensitivities and understanding of artistic statements in general. We consider the intensity of the aesthetic experience to relate to the dynamics of the appreciation process, insight/resonance is not understood as a process of static perception. Embodied interaction offers methodologies and pragmatic technology to develop knowledge of the cognitive processes underpinning deep forms of human-machine interaction. Generally speaking, the manifestation of art can be viewed as an emergent property of a grounded complex dynamical system; a global meaning emerges from local interactions between an infinite number of components. Art exists as a floating network spanning in an unknown number of dimensions in time and space.

---

[1] 12 to the power 144 is a 156-digit number.

References

Beyls, P.: Intimate machine interaction; an illustrated definition. Vis. Comput. **2**, 152–158 (1990)

Beyls, P.: Motivated learning in human machine improvisation. In: NIME2018 Conference Proceedings, Virginia Polytechnic Institute and State University, Blacksburg (2018)

Beyls, P.: Improvisation as speculative computing. In: Proceedings of the Improvisational Creativity Workshop, Prato. ICW2017. Monash University (2017)

Bresson, J., Chadabe, J.: Interactive composition: new steps in computer music research. J. New Music Res. **46**(1), 1–2 (2017)

Bilda, Z., Edmonds, E., Candy, L.: Designing for creative engagement. Des. Stud. **29**(6), 525–540 (2008)

Clark, A.: Gesture as thought? In: The Hand, an Organ of the Mind; What the Manual Tells the Mental, pp. 255–268. MIT Press, Cambridge (2013)

Csikszentmihalyi, M.: Creativity: Flow and the Psychology of Discovery and Invention. Harper Perennial Modern Classics, New York (2009)

Edmonds, E.: The art of interaction. Digit. Creat. **21**(4), 257–264 (2010)

Fels, S.: Intimacy and embodiment: implications for art and technology. In: Proceedings of the ACM Workshops on Multimedia, pp. 13–16 (2000)

Ihnatowicz, E.: Page 38. In: On the Relevance of Mechanical Manipulation to the Process of Perception, pp. 6–7. Bulletin of the Computer Arts Society, London (1977)

Littlejohn, S.W.: Theories of Human Communication, 3rd edn, p. 175. Wadsworth Publishing Company, Belmont (1989)

Mulder, A.: Interact or Die. Dutch Electronic Art Festival, Rotterdam. V2 Publishing/NAI Publishers (2007)

Pask, G.: A comment, a case history and a plan. In: Reichardt, J. (ed.) Cybernetics, Art and Ideas. New York Graphic Society Books, Norwalk (1971)

Resnick, M.: Turtles Termites and Traffic Jams. Explorations in Massively Parallel Microworlds. MIT Press, Cambridge (1997)

Rockeby, D.: Transforming mirrors: subjectivity and control in interactive media. In: Penny, S. (ed.) Critical Issues in Interactive Media. SUNY Press, Albany (1996)

Rothko, M.: The Artist's Reality: Philosophies of Art. Yale University Press, New Haven (2006)

Salen, K., Zimmerman, E.: Rules of Play. MIT Press, Cambridge (2004)

Savasta, D.: Collocated gaming: analysis of social relations in gaming through interaction ecologies. In: xCoax Proceedings (2016)

Waisvisz, M.: The hands. A set of remote MIDI controllers. In: Proceedings of the ICMC, Burnaby, BC (1985)

New Requirements for User Experience on Non-legacy Contemporary Design of Traditional Handicraft Skills

Yu Chen$^{(\boxtimes)}$

University of Jinan, No. 336, West Road of Nan Xinzhuang,
Jinan 250022, Shandong, China
chyu_@163.com

Abstract. In this paper, we will study the non-legacy of typical Chinese traditional hand crafts, study the current development of practice, emphasize the user experience and living inheritance, study the relationship between user experience and contemporary design and the impact on contemporary design and cultural heritage. Through various user experience methods, excavating modern people's cultural psychological appeal and consumer psychology, and putting forward new requirements for the non-legacy contemporary design through user experience research. Therefore, the user experience has a strong research value and practical significance to the new requirements of the modern design of traditional handmade arts. It will have a direct and far-reaching impact on the inheritance and development of the heritage of the culture.

Keywords: User experience · Handcraft extract · Contemporary design

1 Introduction

Intangible cultural Heritage is a valuable cultural property and spiritual treasure of the country and nation, the crystallization of national wisdom and an excellent representative of national traditional culture. Today, with the cultural integration of today's world, maintaining the uniqueness, freshness and difference of national culture is a remarkable feature of a country's ethnic culture, therefore, actively demonstrating the unique charm of national culture, and mutual learning and reference is a manifestation of the world towards cultural pluralism. As General Secretary Xi Jinping pointed out: "To improve the soft power of the country's culture, we should strive to show the unique charm of Chinese culture." "Rather than the material cultural heritage, is concentrating on the essence of Chinese culture, showing the spirit and charm of national culture, therefore, in the future social development to study how to strengthen the intangible cultural heritage of contemporary design and heritage innovation is particularly important."

A. Marcus and W. Wang (Eds.): HCII 2019, LNCS 11583, pp. 34–46, 2019.
https://doi.org/10.1007/978-3-030-23570-3_4

2 The Current Development Status of Traditional Handicraft and Non-legacy in China

In recent years, due to the importance attached by the State to the protection and development of the non-heritage, more and more people have been involved in the protection and inheritance of the non-heritage, and many non-legacy projects have been protected and supported by various aspects, such as government funding and publicity for non Some corresponding development ideas and strategies are put forward, especially for the handicraft technology put forward the strategy of production protection and branding development. Although the non-legacy in the present can be better development, but there are still many shortcomings, in the development process encountered bottlenecks, not timely solution will affect its next step in the sustainable development of the problem. Taking the traditional blue calico technique and tie-dyeing technology as an example: the traditional blue calico technology and tie-dyeing technology are the important representatives of China's intangible cultural heritage, which can be developed and produced by the related products, so as to realize the industrialization and brand management, so as to enhance the connotation and value of its culture, and spread and popularize it widely. So that it is better integrated into contemporary life. As an ancient traditional handmade printing and dyeing technology, blue calico through this traditional handicraft technology finally formed a unique artistic style of material carrier form, was applied in life. It originated in the Song Dynasty Jia ding years, because of its convenience to obtain materials and simple technology, easy to operate and become the ordinary people's favorite printing and dyeing products, the use of the region also spread from Jiangnan to the whole country, mainly affected to China's Zhejiang, Shandong, Anhui, Hunan, Hubei and other places, and gradually formed their own unique regional characteristics and style (Fig. 1).

In view of the development of traditional blue calico technology in China, the overall development is good, but in the development process also encountered some problems, not very good integration into contemporary life, especially in its contemporary design and application did not better play the role of contemporary design, the main problems include: lack of heritage and innovative design of senior talent participation, the user experience is not prominent in the design, life integration is not widely used, cultural publicity and promotion is not enough.

In view of the current inheritance and development problems faced by traditional handicraft skills, we should adjust and explore the strategies suitable for their development in time, the emphasis should be on their contemporary design and life integration research, especially should pay attention to and study the research on user experience, through the user experience research can design excellent suitable for contemporary products, In order to promote the traditional handicraft technology benign and continuous inheritance and development.

Fig. 1. Traditional blue cloth with design in white (Color figure online)

3 The Value and Significance of Studying User Experience for Non-legacy Contemporary Design of Traditional Craftsmanship

User experience as a design concept, as early as the early days of the century by the international famous psychologist, designer, Professor Donald · proposed by Dr. A Norman. User Experience is a concentrated embodiment of the human-oriented design concept. The standards developed by the International Organization for Standardization define the user experience as "people's Cognitive impressions and responses to products, systems or services that are used or expected to be used." That is, the user's full feelings before, during and after the use of a product or system, including emotions, beliefs, preferences, cognitive impressions, physical and psychological reactions, behaviors, and achievements. The user experience is dynamic, environmentally dependent and subjective.[1]

About the traditional manual skills in today's development of the bottleneck of the current situation, how to combine with contemporary design, how to better integrate into the life of modern people, the author believes that it is really necessary to deeply study users, research user experience, only through the user experience to truly understand the user's inner and emotional needs in order to better design and innovation, Then the traditional skills can be attracted and involved, and its related derivative products can be truly integrated into modern life, so the study of user

---

[1] Ding Yi, Guo Fu, Sun Fengliang, User Experience Research Summary at Home and Abroad, Industrial Engineering and Management, 2014, No. 4, pp. 92–97.

experience will have a high academic research value and practical guiding significance for the non-legacy of traditional handicraft skills.

4 A Probe into the New Requirements of the User Experience for the Contemporary Design of Traditional Handmade Craftsmanship

Under the contemporary social environment and aesthetic characteristics, the traditional handicraft class should want to better integrate and develop, need the user's participation, make use of the user experience design concept and method, in view of the traditional handicraft class non-legacy user re-research is very necessary, which opens up a new vision for the contemporary design of the traditional skill category, And it provides the theoretical basis and research direction for the innovation and application of product design, therefore, the user experience puts forward new requirements for the contemporary design of traditional craftsmanship.

4.1 The Consumption Population of Traditional Craft Non-legacy Related Derivatives is Classified and Studied

Traditional craftsmanship is the product of the past era, because of the underdeveloped technology at that time, people in order to meet the needs of life and the invention and use of the skills, can bring convenience to life, such as manual dyeing skills, pottery skills, etc., people dress from the original shame, cold protection function to the gradual pursuit of beauty, began to clothing from the rustic primary More from the nature of the plant to extract pigment for dyeing, and among the most common blue dyeing, especially the rare folk blue printed cloth, because the blue dyeing materials are easy to plant, such as Indigo, Malan, Song Blue and so on, picking the leaves of these plants to extract blue pigment dyeing, this traditional handicraft technology has been handed down for application to date, However, due to the development of the Times and aesthetic changes, most people are now indifferent to this skill, the current young people do not like these "outdated" old objects, therefore, in view of this phenomenon should re-examine and study the relationship between traditional skills and current users, user-centric research. Because the traditional technology is finally presented with the material carrier, that is, its related derivative products, if let its derivative products conform to the current people's use function and aesthetic function must first start from the user classification research, the Consumer Population Division and research, each kind of population to carry on the thorough detailed understanding and the research. For example, for the traditional skills of blue calico, through the craftsmanship of the production is dyed cloth or after the hollowed carving pattern anti-dyeing of the flower cloth, the formation of cloth and according to the use of life to make practical products, such as clothing, bags, table flags, tablecloth, curtain, tea mats, pillow, sofa cushions, computer bags and other supplies, Ancient traditional skills are designed to meet the needs of daily life and continue to develop to the present, but with the development of the times, most of these products can not conform to people's aesthetic, people's impression is earthy, outdated, old, especially the current young people are not much like, therefore, if not to explore change and innovation to adapt to the current society, Perhaps the ancient handicraft skills will not be able to be well passed on and developed, will slowly die out. Therefore, the product derivative strategy based on the traditional skills must be to study the user as the center, study and master the Psychology, personality, preferences, emotions and other aspects of users of different ages. Consumer users can be divided into several categories: children, adolescents, middle-aged, elderly and so on, according to the age division of the study, so that more close to the user, understand the user's habits, education level, hobbies, attention to fashion trends and so on. After the user research, the product can be designed and positioned, such as children's products can focus on toys and apparel products, such as children's small belly pocket, cloth toys, etc., the adult group is more inclined to decorate art or supplies, such as decorative hanging paintings, table flags, pillow, tea mats, clothing products, etc., while the elderly can follow a more traditional flavor, Instead of feeling out of date, they feel that the more traditional and practical they are, the better. Some of these products can be suitable for all ages, such as China's Nantong blue calico heirs Mr. Wu Yuan'wan and his family developed the Blue Calico Zodiac Doll series products and fish and other auspicious fabrics.

Products to blue Calico combined with red fabrics for design and production, cute shape, meaning auspicious, with a sense of decoration, with the Chinese people on the festival, zodiac cultural feelings, can unconsciously touch the heart of people's national culture warmth, can be said to be widely used, this is its use of the user experience in the emotional factors, product design is also relatively successful (Figs. 2 and 3).

Young people, is the focus of the group of users, they are exposed to new things, the most new trends of the group, love to play, have their own personality and preferences, for the traditional handicraft skills are relatively unfamiliar, so study their psychological characteristics, how to make traditional skills can not only arouse their interest, can also make derivative products get their love and resonance, which can be appropriate simplification of traditional skills, with hands-on experience activities to attract, through their own hands-on to create a gift of love to start, stimulate its desire to move the brain, through the experience of activities to understand the skills and culture, deepen the impression, The completion of their own products have a deeper value and significance, which is obviously the best way to experience the user, but also the spread of non-legacy culture and inheritance of an effective way, should be strongly advocated this way of user experience activities. Middle-aged users consumer groups began to attach importance to the quality of life, in addition to the product's practical function, artistic and environmental applicability requirements to improve, but also favored its experience activities brought about by the cultural and emotional psychological resonance and satisfaction, so this kind of people also attach importance to product quality and emotional experience, therefore, It must be carefully designed to develop products for this group of people.

The elderly group like nostalgia and antique objects, then for the traditional skills made by the product more like the original, simple, quaint, quality, there is a rustic flavor, at the same time to have the practicality of life, such as bags, covers, tablecloth, curtain, decorations and so on (Fig. 4).

Fig. 2. Blue Seal Pisces Ornament (Color figure online)

Fig. 3. Ceramic plate creative clock

Fig. 4. Blue dyeing and tie dyeing experience (Color figure online)

Fig. 5. Ceramic craft experience

Therefore, the study of user experience on the traditional manual skills of non-legacy contemporary design of the new requirements first of all, to study the relevant derivative products of various consumer groups, user-centered in-depth research, in the study of people based on product positioning, and then for different users of age characteristics, psychology, preferences and so on to design, Therefore, the user experience under the contemporary design should first be in-depth research on the user-based and center (Fig. 5).

4.2   The User Experience Focuses on Promoting the Needs of Modern People in Terms of Craftsmanship Experience, Cultural Experience, Emotional Experience, Creative Experience, Etc.

The traditional handicraft category is based on the handicraft technology, its core value is the handicraft technology, is also the traditional culture can inherit the essence of the continuation to this day, not only has the historical inheritance, but also has the cultural accumulation, how can the better pass on? The author believes that the traditional skills and contemporary life better integration, so that the general public, especially the younger generation, should be recognized and contact from an early age, gradually in all aspects of the imperceptible influence, such as museums to have, schools have traditional culture classroom, the community has culture and experience space, Industrial park has creative experience space, A variety of handmade workshop experience areas and so on. It is through various forms of experience activities, experience space will make valuable traditional skills better contact with the public, but also to produce better cultural promotion and dissemination. Today, there are more and more such forms, such as non-legacy lecture halls, creative Amoy, blue dyeing experience, wood painting production and so on, in this variety of forms to make the public more accessible to non-legacy traditional skills, which is an important way of user experience, in order to increase the desire to experience demand.

For example, such as tie-dyeing, blue calico, pottery and so on some of the masses of the strong foundation of non-heritage projects, should be in line with the current heritage and development of some of the problems to be solved, such as the aging of the craftsman, the extreme lack of young heirs, lack of innovative design personnel and other right medicine, the government can give it, its original more closed traditional family, the way of teacher can be changed to the public inheritance, for the masses to recruit the heirs. By the relevant departments to plan in an integrated manner, the public recruitment of apprentices, to achieve the purpose of skills inheritance and innovation. As schools, especially colleges and universities, will be the best place to choose the dissemination and inheritance, for those who love traditional culture and innovative sense of design talent, they will be intangible cultural heritage inheritance and dissemination of a strong crowd. Therefore, more and more non-legacy has entered the campus, through lectures, exhibitions, creative experience and other forms to integrate into the campus cultural atmosphere, through the students close contact and personal experience and learning skills, so that the skills of better in the younger generation to have an impact, in order to promote inheritance and dissemination, and to find and cultivate non-genetic innovation people, Find and realize opportunities for the spread of cultural heritage and the transmission of innovation to the non-legacy (Figs. 6, 7, and 8).

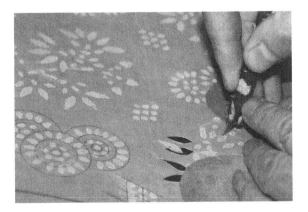

Fig. 6. Blue print engraving process (Color figure online)

Fig. 7. Blue printing cloth squeegee (Color figure online)

Fig. 8. Dyeing process

4.3 Decomposition of Traditional Skills, Simple and Easy to Operate, Stimulate People's Hands-On Desire

How to better integrate traditional skills into public life? Let the public have a desire to experience and learn from traditional skills, which requires a lot of thought in terms of craftsmanship, the original complex technology decomposition, simple and easy to operate, increase their own desire to do. Taking the traditional blue calico printing and dyeing technology as an example, its traditional craftsmanship is manual form, but its final appearance of the external material form of blue printed cloth, but shows the culture, art, aesthetics, function, folklore and many other characteristics, therefore, experience space and places can be diverse, such as entering the school, and the school's visual communication, product design, Cultural communication and other related professional integration for practical teaching experience. As our country blue

Calico inheritors Wu Yuanwan teacher said: "As long as the retention of core skills, such as manual engraving, manual scraping, manual printing and dyeing, manual scraping, manual drying and other These procedures unchanged, other can adapt to the times, in line with the mainstream culture to make changes." Adapt to this era, both national and modern works can be recognized by modern people, in order to be new, and constantly carry on. "Just because Wu Yuanwan recognized the importance of school education, he practiced it and brought blue Calico into the campus, through lectures, exhibitions, lectures, the establishment of institutional partnerships, the establishment of laboratories and other forms of blue calico non-legacy skills into the campus." Therefore, in view of the design of some institutions of higher learning, combined with the relevant design courses to properly integrate the manual skills of non-legacy projects into the classroom, so that students in the course of practice in the process of personal participation and experience of our national traditional culture, stimulate the creative thinking of young designers, driving college students This heritage of people, To create new works adapted to contemporary social life, but also to achieve a better inheritance and innovation of the non-legacy. The concrete implementation process can set up a special traditional manual skills and design courses, while emphasizing the traditional "craftsman spirit", break the traditional "teacher-student system" teaching mode, the use of professional compulsory, elective way, through formal classroom teaching, the application of modern technical means for teaching, popularize the traditional handicraft culture. In addition to entering the regular school popularization and guidance, but also to the social space, such as some handmade workshops, pottery bar and so on. In these experience space, the traditional craftsmanship and process steps should be decomposed, simplified, easy to operate the process, experience the environment has the traditional skills of the cultural atmosphere, consciously stimulate the desire to experience, their own work to create works. For example, tie-dyeing skills, blue calico skills, pottery skills, etc., the skills in accordance with the process of decomposition, simplification, such as tie-dyeing technology can be reduced to the following process: (1) Select the material or finished product to be tie-dyeing → (2) design pattern → (3) According to the design of stitching → (4) Soak in clear water → (5) into a modulated dyeing solution dyeing → (6) Squeeze the dye dry in the air to oxidize → (7) solid color flushing → (8) ventilation place to dry and so on. In this way, the decomposition of a few process steps, at a glance, even in the experience environment according to the process steps to mark, in order, with the relevant tools and equipment, the early preparation and arrangement so that the entire process is simplified, clear, easy to let the audience see just want to sit down to do a thing, stimulate the user to experience the desire. Therefore, this is also one of the new requirements of the user experience for the non-legacy design of traditional craftsmanship.

4.4   Enhance the Functional Experience and Application Environment Experience of the Product at the Consumer Terminal

Any product has its practical function and aesthetic function, etc., in order to better exist and continue, whether the traditional skills continue to be the product or modern science and technology products, if the old skills and products can not adapt to the needs of the current people's various functions, it is bound to gradually be eliminated, therefore, The contemporary design of traditional craft non-legacy products must conform to the present era, with the development of the Times to continue to innovate in order to better be recognized and accepted by the times, and naturally will continue to inherit and develop over time. Non-legacy products R & amp; D is through the early market research, market positioning, user research, product positioning and other work, the final product design innovation and development, from the shape, color, pattern, materials, functions, aesthetics and other angles, repeated consideration of the design plan, and through trial production, trial sales before the final decision to put on the market, Enter the consumer terminal for sale. Product Sales terminal can be a variety of forms of various places, but the most important should be a shop or experience store, in the shop is not only to let customers choose products, but also should be customers to experience products, experience its design, function, as well as the use of physical, psychological and emotional feelings in the process. So in addition to the product itself, for the terminal store is undoubtedly the environment created by the shop, such as shop design, color combination, display collocation, environmental atmosphere, etc., the product in a certain application environment, such as with the use of products in the United States home living environment, so that users into the design of the environment to feel the product in use of life scene, To achieve visual, tactile and psychological emotional resonance, so as to attract recognition and love of the product and create a desire to buy, and ultimately achieve product sales. Therefore, the user experience design of the function and application environment of the product terminal is one of the new requirements of the contemporary design of the traditional craft non-legacy products, which must be paid equal attention to in the product design (Figs. 9 and 10).

Fig. 9. Blue dyed derived household products (Color figure online)

Fig. 10. Blue dyed derivatives (Color figure online)

5   Concluding Remarks

Intangible cultural Heritage is the crystallization of the collective wisdom of the Chinese nation, protecting and inheriting intangible cultural heritage, carrying forward Chinese culture, promoting the prosperity of cultural undertakings and the development of cultural industries, enhancing the country's soft power and realizing the Chinese dream, we must strengthen cultural construction, at the same time, further promote the self-confidence, self-esteem and pride of our national culture Intangible cultural Heritage has "living state", its existence depends on human activities, and its development is in the never-ending changes of man and nature, history and reality. From the user experience, the establishment of intangible cultural heritage of various experience space and heritage base, the establishment of related intangible cultural heritage experience courses, conducive to the cultivation of intangible cultural heritage of a new generation, is conducive to enhancing young people's understanding of China's intangible cultural heritage, the unknown world and things full of curiosity of young people contact, When learning about Intangible cultural heritage, it will be attracted by their diverse culture, rich forms and intrinsic values, resulting in great national pride, thus producing positive cognition and learning of Intangible cultural heritage, in-depth exploration and the interest of inheriting intangible cultural heritage, and helping to arouse people's national consciousness and national identity, Strengthening national cohesion, helping to maintain the blood of the national culture of our country and maintaining the uniqueness of national culture, is conducive to maintaining the pluralism of our national culture and promoting the harmonious development of culture.[2]

---

[2] Han Pingyu and other parts. Inheriting innovation: Promoting the sustainable development of contemporary Chinese cultural construction [m]. Jinan: Jinan Press, 2014:10–26.

In recent years, the government and the Intangible cultural heritage of the relevant departments to work together to introduce intangible cultural heritage to the campus, museums, cultural halls and other cultural spaces, for the community, from the user experience to the contemporary design truly integrated into contemporary life, in the user experience of the living state of the practice way to get better attention, expansion, Research and development.

References

1. Xu, P., Wu, L.S.: Masters of Chinese Arts and Crafts: Wu Yuanxin. Jiangsu Fine Arts Publishing House, Nanjing (2014)
2. Wu, Y.X., Wu, L.S.: Gujiangyingranzhihun - Zhongguo lanyinhuabu. Heilongjiang People's Publishing House, Haerbin (2011)

Cyborg Maintenance: Design, Breakdown, and Inclusion

Joshua Earle[(⊠)]

Virginia Tech, Blacksburg, VA 24060, USA
jearle@vt.edu

Abstract. The lived experiences of common cyborgs are ignored by those who most wish to be cyborg. I push back against the utopic, teleological imaginaries of the Transhumanist movement using a daily concern for actual cyborgs: maintenance. Scholarly work on maintenance is sparse, relatively recent, and generally focused on infrastructure and large technological systems. I merge the work done on these large technological systems with the biopolitical work by disability studies scholars and activists. I show that the common narratives of innovation that insist that technology becomes faster, more efficient, and more durable over time are false, and how upkeep rather than upgrading will be the norm for cyborg bodies. I call for a more deliberate design ethos for producing more accessible maintenance as well. The interfaces between technology and the body are sites of significant breakdown as each degrades the other. Moisture, acidity, and healing processes make it difficult for technological systems to last long within the body, and the intrusion of foreign material into the human body triggers scarification, fibroses, infection, and systemic reactions. Disabled people regularly navigate these concerns, and their description of the sorts of work they do to keep up their techno-bodyminds does not match well with the transhumanist narrative. The concerns of cyborg maintenance need to be considered as technologists continue to produce technological interventions into our bodies, and disabled folks for whom such intervention is already a reality can tell us a lot about how that needs to happen.

Keywords: Cyborg maintenance · Disability · Design · Transhumanism · Breakdown · Care

"The cyborg is the engineer's dream. The engineer steers and manipulates the human to greater performance. As a common cyborg, I subvert that dream. I do not want to sell any of their shit for them. I am not impressed with their tech, which they call 3C98-3, and which I am wearing, a leg that whirs and clicks, a socket that will not fit unless I stay in the weight range of 100-105 pounds... The last one they gave me was a lemon. Maybe this feeling of trial-and-error, repetition and glitch, is part of the cyborg condition and, by extension, the disabled condition.

- Jillian Weise, "Common Cyborg"

© Springer Nature Switzerland AG 2019
A. Marcus and W. Wang (Eds.): HCII 2019, LNCS 11583, pp. 47–55, 2019.
https://doi.org/10.1007/978-3-030-23570-3_5

What is it like to be – to maintain and remain – a cyborg? In this paper I look at design and the lived experience of the cyborg bodymind[1] in order to contrast it with the expectations of those who most want to become cyborg. The theme of cyborg maintenance sits in opposition to simple and tidy futuristic visions. While every "what is it like" is unique and ultimately unknowable to others [27, 41], we need only listen to current cyborgs [28, 39, 40] to understand that the future cyborg imagined by engineers and transhumanists fails to appreciate the cyborg lived experience. In this paper, I investigate what it's like to inhabit (and continue to inhabit) a cyborg bodymind. I do this as well as a non-cyborg can. While I do rely on technology, just as everyone else does – I am lost (literally and figuratively) without my cell phone, I require clothing and housing and a car to live the life I do – I need no technological assistance which is implanted into, or strapped onto my body in the same way that someone with a pacemaker, or a prosthetic limb or wheelchair does. I don't even wear corrective lenses to see, though I expect that will be changing sooner rather than later.

There are different notions of what a cyborg is. Donna Haraway saw the cyborg as an ironic political myth that had no truck with patriarchy, binaries, boundaries, or beginnings [17]. Andy Clark maintains that we are all cyborgs and always have been, that one cannot be human without an intimate relationship with technology [6]. I have a fondness for both definitions as they appreciate the different ways in which we are entangled with the things we make, our social structures, and extensions of our will and ideation [10]. A lot of my work revolves around the notion that we are diffractively inseparable from our material-semiotic contexts, from our technology, and that we become different things in each of these contexts [2]. But, because we are (ontologically, epistemologically, and axiologically) different as contexts change, the context of being a cyborg has relevant situational nuances as well. As such, I take on a narrower definition of cyborg that Ashley Shew has expressed to me in conversation, and that is implicit in her work, as well as the work of Weise [39, 40], Garland-Thomson [15], and Johnson [20]. In this definition, a cyborg is one who needs an intimate connection to a technological artifact in order to go about normal, everyday, actions. These actions can be as mundane as moving between rooms, sleeping comfortably, or even breathing. The artifacts required must be either within the body, strapped to it, or carrying the body in some way. The function of the body itself, not just the body in social context, must be significantly affected by the technological artifact's presence or absence. The technological artifacts must become a part of the infrastructure of the cyborg bodymind. They disappear when working well, and become much more legible,[2] phenomenologically, upon breakdown [37].

---

[1] I use the term "bodymind" here in the tradition of feminist and disability theory which maintains that there is no separation between the body and mind as in traditional enlightenment philosophy.

[2] The legibility of the technological infrastructure of the cyborg body to those on the outside, and the various stigmas associated with those technologies (crutches get stigmatized differently than a motorized scooter, for instance) is of great import, but is beyond the scope of this paper. See: Garland-Thomson (2009), Nelson et al. (Forthcoming).

Thus I turn to disabled bodies, the bodies with ports and stents, with artificial knees and valves, on prosthetics and upon wheelchairs, on crutches and canes and walkers. I look at how they move through the world, and how the world pushes back. I consider how bodies and technologies are maintained, both separately and together, and how that maintenance is ignored by other, relevant groups who dream of cyborgs to come without acknowledging the cyborgs that are [39]. Capitalism, and an individualist bootstrappy society, further marginalizes the disabled cyborg body. I end with a call for greater acknowledgment of our inter- and intra-dependence, and a shift toward care rather than production and individual determination as guiding principles in our cyborg diffractions.

This project was inspired after being regaled with tales from my PhD advisor of her weeks-long adventure to fix a squeaky leg. These tales revealed the lengths to which one must go just to be able to live with a prosthetic leg. Multiple 5-8-h car trips to two different prosthetists in two different States. An appearance at an academic conference was cancelled. Who knows how much family disruption this caused, nevermind having to deal with an incessant squeak following one around, or how much money the entire saga cost (even with decent insurance). This tale, combined with the work done by another colleague of mine, historian of technology Vinsel [32], on maintenance and critiquing narratives of innovation, made me realize that the two issues – maintenance and disability – were not separate. They were of a piece. We maintain our bodies in much the same way we maintain our streets, via projects large and small. Central to maintenance, both toward our bodyminds and toward our infrastructure and technology, is care.

Maintenance is the epitome of care. Designing products in such a way that they can be easily maintained is an important part of such care. We become intimately familiar with the object or body for which we care and on which we perform maintenance. Our hands become covered in the viscera and excreta of the body, technological or biological, on which we work. We become emotionally attached to that which we maintain, and we value that which we maintain over the new or the innovative. We become attuned to the smells and sounds and looks of the bodies we maintain, we understand when they are wearing, when they are unhealthy, when they need more care, or less. To maintain a body is to be in an intimate relationship with it. The more maintenance is required, the more intimacy is also. This is true of objects and bodies both, one's own and another's. Maintenance, both of bodies and of things, constitutes most of human life with them [12, 32].

Because we have traditionally split care from maintenance – the first upkeep of biological subjects, the second upkeep of inanimate or technological objects – the parallels between the two aren't often discussed in the same breath. We socially coded maintenance and care differently, too. Maintenance is generally coded as a masculine pursuit. Your local auto mechanic, your plumber, your handyman,[3] your highway worker. These codes are not, of course, set in stone. You can often find one or two women on a construction site (rarely more than that). My own mother is a master plumber and flips houses as a hobby. My mother also said that she was one of only two

---

[3] Never "handywoman," which kind of sounds like a euphemism.

women (out of hundreds) at her master plumber certification classes. Care, on the other hand is generally coded feminine. Care is ongoing, done in negotiation with a patient, client, or family member, by someone who understands that fragility is a part of life, and someone who refuses to give up on anyone [26]. Nurses, midwives, doulas (for birth and death) [29], secretaries, cleaning services, and more fall under the umbrella of care work, and all are generally populated by women.

Both care and maintenance are culturally stigmatized for similar and dissimilar reasons. The first, which they share, is that the work is dirty. The physical taint of this work becomes social, and sometimes moral, taint [1, 9, 34, 36]. The second, which they also share, is that we consider the work to be for those of a lower socioeconomic class, those with less skill, or those with little to no official education. Care and maintenance are often described as "unskilled labor," even though nothing could be further from the truth. The "unskilled" label attempts to place maintenance and care work in the same socioeconomic category as retail, fast-food, and other parts of the service economy. Care and maintenance work doesn't pay as well as (some) other work, even in similar fields. Nurses, for instance, get paid far less than their doctor counterparts, regardless of their import to the health of patients or the amount of work that they do.

The sorts of embodied skills that care and maintenance require are broadly underappreciated in our socioeconomic system. Engineers who design things with CAD programs and via equations and drawings may look down on "makers" and "tinkers" who do exactly the same thing, but with hands and welding torches. Makers and tinkers are excluded from the category of engineer because they eschew the computerized or theorized way of doing business in favor of getting dirty. This gate-keeping may also be one reason that things are not often designed to be maintained, but rather force maintainers, makers, and tinkers to improvise and "hack" (i.e. get around the official design) the object in order to make it do what is needed. Tech companies actually resist any notion of making their products repairable, preferring forced obsolescence and a discard-and-buy-new society. Apple recently bemoaned that it spent billions of dollars more than expected on repairing iPhones, and many tech companies are spending millions on lobbying efforts to block right-to-repair bills in the European Union and the United States [4, 24].

Similarly, physically and emotionally caring for a person is substantively and phenomenologically different from diagnosing via charts or even repairing via surgery. In the former instance, one must engage on a personal level, touch more intimately; hear, smell, and taste more. These intimacies produce connections, understandings, and emotional closeness that is absent in the more cerebral and detached modes of inquiry. Care, in its ideal, requires you to love the person for whom you are caring.[4] Love is difficult… and stigmatized. Affection is considered a feminine pursuit, and is devalued broadly in our society. Men are often not given (or not allowed to obtain) the sorts of emotional tools which would allow them to step more easily into these care positions [5, 16]. Men are not taught how to love outside of romance and familial contexts.

---

[4] It should be noted that not all care-workers do love those for whom they care, and rates of abuse in supposed care environments, like nursing facilities and rehabs but also with in-home care, are not as uncommon as they ought to be.

Society tells men (particularly straight and cisgender men) that the love of friendship and the love of a care relationship should be foreign, frightening, and avoided: this is one facet of toxic masculinity [25].

At the other end of the relationship, dependency is also stigmatized as weakness and lack of value. When someone is in need of care, particularly if that need is ongoing, they become "moochers," "drains on our system," and part of the "welfare state," all said in sneering tones as if those who get categorized as such ought to just die. The echoes of the eugenic era rings in these narratives, and the valuation of people as capital production units reinforces this view. If only those who needed care could just bootstrap themselves into productivity wouldn't we all be better off? So, when we look at cyborgs – disabled people who need care and maintenance, who care for their own bodies, and maintain the technological infrastructure within and around their body – we end up with multiply-marginalized people. Marginalized for the care they require. Marginalized for the care they (must) give themselves. Marginalized for the dirty work of maintaining a cyborg bodymind. Marginalized for loving the disabled bodymind they inhabit. Marginalized for failing to be as productive a citizen as is considered proper. Marginalized even for fighting against stigmas and exclusions.

But the cyborg must not just maintain their bodymind (as we all do to one extent or another), they must also maintain the technological infrastructure which produces their cyborg-y-ness.[5] They must maintain their prosthetics, their wheelchair, their ports and stents, pacemakers and artificial valves. Each of these technologies experiences wear and tear. They bend and break and need to be bent back and put together, soldered, duct taped, super-glued, and sometimes discarded. They get dirty and need to be cleaned. Ports require flushing, artificial valves and joints require medication to avoid rejection and maintain functionality. Pacemakers require digital updates and replacement batteries.

Much of this labor of repair is done by the user, which probably has a family resemblance to the repair that a handy do-it-yourselfer might make on their house, property, or automobile. But the cyborg's expertise is gained through the necessity of their embodied situation rather than any hobbyist or professional interest (though they may have such interests as well, of course). A handy homeowner will not be prevented from going to work or out in the world if they put off replacing a missing bit of trim, but the same cannot be said for the cyborg who forgets to charge their electric wheelchair, or who fails to properly lubricate joints or sew frayed straps on their prosthetic. One must also have a suite of alternate modes of mobility for when one can't or won't use one's primary cyborg part. Crutches (forearm, always), walkers/rollators, wheelchairs, shower seats and grabby-arms, and all sorts of accoutrement which makes those secondary technologies work as well. Designing these technologies to be easily repaired, particularly by those who will be their most common users (i.e. not requiring individuals to travel a long way or spend a ton of money on specialist repair), should be a first-order consideration of engineers and designers.

For the maintenance that a cyborg cannot do themselves, a vast network of technicians and medical/engineering infrastructure is required. This network is often

---

[5] Technical term.

expensive to access and not available locally, requiring significant travel and the costs associated thereof. My PhD advisor, as I mentioned earlier, had to travel to multiple States just to fix a squeak. Because these are considered medical devices, one also needs a prescription in order to get a new one (this includes wheelchairs, strangely), and it may or may not be covered by one's medical insurance. Cost and insurance are not minor issues. Many disabled people, due to society's focus on capital and productivity, fall below median income levels, and are generally twice as likely to live in poverty as the nondisabled population [8, 21]. Prosthetic legs[6] range from $5000 for basic models, to well over $50,000 for ones with complex, computerized knees and ankles. Wheelchairs also have wide ranges in cost, from around $100-$800 for a manual, hospital-style wheelchair to many thousands for a custom manual chair or powered chair. With wheelchairs, of course, comes the requirement to install ramps in the home, install lifts into vehicles (or purchase vehicles with them), and rigs to get into and out of bed for those with more severe mobility limitations. All of this is expensive and needs maintenance, cleaning, and care.

Once one goes out into the world, one comes up against broken sidewalks, curbs, stairs, heavy doors, and other hostile architecture that makes it clear that the disabled are not welcome [28, 30]. These architectural barriers, in addition to the attitudinal barriers that cyborgs face, produce a being-in-the-world that is different from the nondisabled and the non-cyborg. These material-semiotic contexts necessarily alter the phenomenological experience of moving through the world. We learn and re-learn our embodied contexts throughout life, beginning from a young age [43]. Riffing on Merleau-Ponty, Vivian Sobchak describes the long process of getting to once again 'look where the goal is' and [then get her] 'bodily machine [to do] what must be done for me to get there' in an invisible, unthinking manner [35]. Cyborg existence and experience and movement can be beautiful, pleasurable, and even musical [17, 20, 28]. These existences, experiences, and movements are transmobile[7] and multistable [18, 30], and they are affectively different from the nondisabled way of being-in-the-world.

These contexts and barriers are factors not taken into account by the engineers who build our cyborg presents and futures, nor the transhumanists who want to take on a cyborg bodymind. Zoltan Istvan, former president of the Transhumanist Political Party and popular transhumanist author wrote about how since exoskeletons were going to be available soon, we shouldn't bother fixing sidewalks (19, see also in response: 13, 23, 33). Istvan's article ignores how difficult walking on a broken sidewalk in an exoskeleton might be, or the notion that those exoskeletons themselves might need

---

[6] Arms, counterintuitively, are actually less expensive ($3000 - $30,000). This is mainly because prosthetic arms are less about functional replacement, and more about fulfilling an aesthetic expectation. Because of the limited functional replacement, arm prostheses are less often covered under insurance plans for people who are missing just one, which can make the user's cost exceed that of a leg user.

[7] *Transmobility* (noun): (1) the ability to move between various modes of mobility; use of multiple mobility methods; (2) the ability to move beyond traditional forms of movement and mobility; (3) the existence of free and disabled bodies in motion. Word derived from the prefix 'trans-', meaning beyond, across, through, surpassing, transition, transport, or transcending + 'mobility,' meaning the ability to move or be moved freely. Antonym: Monomobile. Coined by Mallory Kay Nelson. Origins: her experience [28].

repair and upkeep, and that broken sidewalks might exacerbate that need. Also, traveling on broken sidewalks is unpleasant for anyone, not just those in wheelchairs. Failing to maintain our worldly infrastructure simply shifts the onus of maintenance onto individuals who now have to repair broken bicycles, wheelchairs, ankles, and even exoskeletons.

Transhumanists tend to describe cyborg technologies in the same terms as we do our cell phones, that the tech would be replaced upon obsolescence [6, 22] instead of repaired.[8] They also tend toward a very masculine, neoliberal, individualist ethic, which requires them to avoid any grouping of people into groups or demographics [11, 38]. These two beliefs come together to make nearly impossible to consider cyborg maintenance[9] as a part of cyborg being. As Transhumanists also want to end disability [3, 19], they tend to see the disabled body as broken, an object to be fixed, and the person as someone who should only ever be grateful for the interventions, not someone with whom to have an equal and collaborative relationship. By not engaging with cyborgs before producing the technology it is assumed cyborgs want, technologists risk not only producing a technology that will not be taken up, but that the lived experience of the cyborg remains invisible and unexamined. A cyborg could tell a technologist how to build a leg that's easier to maintain, that has the features they want, and that produces a better phenomenological lived experience. Care also runs counter to a lot of transhumanist ethos, since care requires a generous acceptance of interdependence, a dedication to shared values, and a belief in the validity and dignity of the disabled body.

So long as transhumanists and engineers fail to engage with the cyborg bodies that currently exist, or those people who most reasonably may become cyborg soon – in every phase of production, from planning to distribution – they will never produce the kind of cyborg future that they claim to want. Also, so long as transhumanists continue to ignore maintenance and care, advocating instead for a bootstrappy, individualist concept of responsibility, networks and communities which make a cyborg future worth wanting will be limited and insufficient. I end here with a call to transhumanists, engineers, and the rest of us, to take seriously the notion of care and cyborg maintenance. These concepts will help produce a more connected cyborg future, where our architectural context is welcoming of cyborg bodies, and where a wide variety of cyborg (and non-cyborg) bodyminds are valued and share in the pleasures and pains of lives worth living.

---

[8] The problem of externalities and waste from this particular mode of consumption is important, but beyond the scope of this paper.

[9] Among the exceptions is Aubrey de Gray's work on gerontology and turning aging into a chronic condition, able to be treated indefinitely (2007). *Ending Aging* is rife with mechanical, computational, and repair metaphors, with chapter titles such as "Engineering Rejuvenation," "Meltdown of the Cellular Power Plants," and "Upgrading the Biological Incinerators." That this particular wing of the transhumanist movement is particularly non-cyborg in their focus on "hacking" biology is relevant but beyond the scope of this paper.

References

1. Atanasoski, N., Vora, K.: Surrogate humanity: posthuman networks and the (racialized) obsolescence of labor. Catal. Fem. Theory Technosci. 1(1) (2015)
2. Barad, K.: Meeting the Universe Halfway: Quantum Physics and the Entanglement of Matter and Meaning. Duke University Press, Durham (2007)
3. Brashear, R.: Fixed: The Science/Fiction of Human Enhancement (2014)
4. Campbell, M.: Apple Replaced 11M iPhone Batteries Under 2018 Repair Program, 9M More Than Average. Apple Insider (2019). https://appleinsider.com/articles/19/01/15/apple-replaced-11m-iphone-batteries-under-2018-repair-program-9m-more-than-average. Accessed 29 Jan 2019
5. Chaplin, T.M., Cole, P.M., Zahn-Waxler, C.: Parental socialization of emotion expression: gender differences and relations to child adjustment. Emotion 5(1), 80–88 (2005)
6. Clark, A.: Natural-Born Cyborgs: Minds, Technologies, and the Future of Human Intelligence. Oxford University Press, Oxford (2004)
7. de Grey, A., Rae, M.: Ending Aging: The Rejuvenation Breakthroughs That Could Reverse Human Aging in Our Lifetime. St. Martin's Press, New York (2007)
8. DeNavas-Walt, C., Proctor, B.D.: U.S. Census Bureau, Current Population Reports. Income and Poverty in the United States: 2014, Washington, DC (2015)
9. Douglas, M.: Purity and Danger: An Analysis of Concepts of Pollution and Taboo. Taylor & Francis, Milton Park (1966)
10. Earle, J.: Deleting the instrument clause: technology as Praxis. Soc. Epistemol. Rev. Reply Collect. 7(10), 59–62 (2018)
11. Earle, J.: Engineering our selves: morphological freedom and the myth of multiplicity. In: Philosophy and Engineering: Reimagining Technology and Social Progress. Springer (Forthcoming)
12. Edgerton, D.: Shock of the Old: Technology and Global History Since 1900. Profile Books, London (2011)
13. Eveleth, R.: The Exoskeleton's Hidden Burden. The Atlantic (2015)
14. Garland-Thomson, R.: Extraordinary Bodies: Figuring Physical Disability in American Culture and Literature. Columbia University Press, New York (1997)
15. Garland-Thomson, R.: Staring: How We Look. Oxford University Press, Oxford (2009)
16. Guy, M.E., Newman, M.A.: Women's jobs, men's jobs: sex segregation and emotional labor. Public Adm. Rev. 64(3), 289–298 (2004)
17. Haraway, D.J.: Simians, Cyborgs, and Women: the Reinvention of Nature. Routledge, Abingdon (1991)
18. Ihde, D.: Experimental phenomenology: multistabilities. Suny Press, Albany (2012)
19. Istvan, Z.: In the Transhumanist Age, We Should Be Repairing Disabilities, Not Sidewalks. Motherboard (2015). https://motherboard.vice.com/en_us/article/4x3pdm/in-the-transhumanist-age-we-should-be-repairing-disabilities-not-sidewalks
20. Johnson, H.M.: Too Late to Die Young: Nearly True Tales from a Life. Macmillan, London (2006)
21. Kraus, L.: 2016 Disability Statistics Annual Report. Durham, NH (2017). https://disabilitycompendium.org/sites/default/files/user-uploads/2016_AnnualReport.pdf
22. Kurzweil, R.: The Singularity is Near: When Humans Transcend Biology. Penguin, London (2005)
23. Ladau, E.: Fix Discriminatory Attitudes and Broken Sidewalks, Not Humans. Motherboard (2015). https://motherboard.vice.com/en_us/article/d73947/fix-discriminatory-attitudes-and-broken-sidewalks-not-humans

24. Laursen, L.: The 'Right to Repair' Movement Is Gaining Ground and Could Hit Manufacturers Hard. Fortune Magazine (2019). http://fortune.com/2019/01/09/right-to-repair-manufacturers/. Accessed 29 Jan 2019

25. Lawrence, C.L.: We Have to Change the Kind of Masculinity We Teach Our Sons. Role Reboot (2016). http://rolereboot.org/family/details/2016-09-change-kind-masculinity-teach-sons/

26. Mol, A.: The Logic of Care: Health and the Problem of Patient Choice. Taylor & Francis, Milton Park (2008)

27. Nagel, T.: What is it like to be a bat? Philos. Rev. **83**(4), 435–450 (1974)

28. Nelson, M., Shew, A., Stevens, B.: Transmobility: Rethinking the possibilities in cyborg (Cripborg) bodies. Catalyst: Feminism, Theory, Technoscience (Forthcoming)

29. Olson, P.R.: Domesticating deathcare: the women of the U.S. natural deathcare movement. J. Med. Hum. **39**(2), 195–215 (2018). https://doi.org/10.1007/s10912-016-9424-2

30. Rosenberger, R.: Multistability and the agency of mundane artifacts: from speed bumps to subway benches. Hum. Stud. **37**(3), 369–392 (2014)

31. Rosenberger, R.: Callous objects: designs against the homeless. University of Minnesota Press, Minneapolis (2017)

32. Russell, A.L., Vinsel, L.: After innovation, turn to maintenance. Technol. Cult. **59**(1), 1–25 (2018)

33. Sauder, K.: When Celebrating Accessible Technology is Just Reinforcing Ableism. Crippled Scholar (2015). https://crippledscholar.com/2015/07/04/when-celebrating-accessible-technology-is-just-reinforcing-ableism/

34. Slutskaya, N., Simpson, R., Hughes, J., Simpson, A., Uygur, S.: Masculinity and class in the context of dirty work. Gender Work Org. **23**(2), 165–182 (2016)

35. Sobchack, V.: Choreography for one, two, and three legs (a phenomenological meditation in movements). Topoi **24**(1), 55–66 (2005)

36. Stacey, C.L.: Finding dignity in dirty work: the constraints and rewards of low-wage home care labour. Sociol. Health Illn. **27**(6), 831–854 (2005)

37. Star, S.L.: The ethnography of infrastructure. Am. Behav. Sci. **43**(3), 377–391 (1999)

38. Transhumanist Party: Transhumanist Bill of Rights - Version 3.0, 12 December 2018. https://transhumanist-party.org/tbr-3/. Accessed 13 Dec 2018

39. Weise, J.: The Dawn of the Tryborg. The New York Times (2016). https://www.nytimes.com/2016/11/30/opinion/the-dawn-of-the-tryborg.html

40. Weise, J.: Common Cyborg. Granta (2018). https://granta.com/common-cyborg/

41. Williams, D.P.: What It's Like to Be A Bot. Real Life Magazine, May 2018. https://reallifemag.com/what-its-like-to-be-a-bot/

42. Wittkower, D.E.: Lurkers, creepers, and virtuous interactivity: from property rights to consent to care as a conceptual basis for privacy concerns and information ethics. First Monday **21**(10), 1–17 (2016)

43. Young, I.M.: Throwing like a girl: a phenomenology of feminine body comportment motility and spatiality. Hum. Stud. **3**(1), 137–156 (1980)

Application Research of Chinese Traditional Medicine Health Concept in Indoor Environment Design

Ming He[1,2(✉)]

[1] Tianjin University, No. 92 Weijin Road, Nankai District, Tianjin, China
280352020@qq.com
[2] University of Jinan, No. 336, West Road of Nan Xinzhuang,
Jinan, Shandong, China

Abstract. The indoor environment is an important environment in people's lives. The quality of this environment directly affects people's healthy life. With the development of human civilization and the improvement of living standards, how to create a comfortable life and healthy health indoors. The environment is particularly important. The natural concept of TCM Chinese medicine is extremely suitable for this indoor environment requirement. The introduction of TCM concept makes the indoor environment arrangement be adjusted according to the overall view and the natural view, so that people's health starts from prevention and achieves the purpose of healthy living.

Keywords: Chinese medicine concept · Environmental design application

1 Introduction

The indoor environment has become the most important place for human activities. Except for the necessary individual projects, two-thirds of the human activities are carried out in the indoor environment. The design of the indoor environment, the use of materials, decorative articles and plant breeding for humans The health will have an impact, and the natural and holistic view of traditional Chinese medicine has great reference for the health concept in indoor environment design. It can not only realize the basic use function of the indoor environment, but also have the health of the human body. Spleen benefits.

Chinese traditional medicine has maintained the healthy reproduction of the Chinese nation for thousands of years. Apart from long-term wars, turmoil and disasters, there has never been a large reduction in population due to diseases. The traditional Chinese medicine treatment concept has a holistic view and a natural view. The treatment methods and the use of medicines are extremely environmentally friendly. At the same time, they also attach great importance to the "treatment of the disease". In the "Yellow Emperor's Canon", there is "the sage is not cured. Not sick" point of view. Two-thirds of the time in the room can be spent in the "treatment of the disease" of the health care body, so the traditional Chinese medical concept of interior design is absolutely necessary to introduce.

© Springer Nature Switzerland AG 2019
A. Marcus and W. Wang (Eds.): HCII 2019, LNCS 11583, pp. 56–69, 2019.
https://doi.org/10.1007/978-3-030-23570-3_6

Chinese traditional medicine as the main means in China's medical care has great practical significance for us to build green families, green schools, green communities and green lifestyles, which directly reduce the cost of human living environment.

The theoretical system of traditional Chinese medicine comes directly from the ancient Chinese philosophical thoughts–Taoism and Confucianism, and plays a key theoretical guide to the process of constructing traditional Chinese medicine for health prevention, treatment, treatment and post-rehabilitation. effect. The concepts and related contents of "qi", "yin and yang", "five elements", "six kinky" and "corresponding to heaven and earth" as taught by traditional Chinese medicine have also become the core of traditional Chinese medicine and become the basic elements of the traditional Chinese medical theory system architecture. It has gradually formed the theoretical basis of original thinking of traditional Chinese medicine, and has become an important philosophical methodology for guiding Chinese traditional medicine to recognize diseases, prevent diseases and treat diseases, and thus fundamentally different from medicine in other parts of the world.

Traditional Chinese medicine has homogenized the plants, minerals, and animals that exist in nature into medicines, and has been given the natural attributes of traditional Chinese medicine. It is also extremely researching on the wind, humidity, health, hygiene, cold, and fire that cause diseases in human body. These elements are taken into account for body health and disease treatment, and these elements have a high application value in indoor environment design. For example, how to avoid the wind indoors, how to prevent moisture, how to cool, how to dispel cold, how to heat the heat, etc., in addition to the characteristics of plants and minerals for the health care of people of different environments, different ages and different constitutions, etc. It is really preventive for the disease.

2   How to Make a Reasonable Windproof Interior Design

The natural climate phenomenon of wind, cold, heat, humidity, dryness and heat (fire) is called "six gas" in ancient times. Six kinky is a name for the abnormal change of six qi. The ancients believed that abnormal climate change could cause disease (modern science also proved that human beings have different resistance to bacteria and viruses in different climates, and the reproductive and virulence of bacteria and viruses are different. of). Chinese medicine borrows the names of "wind, cold, heat, dampness, dryness, heat (fire)" and its characteristics to summarize all the causes of diseases caused by external factors.

In the interior design, it is necessary to consider not only the functions of practicality, convenience, beauty, and environmental protection, but also the prevention of wind and evil invading the human body when using various types of indoor air. Chinese medicine believes that the wind is the longest disease, belonging to the "six kinky", the wind is the main cause of the spring, and the liver and wood. Wind evil is a disease, and its disease syndrome is wide-ranging and changes rapidly. Its specific characteristics are: all over the body, everywhere, up to the head, down to the knees, skin, internal and internal organs, any part of the body can be affected by wind evil.

Wind evil can be combined with cold, dampness, phlegm, dryness, heat (fire) and so on. The specificity of the disease, the wind disease to go quickly, the course of disease is also short and long, and its special symptoms are also easy to recognize, such as sweating out of the wind, body itching, wandering, numbness and restlessness. When the disease occurs, it will be affected by wind and evil in all seasons, indoors and outdoors, and staying up late. It can be seen that how much wind evil is harmful to the health of the human body and can reasonably avoid the wind and evil.

The human body feels the external factors caused by the external factors, mainly cold and evil, indoors will also be affected by wind evil, such as night wind, air conditioning cold wind, fan direct blow, indoor convection wind, etc. can cause damage to the human body, especially When people are resting, they are most likely to feel the wind and evil.

In the traditional courtyard architecture design in China, the wind-proof design structure has already begun. The courtyard structure we see now is more classic. It has a shadow wall, and the shadow wall has more than just a shadow wall. Avoiding the sight of the outside world, it is more to divert the wind and directly prevent the wind from passing through the courtyard to generate strong convection in the courtyard. The wind diverted by the shadow wall has been reduced, and the wind and the wind have already passed through the doors and windows of each room. It also makes the air circulate continuously in the courtyard, thus taking away the stale atmosphere in the courtyard, and thus achieving the first step of the prevention of wind and evil, which fully embodies the concept of Yin and Yang Five Elements.

Siheyuan

In the area where the indoor convection wind (commonly known as the wind) can not be placed on the bed, sofa, rest seat and other furniture for a long time to rest, so as to avoid the wind evil invade the human body and form a disease. In the whole interior design, the formation of convective wind should be avoided first. If the indoor structure cannot be changed, the screen-like decorative objects can be reasonably used, which can make the placement of the furniture less affected.

Horizontal furniture will generally be placed in a place with good light. In these places, especially pay attention to avoiding the air outlet of the air conditioner. When installing the air conditioner, try to avoid the air conditioning and direct blowing. Modern home air conditioning has become an essential facility. Many diseases are caused by the unreasonable use of air conditioners. This is the wind evil caused by humans, and the refrigeration function of air conditioners can produce cold air, which is easy for people to suffer from cold evil. Therefore, choosing to use air conditioners reasonably can avoid causing air-conditioning diseases.

Freely
placed
screen

Wind evil is the most vulnerable to invading people. The most vulnerable to wind and evil is the human head, limb joints, shoulders and necks. It can cause diseases after being exposed to the wind, and some even form stubborn diseases that have not been going for many years. The body and mind are tortured. Most of the illnesses in these parts are caused by feeling the wind and evil. The old saying goes: Avoiding the wind as a refuge, this is the truth. It can be seen how indoors can avoid how natural and artificial wind evils are important to human health.

3   How to Do Reasonable Cooling in Interior Design

Chinese medicine believes that "dryness is dry" means that the dryness of the transition makes the body's body fluid dry and dry, and the skin is dry and dry. The indoor environment is too dry and can cause harm to human health. The dry air is likely to cause excessive loss of body water and infection. Accelerated aging, easy to cause the spread of bacteria, so we should introduce the humidification device properly in the interior decoration design, not only can prevent the wooden furniture from being chapped due to excessive drying, but also can properly adjust the humidity of the indoor environment. We can usually adjust the indoor environment appropriately. In the setting of several fish tanks, not only can fish culture, self-cultivation, water in the fish tank can naturally evaporate into the environment, so that the humidity in the environment is improved, which can reduce the dryness; we can also place in different areas of the room. Vase flower arrangement can not only beautify the indoor environment, but also the evaporation of water vapor in the vase forms a dehumidifying environment and improves the local air humidity.

Fish tank and vase	

In addition, the appropriate water-absorbing stone placed in the room can achieve the function of humid environment. The water-absorbing stone is also called the water stone. The natural stone of the water-absorbing stone is many, some of them are connected to each other, and the small cave is like a pore. This is the main reason for the strong water absorption. In the cave on the stone, the soil can be planted with flowers, and the large cave can plant trees. Because of the strong water absorption of the stone, the plants grow vigorously and the flowers bloom brightly. The absorbing stone can emit moisture, and it can be used as a fake mountain or bonsai to have a moist environment.

	Absorbent stone	

4 How to Solve the Problem of Air Humidity in Interior Design

The Yellow Emperor's internal classics say that "wet wins and vents". The indoor environment in wet or wet seasons is often plagued by moisture. The indoor ground has a hint of moisture, and the furniture and bedding are not very dry, which not only affects normal family life and Indoor activities, but also cause human health problems, moist is a hotbed of fungi, prone to fungal, fungal infections, skin diseases such as eczema, hand and foot spasm, allergic skin diseases, gynecological diseases, rheumatoid arthritis, itchy skin Diseases such as athlete's foot, and other conditions such as chest tightness, shortness of breath, and depression may occur in hot and humid weather. Therefore, overcoming the damp conditions of the indoor environment is very important to improve the quality of daily life in the room. Besides we use air-conditioning equipment to solve some problems, we can take the following measures to prevent indoor moisture:

1. The candle can make the water vapor condense, so that the indoor humidity is reduced. If there is a musty smell at home, you can choose a candle with natural plant aromatherapy oil, which can make the air dry and remove the musty smell in the room.
2. There is a small space such as a bathroom in the bathroom. It is possible to wrap the quicklime with a cloth bag to absorb moisture. It can also poke a few holes in the washing powder bag, use the washing powder to absorb moisture, and it can be reused, which is economical.
3. Put 5–10 kg of black charcoal in the room, boil for 10 min in advance, filter out the water and ventilate it, put it in a breathable basket after two days, put a small bag and a small bag in the corner, wardrobe, drawer, etc. This will prevent the house from getting wet. It can be reused after drying in the shade, both dehumidifying and deodorizing.

Candle, quicklime, black charcoal

5 Reasonable Application of Chinese Herbal Medicine in Interior Design

5.1 Chinese Herbal Medicines Suitable for Placement and Planting in Interior Design

Chinese Eaglewood, Wood of Chinese Eaglewood, aroma, bitterness, anesthesia, analgesic, muscle relaxation, agarwood still has sedative, antihypertensive, anti-asthmatic, anti-arrhythmia and anti-ischemic effects, for the daily life of the human body Health care has an excellent auxiliary effect, especially for the common diseases of the elderly, such as cardiovascular disease, senile insomnia, high blood pressure and other diseases. Putting a form of agarwood in the room of the elderly can not only play the role of decorating the indoor environment, but also protect the health of the elderly.

Agarwood ornaments

Eucalyptus is an evergreen tree, mainly distributed in the tropics and subtropics, mainly produced in Asia Southeast China, Japan, Korea, Vietnam with India. In other countries, in China, it is mainly distributed in the south of the Yangtze River and in the southwest of China, such as Sichuan and Yunnan. The branches, leaves and broken wooden blocks of eucalyptus can be placed indoors to deodorize, deworm, absorb poisonous odor and achieve the effect of purifying the air. The smell is cool and refreshing. The eucalyptus block or wood chip is placed in the corner of the room, which not only can play the role of insecticide, ants, cockroach, cockroach, cockroach, but also can effectively eliminate harmful substances such as formaldehyde, and can achieve moisture absorption function in indoor humid environment, according to China 2000 The publication of the "Pharmaceutical Code of the People's Republic of China" published in the year is especially effective for patients with rheumatoid arthritis. It can also effectively prevent arthritis and has a good auxiliary therapeutic effect on diseases such as rheumatism, muscle soreness and neuralgia. It is good for human health and does not pollute clothing and the environment. Although it is a good companion for creating a healthy home living environment, it should also be avoided in a non-ventilated bedroom for people with cardiovascular disease. Inside, because the aroma of eucalyptus will make people's heart beat faster, it is not suitable for the elderly who are weaker.

Eucalyptus and eucalyptus blocks

6 Select Natural Materials that Are Already in Place for Decoration

Nowadays, the interior design has been developed to the stage of light decoration and heavy decoration. The concept of nature in the concept of Chinese medicine is one of its core concepts. Human beings are born in nature, and naturally occurring natural substances are the most acceptable to the human body. The building and decoration are made of wood, bamboo and stone, all from nature. The traditional Chinese interior decoration is mainly made of wood materials, bamboo and various kinds of flowers. The natural stones in the interior and exterior decoration are the main decorations. First, trees, bamboo forests, flowers and plants are used to adjust the environment.

Reduce the use of household appliances, reduce the environmental cost in life, humidifiers, air purifiers, etc., plant plants and flowers, the following flowers and plants are suitable for indoor display, not only can beautify the indoor environment, but also beneficial to human health, I do not know Unconsciously prevent disease.

1. Clivia: It is a freshener that releases oxygen and absorbs smoke indoors. An adult Clivia can absorb 1 L of air for a day and night, release 80% of oxygen, and can also cause photosynthesis under extremely weak light, and it will not emit carbon dioxide at night, and there are three in a dozen square meters. Four pots of Clivia can absorb indoor smoke and have a unique effect on preventing smog. Especially in the cold winter when heating in the north, the smog is heavier. In addition, in order to keep the doors and windows closed and the indoor air is not circulated in winter, the Clivia will play a very good air conditioning role, keeping the indoor air fresh and clean.

Clivia

2. African Jasmine: The volatile oil produced by it has a significant bactericidal effect; indoor placement can not only relax the nerves of the human body, but also facilitate sleep, and also achieve the effect of improving work efficiency.

African jasmine

3. White palm: white palm can inhibit the exhaled gases exhaled by the human body, such as ammonia and acetone, and it can also filter benzene, trichloroethylene and formaldehyde in the air for newly renovated indoor space. Its high evaporation properties can reduce the indoor environment, thus preventing the nasal mucosa from drying and greatly reducing the possibility of illness.

White palm
Spathiphyllum kochii Engl. & K. Krause

4. Silver Queen: Known for its unique air purification capacity: the higher the concentration of pollutants in the air, the more it can exert its purification ability, so it is very suitable for dark rooms with poor ventilation.

Silver queen
Aglaonema commulatum cv.Silvcr Queen

5. Adiantum fern: can absorb about 20 μg of formaldehyde per hour, so it is considered to be the most effective biological "purifier". It is necessary to deal with the work of high formaldehyde content such as paints and paints, or at least one pot of ferns in the indoor environment, and it can also inhibit the release of computers and printers. Toluene and toluene can therefore be placed in the study and computer room.

Adiantum

6. Duck feet: For the larger environment of smog, duck feet wood is a standard cleaner, it can absorb the smoke in the air, the room to purify the air. Its leaves not only absorb large amounts of nicotine and other harmful substances from the smoke, but also convert these harmful substances into harmless plant-derived substances through photosynthesis. In addition, the concentration of formaldehyde in the air can be reduced by about 9 mg per hour.

Duck foot wood

7. Chlorophytum: The species of spider plant is diverse and easy to breed. It is very suitable for indoor environment. It can absorb 95% of carbon monoxide and 85% of formaldehyde in the air. Chlorophyll can perform photosynthesis under weak light, and can absorb toxic and harmful gases in the air. A pot of spider orchid is equivalent to an air purifier in a room of about ten square meters. If you raise one or two pots of spider orchids in your room, you can release oxygen all day, and you can also absorb a lot of harmful substances such as formaldehyde, styrene, carbon monoxide and carbon dioxide in the air. Chlorophytum has a particularly strong absorption of certain harmful substances, such as carbon monoxide and formaldehyde. Chlorophytum can also decompose relatively stable benzene, absorb a large amount of

nicotine and other relatively stable harmful substances in smoke, so we call the spider orchid indoor air. The green purifier is both pleasing to the eye and refreshing.

Chlorophytum comosum (Thunb.) Baker)

8. Aloe Vera: Aloe vera is a perennial fleshy herb with low living conditions, strong vitality and variety, but it has a strong function of purifying indoor air. A pot of aloe vera is equivalent to nine sets of bio-air cleaners, so aloe vera has the reputation of air purification experts. Full-bodied aloe can absorb formaldehyde, carbon dioxide, sulfur dioxide, carbon monoxide and other pathogenic substances, especially for formaldehyde absorption; and it can absorb harmful gases such as carbon dioxide and formaldehyde, both day and night, and also absorbs organic volatile substances. It can even absorb some suspended particles that are difficult to clean in the air, and is a cleaning agent for purifying indoor air.

Aloe

9. Monstera: The monstera is not only beautiful in appearance, but also more important in purifying air. It can absorb harmful gases such as sulfur dioxide, hydrogen fluoride, chlorine and ethylene, which are widely emitted from household appliances, plastic products and decorative materials., harmful substances such as carbon monoxide and nitrogen peroxide. At the same time, it can also absorb carbon dioxide while releasing a small amount of oxygen, thereby increasing the content of negative oxygen ions in the air.

10. Ivy: Ivy can be planted on the courtyard and on the balcony, or placed in a potted plant. It can effectively absorb toxic chemicals in the air. Under the conditions of sunshine and light, it can make the living room 90% stupid. Get absorbed. The ivy in the courtyard can also absorb a lot of dust, purify the small environment, and also purify the indoors. It is the natural "air filter" in our home.

11. Rubber Tree: The main function of the rubber tree is to absorb dust. Its thick and wide blades are very suitable for inhaling dust in indoor air. It has a great effect on indoor dust removal and mitigation, so put a rubber tree in the bedroom. Is a good choice. The rubber tree can not only remove dust, but also purify harmful gases such as carbon monoxide, carbon dioxide and hydrogen fluoride in the air. Especially for newly renovated houses, the rubber tree can effectively absorb volatile formaldehyde and purify the air. The bedroom is one of the most popular places for people, so this plant is perfect for the bedroom to clean up the air in time.

12. Bamboo: In addition to absorbing sulfur dioxide, nitrogen dioxide, chlorine and other harmful gases at night, it can also secrete bacteria to kill bacteria. It has a defensive effect on susceptible people and has a good environment for purification. The role is very beneficial to the health of the human body.

13. Brown Bamboo: In a study conducted by the US Space Agency, it was found that brown bamboo is the best plant for purifying the air, ranking second. Yellow coconut is the first to absorb most of the toxic gases in the air, especially ammonia. Gas and chloroform are excellent.

14. Mint: mint taste cool, leaf wrinkles, a lot of hair, can absorb indoor dust, can purify the air, mint breath can also play a refreshing, mosquito repellent effect. And it smells fresh and good, and makes people feel good and happy.

15. Lavender: Lavender plants are evergreen and have aromas. Their fragrance can relax and relieve stress. Sleeping in the bedroom allows you to sleep for one night. Lavender is very rich in color, beautiful and elegant purple, fascinating blue, warm pink and other colors, with high ornamental value, is also a natural ornament in the home.

In summary, the decoration of the indoor environment should be based on the natural concept of Chinese medicine, focusing on the coordination of yin and yang, rationally balancing the five elements of coordination of gold, wood, water, fire and soil. In addition to the use of functional layout, it should pay more attention to indoor health. The creation of the environment, the concept of "treatment of disease" in traditional Chinese medicine is implemented in daily indoor activities or home life. The three pathogenic factors of "six kineses" in cold, heat and heat are harmful to the human body because of space. And how to prevent and avoid in the interior design will not be discussed.

References

1. Ming Ma, W.: Huang Di Nei Jing Su asked to make a statement. Sun Guozhong direction red. Xueyuan Publishing House, Beijing (2003)
2. Ming Ma, W.: The Yellow Emperor's Inner Jing Ling pivoted the certificate. Sun Guozhong direction red. Xueyuan Publishing House, Beijing (2003)
3. Chen, B., Zeng, W.: On the return of humanism in interior design. Sci. Res. **05** (2011)
4. Huang, Y.: Exploring the traditional cultural environment design of traditional Chinese medicine. Mod. Hosp. **06** (2008)
5. Huang, L.: The advantages of indoor ecological landscape design and interior decoration design. Ind. Technol. For. **02** (2019)

Human-Computer Interaction Design in Animation Industry

Xueying Niu$^{(\boxtimes)}$

Zhongnan University of Economics and Law, 182# Nanhu Avenue,
East Lake High-Tech Development Zone, Wuhan, China
15318809121@163.com

Abstract. Motion capture is an important technology in the development of the animation industry combined with human-computer interaction technology. Many problems existing in the field of VR games and somatosensory games in human-computer interaction are derived from the limitations of technological development. At the heart of the somatosensory game is the user experience. Improving the existing technology enables the user have a better experience, while also taking into account the designer's structured modifications. Based on the overall environment of the animation industry, combined with the principle of human-computer interaction technology and user experience supremacy, this paper proposes a scheme to improve the existing motion capture technology, expounds the advantages and disadvantages of this design, the specific design method and its Meaning and specific benefits.

Keywords: Animation industry · Human-computer interaction ·
Real-time systems · User experience · Motion capture design

1 Introduction

The development of human-computer interaction technology in the animation industry has been going on for decades, but most of its practical applications still exist only in science fiction movies. People use 3D scanner and motion capture technologies to capture realistic portraits and track motions for motion capture. After completing these, the data is imported into the computer and edited later into movie animations and even games. This is a kind of human-computer interaction development. The new model is also a new trend that fits the theme. The purpose described below is designed to improve the user experience of the current program, make the device transmission smoother, improve the comfort of the targeted audience and to increase the frequency of use. At the same time, it greatly saves us the time to make animations and movies, and improves the accuracy of the action. If it can be used in more aspects involving human-computer interaction, it will greatly benefit human beings, such as the behavior control of simple intelligent robots. But again, it also has many drawbacks. The main purpose of the current human-computer interaction is people-oriented, so that the user's needs replace other factors as the most important part. Therefore, here we will propose a new and improved form of the original method, improve the use mode, reduce the cost of use, and expand the field of use.

© Springer Nature Switzerland AG 2019
A. Marcus and W. Wang (Eds.): HCII 2019, LNCS 11583, pp. 70–83, 2019.
https://doi.org/10.1007/978-3-030-23570-3_7

2   Learning Theory

2.1   Application of Human-Computer Interaction Technology in Animation Industry

The model of global animation industry development shows that the United States and Japan and other animation powers guide the development of the domestic animation industry. The animation industry is now an emerging industry. Audiences and gamers are equivalent to users in this industry. Paying attention to their feedback and opinions is a prerequisite for correcting development problems and improving the user experience to promote the continuous development of the entire industry.

The animation industry has the characteristics of high investment, high profit and high risk. As a capital-intensive industry, the design of creative and animated characters, the smoothness of animation, and the pertinence of the audience are all important factors for the success of an animation. It is closely linked with technology. The level of animation in different eras will change. The emerging human-computer interaction technology plays an important role in the development. The animation industry has a long marketing cycle, many derivatives, high investment, and high output, so there is a great demand for market purchasing power. At the same time, with the continuous development of science and technology, the improvement of people's living standards, and the increasing demand for products such as animation and games, the animation industry has rapidly increased its position in the global economy, and the demand for talents has increased, which has become a pillar industry in many countries. In particular, China has a strong potential market as a developing country, and the wave of information technology development has created a good foundation for the prosperity of the animation industry (Fig. 1).

Fig. 1. Current VR usage form. (Source: Bing)

At present, VR (Virtual Reality), AR (Augmented Reality) and MR (Mixed Reality) technologies are widely used in the animation industry, and are widely used in the animation industry, especially in games. Most of the virtual VR exists in VR games, bringing vision into the virtual environment, AR brings the virtual part into the real world, and MR is equivalent to the combination of AR and VR, which is a huge flying over in the development of science and technology. There is also CR (Cinematic Reality), which is equivalent to another derivative of MR. These different forms constitute the concept of XR (Extended Reality). Through the development of computer technology and science and technology, the use of wearable devices and the like to create a human-computer-interactive, real-world virtual environment.

In the case of VR games and somatosensory games, the user purchase trend tends to rise steadily and then plummet. The most important reason for the user to abandon the game after purchasing the game is because the user experience is different from the expected one, which results in a huge difference in the magnitude of the difference. Under this trend, adjustment and improvement of technology are indispensable.

2.2   Application of Human-Computer Interaction Technology in VR Scene Design

(1) Analysis of the application status of VR technology
Virtual reality technology was born in the 1960s. It is a process in which users use specific devices to interact with virtual environments in the environment, that is, human-computer interaction. VR has four important characteristics: multi-perception, that is, there should be a sense of visual auditory olfactory touch in human beings in virtual reality; The sense of existence which should be able to make people in the virtual world but unable to distinguish between virtual world and real world; Inter-activity means that people and machines can communicate seamlessly, the operation on the machine should get feedback for the next step. Autonomy means that objects and movements in the virtual world should move according to the laws of motion in the real world [1].

At present, the development of VR technology is mostly used in games, medical, military and other aspects. In terms of life, there is a popular home automation system. In medicine, some nerve systems can be repaired and the brain stimulated appropriately. In terms of games, the equipment uses helmets, glasses or gloves to transmit data from the human auditory vision and other aspects, bringing people into a specific range of virtual environments, giving users an immersive real experience.

(2) Thoughts on the Existing Problems in Human-Computer Interaction in the Practice of VR Technology
In the early stage of technology development, there is a large demand for talents, but most of the VR professional designers gather in the periphery of developed countries and developed countries, which has caused the shortage of talents. At the same time, the defects of image recognition now limit the development of VR, and the accuracy of recognition is low, especially for complex images and dynamic pictures with more details. There is a high demand for game content such as VR games, but the current production content is still limited by capital and technology, and since this is a new technology, many investors do not tend to invest in technology and tend to choose a less risky direction.

The current VR game combines the human sensory system with virtual reality, but can't achieve real human-computer interaction. Most interactions are unilateral interactions. For example, when a person moves in a virtual scene, the machine can only perform a unilateral play operation and a small part of the motion capture to combine the picture with the user's movement path, to convey a predetermined picture sense to the user, and when the person is in motion When you want to stop or dramatically change the virtual scene, you cannot use voice or other forms to interact with the virtual scene.

In terms of somatosensory and game sense, many people are inaccurate like objects and cannot achieve complete real effects. At the same time, if the equipment such as helmets and glasses are worn for a long time, the feeling of dizziness may occur due to the difference in spatial sense. Tactile and gesture recognition is still in its infancy.

In the process of interaction, since the virtual game scene and the actual speed cannot be completely matched, the phenomenon of jamming often occurs during transmission, which affects the user experience. The role of motion capture is essential when interacting in this way. Past research has focused on the capture of facial and body nodes, while ignoring the importance of muscles and bones for motion capture. Among them, for this technology, the problem of somatosensory games is the delay of motion capture; the problem of VR games is the mismatch of transmission speed and the irrationality of some designs; from the designer's point of view, the flaw of this technology leads to Animation is time consuming and costly. When the defects of motion capture technology are improved, these existing problems are likely to be solved.

At present, based on the premise of technological development, many users have become interested in the development of VR virtual technology. Producers seized this opportunity to research and manufacture VR games and somatosensory games, but due to the limitations of technological development, various problems appeared in the later stage, which greatly affected the user experience. The essence of technological improvement is to focus on the user, and the value of the product depends largely on the satisfaction of the consumer. Solve the shortcomings of this technical detail, improve the fluency of the user experience and promote the development of technology.

2.3 The Role of Motion Capture Technology (Based on the User Experience Design)

(1) Relationship between VR and motion capture technology

"In the field of virtual reality, optical positioning technology and sensor-based inertial motion capture technology in motion capture technology are bound together, because if you want to achieve full interaction and true immersion of VR, these two technologies are indispensable" [2]. Motion capture technology is not the only requirement to enhance the VR experience, but its importance is evident. The significance of improving motion capture technology is to raise a fundamental problem in many large areas, focusing on the small details of big problems to more accurately solve the current difficulties.

(2) Explain the application of motion capture technology for games

With the development of technology, motion capture technology has now been widely used, such as somatosensory games. As the most popular gameplay using motion capture technology, it has won the favor of many users in the early stage of entering the market. In terms of animation, many companies use the motion capture of human-computer interaction technology to achieve many shots. The human-based mobile achieves smooth, simulation purposes, and enhances the viewer's experience when watching movies. Currently immersive games, wearable computers and stealth technologies, and emotional computing technologies are still under study (Fig. 2).

Fig. 2. Form description of the somatosensory game. (Source: Baidu)

The motion recognition capability of some control devices has reached the level of consumer application, such as the game console WiiU. The main feature of this remote control is equipped with a motion sensor, which can judge the action on the screen in real time. The action is truly reflected in the game, interacting with the virtual parts of the TV screen. WiiU Gamepad supports near field communication and wirelessly exchanges data with objects, which opens up new possibilities for gaming and interaction. At the same time, motion capture technology is beginning to enter the medical field, and doctors no longer need to manually touch the button to issue commands, but interact through the screen. Then, Microsoft's Kinect does not need to use any controller. It relies on the camera to capture the motion of the player in three-dimensional space. It can be said that Kinect is more dependent on the camera. As the main technology of Natal, Natal is much more advanced than the Wii. It can also perform face recognition at the same time in the process of recognizing human body movements. When the player enters the game, he can also issue commands and voice signals to the game. But on the one hand, Kinect needs a lot of space to achieve motion capture, but few ordinary families can use such a large space to set up space entertainment devices. On the other hand, its game category is only for home entertainment and fitness games, the range of choices is too small, and as a stand-alone program it does not support the import and use of other game programs. So fewer and fewer people use the Kinect somatosensory game console. The Switch, which has emerged in the future, has revolutionized the new way of seamlessly switching between the console and the host mode, and the detachable Joy-con handle, as well as its multiplayer co-game model is a new breakthrough. Overall, some of the achievements in this technology have been achieved. But it also has its shortcomings. For example, the joystick of the handle is not sensitive enough, it is easy to damage, and the pixels of the picture are not high, which affects the user's game experience. In this aspect of the game, the most important thing is the sense of the game, that is, the communication and interaction between people and machines, and the most important part of which I think is the development of motion capture technology.

(3) Questionnaire based on user experience in human-computer interaction games

In response to the current popularity of somatosensory games and VR games among the masses, questionnaires and interviews were conducted. The surveyed population was mainly young people aged 20–30. A total of 200 people were surveyed, most of them are college students, a small number of staff and social service providers. The survey results show that 87% of the survey base (174 people) have played somatosensory or VR games. Among them, 65% (130 people) think that there is a problem in the game experience of this game, such as not smooth, which affects their game experience. For the comparison of ordinary mobile games and somatosensory and VR games, 93% (186 people) tend to choose ordinary mobile games. Through interviews, the reasons for such choices are basically dissatisfied with the built-in fluency of the game, there are delays or catching up in the process of capturing user actions, and there is a lack of portability in such games which is not as easy to play as mobile games. The price is relatively expensive and so on. Only 16% (32 people) in the fifth question tend to purchase somatosensory gaming devices at home. Most people are still on the sidelines of using this device at home. The interview has learned that many people have tried to buy but comments of defects on these devices on the Internet have caused them to abandon their purchases plan. Others have to give up because of the large space required for such devices and the lack of space in the home. The reason why people who have already purchased are not used frequently is because their native games are too less to play. Compared with mobile games, the production process of such games is cumbersome and difficult, so people are generally no longer used after they feel fresh. Finally, 65% of people (130 people) responded that if the above problems can be solved, they may be willing to try more of these devices (Fig. 3).

The conclusion shows that the popularity of somatosensory games and VR games is high, but most people do not choose to purchase because of the current technology, price, space and other considerations. However, the development prospects are huge, and we should focus on solving technical problems and design "user-centered products."

■ QUESTIONNAIRE

MOTION SENSING GAME&VR

1.ARE YOU MALE OR FEMALE?

2.HAVE YOU EVER PLAYED MOTION GAMES OR VR GAMES?

3.DOES YOUR MOVEMENT MOVE SMOOTHLY ACROSS THE SCREEN DURING THE GAME?

4.DO YOU PREFER TO PLAY MOTION GAMES OR REGULAR MOBILE GAMES?

5.DO YOU THINK YOU'LL HAVE A MOTION-SENSING DEVICE AT HOME?

6.WHAT DO YOU THINK IS THE BIGGEST DILEMMA FACING MOTION GAMES AND VR GAMES?

7.IF YOUR PROBLEM WERE SOLVED, WOULD YOU USE MOTION CAPTURE DEVICES LIKE THESE
IN YOUR LIFE?

Fig. 3. Questionnaire questions list. (Source: Author)

(4) Limitations of current motion capture technology development based on user experience

Human-computer interaction technology is similar to film production in many aspects, cinematography and software engineering, editing and design, script writing and information architecture. The most important part is acting, which is the usability of technology. The key to improving the usability of technology is to improve the practical application of this technology, which is closely related to its popularity among the masses. The production of movies and animated games belongs to the same category of production process, and their audience is crowds. Firmly grasping people's preferences and accurately targeting the audience are important parts of the technology development process. Among them, the importance of motion capture technology is self-evident. Nowadays, many movie games use this technology. For example, the most famous ones are "Avatar" and the animated "The Lord of the Rings" series of Gurum (Fig. 4).

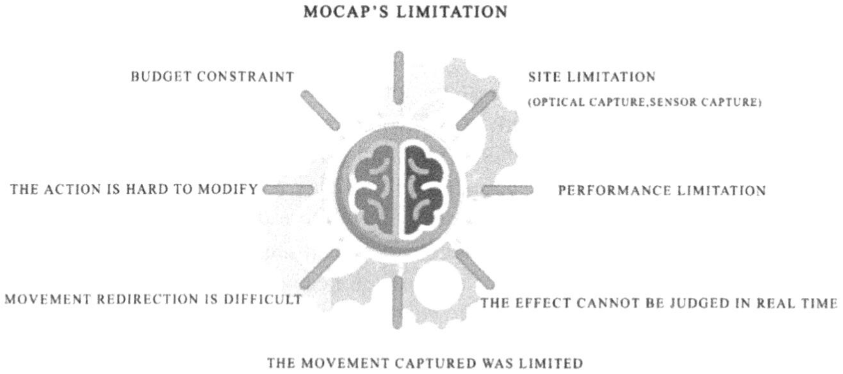

MOCAP'S LIMITATION

BUDGET CONSTRAINT

SITE LIMITATION
(OPTICAL CAPTURE,SENSOR CAPTURE)

THE ACTION IS HARD TO MODIFY

PERFORMANCE LIMITATION

MOVEMENT REDIRECTION IS DIFFICULT

THE EFFECT CANNOT BE JUDGED IN REAL TIME

THE MOVEMENT CAPTURED WAS LIMITED

Fig. 4. Existing problems with motion capture technology. (Source: Author)

At first, the motion capture technology was based on humans, but due to the constraints of science and technology, it could not form a system. Therefore, people use stop motion animation. For example, many pictures in the movie "King Kong" require the animator to debug the scene object one frame at a time to shoot the stop motion animation, but this method is too cumbersome and extremely time consuming and laborious. The mechanical model that emerged later benefited from the development of radio technology, which can control the movement and rotation of the model through controllers such as the joystick. However, the mechanical model itself is difficult to manufacture, and the external type is high, so it takes a long time. At the same time, there will be a pause in the movement process, which greatly affects the smoothness and efficiency of the production process. After that, the frame-by-frame transfer technique solved the problem caused by the mechanical model. At that time, people used this technology to make many famous cartoons. But this way means that the movement of the picture has to be redrawn, the workload is large and it takes a long time, and this method does not constitute a 3D effect. The flatness of painting limits development. But now the motion capture technology has skillfully solved these problems. Measuring, tracking, and recording the trajectory of an object in three-dimensional space is the essence of motion capture, which means the device needs to be measured and recorded. So there are many ways to capture motion, and the pros and cons are obvious. Among them, mechanical and electromagnetic and inertial capture have been rarely used, and optical capture technology is now more used (Fig. 5).

MOTION CAPTURE SYSTEM	STANDARD							
	FTOP	COVER	EXTERNAL DISTURBANCE	ACCURACY	PRICE	RESPONSE DELAY	NUMBER OF PEOPLE	DISADVANTAGE
MECHANICAL	-	NO	NO	INACCURACY	LOW	NO	SINGLE	HEAVY HAVE INERTIA
ELECTROMAGNETIC	120HZ	NO	MAGNETIC METAL	INACCURACY	LOW	LARGE (33MS)	MULTIPLE	LIABLE TO IMPACT BIASED ERROR
INERTIAL	-	NO	NO	INACCURACY	LOW	-	MULTIPLE	RAPID' ACCUMULATIVE ERROR
OPTICAL FIBER	-	NO	NO	ACCURACY	HIGH	SHORT	MULTIPLE	ANGULAR CONSTRAINT
OPTICAL PROFILE (INITIATIVE)	480HZ	YES	RAY	ACCURACY	HIGH	SHORT	MULTIPLE	THE CAMERA IS IN ABSOLUTE POSITION
OPTICAL PROFILE (PASSIVE)	2000HZ	YES	RAY	ACCURACY	HIGH	SHORT	MULTIPLE	THE CAMERA IS IN ABSOLUTE POSITION

Fig. 5. Comparison of different methods of motion capture technology. (Source: Author)

The motion capture technology used today has not been improved and improved for decades, mainly because many objective factors have limited its development, and many problems are difficult to overcome. The current use of motion capture technology is mostly used for animation to the animator as a reference, or as a storyline draft

(Previsulization) and Crowd simulation, and its real role is not fully functional come out. The manner in which the motion capture and feedback and interaction of the few somatosensory games described above has been greatly developed but still has many drawbacks. In response to these problems, an improved idea is proposed.

2.4 Design Ideas for Improvement of Motion Capture Technology in Human-Computer Interaction Technology

(1) Explain the design idea with user experience as the core

As part of the human-computer interaction, to form an effective interaction core, the most important thing is feedback. The feedback contains two aspects, the interaction between the person and the machine. When the button is pressed by the machine, the machine can respond in time. The second aspect is that after this operation, the state of the system itself has changed. A stable expectation is very important for interaction. When the operation is performed and the feedback of the system is contrary to the operation or there is a big discrepancy, the principle of interaction is violated.

The current motion capture technology has been slowly improved, but the fluency and real-time performance are relatively blocked compared to the body's own motion. But suppose that the modeling of human skeletal muscles and skin is combined with the recognition system of the motion capture that has now appeared but is limited, resulting in a direct and rapid scanning of the old form of skeletal muscle instead of bone nodes. In this way, we can solve the problem of low output fidelity of the hinged structure to a large extent and the limitations of identifying the action by marking the position angle. This method can also be input into the current robot as a program, which can improve the interaction ability of the existing robot. At the same time, it solves the shortcomings of losing the ability for the characters when they out of the animation environment (Fig. 6).

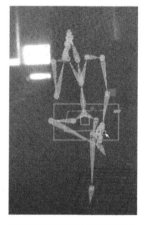
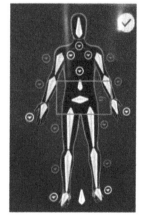

BONE NODES FORMED BY DIRECT IMPORT OF SOFTWARE   INTERFACE THAT COMBINES NODES WITH ANIMATED CHARACTERS

Fig. 6. The actual operation display of the scan generation node in the software. (Source: Author)

- This is a process of transforming the concrete motion into a whole. In appearance, the modification of the person's own clothing device can enhance the comfort of the person when wearing it. The node formed by the person during the motion capture is the state of the node that is diverging from the waist to the head and the foot. So placing the scan point on the waist can form a scan range that diverges from the middle to the periphery thereby scanning the movement path completely and accurately. The Bluetooth transmission system and the auto-scanning system are installed inside the line. Due to the complexity of the center of gravity and scanning, you can choose the belt and other objects as the shape basis. At present, the node generated after scanning is also started from the node of the waist, and scanning as the central node of the body can also better determine the position of the center of gravity of the whole body.

- The form of this scanned body can be transformed from external scan to its own trajectory scan. For example, some existing software (ha you), etc., have already implemented augmented reality technology, and the picture editing can be displayed in the lens of real-time camera through the video painting function. The self-trajectory depiction can be understood as carrying a self-scanning device on the body of the action sender. When moving, the signal is automatically drawn in the connected computer, and the path after the auto-scan is wirelessly transmitted to the switchboard for editing. During the scanning process, the scanning is the self-moving path, that is, the moving curve. The transmission process is a silhouette generated by the combined path after auto-scanning. The separate scanning system of skeletal muscle can only be used to generate a complete human body image when it is generated in the machine after scanning. This method can basically solve the problem of motion capture site limitation. The role in the movement process is simply to trace the path and then feed the trajectory back to the computer which can ensure the scanning body is compact in form and light in size. It can only transmit information as a pipeline between people and computers. This can save energy consumption when the device is moving, reduce the number of feedbacks, and achieve the purpose of drawing the path after one transfer. Reducing the participation of the camera during the capture process can free up space constraints in the technology, and self-transmission replaces the interaction between the sensor and the camera (Fig. 7).

- The transmission process reduces line transmission, and the new technology of 5G equipment is selected. It can support multiple devices for transmission, while the future 5G network can transmit at 10 Gbps and can be transported over long distances. After the scanner carrier self-scans, the information is transmitted through the wireless connection machine, and the data packets such as motion and sound are separately transmitted in the process, thereby reducing the transmission pressure and the jamming phenomenon. Many dynamic data cannot be used directly after the transfer is completed, but require a lot of changes and reorganization. However, the data volume is too large to change, so it is packaged and saved in 20 frames as a compressed file for additional transmission. When it needs to be modified, it only needs to call the compressed folder of the changed folder for later modification. At the same time, the current modulation method has improved the anti-interference ability of the technology to ensure the privacy of transmission. After the transfer,

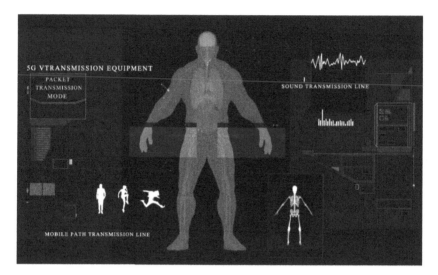

Fig. 7. Interface form when transporting separately in design assumptions. (Source: Author)

the moving path of the program file can be input into the robot's program, so that it can not only improve the accuracy in the animation game, but also improve the defects of the current robot movement.

- When many people are playing the same game, not only to achieve communication between people, but also to ensure interaction between people and machines. The interaction between people is achieved through the voice system, and the interaction between the person and the machine can also be. Data information can be transmitted via Bluetooth during information transmission. Using one of the controllers as a master controller to form a star topology similar to a computer, making the entire line a closed line, forming a private LAN-like game transmission process. But the general controller inside does not take on the real control, but as a central medium to assist in the generation of this topology. When one of them drops, that is, the failure of a single connection will not affect other machines. When there is a problem with the main controller, other connectors will not be affected, thus achieving efficient multi-person transmission.

(2) Design usability analysis

In the design process, the scanner can be divided into industrial use and home use. In terms of industrial use, the accuracy of the capture, the transmission speed, and the like are relatively high, so that the whole body scan can be performed in the program in advance to ensure that the error during the scanning process is smaller. At the same time, program memory can be set separately, and more storage space can be designed for industrial use. Family use is more focused on coherence and real-time. In terms of programming, home capture devices do not require too many complicated functions, while industrial devices require precise and detailed procedures. Based on industrial equipment, simplify the program, retain only the most useful programs and ensure that the interface remains clear and clear. Follow the "ten-minute rule" to achieve the goal of easy learning in the user experience.

As a new way of combining input and output, it has proven to be a practical possibility. For example, the iPhone XS facial recognition system uses motion capture technology for facial recognition. Incorporating this technology into the existing popular household or industrial robot program, the robot's motion control is improved to a greater extent, and its interactive ability is improved. Popularizing popular household robots such as sweeping robots and simple intelligent robots has now entered people's lives. It is undeniable that they can help humans complete some lengthy repetitive work in their own fields, saving time and effort. But from another point of view, the sweeping robot can only judge whether there are obstacles around by a brief and rough perception, and their walking route is not completely independent. So there are often things that sweeping robots repeatedly hit the table corner under your feet. Simple intelligent robots can only do the actions and behaviors set by the system, and this behavior is kind of stiff. Therefore, it is essential to combine the real-time scanning system of bones and muscles with the current human-computer interaction. It can improve the naturalness and smoothness of robot movements as much as possible, so that they can be more beautiful and convenient under the premise of ensuring work efficiency. Now, when you enter this program, you can save the most space by subjecting you to subjectively setting the general direction of movement of a certain behavior to alleviate the burden of simultaneously scanning skeletal muscles. This is the concept of calling, subjectively setting the movement path, or using the movement path after motion capture.

Pre-setting for some fixed actions and fixed positions saves space and saves costs. At the same time, scanning and matching the silhouette of the skeletal muscle can reduce the workload of subsequent operations. For the animator, it is only necessary to adjust the part of the body that fits the body without modifying and making it from scratch. For simple home or medical robots, the accuracy and practicality are greatly improved. At the same time, this way can realize the communication between the ontology and the outside world, and improve the appearance and moving path of the current robot. Through the introduction of the human body's own mobile data, the robot has virtual muscles, and the virtual muscles in the program move the limbs during the movement to complete a series of actions.

This technology can also be applied to the current VR field, using tools to combine virtual world and real world, and can directly perform self-scanning during its work, perfecting the drawbacks of scanning fingers in the current VR scanning process. In the VR field, human-computer interaction can be better realized, and 5G transmission technology and speech recognition technology can be used to make communication between human and virtual world possible. The transmission mode in the improved design is packet transmission, which facilitates the system to separately recognize the voice of the voice, so that the human's willingness can feedback the system's requirements in real time, so that the system can respond in time, thereby achieving a highly efficient multi-person transmission function.

(3) Benefit Analysis Based on Human-Computer Interaction Design

- Economic benefits from improved design

The intuitive benefits of the design come from the direct docking of the animation industry, which improves cost and saves time. At present, the motion capture technology used in the animation industry is expensive, so the design can greatly reduce the cost investment and obtain greater profits after product output. It is easy to form a complete callable action library. The action is not only used by a single person, but also can be modified for a specific number of frames based on the action. At the same time, system maintenance will become easier, reducing the possibility of system crashes and facilitating upgrades. The popularity of 5G technology will provide possibilities for new transmission methods in design. After the popularization of 5G technology, the people's recognition is high, the demand is large, and the purchasing power will inevitably cause the price to drop, so it can also save production costs from this aspect. When the existing problems are solved and then re-entered into the market, the masses will choose to try to purchase, thereby increasing revenue.

- Social benefits derived from user experience

The improved design interface is simple, the system is clear, and its easy learning improves the possibility of high popularity in the future. If the user can accept and enjoy this usage, the design will bring good social benefits. The development of a technology is undoubtedly the best way to drive another technology. This improved technology can simultaneously promote the development of 5G technology and speech recognition technology. Form a parallel state that enhances the comfort of the user experience. The combination of motion capture technology has made it a developmental situation of independent programs. This method can be directly embedded in existing software that needs motion capture technology, combining independence and integration to greatly facilitate people's lives. For designers, this approach is also a more convenient way. The function of separately transmitting is convenient for the modification and upgrade of the program, and the storage method of the compressed package greatly solves the problem that the storage space is insufficient. Therefore, this technology has a good promotion significance and can penetrate current technology equipment from many aspects. The design can greatly improve people's lives, bring convenience to users, and have great social significance.

- Possible defects

At present, it is still impossible to get rid of the shackles of artifacts, and it is impossible to further improve the design using technologies such as thermal sensing. Flexibility is still not enough. When the captured source object is not around, it is impossible to capture the motion for human-computer interaction. Because the solution proposed for the current problem in the design process can not meet the needs of all users to a certain extent, for example, it is difficult for young children to perform self-scanning through the belt during use. Solving the current problems and anticipating possible problems in the future is the most significant way to promote technological development.

3 Future Developments

The future development of human-computer interaction will move toward a more comfortable user experience, a more convenient interaction path and a more efficient interaction. Motion capture technology is always a problem for the current interactive technology. Proposing design ideas, combining modern technology to develop new technologies, improving multi-purpose capture devices, and improving capture capabilities are excellent technological development paths. Multi-purpose use can be combined with the latest technology to stabilize and enhance the development and improve the technical level. The development of the animation industry is not a one-step process, and the combination of the core content of the animation industry and human-computer interaction technology will bring new changes to technology. With the continuous development of human-computer interaction technology, the practical application ability of technology will be greatly improved, thereby bringing a better user experience.

References

1. Liuyuhao: Indoor scene reconstruction technology based on depth information. Yanshan University, Qinhuangdao (2016)
2. Ampoule's small space (ID): Will the high-threshold motion capture technology really become the creator of the VR industry disaster? [EB/OL]. https://baijiahao.baidu.com/s?id=1562109708257277&wfr=spider&for=pc. Accessed 17 Mar 2017
3. Luomingxuan: Talking about the Technology and Application of Motion Capture [EB/OL]. http://blog.sina.com.cn/s/blog_6be92b950101bqtt.html. Accessed 14 Mar 2013
4. OliJiang: Motion capture [EB/OL]. https://wenku.baidu.com/view/65eeb686e53a580216fcfefe.html. Accessed 03 Oct 2012
5. Tai Bohe: VR practitioner: why is the bare hand interaction a pseudo-demand? [EB/OL]. https://www.leiphone.com/news/201611/4FAwT7BCy2Ar4spO.html. Accessed 30 Nov 2016
6. wfbird: Analysis of the development prospect of animation industry [EB/OL]. https://wenku.baidu.com/view/edb410c171fe910ef02df825.html?sxts=1547879965119. Accessed 25 Mar 2014
7. Wangdan: Analysis of the status quo and development strategy of Chinese animation industry. Reform Strateg. **01**, 101–104 (2014)
8. Jiangyajie: Human body gesture recognition and robot control based on Kinect. Shenzhen University, Shenzhen (2017)
9. Zhanqinchuan: Analysis of the application and development status of virtual reality technology. Ind. Technol. Forum 7, 75–76 (2014)

Exploring the Dynamic Aesthetics of Interaction Design

Patricia Search$^{(\boxtimes)}$

Rensselaer Polytechnic Institute, Troy, NY 12180, USA
searcp@rpi.edu

Abstract. In interactive, electronic communication, where information continually changes and users physically interact with objects, there are numerous
elements that define the aesthetic experience. Audiovisual design, dynamic
semantic relationships, cross-modal perception, physical interaction and movement, cognition, and memory impact the aesthetics of the design. Static information hierarchies give way to audiovisual patterns that present information in
parallel, synchronous formats, as well as linear sequences. Diverse sensory
stimuli, interaction in hybrid environments that integrate physical and virtual
spaces, and social networking lead to the formation of discursive semantic
relationships and dynamic perceptual and cognitive networks that also define the
design aesthetics of the work.

Keywords: Aesthetics · Interaction design · Semiotics ·
Cross-modal perception · Embodiment

1 Introduction

The aesthetics of an interface design plays an important role in the quality of a user's
experience. Research has shown that the aesthetics of an interactive, interface design
can impact user engagement, completion time, and error rate [1–3]. Additional research
indicated that the visual appeal of the design encouraged users to stay engaged and
complete tasks, even when the organization and functionality of the interface design
did not yield the fastest time in task completion [4].

Audiovisual design elements contribute to the aesthetics of an object or experience.
The relationships between line, form, color, texture, contrast, rhythm, and audio elements such as timbre, volume, and velocity combine in different ways to communicate
emotions, harmony, resolution, tension, and movement. Design characteristics such as
bright colors, contrast, position, movement, and sound can define audiovisual hierarchies that prioritize information by highlighting specific audio or visual elements. The
Gestalt laws of perception simplify the communication process by helping us group
audiovisual information with similar design characteristics (e.g., size, shape, color,
texture, rhythm, timbre, pitch, volume, velocity, etc.). Discord and tension, as well as
harmony, also impact the aesthetics of an experience. Both define the affective experience, and they can highlight differences and draw attention to specific relationships,
as well as capture the attention of the user.

© Springer Nature Switzerland AG 2019
A. Marcus and W. Wang (Eds.): HCII 2019, LNCS 11583, pp. 84–97, 2019.
https://doi.org/10.1007/978-3-030-23570-3_8

However, the aesthetics of a design is not only defined by the audiovisual characteristics of an object or experience. Aesthetics is not just an affective experience based on emotional reactions. There isn't one definition of aesthetics or specific set of criteria that defines a "good" aesthetic experience. Kant [5] proposed that aesthetics involves logic, as well as the sensory properties of an object or experience. Baumgarten [6] emphasized the importance of sensory perception and cognition in aesthetics. Tuan [7] also highlighted the importance of the senses and cognition in defining the meaning of objects and physical environments, and in turn, the aesthetic experience: "An object or place achieves concrete reality when our experience of it is total, that is, through all the senses as well as with the active and reflective mind" (p. 18).

Artists, designers, philosophers, and psychologists continue to redefine and expand the definition of aesthetics. New electronic technologies that involve interactive, multimedia designs challenge us to define a new aesthetic discourse. The physical interactions of the user in environments where information continually changes, and in hybrid spaces that blend physical and virtual spaces, define the aesthetics of the experience. In these electronic environments, the aesthetics of a design is not static. It continually evolves as relationships change and new experiences are added to our knowledge base.

Research has shown that semantic relationships, sensory perception, cognition, schemas, memory, physical interaction and embodiment, and social discourse impact how we interpret information and the aesthetics of a design. We can gain a better understanding of the aesthetics of interaction design by looking at research in semiotics, cross-modal perception, cognitive psychology, and philosophy. This paper highlights some of the research in these fields that applies to the aesthetics of interaction design.

2   Interactive Semiotics

The semiotics of an interactive, multimedia design is an essential part of the aesthetics of the design. Design can symbolize specific functions. Affordances in design refer to the perceived and actual design elements of an object that suggest how the object should be used [8]. Some affordances that contribute to the aesthetics of the design include:

- Physical Affordance: Design property that makes it possible to physically do something with the object
- Sensory Affordance: Design property that enables the use of the senses
- Cognitive Affordance: Design property that makes it possible to think or know something
- Functional Affordance: Design property that defines the purpose of the design [9, p. 8]

Affordances define layers of signification that become part of the semantic structure of the design, and in turn, part of the design aesthetics. Through experience and interaction with an object, users learn what to expect from a particular design. They form conclusions that can be applied to the interpretation of other designs.

In multimedia computing, the integration of sound and visual design elements expands the semantic structure of a design and creates an interactive dialogue with multiple layers of associations. Research [10] has shown that individuals actively engage in the process of deciphering the relationships between visuals and audio, and derive pleasure from this process, which becomes part of the aesthetic experience. There is "a neurological pleasure in complex processing" because "the brain is pleasurably occupied with the task of simultaneously processing (and perhaps matching) two different visual and auditory codes" [10, p. 53].

In audiovisual design, each sensory stimulus can impact the perception of other stimuli. Research has shown that the perception of visual information is altered when sound is added to the visuals [11–14]. Sound can enhance the detection of specific individual visual elements, as well as improve the detection of motion [11, 15]. The intensity of sound can highlight the perceived contrast and intensity of a visual stimulus [11, 16], and the perception of repetition in visuals is enhanced with the addition of repetitive sounds [17].

O'Leary and Rhodes [18] also discovered that segmenting sensory information in visual stimuli can result in the perception of segmentation in the audio stimuli. For example, their research showed that visual elements that are presented as two separate elements or movements result in the perception of two separate audio tones when concurrent sounds are introduced. Vroomen and de Gelder [11] discovered that if a tone separates from an auditory stream, visual elements also separate from synchronized visual stimuli. However, when continuous visual elements are present in an audiovisual design, the sounds will also be perceived as continuous [18].

A multimedia design is a synthesis of different semiotic structures that enables users to transcend the limited perspective of specific media and actions. Layers of spatial, temporal, and sensory networks continually change. There are parallel, synchronous formats and linear progressions through the content. A new audiovisual semantic structure integrates the syntax of the media into complex affective and cognitive models. The integration of different media results in an overarching metasyntax that is transmodal [19, 20]. The metasyntax integrates the semantic, spatial, and temporal modalities of words, images, sound, and movements into a holistic, multisensory experience. This pluralism results in a polysemiotic semantic structure that defines a discursive communication experience. The different media and movements create an enactive, iconic, and symbolic space in which semiotic structures overlap [21]. The metasyntax creates a fluid semiosis and design aesthetic by defining sensory and cognitive relationships that transcend the meaning of individual elements.

With interaction design, causality also contributes to the semiotics and aesthetics of the design. Actions lead to specific audiovisual responses, and audiovisual events can trigger other events. There is a lack of closure that keeps the semantic structure and aesthetics of the design in flux and continually evolving.

In interactive computing, the physical motions of the user also contribute to the semiotics and aesthetics of the design through the spatial grammar of interaction [22]. The movements define rhythm and tempo. The physical interaction leads to additional information and events that define new sensory and cognitive relationships. Djajadiningrat, Matthews, and Stienstra [23] referred to the "semantics of motion" which shifts action from a purely "non-functional" role to an aesthetic role that is "necessary" for an engaging experience (pp. 10–11). In designing interactive environments, there is usually a focus on the specific action or movement that generates a response. However, the movements in between these actions, which symbolize the potential for new ideas and creative exploration, also contribute to the aesthetic interpretation of the interactive experience.

3 Space and Time

Space and time also define the aesthetics of the design. Space and time are flexible entities that describe relationships between events. The process of interaction creates patterns and rhythms that encode space and time into tangible representations of dynamic relationships and the transformation of ideas [22].

Visual elements and sound create sensory responses and impact the perception of space and time. Visuals can define spatial relationships through perspective, color, transparency, and transitions that take place over time. Sound can be both spatial and linear. Melodic sequences are linear, but sound also penetrates space and creates additional layers of depth that expand our awareness of spatial and temporal relationships. Research has demonstrated that audio and visual stimuli can impact the perception of spatial location [24–29]. The velocities [30–33], relative intensities [34, 35], and duration [35] of auditory and visual stimuli also impact the perception of time and whether or not sounds and visuals appear to be synchronized and occur simultaneously.

Silence is a design element that also contributes to the aesthetics of an experience. It is a space that signifies open-ended possibilities. Silence can intensity the experience as the user waits for something to happen. It can also provide an opportunity for the user to reflect on the information and relationships that have been presented.

In interactive programs, the space between events is as important as the space where events actually happen. Space is where sensory and cognitive relationships are formed which lead to new aesthetic and learning experiences. Space defines moments in the continual process of change, demonstrating that "space and time serve as the contexts in which all communication entities exist and unfold" [36, p. 74].

3.1 Hybrid Spaces

In some interactive applications, such as virtual reality and augmented reality applications, there is also the integration of different types of spaces that impacts the semiotics and aesthetics of the design. These hybrid environments create opportunities to explore sensory and cognitive relationships in the physical and virtual spaces from different perspectives. Ross [37] pointed out that augmented reality's "potential innovativeness lies in its ability to generate new ways of perceiving for the spectator or to disclose what was previously unperceived—unseen, unheard, unfelt, unsmelt" (Introduction section, para. 4).

In hybrid environments, the audiovisual information in physical and virtual spaces becomes part of the syntax and aesthetics of the interactive experience. The interface designs integrate the aesthetics of the physical environment with the aesthetics of the virtual world and program functions. Virtual and physical spaces overlap and combine different information and spatial relationships defined by images, sound, and text. The integration of these diverse layers of sensory and cognitive information impacts the semiotics and aesthetics of the interface design. In augmented reality applications, for example, virtual information is displayed on top of images and sounds in the physical environment. The user experience includes the cognitive processing of facts and analytical relationships, as well as the sensory perception of audiovisual stimuli in the virtual and physical spaces [38].

The integration of these layers of cognitive and sensory information presents designers with new challenges in semiotics and aesthetics. In addition, virtual and physical information may appear within a frame formed by the mobile device or other hardware. These frames form boundaries that define the space and how users interpret the information in that space:

> Only select elements from the physical space are visible within the frame, creating a focus on that information rather than the information outside the frame. The frame itself suggests a finite limit because the experience is defined by discrete groups of data and spatial relationships... The technology emphasizes specific units of information at defined moments in time, rather than highlighting the connections between memories and experiences [38, p. 242].

3.2   Temporal Dynamics

The temporal dynamics of an interactive design also define the semiotics and aesthetics of the work. Information and semantic relationships change over time. There is an emphasis on "now" and "immediacy" [39]. Users anticipate immediate feedback and changes. These temporal dynamics drive the interaction as users feel compelled to update and share information on a regular basis [39]. The "present" takes on significance as it represents the current state of affairs in an environment that is continually changing.

There is also an emphasis on non-linear, pluralistic concepts of temporality that emphasize simultaneity. With multimedia design, it is possible to perceive sounds and visuals simultaneously as well as sequentially, resulting in the juxtaposition of different rhythms and sensory experiences. Because we can hear sounds while we look at visuals, we are able to simultaneously explore different temporal connections between the visuals and sound [40].

Rhythm is a design element that exemplifies the temporal dynamics of interaction design and plays an important role in the aesthetics of interactive, multimedia design. Layers of rhythms in the visual designs, sound, animations, and transitions between elements highlight the temporal relationships. Combinations of linear, sequential rhythms, as well as cyclical rhythms, create audiovisual counterpoints and syncopation. Pauses, empty spaces, and silence alter the rhythm and temporal dynamics of the interactive aesthetics [39]. The repetition of specific rhythms can weave individual elements into a coherent whole. Rhythm can create a unifying, overarching structure for the flexible, semiotic codes that characterize the dynamic aesthetics of multimedia design [39].

The physical interaction of the user also creates layers of rhythm. Djajadiningrat, Matthews, and Stienstra [23] referred to this rhythm as the "choreography motion" and "semantics of motion" which is necessary to envision an experience (p. 31, pp. 10–11). Physical movements define patterns in space and time that create a rhythmic counterpoint to the audiovisual patterns [41]. These patterns may repeat or complement the rhythms in the audiovisual elements, or they may be different and create layers of contrast.

4   Perception and Cognition

Sensory perception and cognition contribute to the aesthetic interpretation of an object or experience. Norman [42] noted that there is beauty that "is associated with the object itself" which is processed perceptually at the visceral, subconscious level, and there is beauty that is related to consciousness (p. 314). Referring to this conscious level of aesthetics interpretation, Norman [42] stated:

> It is only at the reflective level that full-fledged emotions reside. This level is intellectually driven. It is conscious and aware of emotional feelings. Moreover, it uses the rich history of prior experiences, one's own self-image, and personal meanings to evaluate any experience (p. 315).

Brunel, Carvalho, and Goldstone [43] cited established research that demonstrated the connection between perception and cognition, noting that the senses generally make it easier to identify [44], detect [45], categorize [46], and recognize [47] information [43, para. 3].

Parallel connections between sensory experiences also contribute to our interpretation of the aesthetics of an object or experience. When sensory experiences are not "congruent," it is possible to assign connections between sensory modalities that the user will later associate with these modalities [48–50]. We learn to integrate these sensory experiences and group them into "multimodal units" through an associative learning process called "unitization" [51, para. 1]. We also integrate current perceptual experiences with past experiences [52, 43]. As the learning process continues, new cognitive and aesthetic interpretations of an action or experience evolve.

Cross-modal perception also plays an important role in cognition and aesthetics. As previously discussed in the section on Interactive Semiotics, sensory stimuli can impact the perception of other sensory information. Cross-modal perception adds multiple layers of complex sensory relationships and interpretations to the cognitive and aesthetic models.

5   Interaction and Embodied Aesthetics

Embodiment is another dimension of interactive aesthetics. Physical movements bridge the physical and virtual spaces and help users create tangible connections to the visual and cognitive relationships defined in the digital world [53].

Merleau-Ponty [54] noted that "we perceive the world with our body" (p. 239), and he highlighted the interrelationship between perception and embodiment in the interpretation of objects and space: "The identity of the thing through perceptual experience is only another aspect of the identity of one's own body throughout exploratory movements; thus they are the same in kind as each other" (p. 215). Klemmer,

Hartmann, and Takayma [55] pointed out that "our bodies play a central role in shaping human experience in the world, understanding of the world, and interactions in the world" (p. 140).

Physical movements help us interpret spatial and temporal relationships and shape our cognitive understanding of objects and experiences [55–57]. Movement through space leads to different viewpoints, resulting in new interpretations that define the aesthetics of an object or experience.

In interaction design, interfaces that incorporate tangible connections to the physical world engage the senses and augment the learning experience [55, 58]. Palmerius [59] pointed out that "our sense of touch and kinesthetics is capable of supplying large amounts of intuitive information about the location, structure, stiffness and other material properties of objects" (p. 154). Dourish [60] noted that interaction with physical objects enhances cognition because tangible computing "is a physical realization of a symbolic reality, and the symbolic reality is, often, the world being manipulated" (p. 207).

The cognitive semantics theory of conceptual metaphor states that logic and reasoning are founded on image schemas formed by "patterns of our bodily orientations, movements, and interaction" that we develop into abstract references [56, p. 90]. Physical movement through space and interaction with tangible objects lead to symbolic representations [57]. Penny [60] pointed out that "the persuasiveness of interactivity is not in the images per se, but in the fact that bodily behavior is intertwined with the formation of representations… This interaction renders conventional critiques of representation inadequate, and calls for the theoretical and aesthetic study of embodied interaction." (p. 83).

Physical interaction leads to new semantic models and new aesthetic interpretations. We gain new perspectives and see additional relationships based on our physical interaction with the objects. Abrahamson and Lindgren [59] noted that "we develop the skill of controlling and interpreting the world through the mediating artifact" (p. 4). For Piaget [61], logic and the cognitive processing of information are derived from physical and mental interaction, and it is the coordination of action that leads to reflective abstraction. With physical interaction, we use reflective practice to work through ideas rather than just think about them [55].

The significance of embodiment and physical actions in interaction design is summed up by Djajadiningrat, Matthews, and Stienstra [23] who felt "the philosophy of embodiment dissolves the mind-body distinction, rather than replacing the Cartesian priority of 'mind over body' with a similarly dualist priority of 'body over mind'… Instead of a belief in mental models to successfully steer our actions, we may need to design for products that support the view that our understanding of the world springs from our bodily engagement with it" (p. 27). Interaction with the physical environment leads to the synthesis of sensory and cognitive information into abstract models that we use to interpret information and define the aesthetics of a design.

6 Cognitive Collages, Schemas, Memory

Sensory stimuli, interaction and embodiment, and experience are the building blocks for semantic and cognitive models. Research has also shown that the creation of semantic models is a dynamic process that changes over time. Hopfield [62] explored dynamic connectionist models where semantic representations change through interaction with other cognitive processes. These models evolve as an emergent process through learning [63, 64], and lead to complex cognitive models and personal interpretations of information called cognitive collages [65]. Turkle and Papert [66] referred to this type of cognitive mapping of diverse perceptual responses as bricolage.

In a non-linear, multisensory information space, layers of events and time, along with affective domains based on sensory experiences, provide a fluid, multisensory information space that supports reflection and the building of personal networks of associations and cognitive collages. These evolving sensory and cognitive models lead to the formation of complex schemas that help us interpret information [67] and define the aesthetics of an object or experience. Schemas play an important role in knowledge construction [68, 69]. As we learn how something works, we build new associations that draw on these experiences and create new schemas that are defined by the assimilation of information from other schemas [70]. For Moriarty, the "process begins with observation and then proceeds in a back-and-forth process of developing hypotheses and comparing the observations with information known and filed in memory" [71, p. 181].

Memory is an important dimension in aesthetics. Kinesthetic memory, derived from physical actions, contributes to the creation of sensory and cognitive models that define the aesthetics of an interactive design. Physical actions and movements create muscle memory or implicit memory that helps us learn and remember how to perform actions [72]. Costello [73] noted, "Therefore, we not only move our body in certain ways when we feel emotion, but also, in moving our body, we can, through this engrained kinetic intelligence, provoke memories of emotions and bodily sensation" [p. 258].

Memory also contributes to the abstraction and synthesis of information that enables us to draw on past experiences and intuition to interpret the meaning and aesthetics of an object or experience [74]. Kant [5] believed that imagination is also a part of cognition that helps us understand objects. He noted that we gain this understanding "from the influence of the senses, from the play of imagination, the laws of memory, the power of habit, inclination, etc." [5, p. 194]. Imagination, like memory, synthesizes information so we can apply it. However, imagination adds another dimension to this process because it leads to the exploration of relationships and contributes to flexible models of interpretation and aesthetics.

7 Social Discourse

Online discussions and collaborations foster the development of social discourse that also defines the aesthetics of an interactive design by adding layers of mediated sociocultural interpretation to the design syntax. This online interaction redefines the social and cultural context for information and leads to new interpretations and aesthetics based on diverse perspectives.

Ingold [75] highlighted the importance of multiple perspectives and the impact the "creative interweaving of experience in discourse" has on the perception of society (p. 285). Jenkins [76] pointed out that social discourse leads to designs that are "shaped by cultural and social protocols" (p. 133). Users expect and define new ways of interacting with each other, which leads to new approaches to interface design. Benkler [77] noted that decentralized methods of collaboration, along with the focus on sharing information in social media networks, lead to the creation of new "patterns of production" that are defined by social interaction protocols (p. 3).

French art critic Bourriaud [78] recognized the significance of social context in defining aesthetics in his book *Esthétique Relationnelle* (*Relational Aesthetics*). Bourriaud [78] considered relational aesthetics "a set of artistic practices which take as their theoretical and practical point of departure the whole of human relations and their social context, rather than an independent and private space" (p. 113). He emphasized the significance of the relationship the object or experience creates with participants which defines the "criteria of co-existence" [78, p. 109].

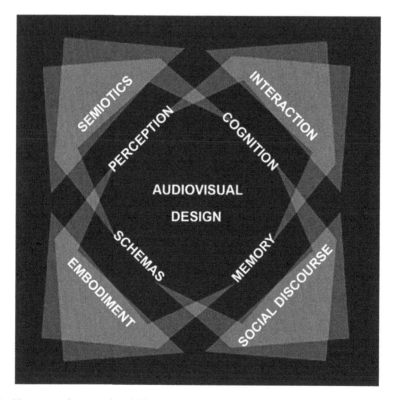

Fig. 1. Numerous elements, in addition to the audiovisual design, define the dynamic aesthetics of an interactive, multimedia program. Layers of sensory and semantic relationships continually change and contribute to the formation of complex cognitive collages. Copyright 2019 Patricia Search. All rights reserved.

With online discussions and collaborations, multiple perspectives lead to a mediated discourse that transforms the meaning of signs and creates a fluid ontology and dynamic aesthetic experience. This type of flexible ontology reflects the following description of the dynamic nature of contemporary society as noted by O'Neill and Hubbard [79]: "If one accepts that mobility, flux and change are normal conditions of our contemporary world, then issues of becoming rather than being appear more in tune with the manifold process by which differences are materialised, embodied and experienced" (p. 47).

8 Conclusion

With interactive technology, the aesthetics of an interface design is defined by numerous factors including semiotics, perception, cognition, schemas, memory, interaction, embodiment, and social discourse (Fig. 1). In interactive programs, where information and events continually change, a discursive, multimedia experience leads to fluid sensory, semantic, and aesthetic relationships. Cross-modal perception and a metasyntax impact the interpretation of these dynamic relationships. Interaction and embodiment define the user's physical relationship to the technology, causal relationships, and the functionality of the design. Each user brings a unique interpretation to the design because of past experiences which create cognitive collages and schemas. Memory and imagination synthesize these experiences into abstract models that define the aesthetic interpretation of the object or experience.

New technologies also impact the aesthetics of an interactive experience. Social media and networking software support social discourse and the creation of collective memory and pluralistic interpretations of interactive designs. Some technologies, such as artificial intelligence agents and cognitive filters, attempt to interpret and anticipate the user's interests by preselecting specific information. These technologies may expand the user's interpretation of the information or limit it by discouraging exploration.

Designers need to be aware of the sensory and cognitive restrictions in technologies and the multiple dimensions of interactive aesthetics, so they can determine the most effective ways to use different media and embodiment in interaction design. The audiovisual design is important, but it is not the only factor to consider. Usability testing generally focuses on evaluating the stylistic, affective domain of an audiovisual design and how the design impacts user engagement and performance. However, there are other factors in the aesthetics of the user experience that should be evaluated. We need to consider how the different dimensions of aesthetics discussed in this paper impact the user's interpretation of the experience and develop research and usability tests to measure those factors. This research can help designers understand how to incorporate the different dimensions of aesthetics into engaging and intuitive interactive experiences.

References

1. Kurosu, M., Kashimura, K.: Apparent usability vs. inherent usability: experimental analysis on the determinants of the apparent usability. In: CHI 1995: Conference Companion on Human Factors in Computing Systems, Denver, Colorado, United States, pp. 292–293 (1995)
2. Ngo, D., Byrne, J.G.: Another look at a model for evaluating interface aesthetics. Int. J. Appl. Math. Comput. Sci. **11**(2), 515–535 (2001)
3. Stasko, J., Catrambone, R., Guzdial, M., McDonald, K.: An evaluation of space-filling information visualizations for depicting hierarchical structures. Int. J. Hum. Comput. Stud. **53**(5), 663–694 (2000)
4. Cawthon, N., Vande Moere, A.: The effect of aesthetic on the usability of data visualization. In: Proceedings of the IEEE International Conference Information Visualization (IV 2007), pp. 637–648, Zurich, Switzerland (2007)
5. Kant, I.: Critique of Pure Reason (P. Guyer, A. Wood). Cambridge University Press, Cambridge (1998)
6. Baumgarten, A.: Metaphysics: A Critical Translation with Kant's Elucidations, Selected Notes, and Related Materials (C.D. Fugate, J. Hymers). Bloomsbury Academic, New York (2014)
7. Tuan, Y.-F.: Space and Place. University of Minnesota, Minneapolis (1977)
8. Norman, D.: The Psychology of Everyday Things. Basic Books, New York (1988)
9. Xenakis, I., Arnellos, A., Spyrou, T., Darzentas, J.: Modelling aesthetic judgment: an interactive-semiotic perspective. Cybern. Hum. Knowing **19**(3), 25–51 (2012)
10. Reason, M., Jola, C., Kay, R., Reynolds, D., Kauppi, J., Grobras, M., Tohka, J., Pollick, F.: Spectators' aesthetic experience of sound and movement in dance performance: a transdisciplinary investigation. Psychol. Aesthet. Creat. Arts **10**(1), 42–55 (2016)
11. Vroomen, J., de Gelder, B.: Sound enhances visual perception: cross-modal effects of auditory or-ganization on vision. Hum. Percept. Perform. **26**(5), 1583–1590 (2000)
12. Mazza, V., Turatto, M., Rossi, M., Umiltà, C.: How automatic are audiovisual links in exogenous spatial attention? Neuropsychologia **45**(3), 514–522 (2007)
13. McDonald, J.J., Teder-Sälejärvi, W.A., Hillyard, S.A.: Involuntary orienting to sound improves visual perception. Nature **407**(6806), 906–908 (2000)
14. Spence, C., Driver, J.: Audiovisual links in endogenous covert spatial orienting. Percept. Psychophys. **59**(1), 1–22 (1997)
15. Beer, A., Watanabe, T.: Specificity of auditory-guided visual perceptual learning suggests crossmodal plasticity in early visual cortex. Exp. Brain Res. **198**(2), 353–361 (2009)
16. Stein, B.E., London, N., Wilkinson, L.K., Price, D.P.: Enhancement of perceived visual intensity by auditory stimuli: a psychophysical analysis. J. Cogn. Neurosci. **8**(6), 497–506 (1996)
17. Chen, Y., Yeh, S.: Catch the moment: multisensory enhancement of rapid visual events by sound. Exp. Brain Res. **198**(2), 209–219 (2009)
18. O'Leary, A., Rhodes, G.: Cross-modal effects on visual and auditory object perception. Percept. Psychophys. **35**(6), 565–569 (1984)
19. Search, P.: HyperGlyphs: using design and language to define hypermedia navigation. J. Educ. Multimed. Hypermedia **2**(4), 369–380 (1993)
20. Macken-Horarik, M.: Interacting with the multimodal text: reflections on image and verbiage. Vis. Commun. **3**(1), 5–26 (2004)

21. Search, P.: Defining a sense of place in interactive multimedia design. In: Avgerinou, M., Chandler, S. (eds.) Visual Literacy in the 21st Century: Trends, Demands, And Capacities, pp. 143–148. International Visual Literacy Association, Chicago (2011)

22. Search, P.: The spatial grammar of interaction design: weaving a tapestry of space and time in multimedia computing. In: Griffin, R., Cowden, B., Avgerinou, M. (eds.) Animating the Mind's Eye, pp. 184–190. International Visual Literacy Association, Loretto (2006)

23. Djajadiningrat, J., Matthews, B., Stienstra, M.: Easy doesn't do it: skill and expression in tangible aesthetics. Pers. Ubiquitous Comput. 11(8), 657–676 (2007)

24. Bertelson, P., Radeau, M.: Cross-modal bias and perceptual fusion with auditory-visual spatial discordance. Percept. Psychophys. 29(6), 578–584 (1981)

25. Vroomen, J., Bertelson, P., de Gelder, B.: A visual influence in the discrimination of auditory location. In: Proceedings of the International Conference on Auditory-Visual Speech Processing (AVSP 1998), pp. 131–135. Causal Productions, Sydney, Australia (1998)

26. Vroomen, J.: Ventriloquism and the nature of the unity assumption. In: Aschersleben, G., Bachmann, T., Müsseler, J. (eds.) Cognitive Contributions to the Perception of Spatial and Temporal Events, pp. 388–394. Elsevier Science, New York (1999)

27. Vroomen, J., Bertelson, P., de Gelder, B.: The ventriloquist effect does not depend on the direction of deliberate visual attention. Percept. Psychophys. 63(4), 651–659 (2001)

28. Lewald, J., EhrenBee, W.H., Guski, R.: Spatio-temporal constraints for auditory-visual integration. Behav. Brain Res. 121(1–2), 69–79 (2001)

29. Leward, J., Guski, R.: Cross-modal perceptual integration of spatially and temporary disparate auditory and visual stimuli. Cogn. Brain Res. 16(3), 468–478 (2003)

30. Neumann, O., Niepel, M.: Timing of "perception" and perception of "time". In: Kärnbach, C., Schröger, E., Müller, H. (eds.) Psychophysics Beyond Sensation: Laws and Invariants of Human Cognition, pp. 245–269. Erlbaum, Mahwah (2004)

31. Jaśkowski, P.: Simple reaction time and perception of temporal order: dissociations and hypotheses. Percept. Motor Skills 82(3, Pt 1), 707–730 (1996)

32. Zampini, M., Shore, D.I., Spence, C.: Audiovisual temporal-order judgments. Exp. Brain Res. 152(2), 198–210 (2003)

33. Zampini, M., Shore, D.I., Spence, C.: Multisensory temporal-order judgments: the role of hemispheric redundancy. Int. J. Psychophysiol. 50(1), 165–180 (2003)

34. Neumann, O., Koch, R., Niepel, M., Tappe, T.: Reaction time and temporal-order judgment: correspondence or dissociation. Z. Exp. Angew. Psychol. 39(4), 621–645 (1992)

35. Boenke, L.T., Deliano, M., Ohl, F.W.: Stimulus duration influences perceived simultaneity in audiovisual temporal-order judgment. Exp. Brain Res. 198(2–3), 233–244 (2009)

36. Monge, P., Kalmann, M.: Sequentiality, simultaneity, and synchronicity in human communication. In: Watt, J., VanLear, C.A. (eds.) Dynamic Patterns in Communication Processes, pp. 71–91. Sage Publications, Thousand Oaks (1996)

37. Ross, C.: Augmented reality art: a matter of (non)destination. In: Proceedings of the Digital Arts and Culture Conference, University of California, Irvine (2009). http://escholarship.org/uc/item/6q71j0zh

38. Search, P.: Information design opportunities with augmented reality applications. Inf. Des. J. 22(3), 237–246 (2016)

39. Search, P.: Relational aesthetics in interactive art and design. In: Aesthetics@Media, Arts and Culture, pp. 632–643. International Association of Empirical Aesthetics, Taipei (2012)

40. Search, P.: Using new media art and multisensory design for information and data representation. In: Tiradentes Souto, V., Spinillo, C., Portugal, C., Fadel, L. (eds.) Selected Readings of the 7th Information Design International Conference, pp. 179–190. The Brazilian Society of Information Design, Brasilia (2016)

41. Search, P.: Multisensory physical environments for data representation. In: Marcus, A. (ed.) Proceedings of HCI International 2016: Design, user experience, and usability, Part III, pp. 202–213. Springer, Cham, Switzerland (2016)
42. Norman, D.A.: Introduction to this special section on beauty, goodness, and usability. Hum. Comput. Interact. **19**(4), 311–318 (2004)
43. Brunel, L., Carvalho, P., Goldstone, R.: It does belong together: cross-modal correspondences influence cross-modal integration during perceptual learning. Front. Psychol. **6**, 358 (2015). https://doi.org/10.3389/fpsyg.2015.00358
44. MacLeod, A., Summerfield, Q.: A procedure for measuring auditory and audiovisual speech-reception thresholds for sentences in noise: rationale, evaluation, and recommendations for use. Br. J. Audiol. **24**(1), 29–43 (1990)
45. Stein, B.E., Meredith, M.A.: The Merging of Senses. MIT Press, Cambridge (1993)
46. Chen, Y.-C., Spence, C.: When hearing the bark helps to identify the dog: semantically-congruent sounds modulate the identification of masked pictures. Cognition **114**(3), 389–404 (2010)
47. Molholm, S., Ritter, W., Murray, M.M., Javitt, D.C., Schroeder, C.E., Foxe, J.J.: Multisensory auditory–visual interactions during early sensory processing in humans: a high-density electrical mapping study. Cogn. Brain. Res. **14**(1), 115–128 (2002)
48. Brunel, L., Labeye, E., Lesourd, M., Versace, R.: The sensory nature of episodic memory: sensory priming effects due to memory trace activation. J. Exp. Psychol. Learn. Mem. Cogn. **35**(4), 1081–1088 (2009)
49. Brunel, L., Lesourd, M., Labeye, E., Versace, R.: The sensory nature of knowledge: sensory priming effects in semantic categorization. Q. J. Exp. Psychol. **63**(5), 955–964 (2010)
50. Brunel, L., Goldstone, R.L., Vallet, G., Riou, B., Versace, R.: When seeing a dog activates the bark: multisensory generalization and distinctiveness effects. Exp. Psychol. **60**(2), 100–112 (2013)
51. Connolly, K.: Multisensory perception as an associative learning process. Front. Psychol. **5**, 1095 (2014). https://doi.org/10.3389/fpsyg.2014.01095
52. Goldstone, R.L., Landy, D., Brunel, L.C.: Improving the perception to make distant connections closer. Front. Psychol. **2**, 385 (2013). https://doi.org/10.3389/fpsyg.2011.00385
53. Search, P.: HyperGlyphs: new multiliteracy models for interactive computing. In: Griffin, R., Lee, J., Williams, V. (eds.) Visual Literacy in Message Design, pp. 171–177. International Visual Literacy Association, Loretto (2002)
54. Merleau-Ponty, M.: Phenomenology of Perception (C. Smith). Routledge, London (1945, repr. 2005)
55. Klemmer, S.R., Hartmann, B., Takayama, L.: How bodies matter: five themes for interaction design. In: Proceedings of Designing Interactive Systems (DIS 2006), pp. 140–148 (2006)
56. Lakoff, G., Johnson, M.L.: Metaphors We Live By. University of Chicago Press, Chicago (1980)
57. Abrahamson, D., Lindgren, R.: Embodiment and embodied design. In: Sawyer, R.K. (ed.) The Cambridge Handbook of the Learning Sciences, 2nd edn, pp. 357–376. Cambridge University Press, Cambridge (2014)
58. Dourish, P.: Where the Action Is: The Foundations of Embodied Interaction. MIT Press, Cambridge (2001)
59. Palmerius, K.L., Forsell, C.: The impact of feedback design in haptic volume visualization. In: Third Joint EuroHaptics Conference 2009 and Symposium on Haptic Interfaces for Virtual Environment and Teleoperator Systems, World Haptics 2009, pp. 154–159. IEEE Press, New York (2009)

60. Penny, S.: Representation, enaction, and the ethics of simulation. In: Wardrip-Fruin, N., Harrigan, P. (eds.) First Person: New Media as Story, Performance, and Game, pp. 73–84. MIT Press, Cambridge (2004)
61. Piaget, J.: Recherches sur l'Abstraction Reflechissante, Vol. I & II. Presses Universitaires de France, Paris (1977)
62. Hopfield, J.J.: Neural networks and physical systems with emergent collective computational abilities. Proc. Natl. Acad. Sci. **79**(8), 2554–2558 (1982)
63. Rumelhart, D.E., Todd, P.M.: Learning and connectionist representations. In: Meyer, D.E., Kornblum, S. (eds.) Attention and Performance XIV: Synergies in Experimental Psychology, Artificial Intelligence, and Cognitive Neuroscience, pp. 3–30. MIT Press, Cambridge (1993)
64. Jones, M., Willits, J., Dennis, S.: Models of semantic memory. In: Busemeyer, J., Wang, Z., Townsend, J., Eidels, A. (eds.) The Oxford Handbook of Computational and Mathematical Psychology, pp. 232–254. Oxford University Press, New York (2015)
65. Tversky, B.: Cognitive maps, cognitive collages, and spatial mental models. In: Frank, A., Campari, I. (eds.) Spatial Information Theory: A Theoretical Basis for GIS, pp. 14–24. Springer, Heidelberg (1993)
66. Turkle, S., Papert, S.: Epistemological pluralism and the evaluations of the concrete. In: Harel, I., Papert, S. (eds.) Constructivism, pp. 161–192. Ablex Publishing Company, Norwood (1993)
67. Rogers, T.T., McClelland, J.L.: Semantic Cognition. MIT Press, Cambridge (2006)
68. Minsky, M.: The Society of Mind. Simon and Shuster, New York (1988)
69. Bergman, A.: Auditory Scene Analysis. MIT Press, Cambridge (1994)
70. Piaget, J.: The Moral Judgement of the Child. Kegen Paul, Trench, Trubner & Co, London (1932)
71. Moriarty, S.E.: Abduction: a theory of visual interpretation. Commun. Theory **6**(2), 167–187 (1996)
72. Meister, M.L.R., Buffalo, E.A.: Memory. In: Conn, M. (ed.) Conn's Translational Neuroscience, pp. 693–708. Academic Press, Cambridge (2016)
73. Costello, B.: Rhythms of kinesthetic empathy. Leonardo **47**(3), 258–259 (2014)
74. Search, P.: A new visual literacy discourse for interactive electronic communication. In: Avgerinou, M., Griffin, R., Giesen, J., Search, P. (eds.) Engaging Creativity and Critical Thinking, pp. 181–188. International Visual Literacy Association, Loretto (2009)
75. Ingold, T.: The Perception of the Environment. Routledge, London (2000)
76. Jenkins, H.: Convergence Culture: Where Old and New Media Collide. New York University, New York (2006)
77. Benkler, Y.: The Wealth of Networks: How Social Production Transform Markets and Freedom. Yale University Press, New Haven (2006)
78. Bourriaud, N.: Esthétique Relationnelle. Les Presses du Réel, Dijon (2002)
79. O'Neill, M., Hubbard, P.: Walking, sensing, belonging: ethno-mimesis as performative praxis. Vis. Stud. **25**(1), 46–58 (2010)

User Experience and Social Influence: A New Perspective for UX Theory

Jan Van Der Linden[1(✉)], Franck Amadieu[2], Emilie Vayre[3],
and Cécile Van De Leemput[1]

[1] Research Center for Work and Consumer Psychology,
Université libre de Bruxelles, Brussels, Belgium
jan.van.der.linden@ulb.ac.be
[2] CNRS, UT2J, University of Toulouse, Toulouse, France
[3] Laboratoire parisien de psychologie sociale,
Université Paris Nanterre, Nanterre, France

Abstract. Research on *User experience (UX)* is mainly focused on the individual user's technological experience. To extend the UX framework and toobtain a better understanding of the psychological processes involved, thisresearch investigates the influence of the social environment (peer students and teachers)on user experience. This UX study is based on the Component of UserExperience model developed by Thüring and Mahlke [1]. A survey was carriedout in a Belgian and a French university to study students' tablet user experience.Results indicate that peer students influence Perceived usefulness, Perceivedease of use, the Aesthetic aspects and the Motivational aspects whileteachers only influence the Aesthetic aspects and Symbolic aspects. Globally, peer students influence instrumental and non-instrumental factors and teachersinfluence only non-instrumental factors. The results may be explained throughthe *Group influence processes* theory. In conclusion, this study offers a newperspective for research on UX. The theoretical framework should extend itsscope to the social environment impact.

Keywords: User experience · CUE-model · Social support · Tablet · University students

1 Introduction

Over the last few years, technology devices have never been so present in our daily lives. People are confronted with technologies in work, learning and leisure contexts. Consequently, it is not surprising that are more and more research efforts aim a better understanding of human-computer interaction from a user point of view. To investigate this matter, the research framework *User Experience (UX)* is particularly adequate. It proposes to understand the psychological processes at stakes when one is confronted with a technological device. However, even if UX related studies became popular over the last few years, not much research has been undertaken to study the impact from the social environment on this user experience. Theories from social psychology and works stemming from other approaches like the Technology acceptance approach have

© Springer Nature Switzerland AG 2019
A. Marcus and W. Wang (Eds.): HCII 2019, LNCS 11583, pp. 98–112, 2019.
https://doi.org/10.1007/978-3-030-23570-3_9

proven the importance of the social surrounding in technology adoption. Therefore, this paper proposes to investigate the influence of peers students and teachers in the context of tablet usage at university.

2 Theoretical Background

2.1 User Experience (UX)

The User Experience approach emerged as a comprehensive framework, which provides a holistic perspective on users' subjective response arising from technology usage. This appraisal can be described as a multidimensional phenomenon that encompasses the judgment of various aspects related to the task accomplishment but also to personal desires, as well as the emotions aroused by technology interaction. In other words, unlike Technology Acceptance Models [2–5] that are based on the assessment of usability, usefulness and ease of use evaluation, the UX approach integrates more than just task-related issues broadening the scope to personal needs, desires and emotional feeling.

The ISO norm 9241-210 defines UX as "a person's perceptions and responses that result from the use or anticipated use of a product, system or service" [6]. Although this definition is rather broad, several attempts have tried to define more precisely the UX concept and to specify its characteristics [7–12]. Based on the aforementioned authors it is possible to summarize the main features of the UX approach in four concepts. First, UX is necessarily subjective and arise from technology usage. Second, UX aims a holistic perspective, including interests in non-utilitarian factors. Third, emotions are fully integrated into the subjective experience. Fourth, the nature of the user experience evolves overtime.

To take these aspects into account, the Components of User Experience model (CUE-Model; see Fig. 1) proposed by Thüring & Mahlke in [1] attempts to define and schematize the core elements of UX. This is one of the most thorough models incorporating several UX features. It has been built from empirical research findings on smartphones and audio players studies. As a result, the CUE-model is particularly suited to empirical research on innovative technologies and allows to test external effects on the several aspects of the user experience [1, 13].

In the CUE-model, the core aspects of the user experience are summarized in three distinct components: the Perceived instrumental qualities, the Perceived non-instrumental qualities and the Emotional reactions. The first component, which concerns Perceived instrumental qualities, focuses on task-related judgments and may be linked to another HCI approach, the technology acceptance framework (e.g. [2–4]). This component takes up Perceived usefulness, and Perceived ease of use as the central elements constituting the component. The second component, which concerns non-instrumental qualities, deals with technological aspects that are not important to task performances but for the user own personal desires and needs. It encompasses the Aesthetics and Symbolic aspects judgments, but also the Motivational aspects that constitute the technology's inherent capacity to motivate its use. The last component concerns Emotional reactions. It is theorized as encompassing the emotional

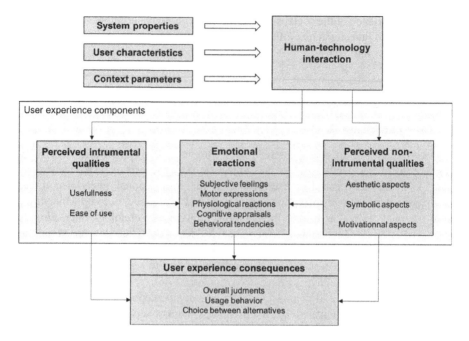

Fig. 1. CUE-model

consequences stemming from the other two components. Moreover, Thüring and Mahlke point out that these three components of user experience will allow one to form an overall judgment and determine technology usage behaviour. Besides, the authors detail the UX antecedents. User characteristics, contextual factors and system properties shape the interaction between a user and a system that is responsible for the user experience's nature. Interestingly, the only direct antecedent of UX is the human-technology interaction.

In conclusion, as Bevan affirms: "user experience focuses on the user's preferences, perceptions, emotions and physical and psychological responses that occur before, during and after use, rather than the observed effectiveness and efficiency. While usability typically deals with goals shared by a user group, user experience is concerned with individual goals, which can include personal motivations including needs to acquire new knowledge and skills, to communicate personal identity and to provoke pleasant memories. User experience also puts emphasis on how the experience changes with repeated use" [14].

2.2   Social Influences

The user's social environment is considered to be a major factor to understand the user's subjective appraisal and behavior. Several psychological theories have proved that a group can significantly affect an individual. For instance, the Reference group theory states that an individual seeks the advice of opinion leaders and/or from a group of experts before shaping his or her own opinion [15, 16]. The Group influence processes suggests that, in order to strengthen relationships with other group members, an individual adopts the behavioral norms of the group [17]. The Social exchange theory explains that an individual acts in a cost-benefit perspective [18]. Where every decision or action is expected to bring personal benefits.

In the specific case of technology usage, the previous theories have also demonstrated a certain consistency between users' opinions and their behavior towards a given technology and the ones that are stemming from his or her social environment. Indeed, *Innovation diffusion* research suggests that technology adoption decisions are impacted by the user's social system, beyond the individual's decision style and IT characteristics [19]. In addition, studies rooted in the *Technology acceptance* approach have shown that social norms and groups play a predominant role in the intention to use a technology. Interestingly, several TAM extensions incorporated social related factors. For example, Hardgrave, Davis and Riemenscneider [20], as well as Venkatesh and Bala [4] included the social norms as explaining factor for Perceived usefulness. Other studies applying the TAM framework show that the appreciation and use of technology by peers and teachers has a positive impact on Perceived usefulness [21, 22].

Based on aforementioned studies and models, it is possible to assume that a direct social impact on an individual user experience must exists. First, as proven by TAM literature, there is a social influence on the Perceived instrumental qualities. Secondly, the Perceived non-instrumental qualities must also be impacted. The *Reference group theory* suggests that the social environment shapes any type of opinions. This must be applicable to the judgment of the non-instrumental qualities, such as technology aesthetics and symbolic attributes. In addition, as more and more everyday technology can be used in a social environment, group influence processes are involved. Accordingly, technology motivational aspects could be influenced. Indeed, to get closer to his or her social group, technology can be used as an expression of group norms adoption.

2.3 Tablet Usage at University

To study this topic, the use of tablets has been chosen as subject. Since the first iPad released in 2010, tablets have become popular devices. They are used in different context, and especially in the educational context. Tablets are considered innovative and user-friendly devices for learning and task management. Some students in order to replace their notebooks or laptops have quickly adopted them. The ease of transport, the need for only finger gestures to control interaction, the autonomy, and their innovative design make these interesting tools suitable for field and laboratory work [23]. Tablets provide the benefits of mobile applications while providing a larger screen than smartphone devices. They are also useful for short or quick interaction and for fun activities at the university [24]. Furthermore, the addition of accessories like an external keyboard or an electronic pencil broadens the range of possibilities and facilitates notes taking, sketches drawing and the marking of electronic documents. Besides, the Bring Your Own Device (BOYD) strategies can be used to reduce in the ICT infrastructure costs and provide students with enhanced comfort of use and the possibility to avoid overcrowded university computer labs. Nowadays, the situation has changed to the point that many students entering higher education expect to use their mobile devices as part of the educational process [25]. And indeed, more and more students are using their tablet to plan and support learning activities.

However, tablets are not only task completion tools. They also reflect the more personal needs and desires of users. In consequence, tablets are perfect study objects to carry out UX research. As mentioned, tablets are not just popular mobile computing devices used for task completion and learning. It may be argued that they also includes self-oriented expectations like an enhanced self-image, or a pleasurable experience. However, these aspects have often been overlooked in studies trying to understand technology usage in educational fields. Frequently, when an innovative technology like a tablet is introduced, the Technology Acceptance Model (TAM) [2], or the Unified Theory of Acceptance and Use of Technology (UTAUT) [3] are used to understand students' acceptance and adoption. As a matter of fact, those studies explain partly the use or the non-use of tablets, and a series of limitations of these approaches have been pointed out [26, 27]. They do not provide an overall estimation of the adoption process. They convey a more rational approach of the user's behavior and focus mainly on the perceived technology's instrumental features. Nevertheless, task related aspects are not always sufficient to explain satisfyingly actual technology adoption. Thus, applying other theories encompassing more aspects, such as the user experience framework, can enhance our understanding of tablet adoption in university context.

2.4 Aim of the Article

According to the above-mentioned literature, a research model has been set up to test the effect of the social environment on a university student's user experience. It proposes to investigate the direct influence of peers and teachers technology appreciation and behaviour on the components of user experience as defined by Thüring and Malhke [1].

3 Methodology

3.1 Study Context

The research is part of an international research project called *LEarning with Tablets: Acceptance and COgnitive Processes* (LETACOP) financed by the French National Agency for research (ANR). It aims a better understanding of the psychological factors and underlying cognitive processes taking place when tablets are used in learning contexts. This paper presents the results of two questionnaire surveys that have been undertaken in a French university and a Belgian university. The two questionnaires included the same scales on UX components and social influence. Only a few questions on the tablet usage have been changed.

3.2 Procedure

The research took the form of an online survey for the Belgian students and a paper form for the French students. The online questionnaire was published with the LimeSurvey 2.5 platform. Several teachers were asked to encourage their students from science, health science and social science to complete the survey. The link to the survey was sent by e-mail or published online on their course learning management system. The paper form questionnaire was given to the French students during courses at university, and students were free to fulfill the questionnaire at the end of the lesson.

3.3   Questionnaire

The used questionnaire comprises four different parts:

- The first part aimed at collecting biographical data such as age, gender, and education
- The second part aimed at collecting information about tablet usage. Students were asked about their tablet ownership, operating system, types of usage, and frequency of use. Belgian students were asked to rate to which extend they use a tablet in hours per day, and French students were asked to rate it on a 5-point frequency scale going from "never" to "very often". It was decided to change the type of question because Belgian students declared that rating the number of hours spent using a tablet was tricky. Besides, to obtain a more detailed picture, a question to assess since when students were tablet owners was also added.
- The third part aimed at collecting data about students' tablet experience and satisfaction. Scales relating to the CUE-model components and subfactors were added (see Table 1). To measure Perceived instrumental qualities based on Perceived usefulness and Perceived ease of use, scales derived from Venkatesh and Bala [4] were used. Examples items are "Using a tablet is usefull for my studies" and "I think that tablets are easy to use for my studies". To measure Perceived non-instrumental qualities, no existent scales satisfying our methodological needs have been found. As a result, items relating to Aesthetic aspects, Symbolic aspects and Motivational aspects were created in a back and forth procedure between scholars. Examples items are "For me, the tablet is an aesthetic device", "Tablet usage is a sign of modernity", and "I feel more motivated to do my activities, because I'm using a tablet". To measure Emotional reactions, it was decided to test the Perceived enjoyment as resulting emotion because it is an easy emotion to assess with a questionnaire. Items for the Perceived enjoyment scale were derived from Venkatesh and Bala [4], an example is "I enjoy using a tablet for my studies". Last, items to measure technology satisfaction were based on Wixom and Todd [28] System satisfaction scale, an item example is "All together, I am satisfied using a tablet". All items were assessed on a 7-point agreement Likert scale going from "I totally not agree" to "I totally agree".
- The fourth part of the questionnaire aimed at collecting data to assess the social influence on user experience. Items about peer and teacher tablet support were used (see Table 1). Example items are: "My friends at university use tablet for during their lessons" and "Professors prompt us to use tablets for our lessons". These scales are based on Martins and Kellermanns [21] scales and were assessed on a 7-point agreement Likert going from "I totally not agree" to "I totally agree".

The figures of Table 1 indicate that quality indicators satisfy all required needs. Each item is highly loaded on its belonging factor, and all factors present an average

Table 1. Quality construct outcomes

Construct	Items	Factor loading	t-Value	AVE	Composite reliability	Cronbach's alpha
Instrumental qualities						
P. usefulness	PU1	0.955	161 766	0.909	0.953	0.900
	PU2	0.952	145 465			
P. ease of use	PEOU1	0.916	112 278	0.818	0.900	0.778
	PEOU2	0.892	63 960			
Non-instrumental qualities						
Aesthetics a.	AA1	0.902	79 014	0.829	0.906	0.794
	AA2	0.919	97 275			
Symbolic a.	SA1	0.863	42 415	0.763	0.866	0.690
	SA2	0.884	48 043			
Motivational a.	MA1	0.888	79 905	0.794	0.885	0.741
	MA2	0.894	74 151			
Emotional reactions						
P. enjoyment	PE1	0.886	70 792	0.726	0.888	0.812
	PE2	0.864	68 257			
	PE3	0.805	34 111			
UX consequences						
Satisfaction	Sat1	0.923	87 528	0.858	0.923	0.834
	Sat2	0.929	108 735			
Support						
Peer influence	PeerInfl1	0.821	31 402	0.714	0.882	0.802
	PeerInfl2	0.845	42 869			
	PeerInfl3	0.869	53 081			
Teach. influence	TeachInfl1	0.784	15 351	0.640	0.842	0.725
	TeachInfl2	0.807	14 765			
	TeachInfl3	0.808	15 950			

variance extracted superior to .5 and a composite reliability superior to .6. Only the Cronbach's Alpha for the Symbolic aspects does not meet the required threshold of .7. Nevertheless, a very close score of .690 has been reached.

3.4 Sample

The characteristics of the respondents are presented in Table 2. A total of 796 students answered completely the questionnaire, 384 students are coming from Belgium and 412 from France.

In Belgium, 56.5% are female and 43.5% are male. In France, 65.3% of students are female and 34.7% are male. The age is respectfully 22.3 years old (s.d. 5.3) in Belgium and 19.6 years old (s.d. 1.8) in France. For Belgian students, 73.7% are bachelor students (first three years at university) and 26.3% are master students (two years after bachelor). In France, 94.9% are bachelor students and 5.1% are master students.

Table 2. Characteristics of the respondents

Characteristics	Belgium	France
Total respondents (n=)	384	412
Gender (%)		
Female	56.5	65.3
Male	43.5	34.7
Age (y.o.)		
Mean	22.3	19.6
s.d.	5.3	1.8
Education (%)		
Bachelor	73.7	94.9
Master	26.3	5.1
Tablet user (%)	49.2	59.2
For leisure	65.1	70.9
For work	30.2	35.7
Operating system (%)		
iOS	47.6	54.3
Android	38.6	32.5
Windows	11.6	11.1
Frequency of use (hours)		
Mean	2.9	
s.d.	2.4	
Frequency of use (%)		
Never		5.0
Rarely		15.9
Sometimes		26.8
Often		32.6
Very often		19.7
Ownership (month)		
Mean		33.6
s.d.		21.8

Concerning technology use, nearly half of students declared possessing a tablet. Indeed, 49.2% of students in Belgium and 59.2% in France. Among those, most of them run an iOS operating system (47.6% in Belgium, 54.3% in France), followed by an Android system (38.6% in Belgium, 32.5% in France), and a bit more than one tenth use a Windows operating system (11.6% in Belgium, 11.1% in France). Frequency of use figures indicate that in average Belgian students use their tablet 2.9 h a day (s.d. 2.4), and that most French students use it often (32.6%), sometimes (26.8%), or very often (19.7%) but several students declared using it never (5%) or rarely (15.9%). In addition, French students also declared that in average they possess a tablet for 33.6 month (s.d. 21.8).

3.5 Data Analysis

Statistical analyses were carried out using SPSS 25 for the descriptive analysis and with SmartPLS 3.2.4 for internal consistency and the calculation of regression scores. Data was processed using the Partial Least Square method because, this method is quite suited to tests complex models with smaller samples. Contrary to the classical structural equation modelling (i.e. Lisrel method, M+), the PLS-method is based on variance analysis [29–33].

4 Results

Results in Table 3 indicate the average scores, standard deviations scores, and minimum and maximum values obtained by each factor. Non-instrumental qualities factors obtain an average that is just below the middle point of the scale, which could show a smaller interest in non-instrumental qualities of tablets. However, all variables present a relatively high standard deviation, which indicate a wide array of responses. Moreover, it is interesting to note that Perceived ease of use obtains a higher average score than Perceived usefulness.

Table 3. Loadings of indicator variables

Construct	Mean	s.d.	min.	max.
Instrumental qualities				
Perceived usefulness	3.92	0.95	1.00	7.00
Perceived ease of use	4.83	1.64	1.00	7.00
Non-instrumental qualities				
Aesthetics aspects	3.76	1.74	1.00	7.00
Symbolic aspects	3.64	1.56	1.00	7.00
Motivational aspects	3.90	1.66	1.00	7.00
Emotional reactions				
Perceived enjoyment	4.16	1.61	1.00	7.00
UX consequences				
Satisfaction	4.54	1.81	1.00	7.00
Support				
Peer support	4.18	1.36	1.00	7.00
Teachers support	3.99	1.35	1.00	7.00

4.1 CUE-Model

The analysis of our variables (Instrumental qualities, Non-instrumental qualities, Emotional reactions, UX consequences), including the links between the sub-factors, validate the CUE Model structure. Globally, the calculation of standardized beta scores of path analysis (see Fig. 2) confirm the effects of Perceived instrumental qualities on Emotional reactions and Satisfaction, as well as the effects of Emotional reactions on Satisfaction, but partially the effects of Perceived non-instrumental qualities on Emotional reactions and Satisfaction.

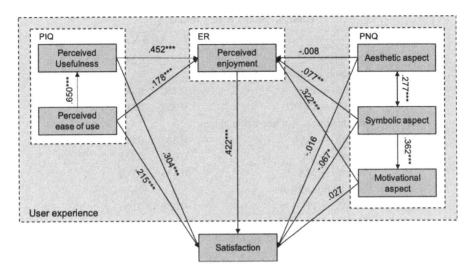

Fig. 2. Results of the research model. Note: *p < 0.05; **p < 0.01; ***p < 0.001

More precisely, the Perceived instrumental qualities factors influence positively the Emotional reactions. However, a significant influence of all three Perceived non-instrumental qualities factors on Emotional reactions has not been found. Indeed, Motivational aspects influence positively Perceived enjoyment, as well as Symbolic aspects but this last effect happens to be quite small. No significant effect has been found from Aesthetic aspects on Perceived enjoyment. Concerning the influence on user Satisfaction, results indicate that Perceived instrumental qualities and Emotional reactions are the highest contributors. The effects of the three Perceived non-instrumental qualities on satisfaction are very small (Symbolic aspect) or not significant. As a matter of fact, it can be established that Perceived non-instrumental qualities has almost no importance in user satisfaction.

4.2   Social Influences

The outcomes regarding the social impact on the different user experience factors are presented in Table 4. The results indicate that the students' user experience is more influenced by their peers than by their teachers environment.

More precisely, the Peers influence affects mainly the Aesthetic aspects (ß = .387; p-value = .000), the Perceived ease of use (ß = .351; p-value = .000), and the Motivational aspects (ß = .335; p-value = .000). In a less extend, Peers influence also affects Perceived usefulness (ß = .182; p-value = .000). To put it simply, our results indicate that Peers influence impacts the Perceived instrumental qualities and Perceived non-instrumental qualities components, but not the Emotional reaction component.

Teachers influence results indicate that two Perceived non-instrumental qualities factors are influenced by their attitude or behavior. The two factors are Aesthetic aspects (ß = .113; p-value = .019) and Symbolic aspects (ß = .142; p-value = .005). Contrary

Table 4. Model testing results

	ß	p-Value
Peer support		
Perceived instrumental qualities		
PeerInfl → PU	0.182	0.000
PeerInfl → PEOU	0.351	0.000
Perceived non-instrumental qualities		
PeerInfl → AA	0.387	0.000
PeerInfl → SA	0.029	0.588
PeerInfl → MA	0.335	0.000
Emotional reactions		
PeerInfl → PE	0.028	0.301
Teacher support		
Perceived instrumental qualities		
TeachInfl → PU	0.007	0.848
TeachInfl → PEOU	0.033	0.574
Perceived non-instrumental qualities		
TeachInfl → AA	0.113	0.019
TeachInfl → SA	0.142	0.005
TeachInfl → MA	−0.034	0.462
Emotional reactions		
TeachInfl → PE	−0.024	0.351

to peer influence, no significant effect as found on the Motivational aspect, nor on the Perceived instrumental qualities (Perceived usefulness and Perceived ease of use).

In addition, no significant effect was found from peers and teachers on the Emotional reactions component, measured by Perceived pleasure

5   Discussion/Conclusion

The *User Experience (UX)* approach has emerged as a comprehensive framework for Human-Computer Interaction studies. It aims at providing a more holistic perspective on user's technology perception that encompasses the perception of the technology's utilitarian and non-utilitarian characteristics and the emotional aspects. However, there is a lack of studies investigating the impact of the social environment on user experience. This study proposes to examine the impact of the social environment on user experience as defined by Thüring and Mahlke [1]. To attain our objectives, a questionnaire was diffused to investigate the university students' experience with tablets. The focus on tablets as technological device has been chosen because tablets, like other mobile technologies, they carry self-oriented expectations, enhanced self-image, or pleasurable experiences. To take into account the social environment influence, two factors have been retained: peer students influence and teachers influence.

Globally, results demonstrate that peer students and teachers (their social environment at university), influence user experience, and by extension, the interests to include social factors to understand user experience.

Our analyses show that the social influence differ depending on the reference group. The impact from peer students is more important that the one from the teachers. Peer students influence perceived instrumental qualities and perceived non-instrumental qualities, and teachers influence only the perceived non-instrumental qualities.

To explain the Peers influence on the Perceived instrumental qualities, we can refer to the Group influence processes theory. Following this theory, individuals adopt behavioural norms in order to strengthen their relationships with other group members. As university teachers belong to another social group, it may be explained that they have no significant influence on Perceived usefulness and Perceived ease of use.

The peer influence on Perceived instrumental qualities confirm partially the results from the *Technology acceptance* approach, and more specifically the results obtained by Martins and Kellermanns [21]. They demonstrated the influence from peers and from teachers on Perceived usefulness. However, in our study, no effect was found for the teacher social influence. Furthermore, our results show a greater impact from peers on Perceived Ease of Use than on Perceived usefulness. This is somehow contrary to the TAM literature, which theorize an effect on Perceived usefulness but not on Perceived ease of use. This could be related to the manner tablets are promoted. Tablets are known to be easy to-use and portable technological devices [23]. Secondly, the teachers' lack of influence on Perceived instrumental qualities can be explained by the fact that students do not usually observe their teacher using tablets. They could ignore how, and why their teacher use tablets. Moreover, students may consider their teachers as belonging to another technological generation, with other kinds of habits and knowledge.

The results regarding the influence of peers and teachers on Perceived non-instrumental qualities also differ in function of the referred group. First, the peers and teachers influence on the aesthetic aspect means that students attribute more positive aesthetics aspects when they perceive an environmental support to tablets at university. Secondly, in line with former conclusion, the influence of teachers on the symbolic aspects means that students judge their tablet as holding a positive symbolic value when they perceive a teacher support to use tablets at university. The absence of effect stemming from peers on the symbolic aspect can be linked to the fact that in our sample more than half of the students own a tablet. Nowadays, tablets are more economically accessible and widely available for university students. In consequence, tablets may no longer considered reserved for a few students and their symbolic values are probably more limited.

Third, regarding the motivational aspects, the *Group influence processes* theory can also be mobilized to explain the willingness of students to use a tablet. As other peers support the use of tablets, adopting the same behavior will allow everyone to strengthen their relationships with others.

Furthermore, the analyses confirm another point regarding the reliability of the CUE-model. There is no significant influence of peers and teachers on Perceived enjoyment. These results corroborate the model structure of the CUE-model. The model theorizes that the Emotional reaction are only influenced by the Perceived instrumental and non-instrumental qualities.

This research presents several limitations. A validation process of the scales could have been useful: some scales have been adapted to the use of tablets at the university, others have been developed for our specific needs. Even though the sample size is quite correct, expanding the database could improve the statistical validity. Moreover, the outcomes need to be verified with other samples, technologies and contexts.

This study focuses on UX factors included in the CUE-model, but accordingly to the UX holistic perspective, it would be interesting to extend this research to other UX factors. In addition, it does not take into account the dynamic nature of UX. More in-depth studies should be carried out to verify if the social influence of peer and teacher remains the same along the technological appropriation process. In addition, it would be interesting to extend this research with personality factors.

In conclusion, this study offers a new perspective for research on UX. The theoretical framework should extend its scope to the social environment impact in order to obtain a better picture on the psychological processes involved. A narrow focus on the individual nature of a user's technological experience, could lead to incomplete insights as technologies are more and more used in the vision of other individuals.

References

1. Thüring, M., Mahlke, S.: Usability, aesthetics and emotions in human–technology interaction. Int. J. Psychol. **42**, 253–264 (2007). https://doi.org/10.1080/002075907013 96674
2. Davis, F.D., Bagozzi, R.P., Warshaw, P.R.: User acceptance of computer technology: a comparison of two theoretical models. Manag. Sci. **35**, 982–1003 (1989). https://doi.org/10. 1287/mnsc.35.8.982
3. Venkatesh, V., Morris, M.G., Davis, G.B., Davis, F.D.: User acceptance of information technology: toward a unified view. MIS Q. **27**, 425–478 (2003). https://doi.org/10.2307/ 30036540
4. Venkatesh, V., Bala, H.: Technology acceptance model 3 and a research agenda on interventions. Decis. Sci. **39**, 273–315 (2008). https://doi.org/10.1111/j.1540-5915.2008. 00192.x
5. El-gayar, O.F., Moran, M.: College students' acceptance of Tablet PCs: an application of the UTAUT Model. Dakota State Uni. **820**, 2845–2850 (2006)
6. ISO 9241-210:2010, http://www.iso.org/cms/render/live/fr/sites/isoorg/contents/data/stand-ard/05/20/52075.html
7. Deng, L., Turner, D.E., Gehling, R., Prince, B.: User experience, satisfaction, and continual usage intention of IT. Eur. J. Inf. Syst. **19**, 60–75 (2010). https://doi.org/10.1057/ejis.2009.50
8. Forlizzi, J., Battarbee, K.: Understanding experience in interactive systems. In: Proceedings of the 5th Conference on Designing Interactive Systems: Processes, Practices, Methods, and Techniques, pp. 261–268. ACM, New York (2004)
9. Hassenzahl, M., Tractinsky, N.: User experience—a research agenda. Behav. Inf. Technol. **25**, 91–97 (2006). https://doi.org/10.1080/01449290500330331

10. Karapanos, E., Zimmerman, J., Forlizzi, J., Martens, J.-B.: User experience over time: an initial framework. In: Proceedings of the SIGCHI Conference on Human Factors in Computing Systems, pp. 729–738. ACM, New York (2009)
11. Law, E.L.-C., Roto, V., Hassenzahl, M., Vermeeren, A.P.O.S., Kort, J.: Understanding, scoping and defining user experience: a survey approach. In: Proceedings of the SIGCHI Conference on Human Factors in Computing Systems, pp. 719–728. ACM, New York (2009)
12. Yogasara, T., Popovic, V., Kraal, B., Chamorro-Koc, M.: General characteristics of anticipated user experience (AUX) with interactive products, p. 12 (2011)
13. Mahlke, S.: User Experience of Interaction with Technical Systems (2008). http://dx.doi.org/10.14279/depositonce-1793
14. Bevan, N., Carter, J., Harker, S.: ISO 9241-11 revised: what have we learnt about usability since 1998? In: Kurosu, M. (ed.) HCI 2015. LNCS, vol. 9169, pp. 143–151. Springer, Cham (2015). https://doi.org/10.1007/978-3-319-20901-2_13
15. Bearden, W.O., Etzel, M.J.: Reference group influence on product and brand purchase decisions. J. Consum. Res. **9**, 183–194 (1982)
16. Park, C.W., Lessig, V.P.: Students and housewives: differences in susceptibility to reference group influence. J. Consum. Res. **4**, 102–110 (1977). https://doi.org/10.1086/208685
17. Goodwin, C.: A social influence theory of consumer cooperation. Adv. Consum. Res. **14**, 378–381 (1986)
18. Blau, P.M.: Exchange and Power in Social Life. Wiley, New York (1964)
19. Rogers, E.M.: Diffusion of Innovations. Free Press, New York (1995)
20. Hardgrave, B.C., Davis, F.D., Riemenschneider, C.K.: Investigating determinants of software developers' intentions to follow methodologies. J. Manag. Inf. Syst. **20**, 123–151 (2003). https://doi.org/10.1080/07421222.2003.11045751
21. Martins, L.L., Kellermanns, F.W.: A model of business school students' acceptance of a web-based course management system. Acad. Manag. Learn. Educ. **3**, 7–26 (2004). https://doi.org/10.5465/amle.2004.12436815
22. Van De Leemput, C., Van Der Linden, J.: Qu'est-ce qui motive les utilisateurs d'un système de gestion des apprentissages? Presented at the (2014)
23. Green, D., Naidoo, E., Olminkhof, C., Dyson, L.E.: Tablets@university: the ownership and use of tablet devices by students. Australas. J. Educ. Technol. (2016). https://doi.org/10.14742/ajet.2195
24. Kobus, M.B.W., Rietveld, P., van Ommeren, J.N.: Ownership versus on-campus use of mobile IT devices by university students. Comput. Educ. **68**, 29–41 (2013). https://doi.org/10.1016/j.compedu.2013.04.003
25. Guhr, D.J.: The Impact of the Rapidly Changing Mobile Devices Market on e-Learning in Higher Education. http://www.ingentaconnect.com/content/doaj/16904532/2013/00000011/00000007/art00011
26. Hong, S.-J., Tam, K.Y.: Understanding the adoption of multipurpose information appliances: the case of mobile data services. Inf. Syst. Res. **17**, 162–179 (2006). https://doi.org/10.1287/isre.1060.0088
27. Kim, J.H., Gunn, D.V., Schuh, E., Phillips, B., Pagulayan, R.J., Wixon, D.: Tracking real-time user experience (TRUE): a comprehensive instrumentation solution for complex systems. In: Proceedings of the SIGCHI Conference on Human Factors in Computing Systems, pp. 443–452. ACM, New York (2008)
28. Wixom, B.H., Todd, P.A.: A theoretical integration of user satisfaction and technology acceptance. Inf. Syst. Res. **16**, 85–102 (2005). https://doi.org/10.1287/isre.1050.0042

29. Chin, W.W.: The partial least squares approach for structural equation modeling. In: Modern methods for business research, pp. 295–336. Lawrence Erlbaum Associates Publishers, Mahwah (1998)
30. Chin, W.W.: How to write up and report PLS analyses. In: Esposito Vinzi, V., Chin, W.W., Henseler, J., Wang, H. (eds.) Handbook of Partial Least Squares. Springer Handbooks of Computational Statistics, pp. 655–690. Springer, Heidelberg (2010). https://doi.org/10.1007/978-3-540-32827-8_29
31. Fernandes, V.: En quoi l'approche PLS est-elle une méthode a (re)-découvrir pour les chercheurs en management? Management **15**, 102–123 (2012). https://doi.org/10.3917/mana.151.0102
32. Lacroux, A.: Les avantages et les limites de la méthode «Partial Least Square» (PLS) : une illustration empirique dans le domaine de la GRH, The Partial Least Square (PLS) approach: an alternative method for SEM models estimation in HRM. Rev. Gest. Ressour. Hum. **2**, 45–64 (2011). https://doi.org/10.3917/grhu.080.0045
33. Yu, J., Lee, H., Ha, I., Zo, H.: User acceptance of media tablets: an empirical examination of perceived value. Telemat. Inform. **34**, 206–223 (2017). https://doi.org/10.1016/j.tele.2015.11.004

Anticipating Ethical Issues When Designing Services that Employ Personal Data

Laura Varisco[(⊠)] ⓘ, Milica Pavlovic, and Margherita Pillan ⓘ

IEX Design Lab - Politecnico Di Milano, Milan 20158, Italy
Laura.varisco@polimi.it

Abstract. Advancements in technology enable cross-device interactions and the creation of complex ecosystems of Internet of Things (IoT). Networked systems support the creation of services for multiple purposes such as smart transportation, health care, wellbeing. The spreading of services based on personal data is shaping current socio-technical systems; it induces innovations that are changing everyday scenarios and behaviors, posing ethical issues that should be taken into account since the very first phases of the design process. As designers, we need to understand the user experience with respect to the usual requirements of usability, acceptability and desirability of the new solutions, and manage delicate issues related to the impacts of these solutions on individuals and communities. This requires knowledge and dedicated design tools enabling designers to make conscious design choices during the design process. In this paper, we present an anticipation method aimed to support awareness of designers about critical issues related to the use of personal data in the project of complex technology-based systems and services. The paper reports the main features of the methods and of the research activity that generated our approach. Furthermore, we illustrate the results obtained applying the anticipation method on a case study, the MEMoSa project. The case study refers to an innovative service offering tailored services for safer driving; this research involved several partners, including a telecommunication company, and insurance offerings services for safer driving. The case study supports the validation of the anticipation method and the discussion of its potentials.

Keywords: Design methods · Anticipation · Ethical elements · Personal data · Social consensus

1 Introduction

Advancements in technological capabilities are enabling cross-device interactions and the creation of complex ecosystems of Internet of Things (IoT). Such networked systems can produce valuable solutions for both individuals and communities [1]: efficient management of energy, lighting and heating systems; smart transportation; collection of data for health purposes; monitoring of physiological parameters for fitness, wellbeing and medical purposes by wearable devices and others, are just some examples of progress produced by the evolution of digital technologies. Connected objects provide the means to create responsive environments and to enable ubiquitous

© Springer Nature Switzerland AG 2019
A. Marcus and W. Wang (Eds.): HCII 2019, LNCS 11583, pp. 113–131, 2019.
https://doi.org/10.1007/978-3-030-23570-3_10

and seamless services: home automation solutions and others, show that IoT can and will enable new ways for people to interact with the world around them [2].

The design and development of personal services and applications based on technology ecosystems involves several different competences: from service design to technology engineering, from business planning to interaction design, UX design, communication and marketing. The design of such systems often requires the collaboration of different stakeholders and partners, each one aiming at specific goals and purposes. Indeed, the challenges of designing new digital services, very often, go way beyond rethinking interaction modalities and interfaces; as connected products and digital services evolve to produce deep modifications of individual behaviors and social organizations through the creation of new paradigms of services, [3, 4] designers face questions about the definition of new values that these connected systems offer to the users [2].

When we design a socio-technical ecosystem [2, 5] with an approach of design for experience, the roles and responsibilities of designers occur on multiple scales: beyond the straightforward requirements of acceptance, acceptability [4, 6], usability, convenience and including physical, digital, individual and social issues [7].

When designing for experiences, we have to consider the diverse levels of significance and impacts involved in our solutions. The ground and primary level refers to the aesthetical meaning: the direct, physical contact with the tangible elements of the designed system. This implies comprehension of functionalities and usability, and it includes ergonomics of the material solutions as well as their pleasantness in direct interaction. The upper level of user experience attends to the creation of the service meaning: valuable utility provided by the designed solution, through convenient modalities of use and involvement, as perceived from the user end. To this regard, an important challenge is posed to the designers concerning the consequences of their solutions. The meaning perceived by the end user, within emerging socio-technical systems, can be of a diverse nature and vary from short to longer-term effects [8]. As designers, we should be able to foresee and manage both, long and short-term consequences of design choices.

As has been pointed out by other approaches like Value Sensitive Design (VSD) [9] and Responsible Research and Innovation (RRI) [10], the design of innovative solutions can be focused on the value provided and perceived by users and the other societal actors. By foreseeing and anticipating the individual and collective consequences concerning the perturbations that the designed solution could have, we can contribute to the design process with reflections, critical thinking and discussion on the values potentially provided to individuals and communities, since in the early stages of the design process. The meanings associated by the users to an innovative solution are difficult to be measured a priori as, rather, they rely on unstable social values that vary over time. Perception of value and meanings continually evolves with the changing society. Therefore, the perception of the society within the project at the concept development phase appears quite labile.

Since the technologies embedded in the society are not neutral, designers play a role in shaping the society itself, starting from an individual level [11].

In our research, we focus on issues related to the use of personal information in the design of connected objects and digital services. Personal information is the fuel for personalized services and the by-product of human activities supported by connected products and web-based services. Digital data supports the production of new knowledge in key social sectors such as healthcare, energy management, transportation planning. Personal information obtained by the processing of raw data supports the creation of personalized services which are capable of reducing cognitive efforts on the user-end, to enhance personal knowledge, improve lifestyles, and provide seamless efficiency. Conversely, the collection and processing of personal data poses complex questions and risks for individuals and the community, that can be briefly indicated in terms of lack of safety, security and privacy, and social engineering. As an example, authors such as Rowland and Goodman highlight the challenges related to issues such as confidentiality and integrity of data and explain how data that seems innocuous can be aggregated to generate privacy breaches [2]. Beyond that, the use of personal information as a central or peripheral element in technology-based systems, can have a wider influence on individuals and communities [12]. We argue that, from the individual point of view, the use of connected products and digital services is deeply affecting not just behaviors, but also perceptions of the world and of the self. We also sustain that, on a social basis, digital services that employ personal data can modify not only organizations and communication tools, but also the codes and principles of human interactions.

In this paper, we offer a contribution to the development of design methodologies aimed to support awareness about possible consequences of design choices suitable in different phases of the design process. The kind of projects we are focusing on are those that bring radical innovation. Anticipating aspects that could shape utopian and dystopian futuristic scenarios, is seen as a potential path for envisioning critical issues regarding consequences a design solution can bring when used long-term [8].

2 Research Background

As the progressive digitization of information [13] is intensifying the process of data production and gathering, the systems that rely on these datasets to provide meaningful services increasingly involve data as the raw material [14] for wellbeing, patterns and behaviors analysis. Data about people, their presence, activities and behaviors are directly created and collected by devices and sensors, as well as extrapolated by data crossing and analysis. While the tracking of personal data can be actively enabled by users through voluntarily logging into devices and platforms, the automatic detection of these data and the analysis performed by technologies to extract personal information is becoming a common practice for many services. The processing performed by the systems of both, voluntary and automatic creation of data about users, provides not only metadata useful to relate elements and actions to the specific users, but also to create service functionalities and provide feedback, reports and task personalization [15].

Many products, services and systems are becoming reactive and proactive according to the information collected from users. The users can access actions and performances through their biodata (e.g. Apple's Touch ID [16]); biodata represent the nourishment of fitness tracking services to create reports and feedback about performances (e.g. Beast Sensor [17]). The voluntary sharing of data can help researchers to cure diseases [11] and the automatic detection of data can support the reduction of energy consumption [18]. Furthermore, reactive materials can use personal information to create proactive products and meaningful physical experiences in the real world [19, 20], by changing in colour, shape, opacity and so on, according to the automatic detection or voluntary input of data.

While the word datafication refers mainly on the use of Big Data as a source of service value and understanding, literature [21, 22] points out the importance of Little Data intended as "based on 'big data' but [...] focus[ed] on individuals, using the vast computing capacity that is available today to collect and analyze what is extremely granular data – such as whether an individual is driving safely or not" [23]. "While using big data and algorithmic decision-making ... this targeting can now be taken further when data are used not to predict group trends but to predict the behavior of a specific individual" [21].

The tensions in the debate on the use of big (and little) data analysis as a creator of value for the creation of services, has been framed on work-practice level, organizational level, and supra-organizational level [24]. The debate is nowadays focusing mainly on the consequences that the use of big (and little) data analysis can bring in the society [23] pointing out the perturbations that it is producing in both organization and work, identifying changes in the nature of professional work (in the practices and skills needed), and in the management of the professional workers (evidence-based management and data-driven approach to managing working). Is so indeed relevant to make efforts in the creation of critical discussion among the possible consequences that the use of data is providing to the society considering not only the possibilities in terms of creation of knowledge and development of functionalities, but also the unintended effects. Literature on information systems are so starting call for actions on this purpose [15], and authors such as Marjanovic and Cecez-Kecmenovic [25] started to identify datafication patterns and their unintended societal consequences.

Designers, researchers and educators in the field of interaction design and HCI [26, 27], are considering the evolution of digital technologies as a new challenge and opportunity to produce creative products and services based on IoT, data processing and cloud computing. On the other hand, the automatic detection of personal information by services is raising issues about data privacy, security and perception of self by the final user and designers [28].

2.1 Envisioning Design Issues Through Scenarios in HCI

From the perspective of design research and practice, the suitability of developing scenarios to envision future conditions and activities enabled by designed services and products, appears undisputed [29]. These future situations unfold and evolve during the design practice and definition phases, and designers involved in complex project processes that require co-design in multidisciplinary project teams are often entrusted to build a common language of communication and to envision the final expected results. Scenarios, therefore, are considered a suitable set of contextual contents for representing and discussing the future possibilities imagined and proposed by designers and other stakeholders. Scenarios articulate description of a design challenge in realistic contexts, and harness existing design knowledge and theoretical frameworks to propose a viable solution to this challenge [30]. A scenario is determined by a narrative, form and function, and it builds a story around target profiles (Personas) recognized for the final design proposal. Scenarios contains elements and factors related to the envisioned situation that enable designers in considering not only the setting in which their solutions will take place, but also possible issues that are worthy of discussion so to create solid and realiable solutions.

In the field of Human-Computer Interaction (HCI), there is a shift from abstract descriptions of computer applications towards prototyping and other interaction representations that allow users to play an active role in an iterative design process [31]. Wider role for scenarios is discussed in HCI, reflecting the idea that scenarios are seen as a basis for overall design for technical implementation. In order to provide effective support in design processes oriented toward the responsible development of radically innovative solutions, the scenarios that are produced should describe the main technological requirements and the user journeys in the best operating conditions. Scenarios should also provide the means for the investigation of worst and limit cases, and to understand all situations of use and operating conditions.

We do believe that, in dealing with services and connected products involving personal information, designers should consider critical issues at the very beginning of the design process, i.e. since the definition of the concept, and, subsequently, while developing the physical features of the systems, considering the technological solutions, the information flows and the functional requirements of the design solution. Furthermore, we believe that the investigation of limit/worst case scenarios should include the realm of possible consequences related to the collection and use of personal data in the operations of the service. In fact, the personal data involved in the service and the ways personal data are collected, managed, shared and processed to generate personalized functions determine the acceptability and desirability of products and services together with the main functionalities and the final characteristics of the interfaces and touchpoints.

In this paper, we present the results of a research aimed at the creation of a design approach (methodology and tools) to support designers in the investigation of potentialities and critical issues related to the use of personal data in digital services.

Our approach is based on a preliminary research aimed at collecting reference information about critical issues related to digital personal data in services; this ample investigation ranges in both the domains of the news about events that happened in the real world as reported in journals and media, and in the realm of imaginary situations extracted from fictions. The collection of these reference information produced the analysis and mapping of several utopian and dystopian consequences connected to the use of personal data in services or technology-based systems. The results of this preliminary research supported the development of a framework of knowledge to be used by designers in the project of services and systems; the framework of knowledge enables indication of possible critical issues that could occur in future scenarios and are related to the use of personal data. The framework and the methodology we suggest provide a method for the anticipation of critical issues, so named Impact Anticipation Method (IAM).

In the following of this paper, we report the main features of the framework and report the process that generated it. Furthermore, we report some results obtained by applying our approach to a project aimed at developing a system for safe driving.

3 Impact Anticipation Method (IAM) for Exploring Digital Utopias and Dystopias

The first activity of our research aimed at mapping the multitude of situations that could be produced by using personal data as they come in connected products, AI based agents, and digital services. Aiming at extracting updated and social validated knowledge, we focused on the use of online content as source of the creation of scenarios and related critical issues. A number of different online sources have been used in this mapping process: case study analysis of emerging products and services, news, ongoing researches, movies and literature.

Within HCI, there has been a great emphasis on the use of fictional narrative in the form of personas and scenarios, and a discussion of how it can influence the work of technology designers [32, 33]. Science fiction writer and futurist Bruce Sterling [33] considers design perspective to be used to inform the creation of fiction that can engage with issues of an imagined or desired future. For these reasons, we choose to collect both information from the real world and imaginary scenarios from fiction.

3.1 Phase 1: Collection of Potential Issues

In our investigation, we considered all the above enlisted sources, so to create the Potential Issues Database that contains the knowledge extracted from real life and fiction.

With respect to science fiction, that we take as a profitable source of meaningful scenarios, we collected and processed data from an online database (IMDb.com [34]) containing information related to movies, short-movies, TV series and games. This provided knowledge from the envisioning of the future made by storytelling and the related validation made by collective intelligence of users that contribute to the database [8].

The queries we performed on the database were initially based on our previous knowledge about scenarios and representations of future in science-fiction storytelling artefacts; the investigation involved several automatic and manual mining of data so to collect the widest information about the science-fiction movies related to utopian and dystopian consequences of the use of technologies. We queried the database using the following keywords so to include both positive and negative narrative scenarios in the research: *dystopian future; dystopia + future; future noir; utopian future; utopia + future; utopian; future utopia; utopianism; future + technology*. This phase produced a First Titles Corpus (508 unique titles). For these titles, we collected both the metadata (title, genre, year, series, season, episode, type, plot, extended plot, language, country) and the data provided by the users (rating and votes). Then we filtered these results to focus our attention on the future related scenarios, and the high ratings (equal or above 6) so to take into account only the valuable results according to the opinion of the collective intelligence.

For the resulting Main Titles Corpus (281 unique titles), we collected all the keywords related to each title and their positive and total votes. The Main Keywords Corpus included more than 17 thousand keywords on which we calculated the related relevance subtracting the negative votes to the positive ones. A further selection was based on the analysis of the relevance of the movie plots; the Final Keyword Corpus, was created eliminating the keywords with negative relevance, and irrelevant references. The Final Title Corpus included 102 unique titles, while the Final Keyword Corpus counting 6.605 keywords (621 of those had positive relevance) and 481 unique keywords. For the entire Final Title Corpus, we carefully read the extended plots to categorize the storytelling settings by similarity. We identified 3 macro-similarities: **Self-perception and self-reflection**, **Machine control and Machine decision**, **Alternatives**. On the Final Keyword Corpus, instead, we organized the 481 unique keywords in 3 main categories: *Technology & Science* (containing all the words related to technological artefacts, research practices and science advancement), *Life Being* (containing all the words related to human social life, actions and life being), and *Reality & Actual* (containing the words related to objects, spaces and times). The categories were not mutually exclusive, so each keyword could fit in more than one of them.

This categorization (see Fig. 1) revealed that most keywords are related to the *Life being* category. Many elements are related to both *Life Being* and *Technology and Science*, showing the relevance between the technologies and people's life. This concerns future scenarios described with technologies that affect the way people live and act as the society. We consider the knowledge produced in this mapping as an investigation of prospective futures as they are produced by collective intelligence. While creating the narration, the storyteller is actively envisioning a hypothetical world where the story will be settled. Science-fiction storytelling provides utopian and dystopian futuristic contexts that are not-yet-real. These contexts are not representing a foreseeing of the future, while they represent the actualization of the current hopes and fears about the future as a realistic projection of what is perceived by the society.

The second step of the creation of the Potential Issues Database is the collection of ongoing discussion about the actual use of personal information in current technological solutions. To do so, we gathered news about technological advancement, about products and services available on the market, and about ongoing research projects that involve the use of personal data by services. The sampling of discussions (101 sources) and the extraction of issues related to the use of personal information provided the qualitative elements that were merged with those extracted from the science-fiction analysis.

To summarize our findings, we created eight different future macro-scenarios that we call **Ethics-oriented-Reference-Scenarios (ERS)** [28] that we describe in the following paragraph. The ERS represent a collection of possible consequences related to the use of personal information by innovative technologies as they are perceived by the society [32]. The eight ERS represent, therefore, situational paradigms linked to the present time and current technological development thanks to the analysis of the current situation extracted by the sampled news [35–43].

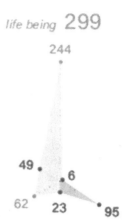

life being 299

244

49
6

62   23   95

technology and science 134   reality and actual 124

Fig. 1. Categories of keywords used for analysing the database of gathered titles of movies, series and games.

3.2   The Ethics Oriented-Reference-Scenarios (ERSs)

In this paragraph we briefly describe the eight ERS formalized as previously described. They are divided into the three macro-categories extracted from the narrative analysis [28]. These macro-scenarios point out some main issues that emerged from our analysis, and they reveal the potential two faceted (utopian and dystopian) impacts of services and products based on personal data.

The IAM method is based on the guided interrogation of the database collecting the potentially different critical issues emerged in the research phase reported above. The ERS provide a main classification of outcomes of the research, and they orient the designers using the database while searching the more suitable reference-cases for the anticipation of the impact of use of digital data with respect to their specific design purposes and goals.

Self-perfection and self-reflection:

1. *Perfect Humanity*: the use of technologies shapes the 'perfection' of the people thanks to the analysis of bio and medical data, and to behavioral analysis on human actions. At the same time, it raises problems related to marginalization, increase of inequalities and suppression of differences.
2. *Pervasive Awareness*: the surrounding systems and services track people's activities thanks to sensors and self-logging. The generated feedback loop [3] make the users more aware of self-state and their activities in the digital and physical environments while it raises overload of information and increase of cognitive effort related to new and possibly useless worries.

3. *Mnemonic*: the use of digital storage solutions enlarges human brain capability, granting ubiquitous access to the memories in real-time. However, the opportunity of ubiquitous and infinite storage raises worries about the permanently available and indelible records.

A. **Machine control and machine decision**

4. *Super Monitor*: the analysis of activities and behaviors made by technological system prevents problems and increase safety while promotes constant surveillance and impossibility to hide.
5. *Automation Box*: AI and proactive systems automatically collect and analyse data to provide services that lower cognitive load and help people in their activities. At the same time they act and react without provide answers and explanation about their decision-making processes, so increasing the perception of a machine-authority that decides on behalf of humans.
6. *Human Behavior Computer*: AI systems learn from people behavior to provide services that are more valuable, human and of natural understanding. However, while they learn from human actions, they also assimilate and use humans' biases and bad behavioral characteristics.

B. **Alternatives**

7. *Stargate*: the use of digital spaces to reduce the distances and time difference helps people to interact each other in ubiquitous ways. At the same time it creates alienation from the reality and the physical world.
8. *Avatar*: the use of alternative identities shapes the experiences and the representation of the self in digital words allowing also a fragmentation of the identity and give people the possibility to voluntarily and involuntarily misrepresent themselves.

The Impact Anticipation Method, employs ERS as a reference to be used during the whole design process. It is intended as an integration of the user-centered design approach; it provides the means to support discussion and awareness about the positive and negative consequences of technology-based innovation with respect to the use of personal data. The envisioning of a scenario in a project process is a creative act that usually leans towards the creation of an ideal world. It aims to explore possibilities, solve problems, identify critical issues and avoid negative and unexpected side effects. The name utopia itself (no place) suggests "impossibility" and the utopian scenarios envisioned by storytellers can reveal how narrow the line that divides utopia from dystopia is. Utopias can be impressive at first, but they can bring problems and implications not always easy to predict. Furthermore, when we consider future scenarios, we should always take into account the variety of needs and attitudes of human beings. As an instance, wellbeing is a subjective dimension [44] - what is a utopian vision for someone may be completely dystopian for someone else.

The design of a new service or product should always be fueled by motivation and effort toward the definition of a convenient and desirable solution; on the other hand, the conscious, instrumented and open discussion of possible critical issues within appears as convenient for both the effectiveness and efficiency of the design process [45].

Starting from the eight ERS, we move to the phase 2 of the Impacts Anticipation Methods: its application on design processes. To illustrate our approach, in the following paragraph we present a case study.

4 Phase 2: Application of the IAM in a Design Process

In this section we report a case study about the application of IAM, so to explain the main feature of the method. The Impact Anticipation Method could be applied in different phases of the design process: analytical phase, creative phase, definition phase, and assessment phase. However, we focus here on its application during the assessment phase; the project we refer to is called MEMoSa and we applied the IAM to inform future iteration of the design process with critical thinking on individual and societal possible impacts of the use of personal information in the service.

4.1 Case Study: MEMoSa

The MEMoSa project aimed at developing a mobile and cloud service to support safe driving and involved several partners and stakeholders, including TIM, the Italian company for telecommunication, some insurance companies, and local shops. The final service is based on personal data about the behaviors (driving and other activities) and the health-state of final users; furthermore, the system also collects and uses data about the vehicle and planning of the trip, offering context-based functions. The service provides feedbacks about the convenience of driving and of the suitable driving-style, in real-time and based on personal information. Insurance companies, selling health and car insurance services, have the opportunity to offer flexible low-cost solutions on-the-spot, and to collect information so to build a better, more comprehensive profiling of their customers. Expected impacts are the reduction of risks connected to driving in unsafe conditions due to lifestyles, health conditions or specific circumstances. Furthermore, the service should reduce insurance costs, and offer additional value based on contextualized needs. The designed system helps users to be more aware of their physiological conditions, increasing health, road safety and reducing insurance and healthcare costs. The development of MEMoSa required the collaboration of several partners, including sociologists, computer scientists, insurance companies, and designers. The authors of the paper participated in the project as designers, contributing to the definition of use-case scenarios, to prototyping and testing, to the communication of the final concept, and the development of the final mobile application.

The MEMoSa system tracks vehicles during use, collecting data about driving styles through an On-Board Diagnostic unit (OBD) in the car; the mobile application collects personal data in regard to health-conditions and users' sleep quality via a wearable device; the cloud platform provides the driver and passengers several value-added services such as on-the-spot insurances, technical assistance, notifications on drowsiness, etc. As it is presumed that a vehicle is used by more than one single driver, the system provides features for creating a community of drivers of the same vehicles for keeping track of the members' activities and vehicle performance.

For its features, MEMoSa is an innovative system concept, and its development required several iterations involving testing with final users'. During the testing activities, several critical situations emerged related to the use of personal data, and the design was progressively refined in order to sync with them [46]. As an example, some issues concern the privacy rights of users sharing the same car: as the application reports on vehicle usage and driving styles, some participants stated that they would use the service only if they could select the exact information to be shared with each particular profile in the community. All in all, the system functions by employing personal data that widely and deeply describe personal characteristics, activities and status. This situation does encourage the creation of useful services, however, possibly accompanied by certain risks that require deep investigation.

For this reason, we consider this project as a suitable test for IAM.

4.2   Application of IAM on the MEMoSa Project

We consider data as the raw material that is detected and processed by the system to extract the knowledge about the individual that is then used to create the service [1]; in the IAM, we classify the data by type, and we cluster type of data under information categories. The categories of information have been defined as following:

- *Identity information*: the information related to physical, biological, medical and biographical aspects of the person;
- *Access information*: the information related to the personal interconnection with the technology-based systems;
- *Behavioral information*: the information related to the actions performed and to the habits of the person;
- *Social information*: the information related to the social representation of the self and to the activities performed in the social life.

As shown in the following table (Table 1), some of the data types appear in more than one information category.

Table 1. Clusters of data types placed inside of information categories.

Information categories	Data type
Identity	Biological, biographical
Access	Presence, activities, network, relationships, conversations
Behavioral	Presence, activities, preferences, network, relationships, contents, conversations
Social	Biographical, preferences, activities, network, relationships, contents, conversations

As a first step for the application of IAM in MEMoSa, we identified the specific personal information and data that are involved in this service and neglected the type of data not used by the MEMoSa system (user contents and conversations) (Table 2).

Table 2. MEMoSa system related classification of data types.

Information categories	Data type
Identity	Biological, biographical
Access	Presence, activities, network, relationships
Behavioral	Presence, activities, preferences, network, relationships
Social	Biographical, preferences, activities, network, relationships

We took this classification as a reference to analyze all the different types of data that are collected, exchanged, processed and employed in MEMoSa; we also made explicit the source of each data type, and its 'destiny' within the system, (see Fig. 2) from the initial data gathering to the final provision of functionalities including insurance paybacks (offers and deals of personalized insurance policy), knowledge for users and stakeholders (car performance, driver's ability analysis, personal performances, community activities) and access modes.

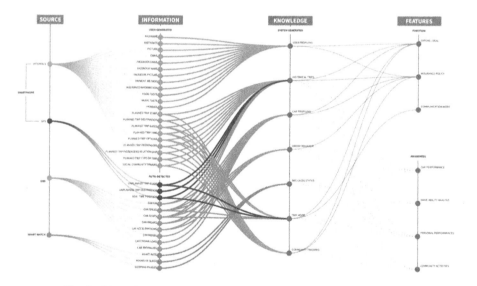

Fig. 2. Map of personal information flows within the MEMoSa system.

The map shows that, in some cases, not all the collected data are used to create the payback to the final users. Some information is collected and stored but it is not actually useful for a specific feedback or functionality.

As a following step in the application of IAM to MEMoSa, we developed a critical analysis of the service based on the cross and comparative checking of different types of data and information flows involved in MEMoSa, compared with the general-purpose knowledge provided by the ERS and the related issues. The analysis revealed which of the main reference scenarios introduced above are potentially relevant for the specific goals of the service: Perfect Humanity, Pervasive Awareness, Mnemonic,

Super Monitor. Furthermore, we extracted from the database the reference issues and mapped them on the specific elements of the features identified in the information-flows diagram generated for MEMoSa (see Fig. 3); the analysis pointed out some potentially critical issues related to four over eight ERS.

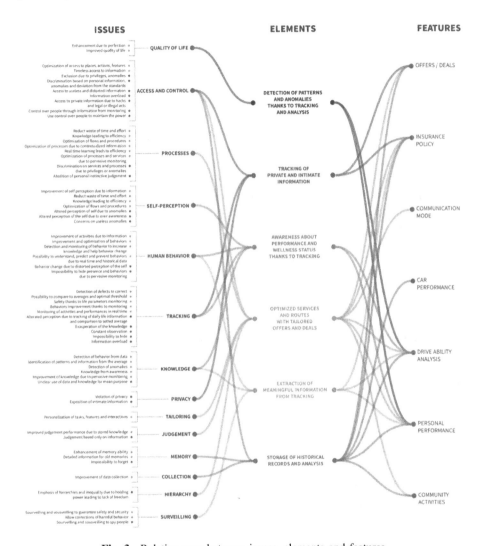

Fig. 3. Relation map between issues, elements and features.

We report here the results of our analysis summarized as a list of "attention points"; these points require further thinking and accurate investigation in order to create a suitable awareness of the impact of the use of personal data in the service and orient the design toward the development of an acceptable and desirable solutions for users on short and long terms.

- *Quality of life (Perfect Humanity).* The system collects biodata to identify behavior patterns and anomalies in the user health. The service creates a payback in terms of awareness of driver's ability and personal performances. This use of personal data involves issues related to the user's awareness about personal health and life-style, with possible changes in the sense of self and in the behaviors to perfection activities and state.

- *Access and Control (Perfect Humanity, Mnemonic, Super Monitor).* The service offers tailored driving itineraries and insurance policies, so inducing choices and behaviors about ways of access to places. The analysis also considers possible exclusion and/or discrimination based on privileged or peculiar service conditions related to the personal data. Data gathered by the system give to the user timeless access to information, but it can also produce information overload; it is important to verify a suitable accessibility to data for different types of users. The delicacy of data managed by the service and the complex system of stakeholders and partners involved in service provision require strict control of the access to the personal data; users should be allowed to understand the destiny of their personal information. The system collects personal data of different types; the processing of these data can produce information far beyond those strictly related to the production of value for users.

- *Processes (Perfect Humanity, Pervasive Awareness, Super Monitor).* The service is based on a continuous monitoring of users, with high sampling of behaviors and personal state in order to produce effective feedbacks and suggest convenient behaviors. The tailoring of functionalities requires a deep monitoring of personal information. The algorithms employed for personalization and the system of insurance incentive could reduce or alter the personal instinctive ability to judge a personal physical state due to transferring the judgement power to the system.

- *Self-perception (Perfect Humanity, Pervasive Awareness).* The system is supposed to provide suggestions about driving styles based on driving behaviors and health (wellness) conditions, so introducing perturbation of the self-perception. Furthermore, the system provides notification of changes in the personal or car conditions and it reveals possible emerged anomalies. This can create concerns in the user, producing stress in some circumstances; it can produce rejection for the excess of information or can lead to over-awareness. The presence of economic incentives offered by insurances can amply these effects.

- *Human Behavior (Perfect Humanity, Pervasive Awareness, Super Monitor).* The awareness about wellness status, performances and behaviors can alter the user's behavior or mental state in a positive or negative way. The pervasive and continuous monitoring can improve and optimize behaviors thanks to the enhancement derived from the possible perfection of actions. It can eventually lead to changes that are not convenient for the users due to the distorted perception of their own behavior. Pervasive monitoring can also create impossibility for the user to hide presence and behaviors.

- *Tracking (Perfect Humanity, Pervasive Awareness).* Biodata and activities tracking are compared by the system with averages or optimal thresholds. This is meant for improving safety and behavior. On the other hand, the awareness of comparative performances and status can have impacts on the perception of self.

- *Memory (Mnemonic).* The storage of information and the knowledge extractable from historical data can enhance the memory ability of the user, enabling him to retrieve detailed information from old memories, but it can also lead to the impossibility to forget information that are useless or even unwanted.
- *Collection (Mnemonic).* The storage of information supports storage information in a non-defined range of time. The storage of the data could be accessible over time for different further purposes even if the user is not aware of its use.

The outcomes of this analysis can be employed for different purposes within the design process. The above reported list of issues can be used to orient the research activities to be performed with users, so to verify the perceived importance of the possible critical impacts of the service. As different clusters of target users can show different attitudes and dispositions with respect to the critical issues and to the costs/benefits features of MEMoSa, the IAM analysis can also support a better definition of the opportunities related to the personalization of services. Furthermore, the issues emerged by the application of IAM provide an overview of aspects that should be taken into account in the physical design of the application as well as in the final communication of it.

5 Assessing IAM: A Comparison of the Method Application Outcomes with the Results of User Studies

Addressing identified issues of MEMoSa system's elements and outcomes, the reflective anticipation directed us to formulate questions related to design principles for supporting designers in developing awareness about the possible consequences in regard to how information is managed.

- Can the solution provide the right transparency on the type of data collected and who is accessing and managing them?
- Can the solution guarantee to the user the complete withdrawal of the consent and the deletion of account, data and information any time?
- Can the solution evaluate the values created for the users by the use of their data, in order to guarantee that it is exceeding the discomfort caused by the collection and use of personal information?
- Can the solution provide freedom in giving and denying the consent on the use of each data and information?
- Can the solution guarantee fairness between users, avoiding discrimination that can emerge from personal information?

For confirming the validity of the outcome of application of the Impact Anticipation Method (IAM) on the MEMoSa system, we refer to the publication of results of user studies conducted during the MEMoSa project [46]. Namely, Pavlovic et al. [46] specified a "need for a social consensus to be considered and directly employed during the design and evaluation process, in order to target and support the area of user values that deal with data and information exchange". The authors have pointed out that in the conducted user studies it resulted that such systems, that rely on the use of personal sensitive data, are desirable, but acceptable under certain conditions.

The issues identified during these user studies mainly overlap with the issues deriving from the application of IAM on the same design concept. In overall, there is a high interest in providing certain personal data for receiving elaborated useful information and features in exchange. This refers to willingness of sharing data with different entities, such as other drivers using the same car, insurance companies, and MEMoSa system agent in general. When it comes to transparency issues, the research of Pavlovic et al. showed that overall transparency in evaluation of a driver's profile, as well as clarity of back-end processes for how the evaluation is conducted, are quite desirable. The freedom of giving and denying consent on the use of each data and information emerged in few observations as well. An example are the situations in which the users pointed out that they would share data on driving style and routes, as well as stops and positioning, only selectively, i.e. only with certain drivers from their community. Fairness and discrimination that can emerge from personal information usage were also addressed in considerations of using sensitive bio-data on behavior, alertness and sleep quality for ratings from the side of the insurance company. Participants of the study "expressed willingness to be familiar with the back-end operations of the system and understand in which way gathered data is being translated into an information, and who has access to such information".

Furthermore, after the final, third, phase of conducted user studies, the participants confirmed that for majority it was clear the purpose of using data collected from cars, smartwatch and smartphone, and that it is also clear who has access to their personal data. After this phase participants were also asked to evaluate the proposed use cases from the initial testing phase once again, and now they evaluated them with higher scores in terms of acceptability and desirability. This directly showed that data treatment is an inevitable factor for assessing design concepts of such nature.

As there is an evident overlap of considerations derived from user studies from Pavlovic et al. [46] and application of IAM in the same project, we can confirm the validity of IAM for anticipating socially acceptable issues, i.e. achieving a social consensus within a design process for complex intelligent systems that employ personal data.

6   Conclusion

We proposed an Impact Anticipation Method for supporting design processes that deal with the use of personal data for creating services of certain user's values. We applied the method to a project of corresponding nature in order to identify potential critical issues. IAM is an approach based on the knowledge of things that have happened in the past and also on "projections" that are imaginary scenarios reflecting fears and hopes that people put into technological innovation. This knowledge is the reference to draw from in order to learn from past mistakes.

IAM does not serve for shutting down ideas related to data usage, rather its purpose is to strengthen the design concepts and values they propose. Therefore, it permits a creation of initial mapping of potential critical issues and aims to channel user studies towards particular aspects that require peculiar attention.

Merging the identification of possible critical issues and with a 'questioning' method to address the emerged design issues from a user-centered point of view, we can stimulate designers' creativity aiming to support them reflect on possible long-term consequences of their choices in use of personal data in the concept generation phase of the design process. The questions that emerge from the application of the proposed approach, aimed to support designers in anticipating issues, are in our opinion relevant and important, being involved as designers and as researchers in different design processes, and as teachers and teaching assistants in design courses.

In conclusion, we believe in the importance of rising and developing a discussion focused on the consequences of design choices within the communities of designers and people engaged in the development of digital infrastructures of our world, and, with our research, we hope to give a contribution to this goal.

Acknowledgements. This work has been partially funded by TIM S.p.A., Services Innovation Department, Joint Open Lab Digital Life, Milan, Italy.

References

1. Lanier, J.: Who Owns the Future? First Simon & Schuster Hardcover edition. Simon & Schuster, New York (2013)
2. Rowland, C., Goodman, E., Charlier, M., Light, A., Lui, A.: Designing Connected Products: UX for the Consumer Internet of Things, 1st edn. O'Reilly, Sebastopol (2015)
3. Young, N.: The Virtual Self: How Our Digital Lives are Altering the World Around Us. McClelland & Stewart, Plattsburgh (2013)
4. Greengard, S.: The Internet of Things. MIT Press, Cambridge (2015)
5. Trist, E.: The Evolution of Socio-technical Systems a Conceptual Framework and an Action Research Program. Ontario Min. of Labour, Toronto (1981)
6. Taebi, B.: Bridging the gap between social acceptance and ethical acceptability: perspective. Risk Anal. **37**(10), 1817–1827 (2017)
7. Winner, L.: Do artifacts have politics? Daedalus **109**(1), 121–136 (1980)
8. Manovich, L.: Trending: the promises and the challenges of big social data. In: Gold, M.K. (ed.) Debates in the Digital Humanities, pp. 460–475. University of Minnesota Press, Minneapolis (2012)
9. Friedman, B., Kahn, P.H., Borning, A.: Value Sensitive Design: Theory and Methods (2002)
10. von Schomberg, R.: A vision of responsible research and innovation. In: Owen, R., Bessant, J., Heintz, M. (eds.) Responsible Innovation, pp. 51–74. Wiley, Chichester (2013)
11. Weitzman, E.R., Kaci, L., Mandl, K.D.: Sharing medical data for health research: the early personal health record experience. J. Med. Internet Res. **12**(2), e14 (2010)
12. Pillan, M., Varisco, L., Bertolo, M.: Facing digital dystopias: a discussion about responsibility in the design of smart products. In: Alonso, M.B., Ozcan, E. (eds.) Proceedings of the Conference on Design and Semantics of Form and Movement - Sense and Sensitivity, DeSForM 2017. InTech, London (2017)
13. Campenhout, L.V., Frens, J., Overbeeke, K., Standaert, A., Peremans, H.: Physical interaction in a dematerialized world. Int. J. Des. **7**(1), 18 (2013)
14. Maude, F.: Data is 'the new raw material of the 21st century. The Guardian, 18-Apr-2012

15. Neff, G., Nafus, D.: Self-tracking. The MIT Press, Cambridge (2016)
16. Apple Touch ID, 2013. https://support.apple.com/en-us/HT204587. Accessed 7 Jan 2018
17. Beast Sensor, 2014. https://www.thisisbeast.com/en. Accessed 27 Nov 2018
18. Martani, C., Lee, D., Robinson, P., Britter, R., Ratti, C.: ENERNET: studying the dynamic relationship between building occupancy and energy consumption. Energy Build. **47**, 584–591 (2012)
19. Chen, X., Olivera, P.G.C.: X.pose, 2014. http://xc-xd.com/x-pose/. Accessed 27 Nov 2018
20. Berzowska, J.: Electronic textiles: wearable computers, reactive fashion, and soft computation. Textile **3**(1), 58–75 (2005)
21. Newell, S., Marabelli, M.: Strategic opportunities (and challenges) of algorithmic decision-making: a call for action on the long-term societal effects of 'datification'. J. Strateg. Inf. Syst. **24**(1), 3–14 (2015)
22. Borgman, C.L.: Big Data, Little Data, No Data: Scholarship in the Networked World. The MIT Press, Cambridge (2015)
23. Galliers, R.D., Newell, S., Shanks, G., Topi, H.: Datification and its human, organizational and societal effects: the strategic opportunities and challenges of algorithmic decision-making. J. Strateg. Inf. Syst. **26**(3), 185–190 (2017)
24. Günther, W.A., Rezazade Mehrizi, M.H., Huysman, M., Feldberg, F.: Debating big data: a literature review on realizing value from big data. J. Strateg. Inf. Syst. **26**(3), 191–209 (2017)
25. Marjanovic, O., Cecez-Kecmanovic, D.: Exploring the tension between transparency and datification effects of open government IS through the lens of Complex Adaptive Systems. J. Strateg. Inf. Syst. **26**(3), 210–232 (2017)
26. Vitale, A.S., Pillan, M.: Products as communication platforms: investigating and foretelling the evolution of product and service systems in the digital era. In: Libro de Actas—Systems and Design: Beyond Processes and Thinking (IFDP-SD2016) (2016)
27. Spadafora, M., Vitali, A.A., Pillan, M.: Objects are not slaves. Envisioning an aesthetic approach to the design of an interactive dialogue with objects. In: Cumulus Conference 2015, pp. 401–412 (2015)
28. Varisco, L., Pillan, M., Bertolo, M.: Personal digital trails: toward a convenient design of products and services employing digital data. In: 4D Design Development Developing Design Conference Proceedings. Kaunas University of Technology, 2017, p. 10 (2017)
29. Selin, C., Kimbell, L., Ramirez, R., Bhatti, Y.: Scenarios and design: scoping the dialogue space. Futures **74**, 4–17 (2015)
30. Luckin, R. (ed.): SNaP! Re-using, sharing and communicating designs and design knowledge using scenarios, narratives and patterns. In: Handbook of Design in Educational Technology, pp. 189–200. Routledge, New York (2013)
31. Bødker, S.: Scenarios in user-centred design—setting the stage for reflection and action. In: Hawaii International Conference on System Sciences, p. 11 (1999)
32. Shapiro, A.N.: The Paradox of Foreseeing the Future, Alan Shapiro
33. Sterling, B.: Design fiction. Interactions **16**(3), 20 (2009)
34. IMDb, Internet Movie Database. https://www.imdb.com/
35. Metz, R.: For $149 a Month, the Doctor Will See You as Often as You Want, 17 January 2017. MIT Technology Review
36. Maroto, F.: Bring Your Own Cyber Human (BYOCH)—Part 1: Augmented humans 04 May 2017. Linkedin
37. McClusky, M.: The Nike Experiment: How the Shoe Giant Unleashed the Power of Personal Metrics, 22 June 2009. Wired
38. Jones, R.: Smart Device Breaks Up Domestic Dispute By Calling the Police, 09 July 2017. Gizmodo

39. Hill, K.: How Target Figured Out A Tee Girl Was Pregnant Before Her Father Did, 16 February 2012. Forbes
40. Gabanelli, M.: Il Patrimonio, Report, 30 October 2017
41. Condliffe, J.: China turns big data into big brother. MIT Technol. Rev. 29-Nov-2016
42. Captain, S.: We Don't Always Know What AI is Thinking—And That Ca Be Scary, 15 November 2016. Fast Company
43. Berman, A.: Bridging the Mental Healthcare Gap With Artificial Intelligence, 10 October 2016. Singularity Hub
44. Diener, E. (ed.): Assessing Well-Being. Springer, Dordrecht (2009)
45. Erwin, K.: Communicating the New: Methods to Shape and Accelerate Innovation. Wiley, Hoboken (2014)
46. Pavlovic, M., Botto, F., Pillan, M., Criminisi, C., Valla, M.: Social consensus: contribution to design methods for AI agents that employ personal data. In: Karwowski, W., Ahram, T. (eds.) Intelligent Human Systems Integration 2019. IHSI 2019. Advances in Intelligent Systems and Computing, vol. 903, pp. 877–883. Springer, Cham (2019). https://doi.org/10.1007/978-3-030-11051-2_134

Research on Application of Interaction Design in Landscape Design

Yanlin Liu[1,2](✉)

[1] University of Jinan, No. 336,
West Road of Nan Xinzhuang, Jinan, Shandong, China
liuyanlin269@163.com
[2] Tianjin University, No. 92 Weijin Road, Nankai District, Tianjin, China

Abstract. With the development of computer science and technology and the application of virtual reality and augmented reality technology, human-computer interaction technology has been widely concerned and applied in many fields. At present, the application of human-computer interaction technology to design and practice urban landscapes has many challenges and new requirements put forward by the trend of the times. First of all, the basic means of human-computer interaction technology include multimedia, augmented reality technology, virtual reality technology, etc., transforming the traditional urban landscape design carrier into the virtual world, and its expression form is more convenient. In addition, the important features of human-computer interaction technology are digitalization and virtualization. By creating design content with strong sense of experience and strong interaction, it brings users a variety of vivid experiences. Therefore, applying it to urban landscape design will bring unprecedented deepening and reform to the field. By applying human-computer interaction technology to the theory, design and application of urban virtual landscape, the future development of this field is studied and explored.

Keywords: Human-computer interaction technology ·
Urban landscape design · Entity user interface · Virtual reality

1 Introduction

In modern times, rapid development of computer science and technology, multimedia, digital imaging technology is also gradually mature. The application of these technologies has effectively improved the imaging quality of electronic devices, increased the transmission speed of electronic data, and promoted the maturity and application of virtual reality technology, augmented reality technology and mixed reality technology. The use and promotion of digital technology in daily life has attracted widespread attention and has increasingly influenced our way of life and concept of life (Fig. 1).

Different times have put forward different requirements for the meaning and content of design. The purpose and object of design is always to take human needs as the primary starting point, to coordinate the relationship between human beings and the environment as the main body, to pay attention to the return of human nature, and to feel a variety of psychological feelings, such as security, domain, belonging and

© Springer Nature Switzerland AG 2019
A. Marcus and W. Wang (Eds.): HCII 2019, LNCS 11583, pp. 132–145, 2019.
https://doi.org/10.1007/978-3-030-23570-3_11

Fig. 1. Interactive cities (source: the author)

identity, which can not be neglected. Visual factors. However, in the information society, the era of media leading everything, people's "sense of participation" should be given great attention. In the landscape design of the new era, the interaction between people and landscape is regarded as the starting point of design. It is one of the ways to adapt to the characteristics of the times and solve practical problems to create new landscape works with modern electronic technology and digital media.

In recent years, the application of digital technology and computer technology has made some achievements in many fields, and its combination with the industry is a new trend of the times. In this context, how to break through the limitations of traditional landscape design and rationally and effectively use digital technology to practice urban landscape design is the direction that designers are gradually thinking and exploring. Especially with the widespread spread of electronic devices such as smartphones and computers into life, people can have multiple experiences without leaving home, making the real experience of outdoor landscapes and people's lives gradually separated. The use of digital technology to transform, adjust and improve the concept and method of landscape design can change the predicament of the current traditional landscape design, and thus meet the needs of people's lifestyle in the digital age of computers.

2 Start of the Art

The development of human interaction technology originated from the concept of entity bits. Tangible Bits (TB) was proposed by MIT's renowned scholars Hirroshi Ishii and Brygg Ullmer at the 1997 CHI conference. Hirroshi Ishii et al. pointed out in their published paper that entity bits enable users to directly access and process bits by combining bits with everyday transactions. Based on this concept, TUI comes into being as the Tangible User Interface (TUI), and is gradually applied in the information and digital world. Users can touch and process digital information, thus making the information exchange more convenient. In addition, Hirroshi Ishii believes that the physical user interface will become the main form of human-computer interaction technology in the future with its convenient application features. Applying it to human-computer interaction systems can fully play its important role in promoting the development of environmental space, building surfaces and atomic coupling (Fig. 2).

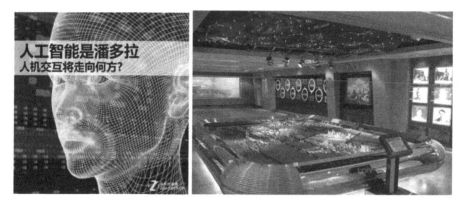

Fig. 2. Human-computer interaction (source: the author)

In view of the great advantages and development potential of physical user interface, practitioners in many different industries at home and abroad have gradually begun to explore the combination and practice of this technology with their own industry. In 2011, Australian artist Rafael Lozano-Hemmer developed the "Tape Recorders" experience device. The principle of the device is that 40 tapes are arranged side by side at equal intervals. Each tape measure can be independently lifted and lowered by motor control. After the information such as the distance between the visitor and the tape measure and the dwell time is collected, it is converted into different heights of the tape measure. When the tape measure rises to a certain height, it will make a sound due to the bending, at this time, the motor will restore the tape measure and circulate the process. Visitors can get interesting experiences by comparing the heights that each other can make the tape measure. This novel art installation brings an unprecedented interactive experience that attracts many visitors. In 2013, Israeli scientists Oren Zuckerman and Ayelet Gal-Oz compared the experience of physical user interfaces and traditional graphical user interfaces (GUIs) based on previous research experience. The study collected 58 subjects, and analyzed the characteristics of TUI and CUI using the statistical analysis of sample characteristics of preference and performance, finally found that most of the subjects were more inclined to use physical user interface of human-computer interaction system, mainly because the entity form of user interface, with a more convenient form of interaction and more abundant information resources. In addition, TANGIBLE GROUP, a scientist from the Massachusetts Institute of Technology, released its research project, the Transform device in 2013. The device is an intuitive experience device based on TUI technology, it is a square matrix composed of many small squares. By collecting and recognizing the user's behavioral intent, the information is transformed into a lifting instruction for each small square. In other words, users can transform the way information is exchanged into a three-dimensional contact and experience. The invention of this device is of great significance for the future use of physical interaction technology in space design, architectural design and landscape design. Another application example of physical interaction design technology is Hexi Wall, a work of art designed by Canadian designer Thibault et al. in 2014. The work is a building wall that can interact with the experience. It is composed of a number of scale devices, each of which can be controlled to perform independent multi-axis flipping. Information such as the distance between the experiencer and the building, and the behavioral intentions of the experiencer can be inadvertently recognized and transformed into scales, bringing intelligent communication experience, and being widely welcomed by the experiencers and highly regarded by designers in many industries.

At present, there are few theoretical and practical applications in human-computer interaction technology and virtual reality in China. The related theoretical works on virtual interactive technology are mostly from the translation of foreign works. The article "Get Real: A Philosophical Adventure in Virtual Reality" by Professor Zhen Zhenming of Sun Yat-sen University is one of the masterpieces of virtual reality technology. In terms of application practice, the National CD Engineering Research Center of Tsinghua University has long started the combination of digital technology and landscape design. They used this technology to realize the virtual reality experience of the Potala Palace. In addition, virtual reality technology has gradually been applied by landscape companies to the performance of landscape design. They display the landscape design through special effects or stereo test demonstration halls, especially before the formal delivery, using this technology to test the effect, saving material costs and increase project adoption rates. In general, the development of digital technology and interactive technology in China is relatively late. Until 2014, related concepts such as virtual reality technology and augmented reality technology gradually entered the public's field of vision, and the combination of digital technology and landscape design still needs to be explored.

Under the background of the rapid development of computer technology, how to combine digital and urban landscape design is an important issue that breaks through the limitations of traditional landscape design under the external conditions of virtual reality, augmented reality and multimedia technology. By incorporating interactive interaction technology into the landscape design concept, the new human-computer interaction and landscape-focused landscape design pattern is fundamentally different from the traditional landscape, bringing the experience to a completely different and vivid experience. This landscape design model is also a new experience for designers, who can enjoy the creative process with more convenient, deeper and more interactive means. This immersive, interactive and digital creative experience is also incomparable to traditional landscape creation methods.

3 Methodology

3.1 Concepts of Interaction Design and Human-Computer Interaction Design

The concept of interaction design was proposed by Bill Mogrich in 1984, who generalized interaction design to the design of product use, task flow and information structure, and applied digital technology to the design process. Since then, interactive design has gradually become an independent discipline that has received widespread attention. According to Alan Cooper, interaction design is a technology that designs the behavior of people, the environment, and the system, and conveys the meaning of its behavior by appearance elements. The purpose of interaction design is to improve the user experience and make the process of using the product more convenient and effective. First of all, the basic starting point of interaction design is the user's feelings, designed around the central goal of user experience, the fundamental purpose of which is to improve the user experience and interaction in the process of work and life. Second, because of the complexity of the discipline itself and the intersection with other disciplines, the research is more extensive, and in the context of the development of computer technology and digital technology, the cross design conforms to the trend of the times, blends and integrates with many fields and many industries. In addition to the most basic computer, virtual reality, augmented reality and multimedia technology, crossover design has been applied in many aspects such as visual effects, artistic creation and service design. Crossover design has gradually become more diverse.

Human-computer interaction technology is a technology for studying the exchange of information between humans and computers, which uses various input and output devices to implement dialogue. It mainly includes two major structures: input device and output device. People can transfer information to a computer by means of an input device such as a mouse, a keyboard, a joystick, a position tracker, etc., and the computer provides a corresponding answer or prompt information through an output device such as a display or a speaker, thereby realizing human-computer interaction (Fig. 3).

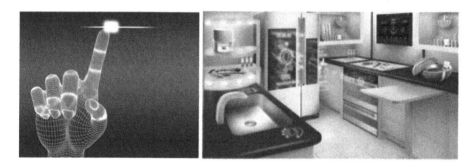

Fig. 3. Application of human-computer interaction in life (source: the author)

The use of human-computer interaction technology has greatly promoted the exchange of information between people and machines. With the continuous development of electronic information technology, people can break through the traditional and single communication mode of "human-mouse-machine" and gradually have a variety of communication options, such as advanced limb posture trackers, visual transmitters, tactile input channels and other advanced equipment to make human-computer interaction more comprehensive, accurate and convenient. This new and diversified human-computer interaction model is constantly integrated into all aspects of people's daily life, which will bring new ideas to the limitations of urban landscapes breaking through traditional design. Especially under the impetus of science and technology, the computer can even intelligently perceive and recognize the interaction behavior and behavior intention of the experiencer, and actively complete the interaction through calculation. With the development of computer technology, the improvement of urban landscape design will receive great motivation (Fig. 4).

Fig. 4. Human-computer interactive information platform (source: the author)

Under the trend of continuous integration of human-computer interaction technology and multiple fields, many urban landscape architects have gradually made relevant attempts. For example, using computer technology such as virtual reality to innovate the experience and communication between people and the space environment, and the designed spatial landscape through the technology to fully display its dynamic development process over time, greatly breaking the traditional landscape design limitations of operability (Fig. 5).

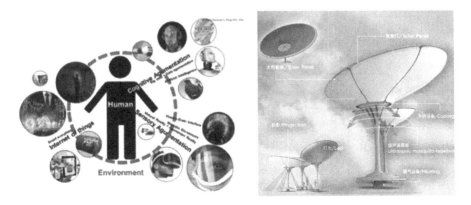

Fig. 5. Human-computer interaction system (source: the author)

3.2   Elements of Human-Computer Interaction in Urban Landscape

The result of the landscape environment being connected to people through a link is called an interactive landscape, basically consisting of three components: interactive media, people and landscape elements. First of all, interactive media can be called interactive information, which is developed by two-way communication of information, such as the process from information sending and receiving to circular feedback. The change of content in the interactive medium is led by different interactive objects, and the output information is implicit and explicit from the perspective of the participants, which basically covers emotions, experience, knowledge and feelings, etc., and the individual has a direct impact on the interaction process after its absorption. While explicit information involves expressions, language, and behavior, and directly interprets and realizes landscape interaction. In addition, based on the perspective of landscape, there are two kinds of output information: image and object image, among which the object image is divided into dynamic scene and static scene: As the name implies, dynamic landscape content, such as image changes and morphological structure; the static scene is the judgment of the naked eye on the static landscape, such as color texture, proportion, scale and morphological structure. Contents such as knowledge, history, and culture can be reflected through intentions, while landscape intentions are the overall perception of the subject's object. Secondly, the participants of the landscape, as the main body of the interactive landscape, can be further subdivided according to quantity, gender, age and socio-economic attributes. Finally, landscape elements are composed of physical form and landscape space, including natural landscape elements such as plants, soil, water, mountains and stones, as well as artificial landscape elements such as landscape sketches, facilities, roads and buildings, as well as immaterial landscape such as values, customs and habits, history and culture. By combing the definitions of the above components and interactive landscapes, a more concrete description can be developed by the following framework diagram, as shown in Fig. 6.

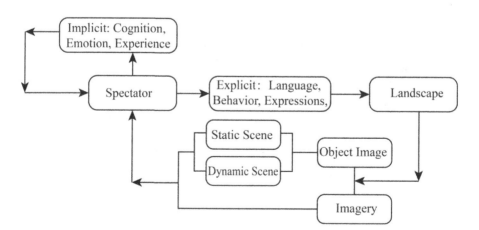

Fig. 6. Schematic diagram of essential element relationship formed by human-computer interaction landscape

4 Discussion

4.1 Principles of Human-Computer Interaction in Urban Landscape Design

The design of human-computer interaction urban landscape basically follows the five principles of intensification, functional visibility, predictability, diversity and people-oriented, as shown in Fig. 7. Firstly, the principle of intensification is mainly reflected in the optimization of comprehensive income, specifically to maximize the role of environmental and ecological benefits, to meet the reasonable spirit and material needs of people, to maximize the conservation of natural resources and resources, so that energy and the utilization rate of resources has been improved to a certain extent, and in order to avoid over-design, the design principle can be maintained intensively, and then the landscape design is guided towards science. Secondly, the principle of functional visibility, that is, in order to facilitate people's control of products and effectively improve the purity and ease of use of products, this principle can be used to design the product form, thereby triggering people to interact in the subconscious. At the same time, when designing interactive landscapes, the design of landscape facilities and landscape forms is basically based on instinctual cognition, which only pays attention to the habit of people to contact the external environment and neglect the behavior of thinking, so as to create interactive opportunities through metaphors. Finally, the predictive principle is that when the designer designs the human-interactive urban landscape, it has certain predictability based on user demand positioning and a large amount of practical research, and the maximum value of landscape output is due to the user's anticipation of historical and cultural foresight, level of demand, psychological expectations and behavioral habits. Judging whether the foresight is successful depends on whether the user's experience goal can be properly catered after the space and material form are designed. If the answer is yes, then the user's expectations match the design of the landscape space, and the design at this time is predictable. The principle of diversity has two aspects, namely, diverse interaction means and diversified landscape design functions. The former is a variety of landscape interactions, based on the experience of different users, while the latter is to meet the needs of different people. The principle of people-oriented can be explained from four points, that is: First, coordinate the relationship between man and nature, the ultimate goal is to create a better living environment for people; second, care for many factors affecting people's physiological psychology, such as social values, lifestyle, history and culture, etc.; third, in order to reflect humane care, fully consider the differences in environmental behavior; fourth, fully understand the user's level of needs.

4.2 Urban Landscape Design Strategy of Human-Computer Interaction

Firstly, the strategy of generating human-computer interaction urban landscape is shown in Fig. 8. Based on the use of digital technology, it is expressed through the design of human-computer interaction urban landscape. The different design features of digital technology play a decisive role in the way the landscape is used, its function and its shape. The following are the different technical advantages from the four levels

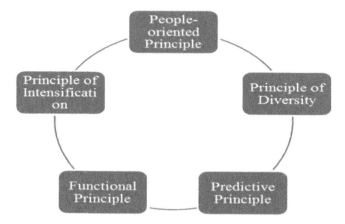

Fig. 7. Principles of human-computer interaction in urban landscape design

of digital projection, mixed reality, augmented reality and virtual reality. First of all, digital projection, which is mostly applied to large public places, the biggest technical advantage is the naked-eye virtual landscape with large volume. Follow by, mixed reality is also to build a virtual landscape. Its working principle is to combine the field with electronic devices, and then present the digital information with dynamic effects. The biggest advantage of this technology application is that it enhances the interaction between users and virtual landscapes, thus enhancing the experience and quality of information acquisition. Next, the biggest difference between augmented reality and virtual reality is that it is closely connected to the site through the super-position of virtual information on the actual site. Therefore, the realization of this technology must rely on the actual site, and then expand and extend the virtual information. Last but not least is virtual reality. The most critical issue in designing a virtual reality system is how to build a realistic virtual environment, including 3D scenes, stereo sounds, and so on. In the human sense, visual ingestion has the largest amount of information, accounting for about 70%, and the response is the most agile. The scene is too simple, it will make the user feel false, and the complex and realistic scene will inevitably increase the difficulty of interaction and affect the real-time. This technology mainly makes the user completely immersed in the scene, the user's perspective is realized by turning the head, and the adjustment of the distance of the viewing angle can be realized by the keyboard direction key, so that the user is immersive. This kind of perspective is very similar to the angle of view of the UAV (unmanned aerial vehicle). When looking at the Western House in mid-air, the advantages and disadvantages of this perspective are obvious. The advantage is that you can see the whole picture, have a certain understanding of the appearance of each part, and even close the place to attract yourself, but the disadvantage is that the experience is not good enough. Since people usually get used to keeping the line of sight and the height of the ground consistent with the height of the human eye corresponding to the ground, this can give a stronger sense of reality in the scene experience, just like walking in the scene, the experience brought by the difference in perspective is different. This fully demonstrates that when a player plays a majority of role-playing games, he usually views the overall scene from a top-down perspective, and then focuses on the role played, so that the entire game screen presents the entire scene according to the perspective of the character or the perspective of the character's height, thereby giving the player a more realistic game experience (Fig. 8).

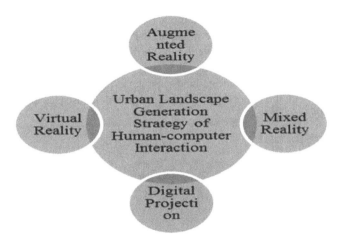

Fig. 8. Urban landscape generation strategy based on human-computer interaction

Secondly, the generation of urban landscape based on human-computer interaction. The generation of urban landscape based on human-computer interaction can be analyzed from three aspects: theme expansion design, use of digital technology equipment, and application of digital technology, as shown in Fig. 9. In the first place, theme development design. This design is reflected in the display of a large amount of additional information in the virtual landscape, taking the virtual landscape design of Nanjing Ming Dynasty City Wall as an example, which shows a series of information related to this theme. For example, the city wall is based on the Nanjing Ming Dynasty City bricks, which is of great artistic value and historical value. The brickwork embodies the history of Chinese ancient bricks, and the masonry and brick structure have important research value, and also it condenses the heavy history in every brick of Ming Dynasty City. In order to facilitate the virtual reality to more accurately present the brick effect, the text information of the city brick is more clearly presented by the scanning of the city wall information and the generation of the digital model by means of the three-dimensional scanning instrument, so that the complete historical information of the Ming City Wall can be better displayed. In addition, using three-dimensional scanning and display, the context information and related historical elements of other historical relics in Nanjing are more fully displayed. In the next place, the use of digital technology equipment is mainly applied to the presentation of virtual reality technology solutions. The hardware facilities that are more common in the application object are virtual reality helmets. HTC VIVE is representative. Users can change the virtual landscape by operating the handle. The viewing angle of the whole screen can be adjusted by rotating the head, and the highly free virtual landscape roaming experience can better meet the user's need for experiential, interactive and immersive virtual landscape scenes. Again, the use of digital technology requires Unity 3D software to implement the urban landscape of virtual reality technology. Unity 3D software has powerful digital model placement capability and convenient operation. The basic working principle of this concept experimental design is that the first step is to prepare the software programming to generate the digital model roaming package; the second step is to put the model in the package; the third step is to adjust the model with Unity 3D. After completing the above operation process, the virtual city landscape file can be presented by reading the virtual reality hardware device. In addition, a major feature of the virtual landscape is the presentation of diverse images, which is reflected in the process of generating virtual landscapes using developer virtual reality devices (Fig. 9).

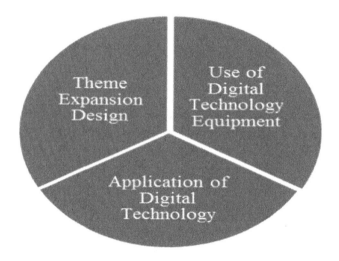

Fig. 9. Urban landscape generation based on human-machine interaction

4.3 Prospects for Human-Computer Interaction in Urban Landscape Design

Kevin Kelly, the founding editor of Wired magazine, wrote in Wired that the human-computer interaction technology will produce the next large technology platform: Mirrorworld. Kevin Kelly predicted that the future of the mirrored world will fundamentally change people's lives.

What is the mirror world? The word mirror was originally promoted by Yale University computer scientist David Gelernter. Objects in the mirrored world not only have the appearance of real things, but also the background, meaning and function of things. We can interact with it, manipulate it, and experience it, just as we do in the real world. The mirrored world will fundamentally change people's lives like the Internet and social media. And this virtual and reality world will eventually be as big as the planet we live in.

In the mirror world, we will be able to search the physical space like searching for text, for example, to help you find "all park benches that can see the sunrise. "We will be able to hyperlink specific objects to a physical network, just like a network hyperlink to a word. All real objects will have a digital twin brother. The development of the mirror world is much faster than we think. Wayfair's "Online Home Product Catalog", a homeware retailer, shows tens of thousands of products, but not all photos are taken in a photo studio. Instead, Wayfair found that creating a three-dimensional computer model for each item is much cheaper. You have to look at every picture on the Wayfair website very carefully to see if it is a virtual object model.

The mirror world is already under development, and although the mirror world is not yet fully existed, it is coming. In the near future, our landscape architects will digitally design in virtual reality space, every place and every thing in the real world, such as every street, every lamp post, every building, every A room will have a full-size digital view in the mirrored world. The mirror world will become the third epoch-making technology platform in the history of the Internet. The first large-scale technology platform is the Internet, which digitizes information and influences knowledge by algorithms. The second largest platform is social media, which is mainly operated on mobile phones, digitizing humans, and subjecting human behavior and relationships to the power of algorithms.

We are currently at the dawn of the third platform, which will digitize all regions of the world. On this platform, everything and territory will be machine readable, and everything will be affected by the algorithm. It takes at least 10 years for the mirrored world to grow to the point where it can be used by millions of people, and it will take decades to mature (Fig. 10).

Fig. 10. Mnirror age of big data collection platform

5 Conclusions

The design of the virtual landscape is more suitable for the reflection of the contemporary landscape from the aspects of technical means, process, regularity and essence. The reason is as follows. First, through the multi-dimensional and development perspective, more types of architectural forms can be digitally designed to facilitate people's understanding and understanding of contemporary landscapes. Second, the contemporary landscape has many design features, and its research involves multidisciplinary theory and method research. Therefore, the design of contemporary landscape by virtual reality technology is an inevitable requirement for exploring the essence, regularity and procedural nature of virtual landscape. Besides, the human-computer interaction urban landscape is different from the traditional landscape design method, and there are differences between the practice mode and the theoretical system in the two design methods. The former can create highly creative ideas and practical cases by adopting digital technologies such as virtual reality and augmented reality in landscape form, landscape function, human-computer interaction, etc. The information elements of virtual landscapes can be obtained through a series of scientific means such as drones, GPS, and 3D scanning. Compared with the traditional landscape and human-computer interaction landscape, the latter pays more attention to the use of modern digital technology, and designers can carry out more extensive creations in landscape forms, functions, human-machine relationships, and even landscapes can be better applied based on the unique expression of the user's re-creation landscape. The rethinking and reflection on urban landscape design has benefited from the new landscape and user relationship and the new urban landscape design thinking mode. With the advent of digital information era, facing the characteristics of contemporary society and contemporary life, designers should adopt coping strategies and expressions that can solve practical problems and challenges. In the new era of environmental art design, the introduction of "interactive design" thinking, from human experience, human and environmental communication as a starting point, the use of new technologies, new materials to create an unusual environmental art and diversified living space. Mutual design emphasizes the usability and user experience of the design ideas make it more advantageous in the future environmental art design, interactive design is a concern about human nature, people-oriented products. This may become the future research hotspot, will also promote the development of China's environmental art design to a certain extent.

References

1. Speights-Binet, J.: Landscape of transformations: architecture and Birmingham, Alabama. Geogr. Rev. **102**(1), 142–143 (2012)
2. Heidmann, F., Schiewe, J.: Human-computer interaction in geovisualization. i-com **16**(3), 203 (2017)
3. Thoss, A.: 3Dsensation: optical technologies are the key for future man-machine interaction. Adv. Opt. Technol. **4**(5–6), 347–350 (2015)

4. Jeremiah, D.: Carscapes: the motor car, architecture, and landscape in England. J. Transp. Hist. **34**(2), 213–215 (2013)
5. Nestler, S.: Evaluating human-computer-interaction in crisis scenarios. i-com **13**(1), 53–62 (2014)
6. Backhaus, N., Brandenburg, S.: Temporal dynamics of emotional activation in man-machine interaction. i-com **13**(1), 63–69 (2014)
7. Lyubchak, V., Lavrov, E., Pasko, N.: Ergonomic support of man-machine interaction: approach to designing of operators' group activities (variational inequality and combinatorial problems). Int. J. Biomed. Soft Comput. Hum. Sci. **17**(2), 53–58 (2012)
8. Nam, Y., Kim, J.: A semiotic analysis of sounds in personal computers: toward a semiotic model of human-computer interaction. Semiotica **182**, 269–284 (2010)
9. Kim, J., Wagner, J., Vogt, T., André, E., Jung, F., Rehm, M.: Emotional sensitivity in human-computer interaction. Methoden und innovative Anwendungen der Informatik und Informationstechnik **51**(6), 325–328 (2009)
10. Le Bigot, L., Terrier, P., Jamet, E., Botherel, V., Rouet, J.-F.: Does textual feedback hinder spoken interaction in natural language? Ergonomics **53**(1), 43–55 (2010)
11. Schmidt, L., Ley, D.: Mensch-Computer-InteraktionsgestaltungzurLuftlagebewertung (Human-computer interaction design for air situation assessment). i-com **7**(1/2008), 12–17 (2008)
12. Holtzman, L., Gersbach, C.A.: Editing the epigenome: reshaping the genomic landscape. Annu. Rev. Genomics Hum. Genet. **19**, 43–71 (2018)
13. Natsuko, H., et al.: Epigenetic landscape influences the liver cancer genome architecture. Nat. Commun. **9**(1), 1643 (2018)
14. Morton, N.: Architecture and landscape in medieval anatolia, 1100–1500. J. R. Asiatic Soc. **28**(1), 195–196 (2017)
15. Benson, A.K.: Host genetic architecture and the landscape of microbiome composition: humans weigh in. Genome Biol. **16**(1), 203 (2015)

Design Theories, Methods and Tools

Sketch Notes, a Non-traditional Way for User Researchers to Take Notes

Maliheh Aghanasiri$^{(\boxtimes)}$ and Grace Phang$^{(\boxtimes)}$

Liberty Mutual Insurance, Boston, MA, USA
{Maliheh.aghanasiri, Grace.phang}@libertymutual.com

Abstract. The User Experience (UX) research team at Liberty Mutual Insurance has implemented a new method of taking notes and sharing notes with the team, Sketch notes. The purpose of Sketch notes is to accurately convey meaning at a glance and facilitate visual memory during collaborative analysis and insight-driven workshop activities. Sketch notes are a condensed visual map of what recruited participants share with the product team in an interview session or a usability test. In the first section, we explain why note-taking is an important part of the work of user researchers. Next, we review the note-taking methods that we use at Liberty Mutual and their advantages and drawbacks. In the third section, we introduce Sketch notes and explain how both the literature and its successful deployment at Liberty Mutual Insurance support this approach.

Keywords: Sketch note · Note-taking methodology · User research notes · Visualized note-taking · Information recall

1 Introduction

1.1 Background

In the process of enhancing Liberty Mutual Insurance digital experiences for customers and prospects, the product and development team including user research has undergone a digital transformation. As part of this transformation in the past two years (starting January 2017), several portfolios and over one hundred squads operating in a customer-centric Agile model were created.

To ensure that products are desirable and usable by customers, the first step is to understand a user's goals and needs. User research activities provide valuable opportunities for designers, product owners, developers, and others in cross-functional roles to learn about user's behavior and how they interact with specific products first-hand [1]. In addition, involving and engaging development teams in research projects encourage stakeholders to develop products that align better with a user's needs and behaviors. It increases empathy for users and creates ownership for usability outcomes.

During Liberty Mutual's transformation journey, the user research team not only implemented new research methodologies into practice, but also incorporated several new data capturing processes and note-taking artifacts. Most of the artifacts were created collaboratively with the research team and Agile squad members.

© Springer Nature Switzerland AG 2019
A. Marcus and W. Wang (Eds.): HCII 2019, LNCS 11583, pp. 149–162, 2019.
https://doi.org/10.1007/978-3-030-23570-3_12

We involved development teams within the research studies we conducted to give them the opportunity to learn about the users and understand their problems. One way to increase stakeholder engagement in research projects was to encourage them to observe user research sessions and take notes [2]. To bring this to realization we used multiple note-taking techniques that varied depending on the study goals, objectives, and research method. Important factors for us were to ensure the accuracy, structure, clarity, and prioritization of data we found during study sessions, such as interviews.

1.2   Note-Taking Methodologies

Note-taking methodologies that we used in different projects included:

- Handwritten sticky notes
- Verbatim note-taking tables
- Video/audio recordings
- Empathy map
- Journey map
- Scorecards
- In-session survey questions
- Sketch notes

Handwritten Sticky Notes. Handwritten sticky notes (see Fig. 1) are the company's most frequently used note-taking method. In every interview and usability test at the company, observers write their top three to five findings on sticky notes. This results in a collaborative and egalitarian process by which each person's top observations are given the same value as everyone else's in the room. Each participant is assigned a different color of sticky notes and separate white pads. At the end of the research sessions, stakeholders stack redundant observations on each white pad for each participant. That is, the same observation by different stakeholders for the same participant counts as one single observation. Stakeholders then affinity diagram common themes across all the participants.

Fig. 1. Examples of handwritten sticky notes created for 13 participants.

Sticky notes are easy to explain, require low effort to set up, and color-coding makes it easy to see specific themes and identify the frequency of specific issues. However, there are a few disadvantages. Handwriting might be difficult to read, sticky notes are difficult to store if not transcribed, and they are limited in scope. They show pieces of information rather than the sequence in which issues happened.

Chronological Note-Taking Tables. Chronological note-taking tables (see Fig. 2) are similar to traditional written note-taking methods. On a grid, note-takers write down information corresponding to specific questions or scenarios.

The note-taking table makes it easy to compare findings across several participants and helps to keep track of certain identified elements. However, it requires preparation time to format and is inflexible, as it is based on the moderator guide.

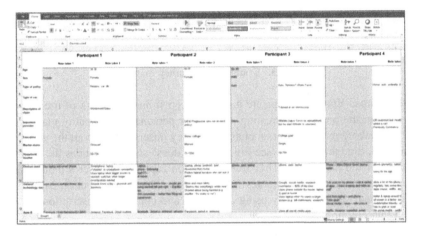

Fig. 2. Example of chronological note-taking table.

Video and Audio Recordings. Video and audio are recorded for every user interview session. A variety of tools are used to take and record videos and audio: Skype, Zoom, GoToMeeting, Validately, and Morae Recorder/Observer.

Videos are the most accurate and exhaustive note-taking method. They can be stored for future use and can be shared with stakeholders who may have missed a session. However, videos require a participant's consent agreement, and it is time-consuming to review and transcribe videos.

Journey Maps. Journey Maps are artifacts that are created in-session, between a participant and a moderator (see Fig. 3). The moderator shares a screen view of a journey map template with the participant and transcribes the participant's explanation of a given process or experience. In our team, journey maps are created in either Microsoft excel files or Google Sheets, measuring several factors: emotion, question/thoughts, and devices. The emotion valence level is measured on a scale of 1 (very negative) to 5 (very positive).

The journey map is a useful tool for the comparison of the same experience across different participants. Because emotions are mapped onto a consistent five-point valence scale, it is easy to visualize the trajectory of emotions through an experience. Journey maps may vary in consistency (for example, number of steps and level of detail) depending on the moderator and participant.

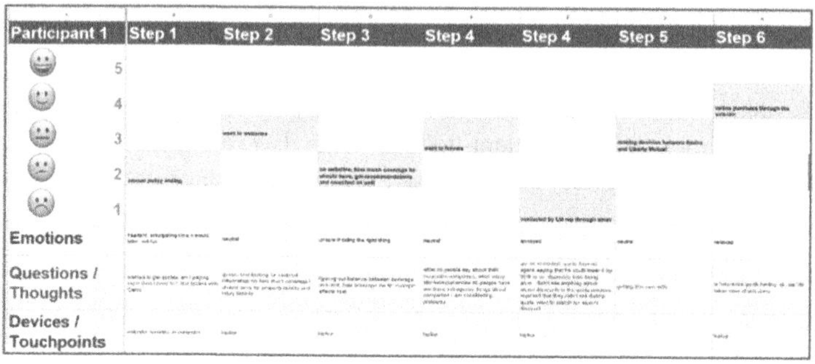

Fig. 3. Example of a journey map.

Empathy Maps. Empathy Maps are a way to deepen understanding of users and are mostly used in the process of creating a customer persona [3]. Empathy maps can be used as note-taking methods that emphasize four key observations about the user - what they said, did, thought, and felt (see Fig. 4). The "does" section includes the behaviors and actions of the participant. The "thinks" section captures the user's thoughts. The "says" section includes direct quotes from the user. The "feels" section captures the user's emotional state, primarily using adjectives and contextual descriptions of what triggered that emotion.

The empathy map is a quick way to organize information about a user's attitudes and behaviors, which aids in the development of personas. However, the distinctions between the sections, such as "says" or "thinks" may appear overlapping or ambiguous. Note-takers must choose the section in which to put an idea, to prevent redundancy. Because information can be stored in multiple sections, this makes finding specific information afterwards more difficult as well.

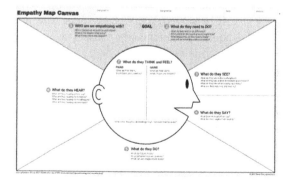

Fig. 4. Empathy map template [4].

Scorecards. Scorecards are a written note-taking method used to yield quantitative data from qualitative interviews. The scorecards are frequently used during user interviews to track metrics such as Likert scale answers, preferences, and experiences across different participants (see Fig. 5).

Scorecards help to quickly identify trends in data, especially regarding points of difficulty for users or perceptions around ease, satisfaction, and usefulness.

Scorecards have a rigid and unchanging design, because the metrics have been incorporated into the study design in advance. Scorecards also take time and expertise to set up, particularly when they include formulas and conditional formatting.

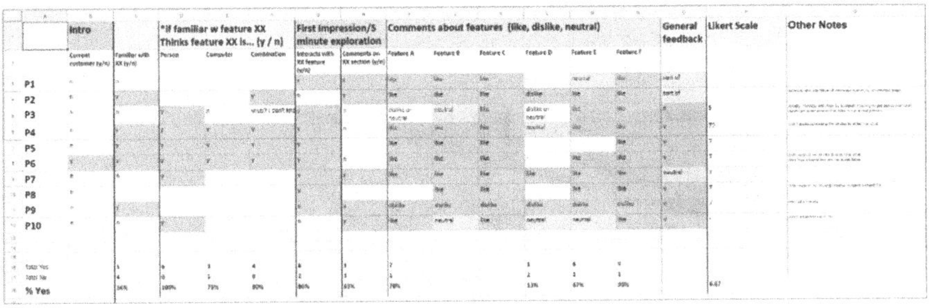

Fig. 5. Example of a score card.

Other Methods. There were other note-taking methods that we used including moderator handwritten notes, an emoji exercise, collages and headshot photos of participants. Moderator notes were used to clarify observer questions and if needed observer notes. We used an emoji exercise to ask participants how they felt in a specific stage of their experience, for example how they felt when they had to file an auto insurance claim. Participants picked 3–5 emojis out of a list of emojis to express their feelings. Collages were created prior to the session by participants to answer a few questions about their previous insurance related experiences (see Fig. 6). The collage is a useful tool in helping participants to recall relevant experiences, so they can better articulate their experiences during the session. Headshot photos of participants were

Fig. 6. Example of a collage.

also recorded. During collaboration sessions, viewing headshots helped many observers to quickly recall and differentiate participants, especially as there are typically 10–15 participants per study.

2   Sketch Notes

2.1   What is a Sketch Note?

"Sketch notes are rich visual notes created from a mix of handwriting, drawings, hand-drawn typography, shapes, and visual elements like arrows, boxes, and lines." [5]

Sketch notes are created in real time while listening to a story, discussion or presentation (see Fig. 7).

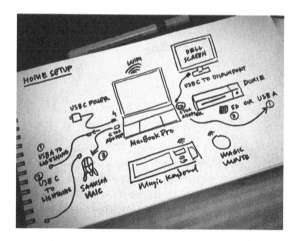

Fig. 7. Example of a sketch note created by [6]

In the process of creating Sketch notes, the note taker listens carefully to the conversation and then draws a visual map of it. The purpose of Sketch notes is to capture the big picture of ideas and discussions using both words and images [5]. Because the note-taker is sketching at the same time the session is happening, she can capture information without having to recall it after the fact; there is also less chance to "misremember" specific details. Although Sketch notes like any other creative products are unique to the note-takers, sketch notes share some common components (see Table 1).

Table 1. Common components of sketch notes

Common components	Example
Simple drawings of people and faces	
Common objects	
Typography to organize the visual map and to represent categories and actions	
Emojis to show feelings	
Quotes to indicate a statement or to draw attention to important points	
Containers to organize the visual components and create categorizations	
Connectors and arrows to show the flow of the processes and the sequence of actions and thoughts	

2.2 Verbal and Visual Channels in Note-Taking

An important part of a user research project is processing the collected data. Sketch notes provide a way for collaborators to use both visual and verbal information to recall and comprehend what a participant shared with them.

To understand why Sketch notes' incorporation of visual and verbal information is important, we can look to research on learning and memory. According to learning styles theory, people differ in their most effective method of instruction [7]. The popular VAK (Visual, Aural, Kinesethetic) model proposes that different people prefer to learn information through different sensory modalities. Thus, a visual learner may prefer to use pictures, images, graphs, and information requiring spatial thinking. An auditory learner may prefer to listen to a session recording. A verbal learner may absorb written information best. A kinesthetic learner prefers to learn through physical actions such as creating tangible items. People express different preferences in how information is shown to them and have different aptitudes for processing and thinking about types of information (visual, auditory, and spatial). Learning theories that focus on these preferences have had a great influence in education from kindergarten to graduate school [7].

According to dual coding theory [8], verbal representations and mental images are processed under distinct cognitive systems. The verbal system focuses on words and speech while the non-verbal system focuses on mental images. An informational unit may be stored in both the verbal and image channels, and recall is greater when the information is stored within the two memory locations. In this theory, the two systems function independent of each other, but may interact depending on how information is activated. Information can be activated directly (representational processing), visual information can stimulate recall of verbal information and vice versa (referential processing), and information can be activated within the same system [9]. As Table 2 shows, different note-methods represent information in different channels - visual, verbal, and auditory.

Table 2. Method vs Information type.

Methods	Channels		
	Visual	Verbal	Auditory
Sketch notes	Yes	Yes	No
Sticky note-taking (individual)	No	Yes	No
Verbatim note-taking table	No	Yes	No
Scorecard	No	Yes	No
Collages	Yes	No	No
Journey maps	Yes	Yes	No
Empathy map	No	Yes	No
Audio/video recording	Yes	No	Yes

3 Methodology

In the past two years, to learn from our customers and prospects' experiences, we interviewed approximately 160 participants in twelve exploratory studies. Each study we conducted had unique goals and objectives and, as a result, distinctive recruiting criteria and participant demographics. For example, in one study we wanted to learn about the motorcycle insurance shopping experiences, so we recruited participants who had recently purchased motorcycle insurance.

Cross-functional teams (marketing researchers, data analysts, product owners, developers, UX professionals) collaborated on these studies. The user research team planned, ran, and executed the research portion of the projects. However, UX designers, developers, and product owners (members of Agile squads) fully engaged in observation of the participant interview sessions, taking notes and finding themes and patterns across qualitative data to build empathy with participants and understand the needs of users.

For each of these studies, the UX research team planned an appropriate note-taking approach to deliver actionable and accurate insights to agile squads for their use in the development cycle. We created note-artifacts for each interview session that not only helped us uncover the experiences of users but also served as valuable reference materials from those sessions.

These artifacts were used in a multi-step collaborative analysis workshop later in the process. The artifacts helped attendees of these workshops (cross-functional team members) perceive and comprehend the information that participants shared with them.

As mentioned earlier in the paper, one of the artifacts we created was Sketch notes. Sketch notes provide a unique, easily comprehensible, visual presentation of content, which facilitates insights for product teams to use in the development of new customer-centric prototypes and applications.

We started using Sketch notes two years ago. During one of the interview sessions about purchasing motorcycle insurance, one of the researchers on the team (also one of the authors of this paper) created a Sketch note. When the observers that had watched the session put their top three findings on the wall, the researcher added her Sketch note drawing next to the sticky notes. Her drawing was simple and included important points about the participant's experience. Observers of the interview session collectively stated that the sketch helped them to recall the session. She was then asked to create Sketch notes for the rest of the sessions of that study. The Sketch notes of that study were so well perceived and shared that stakeholders of other research studies requested them as well (See Fig. 8). Some of the positive feedback about Sketch notes included:

- The visual map helps observers of research studies to recall the details within interview sessions.
- Data is in one place, and as a result, it is easy to review an entire interview session at a glance.
- They show the sequence of events that were shared in a session.
- They are fun to look at compared to text-only notes.
- Sketch notes convey the big picture and don't involve too many unnecessary details.

To enable the creation of Sketch notes for other research projects, we trained Agile team members on how to create Sketch notes. The researcher who originally crafted the Sketch notes led a training session. During that meeting she reviewed Sketch notes from previous studies and gave recommendations and tips: what types of drawing tools and papers to use, what type of information to capture, and what level of details to include.

During the study, we rotated note takers to prevent note-taking fatigue, as creating Sketch notes requires a high level of concentration. For a thirteen-session interview research study, we asked for at least three volunteers to create Sketch notes. Mostly designers, researchers, and content strategists signed up to create Sketch notes. Our team recognized that not all people were confident in their sketch abilities when being

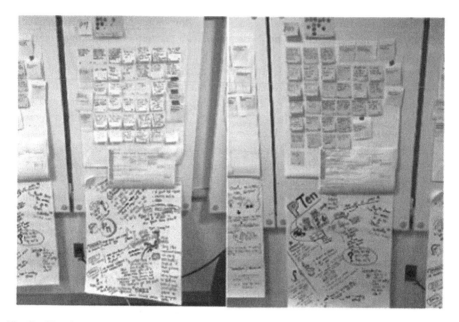

Fig. 8. Sketch notes are exhibited in addition to other note-taking methods for research analysis.

introduced to the subject. However, an advantage of implementing Sketch notes is that it doesn't require high-expertise drawing skills. During the sketch note training process, we emphasized that anyone who can draw circles, squares, triangles, and lines can create Sketch notes.

These Sketch notes were then used in analysis and design thinking activities such as the creation of personas, problem statements, hypotheses, and concepts. For example, when creating personas, development team members would refer to quotes, bolded handwriting, bullet points, and other visualized elements on Sketch notes to recall an important characteristic of a participant and the pain point that the participant had shared during the session. They would then use this information to create distinct personas. Sketch notes were stored as raw data within the main research project folders and were shared with the members of development teams for their reference.

Overall, compared to sticky notes and other text-formatted notes, Sketch notes have been consistently identified by cross-functional development team members as one of the most referred to and valuable artifacts during the collaboration analysis process (see Fig. 9).

As with every note-taking methodology, Sketch notes have unique advantages and disadvantages. In terms of advantages, note-takers must comprehend and summarize top level ideas rather than details. Information is also concise (more concise than typed notes, which can be several paragraphs long). When viewing Sketch notes, collaborators often recall specific memories, information, and participants. Note-takers tend to be more focused and less distracted when using pen and paper than when on their laptops or devices. Creating a Sketch note also requires full attention and focus from the note-taker and as a result, note-takers tend to remember most of the details within a research session. Furthermore, Sketch notes are powerful in multi-disciplinary environments, and their playful nature remind observers of unexpected, off-script moments, which help in team bonding.

As for disadvantages, digitizing Sketch notes requires an extra step of taking a photo or scanning the document. It also requires managing supplies (paper, markers, and pens) and enough desk space for note-takers. Another challenge with Sketch notes is that participants start with low confidence of their drawing ability and not everyone feels courageous enough to try creating a visual map. Lack of ability to search or sort information (as is available in Microsoft Excel or typed notes) is another issue with Sketch notes.

Fig. 9. Observers of research studies review all the notes and analyze the research findings.

4   The Impact of Sketch Notes

To assess the impact and importance of Sketch notes within our current research toolkit, we conducted a multi-factor analysis of all our current research artifacts.

First, we sent out a survey to user researchers to understand and identify the most important factors regarding note-taking methodologies in user research studies. Five user researchers at Liberty Mutual and four outside Liberty Mutual responded to that survey. The result of the survey showed that exhaustiveness, findability, comprehension, sharing, frequency of use, expertise, prep time, quantification of info, and flexibility are the factors researchers and designers keep in mind when it comes to note-taking (see Table 3).

Next, we sent out a survey to UX community members (including researchers and stakeholders who have attended research sessions) to rank the severity of these factors. Twenty-one participants responded to the second survey. The survey asked participants two ranking questions:

1. Choose the top 3 note-taking factors.
2. Group and rank factors: place factors into one of three importance level groups and within each group, place factors in order of importance.

Table 3. Important factors about note-taking methodologies.

Factors	Descriptions
Exhaustiveness	Level of completion as an accurate record (including details like quotes and actions)
Findability	Ability to find a specific fact or piece of information in the notes
Comprehension	Ability to easily understand the notes
Sharing	Ability to share notes with other people
Frequency of use	How often the notes are used/referenced after the study
Expertise	Level of training required to start taking the notes
Prep time	Amount of time required to set up the notes
Quantitative	Ability to quantify the notes (with numbers)
Flexibility	Ability to share the notes under changing conditions

The result from the second survey showed that exhaustiveness, findability and comprehension were the most important note-taking factors, in that order. The second most important factors were sharing, frequency of use and expertise.

After identifying the most important factors regarding note-taking methodologies, in a separate study we asked all seven user researchers on our team in Boston to rate 8 common note-taking methods that we used for interview sessions based on the top 6 factors. We used a 5-point Likert scale for that study. This way we were able to understand the impact of different note-taking methodologies on our research processes. See Table 4 for final scores of all methodologies. The highest scoring methods regarding each factor is highlighted in green.

Regarding the primary factors, the most exhaustive methods were the audio/video recording and the verbatim note-taking table. The ability to find information was highest for the verbatim note-taking table and the scorecard. Comprehension was highest for the sketch notes and journey maps.

Table 4. Methods vs Factors summary table

Factors / Methods	Exhaust-iveness	Findability	Compre-hension	Sharing	Frequency of Use	Expertise	Sum Total
Sketch Notes	2.86	3	4	3.14	2.86	2.71	18.57
Individual Sticky Notes	2.57	2.14	3.14	2.43	2.57	3.43	16.28
Verbatim Note-taking Table	3.86	3.71	3.14	3.86	2.29	3.29	20.15
Scorecard	3.14	3.86	3.43	4	3.14	3.71	21.28
Journey Maps	2.86	3.43	4	3.71	3.43	2.57	20
Empathy Map	2.43	2.14	2.71	2.71	2	2.71	14.7
Audio/video recording	4.29	2	3.29	3.57	2	3.29	18.44
In session survey questions	2.43	3.29	2.71	3.71	2.57	3	17.71
Mean Score	3.055	2.94625	3.3025	3.39125	2.6075	3.08875	18.39125

Regarding the secondary factors, scorecards were rated the easiest to share and the easiest method to train to use. The most frequently referred to method was journey maps.

The biggest strength of Sketch notes is comprehension, which is one of the top 3 important factors in note-taking for user researchers and observers. Journey maps were also highly rated for comprehension, as they are another verbal and visual information method. Sketch notes however, are not as exhaustive as other methods like recordings or verbatim note-tables. The findability of information is also lower than methods such as scorecards, journey maps, and note-tables, and surveys, all of which involve digital, textual documentation that can be filtered or searched.

Sketch notes rank the third lowest in terms of sharing, above sticky notes and empathy maps. Sketch notes may be less frequently shared because the information is not digital, as with other methods, and they need the additional step of being photographed or scanned in order to share. Sketch notes had an above average score for frequency of use, as they are an engaging and frequently used tool. The scorecard and journey maps scored higher than Sketch notes for frequency of use, as these tools have a standard Excel template that is consistently used and can be easily compared across different studies. Sketch notes scored below average for expertise, as people may start off with low-confidence in their sketch skills. Other note-methods like sticky notes and pre-formatted scorecards may allow people to take notes with relatively little training.

5 Conclusion

After using different note-taking methodologies for several exploratory research projects (mostly interviewing participants) at Liberty Mutual, we agree that each methodology has strengths and weaknesses. Depending on the nature of the data collected, purpose of the research study, and the research findings, one note-taking methodology might individually serve better than others. However, a mixed-methods approach works best to capture various types of information and ensure collaborators with different learning styles (visual, verbal, and auditory) can recall and comprehend information effectively.

As the multi-factor analysis of note-methods shows, Sketch notes is not a standalone tool, but it is a valuable complement to other note-methods in a user researcher's note-taking toolkit. The value of Sketch notes also extends beyond user researchers. It facilitates cross collaboration and is highly impactful to engage stakeholders. Implementation of Sketch notes as a research note-taking method has been so successful at Liberty Mutual that they have been continuously requested by stakeholders for several user studies. We recommend Sketch notes as a component of mixed-method note-taking for any user researcher.

References

1. Farrell, S.: Group notetaking for user research. https://www.nngroup.com/articles/group-notetaking/. Accessed 21 Jan 2018
2. Farrell, S.: How to collaborate with stakeholders in UX research. https://www.nngroup.com/articles/collaborating-stakeholders/?lm=group-notetaking&pt=article. Accessed 21 Jan 2018
3. Gibbons, S.: Empathy mapping: the first step in design thinking (2018). https://www.nngroup.com/articles/empathy-mapping/
4. Gray, D.: Empathy map. https://gamestorming.com/empathy-mapping/. Accessed 21 Jan 2018
5. Rohde, M.: The Sketchnote Handbook: The Illustrated Guide to Visual Note Taking. Peachpit Press, San Francisco (2013)
6. Sketch notes for Thinking Things Through. http://rohdesign.com/weblog/category/sketchnotes. Accessed 21 Jan 2018
7. Pashler, H., McDaniel, M., Rohrer, D., Bjork, R.: Learning styles: concepts and evidence. Psychol. Sci. Public Interest **9**(3), 105–119 (2008)
8. Paivio, A., Csapo, K.: Picture superiority in free recall: imagery or dual coding? Cognit. Psychol. **5**(2), 176–206 (1973)
9. Paivio, A.: Mental Representations: A Dual Coding Approach. Oxford University Press, Oxford (1990)

A User-Centered Framework for the Design of Usable ATM Interfaces

Joel Aguirre[1(✉)], Arturo Moquillaza[1,2], and Freddy Paz[1]

[1] Pontificia Universidad Católica del Perú, Lima 32, Lima, Peru
{aguirre.joel,amoquillaza,fpaz}@pucp.pe
[2] Universidad San Ignacio de Loyola, Lima 12, Lima, Peru
miguel.moquillaza@usil.pe

Abstract. Nowadays, the design of usable interfaces is a challenge for every software developer. Little or no consideration of the user-centered design guidelines make systems difficult to use, and the embedded systems in the Automated Teller Machines (ATM) are not an exception to this problem. In order to improve and ensure the usability of the user interfaces of software in this domain, several user-centered design methods and techniques were analyzed and applied to formulate a framework for guiding a design process. The paper provides an analysis of a variety of methods used in the self-service technologies domain and by formal design methodologies; for instance, the standard ISO 13047. In addition, the article describes the process followed to select the most appropriate user-centered design methods that fit the specific ATM domain. This analysis includes surveys and expert judgment, conducted with ATM and usability experts, which show a correct selection of the methods.

Keywords: User interface · Automated Teller Machine · User-centered design · Usability assessment · Framework

1 Introduction

The first bank to place an Automated Teller Machine (ATM) was the Barclays in 1967 in London and nowadays there is practically no bank that operates without one [1]. The demand for cash of every financial client is the most important factor that influences in the nature of an ATM [2]. According to Hellmann [3], despite the fact that the preference for digital accounts is growing, those financial clients continue employing the ATMs as a source of cash, a feature that its digital competitors, web and mobile banking, cannot offer.

According to the studies conducted by Abd et al. [4], the clients appreciate an ATM that really fits their needs as much as they appreciate their time. In addition, according to Camilli et al. [5], for the final user, the interface is the product; usability problems or frustrating experiences could have a negative impact on the institutional brand. In that sense, Gumussoy [6] consider critical the design of usable banking software with the objective of overcome the complex financial system.

In the systematic review conducted by Aguirre et al. [7], is proved the lack of information about how to apply the usability knowledge in the ATM interface design;

© Springer Nature Switzerland AG 2019
A. Marcus and W. Wang (Eds.): HCII 2019, LNCS 11583, pp. 163–178, 2019.
https://doi.org/10.1007/978-3-030-23570-3_13

this problem was noticed first by Moquillaza and Paz [8], who proposed a set of steps, based on user-centered design methods, for the design of ATM user interfaces.

In the same systematic review, Aguirre et al. [7] found that security systems, banking software, and the self-service technologies are domains closely related to the ATM domain.

Only one framework was reported by the systematic review of Aguirre et al. [7]; however, several methods and techniques for designing ATM and interactive interfaces were also found in the literature. In this study, we use the ISO 13047, the standard for designing usable interactive interfaces, as a start point and will expand the mentioned systematic review in order to find the most accurate methods that support ATM interfaces design.

The paper has the following organization: Sect. 2, where the analysis of user-centered design methods conducted by Aguirre et al. is extended to the domain of self-service technologies, Sect. 3???, where we analyze the expert judgment gathered from surveys and interviews, and Sect. 4, where the proposed framework is presented and modeled as a process.

2   User-Centered Design Methods and Techniques

In the present section, a systematic review was conducted following the guidelines established by Kitchenham and Charters [9] in order to extend the review conducted by Aguirre et al. [7] and expand its scope to self-service technologies domain. The articles reported were filtered by quality criteria and grouped by the methods or techniques that they presented, according to the phases of the ISO 13047.

2.1   Quality Criteria

According to the studies of Realpe-Muñoz et al. [10], the related articles to the domain of usable, interactive and secure interfaces are easily classified by six quality criteria. Acknowledging the criteria proposed, we slightly modified them and add a new quality criterion that includes if an article takes into consideration the design of self-service technologies. This made the criteria more robust for the domain we are interested in (see Table 1).

These criteria allow us to filter the articles reported in the literature. The articles with more quality will be compared to the phases of the standard ISO 13047 and serve as a source to obtain methods and techniques for ATM user interface design.

Table 1. Quality criteria

Criterion	Description
Criterion 1	The proposed process makes use of usability guidelines
Criterion 2	There is at least one method that allows users to verify the interfaces meet the initial user requirements
Criterion 3	The proposal has been formally validated
Criterion 4	The author conducts a quantitative analysis
Criterion 5	The author conducts a qualitative analysis
Criterion 6	The article consider user-centered design in its scope
Criterion 7	The main objective of the article is design usable, interactive or user interfaces of banking software of self-service technologies

2.2 Systematic Review

The articles selection was conducted in order to analyze the domains of self-service technologies, interactive user interfaces and secure user interfaces. This was made with the objective of reporting all the frameworks, methods and techniques employed in the mentioned domains that ensure usability or, at least, take it into consideration.

The research questions were based on the PICOC criteria proposed by Petticrew and Roberts [11], which specify Population, Intervention, Comparison, Outcome, and Context. In this case, the objective is not a comparison between frameworks, methods or techniques; hence, we discarded it (see Table 2).

With these criteria, research questions were formulated and are the ones that follows:

Q1. Which usable design processes, methodologies or frameworks are used to design self-service technologies user interfaces?
Q2. What user-centered design methods or techniques are reported in the literature for the design of self-service technologies user interfaces?
Q3. Which usability methodologies or methods are employed in the design of interactive and secure user interfaces?

After defining inclusion and exclusion criteria, the review was started. The consulted databases were the well-known ACM Digital Library, SpringerLink and ScienceDirect.

Table 2. PICOC table

Criterion	Description
Population	Interfaces gráficas de usuario usables para tecnologías de autoservicio
Intervention	Diseño centrado en el usuario para interfaces de usuario usables
Outcome	Técnicas y/o métodos empleados/aplicados en el diseño de interfaces de usuario
Context	Académico e industrial

2.3   Results of the Review

After conducting the review, the most relevant articles that answer the research questions were in total 9 (see Table 3).

Table 3. Relevant articles

Source	Result	Duplicate	Relevant
ACM	270	0	6
ScienceDirect	163	0	1
SpringerLink	200	2	2
Total	633	2	9

The nine selected articles were classified using the quality criteria defined in Sect. 2.1. The articles and the criteria they fit can be seen in Table 4. This classification served as a filter, recognizing the article of Kaptelinin et al. [12] as one with low quality for the purpose of this study.

In the study of Muhammad et al. [13], a commuter line train is redesigned employing methods from the user-centered design methodology. In Moquillaza and Paz [8], the authors proposed an 8 steps process to design ATMs interfaces using an user-centered approach. Siebendhandl et al. [14] redesigned a self-service ticket vending machine using methods from the fourth and fifth phase of the ISO 13047. Camilli et al. [5] made use of user-centered techniques to evaluate and redesign ATMs. Moquillaza et al. [15], proposed UCD methods for the design of an ATM in Perú. RealpeMuñoz et al. [10], proposed a design process based on MPIu+a and expand it to take into consideration the security for authentication systems. In the study of Zhang et al. [16], the authors proposed a six steps process to design interactive and usable public information systems interfaces. Finally, Wong et al. [17], proposed a methodology for the design of graphic interfaces and intangible products used for 8 years, where they used UX methods and a user-centered design approach.

Table 4. Articles classified by quality criteria

Author	C1	C2	C3	C4	C5	C6	C7
Muhammad et al. [13]	x	x	x	x	x	x	x
Moquillaza and Paz [8]	x	x			x		
Siebendhandl et al. [14]	x	x	x	x	x	x	x
Camilli et al. [5]	x	x	x	x	x	x	
Moquillaza et al. [15]	x	x			x	x	
Realpe-Muñoz et al. [10]	x	x			x		
Zhang et al. [16]	x	x	x	x	x	x	x
Wong et al. [17]	x	x			x	x	
Kaptelinin et al. [12]		x					

2.4   Methods and Techniques

The ISO 13047:1999 [18] proposed human-centered design methodology for interactive systems. The term 'human' is used because the design must be centered in all humans (notice that 'human' is more generic than 'user') that interact with the system.

The standard proposed a five phases process and is illustrated as a life cycle in the Fig. 1.

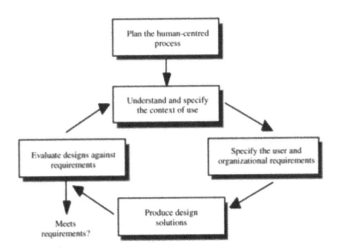

Fig. 1. HCD methodology [18].

The proposed phases by the standard are as follow: Planning, Context of use specification, Requirements specification, Design solutions, Evaluate designs. It is an iterative process aiming for the continuous improvement and correction of errors of the designs.

A correspondence analysis between the methods proposed in the ISO 13047 and the methods employed by every author in the studies reported in the previous section showed that the planning phase is not taken into consideration. The studies reported are focused on the requirements specification, the design of solutions and the evaluation. The objective of this comparison is to use this knowledge to propose a user-centered design process for the design of usable ATM interfaces that uses the methods and techniques proposed in the literature, taking as a baseline the phases propose in the standard ISO 13047. In Table 5 is shown the correspondence between the standard phases and the methods used in the literature.

The articles employed methods and techniques for usable design. For a more extended analysis of these methods, they were also classified under their correspondence to the ISO 13047 phases. For this, the analysis that Maguire [19] made about the ISO 13047 and the methods that support it, serves as a guide to better correspondence analysis.

Some methods and techniques proposed by the articles reported, take into consideration aspects related to hardware design; for instance, Anthropomorphic Needs

Table 5. Correspondence between the standard ISO 13047 phases and the methods used in the literature.

Author	ISO 13047 phases				
	Planning	Context	Requirements	Design	Evaluation
Muhammad et al. [14]		•	•	•	•
Moquillaza and Paz [15]			•	•	•
Siebendhandl et al. [16]	•	•		•	•
Camilli et al. [17]				•	•
Moquillaza et al. [18]	•	•		•	•
Realpe-Muñoz et al. [19]		•		•	•
Zhang et al. [20]				•	•
Wong et al. [21]	•	•		•	•

[13], Posture Evaluation [13] and Hardware Requirements [14]. Because hardware design is out of the scope of this study, these methods were automatically excluded from further analysis.

After finalized the analysis, some methods were excluded and the most accurate for the design of ATM interfaces were left for expert validation. The methods were classified under their correspondence to the phases of the ISO 13047 and are listed in Table 6.

The Planning phase is initially not considered because it is not considered in the literature either. In the next sections, the phases and methods proposed will be validated by expert judgment with aid of Usability and ATM Domain experts.

Table 6. UCD methods proposed for the design of ATM interfaces

Planning	Context	Requirements	Design	Evaluation
	Identify Stakeholders	Competitor Analysis	Brainstorming	Expert Evaluation
	User and Field Observation	Focus Group	Storyboarding	User Tests
	Interviews	Requirements Interview	Parallel Design	Heuristic Evaluation
	User Preliminary Questionnaire	User Profiles	Video Prototyping	Satisfaction Questionnaire
		Escenarios of use		

3 Expert Judgment Analysis

In the present section, the objective is to validate the utility of the methods proposed in the previous section. For this, expert judgment is employed and is supported by surveys addressed to Usability experts and ATM experts. In this way, only the methods that fit the needs of the experts were left for the final proposal.

3.1 Elaboration of the Survey

In every project, the developers that decide using and user-centered design approach in a real project would encounter fundamental questions such as, **what methods do I apply? when? how?**. Even if the methods are selected, how to conduct them, how to manage them and how long would they take in practice are still real questions because there are multiple and heterogeneous definitions [20].

In the study of Maguire [19], he analyzed the ISO 13047 and identified characteristics that make the comparison of the methods easier:

- How and when should the method be applied? - Simplicity
- How long should the method take? - Time
- What benefits that it brings to my project? - Cost vs. Benefit.

A survey was elaborated with closed questions about the participant profile, their experience with ATM usage and UCD design, and a Likert scale questionnaire to allow the participants to qualify the methods proposed in Sect. 2.4.

The survey was addressed to ATM domain experts from a well-known bank in Perú and different Usability experts with a Ph.D. degree from Colombia, México, Chile, and Perú.

3.2 Analysis of the Result

The first phase of the survey shows that the ATM domain experts had, in a majority, master degrees. The Usability domain experts had Ph.D. degrees and are in majority men. The answers about the experience with ATM usage and design showed that the most frequent operation made by the two groups of experts is Cash Withdrawal. The Usability experts use an ATM between 4 and 7 times a month, while the ATM domain experts made use of this self-service 10 or more times a month. In contrast, the Usability experts had more experience with UCD methodologies, 66.7% of the participants know the methodology and applied it before, while the ATM domain experts just the 22% of participants claimed to know the methodology.

The previous information serves as a participant profiler. The second phase is still about the UCD knowledge of the participants; however, is more specific to the methods proposed in Sect. 2.4. From this, is seen that the Usability experts have more experience with evaluation methods due to their academic degree. In the other phases, the ATM Domain experts stated that they know or have applied before most of the techniques.

In that sense, the score given by the ATM experts has double weight than the Usability experts in the first 3 phases proposed (context, requirements, and design) while the opposed happens in the last phase, where the Usability experts have more experience.

The participants were asked to give scores to the methods for answering the questions listed in Sect. 3.1, this way only the more simple methods, that not consume a lot of time and resources will be taken in consideration. Also, the participants were allowed to add other methods they know that are not in the list proposed.

In addition to the questionnaire, an interview with the ATM experts was held in order to contextualize their answers. Some identified considerations to have in mind were:

- The minimum method to consider in the design process must be a decision of the designer/stakeholders.
- The decision of taking into practice simple, fast or low-cost methods depends on the context of the projects, not on the framework.
- Substantial changes are usually analyzed deeply and in a considerable time. Not always is necessary fast methods.

In this sense, four set of methods are proposed after filtering the ones with low scores in the questionnaire and adding the proposed by the participants in the correspondent ISO phase.

Table 7. Methods recommended by the experts

Phase	Methods Recommended
Evaluación	Thinking Aloud
Persona	Persona

In Tables 8, 9, and 10, are listed the simple methods, the fast methods, and low-cost methods. In Table 11, the methods that fit the three characteristics are grouped in an optimal process.

Table 8. Simple methods for the design of usable ATM Interfaces

Phase	Methods
Context	Identify Stakeholder
	Field Study/Observation
	Preliminary Questionnaire/Survey of existing users
Requirements	Competitor Analysis
	User Requirements Interview
	Scenario of Use
	Persona
Design	Parallel Design
	Brainstorming
Evaluation	Heuristic Evaluation
	Satisfaction Questionnaire

Table 9. Fast methods for the design of usable ATM Interfaces

Phase	Methods
Context	Identify Stakeholder
	Field Study/Observation
Requirements	Competitor Analysis
	Scenario of Use
	Persona
Design	Parallel Design
Evaluation	Controlled User Testing
	Satisfaction Questionnaire

Table 10. Low-cost methods for the design of usable ATM Interfaces

Phase	Methods
Context	Identify Stakeholder
Requirements	User Requirements Interview
	Scenario of Use
	Persona
Design	Parallel Design
	Brainstorming
Evaluation	Controlled User Testing
	Satisfaction Questionnaire

Table 11. Optimal methods for the design of usable ATM Interfaces

Phase	Methods
Context	Identify Stakeholder
Requirements	Scenario of Use
	Persona
Design	Parallel Design
	Brainstorming
Evaluation	Thinking Aloud
	Satisfaction Questionnaire

4 The Proposal: Framework for the Design of Usable ATM User Interfaces

Defining a framework involves defining its methods, process, activities, and flow since this adapt the framework to the specific characteristics and context of the ATM interface design and defines the real work to be done [21].

The framework encompasses the process for the design of usable ATM interfaces, which, depending on the context, will apply simple methods, fast methods, low-cost methods, or optimal methods.

The phases proposed by the standard ISO 13047 were used in the framework. The phase of context and requirements correspond directly with the second and third phase of the mentioned standard. The last two phases were group together in the third phase of the framework: design and evaluation of interfaces. The proposal is diagrammed in the Figs. 2 and 3.

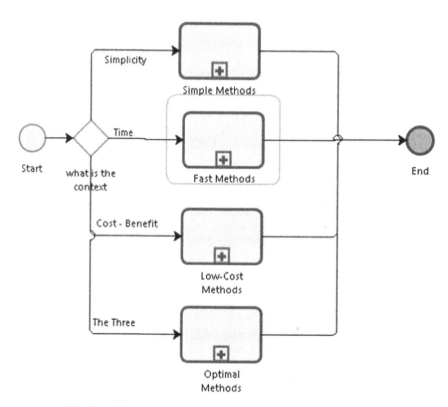

Fig. 2. UCD Framework for the design of usable ATM interfaces

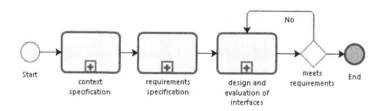

Fig. 3. Detail of the design process for ATM interfaces

The previous diagrams represent the generic view of the framework, which encompasses the 4 proposed processes, the simple, fast, low-cost, and optimal. Each process has the same sub-processes, which correspond to the three proposed phases, context specification, requirements specification and design and evaluation of interfaces.

This process is iterative, the designs could be continually improved through evaluation and redesign. To establish a workflow, the Figs. 4, 5, 6, and 7 detail the workflow that must be followed by the designers and stakeholders.

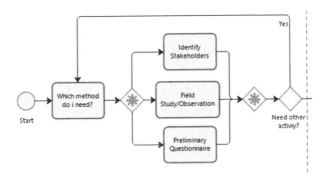

Fig. 4. Context specification details

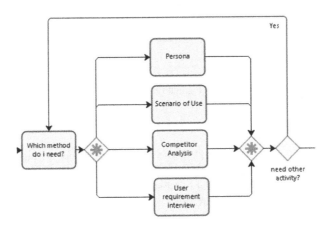

Fig. 5. Requirements specification

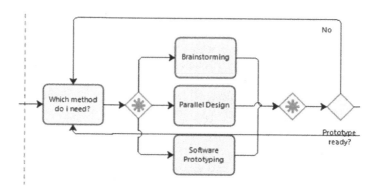

Fig. 6. Design and evaluation of interfaces detail (1)

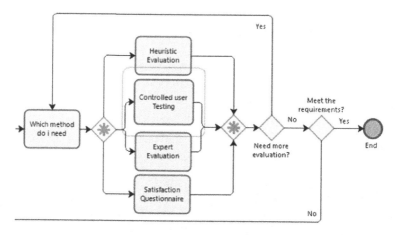

Fig. 7. Design and evaluation of interfaces detail (2)

4.1 Description of the Methods

According to the study of Maguire [19], the methods that support the standard ISO 13047 have an approach to orient the designers on how to apply the method and also an estimated time that it should take. Table 12 simplify the description of every method taken into consideration in the new framework for the design of ATM interfaces.

Table 12. Methods that support the framework for the design of usable ATM interfaces.

Phase	Method	Approach	Support Technique	Time (Max)
Context	Identify Stakeholders	List all user and stakeholder of the system. If possible, a meeting with the project manager and representative users	User Groups	0.5 day
	Field study/Observation	Establish objectives and type of events. The observer must take notes of the performance of the user	User Groups	2 days
	Preliminary questionnaire	Prepare a questionnaire and explained the objective. Use open and closed question	Free	2 days
Requirements	Competitor Analysis	Compare through evaluations the systems that owns the competitors	Free	1 day
	User Requirements Interview	List the problems observed in the context. Each can open wide the view of the designers with their opinion	Libre	5 days
	Scenario of use	Define scenarios with images and explanations	-	3 days
	Persona	Specify typical user profiles, detailing their motivations and activities in a context	User Profile	2 days
Design	Parallel Design	Two or more groups design at the same time multiple ideas. After a meeting, a unique design is elaborated from all the ideas	Interactive Prototyping	5 days
	Brainstorming	In a meeting, each member of the group stimulates the creativity and tell an idea for a solution. There are no bad ideas	Free	2 days
	Software Prototyping	Computer simulations are made by one person only. The objective is to make the test more real	Paper Prototyping	5 days

(*continued*)

Table 12. (*continued*)

Phase	Method	Approach	Support Technique	Time (Max)
Evaluation	Heuristic Evaluation	One or more experts evaluate the design using a set of heuristics	-	2 days
	Expert Evaluation	Experts in the process and workflow try the new design and try to find design errors	Cognitive Walkthrough	3 days
	Satisfaction Questionnaires	An expert elaborates a questionnaire with representative questions. Between 8 and 10 is an ideal number to consider the sample representative	SUS questionnaire	2 days

5   Conclusions and Future Works

In this paper is described how the methods used to elaborate a framework for the design of ATM interfaces were obtained and analyzed. A systematic review was conducted to expand the study of Aguirre et al. [7]. After that, the method found in the literature were classified under the phases of the ISO 13047 to demonstrate that the whole process is not covered in any proposal. With the intention of completing the process, and expert judgment of the methods was analyzed and new methods were proposed by the experts.

Some important information that was gathered from the expert judgment method was that the context is variable and the framework must not limit the catalog of methods available to the designers. The framework does not limit the methods that the designer can apply in each phase; however, established a set of methods as a baseline in each phase.

After obtaining the methods that fit the needs of the experts, the framework was diagrammed as a process, in order to define the real workflow that should follow a real design team. The definition of the framework is complete with the detailed approach of each method that is encompassed in it.

With this framework, the designer would take more into consideration user-centered approaches to reduce the user interfaces usability problems that the ATMs present, improving the phase of design in early stages of a software development process; and improving the user satisfaction strengthening the institutional brand.

As future works, execution of the process by a real team in a real context is necessary to validate the correctness of the framework, it is that it can be executed from start to end without complications. This would demonstrate that the framework is correct and easy to understand. Furthermore, a quantitative validation is left for future studies. The usability scale of an interface designed with the proposed framework has to be higher than the usability scale of an interface designed without a procedural or UCD approach to consider the significant relevance of the framework and formally validate it.

Acknowledgments. This work was supported by the Human–Computer Interaction and Design of User Experience, Accessibility and Innovation Technologies (HCI-DUXAIT) group from PUCP in Lima, Perú. We would also like to acknowledge the support of the experts of the ATM domain who share their precious time to contribute with this study, and Ph.D. André Aguirre, Ph. D. Angela Villareal, Ph.D. Guillermina Sanchéz, Mg. Braulio Murillo and Ph.D. Jaime Diaz, Usability experts who also contributed to this project.

References

1. Mahmood, T., Shaikh, G.M.: Adaptive automated teller machines. Expert Syst. Appl. **40**(4), 1152–1169 (2013). https://doi.org/10.1016/j.eswa.2012.08.022
2. Cluckey, S.: 2017 ATM and Self-Service Software Trends. ATM Marketplace, 31 (2017)
3. Hellmann, R.: In a mobile banking era, the ATM is more important than ever | ATM Marketplace (2018). https://www.atmmarketplace.com/blogs/in-a-mobile-banking-era-the-atm-is-more-important-than-ever/. Retrieved 11 June 2018
4. Abd, R., Aziz, E., Hussien, M.I.: ATM, internet banking and mobile banking services in a digital environment: the Egyptian Banking Industry. Int. J. Comput. Appl. **90**(8), 975–8887 (2014). https://pdfs.semanticscholar.org/7d7a/10baf75f63c8c126cf82a381e3d2fd9825c1.pdf
5. Camilli, M., Dibitonto, M., Vona, A.: User-centered design approach for interactive kiosks: evaluation and redesign of an automatic teller machine. In: Proceedings of the 9th ACM SIGCHI Italian Chapter International Conference on Computer-Human Interaction: Facing Complexity, pp. 85–91 (2011). https://doi.org/10.1145/2037296.2037319
6. Altin Gumussoy, C.: Usability guideline for banking software design. Comput. Hum. Behav. **62**, 277–285 (2016). https://doi.org/10.1016/j.chb.2016.04.001
7. Aguirre, J., Moquillaza, A., Paz, F.: Methodologies for the design of ATM interfaces: a systematic review. ISHED **2018**, 6 (2018)
8. Moquillaza, A., Paz, F.: Applying a user-centered design methodology to develop usable interfaces for an Automated Teller Machine. In: Proceedings of the XVIII International Conference on Human Computer Interaction – Interacción 2017, pp. 1–4 (2017). https://doi.org/10.1145/3123818.3123833
9. Kitchenham, B., Charters, S.: Guidelines for performing systematic literature reviews in software engineering version 2.3. Engineering **45**(4ve), 1051 (2007). https://doi.org/10.1145/1134285.1134500
10. Realpe-Muñoz, P., Collazos, C.A., Granollers, T., Muñoz-Arteaga, J., Fernandez, E.B.: Design process for usable security and authentication using a user-centered approach. In: Proceedings of the XVIII International Conference on Human Computer Interaction – Interacción 2017, pp. 1–8 (2017). https://doi.org/10.1145/3123818.3123838
11. Petticrew, M., Roberts, H.: Systematic reviews in the social sciences: a practical guide. Couns. Psychotherapy Res. **6**(4), 304–305 (2006). https://doi.org/10.1080/147331406009 86250
12. Kaptelinin, V., Rizzo, A., Robertson, P., Rosenbaum, S.: Crafting user experience of self-service technologies. In: Proceedings of the 2014 Companion Publication on Designing Interactive Systems - DIS Companion 2014, pp. 199–202 (2014). https://doi.org/10.1145/2598784.2598798

13. Muhammad, F., Suzianti, A., Ardi, R.: Redesign of commuter line train ticket vending machine with user-centered design approach. In: Proceedings of the 3rd International Conference on Communication and Information Processing - ICCIP 2017, pp. 134–139 (2017). https://doi.org/10.1145/3162957.3162993
14. Siebenhandl, K., Schreder, G., Smuc, M., Mayr, E., Nagl, M.: A user-centered design approach to self-service ticket vending machines. IEEE Trans. Prof. Commun. **56**(2), 138–159 (2013). https://doi.org/10.1109/TPC.2013.2257213
15. Moquillaza, A., et al.: Developing an ATM interface using user-centered design techniques BT. In: Marcus, A., Wang, W. (eds.) Design, User Experience, and Usability: Understanding Users and Contexts, pp. 690–701. Springer, Cham (2017)
16. Zhang, N., Chen, J., Liu, Z., Zhang, J.: Public information system interface design research, pp. 247–259 (2013)
17. Wong, M.L., Khong, C.W., Thwaites, H.: Applied UX and UCD design process in interface design. Proc. Soc. Behav. Sci. **51**(2000), 703–708 (2012). https://doi.org/10.1016/j.sbspro.2012.08.228
18. ISO: ISO 13407:1999 Human-centered design processes for interactive systems. Ergonomics of Human–System Interaction (1999). https://doi.org/10.1006/ijhc.2001.0503
19. Maguire, M.: Methods to support human-centred design. Int. J. Hum. Comput. Stud. **55**(4), 587–634 (2001). https://doi.org/10.1006/ijhc.2001.0503
20. Sánchez, J., Iranzo, R.M., Solé, M.O.: Beyond the wooden knife: Towards an integrated tool for a real design user-centered. In: XI Congreso Internacional de Interacción Persona-Ordenador (2010). (in Spanish)
21. Collins English Dictionary: Framework definition and meaning (2018). https://www.collinsdictionary.com/dictionary/english/framework. Accessed 2 Dec 2018

Design Thinking and Scrum in Software Requirements Elicitation: A Case Study

Rafael dos Santos Braz$^{(\boxtimes)}$, José Reinaldo Merlin,
Daniela Freitas Guilhermino Trindade, Carlos Eduardo Ribeiro,
Ederson Marcos Sgarbi, and Fabio de Sordi Junior

Centro de Ciências Tecnológicas (CCT), Universidade Estadual do Norte
do Paraná (UENP), Bandeirantes, Paraná, Brazil
rafaelsantosbrazpfi@gmail.com
{merlin,danielaf,biluka,sgarbi,fabiodsj}@uenp.edu.br
https://uenp.edu.br

Abstract. Design Thinking is an innovative human-centered methodology that has gained visibility and importance for its great efficacy and efficiency in generating and testing innovative ideas. The present work seeks the application of this method in software development, more specifically in Software Requirements Elicitation. To this aim, the Design Thinking method was adapted by the team through the concepts of the Scrum framework for application in a case study that was conducted within a Brazilian state university. This study has verified this method to design a system for allocating and reserving resources for this university. Through the results obtained, this model can be considered positive, since it was possible to model a solution with 95% of average completeness and 100% of stakeholders' satisfaction.

Keywords: Design Thinking · Scrum ·
Software Requirements Elicitation · Software Engineering · Prototypes

1 Introduction

In the business environment, it is necessary a different way to be ahead of the competitive and dynamic market. Generally, the organizations chose the innovation processes as its differential. In this context, the innovation aims solutions that meet the customers' needs. An innovative solution looks forward to maximizing the products or services quality and to reduce the development time [19]. However, reaching this goal is a complex task because it is necessary to apply multidisciplinary processes and a deep understanding of the client and its working field [1].

This analysis is not limited to the business area since it is possible to find the same problem and definition in other areas, either academical and organizational. One of these areas is software development, which encompasses considerable aspects of creating systems for commercial or non-commercial purposes.

© Springer Nature Switzerland AG 2019
A. Marcus and W. Wang (Eds.): HCII 2019, LNCS 11583, pp. 179–194, 2019.
https://doi.org/10.1007/978-3-030-23570-3_14

In sectors like that, Software Engineering has ruled and concerned about all steps of building systems, from the specification to the maintenance after the deployment [17].

Software Engineering leads to the use of approaches, models, processes, and methods to design and build technological solutions for a specific group of people. Both developing entity and customers long for some innovation. Exactly to attend it, innovative methodologies have been built and used in software processes [1, 17].

The Design Thinking (DT) nowadays practiced has begun in business to improve business innovative processes. DT is a multidisciplinary and human-centered methodology that centers on a target group's needs. It is possible because this approach is design-oriented. Consequently, DT looks forward to the people's experience and well-being [1, 19].

Just as innovation itself, the DT approach can be applied in multiple sectors because of its great effectiveness and adaptability and also its high potential [1]. However, only in the current decade, this methodology is being widely employed in software products developing in the worldwide scope [13]. While the same fact is not a completely valid affirmation in Brazil since initiatives in this area have been slowly promoted in universities and market [14].

As indicated by [1], Design Thinking has high adaptability, and Software Engineering can seize it especially on the Software Requirements Elicitation subarea, which is part of a software lifetime and it is like DT process. The elicitation stage is responsible for collecting, documenting, and checking the system requirements. Abstractly, these requirements describe what the software must do [17].

As mentioned above, a software lifetime corresponds to the steps from beginning to after employing. That whole period is covered by a software project that rules and policies the development of the proposed solution. There are some approaches to manage that type of project, and one of them is Agile Software Development – Agile Methods. These methods have grown significantly in importance and popularity since the ending of the twenty century and, in particular, since the beginning of the twenty-first century because of the Agile Manifest ("philosophical soul" of the Agile Movement) in 2001 [10]. Methods like that aim to deliver software solutions more quickly and also ensuring they meet the costumers' often volatile needs [12].

Within the Agile Context, it is worth mentioning the Scrum framework. Scrum is a mature generalized model within which it is possible to creatively and productively manage the conception of a product, besides maximizing its value by applying the guiding principles of Agile Methods [16].

This work provides an application of DT in software development through the application of a unified Design Thinking and Scrum approach in a case study that has aimed to verify this model's applicability to elicit, analyze and manage the stakeholders and users' needs within a Brazilian state university.

The remainder of this paper is organized as follows. Section 2 presents a bibliographic review and related works. Section 3 describes the Design Thinking method and the Scrum framework. Section 4 describes the research realized, the method adopted and also all its phases. Section 5 presents the whole Case Study conducted, detailing activities and artifacts. Section 6 presents the main results of the study. At last, Sect. 7 presents the conclusions.

2   Background and Related Works

Design as a creative method has been a valuable resource since it was settled as an important factor for organizational differentiation in the second half of the twenty century [18].

Brown indicated in his paper [3] a great first example of applying the Designer's thinking (the design method or Design Thinking): the brilliant inventor and entrepreneur Thomas Edison (1847–1931). Edison was able to create new markets and trends from his ability to imagine how people would long and use his products. That way he could devise products oriented to the customers' needs.

Some decades after Edison, the first generation of DT was started by Bruce Archer (Systematic method for designers [2]) and John Christopher Jones (Design Methods [11]) in 1965 and 1970, respectively. Such studies have been considered the first references to interactive design through multidisciplinary thinking, which is a Design Thinking key requirement [7].

Subsequently, the current DT was born. This approach aims business innovation by creatively soluting problems [18]. Therefore, it is based on the way that designers think during their products conception. This line of reasoning has driven the innovative process, as indicated by Brown [3, p. 85] *"Thinking like a designer can transform the way you develop products, services, processes – and even strategy."* This transformation is due to the fact designers consider a problem everything that impedes the people's experience and well-being. Hence, these professionals identify problems and generate effective solutions [19].

In their paper, Ferreira et al. [8] demonstrate DT in a different context from the business area. The authors indicate this method has been widely used (directly or indirectly) in the health area, frequently in the prevention or diseases treatment stages. In this case, Design Thinking concerns about the interaction between health professionals and their patients, besides checking their real needs and guiding the communication process.

In Grossman-Kahn and Rosensweig's study [10], the authors reported a multidisciplinary design-oriented approach that integrates different innovative methods. It is intentionally directed to Computer Science by employing three different methodologies. The first one is Agile Software Development because it can rapidly build and improve prototypes based on customers' needs during multiple iterations. Furthermore, it deploys the Lean Startup method that predicts importance equivalence between finding the problem and building the solution. The last one is DT for developing the client relationship and efficiently identifying their needs.

According to this train of thought, the authors Alves et al. [1] conducted a case study, in which they directly applied DT in a software project to urban mobility. In their work, they concluded DT is worth for software development. In another study [5], the writers reaffirm this conclusion through a case study for renewing two Brazilian Army's computerized systems.

Paula [14] and Cavalcanti [6] show academic visions on utilizing DT to educational processes in Brazilian's scope. Palacin-Silva et al. [13] write about a similar practice, which DT is placed in international educational context. In both cases, the authors display positive views of employing DT educationally. However, a review on Brazilian's bibliography suggests that DT has not been widely used yet, either academically or entrepreneurially. Initiatives in this area are considerably more recent than internationally. Cavalcanti [6] indicates Brazilian universities began to deeper study the DT applications only around 2013.

At last, the present paper aims to contribute to the above-described context by displaying the results of an applicability case study of Design Thinking and Agile Development Methods unified carried out in a Brazilian state university. The methodology employed during this study is described in the next section.

3   Design Thinking and Scrum

Design Thinking is an innovative methodology to build solutions based on designers' thinking and three main pillars: (1) Empathy, comprehension of other people's feelings and reactions by imagining yourself in similar situations; (2) Collaboration, work-groups realizing collective activities or searching for a common result; and (3) Experimentation, drawing conclusions through different conditions [8].

The basic process used during the case study conducted has been proposed by the consulting American firm IDEO[1]. That process has been broadly accepted as the contemporary DT approach. IDEO has been providing an already consolidated DT method and also presents a number of success stories [1,3].

Generally, the DT process has four non-linear and high adaptable phases. However, there are various ways to apply the designer's thinking since Design Thinking itself is a methodology that has a significant historical path of ideas evolution [3]. Because of it, DT can be applied to different projects, both in its nature and problem [19]. Figure 1 presents the layout of the DT model created by IDEO.

The immersion seeks to approximate the team and the context of the problem from the point of view of the client and users. For this purpose, a reframing and analysis of the problem are done. After that, there is the Analysis and Synthesis stage to examine the information collected. This moment is dedicated to recognizing who are the fundamental people to the problem. Ideation is the phase in which innovative ideas are generated. For this, some tools are employed to stimulate the agents' creativity and participation. Finally, in Prototyping, these ideas are validated trough prototypes that reduce the abstraction of the ideal solution. The way the prototype will be created depends on the project and the available tools [19].

---

[1] https://www.ideo.com/.

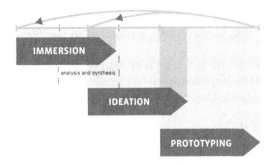

Fig. 1. Stages of IDEO's Design Thinking [19, p. 18].

Agile Methods follow different principles to traditional software development processes, as they have a greater focus on people, and can be satisfactorily adapted to requirements changes [12]. Among the various Agile Methodologies existing, Scrum is a framework that aims to creatively develop products with the highest possible value besides solving complex problems. This methodology has been widely accepted and used both inside and outside universities [16].

Scrum focuses on how the team should interact so that work can be accomplished effectively and efficiently. Through these characteristics of easy comprehension, focus on the agents involved, easy adaptation on requirements, and great management of the software project, the concepts of DT and Scrum were unified in the method adopted during the case study conducted [16].

4   The Method Adopted

According to [9], researches should be classified over its goals and technical procedures. This study can be classified as "Exploratory research" in its goals because it has conceptually detailed Design Thinking and its applications in software development. Besides, it is possible to classify this study as "Case Study" in its technical procedures since it is oriented to explore DT and Agile Methods in the academic context by describing and checking DT applicability to elicit requirements for a real problem in allocating, booking, and organizing university's materials and rooms resources.

Therefore, DT was adapted to the software development context through the Scrum framework. Subsequently, the method adopted was applied to a case study to check if it could satisfactorily specify requirements during the Requirement Elicitation phase.

There are eight different phases in the method adopted, each one of them aiming and manipulating its own artifacts. For the representation of this process[2], the Business Process Model and Notation (BPMN) was used because it

---

[2] Documentation on https://rafaelsantosbraz.github.io/ModeloDT.github.io/.

is a graphic representation that simplifies and standardizes processes modeling and description that is universally recognized in the literature on Software Engineering.[3]

Figure 2 presents the BPMN representation of the process applied, showing all the artifacts and the steps sequence to be followed during a software project. It is plausible to subdivide the steps of the general model into two larger groups: Preparation and Construction. The first one covers all phases from the initial contact to the end of the Prototyping. Construction takes care of the subsequent steps until the end of the project cycle. This separation is important because the Preparation group is responsible for outlining, understanding, analyzing, generating ideas and modeling the solution. The Construction group focuses on coding the specified solution. Because of that, the activities of the preparation group were fully applied in the case study of this research. The sections below describe these activities.

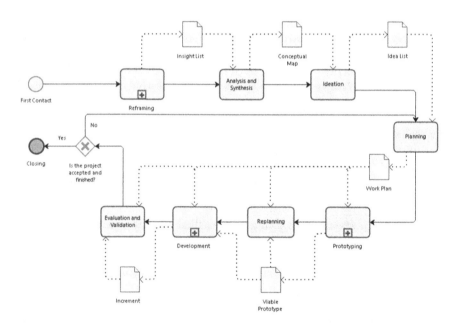

Fig. 2. Graph representation of the method adopted.

4.1   Reframing

The Reframing phase aims to place the work team into the client's work environment and approaches the end users' (client's clients) problem to identify their needs and the opportunities and boundaries of the context studied. This phase

---

[3] http://www.bpmn.org/.

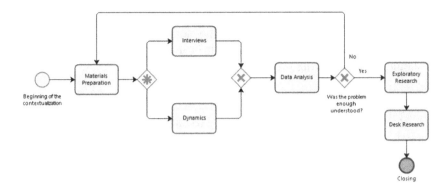

Fig. 3. Activities sequence of the Reframing phase.

is a mix of Preliminary and In-Depth immersions from the first stage of IDEO's DT that searches for different prospects to comprehend the problem identified, besides defining the project boundary.

For this to take place, a number of activities can be done, as shown in Fig. 3. In general, interviews and group or individual dynamics. Besides that, it is necessary to do in-depth research by observing the daily routine of the actors involved. External research for similar cases and their solutions are recommended.

4.2 Analysis and Synthesis

The second phase of the process aims to find patterns, relationships, connections, and challenges that involve the comprehension of the problem established during the Reframing stage. At this moment, it is suggested to synthesize the results obtained. Therefore, a graph representation is selected to ease the understanding of all agents involved. A common way to represent it, it is to create a Conceptual Map that gathers all information generated until the current phase [19].

4.3 Ideation

The Ideation phase is the moment when a large number of new ideas are creatively and innovative generated to solve the problem identified. For this purpose, meetings between the work team and the main actors involved, that can contribute to the ideas generation, is a fundamental activity. Usually, some practices like Brainstorming sessions (all participants are allowed to unrestrainedly contribute new ideas) or Co-Creation Workshops (group dynamics to generate, develop, and present innovative ideas) [1].

4.4 Planning

This is a short-lived phase that acts as a transition moment from all data collected and analyzed to the prototyping process. Then and there, the team has to define which ideas suggested will be taken forward and implemented. Then, it is necessary to create the initial Work Plan that only concern about the prototyping tasks. This document has a time grid for each team member and indicates what should be done during every day of the present stage.

4.5 Prototyping

During Prototyping, the design team has to develop prototypes (models or schemes that represent the ideas in real life) that ease visually and practically demonstrating the features of the expected final product. Thereby, the team can validate the ideas selected and the way they were implemented in the prototypes, checking if they completely meet the users' expectations and if they are applicable. In accordance with the principles of Design Thinking, it is worth highlighting the prototypes can be elaborated in several different and creative ways, therefore, the team has to choose which way is the best one for meeting its own goals. Figure 4 shows the internal activities of Prototyping which follow the creation-validation precept.

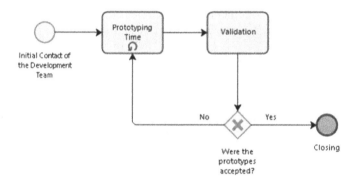

Fig. 4. Representation of the flow of prototyping activities.

4.6 Replanning

This stage is similar to Planning. At this moment, the team has to review and refresh the Work Plan since just.now the Viable Prototypes have been made to guide the construction of the real solution.

4.7 Development

The Development phase is a grouping of activities that have as their common purpose the construction of the specified solution. To that aim, the development is based on Viable Prototypes specifications and the Work Plan. At the end of this, an Increment Done will be obtained. This artifact must be a real, concrete and functional application. Figure 5 details the flow of development activities that follow the same precept of Prototyping (Construction-Validation).

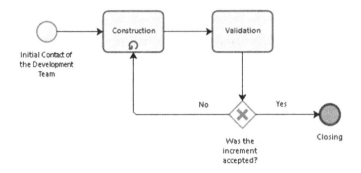

Fig. 5. Representation of the flow of development activities.

4.8   Evaluation and Validation

The current phase is the last one in the Software Project cycle adopted. At this moment, the Increment Done is given to the client and users. Besides this, it is worth pointing a meeting to evaluative review all the main events and actions that influenced the work team or the process. The reviewing could be, for example, a self-assessing and discussion moment to check what actions and behaviors were beneficial to the team and project as well as which ones had better be avoided in the future to optimize the work. The Scrum framework enhance the importance of the review sessions during the whole project [16].

After adapting the Design Thinking process to software development through the Scrum framework, the renewed model was employed in a real situation. The next sections describe the whole case study.

5   Case Study

The case study conducted has covered the Preparation activities group (Sect. 4), which has aimed to verify if the method adopted could be efficiently applied to Software Requirements Elicitation.

The case study was attended by volunteer agents directly or indirectly involved in the problem studied, among them, it is worth citing the participation of professors, students, directors, coordinators, secretaries, trainees, and maintenance, organization and cleaning staff. This multi-stakeholder base follows the Design Thinking precept of observing the problem from the point of view of different people. In this case, the participants were in different hierarchy levels of a Brazilian state university and they acted as clients or users.

At the university in question, the whole process of allocation, reservation, use, organization and control of its resources (material objects or locals as rooms, classes or computer laboratories) was done manually. It generated countless conflicts and a low level of users' satisfaction. Because of that, the team has intended to design a technological solution to help to reduce this problem.

The subsections below expose what activities performed and the artifacts generated during the case study, following the flow presented in Fig. 2.

5.1   Reframing

It was then initiated by the Reframing phase. For this purpose, both individual and collective interviews were applied. The interviews aimed to identify how the manual process of allocation, reservation, and control of the university's resources was realized and what were the main difficulties faced during this process. During the interviews, a simple process of quick conversations guided by a previously prepared questionnaire was followed.

The dynamics applied consisted of conducting activities to better understand the thoughts and the people's point of view about certain aspects as their desires, perceptions, and attitudes. The material used for this was based on the one provided by [15], but translated and adapted by the team. That material[4] is relevant because it creatively stimulates the participants to think about their needs, especially if applied collectively and quickly.

This material is named Hero Profile or Empathy Map and it was chosen because it respects one of the three main pillars of Design Thinking: the Empathy. The work of [4] reaffirms the importance of seeking empathy for clients and users because using this, the team will be able to analyze and understand emotionally and cognitively the needs of its target group. Figure 6 contains a model of the Empathy Map used in the dynamics.

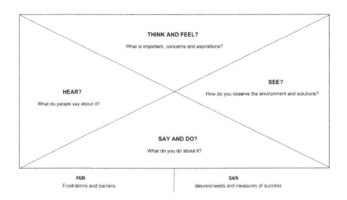

Fig. 6. The Empathy Map model (adapted from [15]).

Subsequently, the team analyzed the data collected during the previous activities. At this point, it was important to extract information that contemplates the needs, opportunities and barriers to the problem studied. This useful information is named insights and the List of Insights is the document that organizes and gathers all those important aspects observed (optimized from [19]).

After the first analysis of the data, the List of Insights drawn by the team had more than thirty items, which were grouped by several themes such as

---

[4] The original material is available on http://www.theservicestartup.com/.

functionalities, acceptance criteria, and norms. The list below contains some summarized examples of these items:

1. Allow dynamic resource allocation.
2. Solve resource allocation conflicts.
3. Efficiently improve the resource allocation process.
4. Seek to decrease the wasting of resources (resources reserved, but without effective use).
5. Allow resources allocation for maintenance and cleaning periods.
6. Pay attention to fixed periods/times for resource allocation.

Consecutively, an Exploratory Research was conducted to understand the client's work context through a Participant Observation, when the daily routine of the main agents of the process was observed. In the end, some more insights were added to the original list. Among them, these two ones are more important:

1. Increase the communication efficiency among the agents involved.
2. Allow all people that participate in the process to be able to use the generated solution.

After this, Desk Research was necessary to broaden the perspectives and better delineate the project boundaries by finding similar solutions in different sources on the Internet. This research is the last one performed in the Reframing phase. At this point, some more Insights were added to norms and opportunities topics.

5.2 Analysis and Synthesis

After Reframing, the work team had to analyze and synthesize the List of Insights drawn, aiming to find patterns and correlations between its items. The results of this stage are usually arranged in a Conceptual Map that is a graphical visualization (simplified, direct, organized and representative) of the information generated and collected during the previous phase. It is possible to build this map starting it from the central problem and branching the information by the main topics. Therefore, this type of representation is useful to discuss the problem with the stakeholders.

5.3 Ideation

That is a significant phase for the remainder of the study since it is the moment to generate innovative ideas to solve the particular problem. As suggested by the original DT, Brainstorming sessions have been realized with clients and users who could participate.

After the sessions, the Idea List was elaborated, which is a catalog of all the ideas generated since the beginning of the process that will be really implemented. That way, this artifact is responsible for guiding the construction of the solution and the Planning and Replanning stages. Generally, this list resembles a restaurant menu or a set of playing cards.

It is worth highlighting this artifact is compared to the Product Backlog because it contemplates the insights and ideas generated in a way closer to the description of software requirements, as mentioned above, but they still maintain their own characteristics.

Finally, the Idea List of the case study has been summarized in the following list:

1. Allow the reservation to be altered, performed or canceled in advance and without direct and personal communication.
2. Allow all users to access the solution through an access validation.
3. Allow viewing of resources in a time grid.
4. Ask users to agree to the term of commitment before the allocation.
5. Enable dynamic inclusion and maintenance of resources and users by users themselves.
6. Allow directly accessing the solution on computers and mobile devices that have a connection to the Internet.

5.4   Planning

For the Planning stage, the team has met with the stakeholders to decide which ideas from the Idea List would be covered in the first cycle of Prototyping. The fundamental items were selected and the Work Plan for the Prototyping cycle was written.

5.5   Prototyping

This step is subdivided into a loop of two main tasks to build a Viable Prototype that has been validated as a concrete application to sufficiently meet the stakeholders' needs and expectations. The first task is the Prototyping Time itself, which is a prototype design cycle. As indicated by the Scrum framework [16], this task always begins with a small meeting to review the Work Plan for the specific day.

During Prototyping, several activities were performed. First of all, paper prototypes were created to represent system wireframes and, subsequently, the digital versions of them were made, aiming to improve the functionalities visualization. The focus of this stage was the needs identified and how to improve the usability.

After the Prototyping Time, it was necessary the prototypes created were validated by the stakeholders, thus, applicable tests were applied to evaluate them by the agents involved in the process. If the prototype was not positively evaluated, it would not be considered feasible and the Prototyping step would be repeated.

In this study, the prototyping and validation sequence has been performed twice until the prototypes presented have been considered viable and reached the ideal satisfaction level. The subsequent section contains the analysis of the satisfaction and the results of the study.

6   Analysis of Results

As mentioned above, some interviews and dynamics were applied to understand the problem and to identify needs. During these activities, participants' satisfaction data were collected to compare the manual process to the solution proposed. In the Design Thinking of IDEO, satisfaction has a strongly qualitative perspective and the dynamics applied to the study through the Empathy Map are also qualitative [19]. For that reason, it is important to emphasize here the predominant qualitative items identified in the process of resource allocation that is summarized in the following list:

1. The existence of general problems and conflicts during the entire resource allocation process.
2. The manual process has been not considered effective as communication, agility, and ease.
3. Participants have indicated a negative view of the environment (the entire context of the allocation method).
4. There is no full organization and control in this manual process, and the participants long for improving it.
5. The method is considered too fixed and difficult to make changes on the time grid.

However, it is possible and preferable to unite these qualitative points with the quantitative ones from the interview questionnaires to outline a general scope of the participants' satisfaction. For this purpose, the Likert scale was employed, which normally has five possible answer options. This pattern was adopted due to the fact it is frequently found and recommended in the literature. In this case, the scale values were enumerated and defined in this way: 1–completely dissatisfied; 2–partially dissatisfied; 3–neutral (neither satisfied or dissatisfied); 4–partially satisfied; and 5–completely satisfied.

Following the Likert scale and statistically analyzing the data collected, the satisfaction level of the participants with the manual process is 2 (partially dissatisfied). This value demonstrates that the current process has not met their needs and expectations. The graph in Fig. 7 indicates the complete distribution of satisfaction that was between values 1 and 3.

After the prototypes validation sessions, more specifically when the prototypes were classified as viable, 100% of the participants indicated the value 5 for their satisfaction level with the prototypes presented. To better specify this satisfaction, the completeness of the prototypes was also analyzed. In this case, this value quantitatively represents how much the prototypes meet the users' needs and defined specifications. This completeness and the level of satisfaction were important for the team to evaluate the prototypes as viable.

The completeness calculation was performed through a mathematical relationship between the fulfilled items and the total number of items previously listed together with the new users' requests. Each value found was classified in one of these three categories of completeness: A (95% to 100%); B (70% to 94%); and C (less than 70%). The evaluation team established the prototypes

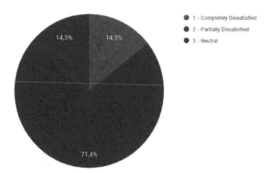

Fig. 7. Participants' satisfaction level with the manual allocation process.

completeness must be in A or B categories (completeness greater than or equal to 70%) to be considered viable, and also at least 80% of the validating agents must be fully satisfied with the prototypes. Figure 8 shows the completeness calculated at the end of the last validation session. As shown, most of the items are above 95% and none of them is below 70%.

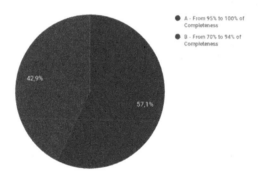

Fig. 8. The final completeness distribution by categories.

7   Conclusion

Design Thinking is an innovative methodology based on identifying people's needs in order to generate innovative solutions. This methodology has a long track of ideas, from the principles of Design to the current method. However, its application outside the business context (the origin of the current DT), more specifically, in software development, became effectively considered only in the late 2000s and at the beginning of the present decade.

DT has been applied in several sectors because this method has a great efficacy and adaptability, and also has a set of well-defined, multidisciplinary and human-centered tasks. Regarding the application of DT in Software Projects, it is worth mentioning its combination to some principles of the Agile Methods because of their apparent compatibility and common objectives.

This work fits in with this context since it presents and discusses the results of a case study conducted to apply the DT method, adapted through the Scrum framework principles, in the Software Requirements Elicitation to model a software product to solute the problem of allocating resources of a Brazilian university.

Through the quantitative and qualitative results obtained, it is possible to indicate Design Thinking as a positive model to the software development area. The unified approach of DT and Scrum has met the team's expectations by successfully identifying needs, opportunities and project barriers, and also modeling the requirements to design prototypes capable of achieving 100% of users' satisfaction and average completeness greater than 95%. Nevertheless, the results of this case study are preliminary ones and it is necessary to keep developing the model employed and reviewing new cases such as complete systems for larger and more complex problems.

Acknowledgments. The authors would like to thank the Universidade Estadual do Norte do Paraná (UENP) and the Fundação Auraucária for allowing the development of the case study and providing financial assistance.

References

1. Alves, A.T., Lima, A.M., de Oliveira Sales, E., da Costa, A.J.S.: Relato da aplicação da metodologia design thinking no projeto de um software para mobilidade urbana. In: SBC (ed.) SBSI. vol. X, pp. 333–344. Londrina (2014)
2. Archer, L.B.: Systematic method for designers. Council of Industrial Design, London (1965)
3. Brown, T.: Design thinking. Harvard Bus. Rev. **52**(6), 84–92 (2008)
4. Callahan, E.: Cross-cultural empathy: learning about diverse users in design thinking process. In: Stephanidis, C. (ed.) HCI 2018. CCIS, vol. 850, pp. 236–240. Springer, Cham (2018). https://doi.org/10.1007/978-3-319-92270-6_32
5. Canedo, E.D., Parente da Costa, R.: The use of design thinking in agile software requirements survey: a case study. In: Marcus, A., Wang, W. (eds.) DUXU 2018. LNCS, vol. 10918, pp. 642–657. Springer, Cham (2018). https://doi.org/10.1007/978-3-319-91797-9_45
6. Cavalcanti, C.M.C.: Contribuições do Design Thinking para concepção de interfaces de ambientes virtuais de aprendizagem centradas no ser humano. Ph.D. thesis, Universidade de São Paulo (USP), São Paulo-SP (2015)
7. Eickhoff, F.L., McGrath, M.L., Mayer, C., Bieswanger, A., Wojciak, P.A.: Large-scale application of IBM design thinking and agile development for IBM z14. IBM J. Res. Dev. **62**(1), 1–14 (2018)
8. Ferreira, F.K., Song, E.H., Gomes, H., Garcia, E.B., Ferreira, L.M.: New mindset in scientific method in the health field: design thinking. Clinics **70**(12), 770–772 (2015)
9. Gil, A.C.: Como Elaborar Projetos de Pesquisa, 4th edn. Atlas, São Paulo (2002)

10. Grossman-kahn, B., Rosensweig, R.: Skip the silver bullet: driving innovation through small bets and diverse practices. In: Leading Innovation through Design: Proceedings of the DMI 2012 International Research Conference. The Design Management Institute (DMI), Boston, MA, USA, August 2012
11. Jones, J.C.: Design Methods, 2nd edn. Van Nostrand Reinhold, New York (1992)
12. Paetsch, F., Eberlein, A., Maurer, F.: Requirements engineering and agile software development. In: International Workshops on Enabling Technologies: Infrastructure for Collaborative Enterprises, pp. 1–6. IEEE Computer Society (2003)
13. Palacin-Silva, M., Khakurel, J., Happonen, A., Hynninen, T., Porras, J.: Infusing design thinking into a software engineering capstone course. In: The 30th IEEE Conference on Software Engineering Education and Training, pp. 212–221. IEEE, November 2017
14. Paula, D.F.O.: Model for the Innovation Teaching (MoIT): um modelo baseado em Design Thinking, Lean Startup e Ágil para estudantes de graduação em computação. Master's thesis, Universidade Federal de Pernambuco (UFPE), Recife-PE, March 2015
15. Pinheiro, T.: The Service Startup: Design Thinking gets Lean: A practical guide to Service Design Sprint, 4th edn. Altabooks, CreateSpace, Hayakawa (2014)
16. Schwaber, K., Sutherland, J.: Guia do Scrum, November 2017
17. Sommerville, I.: Software Engineering, 9th edn. Pearson, London (2011)
18. Valentim, N.M.C., Silva, W., Conte, T.: The students' perspectives on applying design thinking for the design of mobile applications. In: International Conference on Software Engineering (ICSE), vol. 39, pp. 77–86. IEEE/ACM (2017)
19. Vianna, M., Vianna, Y., Adler, I.K., Lucena, B., Russo, B.: Design Thinking: Inovação em Negócios, 1st edn. MJV Press, Rio de Janeiro (2012)

User Interface Prototyping Toolkit (UIPT)

Bryan L. Croft$^{(\boxtimes)}$, Jeffrey D. Clarkson, and Eric VonColln

Naval Information Warfare Center Pacific, San Diego, CA, USA
{bryan.croft,jeff.clarkson,eric.voncolln}@navy.mil

Abstract. A design philosophy implementation in the form of a User Interface Prototyping Toolkit (UIPT) constitutes a software application for use by Fleet users, researchers, designers, and developers to aid in rapid engagement with end users in an agile design process. The toolkit allows rapid development of user interfaces (UIs) for collaborative exploration and validation of new concepts of operations (CONOPS) and new technology for decision-making and situational awareness. This improvement in exploration and analysis of software systems applies no matter the production stage. This product allows researchers, designers and developers to quickly develop new or modify existing UIs as designers work alongside Fleet users in a collaborative design effort. The design effort applies to existing or novel missions utilizing tasks and CONOPs as drivers for meaningful requirements and design input. The UIPT toolkit effort is targeted to Command, Control, Communications, Computers, Intelligence, Surveillance and Reconnaissance (C4ISR) and Cyber missions for the U.S. Navy. UIPT enables the Navy to significantly reduce the risks associated with pursuing revolutionary technology such as autonomous vehicles, artificial intelligence and distributed sensing in terms of the design of the user interface. The UIPT toolkit provides the ability to explore, analyze, develop and test systems that maximize human interaction and efficiency via the interface for these new and evolving CONOPs and systems.

Keywords: Command Center of the Future · Information systems · Rapid prototyping · User Interfaces · Unity3D

1 Introduction

A Naval Innovative Science and Engineering (NISE) project titled User Interface Prototyping Toolkit (UIPT), is exploring the rapid production of high-fidelity user interfaces (UI) prototypes to be utilized by end users, researchers, designers, and engineers working together to develop and validate, new concepts of operations (CONOPS) and emerging technologies.

The objective is to examine the ability to rapidly develop a specific human-machine interface prototype for future Navy information systems that address emerging operational and tactical threats and is currently targeting advanced UI's designs specifically for a large multitouch display device. UIPT is a software development effort to explore rapid prototyping of information systems while standardizing forward looking UI interactions, such as multitouch and augmented reality (AR).

© Springer Nature Switzerland AG 2019
A. Marcus and W. Wang (Eds.): HCII 2019, LNCS 11583, pp. 195–207, 2019.
https://doi.org/10.1007/978-3-030-23570-3_15

To date, software development and technology growth has escalated to meet the business demand. Often a holistic or a "full stack" approach is taken to design and implement an entire software system. This means the frontend or user interface is tightly coupled to the backend or server-side components of the software system. UIPT is taking a split stack approach, separating the frontend from the backend allowing a more focused approach to the creation of the user interface. The UIPT project took the concentrated approach to focus just on the user interface and apply a methodology to mold the interface to specific use cases in an interactive and rapid manner.

1.1 Motivation

The US Navy is increasingly dependent on producing superior information systems in order to create and maintain a decisive advantage over the Nation's adversaries.

As new technologies such as Artificial Intelligence, Machine Learning, and Autonomous Systems grow in importance to the Navy, the ways in which end users will use and control these technologies to maximize user performance gains is largely unknown. More emphasis on the design of future information system's user interfaces in the DoD is critical.

For decades, the lack of emphasis on User Experience (UX) design in software development has resulted in software user interfaces which are non-intuitive, difficult to use, non-task oriented, and have a general lack of form and function required for knowledge and decision support end use. Fortunately, this trend has shifted. Software companies like Apple, Google, Facebook and Amazon have been investing in internal design systems that speed the design process, allowing for product iteration and optimization in early stage prototyping before the commitment to full scale production. As examples, Google's 'Material Design' [1] addresses design style, while tools from companies such as InVision and Figma have been addressing UI prototyping. Currently, UI prototypes which focus on innovative Naval CONOPS development are limited but work in such areas are continuing to increase through efforts such as User-Centered Design [2].

The UIPT toolkit concept when finalized, will allow the rapid production of high-fidelity UI prototypes to be utilized by end users, researchers, designers, and engineers working together to develop and validate CONOPS and new technologies through the use of a scenario driven interactive prototype. This process allows all participants to experience high fidelity user interfaces, that are representative of the desired end product, well before large financial commitments are approved.

1.2 Technical Background

The UIPT technical approach is based on years of experience developing user interfaces for the Navy. Examples range from the 1990s with the Multi-modal Watch Station [3, 4] (see Fig. 1), a touch-screen and task-based application which supported a 3 to 1 plus manning reduction through efficient tasking; to today with a "55" multi-touch work-stations [5–7] for the NIWC Pacific Command Center of the Future VIP demonstration room.

Fig. 1. Multi-modal watch station (MMWS), 1990s

Other NIWC Pacific programs involving mission planning, task-managed designs, decision support aids and visualization have provided a wealth of experience in design and development of user interfaces. This included many user engagements and knowledge elicitation sessions to validate UI concepts and requirements, all of which provided the foundational basis for the UIPT toolkit.

UIPT focuses on UI design and development using a split-stack approach to concentrate on the front-end versus the back-end of the system. Integration of back-end systems is often the focus of DoD software development efforts in lieu of UI design and application. The complexity and effort required for integration can overtake the UI work, therefore UIPT purposely focuses on the front-end while striving to approximate the back-end by simulation. End user and subject matter expert sessions are used to illicit knowledge, data and scenarios, to drive the front end, while the simulation provides enough realistic operational context to process the desired scenario.

UIPT grew out of a mockup demonstration of a future Navy information system as depicted in a NIWC Pacific Vision video, produced in 2015. NIWC Pacific contracted a multi-touch display manufacturer to work with NIWC designers and subject matter experts to design and manufacture the TouchTable hardware and code the mockup application. This mockup (see Fig. 2) was specifically developed for demonstrations to DoD VIP visitors striving to understand the future direction of C4ISR for the U.S. Navy. The mockup provided the foundation for the start of the UIPT toolkit from its first instantiation to the current implementation, which is a rapid prototyping tool for information systems development. The value of a high-fidelity mockup over a PowerPoint presentation was clearly evident and validated by the many VIPs visiting NIWC Pacific.

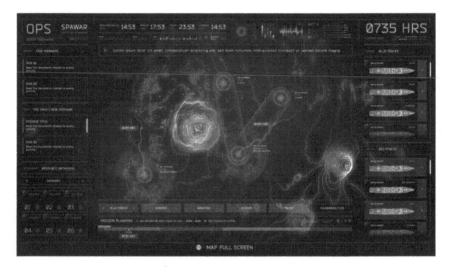

Fig. 2. Advanced user interface prototype design, 2015

1.3   User Interface Display Hardware

User interface designs for UIPT were targeted towards a large 55-in. Table device which is multi-touch enabled. The devices were scaled and positioned ergonomically to be within reach so the user can interact with the system via touch to make a compelling digital interaction for the end user. This device is ideal for 4 to 5 persons to gather around the display and interact with the information via the user interface. UIPT design and development efforts center around this Touch Table Device. User Interface elements within the system were specifically designed to be interactive in a touch environment. Multiple touch commands are recognized by the system to perform standard tasks such as zoom in and out on the map, change the aspect of the map, rotate the map, call up and dismiss data when needed, respond to alerts, initiate commands and set display options. Additionally, users can interact with the system through a series of voice driven commands (Fig. 3).

1.4   Interfacing to Information Systems

The ability to link an existing or legacy information system to an advanced user interface prototyping system, such as UIPT, in most cases requires a significant amount of work to feed the data from the system itself. The question of sensitive or classified information also arises which further complicates such an integration. Often the use of simulated data to fill the display is sufficient for said design purposes. The idea here is not to build the UI as the system is being developed, but to minimize the risk of poor design by doing the design work in front of the development. The UIPT effort seeks to correct this design deficiency by simulating enough data to make a realistic scenario to drive user interactions and converge on an efficient and effective design before software and engineering development starts. This way the end state of the user interaction is already known, and the work focuses on engineering the solution.

Fig. 3. Touch table used by UIPT

2   Objectives

By providing a rapid User Interface Prototyping Tool that allows users to explore the impact of new technology on emerging operational concepts before large program investments are made, the Navy can significantly reduce the risks associated with pursuing revolutionary technology. The Navy is currently investing in new technologies, such as, autonomous vehicles, artificial intelligence, distributed sensing and integrated fires, but the way in which Fleet users will work with and "team" with these new capabilities is largely unknown.

The objective of the UIPT project is to provide users, researchers, designers and developers with a UI toolkit to explore, analyze, develop and test new CONOPs and emerging technology that maximize the human interaction efficiency. Currently, there are no tools dedicated to rapidly testing of CONOPs and technology and the effects on C4ISR decision making through the user interface (UI). The UIPT will enable acceleration of relevant and well-designed capabilities to the Fleet by testing novel CONOPS based on rapid UI testing. Testing UIs before development will save money as Fleet users will already have been informed of and validated the concept.

2.1   Development of the User Interface Prototyping Tool

The UIPT software application allows the quick development of UIs to collaboratively explore and validate new CONOPS and the impact of new technology on the end user decision making process. UIPT also supports the exploration and analysis of improving the usability of deployed, and currently under development software systems used by the targeted audience. This exploration and development targets C4ISR and Cyber mission areas for novel CONOPs and UIs. This results in meaningful requirements and design input into programs of record as well as other projects.

A conversion of the original touch table software from JavaScript was required based on the intended use and objectives for the project. Initial efforts during the first year of UIPT focused on utilizing agile development for development with HTML5, NodeJS, ReactJS, and the REST Framework. The front-end JavaScript engine was used to support the front-end framework with the option of running in the browser. Agile teaming lead to the discovery of the potential difficulty in modifying and rapidly producing the software using the JavaScript/ReactJS technology. Even though this technology is still valid and could provide the same end results, an exploration was made into the use of Unity [8]. Unity is a cross-platform game engine produced by Unity Technologies which is generally used for 2D and 3D game development and simulations. During the exploration of Unity, a faithful reproduction to roughly 80% of the advanced display demonstrated on the Command Center of the Future Touch Tables was developed in less than a month. Further development of new components further validated the selection of Unity by demonstrating the development capability for new features. It became apparent that this rapid and agile development tool would be a natural fit for the project. The outcome using either Unity or ReactJS is the same but the saving and added capability in development validated the switch from ReactJS to Unity.

The development effort, utilizing Unity, provides for dynamic UIs for both web-based applications in a browser (WebGL based compile of Unity) and desktop applications. The development process allows the ability to switch out new user interfaces without complex and costly rewrites. There are many advantages to this approach: UI interactions are faster and use less bandwidth, it allows for developers to specialize and have less dependency of single stack experts, it makes it easier to build automated testing and it minimizes technical debt in agile software development. Furthermore, Unity is proven as a leading gaming engine technology at the current state of the art.

2.2   Employment of the Toolkit

The UIPT tool will provide an interface where designers can work with the users to quickly produce high-fidelity UI prototypes of future naval applications. The high-fidelity UI prototypes will be presented to users in a "mock" command center environment for CONOPS exploration and validation.

The high-fidelity UI prototypes will provide the framework to present new UI components as either real code, animations (animated gifs, etc.), or images. Track data will be presented on the UI screen from a simulator (i.e. NGTS [9], JSAF [10]), but other necessary data and information will be simulated and accessed from the UIPT's internal database and files. There will be a simple messaging capability to allow different UI prototype instances to communication and share information, alerts, and notification. The Fleet user will be able to experience the "New Application" capability as if it were a finished product. Additionally, multiple touch tables will be networked together and co-located to recreate a multi-person staff collaborating on mission objectives and execution.

3   Approach – Design and Development

The technical approach of UIPT has two main goals, first the creations of user interface designs which meet the end users' objectives and requirements, and second the creation of the toolkit which allows that to happen. Both goals are required to meet the objective of the UIPT project. Designers and software developers work hand in hand in an Agile development process with weekly evaluations of the toolkit for both form and functionality.

3.1   User Interface Design

UIPT use a relatively straight forward design process, performing user research, developing multiple design concepts, testing with users and iterating many times. This standard design process to produce a high-fidelity mockup that was used to generate discussions addressing the future direction of Navy information system.

The original mockup research mainly borrowed from current and past NIWC Projects. Since the objective was to create a unique rapid prototyping tool for use to discover how new CONOPS and new technology furthered the Navy mission, there was no available Navy application or Fleet user group to enlist.

The following Figs. 4, 5, 6, 7 and 8 show the progress of the original mockups design to the current UPIT Unity build.

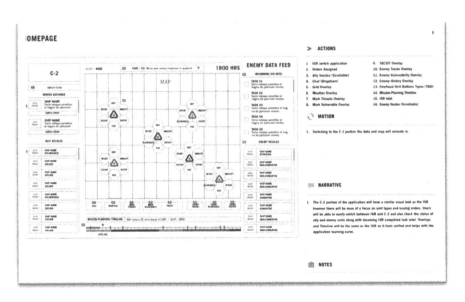

Fig. 4. Wireframe of base design – homepage

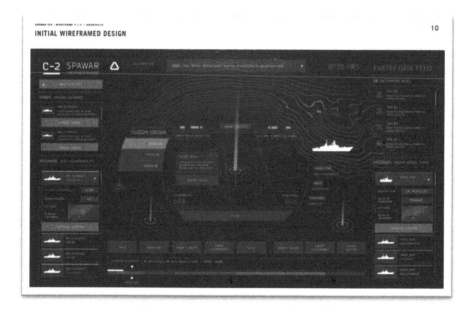

Fig. 5. Early HUD design

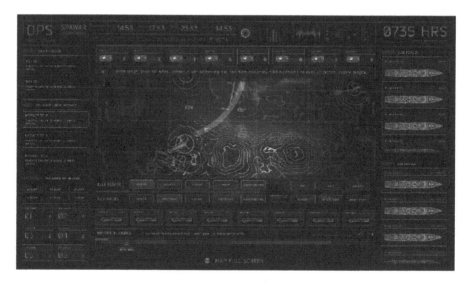

Fig. 6. Early design

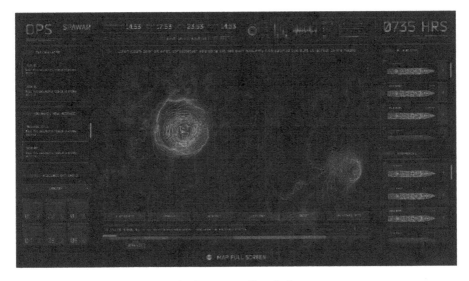

Fig. 7. Intermediate design

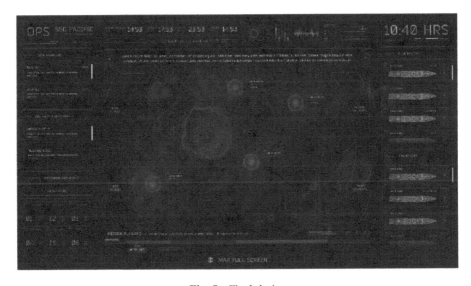

Fig. 8. Final design

3.2 Experimentation Plans and Metrics

UIPT will engage users early in the design process and conduct preliminary user engagements evaluating the prototype. Prior to installation and deployment, UIPT will need to work with users to determine baseline condition. During user events, users will review and comment on a selected Navy Mission domain user interface, as presented in an interactive scenario. User feedback will be reviewed and assessed by the UIPT development team and improvements will be made rapidly during the actual event if possible.

The critical technical parameters will be divided into prototype usability and target concept utility [11]. For prototype usability a combination of the following metrics will be collected during testing (Table 1).

Table 1. Usability metrics

Metric	Description
1. Successful task completion	Each scenario requires the user to obtain specific data that would be used in a typical task. The scenario is successfully completed when the user indicates they have found the answer or completed the task goal. In some cases, users will be given multiple-choice questions
2. Error-free rate	Error-free rate is the percentage of user who complete the task without any errors (critical or non-critical errors)
3. Time on task	The amount of time it takes the user to complete the task
4. Subjective measures	Ratings for satisfaction, ease of use, ease of finding information, etc. where users rate the measure on a 5 to 7-point Likert scale
5. Likes, dislikes and recommendations	Users provide what they liked most about the prototype, what they liked least about the site, and recommendations for improving the prototype

For target concept utility, we will focus on Situational Awareness. The final metrics have not been determined at this time, however a modified Situation Awareness Global Assessment Technique (SAGAT) [12] could be used to collect metrics during the course of testing (Table 2).

Table 2. Utility metrics

Metric	Technical parameter
1. Perception	Object detection time s
2. Comprehension	Object recognition time (s) and quality (scale)
3. Projection	Object intention recognition time (s) and quality (scale)

3.3   Toolkit Development

Software development of the UIPT toolkit is based on an Agile development process which is closely coupled with designs and feedback from the designers of the toolkit. An iterative process is performed to design, develop, test and evaluate the UIPT toolkit. Unity currently serves as the software platform upon which the UIPT toolkit is developed.

Unity used as a development tool gives UIPT developers the ability to create interface elements in both 2D and 3D. The engine offers a scripting/coding API in C# which is used within the Unity editor and other code editors such as Visual Studio. A developer can utilize assets and prefabs, a Unity term for a module, along with scripting/code insertion capability in order to add functionality to the application itself or to the assets and prefabs. The engine has support for the following graphics APIs: Direct3D on Windows, OpenGL on Linux, WebGL on the web. Although Unity is designated as a 2D and 3D game engine, it's set of tools allows the development of advanced user interfaces which provide rich 2D menus and user interface components as well as 3D based visualizations. This permits the overlay of UI components on top of a map-based visualization of virtual real-world space. Many of the Unity 2D features support the generation of rich user interface elements that can be intermixed with the rich 3D display elements. This unique combination provides flexibility in the types of interfaces which can be built. The move from JavaScript to Unity was validated in the faithful recreation of the VIP based demonstrations on the touch tables in the Command Center of the Future. Unity's strong base of third-party development assets and prefabs reduces development costs and saves time. These features of Unity set it as the tool of choice for UIPT based development, but the primary factor was the ability to produce components of equal quality at a much faster rate than using the JavaScript platform.

UIPT requires no network connections for normal operation under the current configuration and development effort, however, there are various prefab add-ons as well as integrated networking capability which becomes essential when driving the user interface with simulated data. All data and processes are installed on the Touch Table workstation and can run with or without a network connection in its current configuration. A simulation generator is currently being developed to drive the system. Initially the simulation generator will be self-contained in the Unity application while a more scalable and flexible approach to a simulation generator is being developed. Unity provides capabilities to move and position entities through built in structures and coding. An example is the use of waypoints which can be placed within the scene and then the use of coding permits a given asset to be moved along a chain of waypoints in a manner prescribed by the functionality added in the code. The use of finite state machines, also part of Unity, is also being used in connection with the built-in simulation generator. The simulation generator permits the creation of scenarios to drive the Unity based user interface and maintains the split stack approach. UIPT provides the ability to switch out new user interfaces without complex and costly rewrites. Typically, all software can be thought of as a stack consisting of many layers. The frontend layer consists of the user interface (UI), while backend layers usually consists of a server, an application, and a database. This split in the software stack development is an architecture pattern that's been developing for several years. Splitting up the backend into several layers for very large complex applications is a common practice, but the new split is frontend to backend. Multiple scenarios can be generated in order to fully explore the domain for the design and functionality created through the rapid prototype toolkit. In this manner the simulation generator can be repurposed for each domain or application that uses the toolkit for UI rapid prototyping.

To date the Unity based development of the UI rapid prototyping tool has made significant progress beyond the initial task of replicating the preliminary JavaScript implementation. Development work will continue with developing common elements of the advanced UI that can be shared across domain implementations as well as the ability to use the toolkit for rapid prototyping. Rapid prototyping concepts consist of allowing the interface to be modified in certain ways as well as providing instantiated options to a given design. This allows the collaborators to relocate and resize components, repurpose components, view components in various optional configurations, and have the ability to change styles, colors or other objects. The development process allows for collaborative feedback to be given upon which the development team prototypes the desired changes. Another collaborative session is then held to further refine the prototype development. An illustration of a work in progress using the rapid prototype UI toolkit is illustrated below in Fig. 9.

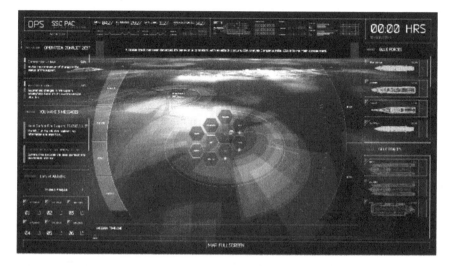

Fig. 9. Example of unity based UIPT screen

4   Conclusions and Future Work

The UIPT project has been in development for just over a year. A portion of that was dedicated to switching the development platform from JavaScript to Unity. The transition to Unity occurred during the last half of the time spent on the project. Not only was the initial JavaScript prototype faithfully implemented in Unity, but its use has been extended to a specific project domain. Several other project domains have since been added to the list of efforts that are porting or creating their project interface via the UIPT toolkit and the advanced display design used in the baseline user interface of UIPT.

The toolkit is still in the process of developing tools and additional views that allows an enhanced end user, researcher, engineer, designer, UCD practitioner, and software developer to collaborate on new user interfaces and CONOPs for a given domain. The value of this new interface has been validated by several domains that have started to incorporate the UIPT designs even before the UIPT Toolkit is completed.

The following describes areas of the UIPT project that require further examination:

1. Complete the elements of the UIPT Toolkit to allow viewing multiple options of a given display. Improve and continue the development of being able to modify the UI for such things as position and size of components or widgets, colors, styles, fonts as well as new components or widgets.
2. Complete baseline user interface along with weekly improvements and bug fixes. An Agile process is in place that lets all team members work together to accomplish this goal.
3. Apply the rapid prototyping of UIs to several new domains. This will validate the extensibility of the designs and the toolkit. One domain is currently being worked with two to three others ready to be worked immediately.
4. Evaluate the effectiveness of the UIPT Toolkit via user sessions from the perspective of the UCD practitioner, the software developer, the designer, and the end user.
5. Continue the iterative process of design and development improvements to the Toolkit to explore new areas not covered or yet to be discovered.

References

1. Google Material Design. https://material.io/design/
2. Van Orden, K.F., Gutzwiller, R.S.: Making user centered design a cornerstone for navy systems. In: Proceedings 144(10-1388), October 2018
3. Campbell, N., Osga, G., Kellmeyer, D., Lulue, D., Williams, E.: A human–computer interface vision for naval transformation. In: Space and Naval Warfare Center Technical Document 3183, June 2013
4. Osga, G.: Building goal-explicit work interface systems. In: Human Systems Integration Symposium, Tysons Corner, VA, June 2003
5. Goldman, K.H., Gonzalez, J.: Open exhibits multitouch table use finding. In: Ideum Open Exhibits Papers, July 2014
6. Hinckley, K., Guimbretiere, F., Agrawala, G., Apitz, G., Chen, N.: Phrasing techniques for multi-stroke selection gestures. In: Ideum Open Exhibits Papers (2006)
7. Schoning, F., Steomocle, F., Kruger, A., Hinrichs, K.: Interscopic multi-touch surfaces: using bimanual interactive for intuitive manipulation of spatial data. In: Ideum Open Exhibits Papers (2009)
8. Unity. https://unity3d.com
9. Next-Generation Threat System (NGTS): Published by NAVAIRSYSCOM on December 9th, 2014. YouTube. https://www.youtube.com/watch?v=3zD52IdI_7I
10. Northrup Grumman, Incorporated: Command, Control, Communications, Computer, Intelligence, Surveillance and Reconnaissance (C4ISR) Modeling and Simulation Using Joint Semi-Automated Forces (JSAF). AFRL-IF-RS-TR-2003-144 Final Technical Report, June 2003
11. The Defense Acquisition Guidebook (DAG). https://www.dau.mil/tools/dag
12. Ensley, M.R.: Situational awareness global assessment technique (SAGAT). In: Proceedings of the IEEE 1988 National Aerospace and Electronics Conference, May 1988. https://doi.org/10.1109/naecon.1988.195097

Effectiveness and Cost-Benefit Ratio of Weekly User Group Sessions

Helmut Degen[1]($\boxtimes$), Gustavo Guillen[2], and Holger Schmidt[3]

[1] Siemens Corporate Technology,
755 College Road East, Princeton, NJ 08540, USA
`helmut.degen@siemens.com`
[2] Siemens Mobility Inc., 700 East Waterfront Drive, Munhall, PA 15120, USA
`gustavo.guillen@siemen.com`
[3] Siemens Mobility Inc., 12735 Gran Bay Parkway,
Jacksonville, FL 32258, USA
`holgerhsschmidt@siemen.com`

Abstract. Early user involvement is a central part of a user-centered design process. In a project to create a UX design for an engineering tool for railways, weekly one-hour user group sessions have been used to elicit domain insights and to gather user feedback for proposed design options. This paper explores the effectiveness of such weekly user group sessions, by answering three research questions: RQ1: How much did the participating users effectively influence the UX design? RQ2: What was the impact of the participating users on efficiency improvements? RQ3: What was the return-on-investment (ROI) for the weekly group sessions? During 18 weekly user group sessions, 64 design decisions were made. Out of the 64 decisions, in 24 cases (38%) the participating users have chosen a different design option than the design option, initially selected by the UX team. Out of the 24 decisions, 14 decisions led to low, 10 to medium and 0 to high efficiency improvements. Comparing the hourly effort of preparing and holding such weekly sessions (cost of investment) with the avoided rework (gain of investment), the ROI is 12%. The conclusion is that weekly user group sessions have been a worthwhile approach to make the user supported design choices early in the development process.

Keywords: User involvement · Participatory design · User groups · Effectiveness · Efficiency · Return-on-investment

1 Introduction

Nowadays, it is expected that software-based systems ("system") are easy and enjoyable to use, and easy to learn. A well-known development approach to achieve such qualities is user-centered design. Involvement of users is a key element of user-centered design [1–3].

The principles of the user centered design process are: Early focus on user tasks, empirical measurement, and iterative design [1]. There are different approaches for user

© Springer Nature Switzerland AG 2019
A. Marcus and W. Wang (Eds.): HCII 2019, LNCS 11583, pp. 208–221, 2019.
https://doi.org/10.1007/978-3-030-23570-3_16

involvement [3]. Users are either exclusively involved in distinctive phases (i.e. analysis, design, evaluation) or across the process [3].

User involvement has the following benefits [4]: Improved system quality, avoiding costly features that the users don't need, improved system acceptance, and greater understanding of the system.

However, in industrial environments, the involvement of users in the system development requires extra effort and budget –someone must pay for it. In an industrial environment, the question arises rather sooner than later: Does it work? Or to reword the question: What is the effectiveness and cost-benefit ratio of user involvement?

This UX case study had the goal to design a configuration tool for interlocking hardware which is used in the railway domain. Since it is a rather complex domain, the UX design of such a configuration tool is not trivial. Therefore, a participatory design approach was chosen. Users should help to inform the UX team about domain background and the users were asked to express their preferences for presented design options. The user participation was organized as weekly user group meetings. The participating users could either select one of the presented design options or they could create an alternative design option, usually based one of the presented ones.

This case study is looking for answers to three research questions, two regarding the effectiveness and one regarding the cost-benefit ratio of participatory design:

RQ1: How much did the participating users effectively influence the UX design? In other words. This question addresses the different view the participating users brought to the table. Let's look at two hypothetical extremes. If the participants always confirmed an initially preferred design choice of the UX team, the influence would be very low. If the participants always rejected the initially preferred design choice of the UX team, the influence would be very high. Note that an initially preferred design choice of the UX team was not communicated to the participants.

RQ2: What was the impact of the participating users on efficiency improvements? One goal of the project was to make the new tool more efficient, compared to the benchmark tool. A question is which impact the user group had on design decisions with low, medium, or high efficiency improvements.

RQ3: What was the return-on-investment (ROI) for the weekly group sessions? This question addresses the mentioned cost-benefit ratio for the effort to let users participate in the design.

The questions were answered in a post-mortem analysis of the industrial project.

The paper is structured into five parts. Section 2 summarizes related work and identifies the research area of this case study. Section 3 introduces the application domain (engineering tool for railway interlocking hardware) and the applied UX process. Section 4 describes the weekly user group sessions which facilitated the participatory design activities. Section 5 describes the methodology to determine the effectiveness and the cost-benefit ratio of the weekly user group sessions. Section 6 summarizes the answers for the three research questions together with lessons learned. Section 7 concludes the results and outlines potential future research.

2 Related Work

There is a significant body of research regarding participatory design (PD) [6–8]. This paper focusses on user participation as "behaviors or activities that the target users of their representatives perform in the system development process" [5, p. 59].

There are different levels of user participation [4]:

- Informative (exchange of information with users)
- Consultative (users comment predefined services/options)
- Participative (users influence decisions)

The way the weekly user group meetings were organized and facilitated addressed all three levels of user participation. Participating users listened to domain related questions and answered them (informative). Users expressed which presented design options they preferred and why (consultative). Finally, the users' preferred choices influenced directly the design direction (participative).

Another way to categorize PD research is to consider contingency variables which are grouped into technical, managerial and user behavioral attributes [7]. The user behavioral attribute has several contingency variables which are applicable to this case study: perceived ease of use, and ease of use (addressing RQ1, RQ2), and system impact (addressing RQ3).

Considering the UX process (see Fig. 1), the participating users are involved in the "Explore and Select" phase to help finding the most appropriate interaction design concept.

Several studies involve users with the intent to improve the quality of requirements [11, 12]. Those participation activities are allocated to step "Define" in the UX process. The requirements are an input into the interaction concept design.

In one study, users were involved to evaluate scenarios of a smart card system use. The evaluation took place with a questionnaire [9]. Scenarios are a result of the "Discovery & Define" phase. Scenarios are not interaction design concepts, but they are one pre-requisite for the design.

In another publication, seven PD studies were analyzed [10]. These studies focused on how the elicitation of user needs can be improved. User needs are a result of the "Discovery & Design" phase.

A main difference to the study described in this paper with many other published studies seem to be the "black-box" vs "white-box" perspective. Many of the above studies look at the effectiveness of PD from a "black-box" perspective. This means the studies measure the impact of PD, applied to some project artifact or activity, on the project outcome, e.g. measured as a subjective rating or on the project success. This study however applies a "white-box" approach to PD. It means that this study looks into the internal mechanisms of a specific participatory design activity and measures the direct impact on key interim results, which are going to have a major impact on the project outcome. However, this study does not consider the final outcome of the project.

So far, the authors could not find a study which tracks the effectiveness of participatory design on single design decisions and their impact and its return of investment.

3   Project Background

3.1   Application Domain: Railway Interlocking Hardware Configuration Tool

The use of railway signals, switches and level crossings control the direction and speed of trains, for safe train rides. Such railroad safety equipment is controlled by interlocking hardware which is installed in the field along railroad tracks. The interlocking hardware needs to be configured for specific track layouts. An application engineer (user) configures the interlocking hardware with an application engineering tool ("tool"). An industrial project had the objective of the development of such a tool.

The configuration tool for interlocking hardware supports the following tasks:

- Task 1: Setup project
- Task 2: Configure system
- Task 3: Define logic
- Task 4: Compile logic

The intent of the first task is to introduce the project parameters. For instance, the railroad is identified which is going to use the interlocking hardware. In addition, it is defined where the interlocking hardware is used and the name of the application engineer. The number and types of chassis are selected. The result of the first task is the basic project infrastructure.

The intent of the second task is the configuration of the hardware (chassis and cards) and software (e.g. network settings). The application engineer assigns hardware cards (e.g. lamp input card, lamp output card) to the chassis slots. When all cards are assigned, system parameters are configured. Afterwards, parameter for each chassis card are configured.

When the system and the cards are configured, the application engineer defines the application logic (task 3). These are complex Boolean equations expressed in ladder logic [13] or relay logic [14] which determine under which condition which devices (e.g. switches, signals, level crossings) are set to which state. For instance, one equation determines under which conditions a red signal light should be turned on or turned off. In a typical project, hundreds or even thousands of such equations are defined.

After all equations are specified, the application engineer compiles the logic (task 4). Under the assumptions that all errors are fixed, the result is a report and an executable file which can be uploaded to the interlocking hardware in the field.

The four tasks require different efforts for an average project. Most of the effort (about 89%) is needed for task 3. Task 2 requires about 10% of the effort. The remaining 1% is distributed to task 1 and task 4.

Depending on the complexity, an application engineering project can last from several days to several months.

The application engineering tool most widely adopted in the industry became our benchmark tool ("benchmark tool") for the project. We articulated the goal that the UX quality of our new tool should make it even more efficient and easy to use for the users.

3.2   Applied User Experience Process

To achieve high user experience quality, a user experience team was tasked with the UX design of the new tool. It applied a user-centered design approach (see Fig. 1).

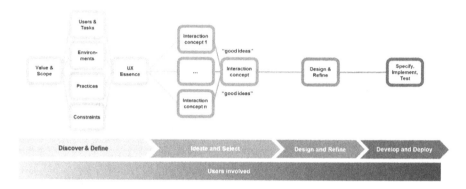

Fig. 1. User experience process

Discover & Define: In an initial "Value and Scope" phase, the UX team understands the business case of the product under design and how UX can support the business case. It also outlined the initial UX scope. Afterwards, the UX team gains an understanding about the involved user roles and their user profiles (e.g. user tasks, user needs, user characteristics), the use environments (e.g. spatial, work flow, social), and relevant good and bad practices (gains and pains). Known constraints (i.e. business, technology, design, and regulatory) are identified. The UX insights are consolidated in a step called "UX Essence" which includes UX goals, optimization use cases, and UX quality and quantity criteria which are used to access explored interaction design concepts.

Ideate and Select: The UX team creates several interaction design concepts and assesses them against the established UX quality and quantity criteria. If the UX criteria are not met, further interaction design concept options will be created. The UX team, together with UX stakeholders, finally settles on an interaction design concept which ideally meets all the defined UX criteria. The interaction design concept is presented as wire frames and screen flows to demonstrate how they support the optimization use cases and how they meet the qualitative and quantitative UX quality criteria.

Design and Refine: The UX team refines the selected interaction design concept, adds missing details and creates the visual design. Users are involved to evaluate the designs. UX designers refine the design according user's feedback.

Develop and Deploy: The UX teams creates optionally a specification or another kind of document as input for the front-end development and implements the front-end. The implementation can be a prototype or a product-quality front-end. The UX teams may evaluate the implemented prototype/front-end (e.g. with usability tests) and refines the design afterwards to address the findings.

Some additional explanations about the outlined UX process:

1) Representatives from identified user groups and project stakeholders (e.g. product manager, project manager, front- and back-end developers) are involved in all phases, so close feedback loops are happening along the way. If users or project stakeholders express concerns, the process may go a step back, e.g. from "Ideate and Select" to "Discover and Define", or from "Design and Refine" to "Ideate and Select". These loops are not displayed in Fig. 1.

2) The outlined UX process can be applied to an entire UX framework (e.g. an Engineering Tool) as well as to a single UX element (e.g. Find and Replace widget). For an entire UX framework, more time is necessary for each phase than when the process is applied to a single UX element.

3) The outlines UX process can be applied to agile, waterfall, or hybrid (called "wagile") product development approaches. It is critical that the first phases ("Discover & Define", "Ideate and Select" and "Design and Refine") are performed before the UX results are implemented.

4) The workshops discussed in this paper took place during the "Ideate and Select" phase. For a given use case, the participants looked at different interaction design concepts and expressed their preference and reasons for one of the presented concepts, or the participants expressed their preference for a give concept with additional change requests.

4   Weekly User Group Sessions

Since the industrial domain was new for the UX team, it has asked the product manager to select a small group of users for weekly user group sessions. The overall intent was to front-load the UX design process as much as possible to avoid late and costly changes, e.g. because of late findings from prototype-based or product-based usability tests. Due to the complexity of the domain, the UX team wanted to establish a communication channel to people who are both domain experts and users, so any kind of questions could be answered in a timely manner.

The group was setup for two reasons:

1) elicit missing domain knowledge, and
2) gather feedback for proposed design options.

The UX team articulated the following selection criteria for the members of this user group:

- Domain knowledge and current user of an interlocking configuration tool
- With different application engineering backgrounds (e.g. freight, commuter)
- Open to new ideas, also from other people
- Team player (no big egos)
- Availability for one hour per week
- Interest in contributing to the development of a new tool

The product manager selected six individuals which met the selection criteria. The weekly user group sessions had a duration of one hour. On average, five users attended the weekly user group sessions. In addition to the five users, the head of the front-end development team attended almost weekly, and the product manager attended some of the meetings. The UX team lead facilitated the weekly user group sessions. Each user group session had a specific UX topic.

There were two types of questions. Only in a few numbers of cases, the UX team asked for additional domain information. In most cases, the UX team asked to express preferences for several interaction design options, presented as wire frames (an example is displayed in Fig. 2).

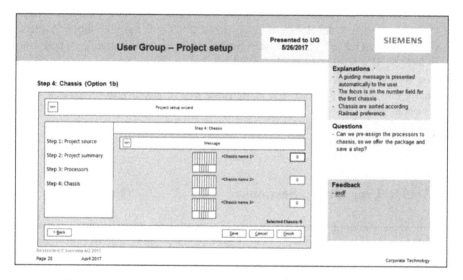

Fig. 2. Example of prepared material for weekly user group meetings

The UX team presented the material to the user group first. The design material was presented on a PowerPoint slides. Most concepts were presented with several options. An option was presented as one or a sequence of wire frames. The UX team introduced the several options and explained the reasons for each option and what distinguishes them. The group was asked to express which option they prefer and why. The group was briefed that they also could adjust presented options ("I like option 2, and would add this or that"), or that they could combine options ("I like option 2 with part x of option 3"). Afterwards, each group member explained which option they prefer and why. The UX team took notes directly on the slide, so the user group members could see what the UX team understood, and response to it when needed. After every user shared their preferences and reasons, the group selected one of the presented options. It also happened that the group selected a combination of several options with additional changes. The decision was noted on the slide.

For this paper, it is important to note that the UX team itself had selected a preferred option, out of the set of options. The UX team did <u>not</u> share its own preference with the user group. In the remainder of this paper, the UX team preferred option is called the "initially preferred option". In some cases, the user group has selected the "initially preferred option" (called the "same" option), in some cases the user group has selected another option (called a "different" option).

5   Methods

To answer the three research questions, we need to introduce methods which allow to measure the effectiveness of the weekly user group sessions (answering RQ1), the efficiency improvements of the made decisions (answering RQ2), and another one to determine the return-on-investment (answering RQ3). All methods are described below.

5.1   Measure Effectiveness of Weekly User Group Sessions

To measure the effectiveness of the weekly user group meetings, all 64 design decisions were analyzed. For each design decision, it was determined whether the user group selected a different option than initially preferred by the UX team ("different") or the same option as the UX team had preferred ("same").

5.2   Measure Impact on Efficiency Improvements of Weekly User Group Sessions

Since efficiency improvements was one of the UX goals, the efficiency of the benchmark tool was compared with the efficiency of the new tool on a use case basis. For this reason, an average interlocking hardware configuration project was defined (including the number and types of chassis and cards, the number of equations etc.).

To perform this average interlocking hardware project, 26 use cases were identified, and determined how often each use case needs to be performed ("frequency") for the benchmark tool and the new tool under design. In addition, it was determined, how many interaction steps it takes to perform each use case ("interaction steps for a single use case") for the benchmark tool and for the new tool under design. To determine the number of interaction steps for the benchmark tools, we counted the actual number of mouse clicks. To determine the number of interaction steps for the new tool under design, we counted the expected number of mouse clicks based on the interaction design concepts (wire frames). By multiplying the frequency per use case with the interaction steps per use case, the number of interaction steps per use case could be calculated (see Table 1).

It was now possible to compare the total number of interaction steps per use case of the benchmark tool with the total number of interaction steps of the new tool under design. The efficiency increase was categorized with the following schema:

Table 1. Determination of efficiency improvements per use case

Use case	Benchmark (Before)			New UX design (After)			Savings		
	Frequency	Interaction steps for a single use case	Interaction steps for all use cases	Frequency	Interaction steps for a single use case	Interaction steps for all use cases	Steps	Percentage	Category
Total	-	-	99	-	-	52	47	47%	
Use case 1	10	5	50	10	4	40	10	20%	Low
Use case 2	4	6	24	2	6	12	12	50%	Medium
Use case 3	5	5	25	0	5	0	25	100%	High

- "Low": If the efficiency increase of the new tool was equal to or less than 33%, compared to the benchmark tool.
- "Medium": If the efficiency increase of the new tool was more than 33% and equal to or less than 66%.
- "High": If the efficiency increase of the new tool was equal to or more than 67%, compared to the benchmark tool.

Example of such calculations are shown in Table 1.

Example calculation for use case 1: For the benchmark tool, use case one is performed 10 times. Each time, it requires 5 interaction steps. This makes 50 interaction steps for use case 1 for the benchmark tool (10 * 5 = 50). For the new design, use case 1 is performed 10 times. However, it only takes 4 interaction steps, which makes a total of 40 interaction steps (10 * 4 = 40). This means the new design is 10 steps (50 - 40) more efficient than the benchmark tool (or 20% = (50 steps - 40 steps)/50 steps).

Each single design decision which was made in the weekly user group was mapped to one of the 26 use cases. The mapping was determined by checking which design decision supports which of the 26 use cases.

In addition, for each design decision, it was checked whether the user group has selected the "same" design option or a "different" design option.

By mapping a design decision to a use case, each design decision inherited the efficiency category "high", "medium", or "low" from the mapped use case (Table 2).

Table 2. Mapping of efficiency category and efficiency category to each design decision

Design decision	Match of user group preference with initial preference of UX lead	Supported use case	Savings category
Design decision 1	Same	Use case a	Low
Design decision 2	Different	Use case b	Medium
...	...	...	...
Design decision 64	Same	Use case c	High

5.3   Measure Return on Investment of Weekly User Group Sessions

To calculate the return on investment (ROI), the following formula was used:

$$ROI = \frac{Gain\ from\ investment - Cost\ of\ investment}{Cost\ of\ investment}$$

To calculate the cost of investment, the effort for planning and holding the weekly user group meetings was determined. We consider the number of hours needed for planning the weekly user group sessions. This included mostly preparing the workshop material by the UX team. For holding the workshop, we count the number of people participating in the workshop and multiply them with 1 h.

To determine the gain from investment, only the effort for potentially changing the design late in the project was considered. Therefore, only "different" design decisions were considered for the cost calculation, meaning that the weekly user group has selected a design option which was different from the initially preferred design by the UX team. The cost estimate considered the cost for a design change, performed by the UX team, and for an implementation change, performed by the front-end development team. The lead of the UX team estimated the effort for designing a different concept (wire frame, visual design, style guide). The lead of the front-end development team estimated the costs for implementing that concept.

6   Results

When we apply the three methods to the weekly user group sessions and their outcome, we get the following answers for the research questions.

6.1   RQ1: How Much Did the Participating Users Effectively Influence the UX Design?

In 18 weekly user group sessions, the user group made 64 design decisions. Out of 64 design decisions, 40 (62%) were identical with the original preferred preference from the UX team ("same"), and 24 (38%) were different from originally preferred design options ("different").

6.2   RQ2: What Was the Impact of the Participating Users on Efficiency Improvements?

Out of the 64 design decisions, 7 were assigned to "high" efficiency improvements, 23 to "medium" and 34 to "low".

All 7 "high" efficiency improvements were the "same" decisions. In other words: the user group did not select a different option which support "high" efficiency improvements.

Out of the 23 "medium" design decisions, 10 were "different" and 13 were the "same".

Out of 34 "low" design decisions, 14 were "different" and 20 were the "same". Table 3 summarizes the results.

Table 3. Distribution of design decisions across efficiency categories

Efficiency category	"Different" design decisions	"Same" design decisions	Total
High	0	7	7
Medium	10	13	23
Low	14	20	34
Total	24	40	64

6.3   RQ3: What Was the Return-On-Investment (ROI) for the Weekly Group Sessions?

To calculate the ROI, we need to calculate the cost and the gain of investment.

Calculating the Cost of Investment. The investment for preparing and conducting the weekly user group sessions were:
Effort for preparing the 18 weekly user group sessions:

- 3-person hours per one-hour session
- Total: 18 sessions * 3-person hours per session = 54-person hours

Effort for conducting the weekly user group sessions:

- 15 one-hour user group meetings with 5 people each: 75-person hours
- 1 three-hour user group meeting with 5 people: 15-person hours.
- Total: 75-person hours + 15-person hours = 90-person hours

Grand total: 54-person hours + 90-person hours = 144 person hours

Calculating the Gain of Investment. The gains consider the avoided late and costly changes. This includes the effort for the design and implementation of all "different" design decisions (where the user group selected a design option which wasn't initially selected by the UX team).
Effort for designing the "different" UX design: 98-person hours
Effort for implementation the "different" UX design: 63.5-person hours
Total: 161.5-person hours

Calculating the ROI. We can now calculate the return on investment:

$$ROI = \frac{161.5 \ person \ hours - 144 \ person \ hours}{144 \ person \ hours} = 0.12 = 12\%$$

6.4   Lessons Learned

Beside the quantitative results, there are some other lessons learned from the weekly user group meetings.

The user representatives reported that it was exciting for them to be part of the design process. Most of them have never experienced such a process before. They enjoyed seeing how the design evolves (from "zero" to "hero") and how many thoughts go into the design process. By contributing their ideas, they developed a strong sense of ownership with the tool under development and the new design.

The product manager appreciated the approach of "fail fast, correct fast". Because of the weekly user group meetings, the project does not work with untested design assumptions for a long time but evaluates each design option in a timely manner. It is a trust building activity which saves money down the road. The product manager also appreciated that the members of the user group started to talk about the user groups and the new tool positively with their peers. They advertised not only the tool but also the project and the process.

The front-end developer understood the user's needs and how they prefer to perform certain use cases first hand. The weekly user group sessions equipped him with the knowledge to make the right development decisions down the road. In addition to learning about the needs, the front-end development lead could identify missing requirements early in the project. This avoided change requests late in the project and reduced project costs and delays.

Because of the weekly user groups, the UX team was always certain that it has a strong foundation for the design. Everything was evaluated quickly and with a rationale, which made the design explainable and defendable to other project stakeholders. For that reason, the UX team gained trust from user groups and the project sponsor. This trust should not be underestimated in a technology focused organizational environment. Another benefit of the weekly user group session was the established communication channel. The UX team could ask any question almost any time. As mentioned earlier, the UX team mostly asked the user group to provide feedback to explored design options. It also used some of the meetings for domain related questions ("Could you please explain this to us?"). In some cases, the UX team could approach individual members of the user group which are specialized in certain topics for further explanation and background information. Finally, the UX team became fully integrated into the project and development team.

One challenge in such group meetings is that everyone should be heard. Due to the selection criteria, strong opinionated individuals were not present. However, depending on the topic and to human nature, some individuals are more vocal than others. To guarantee that every single user was heard, we established the "go-around" method. It simply means we went around and asked every single user individually for his/her preference and the reason behind it ("Darren, which option do you prefer?"). All other users could hear what everyone preferred. We changed the sequence of the go-around method frequently. The method ensured that we collected the preferences of all users systematically for each design decision, and all users knew we want to hear their preference and the reason behind it.

7 Summary and Conclusion

Due to demands from the business to clarify the effectiveness, impact on design decisions on efficiency improvements and cost-benefit ratio of weekly user groups, we analyzed post-mortem the effectiveness and cost/benefit ratio of the weekly user group sessions. The paper articulated the following research questions. And provides some answers:

RQ1: How much did the participating users effectively influence the UX design? In 24 (38%) out of 64 design decisions, the user group has selected a different design option than the design option which the UX team initially preferred. How to interpret this number? We haven't found a comparable number in published research. This number justifies user group sessions and indicates how many of the first design decisions are sustainable. The number is most likely influenced by the amount of domain knowledge of the UX team, and the amount of experience of the users themselves.

RQ2: What was the impact of the participating users on efficiency improvements? The user had different preferences about design options which helped to make the design more efficient in the "low" and "medium" range. The users confirmed all design options with a "high" efficiency improvement. The conclusion could be that users don't need to be involved when it comes to high efficiency improvements. That is probably not a good idea. The increase of efficiency means that some functions are automated and performed by the machine, and not triggered by the user anymore. This means the user loses control. In some cases, this is acceptable, in other cases, it is not. Believing in the principle "control over efficiency", users should be involved in providing feedback to design concepts which significantly increase the efficiency. Otherwise, a new design may have achieved a higher efficiency, but is not accepted by users. The weekly user group sessions helped to address this challenge.

RQ3: What was the return-on-investment (ROI) for the weekly group sessions? The Return on Investment is slightly positive (12%). It indicates that weekly user groups are cost effective. One of the big benefits are the early detection of deviation and avoiding unplanned rework or, due to time constraints, not considering the insights in the development process. The ROI provides an initial cost justification that weekly user group meetings are cost effective.

Overall, weekly user groups meeting can be recommended as a tool for early user participation. It is particularly useful for complex domains and if the UX team is not very familiar with the domain.

Future work can check the "same"/"different" ratio for other domains. It might also be interesting to consider the knowledge of the UX team about a certain domain. It is expected that the "same" ratio goes up the more a UX team knows about a certain domain. A study with a larger number of user group meetings would be beneficial. Another extension is to compare the measured UX quality of the final product with the decisions made in such weekly user group meetings to determine how well it predicts the final UX quality.

Acknowledgements. I thank Christof Budnik and Omer Metel for constructive feedback.

References

1. Gould, J.D., Lewis, C.: Designing for usability: key principles and what designers think. Commun. ACM **28**(3), 300–311 (1985)
2. Norman, D.A., Draper, S.W. (eds.): User Centered System Design: New Perspective on Human-Computer Interaction. Lawrence Erlbaum Associates, Hillsdale (1986)
3. Kujala, S.: User involvement: a review of the benefits and challenges. Behav. Inf. Technol. **22**(1), 1–16 (2003)
4. Damodaran, L.: User involvement in the systems design process—a practical guide for users. Behav. Inf. Technol. **15**(6), 363–377 (1996)
5. Barki, H., Hartwick, J.: Rethinking the concept of user involvement. MIS Q. **13**(1), 53–63 (1989)
6. Bossen, C., Dindler, C., Iversen, O.S.: Evaluation in participatory design: a literature review. In: Participatory Design Conference, pp. 151–160
7. Bachore, Z., Zhou, L.: A critical review of the role of user participation in IS success. In: 15th Americas Conference on Information Systems 2009, AMCIS 2009, Paper 659 (2009)
8. Bano, M., Zowghi, D.: User involvement in software development and system success: a systematic literature review. In: 3rd International Workshop on Empirical Requirements Engineering (EmpiRE), pp. 24–31 (2013)
9. Schaik, P.V.: Involving users in the specification of functionality using scenarios and model-based evaluation. Behav. Inf. Technol. **18**(6), 455–466 (1999)
10. Kujala, S.: Effective user involvement in product development by improving the analysis of user needs. Behav. Inf. Technol. **27**(6), 457–473 (2008)
11. Kujala, S., Kauppinen, M., Lehtola, L., Kojo T.: The role of user involvement in requirements quality and project success. In: Proceedings of the 13th IEEE International Conference on Requirements Engineering, 2005, pp. 75–84 (2005)
12. Emam, K.E., Qintin, S., Madhavji, N.H.: User participation in the requirements engineering process: an empirical study. Requirements Eng. **1**(1), 4–26 (1996)
13. Ladder Logic: Wikipedia. https://en.wikipedia.org/wiki/Ladder_logic. Accessed 5 Feb 2019
14. Relay Logic: Wikipedia. https://en.wikipedia.org/wiki/Relay_logic. Accessed 5 Feb 2019

A Data-Driven Design Framework
for Customer Service Chatbot

Shinhee Hwang[1(✉)], Beomjun Kim[2], and Keeheon Lee[1]

[1] Yonsei University, 50, Yonsei-ro, Seodaemun-gu, Seoul, Republic of Korea
{shinhee,keeheon}@yonsei.ac.kr
[2] Laftel, 14, World Cup-ro 1-gil, Mapo-gu, Seoul, Republic of Korea

Abstract. User experience in customer service is critical. It is because customer service is what a customer first requests for a service. The service fails to satisfactory response will cause a crucial damage. Albeit business includes a chatbot for better responsiveness, customization is still necessary to fulfill the satisfaction from customer service. For customization, a designer performs qualitative research such as surveys, self-reports, interviews, and user observation to pull out key characteristics and to build personas based on the characteristics. However, a small sample size and cognitive limitation of a researcher demand more data to model persona better. Therefore, in this study, we introduce a data-driven framework for designing customer service chatbot that utilizes the past customer behavior data from clickstreams and a customer service chatbot. We apply this framework to a cartoon streaming service, Laftel. In result, we generate three types of customer service chatbots for three personas such as explorer, soft user, and hard user. In the future, we will validate our result by conducting a field experiment.

Keywords: Data-driven design framework · Chatbot · Customer service · Personas · User experience

1 Introduction

It is important for a service provider to increase satisfaction of all the users, especially, in the time when a problem occurs when the user uses the service. Meeting the user problems and providing more customer service than expected improves user satisfaction and competitiveness of the company [18]. Chatbots can answer customers' inquiries cheaply, quickly and in real-time. In the field of CS, chatbots are mainly used to provide answers to repeated questions, and as a result, CS personnel are more practical and cost-effective in that they can give higher value answers to customers [8]. Thus, more and more businesses are choosing chatbots for customer service [19].

In UX design, there are attempts to improve user satisfaction and service completeness by providing a service that covers multimodal user [22]. Also, chatbot has evolved to provide an optimized response for the use [24]. However, the various users are too quick and massive to follow their problems with the present but popular research methods, in designing customer service, to extract key features that may improve user experience. The methods are surveys, self-reports, interviews, and user

© Springer Nature Switzerland AG 2019
A. Marcus and W. Wang (Eds.): HCII 2019, LNCS 11583, pp. 222–236, 2019.
https://doi.org/10.1007/978-3-030-23570-3_17

observation. They usually take a lot of time, effort, and cost. At the same time, the amount of data collection is restricted due to a small sample size and cognitive limitation. It is often not enough to model the actual behavior of responsive users that can be used for customer service customization.

This study is based on the case of Laftel, cartoon streaming service [11]. Laftel is a streaming service that recommends animation and webtoon based on user preference. The service provides contents based on interests with little expertise. Therefore, users change faster because service deviance rate is higher than service that provides professional content, and the main user base is in their 10 s and 20 s. Also, the service provider is a startup that requires an efficient but effective way for customer service so that we choose Laftel as our case.

In this study, we introduce a data-driven framework for designing customer service chatbot that utilizes the past customer behavior data from clickstreams and a customer service chatbot. We apply cluster analysis to user data and segments users to build personas. In order to create a service list of CS, the company's CS data is processed by Natural Language Processing (NLP) to derive words with high frequency of use and words similar to those words. In result, we generate types of customer service chatbots for each personas.

This study suggests a way to provide corporate customer service effectively and effectively, and it is expected that it will contribute to the improvement of corporate value.

2 Literature Review

2.1 Data-Driven Personas

User experience (UX) design is to elicit positive experience by using designs customized to users. In UX design, persona is often used to understand users. Persona categorizes users based on their behavior, goals, needs, and context. Namely, persona is an artificial character that represents various user types in the population of the potential target users. Cooper first utilized Persona concept for Design and User Experience practice [7]. He considered a persona as an archetypal user. Pruitt and Grudin argued that persona is helpful to understand users and their needs because we can perceive user closely as a person [21]. Norman insisted that, in UX design, one can design the experience a person will have when the one empathizes the person totally based on persona [17].

Traditionally, in user-oriented design, personas are built based on collected data from surveys, self-reports, interviews and user observation. But this process generates limited amount of data compared to costs of labor, budget and time. In addition, there is a gap between users' actual behavior and users' realization of their behavior. Additionally, the traditional user research methods are insufficient to support flexible services for fast-changing industry due to 4th industrial revolution and responsive users.

2.2   Telemetry and Click Stream

Clickstream is a digital path of user through a web site. A series of web pages requested by a visitor in a single visit is referred to as a session. Clickstream data includes click path information that shows the goal of service uses and their associated information such as timestamp, IP address, URL, status, number of transferred bytes, referrer, user agent, and cookie data in real time. And thus, collecting and analyzing clickstream data is an effective and efficient way to know user behavior data compared to traditional methods.

We can predict user's needs and the user's behavior by analyzing clickstream data. And, in UX research, clickstream data is utilized in order to understand the users of a website and improve the quality of service [4]. Singh and Cancel used clickstream data to show users of a website have different needs for services and functions [26]. They also showed that the outcome of the service improves when they personalized web designs and product offerings based on a user's path. Mobasher collected and analyzed clickstream data to design a personalized web page [16]. Xiang, Hans-Frederick and Anil made personas based on clickstream data and UX design methodology. They showed that it actually reflects the actual behavior of the users [28].

2.3   Chatbot

Chatbot is a computer program designed to perform certain tasks through communication with humans through text messages, combined with artificial intelligence and messenger functions. Gartner predicted that by 2021, more than 50% of companies will be managing AI-based chatbots within their apps [14]. Chatbots are suitable for providing answers to simple questions, and real-time answers are possible. Therefore, the use of chatbots in the CS field can reduce the labor cost and improve the CS satisfaction of the users because the CS consulting staff can use them in more productive fields [9].

There are two types of chatbots: open type and closed type. Closed chatbots are mainly used when certain functions are limited, or when there are not many data sets. This type of chatbot restricts the user's questions so that the answer is more accurate, but it does not feel as much interaction with the user. Closed chatbots provide a relatively comprehensive service and are used when there are many datasets. This type of chatbot has a high degree of freedom for the user to ask questions, but the accuracy of the answer to a specific question is also low. However, it has the advantage of giving users a sense of interacting with Service. Recently, it is easy to see a mixed chatbot partially borrowing each form in order to take advantage of the closed type and the open type (Tables 1 and 2).

In UX design, there are attempts to improve user satisfaction and service completeness by providing a service that covers multimodal user [22]. Also, chatbot has evolved to provide an optimized response for the use [24]. Makar and Allen studied an algorithm that passes different sentences by each personas in Chatbot Service [1, 15]. Liu classified user types based on postings posted by users, and studied Chatbot, which provides different sentences for each users [13].

Table 1. Comparison of closed chatbot and open chatbot

Type	Input method	Data set	Questions	Accuracy of answer	User interaction
Closed type	Select Options, Simple information input	Small	Limited	High	Low
Open type	Natural language input	Big	Unlimited	Low	High

Table 2. Chatbot by input method

Type	Chatbot	Company	Platform	Service
Closed type	Babylon Health [5]	NHS	App	Health care advice, connectivity to local free services, off-hours medical services
	Leena [12]	Leena	App	HR, Recruitment
	Woebot [27]	Stanford Univ.	App, Messenger	Psychological trace and psychological pattern analysis of patients, improvement of psychological condition, and cognitive behavior therapy
Open type	KAI [25]	Kasisto	Messenger	Financial affairs, common sense Q&A, P2P remittance service
	Astrobot [3]	Astro	App, Messenger	Scheduling, Document management
	Replika [23]	Replika	App	Daily conversation, psychological counseling
Mixed type	Shopbot [20]	Ebay	Web, Messenger	Shopping, ordering, and paying
	Jobpal [10]	Jobpal	Messenger	Recruiting, Interview scheduling, On-boarding, FAQ
	Allo [2]	Google	App, Web	conversation with Google Assistant

3   A Data-Driven Design Framework for Customer Service Chatbot

Basically, we collect clickstreams as data from non-verbal user behavior and cluster them into a several groups that segments users. On the other hand, we collect the conversations of users with CS chatbots as data from verbal user behavior and classify them into a certain number of labels that follows a predefined category system. In this case, the system consists of services that a business provides. Lastly, each user group is defined by a combination of services so that the relationship between user groups and services are one-to-many relationships (Fig. 1).

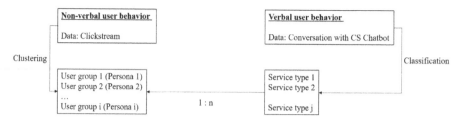

Fig. 1. Data-driven design framework for customer service chatbot

3.1   Identify User Groups (Personas)

We build a persona using hierarchical clustering. Hierarchical clustering is a method of grouping targets based on their similarities using Euclidean distances and is especially useful when the total number of clusters is unknown. The process constructing personas with hierarchical clustering includes following steps.

Step 1: Collecting clickstream data.

To collect clickstream data from the target service, Beusable was used. The tool analyses how the users accessed the web page and whether the users revisited the page or not.

Step 2: Calculating the distances between clickstream.

The clickstream data includes the travel of cursors and their sequences represented with x- and y-coordinate. The distance between two clickstreams is calculated by Euclidean distance method. The resulted distance data can be represented as a matrix where the value of (i, j) in the matrix indicates the distance between the i-th click stream and the j-th click stream.

Step 3: Selecting representative clickstreams using H-Clustering

H-Clustering is applied to the resulted matrix from Step 2 so as to make the clickstreams into several groups, considering the PV.

Step 4: Mapping the representative clickstreams to common workflows

In the last step, the representative clickstreams are mapped with the actual UI of the web page and the personas were drawn from the the grouped clickstream data.

3.2   Identify Service Types

We analyze the conversations of users with CS chatbots in Laftel to format the service provided by CS Chetbot. The process of classifying data and typesetting service type is as follows. In this study, the top 20 nominal words are defined as 'key words' and the top 10 words with high specific word and word vector values are defined as 'related words'. The procedure for defining the service type is as follows. After proceeding step 1 and step 2, make the list in the table as shown in the Table 3. The main contents of the table are key words, the number of times key words are used, and related words of key words.

3.3 Distance Between Clickstreams

Users visited Laftel with ten routes we extracted twenty groups of clickstream data in total which are clickstreams of new visitors and re-visitors from the ten routes (Table 4). However, eight groups whose PVs are under fifty are excluded because of not enough data to analyze. The remaining 12 groups of clickstreams were labeled as Table 1.

Step 1: Extract key words using konlpy and kkma analyzer

1. Separate morphemes and extract noun words

2. Extract the top 20 word frequency of words

Step 2: Extract related words of key words using Word2Vec

1. Generate word vector

2. Extract the top 10 words nearest the distance between words by keyword

3. Delete words with similarity less than 0.9

Table 3. Examples of key words and related words

No.	Key word	Count	Related words
1	Word 1	100	Possession, Inquiry, (Monthly) fee, Automatic
2	Word 2	50	Payment, Inquiry, (Monthly) fee

Second, make a square matrix of the same number of related words between key words. Table b is an example of square matrix of Table a. In Table 3, word1 and word2 have two identical related words, 'Inquiry' and '(Monthly) fee', so the value of (2,1) Finally, the square matrix is classified into n groups by H-Clustering and representative keywords representing each group are selected as shown in Table 5.

Table 4. Example of correcting related words by word

No.	1	2	3	...
1		3	x	
2			Y	

Table 5. Example of selecting representative keyword

Service type	Key words
Representative keyword 1	Possession, Inquiry, (Monthly) fee, Automatic
Representative keyword 2	Payment, Inquiry, (Monthly) fee

3.4   Matching Service List with Persona

The service type defined in Sect. 3.2 and the persona defined in Sect. 3.1 are matched as shown in Table 6 of the receiver.

Table 6. Example of service type matching with person

Persona	Service type
Persona name 1	Representative keyword 1
	Representative keyword 2

4   Result

4.1   Collecting Clickstream Data

We used Beusable to track visiting users to Laftel. Beusable provides basic statistics such as page view, average residence time, dropout rate, device statistics, monitor resolution distribution, and access routes, click stream data by user types (new visit and re-visit). We concentrated on access routes and clickstream data of three weeks. During the three weeks, 30,000 page views and 15,000 unique views are collected.

4.2   Calculating the Distances Between Clickstream

Users visited Laftel with ten routes we extracted twenty groups of clickstream data in total which are clickstreams of new visitors and re-visitors from the ten routes. However, eight groups whose PVs are under fifty are excluded because of not enough data to analyze. The remaining 12 groups of clickstreams were labeled as Table 7.

Table 7. Page View for each type of access routes and user types

Class	New User (PV)	No.	Return User (PV)	No.
search.naver	4442	S1	2335	S2
direct	783	S3	5000	S4
laftel.net	120	S5	150	S6
search.daum	128	S7	81	S8
mangav.zz.am	137	S9	23	-
about.laftel.net	120	S10	31	-
msn.com/sprtan/ntp	4	-	77	S11
laftel.net/preference	2	-	56	S12
laftel.net/accounts/password/	8	-	41	-
laftel.net/freeplus	0	-	29	-

4.3   Selecting Representative Clickstreams Using H-Clustering

We computed the distances between twelve clickstreams using Euclidean distance and generated a n by n matrix as Table 2. The element at i-th row and j-th column represents the distance between i-th clickstream and j-th clickstream (Table 8).

Table 8. The distance between clickstreams

Click Stream	S1	S2	S3	S4	S5	S6	S7	S8	S9	S10	S11	S12
S1		776	1677	1043	1362	1411	1776	2008	1293	2156	1931	1659
S2			1680	1141	1416	1507	1800	1899	1243	2203	1851	1651
S3				1298	1387	1238	2067	2007	1300	2189	2279	1925
S4					1409	1589	987	2000	1293	2175	1626	1091
S5						1351	1254	1186	1033	1670	1642	986
S6							1780	1659	1174	2147	1947	1426
S7								2130	1101	1923	2182	1847
S8									971	2445	2302	2057
S9										1884	1410	1102
S10											2247	1993
S11												1919
S12												

Figure 2 shows the result of hierarchical clustering of the matrix of Table 2. We found six clusters of clickstreams from the result. We regarded the clickstream with the highest PV in a cluster as the representative of the cluster. The access routes and the user types of the selected representatives are S3 (Direct-New), S4 (Direct-Return), S7 (Search-New), S8 (Search-Return), S10 (about.laftel.net-New), and S11 (msn. com/sprtan/ntp-Return).

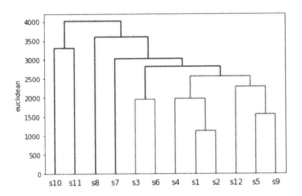

Fig. 2. The result of H-Clustering

4.4   Mapping Clickstreams to Common Workflows

We mapped the coordinates where a certain number of users of the selected click-streams stayed with the functional items in Laftel website. We also recorded the time of stay for each coordinate. And, we compared the trends of six clustered clickstreams each other. We discovered three personas: service explorers, soft users, and hard users as Table 9.

Explorers. These people visited a website through corporate introduction. They traversed the webpage as exploring services. And, they checked if the animations and the cartoons of their interests are provided. Also, they tried to know if purchase of the animations and the cartoons is allowed.

Soft Users. These people came to a web page through a search engine. They tended to consume the animation and the webtoon what they have been consumed. Also, they searched for other contents that can be consumed with the present animation and webtoons. They tended to visit a website in a short time. Within the time period, they consume contents in 50% of the period and watch commercials in the rest.

Hard Users. These people visits a web page through URL. They visit the web page to see the contents consumed before. They had a tendency to stay in the web page a long time, relatively. The 70% of the time is used for content consumption and the others are used for commercials and search).

Table 9. The data-driven personas

Persona	Click Stream no.	Behavior & Time
Explorers	S10	★●★●□□
Soft Users	S7	○★●●
	S8	★●
Hard Users	S3	▲□□●●●●●●
	S4	★●●●●●●●●●
	S11	●●●★★★●●□□

▲ = Registration ● = Content consumption
□□ = Information retrieval ★ = AD ○ = others

4.5   Extract Key Words and Related Words

Laftel is a Korean language service. We use konlpy and kkma, which are Korean natural language processing tools, to find the frequency of words, and Word2Vec, which is a tool to assign word vector values to confirm the similarity between words, was used. As a result of the NLP analysis, 'Key words' are frequently used in the top 20 words, such as Payment (1910), Refund (1103), Point (792), Monthly (714), Purchase (637) Possibility (561), work (539), possibility (405), playback (325), video (278), animation (271), free (of charge) (266), Cancellation (256), Advertisement (243), Viewing (237), Confirm (234), Authentication (228), Cancel (227) and Publication right (225). Table 10 shows the related words for each key word.

Table 10. The key words and related words in CS List

No.	Key word	Count	Related words
1	Payment	1819	Possession, Inquiry, (Monthly) Fee, Automatic, Refund, Use, Subtitle, Purchase, Animation
2	Refund	1103	Payment, Inquiry, (Monthly) Fee, Possession, Purchase, Advertisement, Use, Automatic
3	Point	792	Free (of charge), Month, New work, During, Degree, Experience, Paypal
4	(Monthly) Fee	714	Possession, Publication right, Refund, Inquiry, Way, Animation, Cancel, Authentication
5	Purchase	637	Way, Cancel, Again, Cancellation, Payment, Publication right, Animation
6	Inquiry	601	Publication right, Animation, Refund, Use, Payment, Video, (Monthly) Fee, Possession
7	Possession	561	(Monthly) Fee, Way, Cancel, Publication right, Service, Refund, Animation
8	Work	539	Point, New work, Experience, Voucher
9	Possibility	405	Animation, Service, Account, List, Payment, Cancellation, (Monthly) Fee
10	Playback	325	Advertisement, Addition, Relation, Screen, Function, work, Request, Rental, Count
11	Video	278	Viewing, Again, Inquiry, Service, Animation, Payment, Thought, Login
12	Animation	271	Way, purchase, Publication right, Request, Cancel, Inquiry
13	Free (of charge)	266	Email., Purchase, work, Possession, Inquiry, Animation, Playback
14	Cancellation	256	Screen, Way, Refund, Problem, Payment
15	Advertisement	243	Rental, Playback, Screen, Mistake, Request, Addition, Event, Way, Button
16	Viewing	237	Again, Video, Login, Payment, Answer, Cancel, Purchase
17	Confirm	234	Next, Event, Count, Advertisement, Problem, Webtoon, Mistake, Cancellation, Again
18	Authentication	228	Animation, Service, Account, List, Payment, Cancellation, (Monthly) Fee
19	Cancel	227	Animation, Way, Answer, Payment, Publication right, Screen
20	Publication right	225	Animation, Refund, Inquiry, Cancel, (Monthly) Fee, Payment, possession, Way

4.6 Service Classification and Typing

We grouped words using the similarity of each word and defined the service type. Table 11 shows the similarity between words. The value is the number of the same words among the related words of two words in x and y.

The result of H-clustering the table is shown in Fig. 3. Based on the results, keywords of each service type are selected as shown in Table 12. There are two major

Table 11. Similarity between keywords

No	1	2	3	4	5	6	7	8	9	10	11	12	13	14	15	16	17	18	19	20
1		5	0	5	3	6	4	0	3	0	2	2	5	2	0	2	0	3	2	6
2			0	4	2	5	3	0	2	1	2	2	2	2	1	2	1	2	1	5
3				0	0	0	0	2	0	0	0	0	1	0	0	0	0	0	0	0
4					2	5	5	0	2	0	2	4	3	2	0	1	0	2	4	8
5						3	3	0	3	0	3	2	2	3	0	4	2	3	5	4
6							5	0	3	0	3	2	2	2	0	2	3	3	3	5
7								0	3	0	2	3	2	2	1	1	0	3	4	7
8									1	0	0	1	0	0	0	0	0	0	0	0
9										0	3	1	1	2	0	0	0	7	2	3
10											0	0	1	1	6	1	2	0	1	0
11												2	2	1	0	5	1	3	0	0
12													2	1	2	2	0	1	4	5
13														0	1	1	0	1	1	3
14															2	1	2	2	3	3
15																0	2	0	2	1
16																	0	1	3	2
17																		1	0	0
18																			2	2
19																				4
20																				

service types, 'Content' and 'Account'. There are 3 service types for each major category, 6 for each service type. Content Advertisement, Content consumption, Content etc., Account membership, Account-Authentication, Account benefit'. The key word of the first service type 'Content Advertisement' is 'Advertisement' and 'Confirm'. The second service type 'Content consumption' key words are 'Animation',

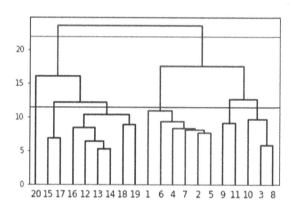

Fig. 3. The result of H-clanging the service list

Table 12. The list of service type classifications and representative keywords selected

Service type		Key words
Content	Advertisement	Advertisement, Confirm
	Consumption	Animation, Free (of charge), Cancellation, Viewing, Authentication, Cancel
	Etc.	Publication right
Account	Membership	Payment, Refund, (Monthly) Fee, Purchase, Inquiry, Possession
	Authentication	Possibility, Video
	Benefit	Point, Work, Playback

'Free (of charge)', 'Cancellation', 'Viewing', 'Authentication', and 'Cancel'. The third service type, 'Content etc.', is the 'publication right' key word. The key word in the fourth service type 'Account membership' is 'Payment', 'Refund', 'Monthly fee', 'purchase', 'Inquiry', 'Consumption'. The key word for the fifth service type, 'Account authentication', is 'possibility', 'Video'. The key words of the last service type 'account benefit' are 'Point' and 'Work'.

4.7   Matching Service List to Persona

Table 13 shows the service types and key words classified according to the needs of the persona. The explorer, a new user of Laftel Service, matched the 'Content consumption' service related to the information of the content provided by Laftel and 'Account membership' which is the service for the membership information. 'Content consumption', 'Content advertisement', 'Account membership', and 'Authentication' service, which is an authentication related service required at the initial stage of the account, are required for a soft user who is an existing user but has a relatively low service utilization degree, authentication'. For hard users who have a lot of service frequency and time, they match 'content consumption', 'account membership', and 'account benefit' which is an additional reward service for each account.

Table 13. Matching service type by persona

Persona	Service type
Explorer	Content consumption, Account membership
Soft user	Content consumption, Content advertisement, Account membership, Account authentication
Hard user	Content consumption, Account membership, Account benefit

5 Conclusion

In this study, we introduce a data-driven framework for designing customer service chatbot. First, we used Beusable to collect clickstream data of Laftel, utilized hierarchical clustering to generate personas representing explorer, soft user, and hard user. In result, explorers visit the website to see if there are animations and webtoons of their interests as well as if they can be purchased. Soft users stay in a website in a short time. The 50% of the time is used for content consumption and the rest is utilized for commercials. Hard users spend a long time in a web site. The 70% of the time is used for content consumption and the rest is utilized for commercials and content search. Second, we defined the CS service type as NLP processing of corporate CS data. We extracted key words with high frequency of use and extracted related words that are close to vector distance from key word. We define that the distance between key words is proportional to the number of related words, and clustering key words by H-clustering the same number of related words. We grouped the service types into 6 groups, and grouped the 6 clusters into 'Content' and 'Account'. The first group, Content, has 3 service types. 'Advertisement', 'Consumption' and 'etc'. Also, the second group, Account, has 3 service types. 'Membership', 'Authentication' and 'Benefit'. In result, we generate three types of customer service chatbots for each personas. Content consumption', 'Account membership' and 'Account authentication' services for Soft users, 'Content consumption', 'Content', 'Advertisement', 'Account membership' and 'Account benefit' Service.

We confirmed the possibility of persona using the data through the literature review. Along with the study of Xiang, Hans-Frederick and Anil [28], this study showed a way to make persona using clickstream data of users. However, not every service can collect every single click stream. Rather, often, a collection of anonymous clickstreams can be accessible and retrievable using tools such as Beusable. And little streaming service users have been analyzed through clickstream data. Yet, Laftel is a popular streaming service that the public uses. And thus, our study can show the potential of data-driven design in general streaming services. We also confirmed the possibility of CS chatbot customized by person. However, previous studies have focused on answering the same answer with different sentences [1, 13, 15]. However, in this study, it is aimed to recognize service which is mainly used for each user and to provide optimized service for each persona.

This study is meaningful in that all of the methodologies used are data, and data processing is applied to UX methodology. It means that we quantify the usefulness of design based on user behavior data. In the basis of our result, Laftel can modify a CS service and validate the usefulness of our approach using A/B testing. We may increase the size of data and see the minimum number of data that can be useful enough for a service provider to have a meaningful result.

**All of the data used in the study are anonymous and there is no Problem to protect users' privacy.

Acknowledgements. This research was supported by Korea Institute for Advancement of Technology (KIAT) Grant funded by the Korea Government (MOTIE) (N0001436, The Competency Development Program for Industry Specialist).

References

1. Allen, C.O., Freed, A.R.: Persona-based conversation. U.S. Patent Application No. 14/557, 618 (2016)
2. Allo Homepage. https://allo.google.com/. Accessed 15 Feb 2019
3. Astro Homepage. https://www.astro.ai/. Accessed 15 Feb 2019
4. Au, I., et al.: User experience at Google: focus on the user and all else will follow. In: CHI'08 Extended Abstracts on Human Factors in Computing Systems, pp. 3681–3686. ACM, New York (2008)
5. Babylon Health Homepage. https://www.babylonhealth.com/. Accessed 15 Feb 2019
6. Beusable Homepage. https://www.beusable.net. Accessed 15 Feb 2019
7. Cooper, A.: The Inmates are Running the Asylum, The: Why High-Tech Products Drive us Crazy and How to Restore the Sanity. Sams, Indianapolis (2004)
8. Cui, L., Huang, S., Wei, F., Tan, C., Duan, C., Zhou, M.: Superagent: a customer service chatbot for e-commerce websites. In: Proceedings of ACL 2017, System Demonstrations, pp. 97–102. ACL, Pennsylvania (2017)
9. Erik, D.: The 2018 State of Chatbots Report: How Chatbots Are Reshaping Online Experiences. https://www.drift.com/blog/chatbots-report/. Accessed 15 Feb 2019
10. Jobpal Homepage. https://jobpal.ai/en/. Accessed 15 Feb 2019
11. Laftel Homepage. http://www.laftel.net. Accessed 15 Feb 2019
12. Leena Homepage. https://www.leena.ai/. Accessed 15 Feb 2019
13. Liu, B., et al.: Content-oriented user modeling for personalized response ranking in chatbots. IEEE/ACM Trans. Audio Speech Lang. Process. (TASLP) **26**(1), 122–133 (2018)
14. Louis, C.: Gartner's Top 10 Predictions For IT In 2018 And Beyond, Gartner. https://www.forbes.com/sites/louiscolumbus/2017/10/03/gartners-top-10-predictions-for-it-in-2018-and-beyond/#2b07633345bb. Accessed 15 Feb 2019
15. Makar, M.G., Tindall, T.A.: Automatic message selection with a chatbot. U.S. Patent No. 8,738,739 (2014)
16. Mobasher, Bamshad: Data mining for web personalization. In: Brusilovsky, Peter, Kobsa, Alfred, Nejdl, Wolfgang (eds.) The Adaptive Web. LNCS, vol. 4321, pp. 90–135. Springer, Heidelberg (2007). https://doi.org/10.1007/978-3-540-72079-9_3
17. Norman, D.: Human-centered design considered harmful. Interactions **12**(4), 14–19 (2005)
18. Parasuraman, A., Berry, L.L., Zeithaml, V.A.: Understanding customer expectations of service. Sloan Manag. Rev. **32**(3), 39–48 (1991)
19. Piccardi, T., Convertino, G., Zancanaro, M., Wang, J., Archambeau, C.: Towards crowd-based customer service: a mixed-initiative tool for managing Q&A sites. In: Proceedings of the SIGCHI Conference on Human Factors in Computing Systems, pp. 2725–2734. ACM, New York (2014)
20. Pittman, R.J.: Say "Hello" to eBay ShopBot Beta. https://www.ebayinc.com/stories/news/say-hello-to-ebay-shopbot-beta/. Accessed 15 Feb 2019
21. Pruitt, J., Grudin, J.: Personas: practice and theory. In: Proceedings of the 2003 Conference on Designing for User Experiences, pp. 1–15. ACM, New York (2003)
22. Reeves, L.M., Lai, J., Larson, J.A., Oviatt, S., Balaji, T.S., Buisine, S.: Guidelines for multimodal user interface design. Commun. ACM **47**(1), 57–59 (2004)
23. Replika Homepage. https://replika.ai/. Accessed 15 Feb 2019
24. Ritter, A., Cherry, C., Dolan, W.B.: Data-driven response generation in social media. In: Proceedings of the Conference on Empirical Methods in Natural Language Processing, Edinburgh, United Kingdom, pp. 583–593 (2011)
25. Say hello to Kai. https://kasisto.com/blog/say-hello-to-kai/. Accessed 15 Feb 2019

26. Singh, M.J., Cancel, D.: U.S. Patent No. 8,095,589. U.S. Patent and Trademark Office, Washington, DC (2012)
27. Woebot Homepage. https://woebot.io/. Accessed 15 Feb 2019
28. Zhang, X., Brown, H., Shankar, A.: Data-driven personas: constructing archetypal users with clickstreams and user telemetry. In: Proceedings of the 2016 CHI Conference on Human Factors in Computing Systems, pp. 5350–5359. ACM, New York (2016)

How to Co-design with Citizens for Successful Living Lab?

Masayuki Ihara$^{(\boxtimes)}$, Mizue Hayashi, Fumiya Akasaka,
Atsunobu Kimura, and Hiroshi Watanabe

NTT Service Evolution Laboratories, NTT Corporation, Yokosuka, Japan
ihara@acm.org, {mizue.hayashi.rt, fumiya.akasaka.cx,
atsunobu.kimura.cv, hiroshi.watanabe.bt}@hco.ntt.co.jp

Abstract. Service design is famous as an effective approach to determine the value to be delivered to users and to reflect that value in a service. Living Lab is one of the service design methods to offer co-design with citizens in actual environments. The main key to the success of Living Lab is co-design with citizens; it is also important to utilize technologies for effective design and the gathering of data for decision making in the design process. This paper introduces questionnaire responses from citizens on workshop difficulty and discusses utilization of technology tools and evidence data as a framework that ensures a successful Living Lab.

Keywords: Service design · Living Lab · Workshop · Survey

1 Introduction

Social businesses to solve social problems are being widely focused on under the influence of the Sustainable Development Goals (SDGs) [1]. In a small city, it is getting more difficult from just the local government to solve social problems, and many private companies are entering the social business field. This seems that both government services and those from private companies are needed for sustainable societies. The government of the United States is improving government services by collaboration between a government organization, the U.S. Digital Service [2], and a private organization, the 18F [3]. The service improvement is based on the design thinking approach [4]. We believe that private companies will have a positive role in resolving the social issues by launching research into methodologies that can create sustainable services for a better society.

2 Living Lab

In order to effectively design social services, service design is famous as an effective approach to determining the value to be delivered to users and to reflect it in one or more services [5]. Living Lab is based on co-design with citizens in actual environments [6–10]. The concept of Living Lab was first proposed in the United States in the 1990s by Lasher et al. [11]. As shown in [12], we have investigated instances of Living

© Springer Nature Switzerland AG 2019
A. Marcus and W. Wang (Eds.): HCII 2019, LNCS 11583, pp. 237–252, 2019.
https://doi.org/10.1007/978-3-030-23570-3_18

Lab held in Japan and Scandinavia and analyzed their use-case data. One advantage of Living Lab is that it makes it easier for citizens to become motivated, and so work together in designing and creating the service that they really want to use sustainably. Figure 1 shows our vision of the society wherein sustainable services created by the Living Lab process are provided to citizens.

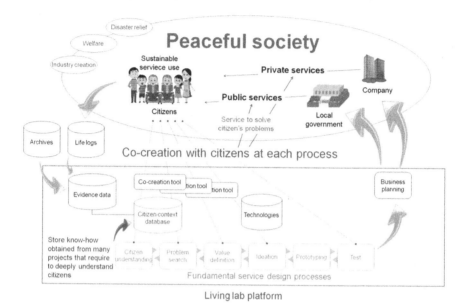

Fig. 1. Our vision of a society wherein sustainable services created by applying Living Lab are provided to citizens

In Living Lab, the service provider starts talking to citizens directly before starting service planning to identify their issues. The provider then co-creates prototypes to resolve the issues, and tests those prototypes in the intended real-life context. Prototyping and testing are conducted again and again. The iterated testing allows the service provider to learn what is deemed necessary by citizens while the citizens acquire new visions of a better life. Through this Living Lab process, a service provider can create a service that citizens truly want and will continue to use.

3   Workshop with Citizens

The main key to a successful Living Lab is co-design with citizens. The typical approach to co-design coordination is a workshop. Unfortunately, citizens are not designers, so it is not assured that they can participate in the workshop effectively. For example, workshop participants may be negatively affected by the facilitator's discussion control failures or by bad behavior of workshop participants such as upsetting the turn taking balance. In this study, we categorize problems in workshop with citizens in Table 1 and analyze them for exploring better designs for Living Lab.

Table 1. Categorization of workshop problems

P1	Problems with the participant himself/herself
P2	Problems with the facilitator
P3	Problems with other citizen participants
P4	Problems with participants from government or commercial entities
P5	Problems with the workshop space
P6	Problems with the topic targeted

4   Questionnaire Survey

We submitted online questionnaires to one thousand citizens in Japan (20's to 70's, male = 578, female = 422) on how difficult they felt the workshop for co-design was. Those citizens were people registered with a database of an online survey company. To determine the types of those citizens regarding "interest in solving social problems", we had those citizens respond to a pre-questionnaire consisting of 4 questions, PQ1 to PQ4, see Table 2.

Table 2. Questions in the pre-questionnaire

PQ1	How strongly do you feel satisfaction with current government services?
PQ2	Which social activity have you participated in?
PQ3	How do you evaluate yourself in social situations?
PQ4	How strongly do you want to contribute to solving social problems by indicating your opinion?

Figure 2 shows the results for PQ1. The citizens fell into two types: mild positive and mild negative. Figure 3 shows the results of PQ2. Most citizens had no experience of a workshop. Regarding psychological factors and activities of citizens (PQ3), Fig. 4 shows that most respondents had a high sense of responsibility, cooperativeness, autonomy and understanding of others' senses of values. Regarding a willingness to make a social contribution, Fig. 5 shows that the respondents expected the government and local communities, not non-profit organizations or commercial entities, to solve social problems.

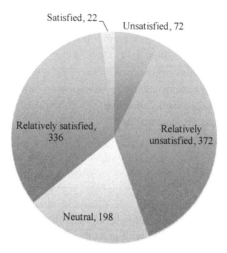

Fig. 2. The results of PQ1: How strongly do you feel satisfaction with current government services?

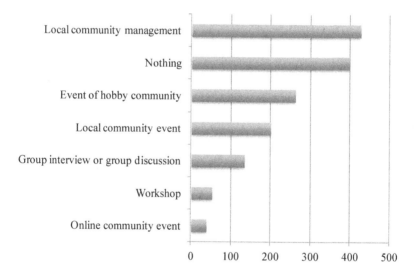

Fig. 3. The results of PQ2: Which social activity have you participated in?

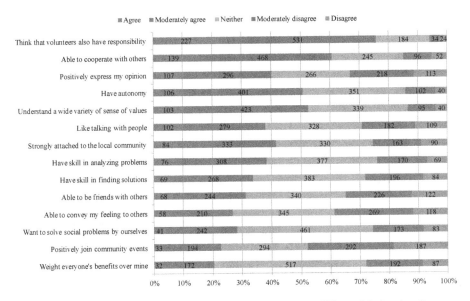

Fig. 4. The results of PQ3: How do you evaluate yourself in social situations?

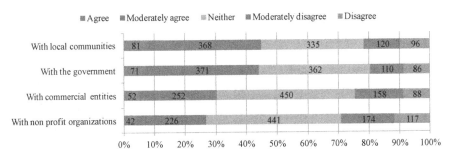

Fig. 5. The results of PQ4: How strongly do you want to contribute to solve social problems by indicating your opinion?

We investigated how people felt about workshops in co-design of social services. In this investigation, we showed some pictures shown in Fig. 6 so that respondents of the questionnaires can imagine a scene of the workshop. First, we posed the question;

Q1: Do you want to join a workshop to co-design a service to solve social problems?

Fig. 6. The pictures shown so that respondents of questionnaires can imagine a scene of the workshop

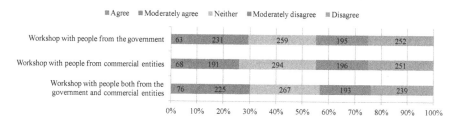

Fig. 7. The results of Q1: Do you want to join workshops to co-design a service to solve social problems?

Figure 7 shows the results of Q1. Most respondents were negative about joining a workshop. In order to know the motivations of those who wanted to participate, we posed the following question;

Q2: Why do you want to join a workshop?

Figure 8 shows that the top two reasons were to contribute to society and secure a benefit for themselves. Next, in order to know why they did not want to join one, we posed the question;

Q3: Why do you dislike the idea of joining a workshop?

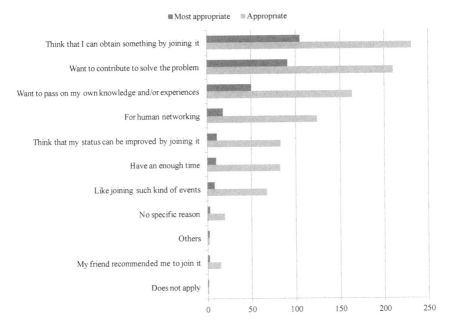

Fig. 8. The results of Q2: Why do you want to join workshops? (N = 301)

Figure 9 shows the three main reasons for their reluctance: a waste of time, no interest, and lack of discussion skills. According to the categorization of workshop problems shown in Table 1, we posed the question;

Q4: Which do you think is the most negative factor inhibiting a successful workshop?

As shown in Fig. 10, we found the following three problems were seen as hindering a workshop;

P1: Problems with the participant himself/herself.
P2: Problems with the facilitator.
P6: Problems with the topics targeted.

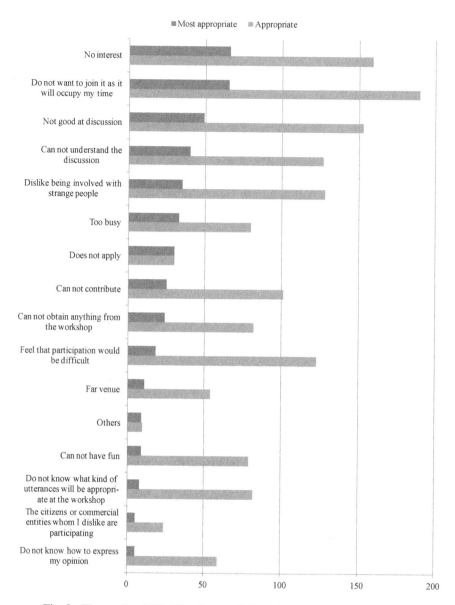

Fig. 9. The results of Q3: Why do you dislike joining workshops? (N = 432)

5 Detailed Analyses

In order to identify, in detail, the reasons of underlying each of the workshop problems, P1 to P6, we conducted an additional questionnaire surveys as follows;

AQ1: What is the main factor creating problems with the participant himself/ herself?

AQ2: What is the main factor creating problems with the facilitator?
AQ3: What is the main factor creating problems with other citizen participants?
AQ4: What is the main factor creating problems with participants from government or commercial entities?
AQ5: What is the main factor creating problems with the workshop environment?
AQ6: What is the main factor creating problems with the topics targeted?

The results of the above 6 additional questions are shown in Figs. 11, 12, 13, 14, 15 and 16. Figure 11 shows that citizens' motivation in joining a workshop is strongly dependent on the topic (social problem) to be discussed at the workshop. Figure 12 shows that many aspects of the facilitator impact the respondent's impression; poor skill in forming an opinion, poor skill of resolving an issue, poor skill in facilitating citizens to speak out, and self-assertive strong prejudicial comments that hinder the expression of citizens' speech. Regarding the problems with other citizen participants, Fig. 13 shows that assertiveness, low flexibility in understanding others' opinions, and no interest in the topic were raised. Regarding the participants from government or commercial entities, Fig. 14 shows that respondents were concerned about terms that citizens could not understand, and being biased by business interests as well as the above problems raised with regard to other citizen participants. Regarding the workshop environment, Fig. 15 shows that the respondents raised the following three problems; discussion flow, sorting out an issue, and time keeping. Regarding the topic targeted, Fig. 16 shows that respondents felt the following; unclear problem definition, excessive difficulty in solving the problem, unknown goal of discussion, confusion as to who would receive the benefit, and the benefit being surreptitiously directed to some unknown party.

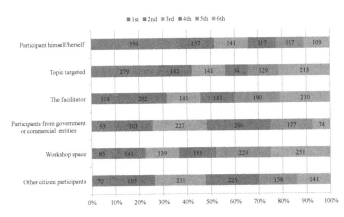

Fig. 10. The results of Q4: Which do you think is the most negative factor inhibiting successful workshops? (Please prioritize)

Finally, in order to investigate the possibility of solving social problems by a holding workshop among citizens, a government and commercial entities, we posed the following question;

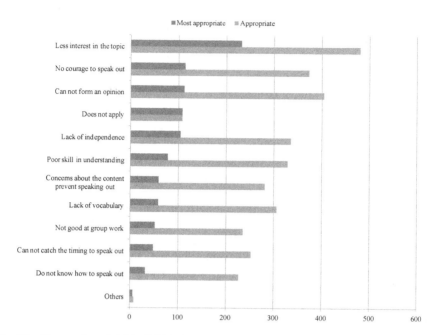

Fig. 11. The results of AQ1: Which is the main factor behind problems with participants (himself/herself)?

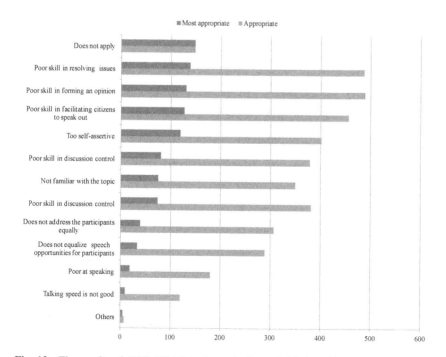

Fig. 12. The results of AQ2: Which is the main factor behind problems with facilitator?

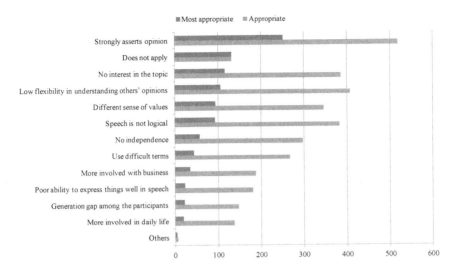

Fig. 13. The results of AQ3: Which is the main factor behind problems with other citizen participants?

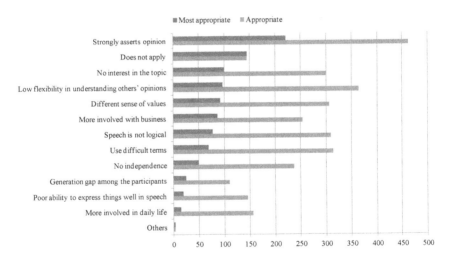

Fig. 14. The results of AQ4: Which is the main factor behind problems with participants from government or commercial entities?

Q: Do you think that social problems can be solved by a workshop among citizens, and government and commercial entities?

As shown in Fig. 17, we found that the respondents had low expectations of solutions coming from government or commercial entities. This is due to the following problems; too systematic discussion style, no passion in discussion, making use of citizens, and making money (see Fig. 18).

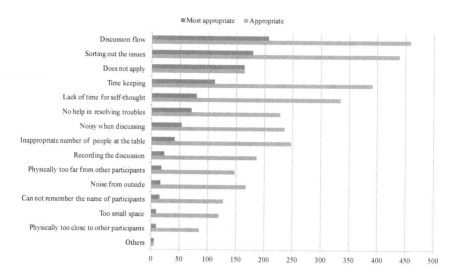

Fig. 15. The results of AQ5: Which is the main factor behind problems with workshop environment?

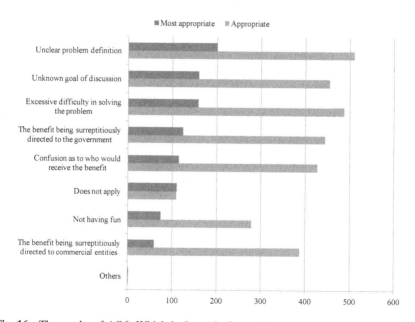

Fig. 16. The results of AQ6: Which is the main factor behind problems of targeted topic?

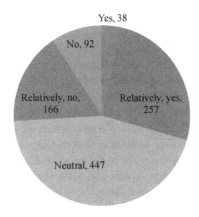

Fig. 17. The results of Q: Do you think that social problems can be solved by workshops among citizens, a government and commercial entities?

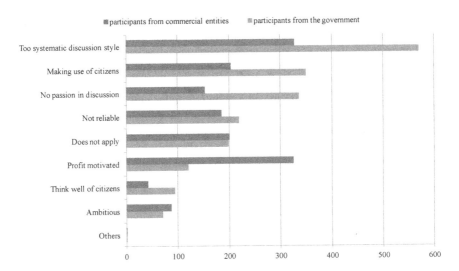

Fig. 18. The results of additional AQ4: How do you feel about participants from a government or commercial entities?

6   Discussion

As shown by the responses to the above questionnaires, workshops involving citizens and government and commercial entities face many kinds of problems. To tackle the difficulties posed by co-designing with citizens, two partial solutions seem likely; one is utilization of technology tools and other is evidence data. In most cases, the success of Living Lab projects strongly depends on individual facilitation skills. It would be very effective to be able to extract and transfer the skills of talented facilitators, to generalize them, and to reflect them in technology tools. Regarding the technology tools, we focused on the following three important functions; process management, streamlining of design processes, and encouragement of participant engagement. We developed a booklet to provide instruction in performing each service design process. The booklet provides novice designers with know-how about "What should I do?" to overcome the types of difficulties raised in the service design processes. With regard to the participants' engagement, we conducted a small Living Lab project where we tried to create an effective service for a community at a disaster recovery public housing complex [13]. The project revealed the importance of presenting many small ideas to citizens. This is because we could extract common factors from citizens' feedback to the many ideas. Note that humorous ideas are needed to relax the citizens enough that they can express their own opinion about the presented ideas. We intend to develop some tools for extracting common factors and generating humorous ideas.

Regarding the evidence data, we focused on utilizing archives of related data and the life logs of citizens. In the service design processes, workshop participants have to make a decision as a group to move forward/backward to the next/previous process. However, each participant may have a different opinion and sometimes they cannot convince the other participants. For example, in deciding which social problem to solve, some will focus on disaster relief while others will focus on the environment. An archive of fact data could help to convince not only other participants but also themselves. For example, it could be effective to present visualized archived data in a shared space while the workshop is in progress. Life logs of citizens such as daily GPS logs are fact data that are very persuasive in convincing participants because they are facts of their own activities. Daily life logs may allow familiar problems to be solved.

Another approach to a successful Living Lab, as an alternative to a workshop with citizens, is utilizing the knowledge acquired by social workers who know the problems that citizens are facing. Social workers care about the daily life of each citizen, so they know the background of the problems such as a trouble with family, physical/mental disability etc. A support tool based on a database of such social workers' knowledge or skills could be effective in solving the problems that citizens have.

7   Contribution to HCI Fields

Finally, as our future contribution to the fields of HCI, we discuss the potential of computation-supported (such as artificial intelligence) Living Lab. One possible utilization of HCI technologies to Living Lab is to support the interaction between participants in co-design by the use of tools or data such as the decision making support mentioned above. Each process in service design is based on analog methods including the facilitator's skills. As mentioned above, some technology tools may help workshop participants in the design processes. For example, a decision making support technology based on artificial intelligence may cover those areas that humans are not good at. For example, automatic evidence data pick-up technology based on artificial intelligence may help workshop participants while the facilitator can understand each participant's emotion and/or sense of values.

8 Related Work

A Living Lab approach is used in several areas. French et al. explored the implementation of Living Lab as a teaching approach in an undergraduate computer science curriculum for innovative thinking [14]. The results showed that Living Lab is effective for students who are not designers. Morgan's paper [15] describes how initial workshops are informing an ongoing process of co-development within two different Living Labs wherein people from public sectors are engaged. Ogonowski et al. highlighted several aspects of Living Lab: the selection of participants, maintenance of participants' motivation, establishment of a trust relationship, and the coordination of collaboration [16]. In Molinari's paper [17], Living Lab is assimilated to multi-stakeholder platforms of Public Private People Partnership. In Sandoval-Almazan's project, Living Lab is used for open innovation of public officials [18]. The project resulted that an innovation process requires a preliminary stage of building trust between governments and citizens. Schelle et al. have studied how to enhance user engagement in creative workshops by a tool [19]. Abel et al. focused on utilizing data in a Living Lab setting [20].

9 Conclusion

Our detailed questionnaires indicated that several workshop issues such as lack of facilitator's skills, behavior of workshop participants, etc. may negatively affect the attendees' impression of the workshop. From the questionnaire results we identified human factors such as willingness for social contribution, motivation for workshop participation, fundamental psychological features, dissatisfaction with government support, etc. Future work will include a design framework to employ technologies and data to enhance the Living Lab process.

References

1. United Nations: Transforming our world: the 2030 Agenda for Sustainable Development, General Assembly (2015)
2. The U.S. Digital Service. https://www.usds.gov. Accessed 1 Feb 2019
3. The 18F. https://18f.gsa.gov. Accessed 1 Feb 2019
4. Brown, T.: Design Thinking, Harvard Business Review (2008)
5. Stickdorn, M., Schneider, J.: This is Service Design Thinking: Basics. Tools, Cases. Wiley, New York (2012)
6. Kareborn, B.B., Stahlbrost, A.: Living Lab: an open and citizen-centric approach for innovation. Int. J. Innov. Region. Dev. 1(4), 356–370 (2009)
7. Almirall, E., Lee, M., Wareham, J.: Mapping living labs in the landscape of innovation methodologies. Technol. Innov. Manag. Rev. 2(9), 12–18 (2012)
8. Leminen, S.: What are living labs? Technol. Innov. Manag. Rev. 5(9), 29–35 (2015)
9. EC ENoLL: European Network of Living Labs (ENoLL) (2015). Openlivinglabs.eu
10. Yasuoka, M., Akasaka, F., Kimura, A., Ihara, M.: Living labs as a methodology for service design – an analysis based on cases and discussions from a systems approach viewpoint. In: Proceedings of the International Design Conference 2018 – Design 2018, pp. 127–136 (2018)

11. Lasher, D.R., Ives, B., Jarvenpaa, S.L.: USAA-IBM partnerships in information technology: managing the image project. MIS Q. **15**(4), 551–565 (1991)
12. Kimura, A., Akasaka, F., Kusano, K., Watanabe, H., Ihara, M.: Hypothesis-search type living lab for effective co-creation. In: Proceedings of the International Conference of Serviceology 2018 (ICServ2018), Taiwan, vol. 3, pp. 315–322 (2018)
13. Akasaka, F., Kimura, A., Ihara, M., Yasuoka, M.: How to make successful Living Labs?: Extraction and description of key know-how for living lab projects. In: Proceedings of the International Conference of Serviceology 2018 (ICServ2018), Taiwan, vol. 3, pp. 307–314 (2018)
14. French, J.H., Cox, C., Murphy, M.A.: A living lab approach for collaboration and innovative thinking in the CS curriculum. In: Proceedings of the 51st ACM Southeast Conference (ACMSE 2013). ACM, New York (2013). Article 38. https://doi.org/10.1145/2498328.2500086
15. Morgan, E., Webb, L., Goddard, N., Webb, J., Carter, K.: Co-designing innovations for energy saving in large organisations. In: Proceedings of the 2017 ACM Conference Companion Publication on Designing Interactive Systems (DIS 2017 Companion). ACM, New York, pp. 50–54 (2017). https://doi.org/10.1145/3064857.3079118
16. Ogonowski, C., Ley, B., Hess, J., Wan, L., Wulf, V.: Designing for the living room: long-term user involvement in a living lab. In: Proceedings of the SIGCHI Conference on Human Factors in Computing Systems (CHI 2013), pp. 1539–1548. ACM, New York (2013). https://doi.org/10.1145/2470654.2466205
17. Molinari, F.: Living Labs as multi-stakeholder platforms for the egovernance of innovation. In: Estevez, E., Janssen, M. (eds.) Proceedings of the 5th International Conference on Theory and Practice of Electronic Governance (ICEGOV 2011), pp. 131–140. ACM, New York (2011). http://dx.doi.org/10.1145/2072069.2072092
18. Sandoval-Almazan, R., Valle-Cruz, D.: Open innovation, living labs and public officials: the case of "Mapaton" in Mexico. In: Baguma, R., De', R., Janowski, T. (eds.) Proceedings of the 10th International Conference on Theory and Practice of Electronic Governance (ICEGOV 2017), pp. 260–265. ACM, New York (2017). https://doi.org/10.1145/3047273.3047308
19. Schelle, K.J., Gubenko, E., Kreymer, R., Naranjo, C.G., Tetteroo, D., Soute, I.A.C.: Increasing engagement in workshops: designing a toolkit using lean design thinking. In: Proceedings of the Multimedia, Interaction, Design and Innovation (MIDI 2015), Article 17. ACM, New York (2015). https://doi.org/10.1145/2814464.2814481
20. Abel, P., et al.: Re-writing the city: negotiating and reflecting on data streams. In: Proceedings of the 2015 British HCI Conference (British HCI 2015), pp. 147–156. ACM, New York (2015). http://dx.doi.org/10.1145/2783446.2783562

Methods for Designing Systems with Benefits of Inconvenience

Hiroshi Kawakami[1(✉)] and Toshihiro Hiraoka[2]

[1] Kyoto University, Yoshida-honmachi, Sakyo, Kyoto 606-8501, Japan
`kawakami@i.kyoto-u.ac.jp`
[2] Nagoya University, Chukusa, Nagoya 4648601, Japan

Abstract. This paper introduces the concept of "benefits of inconvenience (BI)" and proposes ideation methods for designing human-machine interaction (HMI) involving BI. HMI is the superset of HCI. Based on the assumption that convenience means saving time and reducing effort, efficiency, and high functionality provide convenience to users. On the other hand, for discussing HCI, interaction is essential that requires humans' time and efforts. In other words, inconvenience in the sense of above-mentioned assumption is essential for human-machine interactions. In this case, machines do not substitute humans but interact with humans, and inconvenience will be beneficial. This paper categorizes methods for designing systems with benefits of inconvenience into three classes.

Keywords: Benefits of Inconvenience · System design · Human Machine Interaction

1 Introduction

Fuben-eki is Japanese that stands for further benefits of a kind of inconvenience [1]. It does not reflect nostalgia but provides a standpoint of reviewing existing things and designing new systems.

In general, designers tend to pursue designing convenient systems. Convenience may enrich our lives in some ways, but it is not always beneficial for users. Convenient systems may inflate such harms as excluding users, depriving the pleasure of using systems, and eroding human motivation and skills.

Authors of this paper conducted several workshops and practices for designing systems that provide users with benefits of inconvenience. Such practices revealed that ideation (conceiving ideas) processes of designers can be classified into three patterns as reported in Sect. 3 of this paper.

2 Benefits of Inconvenience

2.1 Definition of Inconvenience

Longman dictionary online defined the concept of convenience as "the quality of being suitable or useful for a particular purpose, especially by making something

© Springer Nature Switzerland AG 2019
A. Marcus and W. Wang (Eds.): HCII 2019, LNCS 11583, pp. 253–263, 2019.
https://doi.org/10.1007/978-3-030-23570-3_19

easier or saving you time," and inconvenience as "problems caused by something which annoy or affect you." This paper employs more simple definitions of convenience/inconvenience as follows:

convenience: saving labor to attain a specific task,
inconvenience: being comparatively not convenient, i.e., requiring more labor than convenience,

where the word labor has the following meanings:

physical labor: requiring time and effort,
mental labor: requiring special skills, including the consumption of such cognitive resources as paying attention, memorization, and conception.

Stemming from the fact that labor-derived benefits exist, those simple definitions allow us to think inconvenience does not contradict benefit.

2.2   Fuben-eki Systems

Systems that provide users with the benefits of inconvenience are called fuben-eki systems. A conventional system design that produces convenient systems is evaluated in terms of one axis: the amount of labor. In this case, designers assume that convenience is always beneficial. In other words, as shown in Fig. 1, the axis of convenience/inconvenience and the axis of benefits/harms are identical or in the same direction.

Fig. 1. Conventional understanding the relation between convenience and benefits

Fuben-eki system design, on the other hand, affirms that convenience is independent with benefits and the axis of convenience/inconvenience and the axis of benefits/harms are orthogonal as shown in Fig. 2. In this case, we get the quadrants. The upper right quadrant denotes benefits of convenience, the upper left quadrant denotes benefits of inconvenience, the lower left quadrant denotes harms of inconvenience, and the lower right quadrant denotes harms of convenience.

2.3   Analyzing Fuben-eki Examples

We call examples that provide users with the benefits of inconvenience fuben-eki examples.

Not every inconvenient things have benefits. Somethings are just inconvenient and harmful. Such things are called negative examples and associated with points in the lower left quadrant of Fig. 2. Analyzing negative examples derives necessary conditions for approving fuben-eki systems:

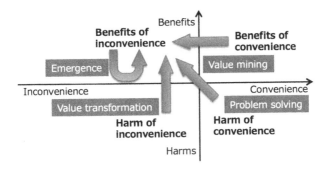

Fig. 2. Four types of ideation for fuben-eki systems

- Benefits and inconvenience belong to the user.
- Benefits are directly derived from the inconveniences.

The former condition means that "your inconvenience is my benefit" is the worst case. The latter condition requires that benefits of inconvenience are not derived without inconvenience.

Analyzing positive examples derives notions that which kind of inconvenience is in what sense beneficial. Those notions can be such support tools as reported in [2] for synthesizing new fuben-eki systems. Positive examples are associated with points in the upper left quadrant of Fig. 2.

3   Synthesizing Fuben-eki Systems

Conventional ideation support methods basically consist of divergence and convergence. At the divergence thinking stage, the quantity of ideas is required rather than their qualities, and criticism is forbidden. They are known as rules of Brainstorming. In this case, inconvenience is passively accepted. Namely, even the ideas are inconvenient, they are not eliminated.

On the other hand, this section positively utilizes inconvenience as a key to ideations. Many design workshops and design practices for designing fuben-eki systems have been conducted. In the workshop, participants are required to design systems focusing on making systems inconvenient. It is not only a requirement but also an activator of ideation.

Observing such activities revealed that ideation processes can be classified into three types that can also correspond to three types of transition of the quadrants as depicted by arrows shown in Fig. 2.

3.1   Ideation Through Problem Solving

The normal way of engineering is based on problem-solving. Roughly, the process consists of two steps: formulating a problem, and solving it by developing a new system. This process can be applied to developing fuben-eki systems as well, i.e., formulating harm of convenience as a problem and solving it by making target systems inconvenient. This process can be called problem-solving based ideation.

The arrow in Fig. 2 from the right lower quadrant to the left upper quadrant illustrates this style of ideation. Namely, it is the transition of harms of convenience to benefits of inconvenience.

Degradation of Navigation System: Degrade navigation system is one example designed by problem-solving based ideation. Navigation systems are generally convenient because they show clear and accurate information of maps. Unfortunately, the convenience deflates our motivation to remember the environment we are walking through. It is known as a problem called Cognitive Disuse Atrophy [3].

By using a navigation system, we only need to follow the fragments of direction to reach our destination, without exploring our surroundings or proactively understanding the area we are moving through. Therefore, we do not remember the roads. Using a navigation system reduce pleasurable explorations to merely idle transportation.

Degrade navigation system was developed as a solution to this problem. The normal navigation system was improved by introducing a novel inconvenience: map degradation [4]. This new system erases gradually the trails followed by users gradually from the map shown on the display of the navigation system. Compared with the normal navigation system, degrade navigation system is inconvenient, because users need to recall the surroundings of the trails when they use the system again; the system encourages users to remember landmarks more precisely. Figure 3 shows the interface of Degradation Navi.

Fig. 3. Screenshot of Degradation Navi interface

Barrie Aree: Barrier-*Aree* (*Aree* is a Japanese word that means existence) is another example of problem-solving based ideation. Compared with barrier-free, barrier-aree is an inconvenient design principle of residence because such minor obstacles as differences in floor levels are introduced to the living space on purpose. Residents are required their time and effort to walk through living spaces but barriers maintain physical and cognitive abilities of residents.

Barrier-aree was designed for solving the problem of physical and cognitive Disuse Atrophy [3] of residents of barrier-free residences.

3.2   Ideation via Value Mining

The second type of ideation methods is called value-mining. The major difference between problem-solving and value-mining is the supposition of problems to be solved. The Value-mining method does not expect problems of the target system.

The upper right quadrant in Fig. 2 represents happy states where the target system is convenient and users feel that it is beneficial. That is, there are no problems.

The Value-mining method starts from this happy state of the target system. At first, the target system is re-designed to be inconvenient one that requires more time and effort for using the system. Then, latent benefits are occasionally mined from the newly designed systems.

Conceptually, such ideation is a shift from the upper right to the upper left quadrant in Fig. 2. Namely, it is the transition of benefits of convenience to benefits of inconvenience.

Prime Number Ruler: Figure 4 shows an example of the results of such ideation: a prime number ruler, which is an original item of Kyoto University. A conventional ruler is only a convenient tool for measuring length, but an inconvenient prime number ruler allows users to devise their own ways to measure length.

At first, a ruler is selected as the target system to re-design. The normal ruler has no problem but participants of the design workshop are required to make rulers inconvenient. One of the ways to force users of rulers more consumption of time and efforts is restricting the tick marks to just prime numbers. The second step is mining benefits from prime number ruler. One benefit is allowing users to make a positive contribution to their tasks. A simple subtraction is required for measuring the length of a non-prime number. As a result, the task of measuring length requires users positive contribution.

Shared Space: Shared space can be seen as a political scheme of traffic designed by applying the value-mining method. It is not just a traffic scheme, but a design philosophy for creating good residential streets. A shared space design removes such traffic controls as traffic lights, excessive signage, and road markings. The easiest way to control traffic is separation. Separating the roads for automobiles,

Fig. 4. Prime number ruler

bicycles, and foot passenger seems to bring safety of the space. On the other hand, shared space design enforce automobiles, bicycles, and foot passenger to share space.

It is inconvenient because the subject of keeping safety is not public administrations but people who exist in the space. This inconvenience leads the "sense of agency" to the people and fosters civility which enables users of the space to move safely through the space using social cues.

3.3   Ideation by Emergence

The third type of ideation is based on the emergent design that is different from both problem-solving and value-mining types. This type of ideation requires designers to shove many fuben-eki designs into their brain and to extract their essences without representing them by linguistic concepts. Then this method generates ideas what pops into the mind of designers.

Conceptually, such ideation is a shift within the upper left quadrant in Fig. 2. Namely, it is the transition of some benefits of inconvenience to a new benefit of inconvenience.

This type of ideation is the most non-systematic one, and practitioners of this ideation method are expected expert skills of ideation. Professional designers call this method one hundred knocks. This style of thought requires accumulated knowledge and the ability to change knowledge flexibly. Analogical thinking or analogical transfer are frequently used in this type of ideation.

Note that the emergent idea may have the opposite which has harms of convenience. The opposite can be the start point of problem-solving type of ideation, but if the process of ideation is based on emergent, the emerged idea is the production of this third type of ideation.

Gesture Unlock System: One of the examples of the production of emergent-based ideation is gesture unlock of smartphone. Considering a method for unlocking a smartphone as the theme of design workshop, we conducted a battle-style brain-storming [5] and got a hundred ideas. Among them, a gesture-unlocking mechanism was proposed.

To unlock her smartphone, the user of this unlocking system has to shake the phone with almost the same movement as she registered in advance. It is an inconvenient system because unlocking is almost impossible when an arbitrary gesture is registered. Muscle memory is required to register gestures.

That is, this system provides users with a subjective benefit called personalization [6]. Muscle memory depends on the body of each person, and the gesture cannot be replicated by others.

Talking-Ally: Talking-Ally [7] can be seen as a result of emergent-based ideation. It is an utterance generation system for communication robots with disfluencies. Generally, convenient communication aims clear, correct, and fluent utterance. From this point of view, disfluency is inconvenient property. On the other hand, the speeches generated by Talking-Ally are not fluent. Based on the assumption that disfluencies were created as a result of the interactions between the speaker and the hearer, Talking-Ally is developed (Fig. 5).

Fig. 5. Talking Ally is a utterance generation system for communication robot with disfluencies [7]

4 Tools for Supporting Synthesize Fuben-eki Systems

4.1 Brainstorming Battle

Brainstorming battle [5] is known as an effective tool for supporting ideation of fuben-eki systems. Brainstorming is one of the most famous divergent thinking methods, where participants have to keep four rules; criticism forbidden, freewheeling encouraged, quantity, and combine and expand. The method has such problems as "participants do not follow the rules," "some participants do not provide any idea," while it is useful for an idea generation. Brainstorming battle is a reformed scheme of brainstorming where participants are divided into some teams and all of them compete for an idea with others in the battle style. It solves the problems of normal brainstorming.

Brainstorming battle is effective for enhancing ideation processes, especially for emergent-based ideation. Namely, it is a scheme for group-work to emerge a new idea of a fuben-eki system.

4.2   Knowledge-Base System and Card-Type Tools for Fuben-eki Design

To support designing fuben-eki systems, we developed a knowledge-base system [8] and a card-type tool [2]. As a result of analyzing almost 100 positive examples of fuben-eki design from the point of view of the relationship between inconvenience and benefit, inconvenience-oriented benefits are classified into eight categories [8]. The green cards (shown in Fig. 6) show these eight categories.

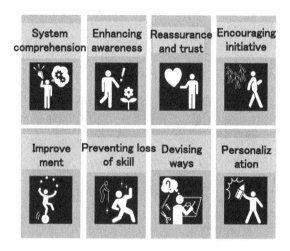

Fig. 6. Fuben-eki cards show example of benefits of inconvenience (Color figure online)

The knowledge-base system is based on TRIZ, which is a theory for inventive problem-solving. The knowledge-base of original TRIZ is the result of analyzing millions of patent claims that provides about 40 principles for technical innovations. A tool for searching for appropriate principles called Contradiction Matrix is also provided.

We extracted 12 principles for designing fuben-eki systems by analyzing positive examples of fuben-eki design and created a tool called Fuben-eki Matrix. The principles are shown on the yellow cards as shown in Fig. 7. The matrix was implemented on a web application [8] and a card-type tool [2].

Yellow cards show the variation of the way to make systems inconvenient. Therefore, they are useful at the first step of the value-mining method where designers are asked to make the target system inconvenient. Green cards show 8 categories of benefits that are derived from inconvenience. Therefore, they are useful at the second step of the value-mining method where designers are asked to mine benefits from the results of the first step.

The problem-solving method also utilizes cards. Green cards help designers to formulate harms of convenience at the first step of problem-solving, and yellow cards help to find the way to make the target system inconvenient for resolving the harms. The web system of Fuben-eki Matrix was designed for supporting designers following the process of problem-solving methods.

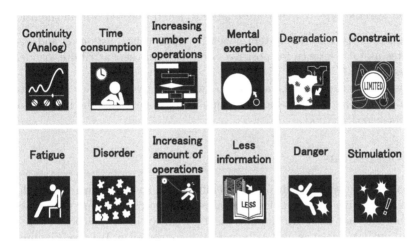

Fig. 7. Fuben-eki principle cards show ways to make system inconvenient (Color figure online)

4.3   Case-Base System for Fuben-eki Design

Fuben-eki matrix and Fuben-eki cards are based on principles that are derived from the abstractions of the examples. In contrast, we developed a case-base system [9] that does not rely on abstract principle but on analogies to examples.

In the case-base, positive examples of fuben-eki design are registered based on the following premises:

factors of inconvenience: fuben-eki must originate from inconvenience,
main task: fuben-eki need to be collateral effects of achieving main tasks,
comparison examples: convenience/inconvenience are comparative.

The positive examples are represented by at least their main tasks, their comparison examples, and the factors that are inconvenient. Embracing these notions, each example is represented by the following three types:

common type (χ): common attributes of the fuben-eki examples and its comparison example,
specific type (σ): objective functions specific to the fuben-eki example,
fuben-eki type (ϕ): subjective functions felt by users who use the fuben-eki example.

The process to use the case-base system is as follows:

1. select common type (χ) that are related to the target system (t) from the list of χ.
2. select desirable fuben-eki type (ϕ) from the list of ϕ.
3. select specific type (σ) that are related to t and selected ϕ from the list of σ.

Through this process, the system generates appropriate lists of ϕ and σ, then generates useful reference for positive examples and their attribute for ideating new design.

This process supports the analogy between positive examples and the target system. Therefore, the case-base system effectively supports the ideation of the emergent-based method.

5   Conclusions

This paper discussed benefits of inconvenience as a new direction of HMI design. It is an alternative direction of uncritical pursuits to convenience. Of course, this direction does not insist on the uncritical pursuit of inconvenience. There exist harmful inconvenience as well as beneficial inconvenience. We need to eliminate the harmful one and to focus on the beneficial one.

This paper showed three types of methods to ideate systems that incorporate the benefits of inconvenience. The types are based on problem-solving, value-mining, and emergence. The start points of three types of thoughts are associated with the three of quadrants that is defined by orthogonal axises of convenience/inconvenience and benefits/harms.

There remains another quadrant that reflects harms of inconvenience. It must be happy to change from the state of harms of inconvenience to the benefits of inconvenience. Some design examples are known as implementations of this state change. A hotel is inconvenient because it is hard to access, but the inconvenience gives us a scarcity premium. A restaurant is inconvenient because it is hidden from main streets, but the inconvenience provides us with a sense of a safe house.

Another design of this fourth type was given by Hiraoka [10]. Based on psychological theories with respect to motivation, an eco-driving system was designed that transform annoying labor into a worthy activity.

References

1. Kawakami, H.: Toward systems design based on benefit of inconvenience. J. Hum. Interface **11**(1), 125–134 (2009). (in Japanese)
2. Hasebe, Y., Kawakami, H., Hiraoka, T., Naito, K.: Card-type tool to support divergent thinking for embodying benefits of inconvenience. Web Intell. **13**, 93–102 (2015). https://doi.org/10.3233/WEB-150312,IOSPress
3. Miwa, K., Terai, H.: Theoretical investigation on disuse atrophy resulting from computer support for cognitive tasks. In: Harris, D. (ed.) EPCE 2014. LNCS (LNAI), vol. 8532, pp. 244–254. Springer, Cham (2014). https://doi.org/10.1007/978-3-319-07515-0_25

4. Kitagawa, H., et al.: Degrading navigation system as an explanatory example of "benefits of inconvenience". In: Proceedings of SICE Annaul Confirmed, pp. 1738–1742 (2010)

5. Hiraoka, T., Hasebe, Y., Kawakami, H.: Brainstorming battle. In: Proceedings of JSAI15 (2015). https://doi.org/10.11517/pjsai.JSAI2015.0_1D4OS22a5

6. Norman, D.A.: Emotional Design. Basic Books, New York (2004)

7. Ohshima, N., Ohyama, Y., Odahara, Y., Silva, P., Okada, M.: Talking-Ally: the influence of robot utterance generation mechanism on hearer behaviors. Int. J. Soc. Robot. **7**(1), 51–62 (2015)

8. Naito, K., Kawakami, H., Hiraoka, T.: Design support method for implementing benefit of inconvenience inspired by TRIZ. In: 12th ETRIZ TRIZ Future Conference, pp. 351–356 (2012)

9. Kawakami, H., Hiraoka, T., Riku, S.: Ideation support based on infomorphism for designing beneficial inconvenience. In: Lavangnananda, K., Phon-Amnuaisuk, S., Engchuan, W., Chan, J. (eds.) Intelligent and Evolutionary Systems. PALO, vol. 5, pp. 255–266. Springer, Cham (2016). https://doi.org/10.1007/978-3-319-27000-5_21

10. Hiraoka, T., et al.: Eco-driving support system to encourage spontaneous fuel-efficient driving behavior. J. Soc. Instrum. Control Engineers **48**(11), 754–763 (2012)

Design Research for Disability: A Case of Airport Service Design

Yi Liu[✉] and Ya Lei Li

Guangzhou Academy of Fine Arts,
No. 257 Changgang Road, Guangzhou, People's Republic of China
64947357@qq.com

Abstract. 1980s, North Carolina State University developed the concept of universal design under the auspices of the federal government of the United States. It has passed through nearly half a century of development. After the concept of barrier-free has come into the field of sociology, it has gained wider social recognition and entered the field of public social policy formulation. Barrier-free design has become the foremost choice of public policy. There are two meanings of barrier-free research in the sociological field: it is the social model of barriers; the second is the birth and research of the universalism of barrier experience; for this reason, the analysis will be carried out from three perspectives: the study of social discrimination against disabilities and the development of barrier-free design research. In today's digital society, digital means and services have covered all aspects of our lives. It covers from public government services to the general social needs of the individual. However, digital products and systems in these fields are designed on the basis of "robust constants". It does not take into account how disabled people integrate into the digital society. Concepts such as universal design and barrier-free design only focus on the relationship between people and objects in physical space. And the interaction between human and physical interface in the process. They have not put forward rational solutions and design ideas for the disabled with digital interfaces and products. Taking the airport service design as an example, this paper tries to put forward new solutions for the disabled on the airport digital travel. From the point of view of system thinking and service, combined with the design method of Internet product experience, the general design based on physical space in the past is moving towards the direction of digitalization and service systematization.

Keywords: Disability · User experience · Universal design · Barrier free

1 Social Concern and Current Situation on Disability

With the development of social modernization, the social "demand" for products and spirit has gradually surpassed the simple material and basic life satisfaction, and then moved to a richer spiritual level. Moreover, the groups concerned by the society are gradually transiting from the mainstream group to the vulnerable group and minority group. The book Fourth Consumption Age (2012), by Miura Atsushi, a Japanese sociological scholar, clearly describes the development and formation of consumer

© Springer Nature Switzerland AG 2019
A. Marcus and W. Wang (Eds.): HCII 2019, LNCS 11583, pp. 264–278, 2019.
https://doi.org/10.1007/978-3-030-23570-3_20

society since the Industrial Revolution. And he divided the consumer society into four stages. The first consumption age defined by Miura Atsushi was the 30 years from 1912 to 1941. In the past three decades, urban population was growing, and the city-centered business model began to take shape, including the birth of department stores, popular magazines, chain stores and modern apartments. The first consumer society formed a city-centered consumption era, which only accounted for one to two percent of the middle class of the society at that time. But from here, a modern westernized way of life has come into being. However, in the first consumer society, most workers provide services for the production of goods for a small number of people above the middle class. That is to say, the enjoyment of services is limited to the middle class living in the city or above. The 30-year period from 1945 to 1974 was defined as the second consumer society. In the second consumer society period, the population gradually gathered to cities. Meanwhile, the mass production Commodities represented by household appliances began to be popularized and promoted throughout the country. If the main object of the first consumer society is still a few elites in society, then the second consumer society benefits from the real development of modern industrialization and the gradual popularization of mass production of goods in all corners of life. Ultimately, it benefits a wide range of mainstream social groups. During the 29 years from 1975 to 2004, economic growth slowed down. The society began to attach importance to the rights and interests of individuals, human rights awareness and so on. As a result, consumption began to shift from family to individual. This kind of individualized change not only exists as a unit of consumption, but also expands the danger of social isolation. Individual egoism has increased. The individualization trend got gradually changed since 2000. Especially the global financial tsunami in 1997, the SARS epidemic in 2003, and the Wenchuan earthquake in 2008, a series of global disasters make people feel the changeability of consumer society. At the same time, people also realize how important it is for families, neighborhoods, society, volunteer organizations, NGOs and other associations to connect. Since then, people have begun to re-examine the consumer society and pay more attention to broader social services. The research on social vulnerable groups has also become the social mainstream concern. Such topics as "fairness", "rights and interests" of vulnerable groups and their convenience in social life have become new research subjects in the academic circles. Also in this period, the design field began to develop interest in "service", and the subject of service design began to be established, which realized the transformation from material to service, and made human beings more concerned.

According to the sociological research and analysis of consumer market, we can divide the market development into four stages macroscopically: National (focusing on the state), Family (focusing on the family), Individual (focusing on the individual), and finally Social (focusing on the society). The word "society" in Latin means "partner" and "connection". However, in the past various stages of market development, with the development of the consumer market, people's personal awareness has increased excessively, and it is more and more difficult for people to realize the connection between themselves and others. While being in society, we do not feel connected to others. Or there are estrangements and communication barriers in social relations. The current service design is the key to solve this contradiction.

The research of this topic is based on the service design of airport public service. In the scope of the study, we focus on the special groups in airport services. As mentioned above, airport service is an important scenario of today's social system which pays attention to society. Therefore, the study of public service design based on airport service has important reference and guiding significance for service design in other fields. Airport scenario is a manifestation of a variety of needs and contradictions. Airports are different from general government public services. General government public services are compulsory, such as taxation, civil affairs, transportation, safety and so on. This type of government public service emphasizes the subjectivity of service institutions, for example, "taxation is the duty of every citizen" - tax declaration work of the tax bureau is more about persuasion. In public service institutions such as airports, the status and role of service providers are weakened. The user in the service chain is the main body. Therefore, in this service system, we need to pay more attention to users 'feelings and experiences. Design and Improvement of Service System shall be centered on traveling users. However, airport services are not the same as general commercial services. Airport services are partly mandatory because of security and other reasons. It is not entirely based on the wishes of consumers. In addition, the airport is a window unit for the outside world, which reflects the values and tolerance of a region and society to various ethnic groups, cultures and strata. Therefore, the degree of concern and care for people with behavioral disabilities at airports has a direct impact on the perception and understanding of the city's tolerance and civility of people for people around the world to a certain extent.

2 Social Policy Concerns for Disabilities

The definition of people with behavioral disabilities includes the elderly, children and the disabled. Since 1999, China has entered into aging society. It is estimated that by 2025, the elderly population in China will reach 280 million, accounting for 18.4% of the total population, and by 2050 it will reach about 400 million. According to the Second National Sample Survey on Disabilities organized by the State Council in 2006, the population of disabled persons in China reached 82.96 million. A total of 70.5 million households with disabilities account for 17.8% of the total number of households in China. The elderly and the disabled are citizens without general behavioral abilities. Therefore, paying attention to the needs of these two groups has a special indicative role in the design of people with behavioral disabilities. At the same time, the elderly and the disabled have many similarities in some characteristics such as lack of physical characteristics, so they can be regarded as one group in study. Children are not exactly equal to adults in mental and behavioral abilities. But they are often accompanied or assisted by adults when they travel. Therefore, in design research, this kind of demand can be regarded as a group behavior.

The state has promulgated many laws and social norms for the protection of the elderly and the disabled since 2010, including the Law of the People's Republic of China on the Protection of the Rights and Interests of the Elderly, the Law on the Protection of the Disabled etc. On the one hand, the promulgation of such laws and regulations has improved the care for special groups in all aspects of social life. On the other hand, it defines the new latitude and direction of public social services for special groups from a more macro perspective. In conclusion, there are five main principles:

(1) Independence Principle: People with behavioral disabilities should be regarded as individual citizens with independent behavioral abilities, and entitled to social services without discrimination. At the same time, they can do things independently without additional assistance.

(2) Participation Principle: to let people with behavioral disabilities participate in the normal group, instead of separating them from other groups. Especially in the interaction of all aspects of public service, they should be involved in the process of experience.

(3) Care Principle: they should be taken care of and protected by family and society. At the same time, to ensure their privacy needs and quality of life;

(4) The principle of self-realization: people in special groups should be allowed to fully seek opportunities to reach out to society and obtain the educational, cultural, spiritual and service resources provided by society;

(5) Principle of Dignity: people in special groups should enjoy dignity and protection of their rights and interests in life. They should be guaranteed not to be abused and treated unfairly, and not to be evaluated on the basis of their economic contribution.

In August 2001, the Ministry of Housing and Construction, the Ministry of Civil Affairs and the China Disabled Persons Federation issued and implemented the Code for Barrier-free Design of Urban Roads and Buildings. In 2012, the latest edition of the Code for Barrier-free Design (GB0763-2012) was issued, which is a compulsory standard throughout the People's Republic of China. It can be seen that our country and society are gradually increasing the attention on people with behavioral disabilities.

Influenced by the government's advocacy and the mainstream orientation of society, various industries in the market have made many new attempts and explorations in the care and services of people with behavioral disabilities. Banks have begun to develop special service processes for users in special groups, set green channels, special counters for special customers, and even provide door-to-door services for customers in need. Railway systems across the country have correspondingly set green channels for special groups. In the international community, accessible facilities such as parking spaces, seats and corridors for the disabled have become the standard configuration of any public service. In the United States, Germany and other places, buses must be equipped with a device called Kneeling bus. Through this device, people with disabilities can easily take public transport. In American supermarkets, shopping carts and elevator fixtures for the disabled have also become standard configurations. In the international community, the introduction boards and guidance systems of scenic spots must include Braille. Moreover, the design and production of each guide plate deliberately makes the graphics into a perceptible concave and convex feeling, which is convenient for blind users to use and recognize through tactile sensation.

Under the impetus of policy environment and social trend, the design of special groups has become an important link and part of consideration of any product or service. However, as for the relevant design of the disabled groups, the existing category still focuses on the exploration of the shallow needs of the disabled groups. There is lack of research and attention on the deep psychological needs of the disabled, such as fairness, participation, dignity and self-realization, which are required by national and international trends. The solution of these problems is not simply the design of a single product, but also systematic study and even changes of the whole service system and process. The research of this subject is based on this point.

In the development and research of foreign enterprises. Softbank also offers new exploration and solutions to the cognitive gap between the elderly living alone and digital products. Old people are "new immigrants" in the digital world. The life style and interaction mode they are familiar with are still in the "simulation" era [1]. From desktop telephones, tape recorders, players to telegrams and newspapers in public services, etc. These old models and products constitute their experience and perception of the world. In the current digital mode. They naturally feel strangeness and distance. Therefore, using the old people's familiar interaction mode and cognitive model to reconstruct the digital world, create a familiar environment for them can let them enjoy long-distance chat of social interaction, the convenience of online video, let them perceive the affection of offspring from other places through the digital world, and let the new technology bring them the joy of being in the digital society again, which is an important Design Proposition in the digital society.

3 Study on Travel of Disabled Persons at Airport

3.1 Methodology

This project adopts participatory design method. By inviting disabilities to participate directly in the field research of the airport, we can directly obtain the measurement data of the physical and behavioral characteristics of the disabled in the scene. At the same time, during the whole process of accompanying the disabled, we pay attention to obtaining the thoughts of the disabled people in the process of traveling. By combining with the objective observation data, we compare the objective observation data with the subjective data of the disabled people to obtain our insight into the travel behavior of the disabled at the airport [2].

In terms of research methods, the research group adopted the method of a combination of observation with interview, while serving multilateral relationship in the process of designing the methodology of the subject. In practice, the disabled affairs in society should include three main aspects: the supervision of service - the government, the service provider - the airport and other service agencies, and the service receiver-the special group. Therefore, in this topic, we have conducted a survey on the various interests of the design of disability services [3]. For the government, which is in the supervision of service, the team interviewed the leaders of Guangzhou Disabled Persons Federation, and made a basic understanding of the protection, regulations and current situation of the disabled in public space. As a semi-official organization, the Guangzhou Disabled Persons Federation naturally has the background of the government. Therefore, interviews with the Disabled Persons Federation can obtain the government's thoughts and opinions on the relationship, importance and development direction of the cause of disability in the government's public service. In the research and investigation of service provider, we interviewed and observed the airports, airlines and the relevant functional personnel of various departments connected with the airport, so as to obtain further operational data and practical insight. For the service receiver, we invited the disabled people on the reception side and visited the whole service flow of the disabilities at the airport, tested and recorded all contacts.

3.2   Travel Procedure for Airport Disabilities

The travel process of the disabled at the airport is not much different from that of the normal people. But in terms of service supervision, service provision and service receiving needs. Although they have implemented their respective work within their respective duties to the extreme, there are still great service misunderstandings. As a result, it has always been difficult to improve services for the disabled in public.

Ideas and Opinions from Service Supervision Side
Service supervision of special population has always been the responsibility of Guangzhou Disabled Persons Federation. During the visits to the Disabled Federation and the focus group research on the disabled, the research group received many valuable advice and opinions.

Relevant needs of the disabled have been the focus of government work in recent years. In terms of public services, the government has promoted barrier-free facilities standards and formulated standards for passengers with disabilities in the field of public transport. In the field of laws and regulations, the government makes every effort to provide relevant laws and regulations to protect the interests of the disabled. However, in terms of standards for service implementation, no relevant implementation norms have been introduced from the government level. For example, although there are service standards for the disabled, but not specific description and definition of the classification standards for the disabled. Therefore, in society, there are many problems that needs of the disabilities are occupied by others, which are often in conflict with other needs in society. At this time, it is more necessary for all disables to work together to screen and analyze the needs, and to make compromises of the relevant needs of the disabilities. For example, in the research, we found that with the popularization and application of modern motor and battery technology, electric wheelchair has been deeply favored by the disabled for its convenience and mobility. However, in the airport travel scenario, the airport's restrictions on batteries are based on the characteristics of power bank products. As a result, all disabled people's electric wheelchairs cannot be consigned or transported by airlines in China.

Views on Service Provider Side
Service providers are mainly divided into two parts in the domestic aviation industry: airlines and airport services. Airport services mainly provide ground services for passengers and docking airlines. Therefore, airlines and airports need a complete process docking. Airport service process for ordinary passengers is a complete set of service process, which has been verified and used for a long time by most airports in the world. It is a mature and efficient service system. This set of processes has been integrated and linked with various systems of airports and airlines and become an

important link for the normal operation of the huge Airport system. However, services for the special population are neglected and missed in the software and hardware systems of airport services.

In recent years, various social service fields have started a large-scale "information" wave of products and services. From domestic tax service, public transport service to all levels of people's social life, "autonomous" and "digital" services have begun. In general, this reduces the time cost and operation cost of the public in the field of public services. However, from the perspective of the disabled, the digital life has brought new difficulties to their already extremely inconvenient accessible social life. Airport travel scenario is also an important example. At present, the airport began to promote "self-check-in" on a large scale, so that ordinary passengers can quickly print itineraries, check baggage and board. However, this "self-help" process has brought many problems to the disabled.

From the perspective of service provider, the self-service they provide for passengers is universal. For the disabled, they think that most of them will be accompanied by people with good mobility because of the inconvenience of travel. Therefore, all the facilities provided by the airport can only be operated by normal people. For the disabilities traveling alone, airports are more inclined to provide one-to-one service for these special passengers. But such services consume more resources and cost more. Therefore, one-to-one airport services need to be booked in advance by telephone and website. For all airports responding to the needs and services of the disabled, the fundamental logic lies in the attribution of the problem of disability and the question of which party should be responsible for the problem. Airports are more inclined to attribute the problem to the disabled themselves: because they do not have the ability to behave, they need to use their own resources to make up for the deficiencies, including accompanying and caring by healthy relatives. At the same time, in order to provide better services for the disabled, the airlines also specifically limit the number of disabled people on different types of aircraft (Table 1).

Table 1.

Model	Limit number of persons	Remark
A330	4 Disable Peoples	Only economy class available for all models. No unaccompanied children are allowed in first class or business class
B737	3 Disable Peoples	
B777	5 Disable Peoples	
A380	8 Disable Peoples	
B787	4 Disable Peoples	
A321/320/319	3 Disable Peoples	
E190	2 Disable Peoples	

The Disabilities 'Views on Airport Travel

Through research, it is found that there are great differences in the aspects of concept consciousness, cognitive behavior and human–machine relationship scale for airport travel between the disabilities and the service providers. Through the perspective of the disabilities, we can see that the designers designed the airport design process for the convenience of the disabilities [4]. But from the perspective of the disabilities, these processes create a lot of inconvenience for them. We elaborate on the study of this group from three parts: concept consciousness, cognitive behavior and human–machine relationship scale (Table 2).

Table 2.

Scene	Pain points	Remark
Metro Exit B	Take a circle to the escalator after leaving the subway gate	Their habit has always been to look for escalators through blind paths
Escalator (No. 1)	1. The button on the middle floor of the escalator shows the arrival of the parking lot it is opposite direction of the people stream when walking out of the escalator 2. No further instructions were given after leaving the staircase or escalator. it is opposite direction of the people stream when walking out of the escalator	
Explosion proof inspection (1st floor)	No signs of how to get to the hall after the explosion-proof inspection, and searching of the escalator	
Escalator (No. 2)	After finding the escalator, the front and back of the escalator are not obvious. At first glance, one cannot tell which side the door is	Walk straight to the door of the escalator, but the interviewee goes around to the back of the escalator before he realizes the position of the door
Departure Hall (3rd floor)	There were no clear instructions when we arrived at the departure hall	Interviewee's demand for arrival at departure hall is to avoid extra roads but to be accompanied by airport personnel during the whole journey is not necessary
Service counter	Without low counter	The back of the escalator is facing the service counter, so when you first see the service counter, you go straight towards it

(continued)

Table 2. (*continued*)

Scene	Pain points	Remark
Enquiry counter	There are high and low counters, but they did not make inquiries there	The inquiry counter is opposite the service counter, that is, ahead of the user's left-hand direction, which is far away, so it is not seen
Self service check-in	1. To get close to the check-in machine, the wheelchair will lean towards the machine, so will the body. One needs to look up at the machine, and you can't see the screen clearly due to reflecting light 2. When looking for self-service consignment, the self-service check-in machine blocked the self-service consignment cabinet and one has to search for a long time. (sight limit for people on Wheelchairs)	
Self service consignment	1. There is a height difference in front of the self-service consignment machine, and the cushion is not suitable for wheelchair movement 2. The baggage tray is a little heavy 3. One has to look up to the machines for self-service consignment	1. A person travels with a backpack (a bag can be held in his hand and a bag hung behind his wheelchair). It is not easy to take out the backpack behind the wheelchair, but she could manage even if it was heavier 2. The machine interface of self-service consignment is operable 3. The existing wheelchair consignment still has to go to the manual counter. If the wheelchair self-service consignment cannot be solved, she will not choose self-service, it is more convenient for her to go directly to the manual counter 4. After taking the tray for luggage, she pushed the checking machine by hand so that her wheelchair could slide backwards

(*continued*)

Table 2. (*continued*)

Scene	Pain points	Remark
Manual counter	1. At the low counter, the staff need to stand up to pass the certificate to the interviewees 2. Check the size, weight and power supply of wheelchair when checking in wheelchairs 3. Wheelchairs can now be assigned for replacement of airport wheelchairs, or can be checked in at the boarding gate after being checked for compliance	1. Interviewees preferred to use their own wheelchairs and check them in at the boarding gate because she felt that the wheelchairs at the airport were unsafe and the size was too large (the same size as international passengers) 2. When choosing to check in the wheelchair at the boarding gate, you need to apply/check/make notes on the check-in system (sit on your wheelchair and check). The batteries of the electric wheelchair needs to be checked. Large wheelchairs also need to be checked at the oversized luggage counter 3. It takes 20–40 min to wait for the wheelchair at the airport 4. Wheelchair consignment is not packaged, only wrapped with tape, many disabled passengers are not confident about wheelchair consignment, especially for expensive folding wheelchairs, they prefer to take on the plane
Barrier-free toilet	1. The interviewees did not find that the barrier-free toilet door was open 2. Barrier-free toilets do not show whether anyone is using them 3. Barrier-free toilet available sign is not obvious 4. At the top of the sign, there was no sign of Barrier-free toilet. The interviewees did not know whether there was a Barrier-free toilet	1. When the interviewees were using the bathroom, two cleaning staff did not notice they were in the bathroom. They roughly tried to open the door handle of the bathroom and made loud noises 2. Interviewees spent 20 min in the bathroom 3. The door needs to be pulled outward, which is more difficult at this time, and it is more convenient to push out
Food and beverage department	1. The restaurant lacked instructions and route guidance 2. The toilet near the restaurant also lacks instructions, and toilet route guidance	Interviewees mentioned that the existing shopping mall K11/Hai zhu City in Jiangnan Xikou is better, and the elevators are fast; while Guangbai does well, but it takes long time to wait for the elevators

(*continued*)

Table 2. (*continued*)

Scene	Pain points	Remark
Security check	1. Security counter service personnel need to stand up and check certificates	1. Wheelchairs can directly pass through Security door 2. During the security inspection, the interviewees supported themselves with hands on wheelchair 3. Family members and special groups of passengers pass security inspection at the same passage
Private inspection room	1. The chairs in the examination room are not safe 2. Lack of relevant auxiliary facilities 3. Lack of warmth	1. Suggested that it was important to resettle special people 2. Some body AIDS need to be disinfected after they are removed and examined
Escalator	1. There are no instructions on the escalator 2. In the elevator, the interviewees were in the opposite direction to everyone else	1. Because there are no escalator and signs, after seeing the hand lift, you can only choose two roads: to the left or right to try to find the escalator
Special passenger rest area	Interviewees prefer to go directly to the boarding gate	1. Special passenger rest area, the middle has more seats, and the chairs are not for wheelchair users 2. The rest area is enclosed 3. At the special passenger lounge counter, you can check the change of the boarding gate and the delay of the plane. Special staff will remind passengers of flight information 4. A little earlier than ordinary passengers to reach the boarding gate for boarding 5. After security inspection, we rely more on the guidance of staff
Boarding gate	1. Face recognition is not suitable (requires more than 1.2 m) 2. Passengers use face recognition and do not know the need to scan tickets to get the tickets out	Special people use manual check-in channels, and enjoy priority in check-in boarding.

- Concept Consciousness: Disabled people do not think they are the weak in the real-life scene. In other words, in their view, they want society to treat them as normal people, rather than special people who need "special care" in society. Therefore, they insist that all facilities, buildings and products in society should meet their needs. what the normal people can handle should also be operated independently by the disabilities. "Help" in society is more like "discrimination" to them in a sense. People with disabilities need the society to treat them as normal people, rather than specialization.
- Cognitive Behavior: In the airport travel scene, the disabled people's perception of information and symbols in the scene is quite different from that of normal people. Navigation is probably the most common problem users face in specific space and scenarios. At the airport, where should we go after the boarding pass and which route can we take to get to the security check-in and boarding gate? All of these require the guidance system in the scene. The information faced by the disabled is often different from that faced by the normal people. For example, consulting before boarding and baggage checking, if the disabled need manual assistance, they need to find a special "low counter" for related operations. Security checks are more different from those of healthy people. Disabled people have special access. Especially for disabled people with prosthetic limbs, there will be special private checkrooms at airports. However, as for the current guidance service system, the airport has not set up a guidance system for the disabled in line with their cognitive style. Just like the "bathroom" sign we often use. The sign of the bathroom for the disabled is different from that of the general one. But the bathroom sign of the disabled did not appear in the general guidance system of the airport. Moreover, wheelchair-bound disabled people usually have low vision. Therefore, the guidance information, flight information and signs set according to the normal value often cause trouble to them because of the problem of sight. The specific contents are shown in the table below.
- Research on Human–Machine Relations: From the perspective of human–machine relationship, we study and analyze every micro-contact in the system, and find that there are many misunderstandings in the use and design of equipment. For example, after ergonomic measurements of boarding pass printing equipment, we found that disabled users would not operate the equipment positively in the way we envisioned. According to their life experience, they will sit sideways in wheelchairs. Which means the data we got changed completely (see Fig. 1).

Fig. 1. The gesture of participator, when they approach to the automatic service machine.

When facing the device frontally, the disabilities need to reach their arms up to 84 cm to touch the bottom of the screen. the line of sight angle and the tilt angle of the screen are 120° [5]. Which makes it almost impossible for the disabled to read the information on the screen.

In addition, the size of wheelchair does not match the standard size of the security channel. Therefore, wheelchairs and people on them need to be separated when the disabled need to pass through the security channel. In this way, it will cause great trouble to the people who carry out security checks and the disabled. Through interviews with disabilities and data acquisition [6]. We have learned that disabilities usually arrive at the airport six hours in advance for relevant formalities and preparations. Which means it is two hours more than that of healthy people. There is still a lot of room for the airport to make adjustments and changes for the travelling of the disabled (see Fig. 2).

Fig. 2. The measurement of the airport security check room

4   Conclusion

Through the research and data acquisition of this subject, the team and the airport sorted out and analyzed the data collected, counted the airport service resources and the service costs that can be invested, and further studied flow characteristics, service demand and matching degree of service resources of peak and normal periods of airport services [7]. Through co-organizing workshops with various departments of the airport, we have agreed on the weight index system composed of several latitudes of "service cost", "importance" and "proportion of service resources", and screened out the executable service contacts. Combining with the improvement of the whole service process, we have obtained a new service design system for the disabled [8] (see Fig. 3).

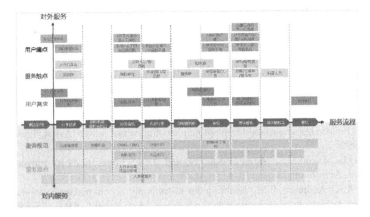

Fig. 3. The new blue print of airport's disable service (Color figure online)

The research of this project is based on the service system of airport. The research team made flexible use of research methods, comprehensive use of interviews, field research, human–machine relationship measurement and other methods into the research process. Based on the literature research methods and the basic theoretical framework of service design adjustment, this paper makes a macro-analysis of service system from a systematic perspective [9]. By integrating the details of the data in the micro contacts with the user's perspective, we can get a rich and complete picture of the service system from different perspectives, so as to provide a complete research framework and data support for the next service system design [10].

Although the airport service system is an individual case, through the design and research of the overall service flow of the airport, we can find many problems in the field of social public services for the disabled. The macro-adjustment of the service system, as well as the improvement and change of the micro-service contacts can all broaden the design thinking and methods of public services and product design. In the past, we tend to treat products as a separate product in barrier-free design. Barrier-free products are more about the "man–machine" relationship between people and products in design thinking. However, in the service system, every contact improvement is linked with other contacts [11]. Therefore, it is a new attempt of this project to consider the needs of the disabled systematically and to provide new design ideas from the design methodology of the system.

References

1. Gummesson, E.: Service design. TQM Mag. **2**(2), 11–20 (1993)
2. Erl, T.: SOA Principles of Service Design. Prentice Hall, Upper Saddle River (2008)
3. Goldstein, S.M.: The service concept: the missing link in service design research. J. Oper. Manag. **20**(2), 121–134 (2002)
4. Zomerdijk, L.G., Voss, C.A.: Service design for experience-centric services. J. Serv. Res. **13**(1), 67–82 (2009)

5. Gordijn, J., Yu, E., Raadt, B.V.D.: E-service design using i* and e^3 value modeling. IEEE Softw. **23**(3), 26–33 (2006)
6. Patrício, L.: Multilevel service design: from customer value constellation to service experience blueprinting. J. Serv. Res. **14**(2), 180–200 (2011)
7. Thompson, S.F., Johnstone, C.J., Thurlow, M.L.: Universal Design Applied to Large Scale Assessments. Synthesis Report, Disabilities, vol. 38 (2002)
8. Burgstahler, S.: Universal Design of Instruction (UDI): Definition, Principles, Guidelines, and Examples. DO-IT 4 (2012)
9. Story, M.F.: Maximizing usability: the principles of universal design. Assist. Technol. **10**(1), 4–12 (1998)
10. Crews, D.E., Zavotka, S.: Aging, disability, and frailty: implications for universal design. J. Physiol. Anthropol. **25**(1), 113–118 (2006)
11. Meyers, A.R., Andresen, E.M.: Enabling our instruments: accommodation, universal design, and access to participation in research. Arch. Phys. Med. Rehabil. **81**(2), S5–S9 (2000)

Interface Design Aesthetics
of Interaction Design

Yan Liu$^{(\boxtimes)}$ and Qiong Zhang

School of Fine Arts, Jinan University, Jinan 250022, Shandong, China
919076097@qq.com

Abstract. Esslinger believed that the 1950s was the era of production, the 1960s was the era of research and development, the 1970s was the era of marketing, the 1980s was the era of finance, and the 1990s was the era of integration, today is the era of intelligence. With the development of science and technology, human–computer interaction become an indispensable dynamic in life. How to strengthen human–computer interaction to make the product design more humanity is very important, so we need to think and research from the user's perspective. Design plays an important role in artificial intelligence – every step from imagination to product cannot be separated from design. It is also very important for interface design in human–computer interaction design. No matter what kind of product it is, the first thing it will show people is the visual experience, and then it will produce interaction and deep experience. Therefore, design can be said to be the explorer, which must be ahead of the public thinking. In other words, design is the visual present one and design is the practitioner of imagination. Only in this way can we design works that satisfy the public. In intelligent interaction, what the design embodies is to allow users to have more in-depth experience and abandon the external form of design. Designers begin to think more deeply about what design means to people, cities and life. What does design shape the user experience? Esslinger once said, "the purpose of design is to create a more human environment. My goal has always been to design mainstream products as art." According to the functions and characteristics of multi-sensory human–computer interaction interface, the design principles of simplicity and aesthetics, unity and diversity, ease of use and interactivity, static and dynamic, and rationality and sensibility are put forward.

Keywords: Interface · Design · Aesthetics

1 Introduction

Interface design is the first visual experience of user's human–computer interaction, so the interface in interactive design is particularly important. The aesthetic experience of interface is not only limited to the interface design elements, but also conforms to the aesthetic principle of human. In the process of designing the interface, the designer should not only follow the habits of the public, but also follow the general aesthetics of users. The principle of applying beauty in the interface design can effectively enhance the aesthetic feeling of the interface and enhance users' deep experience.

© Springer Nature Switzerland AG 2019
A. Marcus and W. Wang (Eds.): HCII 2019, LNCS 11583, pp. 279–290, 2019.
https://doi.org/10.1007/978-3-030-23570-3_21

2 Principles of Human–Computer Interaction Interface Design

Unlike ordinary graphic design, interface design only considers the aesthetics of the work. The work that designers should first do is graphic design. Interface requires not only beautiful, eye-catching in order to achieve good visual effect, but also consider the feelings and experience when users operating software. It needs to make the operation of the software becomes comfortable, simple and easy to use, as well as across different platforms, such as web design, mobile application interface design, etc. The four principles of simple design are consistency, alignment, repetition, and contrast. The four design principles involved in the content and elements including images, icons, line, shape, font, color, size, style, material, spatial relations, etc. Here we are only presenting a simple concept. It still needs to be understood through practical work, as any design concept has a certain value.

Consistency also becomes intimacy, when related items are grouped together into a visual unit rather than isolated elements. It helps to reduce confusion in the organization of interface information and provides a clear structure for users. Alignment principle: nothing can be placed randomly on the interface, and every element should have some visual relationship with any element on the interface, so that the design can keep clear and distinct, and improve the overall readability. The repetition principle: the purpose of repetition is consistency, so that the visual elements of the design are repeated throughout the design. Contrast is used to distinguish what is most important and what is generally important in an interface in order to avoid too much similarity. These so-called four basic principles are the foundation of interface design. Although these four principles are extremely simple concepts, they are often easily ignored. The reason for those rough and problematic designs is here. In the design of the interface, text, instructions, keys and other elements should be arranged according to the aesthetic principle, and then the corresponding arrangement can obtain good results.

3 Principles of Human–Computer Interface Aesthetics

Interface aesthetic experience is not only limited to the interface design elements, but also can exist in each element of the combination of aesthetic principles. In designing the interface, the designer should not only follow the general usage habits of the public, but also follow the common aesthetics of customers, and apply aesthetic principles in the design of human–computer interaction interface. Taiwanese Jiang Xun said that design aesthetic principles is esthematology. The word "aesthetic" comes from the Greek "aesthesis", and beauty is often a kind of feeling comes from the heart. We often think a memory is beautiful, also feel a certain melody is very beautiful, and so on. All the beauty of this is from our inner feelings. We also will integrate these beautiful feelings into the design, so as to make a better design. First of all, more beautiful design should be friendly. Friendly is not only the appearance. The friendly design should think from the heart for users to let them get a better experience, just like the feeling of being friendly when dealing with people in real life. The way that designers put this feeling into design called friendly design, and friendly is to cause the user's emotional resonance.

3.1   Friendly Design

As we all know, UI is the abbreviation of User Interface; the Chinese name is 用户界面, which is the bridge of communication between machines. Most device interfaces we use now are Graphical User Interfaces, or GUI, with which we communicate. However, the initial interface was not so friendly. At that time, the interface was mainly command line interface. If the screen we were facing was such an interface, most people would not choose to use a computer or a mobile phone. It was Jobs who first saw the graphical interface at Xerox in 1979, and he took it to the Macintosh, and he added the mouse. He first presented such a Macintosh with a good GUI to the masses in 1984, and the Macintosh ushered in a new era when interface design laid the foundation for today's computer interfaces. You can find many designs that have been retained over the years. At that time, the boot screen of the Mac was a smile Mac. Even now the development of it is still very interesting and friendly. The icon is called Happy Mac. There is an application called Guided Tour in Mac System 1.0. After opening is a slightly smiling talking man icon. Is it very friendly? It was inspired by Picasso's famous Two-faced Man. After more than 30 years of development, Apple has optimized such friendly icon design and has continued to use it to this day, which is a classic in the rapidly developing digital product design. There is also the classic icon Sad Mac, which is a Sad face that appears when the Mac has serious system problems, making people feel very Sad. When the Sad Mac icon appears on the computer, it will send out the death song, which makes people feel particularly interesting. In 2009, Facebook added a Like button, commonly known as Thumb Up. Thumb Up has become one of Facebook's proudest innovations, one of the defining features of the world's largest social networking platform and one that has been added to many others. Users think Facebook should include options they don't like in their replies. Zuckerberg himself issued a statement saying they were looking into the matter, but he didn't think users needed a button to veto or even disparage others. What users really need is to express their inner feelings through some other symbols. Therefore, they finally launched a brand new emoji reply system, which is a series of emojis to express inner feelings. Users can express their inner feelings directly through these graphics.

Friendly also reflects on some good guidance. A good guidance is like someone kindly showed us the directions and served us as well when we went to a strange place. When using a new application or a familiar application revision, or even updating a function, users need friendly guidance to operate the interface skillfully. For example, Litely, which is one of the most popular retouching apps in iOSrecently. Since its launch, it has been recommended by App Store for many times. Although Litely's biggest selling point is the filter, its visual effect is very good, concise and graceful. In the beginning of using this app, the whole interface was dimmed, which just adding small text tips like photos and some simple and gentle animation of breathing on the plus icon, but friendly guidance was to teach you how to do the most important option. Wood Joints is an extremely good application of craftsman spirit, which was recommended by the App Store as soon as it was published. The designer intends to convey the traditional crafts culture in modern way to more modern people, with a game type of interactive display of mortise and ten on joint structure, materials, tools, and history of mortise and ten on joint is introduced, and so on to tell more public users. Due to the relatively small market of the product itself, the application design is bold and innovative, so it made some friendly tips on the guidance. And the design of the prompt also uses a more traditional style of painting, some guidance can also be used to introduce the function. Therefore, friendly guidance plays a good role in guiding user psychology in human–computer interaction interface design.

The friendliness is also reflected in the boring waiting when the user is waiting for loading. When the user is waiting for loading, it is easy to generate anxiety. The loading design of interesting animation can just fix this point. Yahoo weather, for example, was the winner of the 2013 Apple Design Award. This application has a very wonderful visual effect, and the interface design is very fine and intimate. When the Internet is not great, the page loading animation is also very interesting – the sun icon on the logo appears gradually at the top and then rotates to load, and the ice flower gradually forms at the bottom of the screen, which makes people admire the designer's distinctive design. Of course, there are many more other eye-catching points. These interesting animations can attract users' attention through interesting innovation, which can reduce the bad feelings of waiting and enhance friendliness.

We human like to communicate with people rather than cold machines, which is a very important study in the human–computer interaction discipline. It fully takes into account the psychological feelings of users. When our design is friendly, it can get more favorable impression and resonance from users than the boring and cold design.

3.2   Color

As Steve jobs said, the world is made up of colors. Colors come from nature. We will take color into the design, which will make our design more beautiful. The effective application of color can not only reflect the product's personality, but also affect the users' psychological feelings and behaviors through the understanding, selection, collocation and different ways of use of product attributes. When we think of the beauty of colors in nature, we think of the rainbow on the horizon. Just like Apple's classic rainbow logo, the designer actually designed two schemes at that time, one was black and white stripes, the other was rainbow stripes. Jobs believed that the world was made up of colors, and colors were colorful and rich, which should be returned to people. In addition, it also conforms to Apple's design philosophy. It was Apple's main product at the time, the Apple II, the world's first personal computer that could display colors. Jobs also hoped that computers could attract the attention of teenagers, so he finally adopted the color of rainbow. At that time, most of the logos were white and monochrome, which showed that Apple's design was very avant-garde and bold. In the following decades, apple applied its colorful brand to various levels, such as the original iMac. This was the first time that humans boldly used rich and bright colors on computers, which stood out among the stereotypical and ugly computers at that time. When people buy the same computer, they can choose the color they like. It can be seen that the application of color not only strengthens the product's personality, but also reflects the user's personality. These colorful iMacs also saved apple at that time. Two years ago, the iPhone 5c launched a color revolution in the mobile phone world – not only the color of the body, but also the UI. In addition, Apple has designed the color on the invitation letter of its event for many times as well as the gift card on iTunes. So apple permeated color everywhere it can. After the release of iOS7 by Jonathan, the skeuomorphic style was removed, and the use of colors made us feel the charm of rainbow again, which was the use of colors in iOS7. Whether it is iOS MacOS or WatchOS, I believe that Apple's love and exploration of the beauty of color will never stop. Actually, playing with color is not the patent of Apple. Google, another powerful Internet company on this planet, also displayed its logo in color at the beginning of its establishment. Although several versions of its design were optimized and changed during this period, the color scheme is still retained to this day. The brand color of Google is mainly based on the three primary colors of red, yellow and blue. Since the human eye has three different color sensory bodies, the color space seen can usually be expressed by the three basic colors of red, yellow and blue. The letter L, in particular, uses yellow and blue to get green, which also indicates the non-conformability of Google. We can observe carefully that the new color optimization of Google becomes brighter. Color matching is very important in flat design. It usually uses brighter and more brilliant colors than other styles. The average design contains two to three main colors, while the average flat design uses six to eight colors. Google Material Design is exactly this – different colors are chosen for different options. Through the examples above, we see the richness of color. But the choice of color in the design can be rich and varied, also can be a particular color, this is what we often say the theme color. The choice of theme color is very important, it can not only explain the character of the product, to leave a deep impression, but also to help users understand the product, play a role in guiding the visual.

Through some cases to analyze the application of color in product design, for example, color is the most important part of Instagram, because this product has rich filters and video content with rich colors shared by most mobile users around the world. At present, what users see is the logo of the latest version of Instagram. This is the biggest design change since its release, just like the last one to abandon the skeuo-morphic design and finally open the concise design. If the lens is a bridge into a bolder, simpler design, its design director said, then the rainbow gradient colors are used in the login process, using the animation effect of color gradient, indicating the rich diversity of the product content. It should be noted here that rich colors are usually selected as the background when the interface information is relatively small and the functional entry is relatively simple. Through color, we can make the design more beautiful, and use color to better reflect the character of the product. Even the choice and use of color can help strengthen the product function and improve the user experience.

Color is the first feeling that enters a human eye. In the past few years, more and more designers are using color gradients in their interfaces. The color trend this year is to have the color with flowing gradual change like water, which is popular all over the world. Even if you choose just one color, you can create a rich sense of hierarchy with the help of color gradients and different images to create a pleasing picture. So, the trend toward color gradients is not only sweeping through 2018, but may continue in 2019. In addition, the screen color such as monochrome transparent color plus overlap – font, graphics are monochrome gradient and overlap, not only can make the interface looks more eye-catching, but also can create a sense of space. The overlap of the same elements, supplemented by shadows, will also make the design of the whole interface generate more sense of wonder, which can attract the eye of users. The overlapping of different elements in user experience design may be the color trend of next year.

3.3 Simplicity

Simplicity is not simple, nor is it a simple reduction of elements. Less is more, and layout is blank. The current design is in praise and advocate the beauty of simplicity, and the less is more under the influence of simplicity. Contracted design is reservation normally, often can achieve with little win much. In interface design, simple design can help products to better convey information and highlight content, and help users to better obtain and complete tasks, but the simpler design is often more difficult to do.

The most famous bull is one of representative works of Picasso. It was a very famous one and the simple stone of his oxen works, which draw the outline of the image of a bull with a few lines. In the perspective of art, the no longer simplification bull is the most attractive. while Apple may be the only high-tech company on the planet that dares to compare himself to Picasso. The function and beauty of Apple products comes from the ultimate understanding of simplicity and elegance, which is also a metaphor for Apple designers striving for simplicity, just like Picasso eliminating details to create great works of art. Such as Apple's Mac, since the first Mac was published in 1984, has been through 12 years of development. Its appearance design is more and more simplified. If we look at the side of the iMac, it's getting simpler and thinner, but it's getting stronger. The mouse is also minus the complex appearance, the rest are more powerful and better experience. This concept is reflected in the events of the company, including their product marketing, product design and mouse ergonomics design. Mr. Nelson, Apple's professor, shows a Google TV remote control with 78 buttons. Next, he showed off the Apple TV's remote control, a thin metal device with just three buttons. How did Apple's designers manage to use only three buttons? They started with an idea, Mr. Nelson explained, and debated it until it was clear that the keys were really necessary: a single button to control play and pause; One button to select the channel to watch; One key to enter the main menu. Google TV remote control as a cautionary tale here, with so many buttons, Mr. Nelson said, because every engineers and designers involved in the project want to show that they want, so there are 78 buttons. The fact is that the simplified design is what the user wanted. Apple did it with only three buttons. Bhagalinberg once said, "when you start doing case studies of Apple from now on, there is one thing that comes with your research decades later, and that is Apple's unique and unified culture, where people believe they are doing some of the best products that change people's lives. That's the whole culture of Apple".

Blank space is a common technique in the creation of Chinese art works, which has Chinese aesthetic characteristics. The term "white space" refers to the space left intentionally for the purpose of making the whole painting and calligraphy more harmonious and exquisite. The use of white space can also make the picture to achieve the effect of simplicity, and make our attention focused on the partial focus, such as the fog standing on the roof of the people. When we see such a picture, we will suddenly realize the attention on the body. In the design of some excellent interface, white space will often be used to make it more simple, atmospheric, and perfect. Snapseed uses a minimalist background image to the interface when open the photo. The white space above is the brand information, and there is only a button to open the photo below. While the picture is showed clearly, it also plays a good role in highlighting the brand and guiding functions. In addition to using the minimalist pictures as background, some app also not use, such as VSCO's landing interface. There are only minimalist lines, two icons and text in two places. The most important part of the visual is the prompt to enter an E-mail message. Here you can see white space can use extremely brief picture as the background, you can also use white, even black, also can use the color gradient as the background. In addition to the interface, some icons are also gradually using the principle of white space, such as apple's latest major system icons, and event handling icons. Appropriate white space can improve the overall transparency of the work, the sense of space, and such a work is easier for users to accept, giving people a more comfortable feeling. To win with no more, to win more with less. This is the real artistic conception of white space. The common characteristic of white space is the pursuit of showing reality with emptiness, and the pursuit of "being" out of "nothing". Expanding the creative imagination to realize the flow transition of the image to achieve the promotion which conventional methods cannot achieve.

Blurring the background is an easy and effective way to make the picture elegant and simple. People who love photography like to use a large aperture, because it can get a nice blurred background and make the focus clearer. Frosted glass can achieve a similar effect, and can reflect the good administrative levels feeling and dimensional feeling. Since iOS7, Apple has used a large number of ground glass effects, which is an important way to distinguish the background and information. This is the icloud interface. The effect of white space combined with ground glass is used to blur the background and distinguish the extremely colorful background and numerous icons from the visual focus. Drop-down search in the desktop, iOS uses the method of blurring the background to weaken the dense application icons on the desktop, making the search focus on the input box and a small number of suggested icons. Bluring the background when using Apple's 3D Touch feature to keep the interface simple and focus on the current selection of content. The use of fuzzy background design can reflect the original beauty of the main work, so that every detail of the original show in front of the user, so that we can enjoy the other key elements of the APP interface without any interference.

Simplicity design can help users better use product. We make the design elegant and simple by subtraction, white space, blurring background and other methods, so that the product function and content better show in front of users. But the principle of simplicity design is not blindly advocating minimalism and pursuing style and form, but should pay more attention to function and content. We should pay attention to every detail in simplicity design to better show the state of design and product and maintain the unity of the design as far as possible. Simplicity is just rich concentration, and it is the sublimation of complexity.

3.4   The Proportion of Beauty

We know some characteristics of beauty through our subjective perception of beauty. In addition, beauty in nature has common rules. The proportion of beauty is to explore beauty from the objective world. The golden ratio, also known as the golden section, was first recorded in the 6th century BC. Most people believe that it was first proposed by the ancient Greek mathematician and philosopher Pythagoras. The golden ratio has strict proportionality, artistically and harmonically, and contains rich aesthetic value. The golden ratio is recognized as the most one that can cause the aesthetic feeling. That removal of the shape of the arc form is called the golden spiral, also known as Fibonacci spirals. There exist many such spiral patterns in nature. Such examples are too numerous to list. It is no wonder that Pythagoras called it the law of nature. The golden ratio was praised by Renaissance master Leonardo Da Vinci. Artists of all ages consciously or unconsciously followed such a ratio. *Creation of Adam* is the most famous and moving scene in the creation of *Genesis* painted by Michelangelo in the Sistine chapel of the Vatican. This picture depicts the creation of Adam by God. Where the fingertips of god and Adam meet is actually the golden point of the work. In fact, this point in the entire mural is in the golden ratio position, the overall look is very spectacular. In the iphone6, for example, the search box's position on the screen is exactly the distance from the top of the screen to the width of the screen in a golden ratio. The height of the search box relative to the top of its logo is also the golden ratio, and the height of the title relative to the body area in the same module that loads the recommendation is also the golden ratio. Even the top right to view recent browsing history icon also uses the golden ratio. This shows that Apple is extremely concerned about following the golden ratio.

In fact, there is also the silver ratio, which is similar to the golden ratio, with the ratio of 1.414 to 1, and the exact value is square root of 2 to 1. The silver ratio has been used in some design applications, such as the classic ipad, whose length and width are in line with the silver ratio, and the Google's You Tube icon, whose length and width are also in line with the silver ratio. Silver ratio is also known as "大和比" in Japan. This kind of consciousness has been deeply rooted in the traditional Japanese aesthetic system. Many traditional Japanese buildings contain such proportions. The famous Japanese traditional architecture, such as Horyuji temple, also embodies the silver ratio everywhere. The Sunny tower in Tokyo is also called the Tokyo tree. It is the tallest tower in the world. This Japanese landmark also contains the silver ratio. Not only Japanese architecture, animation silver segmentation is more common. In a 2008 survey by Voice intelligence, nine of the 20 most popular anime characters in Japan, or 45 percent, were silver ratio, with Doraemon being one of them. The silver ratio of the rectangle is closer to the square, which is different from the west's favorite golden ratio, and the east seems to prefer the silver ratio. In addition to gold and silver, there is platinum ratio. Most PC screens are a size ratio of 16 to 9. And there are many more, for example, many of our phones now take photos at the default size of 3 to 4 and so on. In fact, these are strictly proportional, artistic, harmonious, and contain a very rich aesthetic value.

No matter what kind of design you do and what kind of aesthetics do you follow, design something that lets a person feel natural, comfortable and harmonious. It is very effective to use appropriate proportions when presenting a sense of order, rigor, white space, and more complex elements of the design. But these ratios are not a panacea. So, don't go for specific proportions or forms. Sometimes we have to trust our eyes and our true feelings and make different choices according to different scenes, objects and purposes.

3.5   Symmetry

As an old saying goes, "the beauty of a man is not harmful, whether it is from top to bottom, inside or outside, large or small, far or near." It is "beauty" when everything is in balance. Symmetry is such beauty. Like all things in the world, symmetry makes everything balanced and orderly, giving people the beauty of solemnity and harmony. Symmetry as aesthetic principle since ancient times has been the nature of the world with our life. The reason why people feel the beauty of symmetrical design is that human beings have a good impression of symmetrical things. It gives a sense of order, routine, balance and elegance, or of authority, poise, sureness and dependability. Our earth is symmetrical, many beautiful flowers are symmetrical, many animals are symmetrical, and human beings are symmetrical. In addition, there is beauty of symmetry in both western and eastern buildings. The same goes for the Apple, of course. The photo be officially chosen when the 5 k iMac was released. In addition, Apple's hardware products almost always follow the principle of symmetrical beauty. Like the iMac, which is the design of the Mac Pro. What comes is a sense of strength and stability. And many of apple's web interfaces also use a lot of symmetry to achieve proportional symmetry. For example, the default album of iOS, such a design expresses the authenticity. There's also the default email, fancy's Popsicle icon, and more. You can see that these symmetrical ICONS are actually the way they are in nature, and the designers have made them simple and graphical. Let's take a look at the Moment application. The letter M itself is symmetric with two semi-circles attached to it. In addition to the icon, let's look at the startup screen in the Moment interface. The welcome page also uses a symmetrical design. In fact, the welcome page and login page of many applications are designed with a symmetrical structure. The beauty of symmetry also lies in balance and peace of mind. Symmetrical beauty, people will have a sense of peace of mind. Everything seems to be in order, like the stars in its own track, not fast, slowly but firmly. Symmetrical beauty is an art of balance. Symmetrical beauty is also a perfect and auspicious poem, always in pairs, "the sky to the earth, the sun to the moon, the floor to the pavilion, the evening light to the clear sky... Every antithesis is the pursuit of perfection and the balance of Yin and Yang.

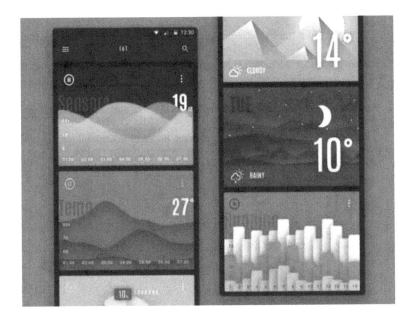

From an aesthetic point of view, symmetry is beautiful, but it does not mean that asymmetry is not beautiful. In human–computer interaction interface design, symmetrical design can better maintain consistency and sense of integrity. The symmetrical design of relatively free style often can give a person the philosophy feeling that lasts long often new, atmosphere, balance, order, be like Yin and Yang to mediate so. Reasonable choose and balance symmetry according to different situations.

4 Conclusion

In the design of human–computer interaction interface, aesthetic principles should be reasonably applied to improve the user experience of the interface. Whether the user experience is good or bad depends on our design. Good design could endure the test of time. Many good designs seems very naturally. What's more important is to design according to the real needs of users. Design aesthetics is actually a course with a large amount of information. In fact, there is no right or wrong in design as long as it is suitable. Most of the time it depends on the choice. Interface design should have an open art and thinking, sharing and creating vitality, sense of reality and power. Design aesthetics can transcend space, nationality, race, language and ideology, transcend the ordinary appearance of things or complex social landscape, and bring people emotional and love dialogue. Get to know the real friendly human–computer interface design with temperature and emotion, as well as the deeper and high-end intelligent challenges it faces.

References

1. Song, F.: An analysis of the aesthetic expression of the human–computer interface. Netw. Inf. Eng. (05) (2016)
2. Ma, H.: Human–computer interaction that connecting future. Internet Week (07) (2010)
3. Hu, J.: Study on the human–computer interaction interface of digital products. Packag. Eng. (9) (2014)
4. Wei, Y.: Application of human–computer interaction design in mobile terminals. Inf. Comput. (20) (2015) (theory edition)
5. Zhou, L., Lv, Q.Q.: Research on human–computer interaction harmonious design method based on intelligent technology development. Res. Art Educ. (06) (2013)
6. Liu, T., Zhang, X.: Research on interface interaction design of intelligent home appliance system based on emotion. Res. Art Educ. (2015)

Design Thinking Versus Design Sprint: A Comparative Study

Carlos Magno Mendonça de Sá Araújo, Ivon Miranda Santos,
Edna Dias Canedo$^{(\boxtimes)}$ (iD), and Aleteia Patricia Favacho de Araújo

Computer Science Department, University of Brasília (UnB),
Brasília, DF 70910-900, Brazil
carlos.magno@gmail.com, ivon.miranda@gmail.com,
{ednacanedo,aleteia}@unb.br
http://ppca.unb.br

Abstract. Design Thinking methodology is being increasingly used by the software industry in an attempt to reduce the problems with requirements elicitation. In the literature it is possible to find several papers addressing the use of this methodology in the analysis and specification of software requirements. In order to help reduce existing problems that have not yet been fully resolved through the use of Design Thinking, Google has launched Design Sprint with the goal of eliciting requirements quickly and efficiently. There are very few academic papers reporting on the use of this technique and what its advantages and disadvantages are. This paper describes a comparative study of the two methodologies used to minimize the problems faced by companies in eliciting the requirements of their software, presenting their phases and how they can be used.

Keywords: Design Sprint · Design Thinking · Methodologies · Requirements elicitation · Comparative study

1 Introduction

Requirements engineering is the science that studies and defines which tasks a software should perform and how [14]. In this process there are several methodologies, the oldest of which is the traditional methodology which become, very widespread due to RUP - Rational Unified Process, a methodology created by Rational [13]. However, this methodology employs a method in which all requirements are raised at the beginning of the project, and problems in the requirements specification will only be identified late in the software development phase, raising the cost of corrections. Encouraged by these problems the studies point out that not only should software development be agile, but so should the gathering of requirements. For this reason, several agile methodologies and processes are being developed to determine software requirements.

The agile methodology emerged from the techniques used by innovative Japanese companies in the 1970s and 1980s (become popular such as Toyota,

© Springer Nature Switzerland AG 2019
A. Marcus and W. Wang (Eds.): HCII 2019, LNCS 11583, pp. 291–306, 2019.
https://doi.org/10.1007/978-3-030-23570-3_22

Fuji and Honda) [12]. These agile methods have in project management because of their high success rates.

The most widespread methodology currently is SCRUM, which works with Sprints to develop the project as a whole [15]. There are however methodologies that complement and even replace SCRUM. We need to think about product development to make the project a success. This paper presents a comparative study between two of the most popular agile requirements analysis techniques:

- **Design Thinking:** a methodology that contrasts with the traditional scientific methodology where it relies on the collaboration of a multidisciplinary team to solve complex problems through the application of design knowledge [16].
- **Design Sprint:** a unique five-day Google Venture process used to solve critical issues through prototyping and brainstorming with customers [3,4]. All the best ideas are condensed and organized in a short space of time for the creation of an excellent idea. In this process, a step-by-step description of what is to be done in each of these five days is given in detail. That, at the end of these five days, we have a validated product that we believe or we are determine that the project, in the way it was designed, is not ideal [11].

This comparative study allowed us to verify that the two methodologies are being widely used, both in the software industry and in case studies developed by the academy to validate its use. Therefore, with this work it was possible to identify that they are both appropriate approaches when using an agile development methodology. Being appropriate and providing benefits to the requirements elicitation adheres to the needs of stakeholders.

This paper is organized as follows. Section 2 contains the concepts needed for around the Design Thinking and Design Sprint methodologies. Section 3 presents a comparative analysis of the two methodologies and Sect. 4 presents the conclusions and the future works.

2   Background

Software methodologies have been developed to facilitate, as far as possible, the software development process. Few methodologies were known until recently. The traditional methodology is one of them, iterative development another among a few others. Nowadays, many software methodologies have emerged that are more flexible than existing ones and this is one reason they are called agile [2]. These methodologies, unlike traditional ones, bring the end-user closer to the software development team, whether it is an internal or external customer [9]. With this type of methodology, approvals are often made in short periods of time, usually 2 to 4 weeks, resulting in several shorter deliveries until the final product is reached [8,10].

The software is gradually being delivered and it is possible to make occasional changes during its construction. Among these emerging methodologies are Sprint Design [4] and Design Thinking [16].

2.1 Design Thinking

Brown [16] believes that the idea that drives Design Thinking is a collaborative process that uses sensitively and creative techniques to meet the needs of people not only with what is technically visible, but with a viable business strategy. Design Thinking aims to convert a need into demand. It is a human-centric approach to problem solving and helping people and organizations to be more innovative and creative.

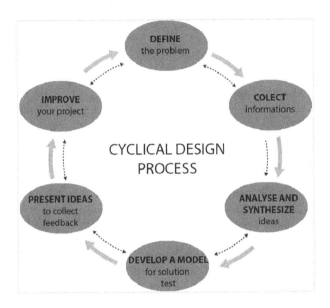

Fig. 1. Design Thinking process, adapted [17]

Although the term design usually refers to something visual, the concept can mean much more than that. Design means planning or making decisions about something that is being created, as well as planning, making, or executing a plan to produce something for a specific purpose [7]. The concept of design is much closer to a project than to a visual design. Design brings a more human-like perception to problem-solving, caring about individuals before tools to solve a problem [6]. New ways of thinking about a problem are established from Design Thinking, seeking to understand a number of contextual factors in thinking about a solution:

1. Who are the individuals we are serving?
2. What are their needs and desires?
3. How do they live? 4. What are their personal experiences?

The design makes it clear that it is an approach focused on **people**. By following a design process, we go through procedures that depart from the definition of the scope of a problem, collecting information that can help solve this problem, experimenting with and testing different solutions and refining them through feedback until achieving a effective solution that addresses the people affected by the problem, as shown in Fig. 1. Design Thinking is based on three pillars focused on people and their needs, enabling human factors to be in focus as protagonists throughout the process [5] namely:

- **Empathy** - the ability to put yourself in another's place, understanding their context and their point of view, including their needs, fears and longings.
- **Collaboration** - integration of multidisciplinary and multifunctional teams. It promotes a richer development process through diversity of experience and specialities.
- **Experimentation** - offering the solutions to be evaluated in the real world, and learning from feedback, refining the product or service.

The Design Thinking approach aims to answer the following questions [6]:

1. **Who** are we solving this problem for?
2. **What** are the needs of these people?
3. **How** will this problem be resolved?
4. **Why** does this job or solution matter to people?

According to [6], these questions are structured into a model. Within this model design thinking starts at the discovery phase that generates options which, after choices are made, converge on what was observed to best the resolve the problem, and then diverge again into a range of development options to build the solution. There are two distinct moments of analysis of the process: during the definition of the problem and during the development of solutions.

Design Thinking is an iterative methodology that brings a new approach to solving complex problems by applying Design knowledge. It has five distinct and well ordered steps so that the predecessor is an input to the successor. The evolution of these steps up until the conclusion of each iteration cycle in this process are [1,16,18]:

1. **Discovery:** immersion (empathy or exploration). At this stage the team should immerse themselve in the problem to get to know it better, using several techniques, to do at complete mapping of the problem. The immersion can be performed in a Preliminary stage and another one in Depth [6]. Reframing, Exploratory Research and Desk Research are part of the preliminary immersion, having the objective of reframing and developing an initial understanding of the problem. The immersion in Depth is intended to identify the needs and opportunities that will guide the generation of solutions for the next phase of the project, to define the scope of the project and its boundaries, as well as to identify the user profiles and other key actors that should be addressed [6].
2. **Interpretation:** analysis and synthesis (definition of the problem). After the immersion stage it is necessary to structure and group the collected data to begin the analysis and synthesis phase. Some techniques are used, for example: affinity diagram, insight cards, mental maps, conceptual maps, personas

and proto-personas and the user's journey. The objective of the analysis and synthesis stage is to organize the collected information and to obtain a synthesis of the desires, needs and motivations of the interested parties, broadening the understanding of the problem that the team intends to solve [6]. At this stage the project team should focus on analyzing all the data collected in the dive immersion stage, and produce a number of ideas. In addition to the wealth of information, team experience and creativity are essential elements for having good **insights**. Another key factor is to form a multidisciplinary team, the more diversified, the greater the wealth of ideas generated [16].

3. **Ideation:** In the ideation stage the team proposes several solutions, using techniques such as *brainstorming* and co-creation workshops. Once all the contributions have been made the group should analyze them together to refine them and decide which will be used in the process [6]. At the time of the synthesis the solutions will be analyzed deeply and many can be eliminated for lack of viability; others are disregarded because better exist; these better will be refined and perhaps even merged with other equally good ones, improving them further [16]. This phase aims to generate innovative ideas for the project theme, stimulating creativity to generate solutions that are in accordance with the context of the subject worked. It is good practice to include in the team those people who will make use of the solution after the final implementation [16]. Thus, in addition to the multidisciplinary project team, other members are selected as users and professionals of areas that are convenient to the topic under study, usually through Workshops co-creation. The objective of bringing together different expertise is to contribute different perspectives, thereby making the final result richer and more assertive [6].

4. **Experimentation:** the prototypes begging with all the materials that were created in the previous steps: personas, user's journey, ideas generated in brainstorming, etc. Ideas are converted into a more concrete deliverable for evaluation. Prototyping has the function of assisting the validation of generated ideas and although presented as one of the last phases of the Design Thinking process, can occur throughout the project in parallel with Immersion and Ideation [6]. Prototypes are classified into high and low fidelity, also called functional prototypes. In this step, a prototype will be constructed that can provide a tangible or intangible experience of the tool through the implementation of a presentation or a prototype [16]. You can use tools such as Storyboard, Video, Innovation Fair, Storytelling, Role play, Magic of Oz (Wizard of Oz Prototyping), among others [16]. Similary, design thinking teams should regard the critiques of their solutions positively and constructively. They should not take personally people's negative comments about their proposed solutions. Instead, they should remember the adage, *"The customer is not always right but always has a point"* [6].

5. **Evolution:** the prototypes should be evaluated in a real-use scenario for field comparison and validation [6]. In the evaluation phase, Design Thinking teams test their prototype solution with the users representing target **personas**. They then update the solution in an iterative manner until the solution meets the needs of the user and exceeds the challenge set in the

initial design phase [6]. Design Thinking team members should always thank users for their criticisms of solutions. Criticism is a natural part of many team efforts, including design and artistic aspects. In history, criticism has even contributed to the emergence of some artistic movements. These artists did not give up because of criticism; instead, they used them to improve their artistic styles and perspectives. Likewise, Design Thinking teams should receive the criticism of their solutions positively and constructively. They should not take people's negative comments about their proposed solutions personally. Instead, they should remember the saying: "**The client is not always right, but always has a point**" [6].

After the evaluation it is possible to use the results obtained to start a new cycle from the immersion stage, making the process repeatable until the desired level of refinement is reached.

2.2   Design Sprint

A Design Sprint is a unique, five-day process created by Google Venture [4] to solve critical issues through prototypes and brainstorming with customers. The methodology and its application include the following activities:

1. **It's time to prepare the environment for everything that will happen:** Before we start a Sprint, we need the team the defined challenge set, and space and time for a Sprint to take place. As previously mentioned, you need a well-defined challenge before you start the 5- day Sprint's 5-day in order to generate a prototype that will lead to a successful product. Besides the goal, it is necessary to choose a team, perhaps a maximum of 7 people and a comfortable space for everyone to make the game happen. Figure 2 presents the phases of Sprint Design.
2. **The Challenge:** Sprints can be useful in challenging situations, such as high-risk projects. A Sprint is a good time to check out initial ideas and change direction in a short time frame. It also fits in well when you are short of time to test the outcome of a project. In five days you will need to find good solutions quickly. One tip the experience with Sprints has given us: Do not

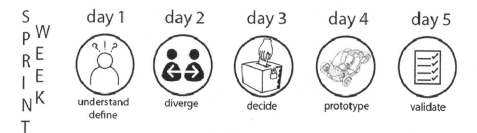

Fig. 2. Phases do Design Sprint [4]

get hung up on details, worry about the bigger picture. It is what will be visible to and attract customers. A poorly-made prototype or product has a good chance of failure. After worrying about the and completing its prototype we will worry about the internals. Now that we know how to choose a good challenge, it's time to choose one. Once we have chosen the challenge, we will have to choose the team. We know that it is not easy to select a team [4].

3. **The Team:** For a Sprint to have a chance of success, it is advisable to set up a team of 7 people or less, preferably including people with the following roles in the company: Definer; Finance Specialist; Marketing Specialist; Consumer Specialist; Technology Specialist; Design Specialist. When choosing the team it is important that people with good relationships are included, because they will work together full time for 5 days. Despite the need for a relation, it is important that you have a person on the team who is by nature a "problem maker". There is a reason to include a person with this profile on the team. Usually these people are intelligent and see problems differently than anyone else. If you feel that 7 people is too few to run the project, you could include other experts to be consulted at the start of the sprint. A good time is Monday afternoon. During this visit, they will be able to tell the team what they know and share their opinions. Now that the team is assembled, we need a facilitator. A facilitator should be a person who manages time, debates and the process in general very well. They must have experience in conducting meetings and know how to arbitrate the discussions, enforcing the time to stop and move on to another subject. The facilitator must always be impartial about decisions. The specialists included in the team should be from different areas and positions as each of them will make an essential contribution, be it with basic information, a new idea, or even useful information about your customers' vision [4].

4. **Time and Space:** To do a week of Sprint Design, you need a team willing to devote their entire time to being fully dedicated. By doing so, you will be able to generate one of the best aspects of Sprint: freedom to work the way you want, with an uncompromising schedule and a challenging goal to be met. On a typical day of a sprint, the team devotes 6 hours to be in the same room from 10am to 5pm, Monday through Thursday. The Friday will be dedicated to testing with users. Electronic devices are banned in the sprint room. There are studies that prove that when a person has their thoughts interrupted, it takes some time to return to the same point of thought. So the ban on electronics is useful in the sprint room. It is important to drive the sprint in the same room throughout the week so we can have white-boards that help us keep the best ideas and check if the focus of the work is not distancing itself from the main idea. White boards are best for viewing these goals. We can not just rely on our brains. Now that we have the team, time and space defined, it's time to start the Sprint [4].

5. **Start at the End:** To help chart the purpose and goal of the sprint, the team should ask themselves: Why are we doing this project? Where do we want to be in 6 months, 1 year or even 5 years? The discussion to get these

answers and the purpose of the Sprint should not be extensive and, to help, you can ask some questions:
(a) What questions do we want to answer in the sprint?
(b) To reach our long-term goal what do we need to do?
(c) What can cause the project to fail?

Activities by day of the week:

– **Monday:** on Monday, you must choose the viable goal to be achieved and draw a map to achieve this goal. You should also ask for help or confer with experts who are not part of the team. After all this discussion one must draw a target to be reached. **Map** During the sprint week, it's very easy to get lost if we have not mapped our idea. On Monday we should already draw an initial map of what we think is the solution to the challenge. Alongside the map will help us choose a more realistic target within a broader challenge. In the same chart that is the map we should:
  1. List the actors: Who are the important actors of our story?
  2. Writing the end: It is easier to write the end than the path we will take to reach this end.
  3. Words and arrows in the middle: write an initial flowchart of how we will achieve this goal.
  4. Keep it simple: The map must have a few steps that everyone agrees on.
  5. Ask for help: we should ask the team if the map seems correct and, based on the answers, reach a map that adheres to the goal.

  The first map of the day may seem simple, but it will have improved over the course of the day's discussions. Once the map is created, we will interview the specialists who are not part of the team to gather more information about the problem. We have to keep in mind that it is necessary to get the maximum information from expert interviews. To do this, each member of the team should have a white-board to jot down questions that came up in the interviews. At the end of the day, we'll have more questions about how to solve the problems we'll face in order to achieve the goal. The team will also have lots of extra information on the problem and several questions to answer when looking for solutions to reach the goal [4]. **The target.** The last task on Monday is to choose the target for the sprint. What is the most important audience and what is their crucial moment in the experience of this audience [4].
– **Tuesday:** The day begins with reviewing existing ideas to fit and perfect. In the afternoon each member will sketch what they think is the best solution to the problem. Sometimes the best way to broaden your search is to look within your own organization. Great solutions come at the wrong time, and the sprint can be the exact time to rescue them. Also, look for ideas in progress, but that are unfinished. Make a list: Ask everyone on staff to create a list of products or services to be analyzed for inspiring solutions. Do three minute demonstrations: The people who suggested the products make a presentation to show the team the interesting points. Make a note of good ideas as the presentations are made. The day begins with reviewing existing ideas to adjust and improve. In the afternoon each member will sketch what they think is

the best solution to the problem. Sometimes the best way to broaden your search and look inside your own organization. Great solutions come at the wrong time, and the sprint may be the exact time to rescue them. Also, look for ideas in progress, but that are unfinished [4]. Make a list: Ask everyone on the team to create a list of products or services to be analyzed for inspiring solutions. Make three minute demonstrations: The people who suggested the products make a rush to show the team the interesting points. Post good ideas as presentations are made [4]. **Draw sketches** Explaining with words only is sometimes quite complicated and it is not so easy to make yourself understood. Ideally, one should use sketche. It is advisable to use the sketch technique in 4 steps. The steps are: Make notes: In this first step, you and your team will walk through the room, check the white boards and make notes. These notes are basically the best ideas of the last 24 h, put together. Have ideas: in this step you should write the ideas that came up about solving the problem. Write down everything that comes to mind. Crazy 8's: This is an accelerated exercise. You should get your most interesting ideas and create 8 variations of these ideas in 8 min. Making the variations of an idea helps you to improve it by thinking of several solutions. Outline of solutions: Now it's time to create something to show the team. You should create a sketch of your best idea and put it on paper. Each sketch is a hypothesis for solving the problem. These sketches will be examined and judged by the rest of the team. The sketch created should: be self-explanation; be anonymous; be detailed, well thought through and complete; use words; have a striking title.

- **Wednesday:** on Wednesday morning the team will make a decision to select the most promising projects. The Battle on Wednesday morning, your team will make a joint decision to choose the most promising drafts. What if there is more than one winning sketch? If it is not possible to unite them in just one solution, the team will the prototypes and the client will decide which is the best, on the Friday. Having made the choice of the sketches, it is time to turn all decisions into a plan of action so that the prototype is ready on Friday. In order not to get lost and have a sketch ready by the end of Wednesday, the following tips are provided: Work with what you have: Work on the ideas that have come to you so far. Do not try to get new ideas. Do not write together: Your prototypes should have simple headers and important phrases. Include only simple details: Add enough detail to leave no doubt about the next step or where to go. One should not be too specific, a prototype does not have to be perfect. The Definer defines: On the Wednesday afternoon the team will be tired and it is very important that the Definer does not let the discussions go on and defines some points that he thinks is the best decision. The Definer can ask for opinions or help from the specialists.

If you are in doubt, take risks: leave aside simple solutions and those have been tested elsewhere, seeing these solutions in prototype will not help much. Prefer to prototype large and bold ideas. Limit the story to fifteen minutes or less: You'll need to set aside time for iteration with customers. If we spend 15 min with the story, surely the presentation will take much more [4]. After all the sketches are included, the storyboard is finished. We will have overcome the hardest part of Sprint. Decisions have been made and the plan is outlined for the construction of the prototype [4]. **Storyboard:** It's time to draw up a plan and the schedule is short. It is possible to see customers testing the prototype and the desire to start is high. If the team starts without a plan, they may trip over small unanticipated obstacles, and the project may collapse. One should put the winning drawings on the wall and begin to think and draw what one imagines the finished prototype to be. This prototype, even on paper, should be rich in detail and depict not just the prototype but all the iterations you imagine for Friday.

– **Thursday:** After the storyboard is finished, it's time to be creative and turn the storyboard into a realistic prototype. **The prototype:** After much time spent testing, failing and succeeding, we have some tips to give for the prototype to come out in just one day: Choose the right tools; Divide and conquer; Sew everything together; Test. **Choose the right tools** Forget the day-to-day tools, they're just too perfect... and slow. Use something simple like Power-point or Keynote. You need to prototype, and doing that in a slide-show template and presentations sounds like a good idea. If it is not possible to do your prototype in a slide show, follow this advice: 1. For software, websites, applications, brochures, etc. Use Keynote, Power point or even Word. 2. If it is a service write a script and use the team as actors. 3. If it is an object, modify a pre-existing object, print on 3-D material, or prototype a marketing material [4]. **Divide and conquer:** The Facilitator should help the team divide into the following roles: Executor: 2 or more; Compiler: 1; Writer: 1; Resource Collector: 1 or more; Interviewer: 1. Executors create the individual components of the prototype. Usually designers or engineers. The compiler is responsible for assembling the components of the executors into a cohesive model. The writer is responsible for the impact words of the prototype. It is very important to have simple, straightforward phrases. Usually a product manager from the prototype end area. The resource collector is the role that will scan the web, image libraries, company products and all the possible places to find photos, icons or content samples that you did not need to create from scratch in order to illustrate the prototype. The interviewer is the one who will write an interview script that will be done with clients on Friday. After everything is ready, it's time to test. Around mid-afternoon re-convince the whole team and revise the prototype. You will still have time to compare it with the storyboard and make minor adjustments [4].

– **Friday:** After an incredibly productive week, you'll be face-to-face with the customer to present the product prototype. This test makes the whole sprint worthwhile: at the end of the day you'll know what to do next. **Interview:** An interview with the client can reveal a lot about the people who will use your product, problems where you did not think they existed and the reasons behind everything. The structured interview in the way that follows helps the client to feel comfortable and ensures that the entire prototype is analyzed: A friendly word of welcome; Context questions about the customer; Presentation of the prototype; Tasks for the client; Record customer's thoughts and impressions. Friday's action occurs in 2 environments. In the sprint room the team watches the interviews while they take place in another room that makes the client feel more comfortable. Once the presentations are over, it is time to look at interview videos, study user reactions, improve what needs to be improved and get to work. It's time to create the real product [4].

3   Comparative Analysis of Thinking Design and Sprint Design Methodologies

Technology is advancing all the time. With each new cycle, new transformational products are launched. To keep pace with these changes, it is necessary to evolve the process for building software. When the Rational Unified Process (RUP) [13] was released, it recorded a cycle of evolution that organized the way to develop software, bringing a methodology with remarkable practical efficiency, while maintaining a good theoretical wealth.

During good times the RUP was the standard methodology used by most software development companies. It would be remiss to not observe how much this methodology contributed to the quality of good software produced to the present day. Nowadays, in order to meet the need to increase speed without giving up quality, demand has arisen for more agile methodologies with fewer bureaucratic processes and consequently more lean ones.

It is from this demand that we observe the appearance of studies that propose the implantation of methodologies preaching agility and speed, with the reduction of bureaucratic processes which are considered, in some moments, unnecessary. We discuss two methodologies in this paper that propose to be more agile through the use of Design techniques. They are Design Thinking and Design Sprint. When observing how the two methodologies work, it is noticeable that they share many principles and techniques, as shown in Fig. 3. The similarities between the two methodologies are so similar that one could erroneously believe that they are identical.

What Are Their Most Striking Similarities and Divergences Between Methodologies?

Design Sprint proposes a model of formation of the structure and the profiles of the members for each role, each task having a predetermined proposed time of execution understood as ideal. The format of a Design Sprint gives teams a way to focus the attention of the team on a very specific problem. The exercises embedded in the five phases are designed to reduce politics, increase collaboration across functions and put the focus on answers (outcomes) and not just assets (outputs). The Understand phase of a Design Sprint is used to discover, understand and define the problem that your customer is dealing with. If there's not enough user research or access to customers to make this worthwhile then a Design Sprint might be premature. Design Thinking does not impose this obligation of appear, being in charge of its members defining the time that will be spent in each activity, and specifying which profiles should execute each task.

Design Thinking proposes to solve complex problems through the mobilization of a multidisciplinary team, where the opportunity to gather knowledge and diverse experiences in the same team tends to enrich the solution found for the problem. The idea behind Design Thinking is to change the mental model in which companies are invested, to create products without first knowing the real needs of their target audience and the key players involved in the process. In theory, it can be represented in four phases: immersion, where the team delves into the implications of the challenge; ideation, in which there is a collaborative brainstorm with the use of practices of stimulus to creativity; prototyping, the phase used for the development of several models in search of the ideal product; and testing, in which the product will be validated with the users. The time can vary from weeks to months. In addition, Design Thinking is not a fixed methodology, so it does not have a step by step to be followed or a specific deadline in which it should be done.

Design Thinking really shines when we need to better understand the problem space and identify the early adopters. There are various flavors of Design Thinking, but they all sort of follow the double-diamond flow. Simplistically the first diamond starts by diverging and gathering lots of insights through talking to our target stakeholders, followed by converging through clustering these insights and identifying key pain-points, problems or jobs to be done. The second diamond starts by a diverging exercise to ideate a large number of potential solutions before prototyping and testing the most promising ideas. Design Thinking is mainly focused on qualitative rather than quantitative insights. For each phase of Design Think, there is a possibility of using a technique chosen for the situation. For example, in immersion phase, it could be research search, ethnographic research, check list, among others.

Design Sprint, on the other hand, is a method based on Design Thinking itself and created by Google Ventures. Beyond the theory, Design Sprint has a systematic application. The method is divided into five phases, designed to be performed in a short period of one week. The goal is to flexibly conceptualize and tangibility an idea, its implementations and macro functionalities in a short time. Design Sprint comes as a way to make projects on paper and focus on the ideas that come up but end up being "shelved". It is a fast and efficient method which, through a deepening of the problems that need to be solved, results in a solution ready to be implemented. Design Sprint is a process created by Google and that today has become routine within the work processes performed by them. It's a bit of the recipe behind the magic of the internet giant.

For the organization and the people, it serves as an impetus for the company to mobilize human resources and allow time for an idea to be made viable and validated. From a cultural point of view, Design Sprint is a way to bring agility and unity of teams and multidisciplinary teams and an incentive to activate an innovative organizational culture. It appears that the Google Venture-style Design Sprint method could have its roots from a technique described in the Lean UX book [19].

The key strength of a Design Sprint is to share insights, ideate, prototype and test a concept all in a 5-day sprint. Given the short timeframe, Design Sprints only focus on part of the solution, but it's an excellent way to learn really quickly if you are on the right track or not. Thus, it is up to each organization to define the sprint rules, including timing and extension. What is essential is that there is a focus, a specific problem that the organization or the team wants to address. If necessary, unmask macro challenges on micros. This is a way to address complex problems and achieve solutions.

The two methodologies are suitable for most situations, the choice will depend on the team profile, Sprint Design prevails a more formatted method with more defined deadlines. In Design Thinking, greater flexibility prevails in the process itself, which has a baseline that shows the main direction, but allows the team to do the way that suits them best. Choosing the ideal model to develop the project is critical to the success of the final product. Therefore, it is necessary to analyze the stage of maturity of the idea and the availability of time and resources of the client.

If You Need to Develop Solutions. Well, if you need to develop a solution or want to build something totally new, it's better to opt for Design Thinking, an approach focused on immersing and understanding a holistic context that complex problem is embedded in. Now, if your goal is to co-create the team to find the workable solution, Design Sprint is more recommended, since it is more objective in the process.

Runtime. One of the great villains for innovation is perhaps the time, both for the dedication that your team has to have and for the level of innovation they must present. If the team needs to develop the solution or at least a Minimum Viable Product (MVP) quickly, Design Sprint is recommended. Now, if the idea is to understand the context in depth and then create a solution, Design Thinking fulfills this role well.

Learning. Although the two approaches are based on collaboration and experimentation, Design Thinking has a more "learn by sharing" character, since Design Sprint is more "learning by doing" due to the sprints' time and the speed one must have to create one MVP (Minimum Viable Product). Both Design Thinking and Design Sprint are approaches that significantly leverage the ability of people involved in being creative. Both approaches in fact, are characterized by tools and methodologies supporting idea generation like How Might We for Design Thinking or Crazy' s 8 for Design Sprint. The Design Sprint methodology promotes a more critical approach providing for a higher number of sessions dedicated to individual thinking compared to what is suggested by Design Thinking.

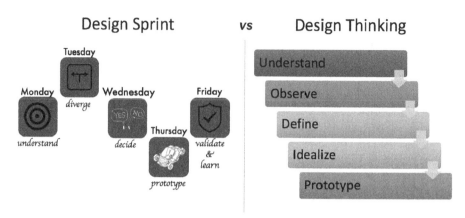

Fig. 3. Comparing Design Sprint versus Design Thinking

Learning by Prototyping. The second aspect the two approaches have in common is undoubtedly the role of prototyping. Both methodologies don't just define the steps needed to imagine an idea, a solution, but enable the work team to reach the implementation through the development of a prototype. As regards Design Sprint these solutions appear to be much more concrete, as if aiming to simulate working prototypes, whereas in Design Thinking projects, prototypes sometimes are just Roadmaps describing how the solution will be developed, without providing physical evidence of the solution itself.

User Contribution. Another difference regards the role that the end user has in the innovation process. The difference of involvement is connected to the fact that the Sprint comes from an internal company challenge while the Design Thinking process stems from the will to look at the needs users are facing and helping them to solve them. This is the reason why the tools used are different. With Design Thinking broad use is made of ethnographic research while in Design Sprint users are involved in tests such as the AB Test.

Process Dynamics. This is one of the aspects that most differentiates the two approaches. If Design Thinking processes can last hours, days, months or even years, with Design Sprint they have a defined duration: 5 business days, from Monday to Friday. This difference in duration has repercussions on process dynamics. In fact: Design Thinking prefers diverging phases that generate innumerable new ideas through brainstorming moments. Design Sprint focuses on convergence to the point of dedicating three days out of five to it and places strong emphasis on decision making moments that are often dealt with through elections. Understanding in just five days (Design Sprint) activities which usually require a greater timeframe (Design Thinking) leads to reducing uncertainties and increase the potential success of a project. This test, which takes place on the fifth day and not after months, enables the team to understand the pros and cons of the solution and learn from it while avoiding that the team becomes enamoured with the solution developed internally and not being open to variations and ascendancy provided by users.

4   Conclusion

Design Thinking is a new way of thinking and approaching problems or, in other words, a people-centered thinking model.

Design Thinking was first cited in 1980, and popularized by the American design and innovation company, IDEO, which began using that approach to solve problems in a more humane way and spread the word around the world so that other companies could discover the power of design in the face of the problems they encounter.

Design Sprint was developed by Google Ventures - Google's Venture Capital arm - based on Design Thinking and agile methodologies, with the main goal of prototyping solutions in a much faster and more dynamic way.

Design Sprint is a five-day process for answering critical business questions through design, prototyping, and testing ideas with customers.

Both Design Thinking and Sprint Design have enormous power of innovation, but aligning expectations and defining why you're doing it will make the whole process clearer for all participants.

References

1. Tillberg-Webb, H., Collier, N.: Using the design thinking cycle to tell the story of innovative learning spaces. In: Hokanson, B., Clinton, G., Kaminski, K. (eds.) Educational Technology and Narrative, pp. 141–153. Springer, Cham (2018). https://doi.org/10.1007/978-3-319-69914-1_12
2. Maruping, L.M., Venkatesh, V., Agarwal, R.: A control theory perspective on agile methodology use and changing user requirements. Inform. Syst. Res. J. **20**(3), 377–399 (2009)
3. Keijzer-Broers, W.J.W., de Reuver, M.: Applying agile design sprint methods in action design research: prototyping a health and wellbeing platform. In: Parsons, J., Tuunanen, T., Venable, J., Donnellan, B., Helfert, M., Kenneally, J. (eds.) DESRIST 2016. LNCS, vol. 9661, pp. 68–80. Springer, Cham (2016). https://doi.org/10.1007/978-3-319-39294-3_5
4. Knapp, J., Zeratsky, J., Kowitz, B.: Sprint: How to Solve Big Problems and Test New Ideas in Just Five Days. Simon and Schuster, New York (2016)
5. Padmanabhan, P., et al.: Design thinking and computational modeling to stop illegal poaching. In: 2017 IEEE Integrated STEM Education Conference (ISEC), pp. 175–181. IEEE (2017)
6. Vianna, M.: Design thinking: inovação em negócios. Design Thinking (2012)
7. Du, J., Jing, S., Liu, J.: Creating shared design thinking process for collaborative design. J. Netw. Comput. Appl. **35**(1), 111–120 (2012)
8. Chamberlain, S., Sharp, H., Maiden, N.: Towards a framework for integrating agile development and user-centred design. In: Abrahamsson, P., Marchesi, M., Succi, G. (eds.) XP 2006. LNCS, vol. 4044, pp. 143–153. Springer, Heidelberg (2006). https://doi.org/10.1007/11774129_15

9. Awad, M.A.: A comparison between agile and traditional software development methodologies. University of Western Australia (2005)

10. Sharma, S., Sarkar, D., Gupta, D.: Agile processes and methodologies: a conceptual study. Int. J. Comput. Sci. Eng. **4**(5), 892 (2012)

11. Banfield, R., Lombardo, C.T., Wax, T.: Design Sprint: A Practical Guidebook for Building Great Digital Products. O'Reilly Media, Inc., Newton (2015)

12. Morien, R.: Agile management and the Toyota way for software project management. In: 2005 3rd IEEE International Conference on Industrial Informatics, INDIN 2005, pp. 516–522. IEEE (2005)

13. Kruchten, P.: The Rational Unified Process: An Introduction. Addison-Wesley Professional, Boston (2004)

14. Pohl, K.: Requirements Engineering: Fundamentals, Principles, and Techniques. Springer, Heidelberg (2010)

15. Higuchi, M.M., Nakano, D.N.: Agile design: a combined model based on design thinking and agile methodologies for digital games projects. Revista de Gestão e Projetos **8**(2), 109 (2017)

16. Brown, T., Wyatt, J.: Design thinking for social innovation. Dev. Outreach **12**(1), 29–43 (2010)

17. Talita, P.: Design thinking. SENAC J. 109 (2018)

18. Canedo, E.D., Parente da Costa, R.: The use of design thinking in agile software requirements survey: a case study. In: Marcus, A., Wang, W. (eds.) DUXU 2018. LNCS, vol. 10918, pp. 642–657. Springer, Cham (2018). https://doi.org/10.1007/978-3-319-91797-9_45

19. Gothelf, J.: Lean UX: Applying lEan Principles to Improve User Experience. O'Reilly Media Inc., Newton (2013)

Game Design Model for Educational History Videogames

Ricardo Navarro Fernandez, Sergio Martinez Palomino,
Vanessa Vega Velarde, Claudia Zapata Del Rio[✉],
and Victor Chiroque Landayeta

Pontificia Universidad Católica del Perú, Lima, Peru
{ricardo.navarro, smartinezp, vanessa.vega}@pucp.pe,
zapata.cmp@pup.edu.pe, echiroq@pucp.edu.pe

Abstract. The objective of this study is to apply and validate a game design model for educational video games. For this purpose, a theoretical review has been carried out on the relevant factors that must be considered when designing an interactive educational experience such as video games. Then a model, previously used in the educational context, was applied to design and develop an educational video game about the independence of Perú. To validate this model, a population of 7 university students between 17 and 19 years played for 45 min the designed video game. Immediately, in-depth interviews were conducted with the validation participants to finally analyze the results and contrast them with the process that was used in the design of the game and the didactics of the story. Additionally, a user evaluation was applied to verify the usability level of the game in order to know if the game is pleasant for people.

Keywords: Game design · Education · Video games

1 Introduction

Since its invention until today, video games have played an important role in our society, as they have promoted the emergence of various social and cultural phenomena that do not go unnoticed by public opinion. In this sense, opposing positions on its impact can be found. On the one hand, a large sector of society considers that this means of entertainment is negative or harmful [12, 19]. While on the other, there are competitive spaces, followed by millions of spectators, where players face each other, considering this activity as a sport that currently involves large sums of money [9, 18].

In the midst of these opposing positions, the results of academic research suggest that video games provide benefits for the cognitive, affective and social development of people [16, 27, 10]. The impact of videogames on cognitive development shows that they can serve as interactive technological tools for education, so that they influence students' motivation and academic performance as shown by several examples found in: [11, 28, 14, 20, 15, 34, 3, 33, 13, 8]. However, these results generate new questions such as what aspects of video games are those that influence the interest of the players and their learning? The answer to this question lies in the design of video games (the "game design").

© Springer Nature Switzerland AG 2019
A. Marcus and W. Wang (Eds.): HCII 2019, LNCS 11583, pp. 307–323, 2019.
https://doi.org/10.1007/978-3-030-23570-3_23

2   Game Design for the Educational Context

Different authors have approached Game Design from different perspectives as stated in [1, 29]. For example, some authors consider the design of video games as an artistic process that becomes a source of creativity and, consequently, considers artists as designers [1]. However, other authors, possibly more associated with the development of technologies, consider Game Design as an engineering process that comes from a systematic methodology and a balance in the game's rules [1]. Each of these perspectives shows essential aspects of the design of a video game. However, none of these perspectives alone can address a comprehensive picture of what Game Design is [1], since it requires creativity and orderly and methodical planning.

Several models have been proposed for the development of Game Design, but most of them in the entertainment industry and not in the educational context. There are relatively useful guides for the educational videogame design process, but they tend to focus on specific aspects of the process with little or no connection to the overall design landscape. For example, it has been pointed out that the mechanics of games can influence the cognitive functions of the user, that narrative resources have a more significant impact on knowledge and that visual effects favor player immersion [7, 22, 4]. These contributions enrich the data accumulation; however, they are limited if you intend to address the complete design of an educational video game. Therefore, it is necessary to develop general models of game design for the educational field that consider the educational aspects, the aesthetic and the entertainment. One of these models for the design of educational video games is the one proposed by Navarro [24] (see Fig. 1).

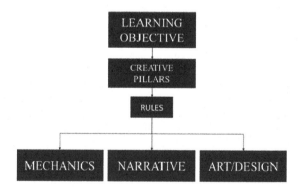

Fig. 1. Game design model revisited base on the structure of Navarro [24]

2.1   Game Design Model

In this regard, an important point to note is that the main purpose of a video game is to entertain [1, 6]. The model proposed by Navarro [24] starts from this premise and considers that entertainment should be oriented or feed a learning objective. The model defines "learning objective" as a set of knowledge, aptitudes, abilities, behaviors or competencies that the user has to learn through the educational video game [35]. Likewise, the model used in this study is based on classic Game Design components in its model: mechanics, narrative and art, to which it adds two components that should guide the design: the learning objective and the creative pillars. In this way, it establishes that the learning objective is the main axis that will guide the development and design of the video game.

From this, the creative pillars are established and, then, all the other components for the design of the game. Below, some general ideas about these five components are developed.

Learning Objective

The first component of the model is the learning objective, which guides the entire design, therefore the process for define it should be serious and diligent. In order to establish the learning objective, it is necessary to carry out a theoretical review on the subject to be addressed, so that specific elements of the topic to be worked on are chosen. Also, the proposed objectives should be clear and specific, avoiding using generalities such as "talk about history," "learn from mathematics," "solve exercises," etc.

Creative Pillars

The Creative Pillars can be understood as guidelines for each decision made in the design of the video game and are established based on the Learning Objective. Thus, these pillars will filter the elements and contents that are addressed in the game. This component is essential for the design of an educational video game for two reasons: (1) it allows to disaggregate the learning objective in specific points that will be retaken throughout the design and (2) it allows to approach the learning objective creatively and attractively. It must be considered that the video game must be entertaining and, at the same time, teach something. Entertainment should not be sacrificed for learning or vice versa; a balance should be found. Likewise, to develop the creative pillars, it is necessary to master the specific theme established in the learning objective and filter those contents that are not relevant [24].

Mechanics

Mechanics can be defined as the basic and main rules of a video game [1]. This element is one of the most important aspects of Game Design in general, so its role in the development of an educational video game is crucial. For its development, it is necessary to consider that the design of a video game, educational or not, is an interdisciplinary work [24]. The mechanics of the video game must contribute to the learning objective [24], although not necessarily directly, but seeking to achieve what is proposed in the creative pillars. When working with mechanics for an educational video game, it is important to point out that there are pedagogical and didactic aspects related to the subject that is to be taught, and they must be taken into account when designing.

Narrative

The narrative is defined, in simple words, as the story in which the video game will be immersed [1]. In no way should the narrative be understood as solely textual; On the contrary, the narrative can be developed from the art of the video game, the mechanics and, of course, the sections in which a story can be explicitly presented in a visual, oral or both.

Art

This component, like the others, must respond to the learning objective. If the thematic of the game is based on symbolism, or allegories to an object or history, the art must respond with more abstract and not so direct designs. If the game is direct and focuses on real contents, art should be as real as possible [24].

Rules

In the present study, the rules can be understood as objectives within the game that determines the scenario where this takes place; and these can assimilate the symbolism expressed in the art and the characters [24].

However, the hierarchy that may exist between this aspect and the mechanics, narrative, and art, is not clear. Therefore, the present study suggests hierarchizing the Rules, placing it below the Creative Pillars, but above the mechanics, narrative, and art (see Fig. 1). This will allow a relationship that can feed the Creative Pillars and the other elements of the game.

2.2 History Learning

The importance of how a subject is taught is essential in the design of an educational video game. It is not the same to teach mathematical content as history content or physics. In this sense, this study is based on pedagogical and didactic bases of history teaching, so a review of the research on history learning is carried out below.

Learning and analyzing historical facts entails various benefits at a cognitive and social level [25, 26]. However, several obstacles hinder the teaching of history. One of the most common is the tendency to memorize historical facts [8, 21]. This type of teaching does not achieve the objectives of this subject and can even be harmful to students [8]. On the contrary, the teaching of this thematic area should focus on developing students' historical thinking [21], that is, helping students understand the processes of change in historical time and the influence they exert.

Historical thinking is a construct composed of six thematic axes [21, 30, 31, 17, 23, 32]:

1. Historical relevance, which refers to the reasons why they are considered as critical specific events;
2. Evidence, which refers to the methodology used to select and interpret the sources of a historical argument;
3. Continuity and change, which refer to temporal processes intertwined and not as opposites;
4. Cause and consequence, which refers to understanding that there are various reasons why specific actions and conditions happened, and in which the social conditions of the moment and the actors themselves are considered;
5. Historical empathy, which refers to identifying the influence of the social, cultural, intellectual context in the actions of the characters; and
6. Historical awareness, which refers to moral obligations on actions considered illegal or criminal carried out in the past and that have had repercussions up to the present.

Based on the literature reviewed, the present study aims to design and validate an educational video game based on the model proposed by Navarro et al. [24], with university students. For this, a qualitative study was carried out, analyzing the users' perception of the video game. The results of this application will be presented and discussed considering the proposed theoretical framework.

3 Developing the Video Game

Video game "1821: la Lucha por la independencia" [1821: The fight for Independence]: is an educational video game that deals with the process of declaration and consolidation of the independence of Peru between 1821 and 1824 (see Fig. 2). The main elements of the game design are described, using the proposal by Navarro [24] as frame of reference.

Fig. 2. Title screen of the video game

3.1 Application of the Model

In this study, the component of Rules is being used as a hinge between the game design elements, the Creative Pillars and the Learning Objective:

Learning objective
In the first instance, the learning objective of the game was established, so that all subsequent design elements would aim at achieving it. In this way, and the function of the revision of material on teaching and pedagogy of history teaching, the following learning objective was proposed:

- "Promote historical thinking in students."

In addition, three specific areas of historical thinking that the video game sought to promote were selected:

- Cause and consequence,
- Historical empathy and
- Historical relevance.

Creative Pillars

Once identified the areas of the learning objective, the next step is to establish creative pillars that address them creatively and entertainingly. The participation of the game designer, in coordination with the educational experts, is especially meaningful in this aspect, since it is important to develop a video game that is entertaining and that also teaches. In this case, three creative pillars were established:

- Choose your destiny: it deals with the area of cause and consequence of historical thought;
- Listen to time: approach the area of historical empathy;
- Do not judge without knowing: it deals with the area of historical relevance.

Mechanics

For the development of mechanics, the educational expert must explain to the game designer what the learning objective is and what the creative pillars of the video game consist of (in case this has not been involved in the development of the same). For this video game, many mechanics were developed; nevertheless, we will mention only some of them below, in order to exemplify the connection between these and the creative pillars.

For the creative pillar "Choose your destiny", the mechanics of "decision-making" was developed (see Fig. 3). This consists of allowing the player to realized various decisions throughout the game.

Fig. 3. Decision making scenes (The translation of the text is: Main text: how would you respond? Text to the left: Friendly greetings, Text in the center: Hostile greetings, Text to the right: Greetings)

Fig. 4. Information Cards (The main title can be translated to: Know more about the intentions of every character)

For creative pillars "Listen to time" and "Do not judge without knowing", the mechanics of Information Cards was developed, which consisted in that before a battle the user had access to cards with data about the context in which it was developed (see Fig. 4).

Narrative

Being a video game based of real history events, the narrative becomes essential. However, the present study has focused on presenting history in a way that encourages historical thinking and not rote learning.

For this, three types of cinematics have been developed that address the Creative Pillars: "Listen to Time" and "Do not judge without knowing", because socio-cultural and personal characteristics of the actors of the Independence of Peru are exposed:

– Initial cinematics: It presents through images and voice-over the social and political context that unleashes the independence of Spanish America. The cinematics cannot be skipped and is subtitled.
– Cinematic by event: As the game progresses, this cinematics expose chronologically the most important events of the independence of Peru, as a preamble to the new section that the user will play.
– Explanatory cinematics: Cinematics that are exposed after the player has made a decision that may affect the development of the game. In this way, these scenes describe the new political, social and/or economic context resulting from the chosen decision.

Art

Finally, for the art of video game, we worked together with an artist, who designed cinematics that presented static images that depicted what was narrated by the voice-over. This is expected to allow concentration on the information presented rather than on other factors that could distract the user. Likewise, the colors used, the shapes and the textures of the elements were designed in such a way as to allow the user to understand how Peru looked in those years. The art was developed in close relation to the narrative, and it was emphasized in crucial aspects such as scrolls for the decisions that must be made, a map of Peru as a driving interface between the events, etc.

3.2 Development Process

Like any other software, a video game can be developed using known methodologies. If the application of the described model is taken as the development needs, then it is necessary to translate these needs into requirements in order to apply the known software development methodologies.

Given the size and interdisciplinarity of the team and the product to be developed, the adaptation of Scrum was considered as a development methodology integrated to usability techniques that allow building a more attractive game for people (see Fig. 5).

We used an adaptation based on a case study by Aguilar and Zapata [2], in which the XP design process is improved through the use of UCD tools. The difference in the present work is explained in Daly et al. [5] where Scrum is used instead of XP as shown in Fig. 5. In this sense, "Interviews" will not be used because the requirements

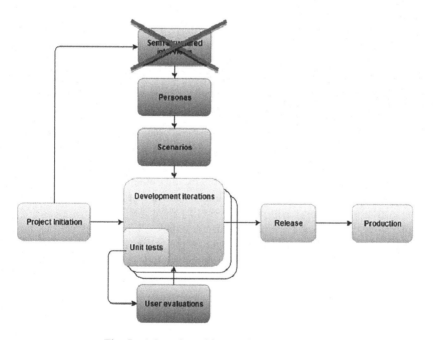

Fig. 5. Adaptation of integration proposed [5]

were obtained from the game design but "Personas" and "Scenarios" were used because they helped to represent the development needs.

For the application of the Game design model, a high-level design was developed that included the components of the model. As part of the iterations of development, the mechanisms of interaction, dialogues, facts to narrate, pieces of art and music were derived, thus allowing an incremental development.

4 Validating the Model

Once the video game was developed, the application of the model was evaluated through a validation that had the purpose of knowing if the players reached the proposed learning objectives.

4.1 Participants

The participants were 7 freshman students at a Peruvian university, whose ages ranged from 17 to 19 years old.

4.2 Instruments

Interview guide: A qualitative interview was developed that explores the mechanics, the narrative and the art of the game and how these influenced or not the achievement of the learning objective. The interview guide was made up of the following areas:

- General impressions: This area explored the general impressions of the users regarding the video game.
- Narrative: This area explored different aspects of the video game narrative. Thus, information was collected on the opinion of the cinematics, the information cards, etc.
- Mechanics: This area explored the way in which users respond to the mechanics in the game, and the rules identified while playing the game.
- Final impressions: This area explored the users' perceptions about the possibility of obtaining multiple endings and if they had understood how to unblock them.

4.3 Procedure

To evaluate if the design of the educational video game was effective, 7 people were asked to play it for 45 min. Then, they answered the usability questionnaire. After that, a total of seven interviews were conducted that explored the various aspects of the game design of "1821: The Fight for Independence", so that it could be evidenced if this had achieved the proposed design objectives. The application was made in a laboratory with four computers, and three sessions were developed in total. First, the participants played the game, without any interference from the researchers. Then, after the time ended, the researchers proceed to perform the interview to the participants.

4.4 Results

The objective of this research was to analyze the design of a video game for the teaching of history based on the game design model proposed by Navarro [24]. To do this, it was explored to what extent the Mechanics, the Narrative and the Art, in harmony with the Creative Pillars and Rules, achieved or not the proposed learning objective. Next, the information gathered in the interviews conducted will be analyzed.

Choose Your Destiny
Concerning the creative pillar "Choose your destiny" it was proposed that users can make different decisions throughout the game, decisions that could change the end of the game, becoming able to unlock six different endings. It was expected that the user would be able to understand that a historical event depends on different causes and that it will have repercussions on a series of future events. Indeed, it has been found that mechanics, narrative, and art have achieved what is proposed by this pillar.

Thus, various users have referred to the importance that the game gives to decision making and that these are what determine the events that will happen later. For example, the results suggest that the mechanics of dialogues and crucial decisions have favored the idea of cause and consequence mentioned above.

Interviewer (I): What do you think is the goal of the game?
Participant(P) 1: (...) give us information to reach a decision, can reach a specific end, with a decision making either in the same game or in the same dialogs that appeared

In the previous quote, it can be seen that the participant realized the importance of decision making and its impact for the future from the mechanism proposed in the video game, specifically from the dialogues and crucial decisions. This provides relevant information because it suggests that mechanics work as expected.

Also, the mechanics allowed users to analyze the situation that would result from the choices they made. Thus, they were able to use the information given, analyze it and ramble about the possible consequences that they entail.

I: (...) The moment you made a decision, what were you doing? What things did you take into account when you made decisions?
P1: Especially the effect that could later have (...) you had to choose if you could talk kindly, neutrally or as an enemy, let's say. Also, depending on that it could be that it is triggered... like, for example, that La Serna retires to the mountains and that La Serna leaves.

In the previous quote, it is observed that the mechanics of dialogue encourages the participant to be aware that the decision he/she will make will influence the possible future situations. Also, it is observed that the mechanics do not work independently of the other components of the video game since the user indicates that he uses the information provided in the proposed Narrative. This suggests that the video game design is an integral product and that it allows an adequate interaction between its elements.

In the same way, the crucial decision mechanics favored, in the users, the conception that the decisions that they make could have repercussions not only in the immediate future of a character but also in the future of other actors that relate directly or indirectly with them.

I: Did you like to make decisions?

P3: It is one of the parts that, like, I did a lot… Because sometimes I am afraid of making decisions, but I had to take one (…) And [the game] put me in a situation of the soldiers and their commander, and it makes me feel like I have a big responsibility. That is, it gave me an enormous responsibility to be leading a whole group, but I had to choose one.

In this way, it can be seen that this mechanism allowed the user to understand the responsibility of deciding for one or another possibility and that this decision would affect various people in different areas. Furthermore, it is pertinent to point out that, in this case, the user comments that he does not feel comfortable making decisions, which could suggest that this mechanism allows observing an action that the user would not be willing to perform in any other learning situation.

The proposed mechanics favor the understanding that a situation can be modified and influenced by the interaction of different facts, as opposed to a linear view of history:

I: Did you like to make decisions?

P2: I mean yes, that is always a plus I think (…) practically all that has repercussions, it is not always going to follow the same line and I think I like it a lot, I always like that.

I: What things did you take into account when making the decisions?

P2: I was thinking about both possibilities: which was the best possible situation and which was the worst possible situation (…) sometimes I chose the worst (…) because I thought I would be able to overcome those adversities in the battle.

In the first quote, it can be observed that the decision mechanics favor the understanding that a story will not always be linear but will depend on the different decisions that are made. However, in the second citation it can also be observed that the mechanics do not promote the idea that a decision will inevitably turn into a specific situation; on the contrary, the user suggests an understanding that following situations also depend on other crucial aspects and therefore, they are modifiable. Thus, he understood that the future of the Independence of Peru depended, at least, on two crucial aspects: (1) the political aspect (addressed by the decision-making mechanics) and (2) the military aspect (addressed by the mechanics of battles to which it refers).

Listen to Time and Do Not Judge Without Knowing
On the other hand, it was hoped that the creative pillars "Listen to time" and "Do not judge without knowing" allow us to understand that the social, political and economic context influences the development of subsequent events, together with the individual actions of the great historical actors. For this, both cinematic and information cards were used.

The results suggest that the cinematics provided information about the social, political and economic context of that time that was useful for the user when making decisions.

I: Did the cinematics help you to understand the history of the game?

P1: Yes, yes. (...), because they give you a context, they give you a context for what you are going to... for the different battles that you are going to have, the different decisions that you are going to have to make.

I: Did the cinematics help you to understand the history of the game?

P2: They give you the social context that is being lived and the functions that each one had.

I: What did you take into account to make the decisions?

P3: I took into account the social context and what could come later (...) That is, what consequences that decision would bring me.

From this, it is possible to assume that (1) the cinematics contained useful information about the context in which the events took place and (2) that this information was considered when making decisions. In this way, we observed that cinematics could allow the user to understand that future events not only depend on the decisions they make but also on the context in which they are immersed.

In contrast, the results suggest that, although the information cards also presented useful information about the context of the events, in some cases they were not considered at the time of making decisions. Also, some of the users did not read all the information cards.

I: Did you read all the information cards?

P1: Not so much. 70–80% of all

I: Did you read all the information cards?

P2: Superficially. I never read them in detail.

However, other users did consider that information cards provided useful information to contextualize and to understand the objectives of the various parties involved in historical events.

I: Did the information cards help you understand the context of the events you played?

P2: The truth, I think so. They told you the date; they told you where I was located and what... from Spain, what was your objective and from Peru what was your objective.

I: Did the information cards help you understand the context of the events you played?

P3: Yes, because they gave you as the context in which the historical context was, the objective of the Patriots, the objective of the realists

Because these results suggest that the information on the cards was useful to understand the context and, in addition, they allowed to understand more deeply the position of the actors when presenting the objectives of each of them, it is possible that the fact of not reading them lie more in the way in which they were presented than in the quality of the information they exhibit. In that sense, it is likely that modifications of art and style are required rather than content.

On the other hand, it was proposed that two main rules would characterize the game: unlock different alternative endings and face the Realist side. Thus, the results suggest that both rules were fully understood and that both mechanics, art, and narrative contributed to this achievement.

I: Why do you think that there are different endings within the game?

P3: [Its because of] how many points you won on the patriotic side, because not everyone can win. Not in every event. This is because of the strategies you can use, because you may have made a bad strategy and lost, then you subtract points and leads you to another end. Another would be the decisions you made or, well, in this case, that I took at the time of talk with a general or something.

Thus, we observed that the users not only understood the rules but that they were able to identify and describe them as expected. Also, the rules allowed an adequate interaction between the mechanics and the narrative. This favors the creative pillars because it allows understanding the video game as an integral and coherent product.

On the other hand, it was mentioned that an educational video game should not be limited to presenting educational content, but that it should be fun and entertaining. In this case, most users suggested that "1821: The Struggle for Independence" is an entertaining video game that is not tedious.

P1: Interesting, interactive (...) summarize, let's say, the history, in a way that is understandable and not so heavy to understand.

P2: Quite interesting. I had not previously played the games to make decisions, so, that influence your adventure, because it left me with the desire to continue seeing what would take my decisions.

P3: (...) Also, then I could go maybe so upset by the decision that took the game right? It is also entertaining to see what happens.

5   Usability Evaluation

As part of the development methodology, user evaluations were applied in each iteration. The final user evaluation is described below, which allows observing that using the described model and usability techniques, an educational video game can be obtained that not only meets the educational objectives but is also usable.

5.1   Participants

The participants were 9 university freshmen students, whose ages ranged from 17 to 19 years old.

5.2   Instruments

Questionnaire: Users resolved a questionnaire that included closed-ended and open-ended questions.

These questions were aimed at verifying if the information provided by the game is clear and if the mechanics of the game are easy to use. We also consulted which aspects of the game are nice and which are not. And finally, he asked the users if they consider the game useful and if they would play it again.

5.3 Procedure

During the 45 min of validation of the game, users of the game were observed to use it and before applying the in-depth interviews they completed the user test questionnaire. In this way, the same users were used in the same session, in addition two more people were added because the time they had only allowed to complete the usability evaluation but not to apply the interview.

5.4 Results

As can be seen in Table 1 corresponding to the results of the questionnaire, users answered positively to each aspect of the game. In this questionnaire, a liker scale from 1 to 5 was used from negative to positive.

– Cinematics: refers to the clarity that the cinematics of the game offer.
– Objectives and context: understandable and clear.
– Characters: identifiable characters and battle sides.
– Movement, attack, and dice: It is easy to interact with these options and use them.
– Decision events: are important.
– Decisions taken: have an impact on the game.

We can observe that the aspects of the battle as easy to attack and use of the dice obtained lower scores which are directly related to the difficulty of understanding these mechanisms at the first opportunity.

Despite the majority considered the stage of decisions important, many did not see clearly the consequences of their actions in the execution they did.

Table 1. Results of questionnarie

User	Cinematics	Objectives and context	Characters	Movement	Attack	Dice	Decision events	Decisions taken
1	5	5	5	5	4	3	5	5
2	5	5	4	5	3	4	2	3
3	4	4	3	3	2	2	3	3
4	5	5	5	5	4	3	4	4
5	5	4	5	3	3	4	4	4
6	5	5	5	5	5	5	5	4
7	5	4	3	3	4	5	4	3
8	5	5	5	5	3	5	5	5
9	5	5	4	4	4	4	5	4
	4.89	4.67	4.33	4.22	3.56	3.89	4.11	3.89

8 of the 9 users considered the game entertaining. All highlighted the usefulness and importance of having a videogame of this type and 7 of the 9 said they would play again especially for the interest of knowing the other possible endings. The aspects that were indicated as positive were:

- The cinematics allow to contextualize the story in an entertaining and clear way.
- The different endings make the game more interesting because the end is not always known in advance.
- Graphics and music are nice.
- The negative aspects found were:
- Difficulty in the interaction in the first opportunities.
- The battle could be made long depending on the results of the dice.
- In some cinematics the narrator's voice is softer than music.

6 Conclusions and Future Works

It is pertinent to point out that the mechanics have favored approaching history from an original perspective, which does not appeal to rote learning. Also, it is possible that the mechanics allow some independence to the user in front of a story that they have usually conceived as immovable (for example, "getting angry" from a decision that the game has taken). Besides, it seems that the historical content has been exposed in a non-boring or tedious way, which may be because the narrative is not overwhelming and that the elements of art, such as music, colors, interface, etc. could be beneficial to reduce this type of situations.

The objective of this research was to analyze the design of an educational video game based on the review of the game design model used by Navarro. The proposed model was characterized by establishing a learning objective and creative pillars that were the guides for the development of rules, mechanics, narrative, and art. From the above, it is possible to conclude that the rules, mechanics, narrative, and art allowed to achieve what is proposed in the creative pillars. This, in turn, made it possible to achieve the learning objective. Also, the results suggest that the video game was considered fun and entertaining by users, a fundamental aspect for the success of any video game and, especially for an educational video game.

The main contribution of this design is the revision and precision of the model proposed by Navarro, emphasizing the importance of establishing a theoretically supported learning objective and the articulation of this objective with the elements of the video game. Finally, the application of the proposed framework is suggested to verify its effectiveness and viability, as well as the limitations it presents.

R. Navarro Fernandez et al.

References

1. Adams, E.: Fundamentals of Game Design. New Riders, Berkeley (2013)
2. Aguilar, M., Zapata, C.: Integrating UCD and an agile methodology in the development of a mobile catalog of plants. In: Soares, M., et al. (eds.) Advances in Ergonomics Modeling, Usability and Special Populations: Proceedings of the AHFE 2016 International Conference on Ergonomics Modeling, Usability and Special Populations, pp. 75–87. Springer International Publishing, Cham (2017). https://doi.org/10.1007/978-3-319-41685-4_8
3. Alarcia, D.T., Barco, D.I.: Videojuegos y aprendizaje de la Historia: la saga Assasin's Creed. Contextos Educ. Rev. Educ. **17**, 145–155 (2014)
4. Clark, D.B., et al.: Digital games, design, and learning: a systematic review and meta-analysis. Rev. Educ. Res. **86**(1), 79–122 (2016)
5. Daly, C., Zapata, C., Paz, F.: Improving the usability in a video game through continuous usability evaluations. In: Marcus, A., Wang, W. (eds.) DUXU 2017. LNCS, vol. 10289, pp. 387–397. Springer, Cham (2017). https://doi.org/10.1007/978-3-319-58637-3_31
6. Deterding, S., et al.: From game design elements to gamefulness: defining "Gamification". In: Proceedings of the 15th International Academic MindTrek Conference: Envisioning Future Media Environments, pp. 9–15. ACM, New York (2011)
7. Dickey, M.D.: Game design narrative for learning: appropriating adventure game design narrative devices and techniques for the design of interactive learning environments. Education Tech. Res. Dev. **54**(3), 245–263 (2006)
8. Evaristo Chiyong, I., et al.: Uso de un videojuego educativo como herramienta para aprender historia del Perú. RIED Rev. Iberoam. Educ. Distancia **19**, 2 (2016)
9. Gamepedia: 2018 Season World Championship. https://lol.gamepedia.com/2018_Season_World_Championship
10. Granic, I., et al.: The benefits of playing video games. Am. Psychol. **69**(1), 66–78 (2014)
11. Gros Salvat, B., Garrido Miranda, J.M.: "Con el Dedo en la Pantalla": El Uso de un Videojuego de Estrategia en la Mediación de Aprendizajes Curriculares. Teoría de la Educación. Educ. Cult. Soc. Inf. **9**, 3 (2008)
12. Henríquez, F.P., Zúñiga, T.A.: Hacia una conceptualización de los videojuegos como discursos multimodales electrónicos. Anagramas: Rumbos y Sentidos de la Comunicación **15**(30), 51–64 (2017)
13. Irigaray, M.V., del Rosario Luna, M.: La enseñanza de la Historia a través de videojuegos de estrategia: Dos experiencias áulicas en la escuela secundaria. Clío & Asociados **19**, 411–437 (2014)
14. Gee, J.P.: Lo que nos enseñan los videojuegos sobre el aprendizaje y el alfabetismo. https://www.uoc.edu/uocpapers/dt/eng/gee.html
15. Valverde, J.: Learning to think historically with information technology supports AU. Cult. Educ. **20**(2), 181–199 (2008)
16. Kato, P.M.: Video games in health care: closing the gap. Rev. General Psychol. **14**(2), 113–121 (2010)
17. Levesque, S.: Thinking Historically: Educating Students for the 21st Century. Scholarly Publishing Division, University of Toronto Press, Toronto (2009)
18. LoLSports: Las cifras del Mid-Season Invitational 2018 | LoL Esports LAS. https://las.lolesports.com/noticias/las-cifras-del-mid-season-invitational-2018-105989
19. Marín, A.A.L., et al.: Qué concepciones tienen los docentes en ejercicio y en formación inicial, sobre el uso didáctico de los videojuegos? (2016) http://files.bartolomevazquezbernal.webnode.es/200000096-4b7664d6a0/Lorca_version%20autor%2027edce.pdf

20. Marín Díaz, V., García Fernández, M.D.: Los videojuegos su capacidad didáctico-formativa. Video Games Didact. Form. Capacity **26**, 113–119 (2005)
21. Carretero, M., Montanero, M.: Teaching and learning history: cognitive and cultural aspects AU. Cult. Educ. **20**(2), 133–142 (2008)
22. Young, M.F., et al.: Our princess is in another castle: a review of trends in serious gaming for education. Rev. Educ. Res. **82**(1), 61–89 (2012)
23. Mora Hernández, G.D., Ortiz Paz, R.: El Modelo de Educación Histórica. Experiencia de Innovación en la Educación Básica de México. Enseñanza de las Ciencias Sociales: Revista de Investigación **11**, 87–98 (2012)
24. Navarro, R., Zapata, C., Vega, V., Chiroque, E.: Videogames, motivation and history of Peru: designing an educational game about Mariano Melgar. In: Ahram, T.Z. (ed.) AHFE 2018. AISC, vol. 795, pp. 283–293. Springer, Cham (2019). https://doi.org/10.1007/978-3-319-94619-1_28
25. Perafán Cabrera, A.: Reflexiones en torno a la didáctica de la historia. Revista Guillermo de Ockham **11**(2), 149–160 (2013)
26. Prats, J., Santacana, J.: Principios para la enseñanza de la Historia. Enseñar Historia: Notas Para Una Didáctica Renovadora, pp. 13–55 (2001)
27. Primack, B.A., et al.: Role of video games in improving health-related outcomes: a systematic review. Am. J. Prev. Med. **42**(6), 630–638 (2012)
28. Requena, B.E.S., McMullin, K.J.: Videojuegos para la inclusión educativa. Digit. Educ. Rev. **27**, 122–137 (2015)
29. Schell, J.: The Art of Game Design: A Book of Lenses. CRC Press, Amsterdam (2008)
30. Seixas, P., et al.: A design process for assessing historical thinking: the case of a one-hour test. In: Ercikan, K., Seixas, P. (eds.) New Directions in Assessing Historical Thinking. Taylor & Francis Group, Abingdon (2015)
31. Seixas, P., Morton, T.: The Big Six Historical Thinking Concepts. Nelson Canada, Toronto (2012)
32. Serrano, J.S., López-Facal, R.: Competencias y narrativas históricas: el pensamiento histórico de estudiantes y futuros profesores españoles de educación secundaria. Rev. Estud. Soc. **52**, 87–101 (2015)
33. Vivancos, A.E., et al.: Videojuegos, historia y patrimonio: primeros resultados de una investigación educativa evaluativa en educación secundaria (2017)
34. Watson, W.R., et al.: A case study of the in-class use of a video game for teaching high school history. Comput. Educ. **56**(2), 466–474 (2011)
35. Preguntas frecuentes sobre Schoology – Centro de Ayuda. https://support.schoology.com/hc/es/sections/200216583-Preguntas-frecuentes-sobre-Schoology

Interaction Design of the Family Agent Based on the CMR-FBS Model

Jingyan Qin[1]([✉]), Wenhao Zhang[1], Zhibo Chen[1], Daisong Guan[2], Moli Zhou[2], and Shiyan Li[2]

[1] School of Mechanical Engineering, University of Science and Technology Beijing, Beijing, People's Republic of China
qinjingyanking@foxmail.com
[2] Baidu AI Interaction Design Lab, Beijing, People's Republic of China

Abstract. The paper explores the function and contents design ontology for the interaction design of the family agent through design prototypes and models. Except for the FBS (Function + Behavior + Structure) Design Model for the agent product function design, the paper proposes the CMR (Contents + Mental/ Interaction Model + Relationship/Requirements) Design Model for the intelligent agent and users Human-Robot Interaction contents design. For the Baidu Brand smart speakers case study, interaction design for agents' wake-up word modes combines FBS and CMR Design Models and also analyzes the transformation relationship between the function task and the description contents. The results show that the combination of FBS and CMR supports high agile live intelligent agent product design and data service interaction design, CMR is the key factors for providing high satisfaction user experience. Finding function and task requirements and construct HRI interaction relationship with the User Generated Contents creation is the new interaction design method for the intelligent products interaction design.

Keywords: Interaction design · Family agent · CMR-FBS model

1 Introduction

The interaction design of the family agent is divided into two parts: function and content. The FBS (Function + Behavior + Structure) Model is an ideal model proposed by Professor Gero et al. to describe the product conceptual design process [1, 2]. Since the FBS Model was proposed (1990), it has been widely studied, used in design and improved by scholars. Although it has solved the problem of fuzzy demand in the early stage of design and development, it mainly focuses on engineering design, architecture, architecture and product design. The field of software design, and mainly for product design of functions, lacks design for the family agent [2–9]. As to the intelligent agent product service system design, designers need expand FBS into the ontology to deal with the function design and contents design. For the lack of design method and model for the contents design, this paper proposes CMR (Contents + Mental/Interaction Model + Relationship/Requirements) Model for the intelligent agent and users Human-Robot Interaction contents design. Through the use of CMR-FBS ontology of designing

© Springer Nature Switzerland AG 2019
A. Marcus and W. Wang (Eds.): HCII 2019, LNCS 11583, pp. 324–334, 2019.
https://doi.org/10.1007/978-3-030-23570-3_24

model, the information communication and fusion of the material world and the digital world can be better realized, and a unified and consistent user experience can be created.

2 Function and Content Design

The scope plane in *Elements of User Experience* contains the functional specifications of product as functionality and the content requirements of product as information (see Fig. 1) [10]. Content is an important part of the user experience that can't be ignored, but we often lack the awareness of content experience in the design process. Content is the essence or meaning contained in things, and it is the sum of internal factors. The four major roles of interaction design are the exchange value of information, the communication medium of the interface, the sympathetic means of function, and the traffic evaluation of content [11].

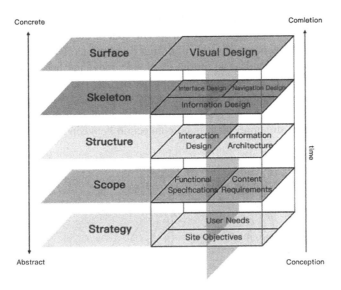

Fig. 1. The elements of user experience [10]

High-quality content can not only solve the needs of users, but content presentation is also a part of user consumption. Alibaba's design team defines content as pan-product information formed by processing and reorganization, which mainly includes four parts of text, goods, pictures and multimedia. The content itself is the flow of communication: from the production of content, to the reorganization of various platforms, to the presentation of content, and finally the content is consumed and transferred by users (see Fig. 2) [14].

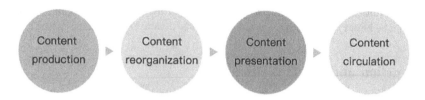

Fig. 2. The elements of user experience [14]

3 The FBS Design Model and Its Optimization

The FBS ontology framework (Gero 1990) models designing in terms of three basic classes of variables: function, behaviour, and structure [1, 12]. In 2004, Gero et al. improved the model and introduced the concept of design requirements. Later, Cascini added the concept of requirements and requirements to the problems in the FBS Model [22]. Gero further described the FBS framework and its relationship to design and design ideas in a 2009 paper (see Fig. 3) [12]. The goal of the design of this process is to transform a set of functions into a set of design descriptions (D). The function (F) of a designed object is defined as its purposes or teleology; the behaviour (B) of that object is how it achieves its functions and is either derived (Bs) or expected (Be) from the structure, where structure (S) is the elements of an object and their relationships [12]. The three ontological categories are interrelated: function is linked to behavior; behavior is linked to structure; there is no connection between function and structure.

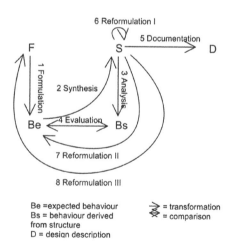

Fig. 3. The FBS ontology of designing (after Gero 1990) [12]

Based on these articulations, the FBS framework proposes the basic processes in eight designs, specifically: [12]

1. A formulation which transform functions into a set of expected behaviours;
2. A synthesis, wherein a structure is proposed that is likely to exhibit the expected behaviour;
3. An analysis of the structure produces its derived behaviour;
4. An evaluation process acts between the expected behaviour and the behaviour derived from structure;
5. Documentation, which produces the design description;
6. Reformulation type 1: modifies the structure state space, based on a re-interpretation of structure;
7. Reformulation type 2: modifies the behaviour state space, based on a re-interpretation of structure;
8. Reformulation type 3: modifies the function state space, based on a re-interpretation of structure and subsequent reformulation of expected behaviour.

Since the FBS design model was proposed (1990), the model has been used as the basis for modeling design (design results) and design processes (design activities) in many design disciplines, including engineering, architecture, architecture, and software design [2–9]. The FBS Model solves the problem of "how to do it", which starts with the function and ends with the structure, and does not cover the content requirements well [15]. And the expression of the concept of variables in the FBS Model is rigid, that is, the expression of non-zero or 1, so in the design and development process of the model, the demand must be clear [2]. However, in fact, the iterative update of technology, the ever-changing relationship between people, things and things makes the user demand multi-level and dynamic change characteristics, so the design front-end needs have certain ambiguity [2]. To this end, the majority of scholars have carried out extensive research and development, mainly through the introduction of other theories and supplements with other models in the early stage of user demand, such as used natural interaction as a solution to fuzzy requirements, and used QFD models to establish a direct mapping between user requirements and product design requirements to ensure a high degree of consistency between user requirements and product design requirements [2, 16]. However, the current application of the FBS Model is mostly for functional entity products, and research on information products is lacking. User needs include not only functional aspects, but also physical, psychological and subjective feelings. This makes the FBS Model have a vague boundary between the interpretation of the objective material world and the thinking space, information space and cyberspace.

4 The CMR Design Model

Because the FBS design model is lacking in content design, Prof. Yan Jingyan found the variable categories corresponding to the content design level for the three onto-logical categories in FBS, and proposed the CMR (Contents + Mental/Interaction Model + Relationship/Requirements) Design Model [4], the corresponding relationship is shown in Table 1.

Table 1. Correspondence relationship between FBS and CMR's variables.

FBS	CMR
Function (F)	Content/Container (C)
Expected behaviour (Be)	Mental model (MM)
Behaviour derived from structure (Bs)	Interaction model (MI)
Structure (S)	Relationship/Requirement (2R)

The CMR Model designs the container of information flow, material flow and capital flow according to the theory of supply and demand (see Fig. 4). C represents the Container carrying the content. C consists of the tangible and intangible (consciousness, ethics and aesthetics) two facets, and the two are in the interactive and balanced relationship. M establishes a mapping relationship between 2R (relationship & requirement) and design requirements of products, with users' mental model of a single line and a double line as the subject, interaction model being the object, which is a five-layer information architecture having two kinds of information, digital information and non-digital information. CMR emphasizes that the content needs matched mental model and interaction model. The defined threshold lead to what users want and need, afterwards the supply-and-requirement relationship is exported, hence forming a moderation relationship among person, things and objects [17].

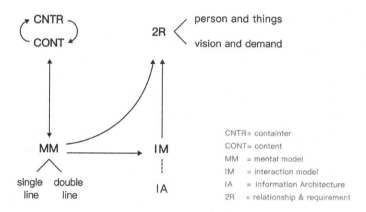

Fig. 4. The CMR ontology of designing

Before using the FBS model for product development, the CMR model is first used to define the threshold, guide the user's vision and needs, derive the supply and demand relationship, and then use it as the functional element of the FBS model, and based on this, develop the FBS model design process. The fusion application of CMR and FBS establishes the connection between user requirements and other variables (F, B, S), making the factors considered in the design process more comprehensive, and it is easy to analyze user requirements from multiple angles [23]. Therefore, the function and content factors of the final design result can be balanced, and the integration of information flow, material flow and capital flow can be realized.

5 Research Methods and Processes

Based on CMR and FBS Model, the "container-contents-function", an integrated application patter of CMR and FBS Model is set. It can guide innovative design of products much more better. The specific research process of in an integrated application of CMR and FBS Model are as follows: (see Fig. 5)

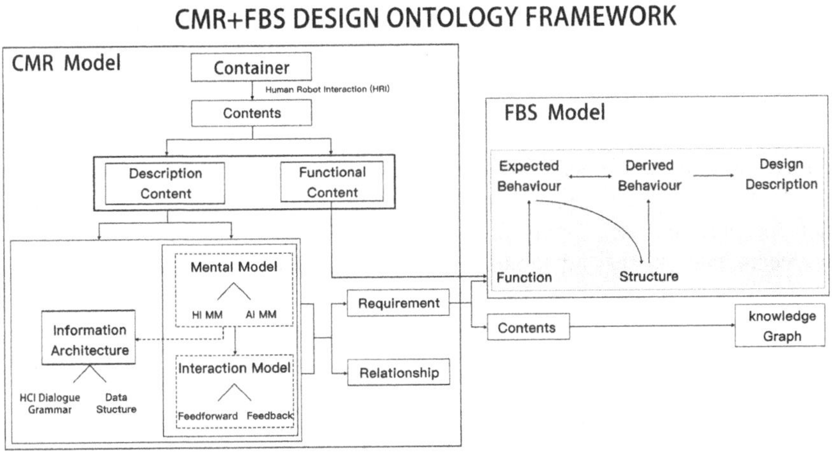

CMR+FBS DESIGN ONTOLOGY FRAMEWORK

Fig. 5. CMR + FBS Design Ontology Framework

1. Establishing a container of human-computer dialogue and calculating the dialogue content;
2. Exploring the user's content requirements and functional requirements from the content of human-computer interaction feedback;
3. The cognitive calculation of functional requirements in the container is conducted according to the FBS method;
4. The dialogue semantic content calculation of content requirements in the container is conducted according to the CMR method;
5. Inductively constructing the user's mental model in the dialogue semantic content and making cognitive judgment decisions on the content;
6. Reorganizing the mental model with artificial intelligence involved according to the user's mental model to form a mental model of the double loop;
7. Matching a human computer interaction model according to the double-loop mental model of human intelligence and artificial intelligence;
8. Defining the content threshold of the human-computer interaction dialogue jointly by the mental model and the interaction model and distinguishing the functional content and description content of the new interaction content;
9. The supply and requirement relationship of the interaction function is exported by the functional content, and feedforward-feedback dialogue relationship of content interaction is exported by description content;

10. Determining the supply and requirement relationship and the dialogue relationship, designing the intelligent robot's supply and requirement relationship between human-robot interaction scene and content of that;
11. Interactive transforming between interaction function and interaction behavior and information architecture transforming between interaction behavior and data structure of are based on requirements and relationships;
12. The HCI dialogue grammar between the user and the agent is jointly defined by MR and FBS, and the function and content of the dialogue enter the next round of HMI feedforward feedback.

The threshold definition in the CMR Model is obtained by matching the content with the interaction model, and transforms it into a supply and demand relationship according to the CMR Model. The content needs to be translated into a specific implementation and user interaction, matching the interaction mode. Construct a link-graph of user supply and demand relationship and design requirements, analyze the relationship between user supply and demand relationship and family agent design requirements, and extract and summarize the key design requirements. Then through the analysis of the relationship data, the key design requirements of the product are determined, and the inductive analysis is carried out to guide the FBS mapping process as a functional element of the family agent. By using the link technique of Goldschmidt (1990), it is possible to identify connections between unrelated fields. We have selected a user dialogue about the family agent design and analyzed it. Then built a link- graph by key design requirements as an example (see Fig. 6).

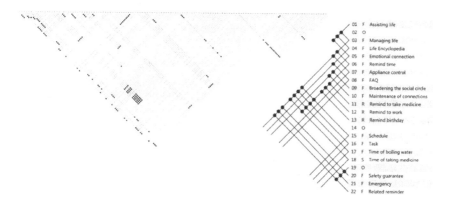

Fig. 6. Linking the segments

In the two mapping process of FBS, the following points should be observed [16]:

1. In the function-behavior transformation process: one behavior conflicts with another behavior, that is, the two behaviors cannot be performed simultaneously; one behavior is similar to the other behavior in form or space, and the two behaviors can be integrated.

2. In the process of behavior-structure transformation, the contradiction between behavior and behavior requires certain restrictions on the execution of these structures to avoid conflicts; a behavior may require multiple parts to be combined, and the user's behavioral scale is required to be considered. Rational distribution of these structures; a structure that can perform multiple functions requires consideration of similarities and differences between two behaviors, using analogy-based reasoning to generate innovative structures.

6 Interaction Design for Agents' Wake-up Word

With the advent of the industry 4.0 era, smart mobile terminals and cloud big data technology have laid the foundation for the new era. The market for skilled products has opened its doors, and now smart products have entered thousands of households [18]. The germination and development of artificial intelligence, along with the development of human-computer interaction technology and interaction design, from human-computer interaction technology to human-centered experience design, to attention consciousness, artificial intelligence to enhance situational awareness and awareness Perception and emotional perception, and finally form a meaning-centered interaction design method [19]. Artificial intelligence can effectively deal with the interaction elements of big data flow, information flow, knowledge flow, material flow and capital flow, and use this data to form subversive innovations from system, information, control and coordination, dissipation, mutation etc. form a subversive innovative thinking [20]. Therefore, in the design of intelligent products, in addition to the traditional function, behavior and structure of the weapon design, it is necessary to fully consider the container design that carries the data information.

As the basic unit of society, the family is the place where the concept of good and evil in the social value system is concentrated. The family agent is a special robot that serves human beings. It is not a simple home or electronic product. It is a family member who is integrated into family life and acts as a "life steward", "intimate friend" and "exclusive nanny". Therefore, the design process of the family agent can not only consider the traditional function-behavior-structure, but also combine the consciousness, ethics and aesthetics of the family form, and use the big data and artificial intelligence algorithms to form the synergistic symbiosis between group intelligence and experience sensibility [17]. However, the design of current home intelligence bodies mostly stays on the realization of functions, and lacks the design of content. From UGC (user-generated contents) to PGC (professional-generated contents) to OGC (occupational-generated contents), there is a lack of knowledge mapping semantic pragmatic grammatical context analysis, environment-aware computing, consciousness-aware computing and emotion-aware computing, lack of storytelling and integrity. The experience of the family agent is poor, and it cannot be well integrated into the family life. Let it becomes a part of the family.

In order to better understand the user's perception and demand for home intelligence, we first received 142 valid questionnaires for the smart product demand survey, covering the consumption level of 18–71 years old, 20 provinces and 4 stalls.

19 groups of three families conducted in-depth interviews and recorded the user's discourse. Through the statistics of the word frequency in the user's discourse, the word size was arranged according to the frequency of occurrence, forming a word cloud (see Fig. 7). With the word cloud of user interviews, we can see the content of users with more demand. From this we can see that users have a large amount of content and information level requirements for family agents.

Fig. 7. Word cloud of user interview

Wake-up as a necessary function of the family agent, the awakening of the speech design needs to be considered from the content level. The family agent acts as a carrier of content, and awakening speech is what it needs to carry. There are two models of mental model and interaction model in the process of interacting with the agent's voice. Only by finding the balance between the two can the user experience be optimized. Therefore, the voice wake-up method of the agent is similar to the way people communicate with each other. For example, one morning, when you go out to see the outside is cloudy, you worried that it will rain and then shouted "Mom" to your mother who is doing housework. When your mother heard it, she stopped doing work and turned his face to you. Then you ask, "Is it going to rain in the sky?", your mother recalled the weather forecast, "No rain, it is cloudy." But the human mind model will actually be more complicated, you may call "Mom", "Mother", or a look of an eye, even without a direct inquiry, your mother can understand that you are talking to her, but the agent is still not as human wisdom, many behaviors can't attract their attention. Therefore, we need to define a word that switches the product from standby to working state, which is the "wake-up word." The wake-up word is the result of matching the mental model with the interaction model.

Take the Baidu Brand smart speakers as an example. When using a smart speaker equipped with the DuerOS system, it is necessary to hand over its name "Xiaodu, Xiaodu" to switch it to work. The success rate and false wake-up rate of the agent identification after the wake-up word is recognized is the most basic consideration for the realization of the wake-up function. In order to improve the recognition rate of the agent and reduce the false wake-up rate, we need to define the threshold of wake-up and wake-up words. For example, you must call two times "Xiaodu" continuously within 3 s, and the interval between multiple rounds of dialogue for a unified task is no more than 8 s. These are all based on the functional level design. If you want to further enhance the user experience, It is necessary to combine content and function design.

After applying the CMR + FBS design ontology model to explore the user's content requirements and functional requirements, it is necessary to summarize the mental model of the user in the semantic content of the dialogue, and make cognitive decision judgments on the content. According to the user's mental model, the mental model of artificial intelligence intervention is reorganized to form a dual-loop mental model, which then matches the human-computer interaction model. For example, in addition to the functional implementation, factors such as the combination of wake-up words and voice intonation can affect the user experience. Studies have shown that the combination of overlapping words and the combination of "Xiao + words" are more likely to be enjoyed by Chinese users [23]. Therefore, the wake-up words of Baidu's smart products are set to "Xiaodu, Xiaodu".

7 Conclusion

In this paper, the application research of the CMR + FBS Design Ontology Framework is carried out for the internal design problem in the process of interaction design. The optimization and improvement of the FBS Model is completed. The application of the CMR Model is studied through the design example of wake-up words of family agent, which is used for user demand extraction. The combination of FBS and CMR supports high agile live intelligent agent product design and data service interaction design, CMR is the key factors for providing high satisfaction user experience. Finding function and task requirements and construct HRI interaction relationship with the User Generated Contents creation is the new interaction design method for the intelligent products interaction design. It provides a new design idea and method to help the user's user needs analysis method in the interaction design process, and expands the application of the FBS model.

References

1. Gero, J.S.: Design prototypes: a knowledge representation schema for design. AI Mag. **11** (4), 26 (1990)
2. Hu, Z., Wang, Y., Wu, Q., Zhou, H.: FBS design model based on natural interaction. Packag. Eng. (2), 127–130 (2017)
3. Deng, Y.M.: Function and behavior representation in conceptual mechanical design. Artif. Intell. Eng. Des. Anal. Manuf. **16**(5), 343–362 (2002)
4. Christophe, F., Bernard, A., Coatanéa, É.: RFBS: a model for knowledge representation of conceptual design. CIRP Ann. Manuf. Technol. **59**(1), 155–158 (2010)
5. Clayton, M.J., Teicholz, P., Fischer, M., Kunz, J.: Virtual components consisting of form, function and behavior. Autom. Constr. **8**(3), 351–367 (1999)
6. Kruchten, P.: Casting software design in the function-behavior-structure framework. IEEE Softw. **22**(2), 52–58 (2005)

7. Howard, T.J., Culley, S.J., Dekoninck, E.: Describing the creative design process by the integration of engineering design and cognitive psychology literature. Des. Stud. **29**(2), 160–180 (2008)
8. Yan, M.: Representing design knowledge as a network of function, behaviour and structure. Des. Stud. **14**(3), 314–329 (1993)
9. Colombo, G., Mosca, A., Sartori, F.: Towards the design of intelligent CAD systems: an ontological approach. Adv. Eng. Inform. **21**(2), 153–168 (2007)
10. Garrett, J.J.: Elements of User Experience, the: User-Centered Design for the Web and Beyond. Pearson Education, Upper Saddle River (2010)
11. Qin, J.: Grand interaction design in big data information era. Packag. Eng. **36**(8), 1–5 (2015)
12. Kan, J.W., Gero, J.S.: Using the FBS ontology to capture semantic design information in design protocol studies. In: About: Designing. Analysing Design Meetings (pp. 213–229). CRC Press (2009)
13. Gero, J.S., Kannengiesser, U.: The situated function–behaviour–structure framework. Des. Stud. **25**(4), 373–391 (2004)
14. Alibaba Design. http://www.zcool.com.cn/article/ZNDc1OTI4.html. Accessed 2018
15. Meng, X., Sun, S.: Research on product conceptual design process model of integrated semantics. Mech. Des. (02), 114–118 (2017)
16. Xu, Y., Song, D., Yan, J., Feng, W.: Research on the versatility design of toilet based on QFD and FBS model. Packag. Eng. (24) (2018)
17. Qin, J.: Research on the impact of aesthetic consciousness on artificial intelligence and innovative design. Packag. Eng. (4), 1–13 (2019)
18. Yan, J.: Research on FBS Model of Smart Home. Diss (2018)
19. Qin, J.: Grand interaction design in big data information era. Packag. Eng. (8), 1–5 (2015)
20. Qin, J.: Research on the impact of artificial intelligence on interaction design. Packag. Eng. (20), 39–43 (2017)
21. DuerOS, Artificial Intelligence "Awakening Words" Research Report https://mbd.baidu.com/. Accessed 2018/1/31
22. Cascini, G., Fantoni, G., Montagna, F.: Situating needs and requirements in the FBS framework. Des. Stud. **34**(5), 636–662 (2013)
23. Zhang, Q., Chen, D., Yu, Y.: User requirements analysis method based on FBS model in product design. Mech. Des. (7) (2018)

Mind Maps in Requirements Engineering:
A Systematic Mapping

Eder Quispe Vilchez[(⊠)] and José A. Pow-Sang Portillo[(⊠)]

Pontificia Universidad Católica del Perú, Lima, Peru
eder.quispe@pucp.edu.pe, japowsang@pucp.pe

Abstract. Many of the mistakes that can be found in software products have their origin in the requirements definition and preliminary design stages; likewise, the correction of these demands a greater effort than those generated in the following stages. The lack of effective and transparent communication between those involved in the process (users, experts in the business domain, analysts, developers, etc.) is one of the main causes for the introduction of these errors, which is why a well-defined method and information exchange are necessary. In this way, a validation and early correction of the requirements could be done with the help of those involved, so that the functionalities implemented can be verified in later instance. Through the process of systematic mapping of the literature, fifteen research studies that consider the use of mind maps as facilitators in the exchange of communications of ideas developed in the requirements engineering processes were selected. Concluding that, the inclusion of the development of mental maps is evidenced more frequently in the processes of elicitation, analysis and validation of the requirements, this as a result of the activities developed in these processes involve a constant interaction and communication between expert users of the business domain and the analysts.

Keywords: Mind maps · Requirements engineering ·
Requirements elicitation · Communication · Software

1 Introduction

Part of the motivation in software development projects is to determine "what to build?". This stage is performed in the phase of defining the requirements of the software life cycle, which is where the functionalities that the system should provide and that are related to the client's needs are identified [5]. It is in the development of software requirements engineering processes that one must ensure that the analyst understands the premises, business rules, protocols, validations, restrictions and decisions indicated by users during the designing of the software [10]. Ensuring consistent communication promotes consistency between what the user knows and what the analyst ultimately represents in the software design [5, 16]. The purpose of the present work is to identify research studies in which the use of mind maps is proposed as part of the requirements engineering process and how they intervene in communications between users and analysts during elicitation, specification, analysis, validation and management of requirements [13, 15, 16]. After the present introduction, this work is

© Springer Nature Switzerland AG 2019
A. Marcus and W. Wang (Eds.): HCII 2019, LNCS 11583, pp. 335–350, 2019.
https://doi.org/10.1007/978-3-030-23570-3_25

structured as follows: Sect. 2 provides the theoretical framework regarding requirements engineering, mind maps and mind maps in requirements engineering; Sect. 3 presents the systematic mapping of the studies available in the literature during the years 2010 to 2016 and finally Sect. 4 lists the conclusions and suggests other studies or related future works that could prove useful.

2   Theoretical Framework

2.1   Requirements Engineering

Requirements engineering (RE) establishes the processes for defining the requirements. These processes must involve different actors and their different points of view. Among these actors, there is the analyst, responsible for the creation of models based on the information gathered from expert users in the business domain [16].

Among the processes considered in the RE are [3, 16]:

- Elicitation of requirements
- Specification of requirements
- Requirements analysis
- Verification, validation and evaluation of requirements
- Requirements management

2.2   Mind Maps

A mind map is a diagram used to view, classify and organize concepts, and to generate new ideas. It is used to connect words, ideas and concepts to a central idea or concept [4].

The main benefits of the use of mind maps are [4]:

- Organization of ideas and concepts
- Emphasis on the relevant keywords
- Association between the elements of the branches
- Grouping of ideas
- Support of visual memory and creativity, innovation ideas driver

An example of a mind map diagram developed by Buzan is shown in Fig. 1 [4].

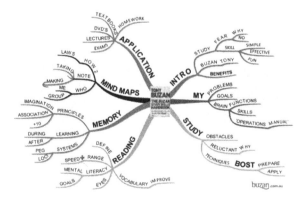

Fig. 1. Buzan's Mind map [4]

2.3 Mind Maps in Requirements Engineering

The use of mind maps in RE contributes to improving the quality and traceability of the requirements. This is due to the fact that mind maps allow the capture of information in multiple layers, therefore, it provides the participants in the RE process with the information captured by others interested in the development of the software product. In addition, iterating the activities of the RE processes helps to gradually grow the knowledge and information captured and, consequently, facilitates the production of an initial set of better quality requirements [18].

3 Systematic Mapping

3.1 Reviewing Process

The objective of the systematic mapping of the literature is to provide information on the state of the art of the different methods or techniques used in the RE that consider the elaboration of mind maps as part of the activities of the process.

3.2 Research Questions

For this research, the following research questions have been defined:

Question 1: Is the development of mind maps in Requirements Engineering included in software development projects?

The objective of this question is to attain the state of the art of the total number of publications in the population of software development projects that mention the development of mind maps in the RE processes.

Question 2: Regarding the development of mind maps in Requirements Engineering, do they take into account functional and non-functional requirements?

Considering the previously obtained results, the question seeks to determine if mind maps consider the lifting of the functional requirements and non-functional requirements of the software development projects.

Question 3: Regarding the development of mind maps in Requirements Engineering, has this been validated or is it currently used in the industry?

The aim of this question is to limit the results obtained with question 1 and verify if these are in the categorization of publications to be evaluated, proposal of solution, validation, case studies applied to the industry, opinion and personal experiences. The answer to the question will allow determining if the development of mind maps in the RE has been validated within an academic environment or evaluated after its application in the industry.

To answer these questions, a search string was built based on the criteria of the PICOC method (Population, Intervention, Comparison, Outputs, and Context) that are shown in Table 1.

Table 1. PICOC

Criteria	Description
Population	Development of software or software projects or software engineering or application development
Intervention	Mind maps or mental modeling
Comparison	Requirements engineering or software requirements
Outputs	Specification of functional requirements or non-functional requirements
Context	Academic environment or case of study or application in the industry

3.3 Search Strategy

In order to carry out the search and selection of the research studies, 5 stages were defined, which are detailed in Table 2.

Table 2. Stages

Stages	Description
Search chains elaboration	It is elaborated based on the terms presented in Tables 1
Consider synonyms	Consider synonyms for the terms used in the search
Combining the search terms	It makes use of the 'OR' connector to combine synonyms and the 'AND' connector to interconnect the main search terms
Divide the search strings	Divide the string into several substrings so that they can be applied to different data sources
Manage references	Mendeley tool is used

Search String. The search string is defined in Table 3, which will be used as the input value in the search engines of the digital data sources listed in Table 4.

Table 3. Search string

Search string
(((("software" OR "application" OR "applications" OR "system" OR "systems") AND ("development" OR "construction" OR "project*" OR "process" OR "processes" OR "engineering")) OR "software requirement" OR "requirements engineering") AND ("mind map*"))

Search Process. The search was performed using the data sources specified in Table 4, which contains the references of scientific articles and journals, conference proceedings and technical documents. The searches were performed on the titles, abstracts and keywords of the publications that provide the digital data sources.

Table 4. Consulted digital data sources

Identifier	Data source	URL
SS	Sciverse Scopus	http://scopus.com/
IEEE	IEEExplore	http://ieeexplore.ieee.org

3.4 Inclusion and Exclusion Criteria

A set of selection criteria classified as inclusive and exclusive has been defined in order to identify the most appropriate studies for the systematic mapping. The inclusion of the studies was determined by the following criteria:

Inclusion Criteria

- The publications must be written in English or in Portuguese.
- Access to the content of the publication must be available.
- The published works should be reviews, solution proposals, validations or evaluations.

Exclusion Criteria

- Publications that do not propose the development of mind maps in the RE.
- Publications that do not validate or evaluate the development of mind maps in the RE.
- Articles based on opinions.
- Duplicate publications. In case there are duplicate results, those whose content can be accessed will be considered.

3.5 Synthesis Strategy

The search resulted in 144 publications between the years 2010 and 2016, of which six were duplicates. The list of selected studies is classified in Table 5.

Table 5. Studies selected according to data source

Identifier	Data Source	Total publications	Relevant publications
SS	Scopus	107	14
IEEE	IEEExplore	37	7

After applying the inclusion and exclusion criteria, fifteen studies without duplication were selected which are listed in Table 6.

Table 6. Selected studies

Year	Identifier	Source	Authors
2010	[2]	SS	Bia A., Muñoz R., Gómez J.
2011	[8]	SS, IEEE	I. Mahmud; V. Veneziano
2012	[16]	SS, IEE	F. Wanderley; D. S. da Silveria
2012	[13]	SS	Wanderley F., Da Silveira D.S., Araujo J., Lencastre M.
2013	[15]	SS, IEE	F. Wanderley; D. S. da Silveira; J. Araujo; A. Moreira
2013	[18]	SS	Zayed R., Kossmann M., Odeh M.
2014	[14]	SS, IEE	F. Wanderley; A. Silva; J. Araujo; D. S. Silveira
2014	[12]	SS	Wanderley F., Silveira D., Araujo J., Moreira A., Guerra E.
2014	[1]	SS	Alrobai A., Phalp K., Ali R.
2015	[6]	IEEE	A. S. Duarte; J. A. Fabri; A. L'Erario; E. C. Genvigir
2015	[7]	SS, IEEE	T. Kakeshita; S. Yamashita
2015	[11]	SS, IEE	F. Wanderley; A. Silva; J. Araujo
2016	[10]	SS	De Oliveira S.F., Martinez P.V., Fabri J.A., Erario A.L., Duarte A.S., Goncalves J.A.
2016	[5]	SS	Ceballos A., Wanderley F., Souza E., Cysneiros G.
2016	[9]	SS	Natarajan S., Kumar K.A.

3.6   Quality Assessment of the Study

The 15 studies selected were subjected to a quality evaluation process. The evaluation instrument applied is based on the proposal of Zarour et al. [17], which uses a rating scale of 3 levels of compliance. If the study submitted for evaluation satisfies the quality assurance question (Yes), 1 point is assigned, if it does not comply (No), a score of 0 is assigned and if it is met Partially it is assigned 0.5 points.

After having applied the evaluation instrument presented in Table 7. Table 8 shows the results of the quality assessment of the selected studies.

Table 7. List of questions for quality assurance

Identifier	Question
QA1	Has the objective of the investigation been sufficiently explained?
QA2	Has the idea or approach presented been clearly explained?
QA3	Have they been considered threats into the validity?
QA4	Is there an adequate description of the context in which the investigation was performed?
QA5	Are the study findings clearly mentioned?

Table 8. Results of the quality evaluation of the selected studies

Identifier	QA1	QA2	QA3	QA4	QA5	Total score
[1]	1.0	1.0	0.0	1.0	1.0	4.0
[2]	1.0	1.0	0.0	1.0	1.0	4.0
[5]	1.0	1.0	1.0	1.0	1.0	5.0
[6]	1.0	1.0	0.0	1.0	1.0	4.0
[7]	1.0	1.0	0.0	1.0	1.0	4.0
[8]	1.0	1.0	1.0	1.0	1.0	5.0
[9]	1.0	1.0	0.0	1.0	1.0	4.0
[10]	1.0	1.0	0.0	1.0	1.0	4.0
[11]	1.0	1.0	0.0	1.0	1.0	4.0
[12]	1.0	1.0	1.0	1.0	1.0	5.0
[13]	1.0	1.0	0.0	1.0	1.0	4.0
[14]	1.0	1.0	1.0	1.0	1.0	5.0
[15]	1.0	1.0	0.0	1.0	1.0	4.0
[16]	1.0	1.0	1.0	1.0	1.0	5.0
[18]	1.0	1.0	1.0	1.0	1.0	5.0

All relevant publications with a total score equal to or less than 5.0 and greater than or equal to 2.5 are considered accepted; while those with a score lower than 2.5 are discarded. From the final results we can see that the scores reached by each study are not less than 4.0, the average score is 4.4. The result of the quality assessment shown in Table 8 shows that all 15 studies are acceptable.

3.7 Data Extraction

The search was conducted in November 2016, considering the inclusion criteria of studies performed between 2010 and 2016. Table 9 shows the number of publications per year.

Table 9. Studies per years

Year	Publications	Number of publications
2010	[2]	1.0
2011	[8]	1.0
2012	[13, 16]	2.0
2013	[15, 18]	2.0
2014	[1, 12, 14]	3.0
2015	[6, 7, 11]	3.0
2016	[5, 9, 10]	3.0

The types of sources of the selected publications are: conferences, symposia, magazines and workshops. Table 10 shows the publications with their respective types.

Table 10. Sources of publications

Identifier	Publication source name	Type
[1]	20th International Working Conference on Requirements Engineering: Foundation for Software Quality, REFSQ 2014	Conference
[2]	14th European Conference on Research and Advanced Technology for Digital Libraries, ECDL 2010	Conference
[5]	16th International Conference on Computational Science and Its Applications, ICCSA 2016	Conference
[6]	2015 Latin American Computing Conference (CLEI)	Conference
[7]	2015 3rd International Conference on Applied Computing and Information Technology/2nd International Conference on Computational Science and Intelligence	Conference
[8]	14th International Conference on Computer and Information Technology (ICCIT 2011)	Conference
[9]	International Journal of Economic Research	Magazine
[10]	11th Iberian Conference on Information Systems and Technologies, CISTI 2016	Conference
[11]	2015 IEEE 9th International Conference on Research Challenges in Information Science (RCIS)	Conference
[12]	14th International Conference on Computational Science and Its Applications, ICCSA 2014	Conference
[13]	16th International Software Product Line Conference, SPLC 2012	Conference
[14]	2014 IEEE 4th International Model-Driven Requirements Engineering Workshop (MoDRE)	Workshop
[15]	IEEE 7th International Conference on Research Challenges in Information Science (RCIS)	Conference
[16]	2012 Eighth International Conference on the Quality of Information and Communications Technology	Conference
[18]	23rd Annual International Symposium of the International Council on Systems Engineering, INCOSE 2013	Simposium

3.8 Synthesis of Publications

From the selected works, RE processes that consider the use of mind maps have been identified. Table 11 details the RE processes [3] that make use of these mind maps.

Table 11. Requirements engineering process

Elicitation	[1, 2, 5–16, 18]
Analysis	[1, 2, 5–16, 18]
Specification	[1, 5, 6, 8–16, 18]
Validation	[1, 5–7, 9–16, 18]
Management	[6, 8, 18]

Based on the data in Table 11, it can be assured that there is evidence of the inclusion of mind maps in the development of the processes of elicitation, analysis, specification, validation and management of requirements. This finding occurs more frequently in the elicitation, analysis and validation of requirements since it involves a constant interaction and communication between expert users of the business domain and analysts.

In order to ensure a correct communication and understanding of what the user expects to obtain as a final software product, techniques such as "Zaltman metaphor elicitation technique (ZMET)" [9] are applied to structure the phases of an interview. Likewise, methods are combined to group and hierarchize the details of the most relevant data or attributes that represent the needs of the users. The information obtained can be represented in a mind map that allows the user to validate that the analyst has correctly understood their needs.

Another method to validate communication among those interested in software development is the "Method of semiotic inspection (MSI)" [10] which describes a flow of communication in which (1) the user requests the construction of the software, (2) identifies the functional requirements using elicitation techniques and complements it with the development of mind maps, (3) validates the requirements with the user (4) requests the construction of interfaces, (5) presents user interfaces or prototypes and (6) validates the communication method. The flow of communication is represented in Fig. 2 proposed by De Oliveira et al. [10], in each phase is modeled in a semi-structured way: the data, ideas and restrictions of the needs of the users [2], the mind map is increasing and improving in each interaction and transfer in the flow of communication.

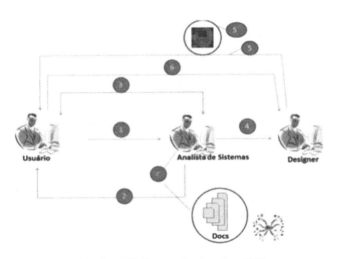

Fig. 2. MSI Communication flow [10]

The studies describe software tools such as "REMEST (Requirement Management Education Support Tool" [11], which propose mind map templates for the development of the activities included in the requirements elicitation process, Fig. 3 represents the template for Identification of the interested parties. Figure 4 represents the template to identify the problems and their possible causes. Figure 5 represents the template for the analysis of the objectives for the resolution of problems. Figure 6 represents the template for the Identification of the means to achieve the objective. Figure 7 represents the template for the identification and specification of requirements. The elaborated templates are developed in the tool and processed to make a comparison with a template that has the mind map of correct answers and returns the inconsistencies that may have been detected by the analyst. Figure 8 represents the result of the comparison of the map proposed by the analyst and the map with correct answers.

Fig. 3. Template for the identification of interested parties (Stakeholders) [7]

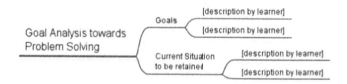

Fig. 4. Template for identifying problems and their possible causes [7]

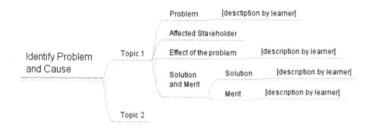

Fig. 5. Template for the analysis of objectives for the resolution of problems [7]

Fig. 6. Template to identify the means to achieve the objectives [7]

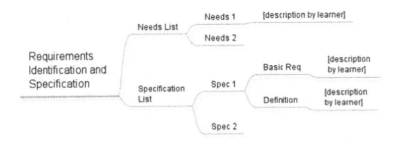

Fig. 7. Template for the identification and specification of requirements [7]

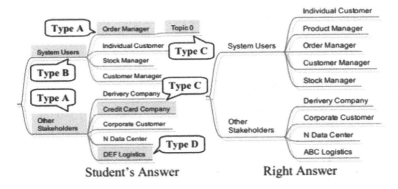

Fig. 8. Comparison result of mind maps [7]

The development of mind maps contributes to a significant improvement in the quality of the specification of software project requirements developed with agile methods [8, 13, 16]. The use of user stories is considered as a technique for eliciting software requirements [3]. Wanderley et al. [11], proposes the specification of user stories using the tool "BehaviorMap", the mind map developed describes an example scenario in which, provided that the ship "Seal" is in a determined position, a coast-guard, visualizing an area of the map limited by the start and end points, you will see this ship within this area. Figure 9 graphically represents the specification of user stories using mental maps.

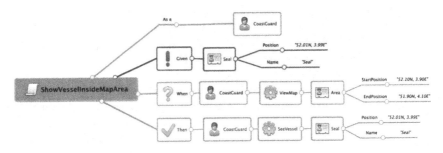

Fig. 9. Graphical representation of user stories by mind maps [11]

In reference to the processes of analysis, specification and validation of requirements, studies propose the use of automated tools such as "MindDomain" [5, 12], "SnapMind" [14], "MindMappingModeler" [16] these tools provide graphic interfaces for the development of mind maps for later with tools such as "DomainModModel" [16] generates the conceptual or business domain models. Then these models are used by the analyst in order to validate the requirements with the users. Wanderley et al. [16], proposes the transformation process is observed between the elicitation of requirements, the development of the mind map, the generation of the conceptual model that using UML class diagrams [15] represent the business entities with their respective attributes and relationships between them [13, 16]. The advantage of transforming the requirements expressed in mind maps into conceptual models or as UML class diagrams create a common vision of the business domain between developers and clients, defining a shared vocabulary [12]. Figure 10 graphically represents the generation of conceptual or business domain models.

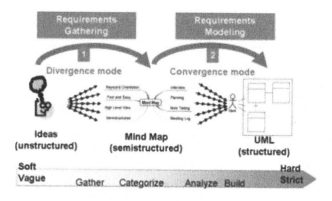

Fig. 10. Generation of conceptual models or business domain [16]

The mind maps developed using the aforementioned tools are graphic representations that visually consider a central element that represents the main idea and around it different nodes that complement the explanation of the context in treatment [2]. These tools automatically organize the graphic elements and structure them in hierarchical mode. These elements represent the different nodes that make up the mind map [2]. They also provide visual editing functions that allow to: hide, show, copy, paste, move, drag and drop the different nodes that make up a mind map. Amongst other functionalities, the possibility is also considered that the nodes register hyperlinks to external files or even references to other mind maps [2].

The methodology "OntoREM" (Ontology-driven Requirements Engineering Methodology), jointly developed by the company Airbus and the University of the West of England (US Patent pending), is an example of adoption of the development of mind maps to facilitate the modeling of the business domain and the specification requirements. The methodology improves the RE processes and allows managing the changes of the business domain including the specification of the requirements over time [18]. Duarte et al. [6], proposes to use mind maps for the registration of the traceability of the addition or modification of the requirements and how these are linked if it is the case.

From the selected works, it was identified that the requirements elicitation techniques consider in greater number the development of mental maps as a complement to the development were identified. Table 12 lists the requirements elicitation techniques [3] that do develop mind maps.

Table 12. Elicitation techniques that include the use of mind maps

Traditional interviews	[1, 5–16, 18]
Scenarios analysis	[1, 2, 5–16, 18]
Prototypes	[10]
Assisted meetings	[1, 5–15, 18]
Observations	[1, 2, 5–16, 18]
Usage cases	None
User stories	[11, 14, 16]
Conceptual models or business domain/Class diagram	[5, 6, 12–16, 18]

3.9   Discussion of Results

In order to answer the research questions that have been previously defined (see Sect. 3.2), this section describes the findings based on the selected studies.

Question 1: Is the development of mind maps in Requirements Engineering currently included in software development projects?

Answer 1: Based on the evidence obtained from the systematic mapping (see Table 11), it is possible to conclude that RE processes do include the development of mind maps. From the findings, it is possible to list the elicitation techniques that include the development of mind maps such as: traditional interviews, analysis of scenarios, assisted meetings, observations, development of user stories, conceptual models or business domain/class diagram (see Table 12).

The inclusion of the development of mental maps is evidenced more frequently in the processes of elicitation, analysis and validation of the requirements, this as a result of the activities developed in these processes involve a constant interaction and communication between expert users of the business domain and the analysts.

There are software tools that allow to develop mental maps and that applying RE elicitation techniques, it is possible to represent the needs of the users in a graphic way, allowing to validate that these have been correctly understood.

Question 2: Regarding the development of mind maps in Requirements Engineering, do they take into account functional and non-functional requirements?

Answer 2: Of the studies presented in Table 6, the inclusion of only the functional requirements is mentioned and referred to and there is no evidence to consider the non-functional requirements during the development of the mind maps.

Automated tools such as "MindDomain", "SnapMind", "MindMappingModeler", provide graphical interfaces for the development of mental maps and later with tools such as "DomainModModel" generates conceptual or business domain models that complement the definition and specification of the software requirements.

Question 3: Regarding the development of mind maps in Requirements Engineering, has this been validated or is it currently used in the industry?

Answer 3: The resulting studies (see Table 6) describe cases of studies that have been validated in controlled environments, as well as their performance in real scenarios in the industry.

The "OntoREM" methodology used in the Airbus company, adopts the development of mental maps to facilitate the modeling of the business domain, the specification of requirements and allows to manage the changes of the business domain including the specification of the requirements over time.

3.10   Threats to the Validity of the Study

Four possible threats to the validity of the results obtained were obtained.

Validity of the Construct. The main construct used in this study is the search chain developed for research. This search string was built using synonyms associated with the terms that were part of the proposed PICOC. Likewise, the chain has been executed on a set of previously selected digital sources. There is the possibility that some relevant studies have not been considered if they were indexed in one of the non-reviewed digital sources or if they contained terms other than those selected to build the search chain.

Internal Validity. It is possible that a bias was introduced when extracting and analyzing the data from the study prepared by the researcher. In order to mitigate this risk, revisions were made by the study advisor to validate the analysis of the selected studies.

External Validity. It is associated with the ability to generalize the results obtained in this study. In order to mitigate this risk, the search process is performed several times.

Validity of the Conclusions. It is possible that some of the studies were incorrectly excluded in this review. In order to mitigate this risk, a careful construction of the inclusion and exclusion criteria and a subsequent validation of the quality of the selected studies were performed in order to avoid the exclusion of relevant studies.

4   Conclusions and Future Works

In the systematic mapping carried out, fifteen relevant articles formed by the results of the searches were identified. From these works, five RE processes were identified that include the development of mind maps: elicitation, analysis, specification, validation and requirements management.

The usage of mind maps to represent conceptual or business domain models helps to reduce the communication gap in users and software analysts, which is evidenced by the understanding of what is desired and what is developed as a product of software [1, 13, 15, 16].

The technique of developing mind maps could be conciliated with a more robust requirements management perspective and, at the same time, mitigate most criticalities and unwanted side effects due to inadequate control of changes in their specification [8].

The usage of the software product efficiently depends on the level of user knowledge and how this is related to the design of the software and the functionalities it offers to meet the business needs expressed in the elicitation stage [10].

Mind maps, being a graphic element, contribute to facilitating interaction in communication and the exchange of ideas between business users and analysts who will design the software product.

As future work, it is proposed to develop a proposal of method of inclusion of mental maps in the requirements engineering for software projects related to the industry. As well as investigating the inclusion of mind maps in the technique of prototyping interfaces and how they complement the premises of usability and considerations so that the user experience is benefited when users interact with the software product. Achieving in this way evidence within a mental map node the non-functional requirements that will limit the functional scope of the software.

References

1. Alrobai, A., Phalp, K., Ali, R.: Digital addiction: a requirements engineering perspective. In: Salinesi, C., van de Weerd, I. (eds.) REFSQ 2014. LNCS, vol. 8396, pp. 112–118. Springer, Cham (2014). https://doi.org/10.1007/978-3-319-05843-6_9
2. Bia, A., Muñoz, R., Gómez, J.: Using mind maps to model semistructured documents. In: Lalmas, M., Jose, J., Rauber, A., Sebastiani, F., Frommholz, I. (eds.) ECDL 2010. LNCS, vol. 6273, pp. 421–424. Springer, Heidelberg (2010). https://doi.org/10.1007/978-3-642-15464-5_47
3. Bourque, P., Fairley, R.E.: Guide to the software engineering body of knowledge (SWEBOK (R)): version 3.0. IEEE Computer Society Press, Washington (2014)
4. Buzan, T., et al.: The Mind Map Book: Unlock Your Creativity, Boost Your Memory, Change Your Life. Pearson BBC Active New York, New York (2010)
5. Ceballos, A., Wanderley, F., Souza, E., Cysneiros, G.: MindDomain: an interoperability tool to generate domain models through mind maps. In: Gervasi, O., et al. (eds.) ICCSA 2016. LNCS, vol. 9789, pp. 469–479. Springer, Cham (2016). https://doi.org/10.1007/978-3-319-42089-9_33
6. Duarte, A.S. et al.: Mind maps in the requirements traceability. In: 2015 Latin American Computing Conference (CLEI), pp. 1–7 (2015)
7. Kakeshita, T., Yamashita, S.: A requirement management education support tool for requirement elicitation process of REBOK. In: Proceedings - 3rd International Conference on Applied Computing and Information Technology and 2nd International Conference on Computational Science and Intelligence, ACIT-CSI 2015, pp. 40–45 (2015)
8. Mahmud, I., Veneziano, V.: Mind-mapping: an effective technique to facilitate requirements engineering in agile software development. In: 14th International Conference on Computer and Information Technology, ICCIT 2011, pp. 157–162 (2011)
9. Natarajan, S., Kumar, K.A.: Methodology to capture the content of customer thought: review on application of Zaltman Metaphor Elicitation Technique (ZMET) and Laddering methodology. Int. J. Econ. Res. 13, 4 (2016)

10. De Oliveira, S.F., et al.: Proposal for semiotics inspection method application in coming artifacts requirements survey activity. Proposta de Aplicação do Método de Inspeção Semiótica em Artefatos Provenientes da Atividade de Levantamento de Requisitos. In: Iberian Conference on Information Systems and Technologies, CISTI (2016)
11. Wanderley, F., et al.: Evaluation of BehaviorMap: a user-centered behavior language. In: Proceedings - International Conference on Research Challenges in Information Science, pp. 309–320. IEEE Computer Society (2015)
12. Wanderley, F., Silveira, D., Araujo, J., Moreira, A., Guerra, E.: Experimental evaluation of conceptual modelling through mind maps and model driven engineering. In: Murgante, B., et al. (eds.) ICCSA 2014. LNCS, vol. 8583, pp. 200–214. Springer, Cham (2014). https://doi.org/10.1007/978-3-319-09156-3_15
13. Wanderley, F., et al.: Generating feature model from creative requirements using model driven design. In: Proceedings of the 16th International Software Product Line Conference on—SPLC 2012, vol. 1., p. 18 (2012)
14. Wanderley, F., et al.: SnapMind: a framework to support consistency and validation of model-based requirements in agile development. In: 2014 IEEE 4th International Model-Driven Requirements Engineering Workshop, MoDRE 2014 – Proceedings, pp. 47–56 (2014)
15. Wanderley, F. et al.: Transforming creative requirements into conceptual models. In: Proceedings - International Conference on Research Challenges in Information Science (2013)
16. Wanderley, F., Da Silveria, D.S.: A framework to diminish the gap between the business specialist and the software designer. In: Proceedings - 2012 8th International Conference on the Quality of Information and Communications Technology, QUATIC 2012, pp. 199–204 (2012)
17. Zarour, M., et al.: An investigation into the best practices for the successful design and implementation of lightweight software process assessment methods: a systematic literature review. J. Syst. Softw. **101**, 180–192 (2015)
18. Zayed, R., et al.: Bridging the gap between human thinking and machine processing in developing and maintaining domain knowledge. Presented at the (2013)

Research on the Design Principles for Intelligent Products

Jiarui Wang, Yan Yan, and Liqun Zhang[(✉)]

School of Design, Shanghai Jiao Tong University, Shanghai, China
zhanglliqun@gmail.com

Abstract. With the rapid development of technology, more and more intelligent products have emerged. They perceive the external environment and internal state, automatically analyze and make decisions based on real-time data to provide people with a more convenient way of life. Compared with traditional products, the main difference is that intelligent products can be combined with technology such as the Internet and artificial intelligence to form a software and hardware service system not just hardware functions or virtual network space. Intelligent products have become one of the focus issues discussed at present. This research explains the definition and classification of intelligent products and discusses their current status and trends from the technical, commercial and user perspectives through quantitative text analysis and literature review. Then expound the current status and trends of intelligence products from the perspective of design. Based on the work above, this research identifies the design principles for intelligent products, which academics can do further investigate on this topic and practitioners may find something helpful in the process of design work. It is foreseeable that the wave of intelligent products is no longer limited to the deepening, generalization or internalization of the mobile Internet, but the terminal form of the service output and information perception in the age of artificial intelligence.

Keywords: Intelligent products · Design principle · Artificial intelligence

1 Introduction

In the era of the Internet of Things and big data, artificial intelligence will become the main force driving economic growth. Both the government and enterprises regard it as an important area of innovation. In terms of the growth of total investment in the industry, 2014 was regarded as the outbreak of smart products in China, which was 503% higher than that in 2013. From the perspective of market size, China's intelligent hardware market reached 331.5 billion yuan in 2016. The intelligent hardware market scale has maintained a stable growth trend. It is estimated from the Fig. 1 that by 2019, China's smart hardware market scale will reach 541.4 billion yuan.

According to the white paper of intelligent hardware industry development released by the China Academy of Information and Communications Technology, the number of worldwide mobile users has reached 7.6 billion in the first quarter of 2017. The number of globally connected intelligent hardware (smart phones) has reached 8 billion

© Springer Nature Switzerland AG 2019
A. Marcus and W. Wang (Eds.): HCII 2019, LNCS 11583, pp. 351–367, 2019.
https://doi.org/10.1007/978-3-030-23570-3_26

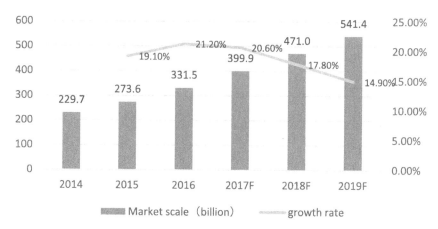

Fig. 1. The market scale of china intelligent products from 2014 to 2019

units, with a per capita possession of 1.1 units, which will rapidly increase to 1.5 in the next five years. From the perspective of data traffic, the mobile networking rate has reached 6.8 Mbps at the end of 2016 and will increase by three times in five years. From 2016 to 2021, the global public WiFi hotspots (including home hotspots) will grow six times [1]. All of this provides an excellent environment for the development of intelligent hardware.

However, in the design process of intelligent products, some problems have not been clarified: what kind of products are intelligent products and what kind of principles should be followed in the design of intelligent products. This study explores the intelligent products from the perspective of design by exploring the status and trends of intelligent products, and finally puts forward relevant design principles.

2   Theoretical Background and Literature Review

This section explores the definition and classification of intelligent products through literature review, and then analyzes the status and development trend of intelligent products from the perspective of technology, business and users. Figure 2 outlines the structure of this section, and gives an overall view of the topics discussed in the section.

2.1   Definitions and Classification of Intelligent Products

Compared with the traditional products, the major difference is that the intelligent products can be combined with technology such as the internet and big data to form a service system of software and hardware. The expectations of the consumer are the services and information provided. Therefore, Wuest et al. pointed out that the intelligent products allow the communication of large amounts of information from various product categories [2]. McFarlane et al. described that the intelligent products are physical and information-based items that may be processed or used and that generate the ability to act in an intelligent manner [3]. Apart from these definition, there are many other ways to define the intelligent products.

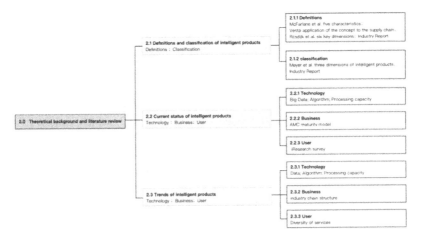

Fig. 2. An overview of the definition and classification of intelligent products

Definitions

The definitions of intelligent products vary from scholars and researchers. McFarlane et al. held the view that there are five properties for intelligent products: (1) possesses a unique identification; (2) is capable of communicating effectively with its environment; (3) can retain or store data about itself; (4) deploys a language to display its features, production requirements, etc.; (5) is capable of participating in or making decisions relevant to its own destiny [3]. McFarlane's theory didn't cover the embedded processing of products but only describe from the perspective of using RFID, which mainly used in the manufacturing and supply chain purposes.

Ventä describe the intelligent products from another four aspects: (1) Continuously monitor their status and environment. (2) React and adapt to environmental and operational conditions; (3) Maintain optimal performance in variable circumstances, also in exceptional cases; (4) Actively communicate with the user, environment or with other products and systems [4]. This definition considers the sufficient embedded computing power, which makes it possible to communicate with other information systems.

Rijsdijk et al. explored the relationships between product intelligence and consumer perception, conceptualizing product intelligence and smartness as comprising six key dimensions: autonomy, ability to learn, reactivity, ability to cooperate, human-like interaction, and personality [5].

Above these academic definition, some industry report also define the intelligent products in their own ways. Analysis define that intelligent products are a technological concept which through the combination of software and hardware to make the traditional devices to get intelligent function [6]. The hardware has the ability to connect and realize the surroundings to analyze and react. IResearch point out that intelligent products should do things in the human way such as reading, listening, thinking and acting via some technology support like Machine learning and etc. [7].

Thus, the intelligent product is a device that can retrieve data automatically and have the ability to learn, react and interact in the human-like way. In the next section, the classification will be discussed from the perspective of academic research and thematic report.

Classification

Based on the definitions from McFarlane and Ventä, Gerben G. Meyer et al. define a classification model of intelligent products shows in Fig. 3. which consist of three dimensions: level of intelligence, Location of intelligence and Aggregation level of intelligence. This model based on three orthogonal dimensions gives a more comprehensive classification of intelligent products which covers all the aspects of the field [8]. The level of intelligence descripts the ability of self-control from the basically manage its own information to completely manage its own life. The location of intelligence distinguished network and object like the relationship between application and hardware. The aggregation level of intelligence describes the difference between item and container, like the engine in the vehicle. This model is a more comprehensive classification and covers aspect from product itself to product lifecycle, which can be used to classify the products even it is brand-new.

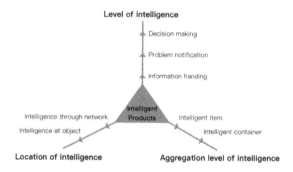

Fig. 3. Classification model of intelligent products by Gerben G. Meyer et al.

2.2   Current Status of Intelligent Products

At present, intelligent products are still mainly in the monitoring and control stage (Fig. 4). The development of intelligent products relies on the support of technology and the promotion of business power to provides a good experience for the majority of users. Therefore, this section discusses the current state of intelligent products from the perspective of technology development, business status and users.

Intelligent Products View of Technology

The underlying support of intelligent products is artificial intelligence technology. When it comes to technology, it is inseparable from big data, algorithms and computing power.

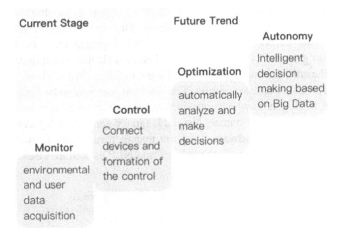

Fig. 4. The development of intelligent products via iResearch report

- *Big Data.* The famous consulting firm McKinsey pointed out: "Data has become an important production factor through the penetration of various business areas in various industries." The properties of "Big Data" have been concluded as "5Vs theory" and the most famous 3Vs are volume, variety, and velocity, which were introduced by Gartner analyst Laney D in a 2001 META Group research publication [9]. Recently the other 2Vs, called variability and value is added. The explanation of 5Vs are as follows in Fig. 5. Intelligent products are the main source for obtaining big data of users in the era of IoT. By collecting and concentrating data, a large amount of data is formed, sometimes even the sample is the whole data. The analysis result of big data may not only create a better user experience, but even achieves commercial success.

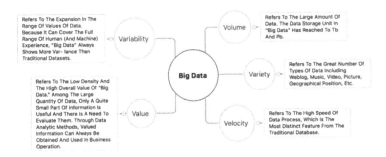

Fig. 5. 5Vs model of big data

- *Algorithm.* While science fiction often portrays AI as robots with human-like characteristics, AI can encompass anything from e-Commerce prediction algorithms to IBM's Watson machines [10]. The engineering approach and modeling approach are two ways to improve AI and the mainstream algorithm is machine learning. The algorithm of machine learning is very different. The input is the data and the desired results, and the output is the algorithm model. Through machine learning, the computer can generate its own model, and then provide the corresponding judgment to achieve the artificial intelligence [11]. We put together a list of classical algorithms in Fig. 6. Based on those algorithms, Forrester has just released a TechRadar report on artificial intelligence, which introduce the 9 aspects that using artificial intelligence to support decisions, namely Natural language generation, Speech recognition, VR/AR, AI-optimized hardware, Decision management, Deep learning platforms, Robotic process automation, Text analytics and NLP as well as Visual recognition.

Fig. 6. The list of classical algorithms

- *Processing capacity.* Apart from data and algorithm, another basic condition of AI is processing capacity. Graphics processing units (GPU), general purpose processors (GPP) and field programmable gate arrays (FPGA) are required to efficiently run AI-oriented computational tasks [12]. Nowadays GPU have evolved aggressively due to Moore's speed. For example, the number of NVIDIA TeslaV100 core transistors has reached 21.1 billion in 2017 exactly for deep learning, which increase 40% from Pascal (15.3 billion) released one year ago. The performance of Tensor floating-point computing is 12 times than that of Pascal; the cost is also significantly reduced. For example, the GTX1080 chip widely used in the market, the cost of one billion floating-point operations per second has been drop to a few cents according to its release price and nominal peak performance.

Intelligent Products View of Marketing

From the marketing perspective, the AMC model proposed by Analysys can be used to classify the intelligent products [6]. This model distinguishes the products by four development stage: exploration period, Market start-up period, high speed development period and market mature period. In this perspective, the Health Care, Consumer Robots, Domestic Robots, Smart Cars, UAV and AR devices is bracket in the exploration period. The VR devices, Industrial Robots, Wearable Devices and Smart Home are grouped in the stage of Market start-up. This classification is in market view and show the development of great potential for different products. As the intelligent products industry chain extends to various fields, more possible profit models will be explored in the future (Fig. 7).

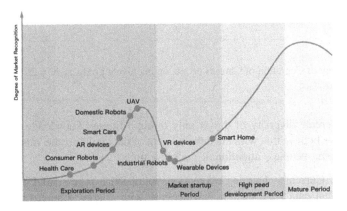

Fig. 7. The AMC curve of intelligent products in china (2017)

Intelligent Products View of User According to the iResearch report about Chinese intelligent products [7], about 40% of people show great concern about the intelligent products and 20%–34% of people have direct contacted with products. The top 2 products ranked by sales volume variance are wearable deceives like Band and smart home products like Robot vacuum cleaner and etc. and just accordance with the curve of ACM. The 70% of intelligent products consumers is male aged from 25 to 35, who are the High-income Groups and have strong consumptive power. The consumer focus on the better quality of life and fashion trend. Therefore, the intelligent products just provide a new experience and convenient way of life (Fig. 8).

2.3   New Trends of Intelligent Products

As mentioned above, the future tend of intelligent products will focus on how to achieve Optimization and Autonomy, which means the products will be smarter to automatically analyze and make intelligent decisions.

The View of Technology

- *Data.* On the one hand, comprehensive data will be collected through the development of IoT to train the model and boost the performance. While on the other hand, some scholars believe that current AI are overly dependent on big data, lack a self-idea function, and are complicated [12]. In the reality word, human being can

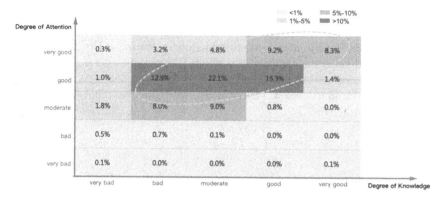

Fig. 8. A survey of Cognition of Chinses people on intelligent products, N = 2019, from online questionnaire in 2015

learn and create diversity of things only through limited knowledge and information. So, we believe that with the development of data volume, the value of data will also get some people's attention at the same time.

- *Algorithm.* Currently, learning expressions extracted from essential information of observational data via a deep neural network with a large number of layers is the mainstream on deep learning research. While in the situation of multitask learning and divert learning, it is still insufficient. For this reason, AI models based on unsupervised learning and shallow neural networks will become trends in future [12]. As mentioned above, the engineering approach and modeling approach are two ways to improve AI performance. The modeling approach simulates the biological mechanism of human and other creatures will inspire people to create greater algorithm (Table 1).

- *Processing capacity.* The core requirements of computing are energy efficiency and low latency. Therefore, infrastructure upgrades such as system clusters, as well as instruction sets, dedicated function libraries, and software frameworks need to be deeply integrated with specific applications to improve the computing power of single-chip platforms to meet the needs of complex intelligent hardware application scenarios such as low power consumption and real-time performance. The general chips like CPU and GPU will develop the interface and processing capacity even integrate the quantum computing to laying the foundation for the construction of computing framework system.

Table 1. Two ways to improve the performance of artificial intelligence

Engineering approach	Modeling approach
Traditional programming and data processing experience to improve performance	Simulates the biological mechanism of human and creature like genetic algorithm and neural network

The View of Business

As the AMC curve shows, the market scale of intelligent products will gradually increase and the corresponding business model will emerge. Take several companies in China as an example: JingDong (JD) Ecology provides a full aspect of support services for hardware entrepreneurs and helps the development of the hardware industry with an open and win-win mentality; Xiaomi uses the mobile phone ecological chain to take the Xiaomi box as the entry point to enter the field of intelligent product industry; Firebird connects designers and consumers with design innovation mode, and has already obtained Pre-B round investment and initiated joint acceleration plan. Rokid also launched full-stack voice open platform to provide one-stop voice solutions for the industry. 1 On the one hand, artificial intelligence enterprises with technical capabilities provide intelligent services to downstream enterprises by providing AI API, open source AI development framework, and open cloud computing capabilities, and become terminal industries together with component companies and OS enterprises. On the other hand, the influence of intelligent service providers will gradually increase. Just like the OEM companies have the same relationship with upstream storage, display and other device manufacturers. Large enterprises can create a smart ecosystem through their own resources, and SMEs can also participate in it as a member of the industry chain (Fig. 9).

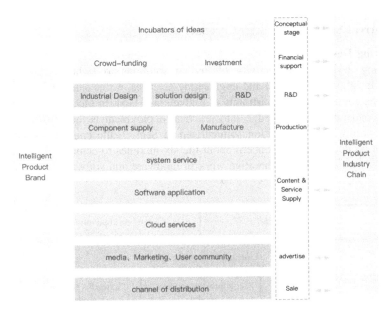

Fig. 9. The industry chain structure of Intelligent product

The View of User

There is no doubt that the number of users using other intelligent products is much less than the that use of smart phone. Therefore, smart phones are still the core terminals in the intelligent hardware system, and there is no precursor to being replaced by new terminals [1]. While the intelligent products that follow human's perception, assist human computing and rely on human knowledge models and decision-making experience will appear in large numbers. As intelligent products will provide diversity of services based the daily life, more and more people will use intelligent products. For example, in a scene where keyboard input and screen attention cannot be performed for a long time, speech recognition and gesture recognition can be used to help people operate, which greatly expands the usage time of home appliances, automobiles, drones, and consumer robots. Moreover, with the attention to user perception and emotion, the services and content provided by intelligent products will more evoke the resonance of users. For example, previous research in our institute is to integrate the factors of user's emotional expression and cognition to the intelligent information recommendation system [13, 14].

3 Current Status and New Trends of Intelligent Product Design

Since the intelligent products are different from traditional products, the design process and design content also show certain uniqueness. This chapter will discuss the design activities of intelligent products from the perspective of current status and trends.

3.1 Current Status of Intelligent Product Design

Engineering Design

Engineering design is the activity of finding solutions to technical problems by applying insights from natural and engineering sciences, at the same time taking into account the conditions and constraints of a given task [15]. In other words, transform empirical and rational knowledge into practical deployment is the primary function [16]. According to the definition summarized in Sect. 2, the engineering design of intelligent products need to concern about the six modules to achieve certain specific functions as well as the collaborative work of hardware and software (Fig. 10).

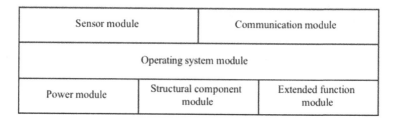

Fig. 10. Six modules of intelligent products

Industrial Design

Design is an interdisciplinary subject that involves many fields of knowledge. The main contains of industrial design is the practicality and beauty of the products. It combines art and technology from the very beginning. For the design of intelligent products, the biggest difference from traditional products is the technological factors. In the concept stage of the product, it is not only a creative sketch to illustrate the shape and structure, but also needs to consider the application of technical elements. At present, the intelligent transformation of product is still at the functional surface, and has not yet touched the revolution of human basic computing needs. New hardware such as VR/AR, intelligent robots, and drones cannot challenge the status of PCs and smart phone in general computing terminals in the short term [1]. Therefore, taking the smart phone as an example, there is no significant difference in appearance of phone. The full screen design and multi-camera design based on technical support have become the hot topic at present.

User Centered Design
Features that a product receive during the manufacturing process, even if they fulfill technical and functional requirements, are not worth much if they do not respond to a client's expectations [17]. Some failed products add many grandiose features but of no practical use, such as Baidu smart chopsticks. Therefore, user-centered design emphasis the important of user research to find out what is user demand. The general methods of user research are summarized in Fig. 11. Designers often do market and design research, pay attention to the feedback information, summarize and summarize, and constantly think about how to do the good design.

Fig. 11. General methods of user research

3.2 New Trends of Intelligent Product Design

Engineering Design
As Jonson suggests, "CAD may foster new patterns, relationships, or aesthetics expanding, rather than reducing designers' creative options". To do this, however,

future systems need to help the visualization of function in the early stages when the geometry is not fully defined [18]. In the case of rapid prototyping techniques, a prototype is produced directly from a digital model of a product and the time of obtaining the prototype is usually much shorter than by use of conventional manufacturing technologies [19]. While using the VR technology, the time shortening effect is achieved mostly through implementation of so-called virtual prototyping, meaning creating a digital prototype highly similar in some aspects to a real product, and then performing necessary tests and studies on it, without the necessity of building a physical prototype [18, 20].

Industrial Design
The important mission of industrial design is to create a product or system with practical value in social life. When intelligent products change the way of information acquiring and cognitive, the complexity of intelligent products sets several challenges to the designer. This increasing complexity need more collaborative work. Designers are no longer merely exchanging geometric and mathematical data, but more general knowledge about design and the product development process, including specifications, design rules, constraints, and rationale [21]. Moreover, they also need to expand into considerations of product complexity, multidisciplinary, integration of domains, and consideration about globalization trends, etc.

User Centered Design
The future trends will be the construction and development of specific and precise models to offer more insight into the cognitive processes [22]. In the process of getting information about the user, the researchers began to introduce the implicit measurement methods in the basic research fields such as psychological mechanism and neural mechanism into the user research to explore the real needs in order to compensate for the weaknesses of explicit measurement and enhance the reliability of user research [23]. There are some common methods of implicit measurement like implicit association test (IAT), electroencephalograph (EEG) and functional magnetic resonance imaging (FMRI) [24]. While these methods are confined to laboratories, the more effective way to get the intention of user is collect data through user behavior log mining. The product collect the information through user's input and sensor part to generate the user behavior log to help people analyze the correlation between each point of behavior. Moreover, there are some new attempts the like generate design process that transfer user-centered design to user participation design. "Thanks to the support of ICT (Intelligence Computing Technology) technology, Generative Design, which is currently taking shape, is triggering a new generation of behaviors, based on protocols and rules, based on digital manufacturing conditions. Design approach to deep involvement in the product generation process: the designer uses a system, such as a modeling grammar rule set, a computer program, with mathematics, with user intervention or some degree of autonomy or self-organizing features of the system itself. A product that defines functionality and meaning. Generating rule design and parameterization are its main technical features [25].

4   Design Principles for Intelligent Products

Based on the review of the definition, trends and design of intelligent products, this paper proposes the following three dimensions of intelligent product design principles (Fig. 12). From the individual point of view of the product, technical support is needed to give the product the ability to be smart and interact naturally; from the perspective of the overall network, products need to be interconnected to form a service network; from the perspective of service content, it is necessary to determine the real pain points and user needs in order to avoid bad user experience and service quality.

Fig. 12. TIS model of design principles for intelligent products

4.1   Technical Assistance

AI Empowerment
Terminal devices will also be coupled with AI technology. Traditional electronic devices simply use the sensors to collect data with not analyzed. The application of deep learning technology accelerates the development of artificial intelligence sensing technologies such as speech recognition and image recognition, enabling intelligent products to initially possess visual, auditory, tactile and other active observation and sensing capabilities, such as cameras, laser radar, millimeter wave radar, microphones, fusion sensors, etc. The device directly acquires external data such as images, video, audio, and position, thereby implementing functions such as face recognition, speech recognition, video analysis, and semantic understanding.

Natural Interaction
Donald A. Norman pointed out that the mouse and keyboard seem to interact naturally but actually they are not natural, and intelligent products bring us more possibilities to explore. Steve Ballmer, CEO of Microsoft pointed out that we expanded beyond the mouse and keyboard and started incorporating more natural forms of interaction such as touch, speech, gestures, handwriting, and vision [26].

- Data interaction is not just about numbers, but about all the resources that can be digitized, including text, images, sounds, and more. The data stream is passed through the input of the intelligent products, causing the system to respond, manipulating the device or feeding back the output information to the user.
- Image interaction is based on the development of technical support for machine vision systems. Intelligent devices obtain the perception of the content itself through image recognition, thereby further analyzing the relevant target attributes and guiding the next judgment and behavior. At present, the widely-used applications are OCR, face recognition and so on.
- Voice interaction is a natural way of interaction. About 75% of human communication is done through voice interaction. Therefore, if the intelligent products have natural language recognition function, it can greatly reduce the operating cost of the smart device and enhance the user experience.
- Behavioral interaction is based on human motion capture to obtain information. Through natural gestures and physical location information acquisition, intelligent products can quickly understand the user's intentions. Touch-based products are almost always designed to let users zoom by finger through the screen.

4.2   Interconnection

Data Acquisition

Various intelligent products perceive different data to form a multi-dimensional intelligent perception network. Through data uploading, data analyzing, data storage in the big data cloud platform, the platform gives feeds back, achieving the integration of calculation and information (Fig. 13). When massive data is transmitted to the big data platform, it need to be calculated by the processing framework and the processing engine, which involves technologies such as cloud storage, distributed scheduling, distributed computing, and finally data interaction through the form of an interactive interface.

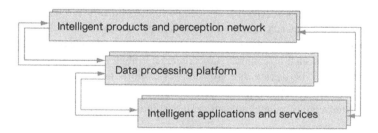

Fig. 13. The framework of Intelligent products and data processing system

Transparency

Only by achieving interconnection and interoperability can a powerful functional system be formed. Enabled by the increasing number of interconnected objects and people, the fusion of the physical and virtual world enables a new form of information transparency [27]. Through linking sensor data with digitalized plant models, a virtual copy of the physical world is created. Context-aware information are indispensable for IoE participants to make appropriate decisions. Context-aware systems accomplish their tasks based on information coming from the virtual and physical world. Examples for information from the virtual world are electronic documents, drawings, and simulation models. Examples for physical world information are the position or conditions of a too [28]. In order to create transparency, the data analytics' results need to be embedded in assistance systems that are accessible to all IoE participants [29].

Sharing

As we mentioned above, the communication module is one of the most important part of intelligent product, which make it possible to connect objects and share information. Based on the IoT, products can interact with each other, cooperate with their neighboring "smart" components to reach common goals through unique addressing schemas. The communication module is the node of data transmission between independent devices. Currently widely used communication technologies include Wi-Fi, Bluetooth, ZigBee, RIFID, ultra-wideband (UWB) and mobile communication like GPRS, 3G, 4G and even 5G technologies. Through the multi-method communication technology applications, a diverse network of perceptions will be created. Machines, devices, sensors, and people are connected over the IoT and IoP (internet of people) and form the IoE (internet of everything) [30, 31].

4.3 Service Content

At present, one of the most familiar intelligent product is Xiaomi bracelet, which has the embedded three-dimensional rhythmic motion sensor to collect user's motion information, and the data such as the amount of exercise, the number of steps, the quality of sleep, and the calorie consumption. When users use such wearable devices, their own various sensory data, psychological data, and experience data will be transmitted to the back end, and give user feedback about how to improve the health status through the analysis and calculation of the server. Sometimes even recommend related products and more through shopping channels. With the development of intelligent products, the services provided will cover more aspects of life, from smart traffic to health care and etc. The assistance of intelligent devices gradually extends from simple operations in complex environments to fine work to liberate the labor.

5   Conclusion

This paper contributes to the ongoing discussion about intelligent products within both the scientific and the practitioners' community. The paper's practical contribution is put forward the design principle of intelligent products to help people avoid many problems of existing products, such as over-reliance on mobile phone, failure to make full use of the data, frustrated with the user experience and etc. The limitation is that we do not focus on specific product or industry but give the general conception. For example, it is quite different to design a smart car and wearable devices. All in all, Intelligent Products will have a visible impact on humans and society in the future.

References

1. China Academy of Information and Communications Technology. The white paper of intelligent hardware industry development (2017). http://www.199it.com/archives/640124.html (in Chinese)
2. Wuest, T., Hribernik, K., Thoben, K.D.: Digital representations of intelligent products: product avatar 2.0. In: Abramovici, M., Stark, R. (eds) Smart Product Engineering. Lecture Notes in Production Engineering. Springer, Heidelberg (2013). https://doi.org/10.1007/978-3-642-30817-8_66
3. Mcfarlane, D., Sarma, S., Chirn, J.L., et al.: Auto ID systems and intelligent manufacturing control. Eng. Appl. Artif. Intell. 16(4), 365–376 (2003)
4. Ventä, O.: Intelligent products and systems: technology theme- final report. VTT Technical Research Centre of Finland, Espoo (2007)
5. Rijsdijk, S.A., Hultink, E.J., Diamantopoulos, A.: Product intelligence: its conceptualization, measurement and impact on consumer satisfaction. J. Acad. Mark. Sci. 35(3), 340–356 (2007)
6. Analysys: China Intelligent Hardware Industry Development Analysis (2017). https://www.analysys.cn/article/analysis/detail/1001082. (in Chinese)
7. IResearch: China Intelligent Products Industry Research Report released by iResearch and JD. http://report.iresearch.cn/report_pdf.aspx?id=2482. (in Chinese)
8. Meyer, G.G., Främling, K., Holmström, J.: Intelligent products: a survey. Comput. Ind. 60(3), 137–148 (2009)
9. Laney, D.: 3D data management: controlling data volume, velocity and variety. META Group Research Note. http://blogs.gartner.com/doug-laney/files/2012/01/ad949-3D-Data-Management-Controlling-Data-Volume-Velocity-and-Variety.pdf
10. IBM Watson. https://www.ibm.com/watson/. Accessed 20 Apr 2017
11. IResearch. China Business Intelligence Industry Research Report (2017). http://report.iresearch.cn/report/201706/3010.shtml. (in Chinese)
12. Lu, H., Li, Y., Chen, M., et al.: Brain intelligence: go beyond artificial intelligence. Mobile Netw. Appl. 23(2), 368–375 (2017)
13. Zhong, K., Zhang, L., Guan, X.: Research on information recommendation optimization mechanism based on emotional expression and cognition. In: Marcus, A., Wang, W. (eds.) DUXU 2018. LNCS, vol. 10920, pp. 133–146. Springer, Cham (2018). https://doi.org/10.1007/978-3-319-91806-8_11
14. Tang, C., Zhong, K., Zhang, L.: A study on the differences in the expressions of emotional cognition between bloggers and users based on the "cloud pet keeping" phenomenon. In: Meiselwitz, G. (eds) Social Computing and Social Media. User Experience and Behavior. SCSM 2018. LNCS, vol. 10913. Springer, Cham (2018). https://doi.org/10.1007/978-3-319-91521-0_27
15. Pahl, G., Beitz, W.: Engineering Design: A Systematic Approach. Springer, London (1996). https://doi.org/10.1007/978-1-84628-319-2
16. Horváth, I.: A treatise on order in engineering design research. Res. Eng. Des. 15, 155–181 (2004)
17. Zawadzki, P., Żywick, K.: Smart product design and production control for effective mass customization in the industry 40. concept. Manag. Prod. Eng. 7, 105–112 (2016)
18. Taborda, E., Chandrasegaran, S., Kisselburgh, L., Reid, T., Ramani, K.: Enhancing visual thinking in a toy design course using freehand sketching. In: ASME International Design Engineering Technical Conferences and Computers and Information in Engineering Conference (2012)

19. Grajewski, D., Gorski, F., Zawadzki, P., Hamrol, A.: Application of virtual reality techniques in design of ergonomic manufacturing workplaces. In: International Conference on Virtual and Augmented Reality in Education, vol. 25, pp. 289–301 (2013)
20. Gorski, F., Wichniarek, R., Kuczko, W., Zawadzki, P., Bun, P.: Strength of ABS parts produced by fused deposition modelling technology – a critical orientation problem. Adv. Sci. Technol. Res. J. 9(26), 12–19 (2015)
21. The evolution, challenges, and future of knowledge representation in product design systems.pdf
22. Vargas-Hernandez, N., Shah, J., Smith, S.: Cognitive models of design ideation. In: ASME DTM Conference (2007)
23. Dirican, A., Türkktürk, M.: Psychophysiological measures of human cognitive states applied in human computer interaction. Procedia Comput. Sci. 3, 1361–1367 (2011)
24. Xie, W., Xin, X., Hu, W.: Research status on user implicit measurement method in product design. J. Mach. Des. 2, 105–110 (2015). (in Chinese)
25. Zhang, L.: New relations and creative cooperation between designer and user in digital micro-manufacturing context. In: 2013 4th HDCon (2013). (in Chinese)
26. Norman, D.A.: Natural user interfaces are not natural. Interactions 17(3), 6–10 (2010)
27. Lasi, H., Fettke, P., Kemper, H.-G., Feld, T., Hoffmann, M.: Industry 4.0. Bus. Inf. Syst. Eng. 6(4), 239–242 (2014)
28. Lucke, D., Constantinescu, C., Westkämper, E.: Smart factory - a step towards the next generation of manufacturing. In: Mitsuishi, M., Ueda, K., Kimura, F. (eds) Manufacturing Systems and Technologies for the New Frontier, pp. 115–118. Springer, London (2008). https://doi.org/10.1007/978-1-84800-267-8_23
29. Gorecky, D., Schmitt, M., Loskyll, M., Zühlke, D.: Human–machine-interaction in the industry 4.0 era. In: 12th IEEE International Conference on Industrial Informatics (INDIN), pp. 289–294 (2014)
30. Vilarinho, T., Farshchian, B.A., Floch, J., Mathisen, B.M.: A communication framework for the internet of people and things based on the concept of activity feeds in social computing. In: 9th International Conference on Intelligent Environments (2013)
31. Nieto de Santos, F.J., García Villalonga, S.: Exploiting local clouds in the internet of everything environment. In: 23rd Euromicro International Conference on Parallel, Distributed, and Network-Based Processing, pp. 296–300 (2015)
32. Pandilov, Z., et al.: Virtual modelling and simulation of a CNC machine feed drive system. Trans. FAMENA 39(4), 37–54 (2016)

Research on the Development
of Contemporary Design Intelligence Driven
by Neural Network Technology

Yan Yan, Jiarui Wang, Chen Tang, and Liqun Zhang[✉]

School of Design, Shanghai Jiao Tong University, Shanghai, China
zhanglliqun@gmail.com

Abstract. In the innovative age of synergy between design and technology, neural network has been popular in the research community, and has become a huge wave of technology trend for design intelligence, its unique characteristics of knowledge production for the design of intelligent areas to bring more possibilities. This paper provides a comprehensive survey and analysis, focusing on domestic and international research on neural network and design intelligence at present. Method Based on the extensive literature research, this paper analyzes the research progress of contemporary design intelligence driven by neural network. Result on the basis of current literatures related, this paper sums up the intelligent process of design based on neural network technology, three types of design intelligence and their typical application cases. It also briefly describes the intelligent design tool based on neural network technology. Moreover, it reviews in detail industrial application of neural network in intelligent design. Finally, this study highlights the existing problems and challenges in the field of design intelligence and discusses future development prospects. Hope to help design researchers and design workers in the future better apply neural network technology to enhance the design intelligence.

Keywords: Design intelligence · Neural network · Design process · Design tools

1 Introduction

Human beings transform the world through labor, creating civilization, material wealth and spiritual wealth. The most basic creative activity is creating. Design is a purposefully creative activity, which is preconceived, planned by human beings for purposeful creation and innovation activities. It is also an innovative creation with creative system integration. In the long history of human beings, design always follows the pace of industrial civilization and information civilization, also, design is good at transforming the latest scientific and technological achievements into design energy and spawning new design patterns. With the development of the modern information technology, designers began to use computer intelligence to undertake and assist various complex tasks in the process of design activities. But computer can only participate in the process of assisting design expression and presenting design results. In the innovative age of synergy between design and technology, neural network has been popular in the research communities, and has become a huge wave of technology trend for design intelligence, its unique characteristics of knowledge production for the design of intelligent areas to bring more possibilities. This paper provides a comprehensive survey and analysis, focusing on domestic and international research on neural network and design intelligence at present. Method Based on the extensive literature research, this paper analyzes the research progress of contemporary design intelligence driven by neural network. Results on the basis of current literatures related, this paper sums up the intelligent process of design based on neural network technology, three types of design intelligence and their typical application cases. It also briefly describes the intelligent design tool based on neural network technology. Moreover, it reviews in detail industrial application of neural network in intelligent design. Finally, this study highlights the existing problems and challenges in the field of design intelligence and discusses future development prospects. Hope it is possible to help design researchers and design workers to apply neural network technology to enhance the design intelligence better in the future.

2 The Development of Design Intelligence

With the development of the modern information technology, designers began to use computer intelligence to undertake and assist various complex tasks in the process of design activities. The first stage is computerization, in which the designers present the drawing process by the aid of advanced computer techniques. So designers can separate themselves from handwork. For example, computer drawing software such as CAD can assist designers to draw shapes through preset menus. The computer can not only draw the two-dimensional image, but also establish the three-dimensional space model. With the improvement of computing speed of computer hardware and the further development of software functions, computer aided design has entered the second stage: computerization. At this stage, the design software freed designers from simple repeated operations. Parametric visual programming can adjust input parameters intuitively and change a series of related results in real time through calculation method [1]. This stage indicates that design has come into early phases of digital and intelligent era.

Since 2006, neural network technology is rising again, and is widely concerned by various fields. Today it has become a wave in the field of design. Driven by neural network technology, computer-aided design has entered the third stage: intelligent design. As a new dimension in the field of design, neural network technology owns the characteristics of gaining knowledge. This feature will create a new look to intelligent design and will challenge the paradigm of traditional design practice and academic research, for the machine has began to mimic human intelligence, began to learn, and even got their own "idea" and "inspiration".

For example, the Chinese character style transfer model developed by Flipboard software engineer Yuchen Tian uses a top-down neural network with CNN architecture to learn and design new Chinese character fonts, so as to realize the transfer of Chinese character styles and transform standard Chinese fonts into target fonts. Paints-Chainer developed a line mapping model based on CNN neural network, which allows for automatic coloring of black and white illustrations and allows for different illustration styles. Georgia tech's robot Shimon can analyze music in real time and collaborate with humans to improvise music. CycleGAN neural network technology can learn how to convert the characteristics of an image to another image without a double data, including the transformation between horse and conversion, landscape in different seasons. Besides, researchers are currently exploring how to apply this technology to other fields; ChAIr is a design project based on GAN, which can assist artists to carry out more creative design. It uses chair data set for training, and finally gets a model that can generate various chair images, so as to give human designers semi-abstract visual hints.

Current research results show that the neural network technology is accelerating the iterative evolution, more and more professional researchers join the explosion based on the neural network technology. The previous design paradigms are dying out, meanwhile the new design paradigms are gradually rising. How to combine it with design to promote the development of future design intelligence will be an important tendency in the future design field.

3 Introduction to Neural Networks

3.1 The Development of Neural Networks

The neural network is inspired by human understanding of brain biology - the interconnection of all neurons. In 1943, McCuloch and Pits proposed mathematical models of MP neurons. In 1958, the first generation of neural network single-layer perceptron was proposed by Rosenblat. The first generation of neural networks were able to distinguish basic shapes such as triangles and squares, which made it possible for humans to invent intelligent machines that can truly perceive, learn, and remember. The basic principles of a generation of neural networks are limited. In 1969, Minsky published the Perceptron Monograph: Single-layer perceptrons cannot solve the XOR problem. In 1986, Hinton et al. proposed a second-generation neural network, replacing the original single fixed feature layer with multiple hidden layers. The activation function uses the Sigmoid function to train the model using the error back propagation algorithm, which can effectively solve the nonlinear classification. In 1989, Cybenko and Hornik et al. demonstrated universal approximation: any function can be approximated by a three-layer neural network with arbitrary precision. In the same year, LeCun et al. invented a convolutional neural network to identify handwriting. In 1991, the backpropagation algorithm was pointed out to have a gradient disappearance problem. For more than a decade, research on neural networks has been shelved. In 2006, Hinton et al. explored the graph model in the brain, proposed an autoencoder to reduce the dimensionality of the data, and proposed to train the deep belief network in a pre-trained manner to suppress the gradient disappearance problem. Bengio et al. demonstrated that the pre-training method is also applicable to unsupervised learning such as self-encoders. Poultney et al. use energy-based models to effectively learn sparse representations. These papers lay the foundation for deep learning, from which deep learning enters a period of rapid development. In 2010, the US Department of Defense's DARPA program funded a deep learning program for the first time. In 2011, Glorot et al. proposed the ReLU activation function, which can effectively suppress the gradient disappearance problem. Deep learning has made a major breakthrough in speech recognition. Microsoft and Google have used deep learning to reduce the speech recognition error rate to 20% ~ 30%. It is the biggest breakthrough in the field in 10 years. In 2012, Hinton and his students reduced the Top5 error rate for ImageNet image classification problems from 26% to 15%, from which deep learning entered the outbreak [2]. As shown in Fig. 1, the blue marked points in the figure represent important turning points in the development of neural network technology, and the gray marked points represent the important development period of neural network technology.

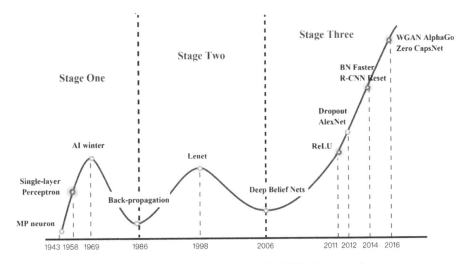

Fig. 1. The history of neural networks (Color figure online)

3.2 The Application of Neural Networks

Neural networks have experienced two waves from shallow neural networks to deep learning. There are important differences between deep learning models and shallow neural network models. Shallow neural network models do not use distributed representation and require artificial extraction of features. Deep learning breaks through the limitations of shallow neural networks. As a feature learning method, deep learning can transform raw data into higher-level, more abstract expressions through some simple but non-linear models. Very complex functions can also be learned with a combination of enough conversions. From a model perspective, current deep learning includes: DBN, CNN, RNN, DLRL, DNN.

With the breakthrough of training algorithms and computational capability bottlenecks (especially for the use of graphics processing and high-performance computing), deep learning is widely used in artificial intelligence-related fields, and has made great progress on many research issues. Typical application scenarios include image processing (image classification, object detection, video classification, scene analysis and shadow detection), speech understanding (speech recognition, prosody prediction, prosody prediction, text-to-speech synthesis), natural language processing (syntax analysis, Machine translation, contextual entity linking) and data mining (sentiment analysis, information retrieval) [3]. For details on neural networks please see the review articles.

4 Neural Networks Drive the Evolution of Intelligent Design

Driven by neural network technology, machines begin to imitate human intelligence and learn to learn, with "ideas" and "inspirations" exclusive to machines. The subject of Design Intelligent has the characteristics of neural network technology: high autonomy, high adaptability. These features are well reflected in the design processes, types of Design Intelligence and design tools. At the same time, the mainstream neural network technology platform builds an ecosystem with the help of the open source model, supporting the industrial application in the design field.

4.1 The Design Intelligence Process Based on Neural Network Technology

Based on the design process theory of academician Youbai XIE and the characteristics of design intelligence, a new process based on neural network is developed (Fig. 2). The design process is divided into three stages – the design task of the proposed stage, conceptual design stage and structural design and detailed design stage [4]. Through its own learning ability, the neural network integrates all the processes and becomes an intelligent design subject which automatically gives design output based on sensory input.

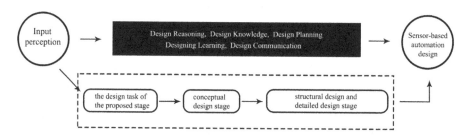

Fig. 2. The Design Intelligence process based on neural network technology

In the proposal phase of a design task, it usually involves the identification of design requirements (including potential requirements) and analysis. The traditional user modeling system focuses on the psychological state of users, and lacks the behavioral orientation of users, such as interaction preference. So it is unable to give timely feedback on the dynamic behavior, preference and psychological attitude of users. Neural network technology can just make up the defect of traditional user modeling, and user modeling is regarded as a dynamic learning process. User knowledge can be acquired by constantly acquiring user behavior, and user assumptions can be obtained more reliably based on the observation of several applications, and they can be applied to multiple applications [5].

On the conceptual design stage, that is, after the design task is defined, the selection stage of design method needs to be carried out. In the traditional design process, designers and researchers will select new design combination methods based on their own experience and case study, which is relatively inefficient for the new design problems constantly arising. However, the research shows that the neural network can bring rich conceptual design results for different design types and problems. For example, in terms of color matching, based on semantic information transfer technology, neural network can generate a large number of completely different but beautiful and reasonable color matching for the same line draft in a short time [6]. In the field of 3d product design, neural networks accelerate the development of generative design by learning the constraints between physical attributes and acquiring professional knowledge. For example, a four-legged helicopter designed by Autodesk needs both good flight performance and strong load capacity, which requires the helicopter to have a light chassis and low aerodynamic resistance. Unlike traditional design processes, machines learn physical constraints and explore possible structures, generating design concepts that human designers cannot imagine.

On the detailed design stage, based on the ability of neural network technology to learn continuously, the machine can test, evaluate, optimize, backtrack and redesign based on the continuous calculation and real-time update of online data. This makes the detailed design more relevant to the conceptual design phase. In addition, the neural network can also help explain the design results. For example, Airbnb uses the neural network technology to explain their pricing model [7, 8].

4.2   Three Types of Design Intelligence and Typical Application Cases

Driven by neural network technology, data sources in the field of design intelligence are very complex, including visual data input, that is identification of visual characteristics, auditory data input, that means conversion from speech to text by recognizing sound fragments of information, such as songs, body movement data input, such as Microsoft kinect and Leap motion, which can use neural network to recognize the user's motion and three-dimensional physical environment. In addition, user behavior can be used as abstract input data, which can be interpreted by neural network technology. Any data that can be converted into electronic signals can be used as input to the neural network [9]. In the design process, there are three types of design intelligence based on different use angles of data: data-driven design intelligence, data-informed design intelligence and data-awared design intelligence. (Fig. 3).

Data-Driven Design Intelligence. Data-driven design intelligence is the direct use of collected data for design decisions. When all the design investigations have been completed, design problems and objectives have been clearly defined, design decisions aimed at specific design details can be made directly based on the results of data collection. A/B test is to obtain users' preferences by providing different alternatives of different products to different users, so as to directly find the design scheme that can yield better effect. Of course, be wary of "micro-optimizations" or "local

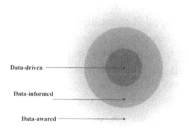

Fig. 3. The relationship between data-driven, data-informed, data-aware design intelligence

maximizations" due to over-reliance on data. When a user creates a site using The Grid, the site asks the user to define the content intent first, then automatically adjust or make changes based on the user's content intent, and then add personalized content based on the user's needs.

Data-Informed Design Intelligence. Data-informed design intelligence refers to taking the data result as an input in the design decision-making process. This is because in many cases, the data analysis results are not completely clear to the decision suggestions of design intelligence. In this type of design intelligence, the data output results are used to enlighten designers on how to view design problems, and help to carry out the next design iteration and in-depth research [10]. For example, Facebook often updates its homepage, even if some indicators become worse, it will not affect them to constantly try to change their products, because the fluctuation of data will not affect their design philosophy. Style AI is to use the neural network technology to capture the inspiration source in life and combine the elements of life, nature and art to help designers explore the inspiration source of various fashion from life for creation.

Data-Aware Design Intelligence. Data-aware design intelligence emphasizes that the design process is a process of innovation, not just design decisions made from instances of data collection. In the design process, what kind of data types and combinations of types need to be obtained is a design problem in itself. Compared with other two types of design intelligence, design intelligence based on data perception is a more strategic way of thinking. Google set up a large number of data centers, most of these data centers are deep learning of the neural network set up by the CPU and GPU, through the data center, data designers and scientists need to work with developers and business strategists, design system actively, in order to collect the right data types or data type combination to solve problem [11]. As shown in Fig. 4, the three types of design intelligence are briefly summarized.

4.3   Design Tool Based on Neural Network Technology

Design tools change as design objects change and technology evolves. RoelofPieters and SamimWiniger analyzed the development history of computers and summarized their three maturity levels as human design tools (Fig. 5): first generation assisted creation system(AC1.0), it can simulate the tools in digital form; then is second

Three types of design intelligence	Introduction	Typical application cases
Data-driven design intelligence	Data-driven design intelligence is the direct use of collected data for design decisions.	Web Page Maker : The Grid
Data-informed design intelligence	Data-informed design intelligence refers to taking the data result as an input in the design decision-making process.	The Style AI
Data-aware design intelligence.	Data-aware design intelligence emphasizes that the design process is a process of innovation.	Google datacenter

Fig. 4. Three types of design intelligence and typical application cases

generation assisted creation system(AC2.0), in this stage people and machinery can work in harmony through real-time feedback loop; and third generation assisted creation systems(AC3.0), negotiate the creative process fine-grained, augment creative capabilities and accelerate skill acquisition time [12].

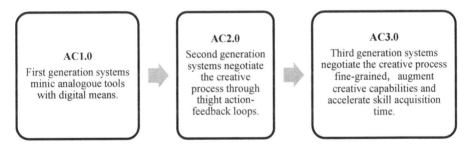

Fig. 5. The development of the generation assisted creation system

Intelligent design tools driven by neural network technology have evolved into the third generation. The strong autonomy and adaptability of neural network technology endow the intelligent design tools with the ability to constantly optimize the design results, and redefine the man–machine collaboration mode: collaborative production, human–machine collaboration and mutual enhancement. Neural network technology can help illustrators draw by modifying strokes, give writers assistance on writing by improving text styles, and help musicians compose music by proposing ideas. At present, the design intelligent tools based on neural network have presented two main types: research type and industrial application type. (Fig. 6).

Research-Based Design Tools. Research-based design tools can make it easier for ordinary users or developers to understand the neural network technology, stimulate the interest of users or researchers, and collect a large amount of training data to continuously improve the neural network technology. Google's AI Experiments are designed to

Two main types	Typical cases	URL
Research-based design tools.	AutoDraw Google AI Painting system	https://www.autodraw.com http://www.idi.zju.edu.cn/project/1178.html
Industrial application design tools.	Alibaba Luban system Project Muse Thread's fashion advice Zoomorphic Design	https://luban.aliyun.com https://muse.jhu.edu/ https://www.thread.com http://www.saikit.org/projects/zoomorphic/index.html

Fig. 6. Design tool based on neural network technology

create cool and interesting products using cutting-edge technologies such as neural networks, so as to explore the possibilities of neural network technologies on a larger scale. Its Autodraw allows users to draw pictures at will, and then, based on the understanding of the patterns drawn by users based on the neural network, vector icons drawn by professional design staff can be matched for users to choose. Users can then paint on this basis and draw to complete their designs. (Fig. 7) AI Painting developed by IDEA Lab of Zhejiang university is a collaborative creation platform between AI and human, which enables users to express the imaginary world into reality. (Fig. 8) The user can use the AI Painting system to create animated stories out of imagination and experience, and create beautiful animated landscapes with just a few strokes of paint.

Fig. 7. AutoDraw Google

Fig. 8. AI Painting system

Industrial Application Design Tools. The progress of neural network technology supports the research and development of innovative tools in the field of design. At present, design tools based on neural network are being widely applied in visual design, clothing design, product design, architectural design and other fields, especially in the realm of visual design.

Neural network technology penetrates visual design industry gradually, which accelerates the development of visual design industry and realizes manpower change into brainpower. Traditional visual design tools output the content of the projected onto a two-dimensional plane space through the communication between the system and the technologists. However, visual design tools driven by neural network can extract the inherent law hidden in the back of data through deep learning and extends more possibilities through reinforcement learning. Through the disassembly and abstraction of a large number of excellent case design patterns, a set of design and development standards, workflow and related tools that can intelligently configure the brand language are constructed. Alibaba's "Luban" system – one-click generated banner advertising system is a typical case, which constructs a set of self-optimizing design process from understanding layer composition to aesthetic and commercial evaluation system through machine (Fig. 9).

	Design Thinking	Data Thinking
Vision	Color, shape, texture	RGB, shape, texture
Space	Location, size, quantity	x, y, w, h, number
Script	design action	index
Aesthetics	Aesthetic quantitative evaluation	style, score

Fig. 9. Alibaba Luban system

The development of neural network technology promotes the transformation of traditional digital clothing design, which is the inevitable trend and result of the new type of industrialization and informatization of the clothing industry. Deep learning algorithm is also applied to recommend personalized fashion collocation for users, help users to match clothes, and generate personalized clothing collocation for users by building a framework to learn semantic information about visual style. That is Thread (Fig. 10). In addition, Project Muse, an artificial intelligence clothing design product launched by Google, supports users to hand-draw and generate personalized fashion dress (Fig. 11).

Fig. 10. Project Muse page   **Fig. 11.** Thread's fashion advice

The development of neural network technology also promotes the transformation of products design. For instance, Zoomorphic Design proposes a way to create morphing shapes by combining artificial and animal shapes. To identify a pair of shapes that are suitable for merging, the Zoomorphic Design team uses an efficient kernt-based technique (Fig. 12). The merging process is formulated as a continuous optimization problem in which two shapes deform together to minimize the energy function combining several design factors. The modeler can adjust the weights between these factors to gain a high level of control over the resulting shape. Thus, it is ensured that the morphing shapes do not violate the design constraints of the artificial shapes. Zoomorphic Design demonstrates the versatility and effectiveness of this method by generating various morphing shapes [13].

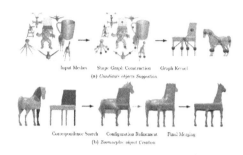

Fig. 12. Zoomorphic designs created by the system

The application of neural network technology in the architectural design industry is deepening, which not only improves the work efficiency, but also makes the characteristics of architectural design better reflected. Gen Nishida et al. put forward the 3D modeling model of architecture applied by neural network: according to the sketch sketched by the user, the system automatically generates 3D architectural model. Based on deep learning, the system finds a set of predefined components that match, then the user selects the appropriate components from the set of components. The system synthesizes the user's options and generates a 3D model of the building [14]. In the future, enhancing the application of neural network technology in architectural design is the inevitable choice for the architectural industry to get rid of the traditional operation mode and move towards intelligent design.

In the future, under the change of new design mode, the design tool based on neural network will become a more widely used tool and an important assistant tool for designers. Neural network endowers tools with recognition ability and natural interaction ability, which will reduce the threshold of using design tools and learning costs, and greatly improve the design expression efficiency of end users.

5   The Development Prospect of Design Intelligence Driven by Neural Network

5.1   Problems Faced by Neural Networks in the Field of Design Intelligence

Neural network technology still faces many challenges in solving design problems. This paper mainly discusses and analyzes from the two main aspects of technical basis and design thinking:

1. Based on the technical level: the rise of the neural network technology was largely due to the wide availability of huge amounts of data. At present, the complex data related to design has growth exponentially and is present through a variety of different morphology (such as text, images, audio, video, etc.), meanwhile it has different distribution. All of this poses challenges to the application of neural network in design. Therefore, how to design effective neural network model and learning theory based on big data, and gain exponential knowledge from the exponential growth of data is now an inevitable challenge in the development process of intelligent design driven by neural network.

2. In terms of design thinking: neural network technology is best at solving problems with clear objectives and rules, such as reasoning, classification, proof and clustering. However, the design is characterized by unclear problem definition, uncertain solution path and unclear evaluation criteria. Design thinking has three characteristics. First, design thinking is a process of cross-media knowledge processing; second, design thinking is the coevolution of problem solutions; third, the whole design process is divergent and convergent. On the whole, the design presents the characteristics of first divergence and then convergence. It can be seen that the problems that neural network technology is good at solving are in conflict with the characteristics of design thinking, and there are many challenges in how to solve design problems through neural network technology.

5.2 Future Development Prospects

The neural network has brought a disruptive change to the field of design. The understanding of "neural network-driven intelligent evolution of design" should not be limited to the technological basis, production organization and lifestyle changes, but the system and management changes at a deeper level. The future development of neural network technology may include:

1. At the technical base level: neural network reconstructs the design data stream and drives the design industry to become technology-intensive. Driven by the neural network, the data-intensive paradigm of design has come. A large amount of unstructured data is generated in the design and production process: consumer data, industry data, design data, designer data, etc. The collection, processing and intelligence of these data is the key to enable design to access data economy. In the future, driven by neural network technology, designers' design works will be precipitated into design data, and the connection between people and data will be realized by constructing knowledge graphs. After the connection of massive data, semantic data and image data will greatly improve the production efficiency of the design industry. Technologies such as neural networks and big data have transformed the design industry from a labor-intensive industry with a lot of low-end repetitive work to a technology-intensive one.

2. At the level of production and lifestyle: neural networks have revolutionized the design process, driving mass customization and human–machine collaborative creation. Designers are no longer using user sampling to find requirements and provide a solution; Instead, it involves itself in the whole production life cycle of the

product and continuously adjusts and optimizes the product in the actual experience of users. Under the new design mode, design is no longer a node in the production chain of products, but an important link in the user-centered design cycle endowed with artificial intelligence, which runs through the whole product life cycle [14]. Neural network technology is a multiplier of efficiency in the process of modern production and life. "digital, intelligent and customized" manufacturing and design have become an important feature of the field. After taking data as the intelligent guidance of computing, mass customization will become the main production organization mode. Design intelligence can realize that results grow and reproduce on their own according to customer's own design intelligence data. Future everyone to get the design result can be different with others, and in the process of the use of the products, based on neural network algorithm of real-time computing user experience, continuously adjust and optimize the product, so as to realize the mass customization of personalization, redefining the man–machine collaboration mode of collaborative production, man–machine coordinated and mutually reinforcing.

3. At the level of management system reform: the neural network realizes the de-elitism of design, drives the role change of designers and the reform and transformation of design education. With the development of neural network technology, contemporary creation-making activities are greatly different from the past in terms of concept and technology. In particular, with the further development and popularization of micro-manufacturing, users can be more deeply involved in the design and generation of artifacts, and the completion activities are transferred from elite entrustment to co-creation. In the design process, users not only provide their own personal views and design knowledge, but also participate in the generation process, showing a trend of acting as part of the role of product design implementer. At the same time, neural network technology will become an important auxiliary tool for designers, and designers will no longer only play the role of traditional product design implementer, but show a trend of gradual transformation to the role of rule definer of product generation. Creativity, the ability to recognize opportunities to deal with complex problems and the ability to think critically will become the core competence for the development of designers. In the era of intelligent design, design education is faced with reform and transformation. It is necessary to upgrade design education and promote interdisciplinary cooperation, so as to cultivate a new generation of design talents with innovative thinking ability.

6   Conclusion

Design always follows the pace of industrial civilization and information civilization, also, design is good at transforming the latest scientific and technological achievements into design energy and spawning new design patterns. At present, neural network technology is vigorously driving the rapid development of design intelligence from design process, design tools, design expression and other aspects, which makes the development of design intelligence enter a new stage. In the future, if the problems faced by neural network technology can be overcome, neural network technology will bring more possibilities to the field of design, and the intelligent ecology of design will be more efficient.

References

1. Ding, J.: Design paradigm in the era of artificial intelligence. Era Archit. **1**, 70 (2008). (in Chinese)
2. Yu, K., Jia, L., Chen, Y., Xu, W.: Deep learning: yesterday, today, and tomorrow. J. Comput. Res. Dev. **50**(9), 1799–1804 (2013)
3. Zhang, R., Li, W., Mo, T.: Research review of deep learning. Inf. Control **47**(4), 385–397 (2018). (in Chinese)
4. Xie, Y.: Research on modern design theory and method. J. Mech. Eng. **40**(4), 1–9 (2004). (in Chinese)
5. Pohl, W.: LaboUr-machine learning for user modeling. HCI **2**, 27–30 (1997)
6. Zhang, L., Ji, Y., Lin, X.: Style Transfer for Anime Sketches with Enhanced Residual U-net and Auxiliary Classifier GAN (2017). arXiv preprint arXiv:1706.03319
7. Kiros, R., et al.: Skip-Thought Vectors (2015). arXiv preprint arXiv:1506.06726
8. Zhu, Y., et al.: Aligning Books and Movies: Towards Story-like Visual Explanations by Watching Movies and Reading Books (2015). arXiv preprint arXiv:1506.06724
9. Hebron, P.: Machine Learning for Designers. O'Reilly Media, Inc, Sebastopol (2016)
10. Tang, C., Zhong, K., Zhang, L.: A study on the differences in the expressions of emotional cognition between bloggers and users based on the "cloud pet keeping" phenomenon. In: Meiselwitz, G. (ed.) SCSM 2018. LNCS, vol. 10913, pp. 375–387. Springer, Cham (2018). https://doi.org/10.1007/978-3-319-91521-0_27
11. Caitlin, T., Churchill, E.F., King, R.: Designing with Data. O'Reilly Media, Inc, Sebastopol
12. Pieters, R., Winiger, S.: Creative AI: On the Democratisation & Escalation of Creativity
13. Duncan, N.: Zoomorphic Design, Interchangeable Components, and Approximate Dissections: Three New Computational Tools for Open-Ended Geometric Design. University of California, Los Angeles (2017)
14. Nishida, G., Garcia-Dorado, I., Aliaga, D.G., et al.: Interactive sketching of urban procedural models. ACM Trans. Graph. (TOG) **35**(4), 130 (2016)
15. Zhang, L.: New relations and creative cooperation between designer and user in digital micro-manufacturing context. In: 2013 4th HDCon (2013). (in Chinese)

Creating Enhanced User Experience Through Persona and Interactive Design: A Case of Designing a Motion Sensing Game

Gui Zhang[✉]

Guangdong Polytechnic of Water Resources and Electric Engineering,
Guangzhou, China
zhangg@gdsdxy.cn

Abstract. Motion sensing games are operated with body movements that are captured dynamically by somatosensory devices so that more authentic experiences can be gained for users compared with the traditional operations with keyboards or joysticks. The motion sensing game design involving interactive design, user cognition, information layout of product, interface, influences nearly every important aspect of user experience. To our knowledge, the main problems exist in the motion sensing game design are as follows: (1) motion sensing games, as new type of video games, lack guiding theories and methods for reference. (2) To enhance user experiences for players, it is necessary to increase the research on user perception of user l behaviors in early stages of the design. Therefore, inefficiency of game design arises due to lack of effective research methods. In addition, (3) it takes a very long time to develop the project and it also costs a lot. Only by determine users' needs in early stages can these problems be resolved. Inspired by current user research methods within human-computer interaction, product design, and architecture, this paper argue that a persona that is created as a design tool can be used in the process of motion sensing game design. This paper ground the persona method through a design project, Ball Game, based on Kinect. This approach opens new avenues for the analysis and practice of user-centered interaction design of motion sensing games and improves the game experience significantly.

Keywords: Persona · Motion sensing game · Interactive design

1 Introduction

Today, motion sensing game, a new type of video game based on somatosensory technology which is one of the most exciting technological achievements in the twenty-first century, has become an attractive form of entertainment. Motion sensing games are operated with body movements that are captured dynamically by somatosensory devices so that more authentic user experiences can be gained compared with the traditional operations with keyboards or joysticks. Studies identified that motion sensing games use images, sounds and videos images to create dynamic and visual interactions also have strengths in improving cognitive function, visual performance

© Springer Nature Switzerland AG 2019
A. Marcus and W. Wang (Eds.): HCII 2019, LNCS 11583, pp. 382–394, 2019.
https://doi.org/10.1007/978-3-030-23570-3_28

skills, hand-eye coordination. Bodies can be used to convey or represent ideas, qualities, forms and other meaningful aspects of the design situation.

Utilization of somatosensory technology, such as dynamic capture, human body photography, face recognition and optical and inertial motion measurement, can make amazing game experiences come true [18]. User actions in the ever-changing environment can be understood through the technology. The combination of somatosensory technology, virtual reality and augmented reality technology will bring tremendous changes to the application of motion sensing games and it will lead to a significantly increased interest in the development of motion sensing games. A team started to use Xbox Kinect and found that the game have its benefits not only on physical but also on emotional functions. Somatosensory video games had its unique characteristics which include immediately feedback, competition, challenges, close to grandchild and fun, to attract older adults to keep involved. With the development of somatosensory technology, the motion sensing game will become one of the most important trends of game developments in the future.

The motion sensing game design involving interactive design, user cognition, information layout of product, interface, is complex and influences nearly every important aspect of user experience [6, 16]. To our knowledge, the main problems exist in the motion sensing game design are as follows: (1) motion sensing games as new type of video games lack guiding theories and methods for reference, on the other hand, (2) to enhance user experiences for players, it is necessary to increase the research on user perception of user l behaviors in the early stage of the design. Therefore, inefficiency of game design arises because of lack of effective research methods. In addition, (3) it takes very a long time to develop and it also costs a lot to develop the project. Only when the user's needs are determined in the early stage can the product be able to solve these problems. The design strategy of 'actions before product' has an emphasis on understanding and exploring physical actions prior to designing " interface mechanisms that afford such actions". Now there are many traditional ways to understand user needs, such as direct inquiry, observation, etc. However, these methods are not easy to cover all user needs, and cannot reflect users' subconscious behaviors in the process of motion sensing game design. In HCI, usability and UX are considered similar but different terms regarding user satisfaction. It is understood that the system's functional characteristics are vital, but the user motivation to keep using the product is critical as well.

2   Related Work

Alan Cooper (1998) proposed the concept of persona in his book *The Inmates Are Running The Asylum*. Later on, the methods are widely used in researching user needs. Based on the data obtained from user interviews and questionnaires, designers build user models, which includes user behavior models and cognitive models. The user cognitive model mainly includes the users' brain activity process and the external conditions in the process of each character operation. Specifically, user operation model is established to describe the action intention in the operation through the perception of external conditions so that users can solve problems they encounter in the operation.

User research can put the users' expectations for product functions, designs and appearance requirements into the product development process through the users' work environment, product use habits and other research, so as to help enterprises improve product design or explore a new product concept in the early stage of product development. However, in the HCI research field, there is some polemic regarding reliability, validity, and sensitivity of these instruments [15].

3 Persona and Interactive Design

3.1 Understanding Persona

Personas are the outline of real characteristics of product target groups and the comprehensive prototype of real users [1]. User goals, behaviors and viewpoints of product are abstracted and synthesized into a set of description of typical product to help designers understand user needs.

3.2 Attributes of Persona

Attributes of persona: goals (what the user wants to do), behavior (how the user does it) and perspective (how the user views the experience and views themselves). The interaction between people and products can be regarded as a dialogue [2]. The conversation starts when the user plays the motion sensing game, for example, users achieve their goals in the process of game operation according to their own cognition. The motion sensing game also can give information to help users quickly achieve the goal of game content, and reasonably response to the users' request [3].

Before designers design motion sensing games, they must be clear about some facts:

(1) The user goals are different from ours.
(2) The user concerns are different from ours.
(3) Users different considerably from each other.

Designers will be more capable of designing usable products after mastering accurate persona and corresponding role scene. At the time of creating persona, it's necessary to ensure that: (1) persona can represent real users to whom designers pay close attention; (2) property and description regarding personas shall be accurate and complete [19].

3.3 Interactive Design

In the past, interaction design was done by programmers, who were good at coding rather than interacting with end users [8]. Therefore, although many software functions are relatively complete, the interaction design is very rough, tedious and difficult to learn and to use [17]. To make software easy to learn, interaction design is separated from programmer's work into a separate discipline, namely human-computer interaction design [4]. In the design of interactive products, approaches are emerging which incorporate movement qualities into product form and interaction [5].

The goal of interaction design is to make the product easy for users to use. The realization of any product function is accomplished through the interaction between human and machine. Therefore, the human factor should be reflected as the core of the design [12].

The principles of interaction design are as follows:

(1) There are clear error prompts. After misoperation, the system provides targeted tips.
(2) Let the user control the interface. "Next step", "complete", facing different levels to provide a variety of options, to provide different levels of users with a variety of possibilities.
(3) Both mouse and keyboard are allowed. The same function can be used with mouse and keyboard at the same time. Offer multiple possibilities.
(4) Allow work interruption. For example, when you write a new text message on your mobile phone, you can still find the new text message you just wrote after receiving the text message or phone call.
(5) Use the language of users, not the language of the technology.
(6) Provide quick feedback. Give the user psychological hint, avoid the user anxious.
(7) Navigation function. Always move from one feature to another.

Essentially, persona is created to represent users with different goals by creating typical users to satisfy user groups with similar goals and needs. Since the persona was proposed, many designers have applied it to product design projects [20, 21]. In this paper, this method has been applied to the design of motion games, and the practice has proved that it can greatly improve the efficiency and quality of the design of motion games.

When creating personas, it is ensured that personas represent the real users, attributes and descriptions of personas should be accurate and complete. Next, let's take a look at the specific ways to create personas.

3.4 Methods for Creating Personas

To find the most accurate model for creating personas, designers will test multiple models at once using statistical analysis. The steps for quantitative persona are as follows:

Step 1: Qualitative research
Step 2: Forming a hypothesis about subdivision options
Step 3: Collecting data of subdivision options through quantitative research
Step 4: Segmenting users based on statistical clustering analysis
Step 5: Creating a persona for each subgroup

After analyzing the subgroups, designers should add the names, photos and stories of the characters, telling them to become real and credible characters to make the characters lively. This method needs to be completed by statistical analysis of "questionnaire". The steps of this methods are as follows:

Step 1: Select user attributes. Gather the goals, behaviors, and opinions of the target users together and classify them according to the priority of primary and secondary attributes.

Step 2: Select the number of subgroups. That is, the number of characters to choose. Generally speaking, each game has 3 to 6 subgroups. Identify segmentation options by analyzing user attributes and the number of personas using the analysis method.

Step 3: Evaluate segmentation options. This process validates and evaluates our resulting segmentation options.

Step 4: Describe subgroups. Put the subdivided groups into two-dimensional table for description. Now designers need to round out our personas by adding names, photos, personal information, industry information, additional information, personas priorities, and complete usage scenarios [22].

There is no such a person as a realistic user, and designers should try our best to enrich and visualize our target user in design decision process. Therefore, it is so necessary to continue to use and update personas that designers need to constantly improve, demonstrate and explain it to each member of the development.

4 Design Experiments: Design Development for a Motion Sensing Game

Inspired by current user research methods within human-computer interaction, product design, and architecture [10, 13], this paper argue that a central persona that is created as a design tool can be used in the process of motion sensing game design. Rather than relying on the imagination of the designer excessively, the approach this paper advocates can be considered as a solution.

Therefore, this paper explores how interactive design and persona can be used to create enhanced user experiences in motion sensing game design. Persona is an abstract user characteristics obtained from user survey, and many key factors of personas are taken into consideration during the creation of this thesis including user study, storytelling, and interactive design principles to enhance their understanding of motion sensing games for users [11].

This project starts with a research on teenagers. This plan employed a questionnaire design in a serious game and recruited N users to participate in our research. A survey was conducted among students in middle and primary schools, and then analyzed the data to describe user's every action, creating a persona for designers to understand user behaviors, finally, grounding the persona through a design project, Ball Game.

4.1 Creating Personas

It is necessary to select the appropriate approach to determine user behaviors, motivation and goals when creating a user segmentation model [14]. Interviewing real users is one of the methods to obtain basic user information, but if investigators want to get more rigorous user data, they need to go to the environment where users use products, and to care about the feelings and expectations of users [7].

In the presented work, this project elaborate our own questionnaire items including more specific questions, one primary school and one middle school in Guangzhou are taken as the sample in the investigation. Distributing questionnaires on the scene and network survey are adopted. 82 questionnaires are taken back of which 11 questionnaires are with data defects and deemed as invalid questionnaires, so there are 71 effective questionnaires in total. The questionnaire is divided into three parts, including basic information on respondents, cognition regarding game objective and game type willingness.

Basic information on samples is as follows (see Table 1):

Table 1. Sample basic information.

Basic information		Number of people	Percentage
Gender	Male	37	52.1%
	Female	34	47.9%
Age	Below 9 years old	6	8.5%
	10–11 years old	15	21.1%
	12–13 years old	34	47.9%
	Above 13 years old	16	22.5%
Average time length of playing games every day	Less than 30 min	35	49.3%
	30 min–1 h	21	29.6%
	1–2 h	8	11.3%
	Over 2 h	7	9.9%

In addition, based on the investigation, more than 88.7% informants agree that playing games can relax and above 78.9% informants have gained some understanding about motion sensing game.

To inspect whether data index is influenced by one factor, we often use variance analysis model for inspection. Fundamental principle of variance analysis is to divide data into a group(s) as per a level(s) of Factor A. In case that sample average level at a level(s) is free from significant difference, it's deemed that Factor A has no prominent influence on data; in case that sample average level at a level(s) is with significant difference, it's deemed that Factor A has a significant To inspect whether data index is influenced by one factor, this paper use variance analysis model for inspection. Fundamental principle of variance analysis is to divide data into a group(s) as per a level(s) of Factor A. In case that sample average level at a level(s) is free from significant difference, it's deemed that Factor A has no prominent influence on data; in case that sample average level at a level(s) is with significant difference, it's deemed that Factor A has a significant influence on data.

Establishment of variance analysis model:

$$SS_T = SS_A + SS_E \tag{1}$$

SST refers to total sum of squares of deviations, reflecting overall variance volatility of data. SSA refers to sum of squares of deviations of Factor A, reflecting the influence of factor A on test index. SSE refers to error sum of squares, reflecting the influence of experiment error on test index.

$$SS_T = \sum_{i=1}^{a} \sum_{j=1}^{b} \left(X_{ij} - \overline{X}\right)^2 \tag{2}$$

$$SS_A = \sum_{j=1}^{b} \sum_{i=1}^{a} \left(\overline{X}_i - \overline{X}\right)^2 \tag{3}$$

$$SS_E = \sum_{i=1}^{a} \sum_{j=1}^{b} \left(X_{ij} - \overline{X}_i\right)^2 \tag{4}$$

Establishment of test statistics:

$$F = \frac{SS_A/df_A}{SS_E/df_E} = \frac{MS_A}{MS_E} \sim F(a-1, \ ab-1) \tag{5}$$

Null hypothesis is refused and factor A is deemed to have an appreciable impact on data at that time:

$$F > F_\alpha(a-1, \ ab-1)$$

Related data of investigation and statistics is brought into variance analysis model (1), (2), (3), (4) and (5) and the following results are obtained:

Table 2. Variance analysis on the time length of people with different sexes playing games

Variance sources	df	MSE	F value	P value
SSA	1	0.08999	0.352239	0.55
SSE	69	0.25548		

Table 2 shows P value $0.55 > 0.05$ and no significant difference occurs to time length of player with different sexes playing games.

Table 3. Variance analysis on time length of people at different ages playing games

Variance sources	df	MSE	F value	P value
SSA	3	0.78	3.376623	0.023
SSE	67	0.231		

Table 3 shows that P value $0.023 < 0.05$, significant difference happens to time length of player at different ages playing games and with the increase in age, progressive tendency occurs to time length of playing games.

Table 4. The time teenagers play games

Time length of playing games	Sample size	Percentage	Class mid-value	Mean value
Less than 30 min	35	49.3%	15 min	44.15 min
30 min–1 h	21	29.6%	45 min	
1–2 h	8	11.3%	90 min	
Over 2 h	7	9.9%	135 min	

Table 4 shows that only 21.1% teenagers play games for more than 1 h and the mean value of player playing games is 44.15 min.

Table 5. Analysis on target expectation when users play motion sensing game

Target expectation	Sample size	Percentage
The game is relatively exciting	27	38.0%
Operation is simple and easy to learn	25	35.2%
Exercise	35	49.3%
Game surface is exquisite	17	23.9%
Only want to experience it	15	21.1%
Interacting with people can be realized	18	25.4%

Table 5 shows top three target expectations when users play motion sensing game are (1) getting the "exciting" game experience in the process of playing games, (2) easy operation and studied, and (3) doing exercise.

User segmentation model is created based on segmentation option data collected by the above quantitative research and statistical analysis. And then designers add names, photos, ages and hobbies to them so as to make them more realistic and reliable as well as vivid and it's necessary to crystallize roles and avoid wrong description as far as possible as well as realize particularity and accuracy. Inaccurate description will cause the designer has less understanding about users and even result in wrong judgment concerning design direction. As for motion sensing game, some stories with content are needed which are like stories in the film and television program or novel. However, users of motion sensing game can have more direct experience and players are personally can play the role in the story.

4.2 Requirement Description of Personas

According to research analysis on target users, motion sensing game to be designed in this paper shall be able to meet the following requirements of users:

Challenging need: "Challenging" of the game can excite users with "excitement" embodied incisively and vividly in the competitive games. With popularity of competitive games, demand of game challenge and satisfaction of challenge demand are very important for players.

"I like exciting games! I like sports!"

Bill

- 13 years old
- Middle School Students
- Lives in Guangzhou
- 2 brothers

After school, Bill would play games with his two brothers for half an hour every day. He thought games were a good way to relax and it had better be challenging.

He knows a little about motion sensing games and VR games. If he has the opportunity, he is willing to try them. It would be even better if motion games could exercise the body while allowing for multiplayer interaction and simple gameplay.

Typical game requirements:

- Exciting game
- Sensitive game operation
- The operation is simple
- Multiplayer
- Exquisite game pictures

Fig. 1. Persona for Ball Game

Aesthetic demand: Aesthetic demand is people's instinct. Exquisite game screen, gorgeous special effects and lifelike persona can enable players to experience beauty.

Interactive demand: Satisfying interactive demand and interaction really can be realized by research on users' psychological need and integration of game factors. In case of game players being able to smoothly communicate with game system, excellent interactive experience will arise. Now, although there are many good multiplayer stand-alone games in the market, they fail to meet players' interactive demand.

Sports demand: Motion sensing game shall be simple and funny and then players can have a happy time in the game freely and easily. In the process of playing games, players often win various awards. Sports is everyone's physiological needs.

4.3   Personas Implementation

At the moment of creating persona (see Fig. 1), there shall be at least one primary persona in the user subdivision group which is the central person to be considered, thus game demand of the main character must be meet. Based on role description, the designers shall reasonably analyze main persona. For example, several main user behaviors (including "head movement", "upper limb movement" and "lower limb movement", etc.) are known by user analysis [9]. Such behaviors is the constitution foundation for one persona model. Satisfaction of user behaviors demand can be realized by recognizing users' effective body language in the motion sensing game finally.

4.4   Process Design of the *Ball Game*

This motion sensing game, Ball Game, is aimed at sport-loving teenagers, who are energetic, loving challenges. Through the analysis of these users, the personas are established, and then the tasks the personas are trying to complete and the feedback of interaction errors are mainly considered in the game design process. Otherwise, users will get lost in the navigation of the game if the reason for the error and the solution are not considered. Therefore, this method can be applied to improve interaction efficiency.

In accordance with main persona established, main users' psychological need and behavior are analyzed. On this basis, the author designs the process of motion sensing game. Based on the method applied for the above persona, one motion sensing game simulating the movement of heading the ball is designed in this paper. In short, motion sensing game design is to conceive game structure and process (see Fig. 2). The design is characterized by emphatically highlighting learnability and repetitive challenge of the motion sensing game-motion sensing football game. For example, the player can get satisfaction of winning by playing the game in several rounds in the link of goaling by heading the ball. In the meanwhile, somatosensory interaction design model established on the basis of persona is used to evaluate problems and solutions from different perspectives, reduces error message prompt furthest and can improve interactive efficiency and solve key problem of interaction model.

4.5   Display of the *Ball Game* Design Example

At the moment of designing the interface of the team member implementing corner kick, the blue is used as background and team members' shirt is red, as a result, team members can be clearly emerged. Characteristics are marked near each team member with highlighting for suggestion, more attention will be attracted from users. Marshalling sequence of team members is set to "s" arrangement which saves interface space (see Fig. 3).

Figure 4 shows the interface of virtual footballer serving a ball which is filled with a very big digit. Such design can facilitate the footballer heading the ball to pay attention to the time and creates nervous game atmosphere.

The scene in Fig. 5 involves character expression of the athlete in the game in the virtual scene. In case of the player in the real scenario moving, the athlete in the virtual scene will also move. Such man-machine interaction is more intuitive and natural. In the virtual scene, each athlete is with one aureole aimed at beauty as well as marking and differentiation.

Figure 6 involves the physical interaction scene where the player is going to head the ball when the ball comes from a distance. Six footballers in the virtual scene correspond to six players in the game. The player goaling by heading the ball is the

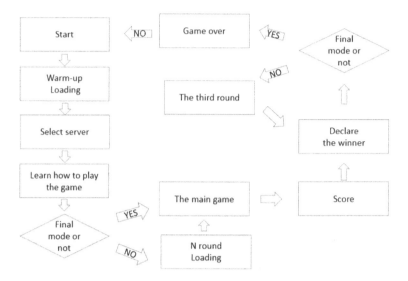

Fig. 2. Interactive flow of the *Ball Game*

winner who can win the game by only judging the best time for heading other than learning other aspects. The game can mobilize the players' enthusiasm and satisfy their mood of aspiring to succeed.

Applying persona to the design of motion sensing games is considered to be an

Fig. 3. Select server (Color figure online)

Fig. 4. Message for kickoff

effec-

tive way and can greatly improve the quality of motion sensing game design. This paper ground the persona method through a design project, Ball Game, based on Kinect and played by teenagers. This approach opens new avenues for the analysis and practice of user-centered interaction design of motion sensing games. The user-centered interaction game design based on personas focuses on the tasks users are trying to accomplish, the feedback of user interaction errors, and what functions the motion sensing game provides, improving the game experience significantly. The results showed users can clarify their ideas based on the interface of motion sensing game.

Fig. 5. Attempt stage   **Fig. 6.** Start the game

5 Discussion and Conclusion

This paper introduces a typical virtual user, persona, to help designers understand game players better. Persona contributes to understanding users better for motion sensing game designers. Additionally, the method of persona reduces the time of game development and the risk of development of motion sensing games relying on designer's intuition or manager's imagination. Finally, users of the game get enhanced user experience. However, survey on more samples should further inquire on the potentially critical relation between the information available of the interactive design of motion sensing games and user behaviors. In addition, further adjustments and additional test iterations are warranted to validate its use as a reliable usability evaluation.

References

1. Friess, E.: Personas and decision making in the design process: an ethnographic case study. In: Proceedings of the CHI 2012. Presented at the CHI 2012, pp. 1209–1218. ACM Press, Austin (2012)
2. Löwgren, J.: Toward an articulation of interaction esthetics. New Rev. Hypermedia Multimed. **15**(2), 129–146 (2009)
3. Hallnäs, L., Jacobs, J.K., Petersen, M.G.: Introduction to special issue on the aesthetics of interaction. ACM Trans. Comput. Human Interact. **15**(3), 1–5 (2008)
4. Hallnäs, L., Redström, J.: Interaction Design: Foundations, Experiments. University College of Borås, Borås (2006)
5. Landin, H.: Digital myths and delusions: an approach to investigate interaction aesthetics. Digit. Creat. **19**(4), 217–232 (2008)
6. Liang, R.-H.: Designing for unexpected encounters with digital products: case studies of serendipity as felt experience. Int. J. Des. **6**(1), 41–58 (2012)
7. Lin, M.H., Cheng, S.H.: Examining the "later wow", through operating a metaphorical product. Int. J. Des. **8**(3), 61–78 (2014)
8. Locher, P., Overbeeke, K., Wensveen, S.: Aesthetic interaction: a framework. Des. Issues **26**(2), 70–79 (2010)
9. Ju, W., Takayama, L.: Approachability: how people interpret automatic door movement as gesture. Int. J. Des. **3**(2), 1–10 (2009)

10. Landin, H.: Anxiety and trust and other expressions of interaction [Doctoral dissertation]. Chalmers University of Technology, Göteborg (2009)
11. Lim, Y.-K., Stolterman, E., Jung, H., Donaldson, J.: Interaction gestalt and the design of aesthetic interactions. In: Proceedings of the 3rd Conference on Designing Pleasurable Products and Interfaces, pp. 239–254. ACM, New York (2007)
12. Lewis, J.R.: Critical review of "the usability metric for user experience". Interact. Comput. **25**(4), 320–324 (2013)
13. Lewis, J.R., Utesch, B.S., Maher, D.E.: UMUX-LITE: when there's no time for the SUS. In: Proceedings of the SIGCHI Conference on Human Factors in Computing Systems (CHI 2013), pp. 2099–2102. ACM, New York (2013)
14. Muñoz-Merino, P.J., Fernández-Molina, M., Muñoz-Organero, M., Delgado Kloos, C.: An adaptive and innovative question-driven competition based intelligent tutoring system for learning. Expert Syst. Appl. **39**(8), 6932–6948 (2012)
15. Pribeanu, C.: Comments on the reliability and validity of UMUX and UMUX-LITE short scales. In: Proceedings of the ROCHI Conference in Human-Computer Interaction (ROCHI '16), Iasi Romania, pp. 2099–2102 (2016)
16. Finstad, K.: Response to commentaries on "the usability metric for user experience". Interact. Comput. **25**(4), 327–330 (2013)
17. Satar, N.S.M.: Does E-learning usability attributes correlate with learning motivation? In: Proceedings of the 21st AAOU Annual Conference, Kuala Lumpur, pp. 29–31 (2007)
18. Vermeeren, A.P.O.S., Law, E.L., Roto, V., Obrist, M., Hoonhout, J,. Väänänen-Vainio-Mattila, K.: User experience evaluation methods: current state and development needs. In: Proceedings of the 6th Nordic Conference on Human-Computer Interaction: Extending Boundaries (NordiCHI 2010). ACM, New York (2010)
19. Aquino Jr., P.T., Filgueiras, L.V.L.: User modeling with personas, In: Proceedings of the CLIHC 2005. Presented at the CLIHC 2005, pp. 277–282. ACM Press, Cuernavaca (2005)
20. Bødker, S., Christiansen, E., Nyvang, T., Zander, P-O.: Personas, people and participation: challenges from the trenches of local government. In: Proceedings of the 12th PDC. Presented at the 12th PDC, ACM Press, Roskilde, Denmark, pp. 91–100 (2012)
21. Clemmensen, T., et al.: CHI 2013 human work interaction design (HWID) SIG: past history and future challenges, In: Proceedings of the CHI 2013. Presented at the CHI EA 2013, pp. 2537–2540. ACM Press (2013)
22. Cabrero, D.G., Kapuire, G.K., Winschiers-Theophilus, H., Stanley, C., Rodil, K., Abdelnour-Nocera, J.: Reflecting user-created persona in indigenous Namibia: what NOT to do when working in Foreign Land. In: Proceedings of the C&T 2015. Presented at the C&T 2015. ACM Press, Limerick (2015)

User Requirements, Preferences
Emotions and Personality

Extending the Concept of User Satisfaction from Customer Experience

Andrés F. Aguirre[1]([✉]), Angela Villareal-Freire[1]([✉]),
Jaime Diaz[2]([✉]), Rosa Gil[3]([✉]), and César A. Collazos[1]([✉])

[1] IDIS Research Group, University of Cauca, Popayán, Colombia
{afaguirre, avillarreal, ccollazo}@unicauca.edu.co
[2] Department of Computer and Information Sciences, University of La Frontera,
Temuco, Chile
jaimeignacio.diaz@ufrontera.cl
[3] Research Group on Human Computer Interaction and Data Integration,
University of Lleida, Lleida, Spain
rgil@diei.udl.cat

Abstract. Current trends in the development of applications bring new challenges that re-quire both a rapprochement and an understanding of the elements implicit in the interaction of this type of system and the users who use them. One of the most relevant aspects in this interaction is user satisfaction; as a result, it is necessary to establish a broader and more precise definition of user satisfaction in interactive systems from customer experience (CX), at the same time giving thought to the different constructs that characterize the software. This article presents a proposal that extends the concept of the user satisfaction to establish the characteristics that derive from the CX, along with traditional approaches that support user satisfaction. From this characterization, it is intended to propose a construct through which the different factors that influence user satisfaction are understood, how these factors condition it and how they converge to impact it.

Keywords: User satisfaction · Customer Experience · User experience

1 Introduction

User satisfaction is one of the determining components in the quality of interaction in any digital system, an aspect that is directly reflected in the competitiveness and positioning of digital resources through which companies relate with their customers. In fact, if the Customer Experience (CX) limits the achievement of the user's objectives or does not meet their needs, it generates not only a rejection of the services or products that originated that experience but also a point of non-return that leads the user to the competition or to the search of other alternatives [1]. Moreover, this can lead to a decrease in potential users, due to the negative impact on reputation [2]. This situation shows that user satisfaction becomes the main parameter that defines the success or failure of a product or service [3].

User satisfaction is a complex and diverse topic, which has led to the existence of different interpretations and approaches related to user satisfaction, which, although

© Springer Nature Switzerland AG 2019
A. Marcus and W. Wang (Eds.): HCII 2019, LNCS 11583, pp. 397–407, 2019.
https://doi.org/10.1007/978-3-030-23570-3_29

they provide a starting point, sharpen the problem of subjectivity inherent in the conception of what should be understood as user satisfaction [3]. This generates the risk of including characteristics that lack significant relevance in user satisfaction, while those characteristics that support it can be omitted. To this problem, the continuous changes and advances in information technology are added, as well as the constant increase of users that use technology, their diverse needs, preferences, perspectives, objectives and other aspects arising from the heterogeneity of the users [4].

Due to the importance and challenges that constitute user satisfaction in the field of design and evaluation of products and services, constant efforts have been made to know which factors are the ones that determine user satisfaction. However, the diversity of strategies arising from the different approaches around user satisfaction are usually dispersed among them, which makes it difficult for them to adjust to a certain business model, or to the particular interests of a company [5]. This lack of convergence represents a lack of objective parameters to understand and develop products and services that respond assertively to user satisfaction. In this sense, it is necessary to consolidate (from a holistic approach) what is that with which user satisfaction is represented, as well as its dimensions and constraints, which lead to an expected CX or higher than expected [1].

For this reason, knowing and understanding the qualities (attributes) of user satisfaction is necessary for the design and/or evaluation of interaction. In this sense, the CX allows a more broad and accurate view to characterize user satisfaction [4]. The CX offers the possibility of covering and integrating each component of the user experience, which plays a determining role in the overall user satisfaction. This aspect not only complements the conceptual structure of the components that influence user satisfaction (derived from traditional perspectives that exist around user satisfaction) but also complements the methodological characteristics necessary for the design and evaluation of products and services [6]. In the same way, the CX allows to increase the threshold of user satisfaction, through innovations that reflect the needs and behavior of new customers, but at the same time, it allows to accentuate the loyalty values of the users.

The conceptualization of user satisfaction, aims to generate consensus among researchers, and thus have a theoretical framework that provides a clear understanding not only of the ostensible components that make up user satisfaction, but also those that underlie their behavior and that condition the interaction with a system [7]. Moreover, the importance of these components not only serve to model user satisfaction, but also lay the foundations that support the design and evaluation of systems focused on the CX [7].

The motivation of this study focuses on the need to establish a characterization of user satisfaction that derives from the conceptual sphere of CX, along with tradition-al approaches that support user satisfaction. From this characterization, it is intended to propose a construct through which the different factors that influence user satisfaction are understood, how these factors condition it and how they converge to impact it.

2 User Satisfaction from Traditional Approaches

2.1 Conceptualization of User Satisfaction from Traditional Approaches

One of the most important issues in which the HCI community works around the quality of interactive systems, and in particular their quality of use, is user satisfaction. However, because technology has flourished in almost all human activities, there are different approaches to user satisfaction that limit the formation of a consensus between them. Much of what is known about satisfaction is based on relatively small empirical work and represents an opinion rather than a fact [8]. Different definitions or approximations found in the literature that describe the concept of user satisfaction are shown below.

Lindgaard and Dudek [9], argue that user satisfaction is the subjective sum of the interactive experience, and therefore, it is likely that this experience involves some affective component that influences the level of user satisfaction. Similarly, Hassenzahl [10] alludes to the emotional reactions that a product can generate, depending on how it meets the expectations of users in particular situations.

On the other hand, McNamara and Kirakowski [11], point out satisfaction as a set of beliefs that individuals have about their interaction with a product in a context of use.

For Xiao and Dusgupta [12], satisfaction includes ease of use, content, format, timeliness and accuracy.

Some definitions that were used to define user satisfaction are shown below:

For Ives *et al.* [13], satisfaction is "the extent to which users believe that the information system available to them meets their information requirements".

Doll and Torkzadeh, [14] define satisfaction as the user's opinion about a specific computer application that he uses. In The End User Computing Satisfaction Instrument [14, 15], they point to satisfaction as a higher order construction, which includes the content and accuracy of the information provided, ease of use, timeliness and format of information.

Finally, Ang and Koh [16] argued that user satisfaction as a perceptive or subjective measure of system success.

The definitions of user satisfaction shown below are used in different contexts such as e-learning, e-commerce, e-government and e-culture, respectively:

For authors such as Capece and Campisi [17] and Yeh and Lin [18], user satisfaction is related to how users believe or feel positively about the system, especially as it meets their expectations and their requirements. Other researchers such as Tsai et al. [19], define user satisfaction as the gap between the expected and the real gain when using the system.

For Ha and Janda [20], customer satisfaction means how a company provides, supplies or delivers products or services to meet the needs and desires of customers.

Alawneh *et al.* [21], point out user satisfaction as the ability for an interactive system to be compatible with the needs, wishes and expectations of citizens.

Finally, Zahidi *et al.*, [22] argue that user satisfaction is subjective and is closely related to the needs, expectations and exciting experiences of users.

2.2   Characteristics of User Satisfaction from Traditional Approaches

One of the most important issues in which the HCI community works around the quality of interactive systems, and in particular their quality of use, is user satisfaction User satisfaction can be considered as the main parameter in the use of interactive system [8]. From this point of view, various efforts have been generated to establish the factors that influence satisfaction, and thus manage them appropriately in the design of interactive systems [23]. However, given the numerous definitions offered by the literature on úser satisfaction [11], this becomes a concept that lacks a systematic and confluent approach [8, 24]. This lack of conceptual clarity makes it difficult to establish pillars to support the evaluation of user satisfaction [11], especially in the need to define what and how to evaluate it. Certainly, the different approaches about user satisfaction are essential for understanding, especially given the growing massive use of technology [11]. However, the diversity in approaches and scope that exist on user satisfaction, could controvert the objectivity of its construct and therefore its evaluation -*numerous studies that aim to measure different aspects of satisfaction appear in the literature as part of the new metrics of satisfaction* [24]. It is unlikely that all the studies contemplate the same variables, which makes it difficult to find a correspondence between the definition and evaluation parameters around user satisfaction. The following Table 1 shows some of the characteristics widely found in industry and academic environments.

Table 1.   Traditional characteristics of user satisfaction.

Usability	Effectiveness	Pleasure
Utility	Efficiency	Emotional
Ease of use	Comfort	Enjoyable
Accessibility	Reliability	Consistency
Functionality	Attractiveness	Flexibility
Learnability	Security	Privacy

User satisfaction is evaluated predominantly through questionnaires, then Table 2 shows some of the questionnaires widely used in the academy and in the software industry, and the most important user satisfaction characteristics that are evaluated in these questionnaires.

Contrasting the definitions found about user satisfaction, with regard to the aspects that are evaluated questionnaires shown above, shows that these questionnaires do not address aspects related to the emotional impact that they could evoke in the users when interacting with an interactive system. These questionnaires have an approach (almost exclusive) in the usability and other objective aspects of user satisfaction [36], which although they are important and impact on user satisfaction in general, do not have the holistic scope that would be expected when using user satisfaction evaluation tools.

Table 2. Characteristics of user satisfaction evaluated by different instruments.

Instrument	Description	Characteristics evaluated
QUIS	*Questionnaire for User Interaction Satisfaction* is a tool developed by researchers at the University of Maryland Human-Computer Interaction Lab. Designed to assess the subjective satisfaction of users on specific aspects of the human-computer interface [25]. The current version, QUIS 7.0, assesses the user's overall satisfaction in 6 hierarchically organized facets in each of the nine interface-specific factors defined in this tool. Each facet, in turn, consists of a pair of semantic differentials arranged on a 10-point scale [25, 26]. The questionnaire is designed to be adjusted according to the analysis needs of each interface, in which only sections of interest can be considered	Screen factors, terminology and system feedback, learning factors, system capabilities, technical manuals, online tutorials, multimedia, teleconferencing and software installation [27, 28]
SUMI	*Software Usability Measuring Inventory* is a method of evaluating the quality of software that allows measuring satisfaction and assessing user perception [29]. SUMI is a commercially-available questionnaire for assessing usability of software developed, validated and standardized on international databases [29, 30]. This method is referred to in standards ISO 9126 [31] and ISO 9241 [32] as a recognized tool for evaluating user satisfaction via five dimensions of usability. This tool is also available in several languages [29, 30]	Efficiency, affection, utility, control, and learning [30]

(continued)

Table 2. (*continued*)

Instrument	Description	Characteristics evaluated
WAMMI	*Website Analysis and Measurement Inventory* is an online service that emerged from SUMI. Both were developed at the Human Factors Research Group (HFRG) at University College, Cork. Unlike SUMI, which is designed for the evaluation of desktop software applications, WAMMI focuses on evaluation of websites [26, 33]. This instrument consists of 20 questions that use 5-point Likert scales as answers [9, 26], and makes it possible to create a questionnaire and link it to WAMMI classification scales [26]. The result of a WAMMI analysis is a measure of "global satisfaction" [9], that is divided into 5 dimensions	Attractiveness, control, efficiency, utility and learning, usability [9, 26]
MUMMS	*Measuring Usability of Multi-Media System* was developed by the same group that designed SUMI and WAMMI. MUMMS consists of a questionnaire that enables assessment of quality of use for multimedia software products [34]. Measurement aspects are the same as those SUMI takes account of and it incorporates a new one related to the user's emotional perception toward the use of the system. This tries to capture information about the fascination the multimedia application exerts on users [34]	Attractiveness, Controllability, Efficiency, Helpfulness, and Learnability [26]
SUS	*System Usability Scale* is an interesting variation of the traditional questionnaires. It presents a combination of statements written positively and negatively, so that the user really pays attention to each of their answers [35, 36]. SUS consists of a 10-item questionnaire, each with a Likert scale of 5 (or 7) points, which provides an overview of satisfaction with the software [35]	Ease of use, Usefulness, Helpfulness, Functionality, and Learnability [26]

3 User Satisfaction from ISO Standards

3.1 Conceptualization of User Satisfaction from ISO Standards

The ISO 9241-11 standard [32] refers to user satisfaction as an attribute of usability, and defines it as positive attitudes towards the use of the product and freedom from discomfort. On the other hand, the ISO 9126 standard [31] point out to satisfaction as the ability of the software product to satisfy users in a specific context of use. The user satisfaction in this standard refers to the users' perceptions of their interaction with the software product. Subsequently, in the ISO/IEC 25010 standard [37], user satisfaction is defined as "the degree to which user needs are satisfied when a product or system is used in a specific context of use". In this standard, satisfaction is also directly related to the user's response to their interaction with the system. User satisfaction in these standards is fully applicable to the human-computer system.

3.2 Characteristics of User Satisfaction from ISO Standards

Although the definitions of user satisfaction raised in the standards mentioned above are practically the same, the ISO/IEC 25010 standard (the most up-to-date), categorizes user satisfaction in characteristics. Below is Table 3 showing the characteristics that shape user satisfaction according to the aforementioned standards. It should be noted that in the quality model in use proposed in the ISO 9126 standard, it does not directly and explicitly define the characteristics of user satisfaction, therefore an abstraction of characteristics was made from the defined metrics.

Table 3. Characteristics of user satisfaction in ISO standards

Characteristic	Description of the feature	Standard
Usefulness	Degree to which a user is satisfied with their perceived achievement of pragmatic goals, including the results of the use and the consequences of the use	ISO/IEC 25010
Trust	Degree to which a user has confidence that a product or system will behave as intended	ISO/IEC 25010, ISO 9241-11[a]
Pleasure	Degree to which a user obtains pleasure from fulfilling their personal needs	ISO/IEC 25010, ISO 9241-11[a]
Comfort	Degree to which the user is satisfied with the physical comfort	ISO/IEC 25010, ISO 9241-11
Motivation	Degree to which a user is interested in using the system	ISO 9126, ISO 9241-11[a]
Performance	Degree to which a user is meet with the performance of the system and its specific characteristics	ISO 9126
Preference	Degree to which the user would prefer to use a system over other competing systems	ISO 9126, ISO 9241-11[a]

[a]The "positive attitudes" (alluded to above-ISO 9241-11) are related to those characteristics that are considered to have an emotional component.

4 Relationship Between User Satisfaction and CX

4.1 User Satisfaction from a New Approach

Each of the characteristics of user satisfaction (regardless of their origin: traditional approaches or ISO standards), have two components: *expected* and *perceived*. Given that these characteristics conform user satisfaction, its dualistic nature should also extend to what is understood as user satisfaction, and therefore, it would be logical to define *expected satisfaction* and *perceived satisfaction*. In the first case, *expected satisfaction* refers to those needs and/or expectations that are generated before the interactions with the system and the product or service. These needs would also represent in some way the parameters of evaluation: the product met the expectations of the use. On the other hand, in the case of *perceived satisfaction*, this is generated when the user has interacted with the system, and it extends until after having interacted with the system. The following Fig. 1 represents this proposal.

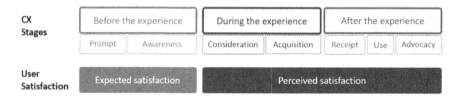

Fig. 1. Relationship between user satisfaction and CX

4.2 CX Stages that Affect User Satisfaction

In this article, the existence of a consubstantial adherence between user satisfaction and CX is established. For this reason, user satisfaction occurs in each of the stages that make up the CX. This with the purpose of giving a broader and clearer view of the different components that are involved in the general user satisfaction. The stages of the CX that were adapted for the purpose of this work are described below [38, 39]:

Before the Experience

Prompt. This is the first step of the experience, it is where the need is generated. Some examples of this stage make reference to the recommendations that the user receives through friends, family, social media, advertising, search results on Internet, etc.

Awareness. This stage refers to the fact of carefully considering something, and will depend on the intensity and value that the user perceives with respect to a given stimulus, *e.g.*, if the perceived stimulus by the user was positive, it is likely that the user will be interested in the use and/or purchase of the product or service.

During the Experience

Consideration. Once the user has decided to acquire a service or product, begins to interact with the site or system, *e.g.*, the user ensures that the site is reliable and secure.

Acquisition. This stage consolidates all the actions and components that are part of a purchase, *e.g.*, making a purchase, purchase confirmation, receiving confirmation email of the purchases, security protocols, etc.

After the Experience

Receipt. Provision of relevant mechanisms for an adequate installation or reception of the system, product or service, *e.g.*, appropriate logistics for delivery, multiplatform installation, etc.

Use. It refers to the use of the product and/or service purchased. In this stage, interactions that involve the "consumption" of the service or product will flourish, *e.g.*, the customer (or in some cases a user who is not the customer) becomes familiar with that product: they learn how to use it and how to consume it.

Advocacy. The experience of the use of the product or service acquired triggers a series of positive and/or negative perceptions, which can generate in the user values of loyalty, rejection or neutrality *e.g.*, the user could show a greater disposition to promote and recommend the product or service, if his experience of using it was positive; in the same way, this experience would promote loyalty towards the product or service.

5   Conclusions

The technological advances have allowed a substantial improvement in the quality of the interactions between users and systems. This has favored the widespread growth of advanced users (sophisticated users), who hope to find experiences that are up to technological advances. This supposes an increase in the efforts that must be made to define parameters of user satisfaction that allow addressing the entire UX.

It is necessary to reassess the considerations surrounding the conceptualization of user satisfaction or what most seem to understand about it. User satisfaction should be a holistic view of the user's perception, and not a value that the user gives to a certain component of the interaction with a system. User satisfaction should be considered as the set of satisfactory perceptions, resulting from the phases of the user experience *e.g.*, a user may be satisfied with the ease of use of the system (expected and perceived), but not necessarily with its utility or with the answer to his needs in general (only expected).

To make an analysis focused on user satisfaction and how it is affected in each phase that shapes the CX, allows obtaining valuable quantitative and qualitative data of the user's satisfaction over time, since it allows extracting representations of the real experiences of the users, a compilation of judgments and other actions that are part of their experience from beginning to end. This would allow covering a wide spectrum of details about the levels of satisfaction that are part of the general user experience, and thus have a more accurate, objective and real analysis about user satisfaction.

References

1. Shin, D.H.: Effect of the customer experience on satisfaction with smartphones: assessing smart satisfaction index with partial least squares. Telecommun. Policy **39**(8), 627–641 (2015)
2. Caruana, A., Ewing, M.T.: How corporate reputation, quality, and value influence online loyalty. J. Bus. Res. **63**(9–10), 1103–1110 (2010)
3. Aguirre, A.F., Villareal, Á.P., Gil, R.M., Collazos, C.A.: Extending the concept of user satisfaction in E-learning systems from ISO/ IEC 25010. Des. User Exp. Usability Underst. Users Contexts **1**, 167–179 (2017)
4. Morgan-Thomas, A., Veloutsou, C.: Beyond technology acceptance: brand relationships and online brand experience. J. Bus. Res. **66**(1), 21–27 (2013)
5. Brakus, J.J., Schmitt, B.H., Zarantonello, L.: Brand experience: what is it? How is it measured? Does it affect loyalty? J. Mark. **73**(3), 52–68 (2009)
6. Sheng, M.L., Teo, T.S.H.: Product attributes and brand equity in the mobile domain: the mediating role of customer experience. Int. J. Inf. Manag. **32**(2), 139–146 (2012)
7. Seckler, M., Heinz, S., Forde, S., Tuch, A.N., Opwis, K.: Trust and distrust on the web: user experiences and website characteristics. Comput. Hum. Behav. **45**, 39–50 (2015)
8. McNamara, N., Kirakowski, J.: Measuring the human element in complex technologies. Int. J. Technol. Hum. Interact. **4**(1), 1–14 (2008)
9. Lindgaard, G., Dudek, C.: What is this evasive beast we call user satisfaction? Interact. Comput. **15**(3), 429–452 (2003)
10. Hassenzahl, M.: The thing and I: understanding the relationship between user and product. In: Blythe, M., Overbeeke, K., Monk, A., Wright, P. (eds.) Funology, vol. 3, pp. 31–42. Springer, Netherlands (2005)
11. McNamara, N., Kirakowski, J.: Measuring user-satisfaction with electronic consumer products: the consumer products questionnaire. Int. J. Hum. Comput. Stud. **69**(6), 375–386 (2011)
12. Xiao, L., Dasgupta, S.: Measurement of user satisfaction with web-based information systems: an empirical study. In: Proceedings of the 8th Americas Conference on Information Systems, pp. 1149–1155 (2002)
13. Ives, B., Olson, M.H., Baroudi, J.J.: The measurement of user information satisfaction. Commun. ACM **26**(10), 785–793 (1983)
14. Doll, W.J., Torkzadeh, G.: The measurement of end-user computing satisfaction. MIS Q. **12**(2), 259–274 (1988)
15. Harrison, A.W., Rainer, R.K.: A general measure of user computing satisfaction. Comput. Hum. Behav. **12**(1), 79–92 (1996)
16. Ang, J., Koh, S.: Exploring the relationships between user information satisfaction and job satisfaction. Int. J. Inf. Manag. **17**(3), 169–177 (1997)
17. Capece, G., Campisi, D.: User satisfaction affecting the acceptance of an e-learning platform as a mean for the development of the human capital. Behav. Inf. Technol. **32**(4), 335–343 (2013)
18. Yeh, Y., Lin, C.F.: Aptitude-treatment interactions during creativity training in e-learning: how meaning-making, self-regulation, and knowledge management influence creativity. J. Educ. Technol. Soc. **18**(1), 119–131 (2015)
19. Tsai, P.C.F., Yen, Y.F., Huang, L.C., Huang, I.C.: A study on motivating employees' learning commitment in the post-downsizing era: Job satisfaction perspective. J. World Bus. **42**(2), 157–169 (2007)

20. Ha, H.Y., Janda, S.: An empirical test of a proposed customer satisfaction model in e-services. J. Serv. Mark. **22**(5), 399–408 (2008)
21. Alawneh, A., Al-Refai, H., Batiha, K.: Measuring user satisfaction from e-government services: Lessons from Jordan. Gov. Inf. Q. **30**(3), 277–288 (2013)
22. Zahidi, Z., Lim, Y.P., Woods, P.C.: Understanding the user experience (UX) factors that influence user satisfaction in digital culture heritage online collections for non-expert users. In: Proceedings 2014 Science Information Conference SAI 2014, pp. 57–63 (2014)
23. Jang, J., Yi, M.Y.: Modeling user satisfaction from the extraction of user experience elements in online product reviews. In: Proceedings 2017 CHI Conference Extended Abstracts on Human Factors in Computing Systems—CHI EA 2017, pp. 1718–1725 (2017)
24. Hornbæk, K.: Current practice in measuring usability: challenges to usability studies and research. Int. J. Hum. Comput. Stud. **64**(2), 79–102 (2006)
25. Chin, J.P., Diehl, V.A., Norman, K.L.: Development of an instrument measuring user satisfaction of the human-computer interface. In: SIGCHI Conference on Human, pp. 213–218 (1988)
26. Tullis, T., Albert, W.: Measuring the User Experience: Collecting, Analyzing, and Presenting Usability Metrics. Morgan Kaufmann, Burlington (2013)
27. Chin, J.P., Diehl, V.A., Norman, K.L.: Questionnaire for user interaction satisfaction (QUIS). In: Human–Computer Interaction Lab, University of Maryland at College Park (1988). https://isr.umd.edu/news/news_story.php?id=4099. Accessed 19 Nov 2018
28. Johnson, T.R., Zhang, J., Tang, Z., Johnson, C., Turley, J.P.: Assessing informatics students' satisfaction with a web-based courseware system. Int. J. Med. Inform. **73**(2), 181–187 (2004)
29. Kirakowski, J., Corbett, M.: SUMI: the software usability measurement inventory. Br. J. Educ. Technology **24**(3), 10–12 (1993)
30. Software Usability Measurement Inventory (SUMI). Human Factors Research Group, University College Cork (1993). http://sumi.ucc.ie/index.html. Accessed 22 Jan 2015
31. "ISO/IEC TR 9126-4: Software engineering – Product quality – Part 4: Quality in use metrics." 2004
32. ISO 9241-11: Ergonomic requirements for office work with visual display terminals (VDTs) —part 11: Guidance on usability (1998)
33. Kirakowski, J., Claridge, N., Whitehand, R.: Human centered measures of success in web site design. In Proceedings of the Fourth Conference on Human Factors & the Web (1998)
34. Measuring the Usability of Multi-Media System (MUMMS). In: Human Factors Research Group, University College Cork (1996)
35. Brooke, J.: SUS—a quick and dirty usability scale. In: Jordan, P.W., Thomas, B., Weerdmeester, B.A., McClleland, I.L. (eds.) Usability evaluation in industry, pp. 189–194. Taylor & Francis, London (1996)
36. Hartson, R., Pyla, P.: The UX Book: Process and Guidelines for Ensuring a Quality User Experience. Morgan Kaufmann, Burlington (2012)
37. ISO/IEC 25010 - Systems and software engineering—Systems and software quality requirements and evaluation (SQuaRE)—System and software quality models (2011)
38. Marquez, J.J., Downey, A., Clement, R.: Walking a mile in the user's shoes: customer journey mapping as a method to understanding the user experience. Internet Ref. Serv. Q. **20**(3–4), 135–150 (2015)
39. Lemon, K.N., Verhoef, P.C.: Understanding Customer experience throughout the customer journey. J. Mark. **80**(6), 69–96 (2016)

Evaluating the User Experience: A Study on Children's Interaction with Socio-enactive Artifacts in a Hospital Context

Camilla V. L. T. Brennand[(✉)], Celso A. R. L. Brennand,
Vanessa R. M. L. Maike, José Vanderlei da Silva,
and M. Cecília C. Baranauskas

Institute of Computing, University of Campinas (UNICAMP),
Campinas, São Paulo, Brazil
camillatenorio123@gmail.com, celsobrennand@gmail.com,
vanessa.maike@gmail.com, vander.vander@gmail.com,
c.baranauskas@gmail.com

Abstract. Digital technologies are currently present in many areas of our lives and are used for various purposes. The omnipresent technology scene through ubiquitous and pervasive technologies has brought new forms of interaction. These interactions have become spontaneous and natural, in the sense of being infiltrated in the physical landscape. Considering the new forms of interaction, we believe that quantitative measures mainly those related to pre-defined tasks are not enough to evaluate the current technological contexts. User eXperience (UX) brings with it new perspectives for evaluation and is now widely recognized as an aspect to be considered and understood in the creation of interactive technologies. In this study, we evaluated the UX of children aged 7 to 12 years old who undergo treatment at the Sobrapar Hospital (Brazilian Society for Research and Assistance for Craniofacial Rehabilitation). Two workshops were carried out with the inclusion of plush animals with ubiquitous and pervasive characteristics in a socio-enactive scenario. The results showed that adapted methods were able to capture essential aspects of children's experience, such as emotions. In addition, the use of drawings for data collection was also useful, since the drawings represent greater spontaneity on the part of the children, validating the emotional responses given by the children through the Emoti-SAM and the Laddering interview. The triangulation of the data analyzed with the different methods was effective for the evaluation of children's UX.

Keywords: Evaluation user experience · Socio-enactive systems ·
Ubiquitous computing · Pervasive computing

1 Introduction

In the past, computer use was confined to the organizational environment and the performance of well-defined tasks. Nowadays, the omnipresent technology scene through ubiquitous and pervasive technologies has brought new forms of interaction. These interactions have become spontaneous and natural, in the sense of being infiltrated into the physical landscape. According to this new panorama, the concept of

A. Marcus and W. Wang (Eds.): HCII 2019, LNCS 11583, pp. 408–422, 2019.
https://doi.org/10.1007/978-3-030-23570-3_30

"enactive system" may be more appropriate to the current technological scenario. According to Kaipainen et al. [12], enactive systems are defined as computational systems made up of human and technological processes dynamically linked, i.e., forming loops of feedback using sensors and data analysis, allowing a perfect interaction between the human and the computer. This work is part of a project that explores the social nature of the mutual influences of interaction between people in the enactive cycle, we name socio-enactive systems [2]. Considering the new forms of interaction provided by this type of system, we argue that evaluation methods, especially those related to predefined tasks, are not enough for the current technological contexts. Invisibility of technology, the lack of conscious actions and the inclusion of technology in the user's natural environments, create potential challenges, above all, for the evaluation of the user experience in those environments.

Despite the increased interest in User Experience (UX) assessment [24], few studies are directly related to the evaluation of UX with children [1, 22, 23]. In view of the increased use of technology by this audience, whether spontaneous or "invisible", in this study we investigated the user experience of children aged 7 to 12 years old, who are treated at Sobrapar Hospital (Brazilian Society for Research and Assistance for Craniofacial Rehabilitation), interacting with socio-enactive artefacts. Two workshops were carried out in the study, with 6 children in each one, accompanied by their parents and some hospital professionals. The first workshop had as main objective to introduce the SOBRAPets (plush animals with some type of technology coupled) to the context of the hospital. One of the plush artefacts called Chico (a monkey) has the function of measuring the intensity of the hugs (hugmeter), through a pressure sensor. The intention was to convey affection through the hug. The other animals: an owl (corujita) with a camera coupled and communication via wifi with Chico, has the function of photographing hugs with greater intensity. The pictures taken are arranged in a display. The second workshop is an extension of the first, also held in Sobrapar aimed at introducing other Pets in communication (through the speech, also indicating the next steps of the activity) and among the children, encouraging the affection through the hug and the socialization.

Considering that positive emotions affect the interaction as a whole [8, 14], the evaluation with the children was done using the emoti-SAM [11] a pictographic instrument that uses emoticons to collect affective responses. The emoti-SAM consists of 15 emoticons, in three dimensions: pleasure, arousal, and dominance. In addition to the emoti-SAM, children were asked to draw about their experience in the workshop, considering that drawings have been used in several areas to capture feelings [5], besides being easily produced by children who are not proficient at writing and are usually accepted by children [15]. The parents/guardians and educational psychologists who also participated in the workshops, evaluated their experience through the AttrakDiff [10] that seeks to capture hedonic, pragmatic and attractiveness qualities of the experience.

For the second workshop, in addition to the emoti-SAM, an interview based on the Laddering technique [19] adapted to the children's context was applied. In both workshops, aspects of ubiquitous, pervasive computing were present, and therefore, the socio-enactive aspects, through the use of the body during the interaction, and the change of the environment through these mutual dynamics.

The results showed that the use of the technology through the SOBRAPets positively affects the UX. One of the factors we believe to have led to the capture of experience is that in both scenarios participants were asked to take the experience as a whole into account, not focusing on a device alone. The triangulation of data through the use of three methods proved to be effective for evaluation in the situated scenarios.

In this paper, we describe in detail both the study scenarios, the methodology including the description of UX evaluation methods used, as well as the analysis and main results. The rest of this article is divided: Sect. 2 describes the workshops used in the experiments. Section 3 shows the methods and the results obtained. In Sect. 4 a discussion is made on the results obtained. Finally Sect. 5 presents the conclusions and future work.

2 The Workshops

The workshops were hosted by SOBRAPAR - Brazilian Society for Research and Assistance in Craniofacial Rehabilitation, the first workshop was held on June 18, 2018, in the hospital auditorium, in the morning, for approximately two hours. Six children, aged 7 to 12 years old, participated with the parents or guardians of each child and health professionals.

The purpose of the workshop was to present the SOBRAPets (stuffed animals incorporated with some type of technology) in the context of the hospital. The children who attended the workshop are treated at the hospital. In a room, previously prepared, several Pets were arranged, some with embedded technology and others not. Among those with technology were Chico and Corujita (See Fig. 1).

Fig. 1. Chico and Corujita

Chico is a plush monkey that has the function of measuring the intensity of the hugs (hugmeter), through a sensor; when embraced with little intensity, a sound message is emitted, requesting a stronger hug. Corujita is an owl-shaped plush animal with a small camera to take pictures of some activities, for example, when a strong hug in Chico is detected. With this situation, Corujita is notified and, in 4 s, takes a photo of what is watching. The photos are arranged on the TV screen, with an interface composed of the intensity of the hug and the last 17 pictures taken. In addition to the stuffed animals, hats representing different animals were distributed. Each child chose one of the hats to attend the workshop.

To contextualize and create a playful environment for the children, a story was told of how the SOBRAPets arrived at the hospital.

The workshop consisted of 4 steps:

Welcome: Contextualization of the project and what would be the proposal of the workshop. At this stage, the children's parents and other participants signed the terms of consent and assent required to carry out the project.

Discovery: There was the delivery of caps (representing animals), the narrative of the introductory story, all the children were invited to embrace the SOBRAPets. This activity was intended to familiarize the children with the SOBRAPets and to satisfy their curiosity regarding the Pet that contained the technological devices.

Experimentation: Chico (who has the device that measures the intensity of the hug) was passing from child to child, arranged in a circle. So, they were invited to hug Chico if they wanted to. Depending on the intensity of the hug, a photo was taken by Corujita (Pet that contained a camera).

Reflection: At this point, the children were asked informally if they liked the activity, and if they liked the SOBRAPets.

Finally, there was the evaluation of the UX; in this workshop, three methods were used to evaluate the UX. AttrakDiff was used to evaluate the UX of the companions and health professionals present in the workshop, although they did not participate directly in the dynamics, we considered that they were participants in a certain way. The UX of the children was evaluated with emoti-SAM and by drawings made by the children.

The second workshop took place on October 8, 2018, at 7:30 am, in the Multimedia Room/Auditorium of SOBRAPAR. This date coincided with the children's week (October 8–11), which somewhat favored the activity.

The dynamics of the workshop involved a narrative for liberating the Teddy (Bear) that was hidden in a box. For this, in each round the Chico (monkey) was passed between the children, and when the force of the hugs given to the Pet reached the maximum level, an emoji was displayed on the TV screen and lights on the Christmas tree lit a level of lamps. The child who was with Chico was supposed to perform a task, asked by Chico himself (e.g. hug your friend at left). The dynamics continue until all children have performed a task and all lamp levels have been lit. At this point, the Teddy was released from the box and the children received the reward, which would be the gifts under the tree.

The workshop started with the environment assembly and configuration of the technological artefacts and systems. After the assembly of the environment, there was the reception of the participants; at this stage, the researchers presented themselves and distributed the terms with consents necessary for the workshop. Then the children and companions had explained the dynamics of the workshop; the children were asked to sit in a circle shape on a carpet arranged in the room. One of the researchers explained the dynamics of the activity. At the end of the workshop, the UX evaluation of the children was carried out; a sheet of paper requesting responses from the children about what they liked the most in the workshop. In addition to the evaluation through the drawings, the Laddering interview was conducted.

3   Methods Used in the Evaluations

AttrakDiff

AttrakDiff, possibly one of the best-known user experience assessment methods [10], consists of a measuring instrument in the form of semantic differentials. It is composed of 28 items distributed in seven pairs whose poles are opposing adjectives (e.g., "Isolating - Connective" "Confused - Clear", "Good - Bad"). Each pair of adjectives is ordered in a scale of intensity (Fig. 1). Each of the average values of a group of items creates value for pragmatic quality (PQ), hedonic quality (HQ) and attractiveness (ATT). The Pragmatic Quality Scale (PQ) has seven items each with bipolar "bases" that measure the pragmatic qualities of the product. This includes "bases" such as Technical - Human and Complicated - Simple. HQI has anchors like Alienating-Integrating and Cheap - Premium. HQS has anchors like Unimaginative - Creative. The Attraction Scale (ATT) with anchors like Ugly - Attractive and Bad - Good. The anchors are presented on a scale, ranging from −3 to +3, where zero represents the neutral value.

Emoti-SAM

The Emoti-SAM consists of 15 emoticons, representing the three dimensions: pleasure, arousal, and dominance. Each line represents a dimension with 5 emoticons that vary in a scale of 5 points, going from the most positive to the most negative - or the opposite, for the dominance dimension. In the dimension of pleasure, the most positive option is the happy face with the thumb up, while the more negative portrays a rabid face with the thumb down. In the excitement dimension, the most positive choice portrays a happy face with hearts and bulbs around representing excitement and inspiration; the most negative response brings a face with closed eyes, simulating someone sleeping or bored. In the dimension of the dominance, the representation sought to translate the sense of dominance in the sense of ease and mastery of the subject (Emoticon representing intelligence, with graduation hat) or difficulty of use (Confused Emoticon) [11].

Laddering

The technique of ladder interviews has its origin in the theory of means and ends proposed by Gutman [18]. This theory is based on the premise that people choose products because they have appropriate attributes, these would be the means. Means would be the way they would achieve the goals that would be the ends. In other words, the choice of products by users depends on how they perceive the attributes as more likely to achieve the desired consequences, which represent individual values. Thus, in general, the means-to-purpose theory consists of Attributes (A), Consequences (C) and Values (V) [18]. Concrete attributes are the perceptible aspects of a product, for example, size and color. Abstruse attributes are the intangible characteristics of a product, such as style. The attributes remain invariant while the consequences are dependent on the individual judgment of the user, they are due to the interaction.

Finally, the values refer to personal values rather than the characteristics of the product, for example, "Why it is important to treat people well". The consequences are classified as Functional Consequences (FC) and Psychosocial (PSC), and Values are Instrumental Values (IV) and End Values (TV). The functional consequences are related to the use of a product or service, for example, "Because of the bad animals talk". The psychosocial ones go beyond the use and are related to the social or psychological level. For example, "Why pets teach me something." Instrumental or terminal values to the individual benefits of the interaction [18]. The Laddering technique [19] uses this theory. The basic feature of a ladder interview is that the discussion begins with concrete features of the product and evolves to a more abstract level. In this way, the topic of conversation evolves naturally. This in-depth interview technique is based on repeating the question, "Why is this important to you?"

One of the motivations for using Laddering in UX evaluations is because the technique is based on the values, Cockton [4]. In addition, Laddering is a method that corresponds well to the ISO conception of User eXperience. We consider that the UX has a subjective nature and, therefore, corroborates with the methodology of the technique Laddering that seeks to analyze experiences of people based on self-reports and, therefore, loaded with frank perceptions about the evaluations.

When using the Laddering technique, we try to understand if the presence of the plush in the routine of the children who attend the hospital conveys some kind of affection. In addition, we seek to understand if the technique can capture aspects of the children's experience with the workshop. The interview questions were: 1. Did you like the Workshop (Activity)? 2. What did you like most? 2.1. Why did you like it? 3. Did you like animals? 3.1 Why did you like them?

Drawing

One of the methods used to evaluate the experience with children is their drawing [22]. This method is suitable for young children because when drawing, children are relaxed and generally do not consider it a task or a duty, but a fun. Children's drawings incorporate a variety of information about the child and their experience [17]. Xu et al. [23] argue that children's drawings are reliable, especially by the fun factor. The same authors argue that the use of drawings in evaluating technologies for children is effective because they can produce drawings even if they are not able to write proficiently. They can also capture some of the user experiences in a way that cannot be easily expressed in words.

In this context, the drawing is examined by "things" that convey understandings of a situation. As a child-centered assessment tool, they can be advantageous as they are: attractive and universal activities, easily produced by children, in addition to diminishing the insecurity of verbal communication as pointed by Xu et al. [23].

Drawings have been used in several contexts and can be used as research methods [7]. Children learn very early to express themselves through drawings, even before writing. Drawings can be used to clarify ideas as well as to encourage discussion. However, drawing alone is not enough as a research method, it must be complemented [9, 16]. However, we believe that drawings can be used to capture the experiences of children, because of the subjectivity of the experience and the spontaneity of the drawings. In addition, we consider that emotional factors are essential to the experience as well as its evaluation. Authors Kearney and Hyle [13] have identified some benefits in using drawings to investigate emotional aspects. 1. Drawings reveal emotional aspects that would not be included in communication in words; 2. Focus on the participant and consequently on individual aspects; 3. The lack of limitation in the drawings provides freedom of expression to the participants; 4. The use of drawings is suitable for data triangulation when used in addition to other research tools.

4   Results

In this section we present the methodologies and the results of the methods used to evaluate the UX in this work.

4.1   AttrakDiff Procedure and Results

The AttrakDiff was used to evaluate the UX of the participants of Workshop 1. The method used here was adapted, the adaptation consisted of the reduction of pairs of words considered inappropriate to the context and the translation into the Portuguese language. In addition, the mode of application was changed to pen and paper, so that people would respond soon after the workshop so that the impressions were not lost. Then the data collected was inserted into the online tool for generating graphical results (http://attrakdiff.de/). This questionnaire has already been used successfully in [3].

AttrakDiff Results
AttrakDiff works with pairs of words in a seven-level semantic differential. Having the center point with a score of 0, the values positioned to the right are scored as 1, 2, and 3, and the values punctuated to the left as −1, −2, and −3.

The results are presented through the Word Pairs Diagram (Fig. 2 located to the left of the figure) and the Results Portfolio (located to the right of the figure). Regarding the User Experience, the Word Pairs Diagram demonstrates that the line formed by the bonding of the blue dots is located significantly to the right, which indicates an excellent experience. The graph shows for the Hedonic Quality - identity (HQ-I), in the items (separates me, brings me closer), all the voters chose "bring me Closer"; this shows that the workshop had high hedonic qualities. The users' perception about attractiveness (ATT), presented all the items positioned to the right of the line with highlight to the adjectives (good - bad) all considered the experience as good. In general, it was considered quite attractive.

The Results Portfolio (located to the right of this figure) shows the positioning of the mean values of the dimensions: Pragmatic Quality, and Hedonic Quality. The representation of Hedonic Quality values is done vertically, and those of Pragmatic Quality horizontally. The workshop experience was evaluated as desired. In terms of pragmatic quality, the experience was evaluated positively. As far as hedonic quality is concerned, the results show that users are significantly stimulated by the novelty of the product.

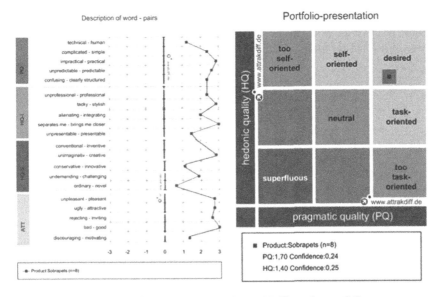

Fig. 2. Word pairs diagrams and AttrakDiff results portfolio

4.2   Emoti-SAM Procedure and Results

The evaluation with the emoti-SAM was performed after the workshops. The emoticons were printed on paper and were arranged in a wooden box with places for each emoticon. Participants were invited to choose one or more "face" or emoticon that represented their overall experience with the workshop, to put it in a closed box.

Emoti-SAM Results
Workshop 1: The figures entered in the closed box were counted manually, all the children who participated in the workshop chose an emoticon (Fig. 3 left image).

We collected 6 emoticons, one of which belongs to the pleasure dimension, with the second most positive response, the smiling face. In the excitement dimension, an emoticon was selected, this being the most positive response, i.e. the face with drawings of hearts and bulbs around. For the dimension of the domain an emoticon, similarly the most positive response, the face with graduation hat. In addition, a smiley emoticon, which belongs to the dimensions of pleasure and dominance was chosen. All collected emoticons are positive; these results suggest that the children had a pleasant experience, which provoked affective responses notably positive.

Workshop 2: Similarly to the previous workshop, we asked each child to choose an emoticon that most represented their experience with the workshop. However, more than one emoticon per child was chosen, this demonstrates the excitement of the children during their choice. In this workshop 19 emoticons were collected of which six belong to the pleasure dimension, with the most positive response and two emoticons that is the second most positive face. Nevertheless, an emoticon that represents sleep or fatigue was also found. In the excitation dimension, four emoticons were chosen, the latter being the most positive response and a happy face, the second face being more positive. For the dimension of the dominance, four emoticons were chosen, these being the most positive answers. In the same way, we can say that the workshop aroused positive emotional reactions in children (Fig. 3 right image).

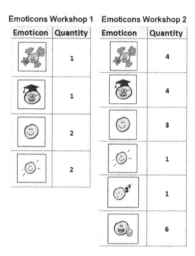

Fig. 3. Emoti-SAM results

4.3   Drawings Procedures and Results

In the first workshop, a paper sheet organized in two parts was delivered to the children; in one part we suggested that the children draw themselves and in the other half draw what they liked in the workshop.

In the room where the workshop took place, there was a table, in which colored pencils and the forms (sheet with white space for drawing) were available. The children could draw and they seemed willing and interested in the drawings.

In the second workshop, the children were invited to draw what they liked most in the workshop. It was delivered a blank sheet with the words "Draw what you liked in the workshop".

Drawing Results

The first step in the analysis of the drawings was to interpret participants' responses and identify trends and categories. To evaluate the results, the drawings were quantified and analyzed by the authors. Aspects such as color, repetition, textual representation and self-representation were analyzed.

Regarding the choice of colors, it can reveal the mood and personality of the children [6]. For example, the drawings made by the children participating in the workshop had a great concentration of colors, suggesting that the children were concentrated and excited.

The evaluation of the drawings can also be made through the repetition of forms and details, these can point to meanings. In the workshops, the plush was portrayed by six children. This indicates that they were important elements in the workshops.

Farokhi et al. [6] stated that the drawings of young children are secondary, while the slightly older children the theme becomes more important. When a single symbol or theme appears repeatedly in a single drawing, it deserves attention, and there are cases where there are hidden meanings behind them. This is because Unconscious thoughts, feelings, and actions are the source root of symbols and themes [6].

In addition, to analyzing children's drawings, it is important to consider the first impression that the drawing brings. The first feeling emphasized by the image should be saved for the final analysis. Sometimes there is the possibility that the first impression felt means that it was in close contact with the unconscious world [6]. Instead of focusing on finding symbols, it is a necessity to look at the image as a whole. The integrated whole is greater than the sum total of its parts. This is called the "pre-eminence of the whole."

With regard to free design, the individual interests and needs of the child can be understood by the chosen themes. For example, in our work, we aimed to analyze the children's UX in the workshop. For this we asked the children to draw what they liked the most in the workshop, at no time was imposed or suggested what the children should draw.

In the first workshop, the children were asked to draw themselves and what they liked the most in the workshop. All the children made drawings, the drawings were quantified and analyzed. In total, three designs by Chico and Ted, this shows that they were important to children during the workshop.

Other elements were also found, such as sun, clouds, and rainbows. Concerning the request that the children should draw themselves, four of the six children designed themselves without the use of the characterization made by the hats¿ delivered at the beginning of the workshop. Two children were drawn with this characterization. Two children were designed completely as the pet to which they wore the cap, this fact may

Fig. 4. Collected drawings

suggest that the children strongly identified with the characterization. In the second workshop, it was suggested that the children draw what they liked best in the workshop. Four of the six children designed Chico, Ted was represented 3 times. The gifts under the tree were drawn three times, and the tree three times too. Two children designed themselves, one of them was designed in the workshop, with the Christmas tree, presents, and panettones; the self-representation of the children may be related to acceptance of their own appearance. Some children wrote "Merry Christmas" texts in their drawings, this may be due to the theme of the workshop, or the time when it was done. Five children wrote their own names on the sheet they drew. Some examples of children's drawings are in the Fig. 4.

4.4   Laddering Methodology and Results

The interviews were conducted after the workshops. Each child was interviewed by an individual researcher in the same workshop environment as an informal and relaxed atmosphere. The researchers were instructed not to press and try to avoid biases. If the children did not wish to respond they would not be obliged.

The questions were directed to the workshop, with questions such as "did You like the Sobrapets (Pelucias)" and "Why did you like them", in order to achieve levels of subjectivity relevant to the experience. Interviews lasted an average of 3 min per child. The interviews were carried out using the pen and paper method, the researchers who participated in the workshops asked the questionnaire questions individually to each child. The data were then independently analyzed by the authors for the purpose of identifying the elements (Attributes, Consequences, and Values).

Laddering Results

The analysis of interview data involves a qualitative and quantitative approach. Qualitative analyses are performed through the transcription of the elements (Attributes, Consequences, and Values). At this stage, the elements cited by the interviewees are coded. These elements emerge from the interviews, are categorized, and must have been cited by more than one user. Cross-referencing of qualitative data allows the collection of quantitative data.

Workshop 1: Six children answered, the first question in the interview is a direct question: Did you like the workshop? All the children answered "YES" to the question, some children answered in addition to the "Yes" or "No" answer and gave feedback like "I liked it a lot" and "I found it to be super cool".

The responses were quantified and categorized in terms of Concrete Attributes, Abstract Attributes, Functional Consequences, Psychosocial Consequences, Instrumental Values (IV), Final Values (TV), according to Vanden and Zaman [20]. These categories were then quantified.

Five concrete attributes were collected, which usually describe the product, for example: "I like teddy bears that speak". Five abstract attributes, which are impalpable attributes, for example: "Bugs are cute" which are characteristic of plush. In the same way, 5 functional consequences were collected: "Because the animals talk and we can hug".

Six Psychosocial Consequences are those related to psychological aspects, for example, "I had a lot of fun with the animals". Only one Instrumental Worth was found "Because I hug the little critters."

Four Final Values were derived, for example: "He liked the monkey because he likes bananas".

Workshop 2: Similarly to Workshop 1, six children attended the workshop and answered the interview, all of them answered "Yes" to the question of whether they liked the workshop. The evaluation criteria were the same as those of the previous workshop. They have derived six concrete attributes, such as: "I liked the tree". Five abstract attributes, like those of the previous workshop, for example: "Ted and the little monkey are fluffy." Three functional consequences, for example: "I liked the tree because it lights.". Four Psychosocial Consequences "Because it is cool, and I can be accompanied by my colleagues." Four Instructional Values were derived, (e.g., "I liked the little critters I hugged them"). And finally, three Final Values were collected, for example: ("I liked that embracing is cool").

5 Discussion

UX assessment of children is a complex task, in part because of their subjectivity, partly because of the lack of specific methodologies for such assessments.

In this context, authors such as Jolley [17] argue that to suggest improvements in design regarding usability or user experience, care should be taken in drawing conclusions about children's behaviors and reactions. One should always critically question whether children's enthusiasm is actually caused by positive experience and not, for example, by the fact that, in general, people are more likely to report positive product emotions than negative emotions [17]. In this paper, we try to circumvent these prerogatives by adapting methods and procedures.

The AttrakDiff questionnaire, adapted to the context of the workshop, proved useful for evaluation. It brought positive results regarding interaction with the artifacts exposed and the use of the pen and paper model, different from the traditional online questionnaire, was effective because it promoted more spontaneity of the participants. The fact that the assessment was made immediately after the interaction also allowed the overall impression of the interaction not to be lost.

The evaluation of affective responses through emoti-SAM was also efficient to capture aspects of the children's experience. The figures were easily understood by the children, with only a questioning about the emoticon with a hat. However, this did not cause any loss to the participants' interpretation.

Regarding the evaluation of the experience through drawings, we sought to understand whether it was possible to evaluate the UX of children by means of drawings. We wondered whether the plushies of the workshops would wake the children emotionally and whether this would be captured by the drawings. The results showed that the drawings can be used as a research method and aid in the evaluation of UX, especially when corroborated by other methods. The use of UX evaluation drawings showed the following results: It helped create a relaxed and comfortable environment, improved communication between the researcher and the children, providing a deeper insight into the perspective of the children, likewise offered to children the possibility of expressing their personal experiences through the drawings.

With regard to the evaluation made through the interview based on the Laddering technique, both psychosocial aspects were detected in both workshops. Regarding the manifestation of social interaction, one of the children expressed it in his answer: "Because it is cool, and I can be accompanied by my colleagues". Likewise, mood tendencies have been identified (e.g. "teddy bears are very funny"). Tendencies of affection have also been detected, (for example, "I loved the hugs").

When using the Laddering technique, we tried to understand whether the presence of the plush in the routine of the children who attend the hospital conveys some kind of affection. Whether the technique is able to capture aspects of the children's experience in the hospital context.

We asked ourselves whether the interview based on the ladder methodology would be able to capture aspects inherent to the user experience. The results of the interviews through the psychosocial consequences showed that key aspects of UX could be observed. With regard to the emotional aspects of the interaction, we in-tended that the hug stimulated by the dynamics of the workshop could provide affection and trust between the child and the "plush" objects.

Laddering data provided insight into children's perceptions of the workshops, for example, which elements were the most relevant to them. In the initial dynamics it was proposed that through the hugs given in the pets, levels of the Christmas tree would be lit; however, only one of the children mentioned the lighting of the lamps and their relationship with the hugs. In fact, the tree was not their central object of attention.

In this study we could perceive the potential of the techniques to evaluate the UX of this audience. Although the original Laddering aims to perform a comparison between products, we believe that it is possible to apply the technique with a focus on inter-action and experience.

Vanden and Zaman [20] argue that reaching the level of functional or psychosocial consequences already provides the UX evaluator with information about meaningful associations between the individual and the attributes of the product.

6 Conclusion

Contemporary scenarios of technology use (ubiquitous, pervasive) present several challenges in evaluating the user experience. This work sought to situate itself in this context, investigating and understanding how the user experience can be evaluated considering the new forms of interaction. Likewise, assessing UX for children is equally challenging, in part, due to the lack of adequate methods to obtain the data.

In this work two UX evaluation methods were used: the AttrakDiff, which seeks to evaluate hedonic, pragmatic and attractiveness qualities, considering that these aspects characterize a product or service. We also used Emoti-SAM, as we consider that affective aspects are relevant to the experience as a whole. Drawings were also used to capture the children's UX, as we consider that drawings reveal emotional and indi-vidual aspects that would probably not be included in word communication. The Laddering interview was used because we understood that UX is subjective in nature and, therefore, the methodology of the Laddering technique that seeks to analyze the experiences of people based on self-reports might be helpful.

The results showed that adapted methods were able to capture essential aspects of children's experience, such as emotion. We believe that the adaptation to the contexts of the case studies as well as the procedures used during the evaluation together with the fact that the evaluation was done immediately after the interaction prevented the aspects of the experience of being lost. The triangulation of the data through four methods proved to be effective for the evaluation of children's UX.

In addition, the use of drawings for data collection was also useful, as they represent greater spontaneity on the part of the children, validating the emotional responses given by the children through Emoti-SAM and the interview Laddering.

Although AttrakDiff has closed questions, when used in conjunction with other methods, it has shown that the results obtained were consistent with the results of Emoti-SAM. We understand the challenges posed by UX's assessment, especially when evaluating the experience of children with technology. Nevertheless, based on the results so far, we believe that the combination of methods explored in this work may be useful for evaluating UX in similar scenarios.

Future work involves extending the results of this study to the creation of a set of guides to evaluate UX in socio-enactive scenarios.

Acknowledgements. The authors thank the FAPESP Thematic Project (2015/16528-0), and colleagues of InterHAD, Institute of Computer UNICAMP.

References

1. Abeele, V.V., Zaman, B., De Grooff, D.: User eXperience Laddering with preschoolers: unveiling attributes and benefits of cuddly toy interfaces. Pers. Ubiquitous Comput. **16**(4), 451–465 (2012)
2. Baranauskas, M.C.C.: Socio-enactive Systems: Investigating New Dimensions in the Design of Interaction Mediated by Information and Communication Technologies FAPESP Thematic Project (2015/16528-0) (2015)
3. Brennand, C.V.L.T., Baranauskas, M.C.C.: Evaluating UX-Case Studies in Socio-enactive Scenarios
4. Cockton, G.: From quality in use to value in the world. In: CHI 2004 Extended Abstracts on Human Factors in Computing Systems, Vienna, Austria, pp 1287–1290. ACM (2004)
5. Denham, P.: Nine to fourteen-year-old children's conception of computers using drawings. Behav. Inf. Technol. **12**(6), 346–358 (1993)
6. Farokhi, M., Hashemi, M.: The analysis of children's drawings: social, emotional, physical, and psychological aspects. Procedia Soc. Behav. Sci. **30**, 2219–2224 (2011)
7. Fleury, A.: Drawing and acting as user experience research tools. In: Proceedings of the 10th Asia Pacific Conference on Computer Human Interaction. ACM (2012)
8. Forlizzi, J., Battarbee, K.: Understanding experience in interactive systems. In: Proceedings of the 2004 Conference on Designing Interactive Systems (DIS 2004): Processes, Practices, Methods, and Techniques, pp. 261–268. ACM, New York (2004)
9. Guillemin, M.: Understanding illness: using drawings as a research method. Qual. Health Res. **14**(2), 272–289 (2004)

10. Hassenzahl, M., Burmester, M., Koller, F.: AttrakDiff: Ein Fragebogen zur Messung wahrgenommener hedonischer und pragmatischer Qualität. In: Mensch & Computer (2003)
11. Hayashi, E.C.S., Posada, J.E.G., Maike, V.R., Baranauskas, M.C.C.: Exploring new formats of the Self-Assessment Manikin in the design with children. In: Proceedings of the 15th Brazilian Symposium on Human Factors in Computer Systems. ACM (2016)
12. Kaipainen, M., et al.: Enactive systems and enactive media: embodied human–machine coupling beyond interfaces. Leonardo **44**(5), 433–438 (2011)
13. Kearney, K.S., Hyle, A.E.: Drawing out emotions: the use of participant-produced drawings in qualitative inquiry. Qual. Res. **4**(3), 361–382 (2004)
14. Hassenzahl, M., Tractinsky, N.: User experience: a research agenda. Behav. Inf. Technol. **25** (2), 91–97 (2006)
15. MacPhail, A., Kinchin, G.: The use of drawings as an evaluative tool: students' experiences of sport education. Phys. Educ. Soc. Sci. **9**(1), 88–108 (2004)
16. Mills, J.E.: An Exploration into How and Why Drawing Works. Virginia Tech, Blacksburg (2010)
17. Jolley, R.: Children and Pictures: Drawing and Understanding. Wiley, Hoboken (2010)
18. Reynolds, T., Gutman, J.: Laddering theory, method, analysis, and interpretation. In: Reynolds, T., Olsen, J. (eds.) Understanding Consumer Decision Making: The Means-End Approach to Marketing and Advertising Strategy, pp. 25–52. Lawrence Erlbaum, Mahwah (2001)
19. Reynolds, T.J., Gutman, J.: Laddering theory, method, analysis, and interpretation. J. Advert. Res. **28**(1), 11–31 (1988)
20. Vanden Abeele, V., Zaman, B.: Laddering the user experience! User experience methods, interact 2009, Uppsala, Sweden (2009)
21. Vanden Abeele, V., Zaman, B., De Grooff, D.: User eXperience Laddering with preschoolers: unveiling attributes and benefits of cuddly toy interfaces. Pers. Ubiquitous Comput. **16**(4), 451–465 (2012)
22. Vissers, J., De Bot, L., Zaman, B.: MemoLine: evaluating long-term UX with children. In: Proceedings of the 12th International Conference on Interaction Design and Children. ACM (2013)
23. Xu, D., Read, J., Sim, G., McManus, B.: Experience it, draw it, rate it: capture children's experiences with their drawings. In: Proceedings IDC 2009, pp. 266–270. ACM (2009)
24. Zarour, M., Alharbi, M.: User experience aspects and dimensions: systematic literature review. Int. J. Knowl. Eng. **3**(2), 52–59 (2017)

Elderly Users and Their Main Challenges Usability with Mobile Applications: A Systematic Review

Lesly Elguera Paez$^{(\boxtimes)}$ and Claudia Zapata Del Río$^{(\boxtimes)}$

Pontificia Universidad Católica del Perú, Lima, Peru
{lesly.elguera, zapata.cmp}@pucp.edu.pe

Abstract. The development of mobile applications has become a means to improve the quality of life of older adults since it is possible to apply to various sectors such as medicine, for example. Also, the population aged 60 or above is growing at a rate of about 3 percent per year. Currently, rapid ageing will occur in different parts of the world as well, so that by 2050 all regions of the world except Africa will have nearly a quarter or more of their populations at ages 60 and above [45]. Likewise, it is known that older people require more time to complete tasks on mobile devices [4] and presents usability problems, so the generic developments of mobile applications do not adapt to their needs and special characteristics. For this reason, this paper addresses which are the main usability challenges that adults face when they interact with de user graphic interface of an application and how they can be made more acceptable to the target population. We summarize the relevant issues in three potential causes: visual, psychomotor and cognitive limitations. In the first category we found problems as the size and sharpness for the visual elements such characters, icons, images, charts and buttons. Also, use hard colors or inappropriate contrast color for the elements represents a significant problem to the seniors. On other hand, we found that the demand for fast and repetitive movements for interaction like moving texts or targets, the maximization in the required number of steps to complete a task and the use of scrollbars represent inconveniences in the second category for the elderly. Finally, in the last category, the most relevant issues are the use of non-significant and irrelevant graphics, or non-meaningful icons with decoration, animation or with no concise text description that goes with it. Besides, use complex texts and navigating through deep, complex and expandable menu hierarchies causes that older persons getting lost within the device menu.

Keywords: Elderly users · Mobile applications · Usability · Systematic review

1 Introduction

The concept of Human-computer interaction can be defined as one discipline concerned with the design, evaluation, and implementation of interactive computing systems for human use and with the study of major phenomena surrounding them [13]. This field of research is directly related to technological changes and evolves constantly in response to them [26].

© Springer Nature Switzerland AG 2019
A. Marcus and W. Wang (Eds.): HCII 2019, LNCS 11583, pp. 423–438, 2019.
https://doi.org/10.1007/978-3-030-23570-3_31

With the emergence of mobile innovation, the way people use technology has changed profoundly and an evident example is the massive use of Smartphones, Tablets, IPad's, mobile devices in general, which have become powerful personal computing devices enabled for interaction through applications that can be used anytime and anywhere thanks to an Internet connection.

Because the use of these mobile technologies have become a trend, several applications are being introduced in these devices in different categories such as entertainment, health, finance, retail, education, social media, etc. [17]. To the first quarter of 2018, Android users were able to choose between 3.8 million apps while Apple's App Store remained the second-largest app store with 2 million available apps [36].

Among the millions of users who use mobile applications, we can find: children, seniors, persons with disabilities and others. Focusing on seniors, in a study conducted in United States during June 2016, this type of users accessed mobile apps via smartphones for an average of 42.1 h and spent an average of 23.4 h in mobile apps via Tablets in contrast with the youngers who used mobile applications on smartphones 95.3 h and 27.6 h on tablets on average [43]. In general, UIs designers have not had the opportunity to work closely with elderly [16]. Failure to design "elderly friendly" interfaces may lead to reluctance to the use of mobile devices by the elderly [15], while a properly designed UI that respects the elderly's needs can tackle this issue [15, 25].

Also, a 2014 report on app users revealed that there are actually only a few apps for elderly people [37] that cater for impairments many seniors suffer from (such as less acute vision or reduced tactile sense) or for missing prior knowledge (such as special gestures or typing on a soft keyboard) [6]. For that reason, many elderly people cannot benefit from the large amount of available mobile apps that could support their activities of daily living [6].

The success of any type of application depends on how well it is being used by the user i.e. the usability [17] Due to the above, there is a need to conduct research through one Systematic Review Literature (SLR), following the guidance of Kitchenham [18], which is focused on synthesizing which are the main problems and challenges usability among elderly users when interacting with the UI of a mobile application. Finally, different actions are recommended that should be applied to ensure that this type of user can easily access the different applications and strengthen the growth of the market for which they have been developed.

The paper is structured as follows:

- Section 2 presents a brief description of the term usability and related concepts.
- Section 3 specifies the context of usability in mobile applications for elderly people.
- Section 4 discusses the search method developed in detail to conduct the systematic review.
- Section 5 reporting the systematic review and presents the results and recommendations on action plans.
- Section 6 presents some conclusions.

2 Usability

Usability is a core terminology in HCI that can be defined by the International Organization for Standardization (ISO) (1998) as "the extent to which a product can be used by specified users to achieve specified goals with effectiveness, efficiency and satisfaction in a specified context of use" [14]. The concept of usability is very important to any kind of products because if the users cannot achieve their goals of a way effectively, efficiently and establishing an easy interaction that is reflected in a positive user satisfaction, they can seek another alternative solution to achieve them. In another words, the interaction interfaces should be friendly enough, that allow users to accomplish their purpose in a native or no difficult way [23]. A usable product seeks to achieve three main outcomes: (1) the product is easy for users to become familiar with and competent in using it during the first contact, (2) the product is easy for users to achieve their objective through using it, and (3) the product is easy for users to recall the user interface and how to use it on later visits [26].

According to Shackel (1991) three things are measured about usability of a technology: size, performance and attitude. Dimensional measurements of a technology have direct physical dimensions (width, height, etc.) to measure and are used to determine the volume of products. However, performance measurement is used to determine the time spent and the numbers of mistakes are made during the use of a technology. Attitude scale is used to determine the positive or negative opinions of ones using the technology [30]. In this context, the user interface design of a product is a very important factor that determines the user experience. The UI must be understandable, in a way that users do not make much effort to use it. Also must be attractive to the end user and must contribute to the easy learning, comprehension and operation of its elements. It is important to achieve these aspects to provide a high degree of usability in the applications, to strengthen their use, and guarantee their success. Otherwise, if a software product is difficult to use, hard to understand, or fails to clearly state what it is offering, the user will not use the application anymore [7].

3 Mobile Applications Usability for Elderly People

What is understood as older people or senior citizen? It depends on the context, in Europe an older person is not the same as in Africa, most developed countries set the age of 65 years to define when a person is older [11]. At the moment, the United Nations (UN) agreed cut-off is 60+ years to refer to the older population [44]. This is the age that this study used to consider who is an older person. It is known that as fertility declines and life expectancy rise, the proportion of the population above a certain age rises as well. This phenomenon, known as population ageing, is occurring throughout the world. In 2017, there are an estimated 962 million people aged 60 or over in the world, comprising 13 per cent of the global population. The population aged 60 or above is growing at a rate of about 3 per cent per year. Currently, Europe has the greatest percentage of population aged 60 or over (25 per cent). Rapid ageing will occur in other parts of the world as well, so that by 2050 all regions of the world except Africa will have nearly a quarter or more of their populations at ages 60 and above [45].

Besides, a high percentage of older people in developed countries (Europe, North America, Japan, Australia and New Zealand) owned mobile devices, however they use only mobile phones for very limited purposes, such as for calling or texting in emergencies [11]. But why they do not use other features like mobile apps? Basically, it is because this technology is not adapted to their needs and special features, so it is required facilitate the use of mobile applications for the elderly, so they can adapt quickly, have access to the services that the apps can offer and can get efficient answer to all the actions that they carry out. Regarding the works that study the usability of mobile technology for senior citizen, Villaseca [33] made a review of different studies in this sense. This study shows that older people require more time to complete tasks on mobile devices [4] and it describes problems such as: the size of the screen to read information, the size of menus and interfaces to enter data such as keyboards, functionalities such as de drag and drop, the size of the target (the older tend to make errors when tapping a small target), etc. In the following section, this study presents the strategy to develop the systematic review of the main problems and challenges that elderly people experience when interacting with the user interface of a mobile application.

4   Research Method

In order to gather evidence on the main challenges usability among elderly user when interacting with the user interface of a mobile application, the present study conducted a systematic literature review (SLR) considering the parameters defined in the study of Kitchenham [41] with the aimed at finding all the existing evidence on the factors that impact in usability of mobile applications in the senior citizens. A SLR is defined as a means of identifying, evaluating and interpreting all variables research relevant to a particular research question, or topic area, or phenomenon of interest [41]. Kitchenham establish a set of activities that facilitate the process of a systematic review in the area of software engineering [23]. The steps of this methodology are presented in the following subsections.

4.1   Research Question

The most important activity during the protocol is to formulate the research question, it is also crucial to make this question meaningful and able to identify and/or scope future research activities [41]. The goal of this study was to determine the main barriers usability among elderly users when interacting with the user interface of a mobile application. In this way, the subsequent research question was formulated:

RQ: Which is the main challenge usability among elderly user when interacting with de UI of a mobile application?

This research question has been structured with the help of the PICOC method as suggested by Petticrew and Roberts [40]. Therefore, the comparison criterion was not considered because the objective of this systematic review is not to find the evidence about comparison of different types of usability problems. Table 1, detailed the definition of the general concepts through the use of PIOC.

Table 1. Definition of the general concepts using PICOC

Criterion	Description
Population	Mobile applications
Intervention	Usability challenges
Outcome	Case studies where the main usability challenges have been determined respect to the user interface of a mobile application among elderly
Context	The context will encompass academic as well as software industry, all type of stakeholders (developers, maintainers, testers, project managers, students, researchers, etc.) and all type of empirical studies

4.2   Search Strategy

The strategy used for deriving search terms is a reference of the one used in [21] and is specified below:

(a) Derive major search terms from the research questions by identifying Population, Intervention, Outcome and Context. See Table 2.

Table 2. Terms derived from PICOC

Population	Mobile application
Intervention	Usability challenges
Outcome	User interface, elderly
Context	Software industry, developers, maintainers, testers, project managers, students, researchers, empirical studies.

(b) Find alternative spellings and synonyms for the search terms with the help of a thesaurus. See Table 3.

Table 3. Terms derived from alternative spellings and synonyms

Mobile application	Application, mobile, smartphone
Challenges	Problems, barriers
User interface	Interface, graphical user interface, mobile interface
Elderly	Older, senior, aging, age

(c) Use Boolean OR to construct search strings from the search terms identified in (a) and (b). See Table 4.

(d) Use Boolean AND to concatenate the search terms and restrict the research.

Table 4. Construction of terms by using Boolean OR

Mobile application OR application OR mobile OR smartphone
Challenges OR problems OR barriers
User interface OR interface OR graphical user interface OR mobile interface
Elderly OR older OR senior OR aging OR age

The resulting search string allows identifying as many academic papers as possible, which describe the main usability problems of the elderly when interacting with the user interface of mobile software. See Table 5.

Table 5. Concatenation of Terms by using Boolean AND

(Mobile application OR application OR mobile OR smartphone) AND (Usability) AND (challenges OR problems OR barriers) AND (User interface OR interface OR graphical user interface OR mobile interface) AND (elderly OR older OR senior OR aging OR age)

4.3   Search Process and Resources

The search process was executed on October 15, 2018 and it was directed towards using search engines and recognized online databases to search for primary and secondary studies. No additional studies were considered. In order to avoid omitting any evidence, the search process will include literature published since 2013 to date. 2013 was chosen as the starting limit because a search test was conducted, and the most relevant results were found in that year. Grey literature was also excluded.

The following electronic resources were chosen because they were used by some examples of systematic reviews from discipline of software engineering [21] and they were suggested by the digital library of the University. All databases were searched using appropriate keywords and headings related to the concepts usability, mobile applications, elderly people and user interface.

Online Database:

- IEEE XPLORE
- SCOPUS
- ProQuest Computing
- ACM Digital Library

4.4   Selection of Studies

Once the articles that met the search string were obtained, an analysis of the title, authors, abstract and keywords of each study was carried out to determine their relevance. Also, a study selection criterion was developed. This study is intended to identify those studies that provide direct evidence about the research question [41]. Inclusion and exclusion criteria should be based on the research question and they should be piloted to ensure that can be reliably interpreted and that they classify studies correctly [41] Papers that satisfy at least one of the following conditions, published between Jan 1st 2013 and September 30th 2018, were included in this analysis:

- Tittle, keyword list, and abstract make explicit that the paper is related to usability problems when the elderly interacting with de user interface of a mobile application.
- The study reports on the analysis of the interface of the any type (domains) of mobile application: health, education, social media, etc.
- The study presents usability problems among senior when interacting with the user interface of any mobile device: smartphone, iPad's, tablets, mobile touch screen devices in general, etc.
- The paper presents recommendations and guidelines to design an appropriate graphical user interface focus on the elderly.
- The paper focuses its analysis of usability of mobile devices only elderly people.
- The study focuses their analysis on specific communities of the world.
- The paper presents comparisons between different age groups (younger, older, middle age) with regard to usability problems in mobile applications.

The studies that met at least one of the following aspects will be excluded from this systematic review:

- Duplicate reports of the same study (the most complete version of the paper was included in the research).
- Informal literature.
- The study is not written in English.
- The year of publication of the study was before to 1st January 2013.
- The publication is not accessible.
- The study has not developed its analysis regarding the use of touch-based mobile devices (for example, tablets, smartphones, iPads) by seniors.
- The paper describes the use of a specific platform or presents how to develop and design a specific application without mainly addressing the problems that the elderly face when interacting with the GUI of the application.
- The study presents the intention of use or the behavior of an older person on a specific mobile application without focusing mainly on the usability of the elements of the graphic interface of the application.
- The study presents an analysis of usability of applications in the following areas: augmented reality, internet of things, web platforms and mobile robots.

The Table 6 summarize the results obtained for each four databases after conducting the search process and selecting them. As a result, we obtained 201 studies of which 24 papers were classified as duplicates. Finally, 177 unique studies were obtained and after the application of the inclusion and exclusion criteria, 28 papers were selected and included in the systematic review.

4.5   Data Extraction Strategy

The objective of this section is to design data extraction form to accurately record the information researchers need from the studies [41]. For this reason, the strategy to be adopted for recording the data is given below:

Table 6. Summary of search results

Database name	Search result	Duplicated papers	Unique accepted papers	Unique rejected papers
IEEE XPLORE	60	5	3	52
SCOPUS	59	4	20	35
ProQuest Computing	25	5	4	16
ACM DigitalLibrary	57	10	1	46
Total	201	24	28	149

- Data Extraction Form

  The design of the data extraction form was performed according to the protocol proposed by Kitchenham [41] and has been designed to collect all the information needed to address the research question, also it form provides standard data. For each resulting paper of our search, we developed the following structure given in Table 7.

Table 7. Data extraction form

Item	Value
Study ID	A unique identifier: <number>
Title	
Type of study	Experiment/Case Study/etc.
Year of publication	
xion	
Database in which the study was found	IEEE XPLORE/SCOPUS/ProQuest Computing/ACM DigitalLibrary

5 Systematic Review Results

According to the studies reviewed, it can be concluded that the usability problems that older people finding when interacting with the graphic interface of a mobile application have their causes in three broad categories: Visual limitations, psychomotor limitations and cognitive limitations. On the following lines will detail which are the problems that constitute each of these groups.

5.1 Visual Limitations

Vision is the most important way how technology can present information to the user. As the limitations of a human eye depend on age, seniors have mostly worse vision [31]. Therefore, the old eye has a slower accommodation between dark and light places. It cannot quickly change the focus, or react to fast-changing brightness [31]. For these reasons, the difficulties that older users have when using a mobile application are:

- Find small and unclear visual elements such characters, icons, images or graphical content, charts, font size on charts and buttons on the screen [2, 3, 10–12, 20, 22, 25, 27, 29, 34, 35, 38]. Also, display text that uses a very small or thin font represents an issue to the elderly [31].
- Find touch targets that are not big enough [5].
- Visualizing and using a keyboard too small [12].
- The size of on-screen buttons has a clear influence on interaction speed and accuracy [22].
- Find inappropriate or hard colors for the icons, images or graphical content, for example those that are too bright [2, 29].
- Visualize an inappropriate contrast color [10, 32], for example a very strong color during the user interaction [11, 12, 24]. Find color combinations with a low contrast [31].
- Don't find a color coding to differentiate and group the elements [38].
- Visualize characters on the keypad that are not clearly visible; especially in the dark and night time [20].
- Don't find a wider space between lines and letter [10] on the GUI. Also it was detected that the performance of elderly was significantly influenced by spacing and location of the target [35].
- Do not understanding and distinguishing the buttons from one another either visually or by touch [24].
- Not visualize sufficiently large gaps between individual elements, particularly between elements such as buttons that are touch targets [5, 20].
- Visualize very small menus sizes and interfaces to enter data such as keyboards (virtual and physical). Also, find that the size of the target it is too small (the older tend to make errors when tapping a small target) represents a problem for the elderly [11].

Recommendations

- In general, older adults found enlarging the text size to be helpful [25].
- Options to zoom in and increase the font size [24].
- Allow to adjust font size and contrasting colors [9].

Likewise, the following recommendations are specified in the Android application development guide:

- By providing increased contrast ratio between the foreground and background colors in the app, it will be easier for users to navigate within and between screens. For large text, 18 points or higher for regular text and 14 points or higher for bold text, you should use a contrast ratio of at least 3.0 to 1. For small text, smaller than 18 points for regular text and smaller than 14 points for bold text, you should use a contrast ratio of at least 4.5 to 1 [39].

- Uses cues other than color to distinguish UI elements within the screens of the app. These techniques could include using different shapes or sizes, providing text or visual patterns, or adding audio [39].
- Color can help communicate mood, tone, and critical information. Use color so that all users can understand the content is fundamental to accessible design. Choose primary, secondary, and accent colors for the app that support usability [39].
- Clear and helpful accessibility text is one of the primary ways to make UIs more accessible. Accessibility text refers to text that is used by screen reader accessibility software, such as TalkBack on Android, VoiceOver on iOS, and JAWS on desktop. Screen readers read all text and elements (such as buttons) on screen aloud, including both visible and nonvisible alternative text [39].

On the other hand, the following recommendations are specified in the iOS application development guide:

- Provide the feature of zoom to magnifies the entire device screen [42].
- Voice Control, that allows users to make phone calls and control iPod playback using voice commands [42].

5.2 Psychomotor Limitations

The general rule is that seniors require about 50–100% more time for completion of a task than adults fewer than 30. Many interfaces require very fine movements. The consequences of an error are frustrating. For example, if a user accidentally removes the file, or s/he is an inaccurate during the drag and drop of the file, so s/he needs to start over and over again [31]. The principal issues that the elderly can find in the interface user of an application mobile are the following.

- Interacting with moving text and targets, when the interface item unexpectedly moves, makes it difficult for the user to interact. Also the elderly has problems with text entry using virtual keyboards [10, 12, 24].
- Demanding fast and repetitive movements for interaction, maximization the required number of steps to complete a task. In other words, the user has difficulty in performing a sequence of actions/navigations [10, 12, 28].
- The use of scrollbars is maximized or do not placed on the side of the phone [24].
- Have to do functions that require user to perform unfamiliar and challenging actions for example, "drag and drop" [11, 29].
- Can't identify *tappable* areas on touchscreens [24].
- Have difficulty in assessing the function of buttons or can have difficulty understanding mobile scroll bars [22].
- Detecting which buttons or target to press, which often leads to long taps of a virtual button or pressing the wrong button on the virtual keyboard. This can be caused by the buttons being very close to each other (to the target button) [1, 35].
- Do not find colorful and not animated icons, which are supported textually. However, it is known that labels are more efficient for older people to initially use icon [1].

- Must do actions of scrolling and tapping are confusing. In addition, pop-up windows for request messages could be stressful for the user [27].

Recommendations

- Reduced number of interactions [38].
- Use a simple menu structure and only essential functionality [34].
- Instead of using interaction concepts such as scrolling and drag and drop, previous research proves that the elderly only likely to use traditional pressing button method [2].

Likewise, the following recommendations are specified in the Android application development guide:

- By providing larger touch targets, it will be substantially easier for users to navigate the app. In you want the touchable area of focusable items to be a minimum of 48dp × 48dp [39].

5.3   Cognitive Limitations

Memory ability declines with age. It has been generally accepted that the capacity of working memory significantly decreases with age. Regarding long-term memory, however, the decline is not global. Whereas semantic memory is trivial, age-related loss is episodic, and procedural memory is common. In addition, deficits in prospective memory, that is, the ability to remember to carry out an intended action, are prevalent among older people [10]. When the interface presents the information in inappropriate way, many people get confused and tend to blame themselves rather than the application. The effective interface is the one that helps users in completing their goals with a little confusion and less errors as possible [31]. The main difficulties that the older users experiment are:

- Use complex texts and navigating through deep and complex menu hierarchies, use moving and expandable menus, which causes that the elderly getting lost within the device menu. Not using standardized menus or one-level navigation causes the user to have difficulty understanding the menu hierarchy [8–10, 12, 35].
- Use of non-significant and irrelevant graphics, many ambiguous pictograms and non-meaningful icons with decoration, animation or with no concise text description that goes with it. All of this causes confusion about the meanings of the interface icons and makes it difficult to know and recognize what each one represents. In addition to that, using similar icons for labeling UI elements playing distinct roles represent a difficulty for the elderly [1, 8–10, 19, 24, 29, 31].
- Use ambiguous uncommon terms (abbreviation meaning), employs terms and expressions that are difficult to understand (inadequate labels), the language used is vague and not meaningful and use over-complicated jargon or use metaphors that look familiar to the elderly but are not [5, 12, 28, 29, 34].
- Do not apply a standard (well-known) icon design configuration, which is consistent in size and shape [28].

- The use of drop down menus is proven to be an issue because precise movements are physically challenging for this population group [38].
- Can´t find the option of refining the search by applying further criteria. When displaying the search results, the availability of sorting options (e.g. according to date, location, and other criteria) is no available [5].
- Find unclear instructions on how to proceed to use a certain function. Lack of instruction, not intuitive instructions, lack of directions and lack of help [27, 35].
- Use long content that requires memory recall affects older adults with cognitive impairments [38].

Recommendations

- Use menu structure must be simple and flattened (menus standardized and customized [11]).
- Use easy-to-use menus should be preferred.
- Information about the current menu item helps users to navigate [5].
- If icons are used for navigational purposes, these should be easily identifiable in terms of their function [5].
- Older adults preferred to use colorful, not animated icons, which are supported textually. Also, their study found that labels are more efficient for older people to initially use icons [1].
- Animation should be avoided because it would interfere with the focus of senior citizens to interact with the computer. Icon design should be simple to understand and refers precisely to the function of the icon [2].
- With regard to the search process, good positioning of the search fields is just as important as transparency [5].

Likewise, the following recommendations are specified in the Android application development guide:

- It is important to provide useful and descriptive labels that explain the meaning and purpose of each interactive element to users [39].
- Developers should arrange related content into groups so that accessibility services announce the content in a way that reflects its natural grouping [39].
- Make sure users can navigate through your app's layouts using keyboards or navigation gestures, avoid having UI elements fade out or disappear after a certain amount of time [39].

On the other hand, the following recommendations are specified in the iOS application development guide:

- Provide a label that very briefly describes the element and begins with a capitalized word [42].
- An accessible user interface element must provide accurate and helpful information about its screen position, name, behavior, value, and type [42].

- Provide the current value of an element, when the value is not represented by the label. For example, the label for a slider might be "Speed," but its current value might be "50%." [42].

6 Conclusions

The main goal of this paper is to know which are the main usability issues faced by the elderly when interacting with the graphic interface of a mobile application. The recognized problems can be part of three large categories: visual limitations, psychomotor limitations and cognitive limitations. These groups represent the causes of the difficulties that older persons find when using the apps.

According to the primary studies reviewed, the usability issue that was identified a greater number of time in the first category was finding small and unclear visual elements such characters, icons, images or graphical content, charts, font size on charts and buttons on the app. Likewise, we found that the demand for fast and repetitive movements for interaction like moving texts or the maximization in the required number of steps to complete a task represents significant problems in the second category for the seniors. Finally, in the last category we found that the main issue was the use of non-significant and irrelevant graphics, many ambiguous pictograms and non-meaningful icons with decoration, animation or with no concise text description that goes with it. All of this causes confusion about the meanings of the interface icons and makes it difficult to know and recognize what each one represents.

Besides, use complex texts and navigating through deep, complex and expandable menu hierarchies causes that the elderly getting lost within the device menu.

Finally, considering the analysis of the Android and IOs guides to develop more accessible applications, it is concluded that although there are several recommendations in each of the three defined limitations: visual, psychomotor and cognitive, many of the applications that are currently sold in the market lack special features for this group of users. For example, it is a fact that color can help communicate mood, tone, and critical information so it is recommended to use color so that all users can understand the content is fundamental to accessible design. Likewise, choosing primary, secondary and accent colors is important for the application to support usability. So, this kind of recommendations should be considered primarily by developers when creating a new application.

References

1. Al-Razgan, M., Al-Khalifa, H.S.: SAHL: A touchscreen mobile launcher for Arab elderly. J. Mob. Multimed. **13**(1–2), 75–99 (2017)
2. Azir Rezha, N., et al.: Tackling design issues on elderly smartphone interface design using activity centered design approach. ARPN J. Eng. Appl. Sci. **9**(8), 1190–1196 (2014)
3. Azuddin, M., et al.: Older people and their use of mobile devices: issues, purpose and context. In: The 5th International Conference on Information and Communication Technology for the Muslim World (ICT4M), pp. 1–6 (2014)

4. Lin, C.J., Hsieh, T.-L., Shiang, W.-J.: Exploring the interface design of mobile phone for the elderly. In: Kurosu, M. (ed.) HCD 2009. LNCS, vol. 5619, pp. 476–481. Springer, Heidelberg (2009). https://doi.org/10.1007/978-3-642-02806-9_55
5. Darvishy, A., Hutter, H.-P.: Recommendations for age-appropriate mobile application design. In: Di Bucchianico, G., Kercher, Pete F. (eds.) AHFE 2017. AISC, vol. 587, pp. 241–253. Springer, Cham (2018). https://doi.org/10.1007/978-3-319-60597-5_22
6. Diewald, S., et al.: Mobile AgeCI: potential challenges in the development and evaluation of mobile applications for elderly people. In: Moreno-Díaz, R., Pichler, F., Quesada-Arencibia, A. (eds.) EUROCAST 2015. LNCS, vol. 9520, pp. 723–730. Springer, Cham (2015). https://doi.org/10.1007/978-3-319-27340-2_89
7. Engel, E., Öncü, S.: Conducting preliminary steps to usability testing: investigating the website of Uluda University
8. Fletcher, J., Jensen, R.: Mobile health: barriers to mobile phone use in the aging population. On-Line J. Nurs. Inform. OJNI **19**(3) (2015)
9. Fletcher, J., Jensen, R.: Overcoming barriers to mobile health technology use in the aging population. On-Line J. Nurs. Inform. OJNI **19**(3) (2015)
10. Gao, Q., et al.: Design of a mobile social community platform for older Chinese people in urban areas. Hum. Factors Ergon. Manuf. Serv. Ind. **25**(1), 66–89 (2015)
11. García-Peñalvo, F.J., Conde, M.Á., Matellán-Olivera, V.: Mobile apps for older users – the development of a mobile apps repository for older people. In: Zaphiris, P., Ioannou, A. (eds.) LCT 2014. LNCS, vol. 8524, pp. 117–126. Springer, Cham (2014). https://doi.org/10.1007/978-3-319-07485-6_12
12. Gonçalves, V.P., et al.: Providing adaptive smartphone interfaces targeted at elderly people: an approach that takes into account diversity among the elderly. Univ. Access Inf. Soc. **16**(1), 129–149 (2017)
13. Hewett, T.T., et al.: ACM SIGCHI Curricula for Human-Computer Interaction. ACM, New York (1992)
14. International Organization Standardization (ISO): Ergonomic requirements for office work with visual display terminals (VDTs)—part 11: Guidance on usability
15. Balata, J., et al.: KoalaPhone: touchscreen mobile phone UI for active seniors. J. Multimodal User Interface **9**, 263–273 (2015)
16. Johnson, J., Finn, K.: Designing User Interfaces for an Aging Population: Towards Universal Design. Morgan Kaufmann, USA (2017)
17. Kalimullah, K., Sushmitha, D.: Influence of design elements in mobile applications on user experience of elderly people. Presented at the Procedia Computer Science (2017)
18. Kitchenham, B.: Procedures for Performing Systematic Reviews. Software Engineering Group Department of Computer Science Keele University and Empirical Software Engineering National ICT Australia Ltd., United Kingdom, vol. 33, pp. 1–26 (2004)
19. Lai, L.-L., Lai, C.-R.: Designing interface for elderly adults: access from the smartphone to the world. In: Lecture Notes in Computer Science (including subseries Lecture Notes in Artificial Intelligence and Lecture Notes in Bioinformatics), vol. 9469, pp. 306–307 (2015)
20. Malik, S.A., Azuddin, M.: Qualitative findings on the use of mobile phones by Malaysian older people. In: International Conference on Advanced Computer Science Applications and Technologies, pp. 435–439 (2013)
21. Riaz, M. et al.: A Systematic Review of Software Maintainability Prediction and Metrics. In: Proceedings of the 2009 3rd International Symposium on Empirical Software Engineering and Measurement, pp. 367–377. IEEE Computer Society, Washington, DC (2009). https://doi.org/10.1109/ESEM.2009.5314233

22. Nicol, E., et al.: Re-imagining commonly used mobile interfaces for older adults. Presented at the MobileHCI 2014—Proceedings of the 16th ACM International Conference on Human–Computer Interaction with Mobile Devices and Services (2014)
23. Paz, F., Pow-Sang, J.A.: Current trends in usability evaluation methods: a systematic review. In: 7th International Conference on Advanced Software Engineering and Its Applications, pp. 11–15 (2014)
24. Petrovcic, A., et al.: Design of mobile phones for older adults: an empirical analysis of design guidelines and checklists for feature phones and smartphones. Int. J. Hum. Comput. Interact. **34**(3), 251–264 (2018)
25. Piper, A.M., et al.: Understanding the challenges and opportunities of smart mobile devices among the oldest old. Int. J. Hum. Comput. Interact. **8**, 83–98 (2016)
26. Punchoojit, L. et al.: Usability studies on mobile user interface design patterns: a systematic literature review. In: Advances in Human-Computer Interaction, New York (2017)
27. Ruzic, L., Sanford, J.A.: Usability of mobile consumer applications for individuals aging with multiple sclerosis. In: Antona, M., Stephanidis, C. (eds.) UAHCI 2017. LNCS, vol. 10277, pp. 258–276. Springer, Cham (2017). https://doi.org/10.1007/978-3-319-58706-6_21
28. Salman, H.M., et al.: Heuristic evaluation of the smartphone applications in supporting elderly. In: Saeed, F., Gazem, N., Mohammed, F., Busalim, A. (eds.) IRICT 2018. AISC, vol. 843, pp. 781–790. Springer, Cham (2019). https://doi.org/10.1007/978-3-319-99007-1_72
29. Salman, H.M., et al.: Usability evaluation of the smartphone user interface in supporting elderly users from experts' perspective. IEEE Access **6**, 22578–22591 (2018)
30. Shackel, B., Richardson, S.J.: Human Factors for Informatics Usability. Cambridge University Press, New York (1991)
31. Slavicek, T., et al.: Designing mobile phone interface for active seniors: user study in Czech Republic. In: 5th IEEE Conference on Cognitive Infocommunications (CogInfoCom), pp. 109–114 (2014)
32. Sookhanaphibarn, K., et al.: Optimum button size and reading character size on mobile user interface for Thai elderly people. In: IEEE 6th Global Conference on Consumer Electronics (GCCE), pp. 1–2 (2017)
33. Urdaibay-Villaseca, P.T.: Usability of Mobile Devices for Elderly People. National University of Ireland, Galway (2010)
34. Van Biljon, J., Renaud, K.: Validating mobile phone design guidelines: focusing on the elderly in a developing country. Presented at the ACM International Conference Proceeding Series (2016)
35. Wong, C.Y., Ibrahim, R., Hamid, T.A., Mansor, E.I.: Usability and design issues of smartphone user interface and mobile apps for older adults. In: Abdullah, N., Wan Adnan, W.A., Foth, M. (eds.) i-USEr 2018. CCIS, vol. 886, pp. 93–104. Springer, Singapore (2018). https://doi.org/10.1007/978-981-13-1628-9_9
36. App stores: number of apps in leading app stores 2018|Statista. https://www.statista.com/statistics/276623/number-of-apps-available-in-leading-app-stores/
37. deloitte-au-tmt-smartphone-generation-gap-011014.pdf. https://www2.deloitte.com/content/dam/Deloitte/au/Documents/technology-media-telecommunications/deloitte-au-tmt-smartphone-generation-gap-011014.pdf
38. Integrating Universal Design (UD) Principles and Mobile Design Guidelines to Improve Design of Mobile Health Applications for Older Adults - IEEE Conference Publication. https://ieeexplore.ieee.org/document/7052509
39. Make apps more accessible|Android Developers. https://developer.android.com/guide/topics/ui/accessibility/apps
40. Systematic Reviews in the Social Sciences: A Practical Guide. https://www.wiley.com/en-us/Systematic+Reviews+in+the+Social+Sciences%3A+A+Practical+Guide-p-9781405121101

41. systematicreviewsguide.pdf. https://www.elsevier.com/__data/promis_misc/525444systematic reviewsguide.pdf
42. Understanding Accessibility on iOS. https://developer.apple.com/library/archive/documentation/UserExperience/Conceptual/iPhoneAccessibility/Accessibility_on_iPhone/Accessibility_on_iPhone.html#//apple_ref/doc/uid/TP40008785-CH100-SW1
43. U.S. mobile app hours by device and age 2016|Statistic. https://www.statista.com/statistics/323522/us-user-mobile-app-engagement-age/
44. WHO|Proposed working definition of an older person in Africa for the MDS Project. http://www.who.int/healthinfo/survey/ageingdefnolder/en/
45. World Population Prospects. https://esa.un.org/unpd/wpp/publications/files/wpp2017_keyfindings.pdf

A New Method of Smartphone Appearance Evaluation Based on Kansei Engineering

Wenjun Hou[1,2], Zhiyang Jiang[1,2(✉)], and Xiaohong Liao[1]

[1] School of Digital Media and Design Art,
Beijing University of Posts and Telecommunications, Beijing, China
janejiang595@gmail.com
[2] Beijing Key Laboratory of Network and Network Culture,
Beijing University of Posts and Telecommunications, Beijing, China

Abstract. As the smartphone market gradually becomes mature, smartphone appearance has become a prime factor in the consumer's decision-making process when purchasing a smartphone. Based on the methodology of Kansei engineering, this paper aims at constructing a Kansei image rating system to evaluate smartphone appearance. Firstly, an initial Kansei image scale was constructed containing 36 word pairs selected from over 700 emotional ideological words from Chinese literature and interview. Secondly, the semantic difference experiment was conducted over 50 subjects to evaluated six smartphones with different appearances using the initial scale. Thirdly, three statistical analyses were applied to the experimental data to further optimize and weight the Kansei image scale, including project analysis, factor analysis, and AMOS structural equation modeling. Finally, we applied the overall weighed Kansei image rating system to evaluate the performance of the six smartphones on four dimensions: exquisiteness, balance, color and reliability. The results show that our weighted Kansei image rating system can be applied to future smartphone appearance evaluation and marketing prediction.

Keywords: Kansei image scale · Smartphone appearance ·
Project analysis · Factor analysis · AMOS structural equation model

1 Introduction

As the modern industrialization matures, consumers are paying more attention to the appearance of products, including home appliances, automobiles, daily necessities, etc. Customers forms their awareness of consumption over their increased experience of purchases, and they are more willing to pay for the products or services that satisfy their aesthetic needs. In addition, consumer demands for products or services have shifted from basic material needs to perceptual needs. Whether products or services bring consumers the sense of pleasure and

A. Marcus and W. Wang (Eds.): HCII 2019, LNCS 11583, pp. 439–449, 2019.
https://doi.org/10.1007/978-3-030-23570-3_32

satisfaction is becoming more and more important. Therefore, it is necessary to study the consumers' perceptual cognition of a product. However, it is difficult for a single human individual to let others understand our senses accurately. Our subjective response to objects can be affected by our past memories, emotions, current environment and state of mind. So for the manufacturers, how to evaluate the response of a new product from the market and from most of the consumers? This paper will conduct a detailed study from this perspective.

Kansei engineering is an approach to derive consumers' affective needs of services and products [1,2,4]. Kansei engineering's ultimate goal is to build up a certain corresponding relationship between a specific product design element and the perceptual reaction of observer, and find the product design which can meet user's different needs the most by studying the influence of different product design elements on human perceptual emotion [5,6]. In a word, as a new research method, the Kansei engineering can do quantitative analysis on the human perceptual emotion [3].

2 Methodology

2.1 Collection and Selection of Kansei Image Word Pairs

Based on Kansei engineering research methods, first we need to describe the consumers' perceptual evaluation on the product appearance systematically, that is to construct a standard set of Kansei Image Scale, which covers as many images when consumers see a product as possible. We collected nearly 100 Chinese literatures related to Kansei engineering to extract the undeleted image vocabulary statistics, as shown in Table 1:

Table 1. Some image vocabulary in chinese literature, translated to English.

elegant—vulgar	concise—complicated
fluent—stiff	light—heavy
trendy—quaint	generous—stingy

In this way, 650 image vocabularies were collected. In order to check its completeness, we chose six smartphones and recruited 15 subjects for interviews, asking them to use adjectives to describe the appearance of smartphone in front of them. Before each interview, the researcher make sure the phone is turned off, wipe the surface of the phone with cotton cloth, and place it on the spinning stand. During the interview, subjects can only observe the phone instead of touching it, and the researcher records the adjectives in the description of a specific product. Based on the results of this interview, we acquired a total of 200 adjectives, in which 150 adjectives overlaps with the previously acquired image vocabularies. As for the remaining 50 words, they also have similar words in the vocabulary, however we still add them at this point. Thus, the image vocabulary has been expanded from 650 to 700.

Second, we sort these Kansei image vocabularies through the card sorting experiment and eight designers from the industrial design areas. There are three principles of the sorting: (1) the selected vocabulary used for describing the product is appropriate; (2) we just keep one word among the words with similar semantic meanings; and (3) the final selected vocabularies should basically contain all possible description of a product. The outcome of this are 36 word pairs, as shown in Table 2. For the convenience of data processing, the words were numbered. We use this as the initial Kansei Image Scale.

Table 2. Initial Kansei Image Scale

w1	rough	exquisite	w19	simple	gorgeous
w2	complicated	simple	w20	dreary	festive
w3	conservative	innovative	w21	easygoing	rigorous
w4	low-end	high-end	w22	business	casual
w5	mild	hard	w23	thick	light
w6	scattered	integrated	w24	bloated	slim
w7	irregular	regular	w25	ugly	beautiful
w8	unbalanced	coordinated	w26	realistic	science fiction
w9	old-fashioned	faddish	w27	trendy	classic
w10	humanities	technology	w28	feminine	masculine
w11	cheesy	elegant	w29	fancy	practical
w12	stingy	generous	w30	cold	lovely
w13	estrangement	affable	w31	calm	excited
w14	childish	mature	w32	difficult	easy
w15	old	young	w33	dim	bright
w16	national	international	w34	squared	rounded
w17	vulnerable	resilient	w35	concrete	abstract
w18	dirty	clean	w36	cheap	expensive

2.2 Smartphone Morphological Analysis and Semantic Difference Experiment

For industrial products, its shape is presented by the appearance of the product image, which is collected from the aspects of visual sense. In order to verify the reliability and validity of perceptual image and vocabulary, we need to choose one product to conduct reverse user test. Therefore, we choose six kinds of models of smartphones for research, as shown in Fig. 1. The reason why we choose smartphones, rather than other kinds of products for research is that the smartphone appearance aesthetic differences is a very large factor in the consumer decision-making process.

Fig. 1. Six smartphones for research

The smartphones to be tested are numbered with phone 1, 2, 3, 4, 5 and 6. The appearance of several smartphones is described by morphological analysis, as shown in Table 3.

Table 3. Morphological analysis on the six smartphones

	Modeling characteristics	Body color	Material
Phone 1	Screen size: 6 in. Thickness: 7.5 mm 2.5D arc glass panel Screen and body rounded together	Gold	Aerospace titanium alloy & leather
Phone 2	Screen size: 6 in. Thickness: 7.9 mm Arc back	Silver	Metal
Phone 3	Screen size: 5 in. Thickness: 8.1 mm All-surrounded back	Black	Plastic
Phone 4	Screen size: 5 in. Thickness: 7.55 mm Dual micro-arc design	White	Magnesium alloy
Phone 5	Screen size: 5.7 in. Thickness: 6.9 mm Hyperbolic side screen	Silver	Metal & glass
Phone 6	Screen size: 4.95 in. Thickness: 7.53 mm	Black	Alloy & high hardness glass

Among them, the body of smartphone 1 has Xiangyun texture (a traditional Chinese texture), and the rest of the phone has no texture pattern. In this study, we recruited 30 subjects to conduct semantic differential experiments. Researchers put the phone in a random order in front of the subject. Touching is prohibited as before, and researchers will help subject when they need to turn smartphones over. The subject is requested to give scores for each word pair (topic) in the Kansei image scale, on the range of $\{-2, -1, 0, 1, 2\}$, on each of the six phones. They should compare all six phones when giving mark on each topic, and it is necessary to give reasons when using negative words. After finish the marking of one topic on all six phones, they move on to the next topic. What should be emphasized is that, before experiment, we use stickers similar in the color of the phone to cover the logos on the surface, in order to avoid the brand effect which influences the experimental subjects and causes derivation in experiment.

2.3 Revise the Scale Using Experimental Data

Project Analysis. The key purpose of project analysis is to test the appropriateness and reliability of the experimental scale or a particular term in the scale. The difference between project analysis and reliability test is that, the purpose of reliability test is to check the reliability degree of the entire scale or concepts containing multiple terms in the scale. The test of project analysis is to explore differences between any two terms of all the subjects, or to test the homogeneity between terms. Project analysis results provide a scientific basis for whether to modify or delete a term in the image scale.

Through the method of project analysis, this experiment examines the reliability of 36 word pairs, and excludes the word pairs with low relevancy. We choose two common project analysis methods to perform this step, namely the critical ratio method and the average Pearson analysis method. The excluded nine word pairs are w5-mild-hard, w22-business-casual, w27-trendy-classic, w28-feminine-masculine, w29-fancy-practical, w33-dim-bright, w34-squared-rounded, w35-concrete-abstract, and w36-cheap-expensive. The Kansei Image Scale remains 27 word pairs.

Factor Analysis. Constructing an ideal Kansei Image Scale can make the product appearance evaluation easier, and can help the evaluation to reach a reasonable conclusion, which has a great reference value in the actual product design iteration process. This step begins with a factor analysis based on the project analysis, transforming factors that affect the aesthetic appearance of the product into a few, and building structural equation models using AMOS.

We conduct a factor analysis on the Kansei word pairs, which are the variables that forms the Kansei Image Scale. The tool for factor analysis is SPSS. First of all, the KMO test and the Bartlett's test of sphericity are performed on the factor analysis data, which are shown in Table 4. The result shows that the KMO value is 0.914. According to the KMO metric, a KMO above 0.90 is considered extremely suitable; 0.80 to 0.90 is considered very suitable; 0.70 to 0.80 are considered suitable; 0.50 to 0.60 are considered less suitable; Less than 0.50 will be considered not suitable. Therefore, the original 27 variables are very suitable for factor analysis. The probability of the significance of the statistic value of x of the Bartlett's test of sphericity in the table was 0.000, less than the significance level of 0.001, thus rejecting the null hypothesis of the Bartlett's test for sphericity, which is considered suitable for factor analysis.

The scree plot of factor analysis visually shows the size changes of 27 eigenvalues, as shown in Fig. 2. Scree plot of factor analysis can also help us determine

Table 4. KMO and Bartlett's test

Kaiser-Meyer-Olkin (KMO) measure of sampling adequacy		.914
Bartlett's test of sphericity	Approx. Chi square	4277.750
	Degree of Freedom	351
	Significance	0.000

the optimal number of factors. The abscissa of the scree plot is represented by the number of factors, while the ordinate is the eigenvalue. The first four eigenvalues are relatively large. From the fifth eigenvalue, the become smaller, and the connected line of the eigenvalues also become steady.

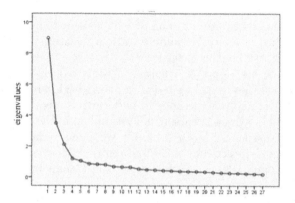

Fig. 2. Scree plot of factor analysis

After the first four factors were extracted, the rotation analysis was performed to reduce the comprehensiveness of the factors. Then, each vocabulary was classified according to the load values on the four factors. The classification results are shown in Table 5. The category represented by factor 1 is exquisiteness, factor 2 is balance, factor 3 is color, and factor 4 is reliability.

Table 5. Classification of the factors

	First-level factor	Second-level factor
Scale	Exquisiteness	w3, w9, w26, w4, w1, w11, w15, w16, w25
	Balance	w7, w32, w2, w8, w6, w13, w18, w24
	Color	w14, w12, w21, w23, w17
	Reliability	w20, w19, w31, w30

Table 6 shows the factorial covariance matrix of the four newly generated factors, which shows that after the rotation, the four factors are still orthogonal.

Table 6. Factor covariance matrix

	1	2	3	4
1	1.000	.000	0.000	.000
2	.000	1.000	0.000	.000
3	0.000	0.000	1.000	0.000
4	.000	.000	0.000	1.000

Scale Revision by AMOS Structural Model. The starting point of the structural equation model is the established quantitative causal relationship between the observable variables according to the assumed causal relationship. At the end point, the relationship between the variables is clarified by the path map with path coefficients. It is assumed that the model is usually established according to the specific background, and each path corresponds to some inter- pretable practical meaning. Therefore, a deep understanding of the practical problems and the correct grasp of the relationship between variables and the constructed variables are the prerequisites for constructing the structural equa- tion model. The path map with path coefficients is essentially a visualization of the linear equations. It clearly presents the relationship between observable vari- ables and latent variables, as well as relationships between each latent variable. It is also a multivariate statistical method whose essence is a generalized general linear equation.

The steps to construct structural equation model are: model identification, model estimation, model evaluation, model modification and model interpreta- tion. Finally, after satisfying all the indicative conditions, the results acquired are as shown in Fig. 3.

From the path map with path coefficients, the correlation between the second- level observable variable and the first-level observable variable, as well as the correlation between the first level observable variable and the overall Kansei Image Rating, can be obtained, as shown in Table 7.

From the path map with path coefficients, we can see that among the first- level variables that directly affect the product's Kansei image, the correlation coefficient of exquisiteness is the highest (1.00), followed by balance (0.41) and reliability (0.36). The correlation coefficient of color is the lowest (0.29).

3 Results

Through the analysis above, we can conclude that there are four dimensions which affects the product's Kansei image: exquisiteness (correlation coefficient 1.00), balance (correlation coefficient 0.41), reliability (correlation coefficient 0.36) and color (correlation coefficient 0.29). In the semantic difference exper- iment, the performance of the six smartphones with different appearances on these four dimensions is evaluated by calculating the score average on each

Table 7. Weighted scale

	First-level latent variables and its path coefficient		Second-level observable variables and its path coefficient	
Overall Kansei image rating	1.00 exquisiteness		1.00	w3-conservative-innovative
			1.31	w9-old-fashioned-faddish
			0.89	w26-realistic-science_fiction
			1.15	w4-low_end-high_end
			0.94	w1-rough-exquisite
			1.26	w11-cheesy-elegant
			1.01	w15-old-young
			0.96	w16-national-international
			1.17	w25-ugly-beautiful
			0.34	w10-humanities-technology
	0.41 balance		1.09	w7-irregular-regular
			0.69	w32-difficult-easy
			1.22	w2-complicated-simple
			1.22	w8-unbalanced-coordinated
			1.33	w6-scattered-integrated
			1.18	w13-estrangement-affable
			1.00	w18-dirty-clean
			0.79	w24-bloated-slim
	0.36 reliability		1.00	w14-childish-mature
			0.89	w12-stingy-generous
			0.69	w21-easygoing-rigorous
			0.42	w23-thick-light
			0.47	w17-vulnerable-resilient
	0.29 color		1.33	w20-dreary-festive
			1.54	w19-simple-gorgeous
			1.03	w31-calm-excited
			1.00	w30-cold-lovely

Kansei image word pairs rated by 50 subjects, multiplied by the corresponding second-level variable path coefficient, and then summed up grouped by four dimensions. The results are as shown in Table 8.

Based on the rating on each dimension for each smartphone, the overall Kansei image rating of 50 subjects on six smartphones are calculated, for example: Overall Kansei Image Rating of Smartphone 1

= Exquisiteness Score (−2.727) * Weight of Exquisiteness (1.00)
+ Balance Score (−0.452) * Weight of Balance (0.41)
+ Reliability Score (2.900) * Weight of Reliability (0.36)
+ Color Score (1.230) * Weight of Color (0.29)
= −1.51222.

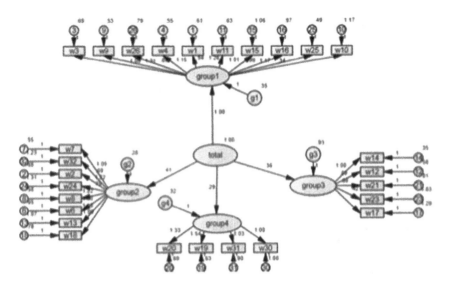

Fig. 3. Model parameters estimation results

Table 8. Weighted ratings on each dimension of 50 subjects

Phones	Exquisiteness	Balance	Reliability	Color
P1	−2.727	−0.452	2.9	1.23
P2	1.575	2.721	3.401	−2.059
P3	5.583	9.644	1.614	−1.759
P4	10.564	3.265	0.508	4.44
P5	−1.271	3.438	−1.907	2.425
P6	1.26	4.564	1.314	−2.104

The overall Kansei image rating of the six smartphones are calculated in Table 9.

Table 9. Weighted overall Kansei image rating

Phones	Overall Kansei image rating
Phone 1	−1.51222
Phone 2	3.317462
Phone 3	9.607388
Phone 4	13.37298
Phone 5	0.155737
Phone 6	2.99374

The range of Kansei image rating is $(-30, 30)$. It can be seen from the table above that smartphone 4 has the highest overall Kansei image rating, for smartphone 4 has obtained relatively high scores in the dimension of exquisiteness and color. Smartphone 3 follows, for its score were high in the dimension of exquisiteness and balance. Smartphone 1 had the lowest overall Kansei image score. Although its score in the reliability dimension was high, but reliability is not the key factor that affects the overall score. Meanwhile, smartphone 1 has a low score in the dimensions of exquisiteness and balance, which is the reason that the overall score is low.

4   The Application of Kansei Image Scale

According to data released by the China Ministry of Industry and Information Technology, the total annual shipments of the Chinese smartphone market reached 492 million in 2017, which was 4% lower than that in 2016. This is the first time that China has seen the total volume of smartphone sales decline. It is expected that competition will be more intense in the next few years.

The saturation of smartphone market forces companies to pay more attention to produce smartphones that are well designed, functional and provide better user experience in order to expand their market.

In this paper, the Kansei Image Scale with path coefficient helps designers or mobile device manufacturers to evaluate the performance of existing products and conceptual products on the perceptual level. Also it can be used for comparison and analysis of competitive products. By assessing the product performance in the four factors which are exquisiteness, balance, reliability and color product, the quality of design can be quantified for future improvement.

Another application of the Kansei Image Scale lies in its relatively accurate prediction. Prediction regards to emotional feedback and market sales. Through the previous semantic difference experiment, we obtained the scores of six smartphones in Kansei Image Rating. Compared with user experience feedback on the e-commerce platform of smartphone, it's found that the two results maintain a high degree of consistency; In addition, we also find that the conclusions drawn from the semantic difference experiment of perceptual images are consistent with the sales of smart phone in 2017. That is to say, the merchants can estimate the market reaction and approximate sales volume of the products that have not been put on the market.

5   Discussion

There are some research points for further discussion as follows:

1. As for the initial scale model, whether the application scope of the initial Kansei Image Scale can be extended to the appearance evaluation of other industrial products? In this paper, the word pairs of initial Kansei image were selected from more than 700 words that covered the field of female cell

phone modeling, iPhone modeling, Nokia cell phone modeling, display modeling, car interiors, car front, tablet, PC modeling, exercise bike, toys, Chinese furniture, microwave ovens, student apartments, ceramic products, web pages, commercial vehicles, clothing, shoes, car seats, door handles, sewing machines. The research and verification only applied to appearance design of smart phones. The results show that the reliability and validity of the scale are good. Therefore, it deserves to be discussed if the scale can play a role in product positioning and prediction of user feedback and market sales volume of other industry products

2. As for improved scale model, the adaptability index of the fitted model can be further optimized and the model can be further adjusted. Currently, there are noticeable difference in the number of the second-level variables corresponding to the four first-level variables.

References

1. Dahlgaard, J.J., Schütte, S., Ayas, E., Mi Dahlgaard-Park, S.: Kansei/affective engineering design: a methodology for profound affection and attractive quality creation. TQM J. **20**(4), 299–311 (2008)
2. Jindo, T.: A study of Kansei engineering on steering wheel of passenger cars. In: Japan-USA Symposium on Flexible Automation, pp. 545–548 (1994)
3. Jindo, T., Hirasago, K.: Application studies to car interior of kansei engineering. Int. J. Ind. Ergon. **19**(2), 105–114 (1997)
4. Nagamachi, M.: Kansei engineering: a new ergonomic consumer-oriented technology for product development. Int. J. Ind. Ergon. **15**(1), 3–11 (1995)
5. Poirson, E., Petiot, J.F., Aliouat, E., Boivin, L., Blumenthal, D.: Interactive user tests to enhance innovation. In: International Conference on Kansei Engineering and Emotion Research, pp. 2021–2030 (2010)
6. Schütte, S.T., Eklund, J., Axelsson, J.R., Nagamachi, M.: Concepts, methods and tools in Kansei engineering. Theor. Issues Ergon. Sci. **5**(3), 214–231 (2004)

User Experience Classification Based on Emotional Satisfaction Mechanism

Jingpeng Jia[(⊠)] and Xueyan Dong

Beijing Union University, Beijing, China
tjtjingpeng@buu.edu.cn

Abstract. The invention of iPhone was a breakthrough in the mobile phone market, since then the values of user experience began to be widely realized. However, the basic theoretical construction of user experience is still incomprehensive. This has been a constraint on the effective implementation of UX studies and design practice for a long time. Clear classification of user experience is one of the theoretical problems to be solved. This study analyzes the emotional satisfaction mechanism reflected in various cases of purchase to define six experience categories which are utility experience, usability experience, aesthetic experience, novel experience, fashion experience, symbol experience. Their relationships and influence are also discussed. Each of these concepts specifies a range of practice for researchers while ensuring its independence. As a result, a systematic user experience classification system is established, which can assist UX investigators specifying their practice objects to effectively conduct their user study.

Keywords: Emotional satisfaction mechanism · User experience · Experience economy · Experience classification

1 Introduction

In 2008 the advent of the iPhone refreshed the definition of mobile phones, more importantly it enlightened business practitioners around the world to re-understand the concept of user experience. According to the demands of user experience research and design in business practice, ISO 9241-210 standard defines User eXperience (UX) as "customers' impression and response to the use or expectations on the product" [2] that is, whether the product is simple to use and how it feels like while being used. From the definition, it is not hard to find that UX is more about subjective feelings customers have when using the product. The advent of first iPhone has passed ten years, now we have entered the era of experience economy [3]. The salient feature nowadays is that the pursuit of perceptual stimulation and pleasure, it means that the need of extreme experience has increasingly become the essence of consumption [4–6]. Observing the concept of user experience against the background of the entire history of human consumption, we can easily see that it is just recent decades that the concept is established and becomes popular. However, the facts of experience have existed for a long time. Since the birth of the first product in the world, this subjective feeling from

© Springer Nature Switzerland AG 2019
A. Marcus and W. Wang (Eds.): HCII 2019, LNCS 11583, pp. 450–459, 2019.
https://doi.org/10.1007/978-3-030-23570-3_33

the use of the product is already made no matter whether the issues on user experience can be clearly recognized.

For a long time, due to limitations in the productivity and industrial technology, products our society supplied have not yet been able to fully meet the customers' needs for basic functions and aesthetics. For the fact, the society environment at that time is not helpful to understand the concept of user experience. It is noteworthy that by the 1990s, the productivity level had risen significantly compared to the early days of the Industrial Revolution [7]. In this context, Donald Norman introduced and promoted the concept of UX in the mid-1990s [8]. In addition, Allan Cooper discussed the issues such as goal-orientation and user's mental model at a similar time [9]. In essence, their work makes great contributions in the study of user experience. However, they fail to make the concept of UX popular.

There are two possible reasons. First of all, customers lack of adequate understanding of the experience values in the consumer market. In the second place, UX researchers, like Norman and Cooper, may have no personal experience in making a product which offers high-quality experience as the Apple Inc. did. But with either the continuous improvement of the overall productivity and purchasing ability all over the world or the contribution of Norman and Cooper on UX study, they are pushing the global consumer market to a threshold of opening an era of experience economy. Apparently, the Apple Inc led by Steve Jobs was aware of these changes in the consumer market in a sensitive and timely manner, so they can constantly invent popular electronic products with obsessive experience to gain advantageous in the competitive market. Due to the global influence of Apple brand and its product, their innovative products greatly catalyze the further cognition and demand of experience values in the market. The formal start of experience times can be attributed to the creation of iPhone in 2008. Compared to previous mobile phones, iPhone offers novelty and extreme experience for customers [10]. Therefore, the values of experience have been greatly realized by customers. It is the smart iPhone which started the Pandora box of making customers, and it explicit the needs on product experience. From then on, more and more companies and customers put their focuses on the values of experience. To date, user experience was first appeared and developed in the electronic industry and internet technology companies, but now it can be found in various industries, such as cars, home electronics and traditional food-making industries and a number of service companies. Many companies even believe that offering products with high quality of experience is a strategy to be competitive.

2   Problem

User experience has received large supports from many business, however, until now it is quite difficult to generate a product offering extreme experience. There are two possible reasons.

Firstly, from the perspective of industry performance, new values are indeed provided to the market with the help of big data and various existing methods on user experience. However, there are two problems in these methods. One is that compared to the overall research and study, those can indeed suit users' needs are less than 5%.

Recall the past few years, a large number of concepts gaining popularity in the market jump into the consumers' sight, but soon most of them fade away because they do not fit the actual needs of users. The other thing is that after Steven Jobs passed, it is hardly to find any company or individual that can create products like iPhone providing such unbelievable experience.

Secondly, in terms of practice of user study and design, many professional and large entrepreneurs set to work seems using the systematic processes in a logic manner. In fact, almost all steps in the process require insight, inspiration and intuition or nature factors to get involved. This makes uncertainty as a property for user experience. It also makes the project failed on the half way so that the designed products iterate with a low efficiency in two ways: one is to revise the design scheme according to the feedback from customers or their expectation. The other case is if customers dislike the product, the company has to try another insight, inspiration and intuition to test their luck. It is approved that these two practices fail to be helpful on establishing high quality of user experience.

In the background, since 2016, some employees and researchers began to reconsider the problems in the popularity of user experience. While business put more emphasize on the value of experience, they lack of basic and deep studies on user experience. This makes the logical refection less possible for those who work in the field of user experience have problems to solve. Thus, they have to put their expectation of being successful into the product iterations, which may never end. In order to improve the efficiency of user experience in practical design, it is an urgent need for researchers to establish a professional and systematic theory that can effectively guide the practice for the purpose. As one study requires defining the objectives in the first place, it is also true in user experience study. Its goal is to establish a concept to cover all experience types. More specifically, a comprehensive classification of use experience is required. However, to date, either in the experience industry or among scholars, there has been no definite consensus on such a classification. This prevents practitioners from looking at the full elements of experience to examine the experience values of a product and the long-term strategy in designing a product.

3   Related Work

Existing concepts on user experience classification come from the source of history reasons. Usability test was firstly introduced to electronic products design through understanding and thinking of the technology-centered [9]. Enjoyment experience firstly appeared in the methodology of design thinking proposed by the department of design at Stanford University [11]. Aesthetic experience and brand experience were originated from the traditional marketing. In terms of guiding experience study and practice, the concepts discussed above have two problems: (1) Current definition of experience are not independent with each other, in other words, they have somehow overlap. This leads to ambiguous borders. It also brings difficulty in exploring the relations among the various types of experience. (2) There is insufficient evidence to approve the existing concept can cover all experience types. To date, in the field of experience either in industry or scholar, there is few study which can give an overall concept to deal with the problems. This paper attempts to bridge the gap.

4 Method

How to better define and understand various types of user experience? First, the idea of classifying user experience is originally inspired by the development of philosophy aesthetic theory. Since the times of Plato, through a large amount of discussion on the essence of aesthetic, researchers finally reach a consensus in aesthetic, it is subjective feelings so that we can analyze the psychology feelings to explore activities related to aesthetic [12]. Accordingly, a conclusion can be easily set up in which beauty can be defined by analyzing the emotional satisfaction logic in aesthetic activities, that is to analyze the psychological activities. Based on such a result, the differences from other subjective feelings can be found. The explanation of aesthetic activities from Philosophy aesthetic reflects human's mental modes and recognition abilities to define emotional experience classes, which can be achieved by analyzing various emotional satisfying logics in customers' psychological activities to define and classify the corresponding experiences.

Second, the process of exploring user needs is that customers should have needs to solve a specific problem. Then the company would make products to meet the needs. When a customer has a purchase, they begin to form experience. User needs and user experience can be regarded as two sides of a coin, each type of experience corresponds to its need. Therefore, to classify various user experiences, the type of needs is supposed to be analyzed first.

Considering the two reasons above, this study uses the observation method and the psychology analysis to differentiate the consumption needs, and analyzes the logic of purchase activity and features. Based on these, we explore the underlying emotional mechanism to classify user experience. By doing this, a user classification system is set up for providing an instruction on user experience study and design practice.

5 User Experience Classification

In this section, we explain the emotional satisfaction mechanism implied in the behavior of buying products and define six different types of experience each subsection.

5.1 Utility Experience

A truth is that except for crafts for appreciation and collection, any product can be sold, unless it has to have some usage. This is the premise to be a product taken into the market. Due to the drive of physical and psychological motives, customers have basic needs for some products primarily because of the fact the products they purchase can solve their practical problems. Such as drink mineral water for thirsty, observe text and video through online website for obtaining knowledge, use a hand nail gun to make a hole on the wall. Corresponding to the experience, it is certain that people would have subjective feeling while they use the product. Jakob Nielsen defined such a value of product as Utility [13], this definition is widely accepted in the worldwide. Thus, it is feasible to define the subjective feeling of customers on practical usage of products as utility experience.

The emotional satisfaction mechanism behind the utility experience is represented two aspects. First, if customers buy products for their practical use and the product can effectively help address the problems, they would recognize the value of product. That means they have a great experience, otherwise their experience is not good. Second, the quality of utility experience is related to the expectation that users have. Such an expectation can be divided into two elements: quality and quantity. Quality refers to expectation on effectiveness of functions. For instance, people tend to have high expectation on the car accelerator. If the practical product outweighs their expectation, they are more likely to have good experience. Quantity means the number of functions that product offers. That is the expectation on the number of functions. If a watch can provide not only the usage of showing time, but also the use of compass, this would also bring enjoyable experience. So far, the emotional satisfaction mechanism above discussed have pointed out the content of utility experience and the boundary as utility experience.

5.2   Usability Experience

In the early days of computers as major interactive products, the products in the market offered new and practical functions to attract customers, however, compared to the earlier ages, the operations become more complicated. Actually, this happens a lot in many products. Some interactive products on the one hand provide powerful functions. On the other hand, the complex of operating steps brings the difficulty in using them for customers. Alan Cooper explained the problem as the difference between operational mode and psychological mode [9]. This makes designers to think about how to simplify the operations so that they can better suit the habitat of users. From then on, usability experience comes to the horizontal line. Up to now, usability experience has been the key to conduct user study in the IT industry, which devotes to develop applications and interactive hardware. In addition, apart from the promotion of usability experience by many consultant companies and academic institutions, the consumption market put more emphasis on usability. Overall, more and more car and family electrical factories began to take the improvement of usability values as their competitive strategy.

The emotional satisfaction mechanism underlying usability experience is brief and obvious. If products bring the convenience and effectiveness for customers to use, users would say they have great experience. This is the base to differentiate usability from other types of experience. Another thing to notice is that the products that primarily aims to improve usability experience can also bring users with other explicit or latent experience. For instance, most of automobile car producers can make shock absorber have sufficient support so that it can deal with side tilt caused by centrifugal pull when car is making a turn. However, due to the improvement of the technological level and the increasing competition in the market, especially the producers of high-end auto-motive products, it is common for shock absorbers to provide enough support force and also an appropriate damping process between the release supportive forces and limit of supportive movements. This allows the driver to feel the support of the shock is not stiff, rough and simple, but soft, delicate, textured, rhythmic and connotation. Apparently, the later experience is not just usability experience any more. By analyzing the satisfaction emotions, such experience can be formed based on usability experience but rely on aesthetic and innovation experience. Even for some customers they also offer symbol and taste experience according to their life environment, knowledge background and incentive.

5.3   Aesthetic Experience

Everyone likes himself or herself to be beautiful. It is human's nature that everyone has the aesthetic need, which corresponds to the aesthetic value in consumption market. Although most of us realize its existence, it is ambiguous that how to recognize and define such aesthetic experience because it depends on the psychosocial activity and is quite complicated. The theory on philosophy aesthetic can give an answer. Baumgarten explained that aesthetic is the components of sensitivity activities, meaning when people use the product, they can be satisfied through the sense channel, such as visual and hearing. He disclosed the essence of aesthetic and the key to aesthetic experience is emotional satisfaction theory [14]. Take a further look, the aesthetic sense is the emotion and spiritual enjoyment on color, appearance and sound. It means that the source of aesthetic not only comes from visibility but hearing, smelling, tasting and touch. In terms of aesthetic experience, costumers can be satisfied from the perceptual recognition on the harmony of modeling, sound and quality, brand and service.

Wang [15] believed that aesthetic experience relies on the emotional satisfaction mechanism by giving three features in aesthetic activities. (1) Beyond-success: It means the aesthetic activities do not have to consider the material success. Here material success related activities refer to nature activity and practical work, as well as psychological and social activities referring to success, greedy, and benefit. (2) Subjective: It means that human beings have self-subjective, abled, free, and intentioned features. These features are subject to natures, ethics, social orders, laws and material conditions. However, aesthetic activities are less subject to restricted rules so that human's nature and subjective can be presented and can represents freedom. (3) Sensitivity: It is contrast to rationality and logic. It more emphasizes on the nature states, such as sense-physical needs, emotions and personalities related. Aesthetic activities tend to have such requirements.

5.4   Novel Experience

Except for usability and aesthetic experience, people expect the product can meet novel needs. In other words, customers hope new products can perform distinctly from old ones by showing new and impressive features. This requires four points to support: (1) Pursuit of innovation, one of the basic incentives. As Peter pointed out any products that brings experience never change would not be enjoyable [16]; (2) The space-time expansion lays the foundation for developing and updating products; (3) Recently, the productivity promotion provides material support on the release and satisfaction of novel needs. (4) Before the 18th century, the novel concept has not been spread. On the modern times, the consumption culture leads the values for most consumers. Different from the traditional Endian culture, it more emphasis on world-in values and encourages people to release our desires and make us believe that obtaining material needs at maximum and reaching self-achievement is the path to success and happiness. Thus, it provides support on culture environment for novelty experience. Under such an environment, to date, novelty can defend itself and prove itself effectiveness and it doesn't have to be confirmed by other concepts. Las believed modern began to be equal to novelty. Customers began to form recognition on liking-novelty [17].

It is obvious that customer can have novelty experience because their emotions can be satisfied. This is to say that if product can offer new design functions or elements, customers would have novelty incentive from sense or recognition, this is called novelty experience. The degree of such an experience tends to have a positive relationship to the amount of difference compared to the old. The emotional satisfaction discussed here can be used to differentiate novelty experience from other experiences. However, it is insufficient for UX researchers on to just know novelty experience, they still need to study its relationship to classic experience meaning the necessary and key values as a product, like functional values and basic appearance structures. It is easy to understand that innovative products are supposed to inherit the classic values and also provide novelty. Only by doing this, we can say novelty experience is great.

In regards to its relations with other experiences, there are two main points: (1) the novelty incentive must rely on the usability, aesthetic and symbol experience. (2) Novelty experience is the necessary carrier for fashion experience. But for symbol and taste experience, novelty is not necessary.

5.5   Fashion Experience

The fashion need is the explicit desire of customers in modern society. Customers want to pursuit how much fashion and the ways they want to show their fashion are distinct from people. In contrast with usability and aesthetic values, needs on fashion is not our human nature, it is the outcome of history and psychological incentive, such as envy, and self-realize. In the late of mid-century, self-recognition began to be awake and human are beginning to pursuit enjoyment, this makes the nobility put much attention on personality of appearance. In social recognition, new concepts on abstraction between males and females are also formed, this enables the appearance become the power of lure. Therefore, People began to pursuit fashion in innovation and differences. Analyzing nowadays fashion, we can easily find its essence lie in the establishment of new products. This brings new concepts that focus on these products. Then, the rate of increase is very fast so that this generation products are over-fitted and the meaning also becomes plain. Then, a new product is shot and the corresponding ideas are given. This whole process was done repeatedly. The key in fashion experience is not satisfying existing needs but creating new needs.

According to the fashion mechanism discussed above, the emotional satisfaction based on fashion experience can be meet based on two pre-conditions. First, users can own products that express new meaning and new concepts. These can be presented by new functions and new styles. Here new is contrast to existing meaning and statement, it means that such innovation can be classic. Second, the new concepts have to be accepted and promoted by the customers. When the two conditions are met, customers can obtain fashion experience meaning their vanity from two aspects: 1. Other people compliment and confirm the products. 2. Owners believe their fashion identity and taste can be confirmed for peers.

From the aspect of relationship with other experience, novel experience is the basis for fashion experience, but they are not equal. Fashion experience requires wide acceptance and promotions. It is distinct from novel experience. Second, fashion can be regarded as a form of taste experience and symbol experience.

5.6 Symbol Experience

Since human in nature tend to have some degree of their vanity and are easily influenced by the modern culture, symbolic consumption becomes an important purchase reason. This concept is inspired by symbolic study. Here symbol refers to that the product can represent a thing that outside itself. For instance, Product A is not only itself but also means another object B. When people mention A, they can know its underlying meaning, B. In a typical scenario of symbol experience, the company stimulates customers with a perceptible thing to enable them know its meaning even when the thing appears or disappears [18]. In this case, when customers decide to purchase a BMW car, they are definitely not only for driving, but more emphasis on the products' underlying meaning, such as luxury and taste. Objectively, there is a relationship between the values that the product reflects and consumers when the purchase behavior happens. Furthermore, products can be regarded as a symbol primarily because Poled found that there is object system existing. Take Mercedes car for example, C model has 180-type and 200-type, E level provide 200-type and 260 types, S level has 300-type and 600-type, such a level former an entire object system. In the system, in contrast with other cars, each type can express the owner's values, like economy status and personality. Every product can have what symbols is decided by its social culture. Thus, Social field determines what the product means.

According to the consumption analysis above, symbol experience relying on the emotional satisfaction logic include two aspects. First, products that customers have can show symbolic value, such as, luxury and elegant. These symbolic meaning can represent customers' social status. Second, the values of these symbols should be accepted widely. These two aspects can offer symbol experience in two various ways. (1) Group identity that product symbol represent can be confirmed (2) Social identity can be established due to symbol experience.

In terms of relationship to other experience, symbol of products is often presented as difference. It has to rely on usability, novelty and aesthetic values. Take a further look, symbol experience can be meaningful only when other experience can be satisfied. When customers' only focus on symbol experience, they would think the fulfillment of other experiences is a must. No doubt a product has a quality problem, symbol experience would not be great.

6   Discussion

This research defines six categories of user experience according to the satisfaction logic reflected in the purchase. According to the definition of aesthetic experience by philosophy aesthetic, we analyze the customers' emotional satisfaction mechanism at the psychological level and divide user experience into six categories. Such a classification method provides an approach to understanding the subjective experience but it really relies on users' previous recognition and background. In contrast with existing experience definition, our classification method is more comprehensive as it aims to list out all possible experiences. There are two main contributions to the UX study. (1) A clear and practical method of user experience classification is introduced. UX researchers can either directly apply our method to their studies so as to better understand users' real needs. (2) A practical way on how to apply each experience type is presented and we also ensure each type is independent with others. This can assist employers in the work of designing best-celling products that can satisfy one or more types of experience. We admit there are limitations in our approach as it is difficult to find out all possible experience. Actually, our work is an ongoing research so our classification may be more comprehensive in the future. Understanding the experience type is the first step, it is more important to make it feasible in real applications. We suggest researchers to have great observation ability and critical thinking to reach the goal.

7   Conclusion

As the times of experience economy has arrived, more companies begin to conduct studies on user experience and try to expand the market. However, until now there is lack of studies on basic theoretic problems. A definite use experience classification is one of problems to be addressed. This problem hinders the study and design of user experience. To address it, this paper gives six types of user experience and their relationships are also illustrated through analyzing the customers' emotional satisfaction logic during the purchase. In theoretic contribution, our research initially establishes a system of user experience classification. In practical contribution, it can provide practical goals for UX studies and design. It can particularly help employers in UX field fully understand all elements of experience and their relationships so that they can rethink the effectiveness of the designed product. In the future, more detailed observation and analysis will be conducted to rich our classification method.

Funding. The publication of this research is supported by the funding project, Premium Funding Project for Academic Human Resources Development in Beijing Union University (No. 12210611609-039).

References

1. International Organization for Standardization: Ergonomics of human system interaction - Part 210: Human-centered design for interactive systems (formerly known as 13407). ISO F±DIS 9241-210 (2009)
2. Norman, D., Miller, J., Henderson, A.: What you see, some of what's in the future, and how we go about doing it. In: Proceedings of CHI (1995)
3. Gothelf, J., Seiden, J.: Lean UX. O'Reilly Media, Sebastopol (2016)
4. Postman, N.: Amusing Ourselves to Death: Public Discourse in the Age of Show Business. Penguin Books, London (2005)
5. Huxley, A.: Brave New World. Harper Perennial, New York (2006)
6. Dawkins, R.: The Selfish Gene. OUP Oxford, Oxford (2016)
7. Backhouse, R.E., Tribe, K.: The History of Economics: A Course for Students and Teachers. Agenda, Newcastle upon Tyne (2017)
8. Norman, D.: Emotional Design: Why We Love (or Hate) Everyday Things. Basic Books, New York (2005)
9. Cooper, A.: About Face 2.0: The Essentials of Interaction Design. Wiley, Hoboken (2003)
10. von Borries, F., Klincke, H.: Apple Design. Hatje Cantz, Berlin (2011)
11. Dorst, K.: The core of 'design thinking' and its application. Des. Stud. **32**(6), 521–532 (2011)
12. Kant, I.: Critique of Judgment. Hackett, London (1987)
13. Nielsen, J.: Usefulness, Utility, Usability: Why They Matter. Video, 20 February 2012. https://www.nngroup.com/videos/usefulness-utility-usability. Accessed 10 Sept 2017
14. Adorno, T.W.: Aesthetics. Polity, London (2017)
15. Wang, X.: The Principle of Aesthetics. China East Press (2012)
16. Gordon, P.: Savour: Salads for All Seasons. Jacqui Small, London (2016)
17. Svendsen, L.: Fashion: A Philosophy. Reaktion Books, Islington (2006)
18. Klenk, V.: Understanding Symbolic Logic. Pearson, London (2007)

The Role of Gamer Identity
on Digital Gaming Outcomes

Linda K. Kaye[✉]

Department of Psychology, Edge Hill University, St Helens Road,
Ormskirk L39 4QP, UK
Linda.kaye@edgehill.ac.uk

Abstract. Social identity theory (SIT) has been widely applied to many contexts as a way of understanding group identity and the associated impacts. However, less research has explored the relevance of SIT to digital gaming. This paper outlines recent studies which have sought to establish a number of psychosocial outcomes associated with gaming identity across a number of gaming domains. Large-scale cross-sectional survey research in this area with varying gamer groups has generally found that positive identity to gaming groups is associated with positive aspects of well-being, such as lower loneliness and enhanced self-esteem and general well-being. Taken together, gamer identity appears to be a positive factor, which can go some way to support players on a psychological level.

Keywords: Social identity theory · Gamer identity · Self-esteem · Loneliness · Well-being

1 Introduction

Digital gaming can be a highly social pursuit, in which players can meet, interact and play with other players (Domahidi et al. 2014; Kowert et al. 2014; Yee 2006). In addition to this, gaming may foster social experiences which are peripheral to gaming itself yet also seem to be very important to players. These social experiences may occur via gaming forums, gaming conventions, and online community pages. As such, these "indirect" social experiences are not necessarily related to gameplay itself but are established through the fact that gaming may be a common activity for a given group of people. In this case, there is something psychological which draws an affiliation between these individuals whereby they experience a collective sense of belonging. This phenomenon can be explained through a well-known framework within the psychological literature, known as Social Identity Theory (SIT).

SIT posits that one's sense of self is determined by an affiliation to a given social group (Tajfel 1978, 1979; Tajfel and Turner 1979), whereby one's "personal self" is merged with the "collective self", by which the strength of affiliation to a social group (i.e. the social identity) has a key influence on one's own personal self-regard (Abrams and Hogg 1988; Ellemers et al. 2003). Three inter-related processes underpin social identity theory (Tajfel 1978):

© Springer Nature Switzerland AG 2019
A. Marcus and W. Wang (Eds.): HCII 2019, LNCS 11583, pp. 460–465, 2019.
https://doi.org/10.1007/978-3-030-23570-3_34

- Social categorisation in which individuals see themselves and others as categories rather than as individuals
- Social identification in which individuals' identity is formulated by their experiences within a social group or situation
- Social comparison in which individuals assess the worth of groups through comparing their relative features

In respect of social comparison, a distinction between "in-groups" and "out-groups" is made, in which solidarity within in-groups is said to promote a sense of self-esteem through such affiliation (Abrams and Hogg 1988).

The core literature on SIT has largely established that social identity fosters a number of positive psychological outcomes. Specifically, previous research across a wide range of contexts, has found that one's strength of social identity is related positively to aspects of psychological well-being, such as enhanced self-esteem (Crocker et al. 1994; Haslam et al. 2009). For example, a positive social identity has been found to foster feelings of belongingness and self-worth (Branscombe and Wann 1991). Until recently, it had not been well established, the extent to which social identity to gaming domains may be relevant to also understand positive psychosocial functioning. However, recent studies have revealed that these outcomes may indeed be relevant (Kaye 2014; Kaye et al. 2017a; Kaye et al. 2017b; Kowert 2015). For example, gamer identity has been found to promote higher levels of social and psychological investment within gaming communities which can foster a sense of belongingness and self-esteem (Kowert 2015). Of course, this area of research should consider the fact that gamer identity may be multi-faceted (Grooten and Kowert 2015), and as such, should be referenced in respect of specific gaming domains or communities rather than to gaming per se. As such, the following sections highlight how identity to specific gaming domains has been explored to understand its role for a range of key psychosocial outcomes.

2 Social Identity in Gaming Domains

Football Manager (Sports Interactive) is a football management simulation game in which players have control of a football club to make decisions and consider tactics. This franchise also provides social experiences in which players compete in online leagues, or can engage in network play with other players. This game format is somewhat distinct from other sports games as it does not proffer many opportunities for direct competitive gameplay such as those derived from games such as FIFA (EA Sports), but instead may foster more "indirect" social experiences which occur outside of gameplay (e.g., social cohesion, conversations relating to the game). As such, the SIT framework is well suited to help underpin the way in which players of this game may establish a collective sense of "togetherness" through their affiliations to this game franchise.

Research by Kaye (2014) pioneered the work to establish the relevance of SIT to specific gaming domains, in which Football Manager was utilised as a starting point. Indeed, through a series of semi-structured interviews with Football Manager players (three male and one female, all between the ages of 19 and 26), it became apparent that the process of social comparison was a particularly key facet of social identity which was relevant. That is, participants made a clear distinction between those who were also Football Manager players (in-group) and those who were not (out-group). For example, they described that non-players did not appear to appreciate or acknowledge the importance of the game. By contrast, the knowledge that there were others who shared the in-group mentality and had a collective understanding of the meanings derived through Football Manager experiences, allowed participants to recognise their in-group affiliation. To follow this up, further research has established that strength of identity to Football Manager is positively related to overall perceptions of one's psychological well-being (Kaye et al. 2017a) suggesting that the collective identity surrounding this domain presents a positive factor to support psychosocial functioning.

However, what it important to further establish is the extent to which identity to specific gaming domains may vary as a product of the context of gaming associates. That is, whether other players who are recognised as sharing a collective identity are those who are "real world" friends or "online-only" friends. To empirically test this assertion, research aimed to establish whether there were differential outcomes for well-being between sub-groups of players of the game FIFA who varied between either playing with their "real world" friends via co-located multi-screen play, or those who played online with random other players (Kaye et al. 2017a). This found that when identity to FIFA was framed in reference to "real world" FIFA friends, this was positively related to deeper and more supportive relationships with these players compared to those who identified more with online-only players. However, irrespective of the context of identity, FIFA identity in general was positively related to players' self-esteem (Kaye et al. 2017a). This echoes the findings of other research exploring types of gamer identity on psychosocial well-being (Kaye et al. 2017b). Namely, for Massive Multiplayer Online (MMO) games, the strength of this identity for these players has been found to be positively related to their self-esteem, as well as favourably to the perceptions of their social competence and loneliness (Kaye et al. 2017b). Further to this, it appears that various levels of involvement in MMOs (e.g., contributing to MMO forums, interacting with other players outside gameplay) and the various social resources these experiences afford, are also related positively to players' sense of collective identity in this domain (ibid). Taken together, it suggests that gamer identity is not just something related to gaming engagement itself, but instead may manifest through these experiences but have more wide-spread and enduring impacts on one's psychosocial well-being even outside the game environment.

This suggests that aspects of gamer identity, in the main part, is experienced as a positive aspect of self-regard, which is reassuring given the usual negative stereotypes which are attributed to gamers as being socially inept, low in social status and isolated (Kowert et al. 2012; Kowert and Oldmeadow 2012). As such, it appears that even if these stereotypes still prevail in the 21st Century, they do not appear to be self-fulfilling or impact on self-regard for players themselves. The same also seems to apply for players who are female, in which under stereotype threat, they do not appear to be impacted detrimentally on either their self-perceptions or performance outcomes relating to gaming (Kaye and Pennington 2016; Kaye et al. 2018; Pennington et al. 2018). As such, it appears that aspects of gamer identity may be a protective factor and therefore may function as a mechanism to maintain positive self-regard.

3 Thinking Forwards

In reference to the aforementioned literature, some ongoing questions remain unanswered which would benefit from further empirical exploration. That is, the first refers to the causation of how gamer identity functions for well-being. That is, the majority of work in this area (including work previously cited), is based on cross-sectional survey methodology, in which it is not clear whether the psychosocial variables reported are actually influenced by gamer identity, or whether there is simply an association which is not causal. Addressing this issue would lend further weight to any endeavours designed to promote gamer identity.

A second issue which would benefit from further exploration is that of how gamer identity may develop in the first place. Considering the three inter-related processes of social categorisation, social identification and social comparison, pragmatically it would be useful to know how these actually are fostered in respect of gaming experiences. Some research has established that the most prominent feature of gamer identity construction is through people's perception of how their gaming behaviours correspond to those stereotypically understood to constitute gaming (De Grove et al. 2015). Further, friendship networks serve as additional contexts to promote gamer identity (ibid). Clearly there is fluidity of identity across contexts and so it does not seem sufficient to suggest that gamer identity manifests itself solely through gameplay. This leads on to a further query about the conditions under which gamer identity is more salient over others. That is, are there "optimal" conditions whereby gamer identity is more pronounced and therefore more impactful than others? This would be an intriguing question to follow up, specifically to recognise how domain-specific identity may be.

Finally, another intriguing area of research to follow up is to explore how gamer identity may interact with other aspects of one's identity, particularly that of gender (Shaw 2012). That is, despite gaming being an activity enjoyed by both men and women (ESA 2015), there is still the assumption of masculinity to the gaming domain (Salter and Blodgett 2012), in which "female gamer" is often needed as an additional descriptor to characterise those who happen both to be female and play games. Based on this, one may propose that gamer and gender may overlap more closely and coherently for those who identify as male rather than female. From an identity fusion perspective, this may be more easily fostered for male gamers rather than female ones. As such, an interesting question is the extent to which women who identify as gamers may be dealing with a potential conflict of competing identities (gamer vs female) rather than men who may be more likely to experience an equilibrium between facets of their identity (gamer = male). See Fig. 1 for illustration of the proposed difference. Research has started to establish the processes through which female players may express their gamer identity (Vermeulen et al. 2017). That is, it suggests that cognitive evaluation of gender categorisation, and feeling closely connected to other women do not relate to gamer identity, yet collective appraisal of womanhood does (Vermeulen et al. 2017). This is interesting and serves a basis for further exploration, particularly in how this may operate for gamer identity in respect of different gaming domains. Exploring the interaction of gender and gamer identity, and comparing this for males and females, is therefore a pertinent issue for further research to more fully establish its psychological and social impacts for different players.

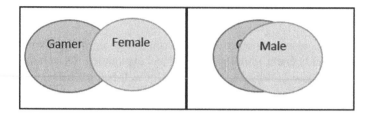

Fig. 1. Illustrative example of the distinctions in how gender and gamer identity may interact/overlap for female versus male gamers

4   Conclusion

This paper has outlined the literature indicating that role of gamer identity on a range of positive psychosocial outcomes, including self-esteem, loneliness and general well-being. Taken together, there appears to be a developing literature base to suggest collective identity to gaming domains serves a positive and in many ways, a protective factor for players in maintaining self-regard. However, there is much still to explore, and this paper has identified a number of key directions which would be of interest to both academic and practitioner audiences. Certainly, there is sufficient evidence to suggest that a psychological enquiry into player affiliation is important to better understand player experiences and outcomes, and thus it is hoped that this helps informs game development and communities.

References

Abrams, D., Hogg, M.A.: Comments on the motivational status of self-esteem in social identity and inter-group discrimination. Eur. J. Soc. Psychol. **18**, 317–334 (1988)

Branscombe, N.R., Wann, D.L.: The positive social and self concept consequences of sports team identification. J. Sport Soc. Issues **15**(2), 115–127 (1991)

Crocker, J., Luhtanen, R., Blaine, B., Broadnax, S.: Collective self-esteem and psychological well-being among White, Black and Asian college students. Pers. Soc. Psychol. Bull. **20**(5), 503–513 (1994). https://doi.org/10.1177/0146167294205007

De Grove, F., Courtois, C., Van Looy, J.: How to be a gamer: exploring personal and social indicators of gamer identity. J. Comput. Mediated Commun. **20**(3), 346–361 (2015)

Domahidi, E., Festl, R., Quandt, T.: To dwell among gamers: Investigating the relationship between social online game use and gaming-related friendships. Comput. Hum. Behav. **35**, 107–115 (2014). https://doi.org/10.1016/j.chb.2014.02.023

Ellemers, N., Haslam, S.A., Platow, M.J., Knippenberg, D.: Social identity at work: developments, debates and directions. In: Haslam, S.A., Knippenberg, D.V., Platow, M.J., Ellemers, N. (eds.) Social Identity at Work: Developing Theory for Organisational Practice, pp. 3–26. Taylor and Francis Group, Hove (2003)

ESA.: Essential Facts about the computer and video game industry. Entertainment Software Industry (2015). http://www.theesa.com/wp-content/uploads/2015/04/ESA-Essential-Facts-2015.pdf. Accessed 25 Jan 2017

Grooten, J., Kowert, R.: Going beyond the game: development of Gamer Identities within societal discourse and virtual spaces. Loading… **9**(14), 70–87 (2015)

Haslam, S.A., Jetten, J., Postmes, T., Haslam, C.: Social identity, health and well-being: an emerging agenda for applied psychology. Appl. Psychol. Int. Rev. **58**(1), 1–23 (2009). https://doi.org/10.1111/j.1464-0597.2008.00379.x

Kaye, L.K.: Football Manager as a persuasive game for social identity formation. In: Ruggiero, D. (ed.) Cases on the Societal Effects of Persuasive Games, pp. 1–17. IGI Global, Philadelphia (2014). https://doi.org/10.4018/978-1-4666-6206-3.ch001

Kaye, L.K., Carlisle, C., Griffiths, L.R.W.: A contextual account of the psychosocial impacts of social identity in a sample of digital gamers. Psychol. Pop. Media Cult. (2017a)

Kaye, L.K., Kowert, R., Quinn, S.: The role of social identity and online social capital on psychosocial outcomes in MMO players. Comput. Hum. Behav., 74, 215-223 (2017b)

Kaye, L.K., Pennington, C.R.: "Girls can't play": the effects of stereotype threat on females' gaming performance. Comput. Hum. Behav. **59**, 202–209 (2016). https://doi.org/10.1016/j.chb.2016.02.020

Kaye, L.K., Pennington, C.R., McCann, J.J.: Do casual gaming environments evoke stereotype threat? Examining the effects of explicit priming and avatar gender. Comput. Hum. Behav. **78**, 142–150 (2018)

Kowert, R.: Video Games and Social Competence. Routledge, New York (2015)

Kowert, R., Domahidi, E., Quandt, T.: The relationship between online video game involvement and gaming-related friendships among emotionally sensitive individuals. Cyberpsychol. Behav. Soc. Netw. **17**(7), 447–453 (2014). https://doi.org/10.1089/cyber.2013.0656

Kowert, R., Griffiths, M.D., Oldmeadow, J.A.: Geek or chic: emerging stereotypes of online gamers. Bull. Sci. Technol. Soc. **32**(6), 471–479 (2012). https://doi.org/10.1177/0270467612469078

Kowert, R., Oldmeadow, J.A.: The stereotype of online gamers: new characterization of recycled prototype? In: Proceedings of Nordic DiGRA: Games in Culture and Society Conference. Tampere, Finland (2012)

Pennington, C.R., Kaye, L.K., McCann, J.J.: Applications of the multi-threat framework of stereotype threat in the context of digital gaming. PLoS ONE **13**(2), e019213 (2018)

Salter, A., Blodgett, B.: Hypermasculinity and Dickwolves: The contentious role of women in the new gaming public. J. Broadcast. Electron. Media **56**(3), 401–416 (2012)

Shaw, A.: Do you identify as a gamer: Gender, race, sexuality and gamer identity. New Media Soc. **14**(1), 28–44 (2012)

Tajfel, H.: Differentiation Between Social Groups. Academic Press, London (1978)

Tajfel, H.: Individuals and groups in social psychology. Br. J. Soc. Clin. Psychol. **18**, 183–190 (1979). https://doi.org/10.1111/j.2044-8260.1979.tb00324.x

Tajfel, H., Turner, J.: An integrative theory of inter-group conflict. In: Williams, J.A., Worchel, S. (eds.) The Social Psychology of Inter-Group Relations, pp. 33–47. Wadsworth, Belmont (1979)

Vermeulen, L., Van Bauwel, S., Van Looy, J.: Tracing female gamer identity: an empirical study into gender and stereotype threat perceptions. Comput. Hum. Behav. **71**, 90–98 (2017)

Yee, N.: Motivations of play in online games. CyberPsychol. Behav. **9**, 772–775 (2006)

Experience Design for University Students' Domestic Waste Management Based on Usability Analysis

Qin Luo, Ruiqiu Zhang, and Zhen Liu[⊠]

School of Design, South China University of Technology, Guangzhou 510006,
People's Republic of China
liuzjames@scut.edu.cn

Abstract. Managing personal domestic waste is a very important part of people's daily life behavior, and inappropriate management style will bring multiple negative impacts on people's life. In the research field of domestic waste management, existing researches mainly focus on material processing, recycling and system, but lack of analysis on users' life management, behavior analysis and product use, resulting in a single research perspective in this field. This study takes it as the focus of analysis, demonstrating the importance of analyzing users' life, behavior and product use in the research of domestic waste management. The principle of the experience design is to improve the user's usability of garbage bags by combining the use of WeChat, so that the users can develop their habit of changing garbage bags every day. It verifies that usability is a special and important perspective to analyze user requirements, which can further improve the design quality. In the design process with user experience as the core, the analysis of users' product usability can indeed help designers better understand users' potential needs in life management, behavior and experience. In addition, by changing the user's product usability, the user's experience in personal domestic waste management can be changed, providing a theoretical basis for the application of usability in user experience design. This paper involves a variety of innovative design methods in the process of usability analysis, which overcomes the limitation of cost and time of traditional analysis methods. This analysis method has methodological reference significance for the application of user experience design in terms of university students' domestic waste management.

Keywords: Experience design · University student ·
Domestic waste management · Usability analysis · Design method ·
Design process

1 Introduction

In recent years, the usage has gradually become a research hotspot in the industry and academia. By analyzing the usage of the products of the target users, it can help designers further clarify the needs of users and overcome the defects of subjective judgment deviation caused by the traditional design process relying on actual design experience or expert knowledge [1].

© Springer Nature Switzerland AG 2019
A. Marcus and W. Wang (Eds.): HCII 2019, LNCS 11583, pp. 466–477, 2019.
https://doi.org/10.1007/978-3-030-23570-3_35

At present, there is a lack of research on the product usage of personal domestic waste management at home and abroad. Most of the research related to domestic waste management focuses on the centralized treatment and sustainable utilization of public waste [2]. Most of the researches concerning personal life management are from the perspectives of ideology and system [3]. Lack of analysis from the perspective of personal life management, so it is necessary to study the management of personal domestic waste from a new perspective. Product usage has been a hot topic in recent years, which can provide a powerful design basis for designers to define design goals.

2   Research Framework

The research framework is shown in Fig. 1. The first step is to obtain the data of the target users. The initial data of the sample users are collected through "A day in the life". The second step is to extract the obtained data and conduct a mind map for the behavior trend, so as to obtain the user's product usage in the aspect of domestic waste management. And through literature research on the current situation of contemporary college students in domestic waste management to get the possible needs of users, and then through in-depth interviews to clarify the needs of the target user group; the third step is to design, after clear the needs of the user group The initial design, first through the "image and mood boards" to get inspiration, form a initial design concept, and then expressed through "sketching", obtained a initial design results. After the design is clearly defined, we need to show the design in a better form. This study first produced "sketching modeling" for the user to experience, and then presented a better visual effect in the "mock up" way; the fourth step is usability testing. The method used in this paper is to make a prototype for sample users to experience, and verify whether the design results meet the requirements put forward in the early stage by analyzing the degree of test completed by users.

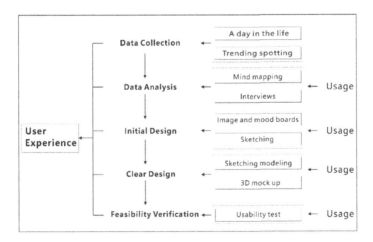

Fig. 1. Research framework.

3 Data Collection

3.1 A Day in Life

"A day in life" is to obtain behavioral data of sample people by following their daily work behaviors. Recording techniques include but are not limited to taking photos, photographing, recording, etc. This design method can reveal unexpected problems that people may encounter in daily life. After recording the behavioral data of the sample population, use "Trend spotting" to summarize the behavioral trends of the sample users. In this study, the two methods were mainly used to obtain data. The first step is to randomly select three working days to take photos and record the main actions of the sample users in the whole day. Table 1 is a data table obtained from the survey. After screening, the relevant pictures of the sample user's domestic waste are extracted for data statistics:

Table 1. A day in life of the user.

Time	Activity	Outcome	Scene photo
12:00	Get up		
12:00-13:00	Washing, Clean up, Point take-away, Dining	Produce garbage	
13:00-15:00	Learning in front of the computer		
15:00-16:30	Make leather goods while watching computer videos, and eat snacks by the way	Produce garbage	
16:30-17:30	Play mobile games		
17:30-18:00	Eat snacks, watch live games	Produce garbage	
18:00-20:00	Learning in front of the computer		
20:00-22:30	Watch the video, Eat some snacks by the way	Produce garbage	
22:30-23:30	Walk around, Chat with roommates, Do hygiene	Produce garbage	
23:30-24:00	Take a shower, Wash her hair, Wash her clothes		
24:00-02:00	Study in front of the computer, drink a cup of milk before going to bed, Eat a little snack	Produce garbage	

The first step is to start from the user's "life behavior" as the center, and analyze the user's data from four aspects: clothing, food, housing and travel, and the obtained mind map is shown in Fig. 2, so as to obtain the product with the highest usage in the domestic waste treatment of the user.

Fig. 2. Mind mapping of a day behavior.

To summarize the mind map, the most used appliances for the user's domestic waste management are garbage bags and garbage cans, among which the most direct domestic waste disposal appliances are garbage bags. At the same time, the proportion of time that the sample users generated domestic waste in daily life can be obtained. As shown in Fig. 3, no matter from the perspective of users' life behavior or time, the use of garbage bags and garbage cans is the highest usage in the aspect of domestic waste management.

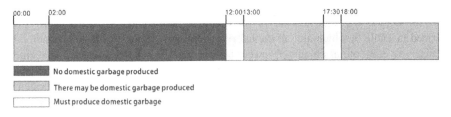

Fig. 3. Time period of generating domestic waste in a day.

3.2   In-Depth Interview

At present, some useful methods to evaluate product usage mainly rely on the data analysis of questionnaire survey [4]. However, in fact, questionnaire survey is limited by cost and time, and sometimes the answer sheet will deviate from objectivity, ultimately affecting the effectiveness of the analysis results. This paper adopts the in-depth interview method [5]. The interview is divided into two parts: interview outline design and formal interview. The interview structure and questions are listed in Table 2. The interviewees are nine full-time graduate students.

Table 2.   The interview structure and questions.

Interview structure element	Interview question
1 Basis of interview	1.1 Is the garbage disposal method in your living/working environment collected in a garbage bag or trash can and thrown away?
	1.2 The garbage generated in your living/working environment is handled by yourself or someone will help you with it?
2 Basic information	2.1 How often do you/the people who help you with your household waste process?
	2.2 In your mind, how often should a healthy household waste be treated?
	2.3 Have you ever forgotten to deal with garbage? How often is the frequency? And what is the reason?
	2.4 When dealing with other things, have you ever seen the same forgotten situation, How did you deal with it?
	2.5 If you have never seen a situation of forgetting to throw away garbage, what is your reminder of the way to deal with it?
3 Exploration of demand	3.1 Do you want to handle your own garbage to the best frequency you think?
	3.2 If there is a product that can help you reach the most healthy living garbage management frequency you think, what do you think it must meet?
	3.3 Please describe your other suggestions on domestic waste management

The interview was recorded by recording, and then the recording was arranged into documents to avoid missing important information raised by users. And the content analysis method was used to analyze the user interview. The results are briefly summarized in Table 3, which are: all the interviewees' daily domestic waste is handled by themselves; eight out of nine interviewees believe that the healthiest waste management needs to process the daily waste on the same day; all of them have experienced forgetting to dispose of waste; all the them have also experienced the same forgotten in other things, including six of them will use sticky notes, memos and other means to remind themselves, but will not use these tools in the waste management, which can be used for reference in design; eight out of nine users expressed the hope that their situation of forgetting to throw waste could be improved; and features of the design objectives include but are not limited to simple, cheap, beautiful and not disturbing daily life.

Table 3. The summary of interview questions' results.

Issue of handling garbage	Key result	Number of users
1 Way	Collect and throw away with garbage bags or trash cans	9
2 Person	Handling it by myself	9
3 Frequency	3.1 Three times a week or more	4
	3.2 Twice a week	4
	3.3 Once a week and below	1
4 The ideal frequency	4.1 All are once a day	8
	4.2 Kitchen waste: once a day Other garbage: 3 to 5 days	1
5 Have you forgotten	Yes	9
6 Similar problem and the solution	6.1 Notes/calendar/alarm/memo, etc.	6
	6.2 No measure	3
7 Hope to be improved	7.1 Yes	8
	7.2 Indifferent	1
8 Requirements for related products	8 Economy, Do not interfere with life, Easy to use, Simple, Small footprint, Can popularize the public	8

The interview results indicate perspective of usage aspects, which are: users' daily use of garbage bags is relatively high; if the user achieves a healthy lifestyle of waste management, the garbage bag shall be replaced at least once a day; users often forget to deal with garbage, reducing the use of garbage bags; and users do not have enough use of auxiliary tools in waste management. Therefore, users can improve their use of garbage bags by increasing the use of auxiliary tools.

4 Design Process

4.1 Concept Design

The design method used for the concept design is the image and mood boards, which is a kind of layout where designers carefully integrate the collected color, text, pictures, images and digital resources [6]. As shown in Fig. 4, relevant materials and data are connected in a tiled way, such as post-it notes, trash cans, snacks, take-out food, and etc., to find the correlation and extract the important relevant factors.

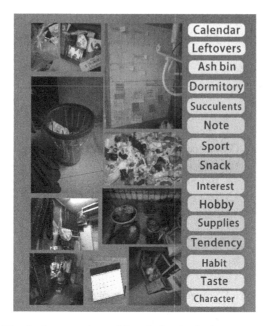

Fig. 4. Image and mood boards for the design process.

By analyzing the available information keywords obtained by the image and mood boards, the design is in line with the elements extracted from the image and mood boards combined with the user's needs in the user interview, which are:

(1) Calendar: record the date, remind the itinerary, update every day;
(2) Trash can: used for garbage and non-disposable use;
(3) Garbage bag: used to hold garbage, updated every day, can be torn;
(4) Food waste: It needs to be packed separately, and the smell is not suitable for direct use of the trash can;
(5) Succulent plants: the user's hobby, decoration, good-looking, quality of life;
(6) Snacks: preferences, environment, meals, smells.

The design outcome of this research is a WeChat applet, and the target users are contemporary college students. As a new communication medium, WeChat has exerted an important influence on college students' life, study, interpersonal communication and values [7]. In early 2018, the applet began to grow explosively. Its simple operation mode and one-touch access greatly reduce the time cost of users, which coincides with the time fragmentation of users [8]. Therefore, it greatly conforms to the design requirements proposed by the target users of this study, such as economy, non-interference with life and low sense of existence. The small program design comes from the calendar notes of the elements, and the official accounts jointly remind users to update the garbage bag every day. As shown in Fig. 5, the official accounts associated with the applet needs to send WeChat message to the user every day to remind the user to replace the garbage bag. Applet needs to have a calendar, sticky notes function, calendar can view the day and other dates; Notes can be added, edited and deleted; Note editing requires a description of the event.

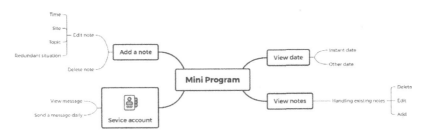

Fig. 5. Applet architecture of the design concept.

4.2   Design Development

"Sketching modeling" can be used to demonstrate the feasibility of the design after the designer has clearly defined the design goal [9]. As shown in Fig. 6, drawing software is used to demonstrate and illustrate the use process of the design prototype.

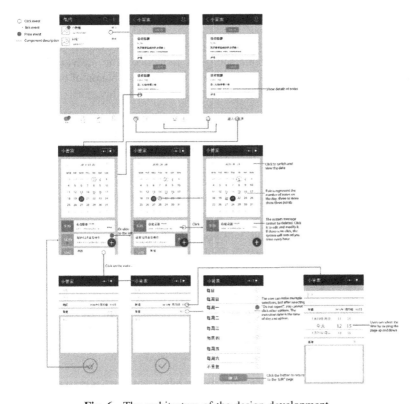

Fig. 6. The architecture of the design development.

5 Feasibility Study

Since the design of this study is aimed at the experience of special samples, the feasibility depends on the user experience. The feasibility verification of this study is divided into two parts. The first is to give the user the usability test in the form of a model. Then the user's usability of garbage bags is obtained through the interview. The focus of usability testing is to record the time and fluency of users in completing test tasks, because fluency is of great concern to users among many factors affecting the experience of intelligent terminals [10]. The object of this usability test and interview is the same as that of the previous interview. The recording is also used in the process, and then the audio file is converted into the transcript for sorting.

This usability test is divided into following three parts:

Task 1: The users have an applet called "little housekeeper", it is associated with a official account of the same name, please enter the applet through the official account now, press the prompt after changing the garbage bag and click the corresponding button.

Task 2: Today is January 1st, 2019. Please add a note on January 20th, with the title: the tutor has a meeting at 12:30. Venue: 3rd floor; Time: today and Monday repeat; Note: the tutor requires the meeting to be held in room 312 on the third floor of the science building.

Task 3: Please delete the new notes in task 2, exit the applet, and return to the front page of WeChat.

The test process are shown in Table 4, in which the user's usability test process was smooth, without discomfort and the time was moderate. The individual tasks were slightly extended due to the network speed and the task distribution of the host, and the overall experience was good. The interview outline of usability test is shown below:

1. Will you click to see all the unread messages on WeChat?
2. Did this product cause any discomfort to you during your use?
3. Is there any discomfort, unaccustomed or repugnance caused by the shape and appearance of this product?
4. In your opinion, does this product remind you to replace the garbage bag?
5. In your opinion, does this product meet your requirements of "simple, easy to use and low cost"?

If this product is made for you, will you use it?

The interview results are shown in Table 5. Through the analysis of the interview results, it is known that the user is positive and acceptable to the design result, so the feasibility of the design is verified.

The interview results indicate the perspective of usage aspects:

(1) All users can use WeChat, the usage of the official account is high;
(2) Meet the user's usage habits and needs;
(3) The user's willingness to use is high;
(4) The associated user will replace the garbage bag, thereby increasing the usage of the garbage bag.

Table 4. The feasibility study process.

User	Task	Time	Obstacle and time	Use test photo
	1.1 The first	21	No obstacle	
1	1.2 The second	38	No obstacle	
	1.3 The third	16	No obstacle	
	2.1 The first	13	No obstacle	
2	2.2 The second	37	No obstacle	
	2.3 The third	14	No obstacle	
	3.1 The first	16	No obstacle	
3	3.2 The second	48	The network speed is too slow	
	3.3 The third	14	No obstacle	
	4.1 The first	19	No obstacle	
4	4.2 The second	36	No obstacle	
	4.3 The third	16	No obstacle	
	5.1 The first	14	No obstacle	
5	5.2 The second	32	No obstacle	
	5.3 The third	18	No obstacle	
	6.1 The first	15	No obstacle	
6	6.2 The second	32	No obstacle	
	6.3 The third	19	No obstacle	
	7.1 The first	19	No obstacle	
7	7.2 The second	40	The network speed is too slow	
	7.3 The third	12	No obstacle	
	8.1 The first	13	No obstacle	
8	8.2 The second	30	No obstacle	
	8.3 The third	12	No obstacle	
	9.1 The first	20	Editing the date:3 seconds	
9	9.2 The second	39	No obstacle	
	9.3 The third	25	No obstacle	

Table 5. The interview results of usability test.

Question	Answer	Number of users
Whether to view all unread messages on WeChat?	Yes	7
Does this product make you feel uncomfortable?	No	7
Are you satisfied with its appearance?	Yes	6
Is it useful for your life?	Yes	8
Whether it meets your previous requirements?	Yes	9
Would you like to use this product?	Yes	8

Therefore, this design drives users to improve the usage of garbage bags through the high usage of WeChat official account, so as to promote users to develop a healthy lifestyle of waste management by changing garbage bags every day. In addition, users have better experience of the design results in usability tests and interviews. Therefore, the experience design method based on product usage is scientifically useful.

6   Discussion

Through literature review, it can be concluded that in the research field of domestic waste management, existing researches mainly focus on material processing, recycling and system, but lack of analysis on users' life management, behavior analysis and product use, resulting in a single research perspective in this field. This study takes it as the focus of analysis, demonstrating the importance of analyzing users' life, behavior and product use in the research of domestic waste management. The case of design practice starts from the brand new perspective of product usage analysis. By analyzing the daily behavior data of users, the user's usage on related products can be obtained, so as to deeply explore the user's needs on the behavior and experience of domestic waste management and design according to the needs. The principle of the final design result is to encourage users to develop the domestic waste management habit of changing garbage bags every day by improving the user's usage of garbage bags in life, neither conflict with the scientific viewpoint of existing research and made up for the inadequacy of the research caused by single angle. It provides a theoretical basis for mixed analysis of design research with user experience as the core. At the same time, the usage is a research star issue in the industry and academia in recent years. It is very valuable in reference. This study combines various international innovative design techniques in the design process to improve the usage analysis method and overcome the use of traditional analysis because of excessive dependence on the questionnaire investigation and cause analysis of subjective and disadvantages such as easily affected by time, and provides a methodological reference for the introduction of usage in other fields.

7   Conclusion

Usage analysis is an important perspective for user needs, which can further improve the quality of the design and change the user experience. Through the analysis of the user's product usage, the potential needs of users in life management, behavior, and experience can be further obtained, and targeted products can be designed to improve the user experience. In this study, by promoting the user's use of garbage bags, the user is encouraged to develop the domestic waste management habit of replacing the garbage bags, and the importance of analyzing the user's product usage in the design with the user experience as the core is demonstrated. At the same time, this study combines a variety of international innovative design methods in the process of usage analysis, overcoming the shortcomings of traditional cost analysis methods that are limited by cost and time. It has a methodological reference for the application of usage analysis, and provides a theoretical basis for the usage in the application of user experience design research.

Acknowledgements. The authors wish to thank all the people who provided their time and efforts for the study. This research is supported by "Guangdong University Students Innovation and Entrepreneurship Education Research Center" (project number 2018A100402), South China University of Technology (SCUT) project funding x2sj/K5180600, and China National Natural Science Foundation (grant number 61803108).

References

1. Liu, P., Wang, L.: Product function usage analysis based on web semantic mining. Appl. Res. Comput. **28**(7), 2580–2585 (2011)
2. Ma, J.: Current status and discussion of urban domestic waste management in China. Jiangsu Environ. Technol. **1**, 33–35 (2005)
3. Jing, K.: Research on College Students' Daily Life Management and Education. Wuhan University, Wuhan (2015)
4. Han, S.H., Kim, J.: A comparison of screening methods: selecting important design variables for modeling product usability. Int. J. Ind. Ergon. **32**(3), 189–198 (2003)
5. Legard, R., Keegan, J., Ward, K.: In-depth interviews. In: Qualitative Research Practice: A Guide for Social Science Students and Researchers, pp. 138–169 (2003)
6. Zheng, Q., Li, S.: Application research of emotional board in interaction design. Packag. Eng. **31**(11), 126–129 (2009)
7. Zheng, X.: Investigation and analysis of the status Quo of College Students' WeChat use—Taking 208 Universities in China as an example. Ideol. Theory Educ. **2**, 83–86 (2014)
8. Qian, Q.: The most practical and innovative five types of WeChat applets. Internet Weekly **19**, 28–29 (2018)
9. Liu, J., Yang, J., Yu, Y.: Concept mold making and its role analysis in product design. Beauty Times **2**, 71–73 (2009)
10. You, Z.: Research and Implementation of Intelligent Terminal Smoothness Evaluation Based on User Experience. Beijing University of Posts and Telecommunications, Beijing (2018)

User-Centered Survey Design: Considering Group Membership Effects on Survey Responses

Kelly C. Roth$^{(\boxtimes)}$ and Dania Bilal$^{(\boxtimes)}$

University of Tennessee, Knoxville, TN 37996, USA
`kelcroth@vols.utk.edu`, `dania@utk.edu`

Abstract. Attending to diversity is an essential factor in interface design [22]. Today, there is a need for understanding the complex factors shaping the design practice of interfaces, instruments, and research tools, including surveys. With growing use of online surveys for data collection, designing surveys that address user diversity is becoming increasingly important [15]. However, there is also an overall trend of declining survey response rate across all modes [1], disrupting the accuracy of responses. While many studies on social identities exist, such as in-group/out-group status of the researcher compared to the respondent and their effect on face-to-face survey responses (e.g., [8, 13], we know very little about whether participants' identities (i.e., university affiliation) affect responses to online survey designs. This study attempts to fill this gap by exploring if college students would agree to continue participating in a survey that uses different university affiliations across design conditions. While findings from this study did not show differential responses based on whether participants saw an in-group member of their own university or an out-group member of a rival university, we believe that it is most likely due to participants who did not agree to informed consent not being analyzed. Whether university affiliation affects participants' willingness to participate in a survey in the first place has yet to be investigated. Practical and methodological implications are discussed in relation to how user-centered survey design could help increase survey response rates and improve diverse representation in samples, advocating for inclusive rather than exclusive participation.

Keywords: Survey method · Theory-method intersection · User-centered design

1 Introduction

Increasing response rate to surveys has been a goal of researchers since surveys were created. One simple method of increasing a participant's willingness to complete a survey is through personalization. For example, dressing similarly to the participant to appear as an in-group member or appearing as a member of a group the participant has a high opinion of are ways to increase response rate when conducting surveys in person [8, 13]. While these studies on personalization have traditionally been applied to in-person surveys, the internet has provided researchers with the option to use online survey designs [4, 17].

© Springer Nature Switzerland AG 2019
A. Marcus and W. Wang (Eds.): HCII 2019, LNCS 11583, pp. 478–491, 2019.
https://doi.org/10.1007/978-3-030-23570-3_36

Today, online surveys are common, convenient, inexpensive, and increasingly accessible in our progressively globalized and internet-connected world. The benefits of online surveys include cross-cultural and expanded geographical reach as well as easily modified formats for greater flexibility (e.g., [7]). With an increasing use of online surveys for data collection, and with an increasingly diverse pool of participants who have access to such surveys, it is imperative that researchers become aware of how best to recruit accurate samples of populations and how to develop user-centered personalized surveys.

Currently, with surveys designed by the majority for the majority, "low-incidence" or specialized subsets of the population are being passed over for survey research or are not responding when recruited [3, 20]. Additionally, there is an overall trend of declining surrey response rate across all modes, be it in-person or online [1]. Online surveys that are distributed via email have had a significantly decreasing response rate since 1986, according to one review [21]. This decline affects the ecological validity of the final survey dataset. Reduced response rate disrupts the accuracy of the final sample, as minority groups of identities may be less motivated to respond, allowing an oversampling of majority group members or specific kinds of groups (i.e., the volunteer bias, which explains people with certain personality traits are more likely to participate in research [12]).

Presently, the literature focuses on how researchers can display in-group social identities to increase face-to-face survey response rate, but whether these same factors affect online surveys is yet to be investigated. Research examining how personalization and in-group/out-group social identities affects online survey responses is lacking. The purpose of this study is to determine if incorporating social identities will improve online survey response rate, much the way traditional pen-and-paper surveys automatically include the researcher's identity due to the in-person nature of the research. Increasing personalization through developing user-centered design surveys could contribute to recruiting a more representative sample of the population as well as an overall increase in response rate. As Cook, Heath, and Thompson [4] state, "Election polls make clear that the *representativeness* of our samples is much more important than the response rate we obtain. A sample of fewer than 1% of the population can be more representative, indeed much more representative, than a sample of 50% or 60% of the population" (p. 821). Findings from this study have implications for designing user-centered online surveys that reach more diverse samples of participants, allowing for a more representative, ecologically valid dataset.

1.1 Increasing In-Person Survey Response

Surveys have been one of the main methods of collecting data for research for decades (see Converse, 2017 for a history on survey research in the United States of America). Originally, recruitment for surveys was in-person as a face-to-face interaction. Groves, Cialdini and Couper [13] have shown in these face-to-face interactions "similarity leads to liking"; that is, if the person requesting information for the in-person survey is similar to the participant, the participant is more likely to participate in the survey (p. 488). They give examples of researchers driving older cars when conducting door-to-door surveys in poorer neighborhoods and dressing up in suits when in richer neighborhoods.

Dell, Vaidyanathan, Medhi, Cutrell and Thies [8] support expanding diversity in HCI research populations. In their study, the researcher interviewed participants and asked if they would be interested in a new technology they were selling. The interviewer was either Indian, like the participants, or a white Westerner. If the in-person interviewer was perceived as a foreigner, then the Indian participants preferred the interviewer's technology, even if it was objectively inferior, due to a heightened opinion of western technology. They concluded that social identities have an impact on participants' responses and willingness to participate.

1.2   Increasing Online Survey Response

Studies on online survey design have shown that including pictures and visual elements beyond simple text facilitates response rate. Historically, Dillman, Tortora, Conradt and Bowker [11] found that pictures reduce participant responses, but this is due to HTML requiring more data and being slower to load in the nineties compared to today's highspeed internet. However, even back then, Dillman and colleagues did recommend graphics as a way to keep participants' attention, such as giving them a visual progress indicator [10].

Couper, Tourangeau, Conrad and Crawford [5] found online surveys that show participants visible options have a better response rate. Much like Dillman et al. [10], this continues a theme of using images to help to engage participant attention. Deutskens, De Ruyter, Wetzels and Oosterveld [9] found that the inclusion of visual elements, such as product images, improved the response rate of online surveys. Daley, McDermott, McCormack Brown and Kittleson [6] reported that their focus group of undergraduates recommended clipart be used within online surveys and a photo of the primary investigator be displayed on the site hosting the survey as a way to add a personal touch to an otherwise impersonal questionnaire. This echoes earlier studies on how the personal interaction in face-to-face surveys can improve response rate [13]. Sauermann and Roach [19] found that personalization via addressing the participant's first name increases emailed survey response rate by as much as 48%, in a study of 24,651 survey respondents. Cook, Heath and Thompson [4] conducted a meta-analysis of online survey response rate and found personalized contacts to be a major factor associated with a high response rate in online surveys.

1.3   Knowledge Gap

It is clear from the reviewed literature that personalization is important to survey participants, and that considering their identities and how they may perceive the person giving the survey has effects on response rate [4, 13, 19]. Many of the reviewed studies on visual elements and personalization of survey design are dated (late nineties to early aughts) or focus on in-person surveys only. Very little research has investigated how the "human element" in face-to-face surveys translates to online surveys in this digital age. This is further expanded upon by Schlesinger, Edwards and Grinter [20] in their call to action to begin including more diverse participant groups and controlling for the multitude of identities an individual can have in HCI (human-computer interaction) studies. Thus, personalization and social identities (i.e., foreigner or native, same income bracket or different) have real effects and should be considered in the context of the respondents' identities interacting with the survey design. With increased awareness of the role of diversity in surveys [2, 20], attention should be given to how online surveys can be personalized on a level beyond simply using the person's name, especially since respondents are not experiencing a face-to-face interaction with survey researchers.

How can survey response rates be increased in online surveys? Does Groves et al.'s [13] "similarity leads to liking" in in-person surveys translate to an online format? Does the presence of faces, either as in-group members or out-group members, affect online survey responses the same way it does in-person surveys? The answers to these questions have the potential to inform researchers of how personalized, user-centered online surveys could increase the response rate and representation of target populations, as well as improve the experience of survey participants.

2 Current Study

This study investigated if participants' identities (i.e., university affiliation) affects responses to different survey designs in an online format the same way these identities affect face-to-face survey responses [8, 13]. The experimental design tested if inclusion of faces with differing social group identities had an effect on participants' willingness to continue answering questions. Participants saw the face of someone they believe attends their university, the face of someone they believe attends a rival university, or a simple text-based survey with no picture. Participants were then presented with two questions that gave them the option to continue participating at no additional benefit to them.

2.1 Research Questions

The following research questions guided the direction of this study.

RQ-1: Does seeing an in-group member versus an out-group member (based on university affiliation) have different effects on participants' responses to online surveys, similar to the effects seen in in-person surveys?

RQ-2: Does the mere presence of a photo of a person, regardless of group membership, impact responses differently than a text-only, photo-less design in an online format?

2.2 Assumptions and Hypotheses

The assumptions that underlie the hypotheses to be tested in this study are that in-group members (members from the participant's own university) have a positive influence on participants' willingness to participate in a focus group and answer an additional survey when asked [13].

Conversely, out-group members (members of a rival university to the participant's university) have a negative influence on participants' willingness to participate in a focus group and to answer an additional survey when asked [8].

Another assumption is that there will be an overall effect of increased positive influence on participants' willingness to participate in a focus group and answer an additional survey when comparing conditions with a photo to the condition with text-only [6, 9, 11]. Based on these assumptions, the following hypotheses were tested:

H_1: Participants are more likely to continue to answer survey questions if they view a picture of someone they believe is from their own university (The University of Tennessee, Knoxville).

H_2: Participants are less likely to continue to answer questions if they view a picture of someone they believe is from a rival university (Alabama or Florida).

H_3: Participants are more likely to continue to answer questions if they view a picture of a person, regardless of university, than if they view only text with no picture.

2.3 Theoretical Framework

This study is grounded in the overarching theory of user-centered design, which gives attention to user characteristics and the environment in designing a product and the perspective of how this product will be understood and used by a user. User-centered design takes into consideration user beliefs, attitudes, and behaviors as they connect to specific tasks the user aims to achieve [16, 22]. Personalization is an important factor of user-centered design [15, 22].

In this study, the design of the survey will be tailored based on two assumptions: 1. participants are more willing to answer additional questions in a survey if they believe the person asking is a member of their "in-group," and 2. university affiliation can be considered an in-group or out-group status. Groves, Cialdini and Couper [13] is a prime example of using in-group status to garner responses by intentionally changing their appearance to appeal to the participants' demographic groups they were surveying. They did so by wearing a suit or by driving a cheaper car depending on whether the potential participants were of a higher or lower income class, respectively.

Within postal surveys, university affiliation has shown to be a marker of in-group status [21]. In a study on own-race bias, participants were more likely to remember the faces of those they believed belonged to their own university than the faces of those they believed belonged to a rival university, regardless of race [14]. Based on existing literature (see [18] for a review), one would have predicted that race would have a stronger effect on face recognition; however, university affiliation was what determined recognition accuracy instead.

2.4 Methodology

This study employed a quantitative method to gather data about participants' perceptions of researcher in-group status and how these perceptions affected responses to online survey questions asking for additional information to be provided. A survey questionnaire was developed by the researchers to collect the data. There were two instances where a participant could agree or disagree to contribute more data. These responses were quantified by coding participants' willingness to answer more questions as a binary response.

Participants. The Psychology Department at the University of Tennessee, Knoxville (UT) has a SONA (Sona Systems Ltd.) database of undergraduate students enrolled in introductory psychology courses, maintained by the head of the experimental psychology department. Undergraduates taking introductory psychology courses at UT are required to enroll in the SONA database and complete studies that researchers post for course credit. Students must complete 5.5 credits worth of studies by the end of the semester, and completing this survey earned the student 0.5 credits. There are approximately one thousand undergraduate students actively enrolled in the database each semester.

Following the IRB approval (granted on November 1st, 2018), all students in this database were recruited to participate in the study. An invitation and a distribution link to the survey was posted in the SONA database, which allowed students to self-select to participate based on interest in a football themed survey; a total of 400 students completed the survey.

Instrumentation. Qualtrics survey software (Qualtrics, Provo, UT) was used to develop survey questions and to collect data from participants. The survey questionnaire consisted of 20 closed questions and 11 open-ended questions, followed by 2 closed questions asking about contributing more data, making the survey 33 questions long at its shortest length. However, if students agree to answer additional survey questions, there was a second set of questions about personality traits that included 2 matrix questions, 3 closed questions, and 1 open-ended question. Students were expected to take fifteen to thirty minutes to complete the survey, depending on whether they agreed to the second set of questions. Estimated completion times were calculated via Qualtrics in-house completion time estimate.

Conditions. The first page of the survey randomly displayed one of five conditions to the participants: a stock image of an actor with UT school logos, the same actor with UT football logos (the 2 in-group conditions, which included a "Go Vols!" in the text); the same actor with Florida University logos, the same actor with Alabama University logos (rival universities, the 2 out-group conditions, which included a "Go Gata!" or "Roll Tide!" respectively), or a plain text box with no images or references to a college football team (a control for picture effects).

Procedure. All undergraduates enrolled in the SONA database as of the fall semester 2018 (approximately 1000 students) were recruited to participate in this study. An invitation with a link to the survey was posted in this database. Students browsing research studies and who were interested in the survey titled "College Football Fan Survey" took the survey. Thus, participants self-selected to participate depending on their interest in the study. This helped ensure that the students were indeed fans of college football and held strong beliefs about their favorite team.

Four hundred students (N = 400) completed the survey. However, only data where students identified the University of Tennessee, Knoxville as their favorite football team and who filled out all open-ended questions were included for analysis ($N = 358$). Data was excluded from analysis if the student identified a different team than UT as the favorite ($N = 38$), or if the student did not fill out the open-ended questions ($N = 4$). Filling out the open-ended questions was used as an indicator of whether the students were paying attention and genuinely answering the questions.

Before filling out any of the questionnaires, participants viewed the experimental condition picture or text-box and were asked to read and electronically sign an informed consent form on the first page of the survey, indicating they agreed to participate. Participants first completed the thirty-one-question survey about college football, which asked questions such as, *which college football team is your favorite*, and *how often do you attend games*.

Next, participants were presented with the experimental condition (picture or text-box) again with a question asking if they would be willing to participate in an in-person or over the phone focus group session at a later date. They were also informed that their answer to this question would not increase nor decrease their participation credit of 0.5 credits. Afterwards, participants were asked if they would be willing to answer 6 additional questions for an unrelated survey about fantasy characters and personality traits, again with no change to their participation grade regardless of their answer. There was no focus group and the additional optional survey was used as "filler," both explained in the debriefing. These questions were to test if participants were willing to continue participating in the research at no additional credit depending on if they thought an in-group member (someone from their own university, UT) or an out-group member (someone from a rival football university) was asking.

After completing the survey, the participants were provided a debriefing explaining that the study was not about football, but rather about in-group statuses of researchers and their effect on responses. This is required by UT's IRB in cases where the experiment uses deception, which was the circumstance in this study. Then, they were asked if they consented to submitting their data for analysis given that they were now aware of the true nature of the study. All participants whose responses were included in the data analysis ($N = 358$) agreed to the debriefing.

2.5   Data Analysis

Responses to the survey were filtered to only include those who agreed to both the informed consent and the debriefing. Of those responses, data was analyzed using those who listed a variation of UT as their favorite football team and who also answered all other text-box questions (e.g., *If you could choose to go back in time to any college football game of your choosing, which game would you want to see in person and why?*). Answers to the text-box questions were not analyzed; they were simply used as a marker to tell if the participant was completing the survey fully or was skipping questions and leaving them blank. This was to ensure that the data from those who listed UT as their favorite team were paying attention to the survey.

Responses were grouped based on the five experimental conditions. Participants either saw a picture of a man with University of Tennessee school logos (UTstudent, $N = 74$), University of Tennessee football logos (UTsports, $N = 67$) (the two in-group conditions), University of Florida school logos (FLstudent, $N = 76$), University of Alabama school logos (ALstudent, $N = 65$) (the two out-group conditions as these are rival football teams to UT), or a simple text box with no images or references to a college team or university (Text-Only, $N = 76$) (the control condition). The picture was a stock image of a young white man, which is the same for all four groups featuring an image. Only the logos on the picture changed between groups. The participants viewed this picture on the first page where they agreed to the informed consent and again before they saw the two questions asking them to contribute more data.

Of question responses, answers to "Would you be willing to participate in a focus group?" and "Would you be willing to answer another questionnaire?" were dummy coded to list affirmative answers ("yes I'd be willing to") as 2, and negative answers ("no I don't want to participate") as 1.

In addition to the five groups based on what picture (or lack of picture) the participants saw, a group coefficient was created based on the group status of the picture. These three groups were created by combining UTstudent and UTsports ("In-group member" group, $N = 141$), ALstudent and FLstudent ("Out-group member" group, $N = 141$), and the text-only condition ("Control", $N = 76$). While the five separate groups allow for possible differences to be seen based on the specific picture or university, combining the UT groups and the rival university groups into "in" or "out" status helped delineate any overarching effect the in-group/out-group status had on responses. Additionally, participants were grouped by whether they saw a photo ($N = 282$) or text only ($N = 76$) to determine if there was an effect of seeing an image of a face, regardless of group membership of the actor.

Using SPSS statistical software, contingency tables were set up and a chi-square test of independence was performed to examine the relationship between condition and answers to each survey question requesting additional information. This study utilized two questions, one about participating in a focus group and one about answering an additional survey. The chi-square tests were used to determine if answers to those two questions were statistically dependent on condition. The answers to these two questions were analyzed separately by condition. The answers to the questions were also tested to see if they were correlated.

3 Results

3.1 RQ-1

Does seeing an in-group member versus an out-group member (based on university affiliation) have different effects on participants' responses to online surveys, similar to the effects seen in in-person surveys?

The relationship between condition (UT sports, UT student, AL student, FL student, Text-only) and answer was insignificant for both questions, X2 (4, $N = 358$) = 0.89, p = 0.93 for the question about participating in the focus group and X2 (4, N = 358) = 3.85, p = 0.43 for the question about completing the additional survey (see Table 1).

The relationship between group status (in-group, out-group, or control) and answer was insignificant for both questions, X^2 (2, $N = 358$) = 0.15, p = 0.93 for the question about participating in the focus group and X^2 (2, $N = 358$) = 1.03, p = 0.60 for the

Table 1. Contingency Table comparing Answers * Condition.

Question	AL student		FL student		Text only		UT sports		UT student	
	n	%	n	%	n	%	n	%	n	%
Group										
No	51	79	57	75	57	75	50	75	59	80
Yes	14	22	19	25	19	25	17	25	15	20
Survey										
No	39	60	53	70	54	71	40	60	51	69
Yes	26	40	23	30	22	29	27	40	23	31

question about completing the additional survey (see Table 2). Since the control group was much smaller than the in-group and out-group, an additional Chi-square test was run only on in-group and out-group effects on both questions. Results were insignificant for both the focus group question, X^2 (1, $N = 282$) = 0.20, p = 0.89, and the additional survey question, X^2 (1, $N = 282$) = 0.02, p = 0.90.

Table 2. Contingency Table comparing Answers * Group.

Question	Control		In-Group		Out-Group	
	n	%	n	%	n	%
Focus group						
No	57	75	109	77	108	77
Yes	19	25	32	23	33	23
Extra survey						
No	54	71	91	65	92	65
Yes	22	29	50	35	49	35

3.2   RQ-2

Does the mere presence of a photo of a person, regardless of group membership, impact responses differently than a text-only, photo-less design in an online format?

The relationship between presence/absence of a photo (photo vs. text-only) and answer was insignificant for both questions, X^2 (1, $N = 358$) = 0.13, p = 0.72 for the question about participating in the focus group and X^2 (1, $N = 358$) = 1.02, p = 0.31 for the question about completing the additional survey (See Table 3).

Given that no condition had an effect on responses, a phi-coefficient analysis was used as a measure of association between the two binary variables to determine if answers to one question were correlated with the other across all conditions. There was a significant moderately positive correlation, $\varphi = 0.45$, p < .01, between a participant's answers to the first and second question. If a participant said "yes" to the first question,

Table 3. Contingency Table comparing Answers * Photo.

Question	No Photo		Photo	
	n	%	n	%
Focus group				
No	57	75	217	77
Yes	19	25	65	23
Extra survey				
No	54	71	183	65
Yes	22	29	99	35

the participant was likely to say "yes" to the second question; likewise, if the participant said "no" to the first question, the participant was likely to say "no" to the second question, regardless of experimental condition (See Table 4).

Table 4. Contingency Table comparing Focus Group Answers * Extra Survey Answers.

		Extra survey		
		No	Yes	Total
		n	n	
Focus group	No	214	60	274
	Yes	23	61	84
	Total	237	121	358

4 Discussion

While there have been studies that have investigated how a researcher's social identity and the survey respondent's social identity interact in face-to-face scenarios [8, 13], and how personalization in online surveys, especially personalization based on university affiliation, can increase response rate [4, 19, 21], no study thus far has investigated the effect of seeing pictures of in-group or out-group university member faces on responses to an online survey.

This study employed a photo of a young white man with university logos around him as a proxy digital representation of the "researcher." Participants who indicated the University of Tennessee, Knoxville was their favorite college team were placed in one of five conditions when taking the survey: two conditions had them view the actor with UT logos, two of the conditions had them view the actor with a rival football university's logos, and the last condition had them view a simple text box instead of an image.

Results showed that the photo the participants saw before the survey and before answering questions about contributing more data did not have an effect on their answers. Similarly, whether or not the participants saw a photo of a person with the instructions did not influence their answers. Instead, it was found that a participant's first answer was moderately correlated with their second answer, regardless of what condition they were in. This may imply that once a participant has agreed to participate, conditions within the survey surrounding identity do not have a large impact on responses.

The most important factor about this study to note was that it was conducted with participants who had agreed to answer the football survey; per the IRB, only data from those who agreed to the informed consent and debriefing were included in the original $N = 400$. While other studies have investigated survey response rate by analyzing whether a participant *agreed or disagreed to participate after initial contact*, this study looked at those who had *already agreed to participate* and tested how the experimental conditions affected their responses within the survey (see [1] for a meta-analysis of quantitative data regarding response rates to surveys). Based on the way this experiment was set up, participants saw the informed consent page with the photo of the actor, and only data from those who agreed to the informed consent after seeing the experimental condition could be analyzed. Thus, whether a participant agreed or disagreed to the informed consent (therefore agreeing/disagreeing to participate in the survey) based on experimental conditions could not analyzed. A future direction for research would be analyzing whether participants agree to take the survey at all if they view a picture of an in-group or out-group member, instead of focusing on answers within the survey of those who already agreed to participate.

5   Implications

These findings have methodological and practical implications. As to the methodology, results indicate that, in analyses of participants who agree to participate in a survey, individual differences between participants, such as different personality traits, may have more of an effect than the perceived social identity of the researcher. If the participant is someone who would be willing to participate in a focus group and answer additional survey questions, the participant is likely to do this regardless of who is asking if they have already agreed to participate. Likewise, if the participant is someone who is unwilling to be a part of a focus group or answer an additional survey, the participant is likely to be unwilling even after they have agreed to participate, regardless of who they believe is asking. Thus, future research should investigate whether a participant agrees or disagrees to begin a survey based on who they believe is asking, instead of looking at which participants continue to participate after they have already agreed to take the survey. Future studies should collect participant demographic data and design surveys that include pictures representing diverse racial or cultural identities to determine if there is an interaction effect of these identities on responses.

A practical implication for these findings is that increasing response rate from participants with diverse backgrounds creates a more representative dataset [3]. This could improve knowledge gained from survey-based experiments about both general and specific subsets of the population. With increased use of online surveys as a method for research, attention should be given to how personalization in the context of user-centered design can be implemented to enhance response rate and quality of responses. By personalizing surveys based on user-centered design principles, participants may be more willing to begin surveys, even if the personalization does not have an effect once they agree to complete the survey.

6 Limitations

One of the main limitations to consider in this study is the population. As data was collected from mostly freshman students, it is possible they did not yet feel strong ties to their university as their college football team, despite indicating UT as their favorite. Hence, seeing a rival university was not as salient or negative. Data was also collected during the latter half of the semester, and since students were taking this survey for a course grade, it is possibly the high number of negative responses was due to a lack of time on the participants' part. Had there been no course grade requirement incentive, responses may have been different.

Additionally, the survey design used a singular white man as an in-group or out-group member. Relevant literature has shown other demographic information to be equally as salient as university affiliation, such as the race of the participant and the researcher. Similarly, studies on whether a person is shown alone or in a group of people has been shown to have an effect on how a participant perceives them [14, 23, 24]. It is possible that showing the participant a picture of a person who is from the same university but is of a different race from the participant may have different effects on responses than seeing someone of the same race and same university [24]. It could also be possible that showing a group of researchers who are all from a university as the "research team" would have a different effect than showing one person as a representative of a university [14].

7 Conclusions

There are many factors to consider when designing a survey. With the decline in online response rates, researchers should employ the best practices and methods to increase responses overall [1, 17]. While some social identities may not affect participants' willingness to respond, other factors may. In this study, use of university affiliation appeared to have no effect on answers to questions within the survey. Previous studies have revealed an effect of university affiliation on participants' willingness to participate in postal surveys [21], and on participants' opinions of whether a person is an in-group or out-group member [14, 24]. Our findings are mainly attributed to the design of the survey in that participants agreed or disagreed to informed consent while viewing the photo of the in-group/out-group member, and those who did not consent to participate were not analyzed. Researchers should include the image of the actor (the "researcher" proxy) on the first page of the survey and analyze whether participants agree to take the survey at all if they see an in-group or out-group member; analyzing those who choose not to participate based on group status of the actor may provide additional insights. These images should be diverse and more representative of participants' backgrounds and cultures.

Future directions should explore the social identities of participants and how this factor interacts, both positively and negatively, with the perceived identities of the researchers. This could include testing the effects of group size as well as other demographic manipulations. Including questions to collect demographic data would allow for matching a participants' race, gender, and university affiliation, among other information, to determine the effect of each of these variables on responses. Researchers should consider using a mixed research method to collect not only quantitative, but also qualitative data. For example, surveys could include questions to explore participants' feelings toward their own university and to gather their opinions about university affiliation and its impact on their responses. Alternatively, such data could be obtained through individual or focus group interviews following the survey.

User-centered survey design is a new and unexplored theory in terms of how personalization can interact with participants' willingness to participate. As online surveys become a more mainstream research approach, studies should focus on effective interface design to motivate participants to complete surveys. Increasing responses from marginalized social identities will provide a more accurate representation of the population in the final sampling, which could lead to enhancing the ecological validity and generalizability of collected data, in addition to improving the experience of the participants.

References

1. Barbier, S., Loosveldt, G., Carton, A.: Measuring the survey climate: the Flemish case. Surv. Methods: Insights Field (2016). https://surveyinsights.org/?p=7430
2. Barreto, M.A., Frasure-Yokley, L., Vargas, E.D., Wong, J.: Best practices in collecting online data with Asian, Black, Latino, and white respondents: evidence from the 2016 collaborative multiracial post-election survey. Polit. Groups Identities 6(1), 171–180 (2018)
3. Berry, J., Chouhoud, Y., Junn, J.: Reaching beyond low-hanging fruit: surveying low-incidence populations. In: The Oxford Handbook of Polling and Survey Methods (2016)
4. Cook, C., Heath, F., Thompson, R.L.: A meta-analysis of response rates in web-or internet-based surveys. Educ. Psychol. Measur. 60(6), 821–836 (2000)
5. Couper, M.P., Tourangeau, R., Conrad, F.G., Crawford, S.D.: What they see is what we get: response options for web surveys. Soc. Sci. Comput. Rev. 22(1), 111–127 (2004)
6. Daley, E.M., McDermott, R.J., McCormack Brown, K.R., Kittleson, M.J.: Conducting web-based survey research: a lesson in internet designs. Am. J. Health Behav. 27(2), 116–124 (2003)
7. Daikeler, J., Silber, H., Bosnjak, M.: Where do web surveys work? A meta-analysis of response rate experiments across countries (2018). https://doi.org/10.23668/psycharchives. 850
8. Dell, N., Vaidyanathan, V., Medhi, I., Cutrell, E., Thies, W.: Yours is better! participant response bias in HCI. In: Proceedings of the SIGCHI Conference on Human Factors in Computing Systems, pp. 1321–1330. ACM (2012)
9. Deutskens, E., De Ruyter, K., Wetzels, M., Oosterveld, P.: Response rate and response quality of internet-based surveys: an experimental study. Mark. Lett. 15(1), 21–36 (2004)
10. Dillman, D.A., Tortora, R.D., Bowker, D.: Principles for constructing web surveys. In: Joint Meetings of the American Statistical Association (1998)

11. Dillman, D.A., Tortora, R.D., Conradt, J., Bowker, D.: Influence of plain vs. fancy design on response rates for web surveys. In: Proceedings of Survey Methods Section (1998)
12. Dollinger, S.J., Leong, F.T.: Volunteer bias and the five-factor model. J. Psychol. **127**(1), 29–36 (1993)
13. Groves, R.M., Cialdini, R.B., Couper, M.P.: Understanding the decision to participate in a survey. Public Opin. Q. **56**(4), 475–495 (1992)
14. Hehman, E., Mania, E.W., Gaertner, S.L.: Where the division lies: common ingroup identity moderates the cross-race facial-recognition effect. J. Exp. Soc. Psychol. **46**(2), 445–448 (2010)
15. Kaneko, K., Kishita, Y., Umeda, Y.: In pursuit of personalization design. Procedia CIRP **61**, 93–97 (2017)
16. Kramer, J., Noronha, S., Vergo, J.: A user-centered design approach to personalization. Commun. ACM **43**(8), 44–48 (2000)
17. McPeake, J., Bateson, M., O'Neill, A.: Electronic surveys: how to maximise success. Nurse Res. (2014+) **21**(3), 24 (2014)
18. Meissner, C.A., Brigham, J.C.: Thirty years of investigating the own-race bias in memory for faces: a meta-analytic review. Psychol. Public Policy Law **7**(1), 3 (2001)
19. Sauermann, H., Roach, M.: Increasing web survey response rates in innovation research: an experimental study of static and dynamic contact design features. Res. Policy **42**(1), 273–286 (2013)
20. Schlesinger, A., Edwards, W.K., Grinter, R.E.: Intersectional HCI: engaging identity through gender, race, and class. In: Proceedings of the 2017 CHI Conference on Human Factors in Computing Systems, pp. 5412–5427. ACM (2017)
21. Sheehan, K.B.: E-mail survey response rates: a review. J. Comput. Mediated Commun. **6**(2) (2001). https://academic.oup.com/jcmc/article/6/2/JCMC621/4584224
22. Shneiderman, B., Hocheiser, H.: Universal usability as a stimulus to advanced interface design. Behav. Inf. Technol. **20**(5), 367–376 (2001)
23. Short, L.A., Wagler, M.C.: Social categories alone are insufficient to elicit an in-group advantage in perceptions of within-person variability. Perception **46**(8), 929–940 (2017)
24. Shriver, E.R., Young, S.G., Hugenberg, K., Bernstein, M.J., Lanter, J.R.: Class, race, and the face: Social context modulates the cross-race effect in face recognition. Pers. Soc. Psychol. Bull. **34**(2), 260–274 (2008)

An Approach to Analysis of Physiological Responses to Stimulus
From Electrodermal Activity to Combined Physiological Responses

Reza Tasooji, Nicole Buckingham, Denis Gračanin$^{(\boxtimes)}$, and R. Benjamin Knapp

Department of Computer Science, Virginia Tech,
2202 Kraft Drive, Blacksburg, VA 24060, USA
gracanin@vt.edu

Abstract. Recent advances in wearable devices capable of measuring physiological signals such as Electrodermal Activity (EDA) support affective computing and related applications. We present an algorithm that uses EDA signals to detect highlights of a stimulus. To test the accuracy of our method, two different mediums, a scene from a movie, as our ground truth, and a scene from a video game, for testing the algorithm, were selected. We conducted a user study with 20 participants, analyzed the differences between mediums and validated the accuracy of our method for detecting the highlights of the stimulus using only EDA signals. Our approach uses commonalities among users based on their phasic responses for detecting highlights. The result of the study shows a F1 score of 0.93 and 0.89 for movie and video game respectively. We are in a process of conducting a user study with several sensory devices to explore combined physiological responses using IAPS data set as a stimulus.

Keywords: Emotion recognition · Affective computing ·
Human Computer Interaction · Electrodermal Activity · Fear

1 Introduction

Our emotions play an important role in our decision making and the outcome of our decisions can change the emotions we experience. This interplay between emotions and decisions plays a crucial role when defining normal and abnormal human behaviors.

Emotion is a sensory or behavioral reaction that is caused by any object or event. In psychology, the term "affect" describes the experience of emotion. The object or event that causes such changes is called "stimulus". The two fundamental dimensions of emotion are valence and arousal. Various studies show that these dimensions are related to physiological aspects and brain activities [14, 18, 26].

© Springer Nature Switzerland AG 2019
A. Marcus and W. Wang (Eds.): HCII 2019, LNCS 11583, pp. 492–509, 2019.
https://doi.org/10.1007/978-3-030-23570-3_37

Extensive research in this field has revealed that it is possible to detect emotion through physiological signals. One study, done by Feldman [11], showed that the degree of arousal is related to the amount of physiological activities during affective experience. Additionally, Chênes et al. [6] stated that physiological signals are difficult to hide or fake and with appropriate biometric sensors, it can be possible to detect the presence of emotion.

For many years, medical and health services have used biometric sensory devices to monitor the behavior of many human organs, such as the heart and brain. These sensory devices are now becoming available to the general public in different forms, including wristbands. Wristband-like sensory devices aid in data collection and can be easily integrated into the process of analyzing physiological signals.

In the field of human computer interaction (HCI), the use of such devices can help enhance user interaction by removing the cognitive load, through solely analyzing affective responses. The current databases used for the majority of emotion recognition systems, such as IAPS [20], are heavily dependent on participants' self-reports. Our goal is to explore methods for detecting highlights of the video stimulus that might cause affective responses, without fully relying on users' self-reports.

2   Related Work

The process of automatically detecting the highlights of a video is a far-reaching subject. With the huge variation in genres and different mediums such as video game, movies, virtual reality (VR) and augmented reality (AR), defining what is considered as a highlight can be diverging. Several studies [6,16] show that it is possible to detect highlights of the stimulus with high accuracy using physiological changes, but designing such a system comes with limitations and it will not be able to handle all possible outcomes.

Studies by Levenson [21,22] show that it is possible to distinguish emotion based on physiological responses. Specifically, fear stimulus will cause significant metabolic demands on the heart, which increases the maximum heart rate, and fear and disgust will cause higher skin conductance compare to happiness.

Joho et al. [16], analyzed facial activities to detect personal highlights of the content. This team developed a real time facial expression recognition system that outputs a vector of motion features of certain regions of the face. In a user study, they used eight video clips from different genres with varying duration and showed the content to ten participants. To extract the highlight, the team searched for a high level of consensus on personal highlights for the different videos. Results revealed one video had a common highlight among all users except one.

Unlike speech recognition and facial expression [7,9,10,12], using biosensors to measure and analyze physiological signals for identifying emotion is not well researched. Chênes et al. [6] present a technique to obtain user-independent summary of a given video. This approach did not require emotion recognition.

Instead, the system concept was based on the physiological linkage between different participants' emotional responses. Four physiological signals were used in the study: Electromyogram (EMG) which measures the activities of the muscles, Blood Volume Pulse (BVP), measures the change of blood pressure, Electrodermal activity (EDA) and skin temperature. The results showed that skin temperature with a window response of eight seconds returned the best correct classification rate (77%) and the EDA signal can be considered the most promising signal for detecting highlights in video clips.

EDA signals are a great candidate to detect highlights; EDA devices are easy for users to wear and it that provides sensory data with high accuracy. Two main components of an EDA signal are tonic and phasic responses. Tonic response, also known as Electrodermal Level (EDL), is the slow background changes. It can be described as slow changes that happen in absence of stimulus or during response-free recording intervals. Phasic response, also known as Electrodermal Response (EDR), is a distinct response to a stimulus [8].

We are using the method proposed by Benedek and Kaernbach [2] to deconvolve EDA signal into two contentious signals of tonic and phasic responses. This method is based on the precondition that there exists a stable Impulse Response Function (IRF). The assumption is that sudomotor nerve activity will show peaks, known as sudomotor bursts, with short time constants which leads to a larger time constant exhibition in EDRs. IRF represents the basic EDR shape that would result from a unit impulse. Further, we focus on the phasic component of EDA signal to find the highlight of the video stimulus.

To validate our model, we used video stimulus that might cause fear. Fear can be described as an evolutionary necessity that notifies a person to proceed on their current direction or take another course of action in order to increase the likelihood of survival. Excessive fright can cause a cognitive dissonance state, which can cause an attitude change, or inconsistent thoughts, that might turn anxieties into phobias. Additionally, fear is an essential emotional response to societal conflicts. For example, the fearful expression is thought to serve as a social cue [24].

The result from the study by Trubanova et al. [31] shows the positive correlation between recognizing fear and perspective-taking abilities, while perspective-taking was not significantly associated with recognition of the other basic emotions. The result shows there is something unique about fear that might separate it from other basic emotions.

A study by Lynch [23] examined fright experiences caused by video games. This study was based on a self-report by 269 undergraduate students; no physiological signal measurements were included in this study. The results showed that elements such as darkness, zombies, being surprised, etc. in video games are causes of fear. There was no significant gender-based differences in experiencing fear. These studies demonstrate that fear could help to detect the cause of affective response with more confidence.

3   Problem Definition

The exponential growth of video media increases the necessity of algorithms to summarize the content of the video. Personalized recommendations from content providers, such as Netflix's "Top picks for you", helps consumers watch the content that they care about and helps advertisement companies by providing them with better insight on what gets watched, and by whom. Additionally, VR and AR are finding their way into the entertainment industry. This industry is growing more than ever and with many variations of this medium, the consumers want the content to be their way.

One approach to put the consumer first in selecting the content is to build a system capable of automatically detecting what a consumer wants to see based on their physiological changes. Detecting the highlight of the media and analyzing the content can help us to take the first step for building a system that is capable of selecting the content based on the users' current affective response.

One of the problems with current approaches for detecting highlight is that the process for collecting signals is often laborious and exhausting for average users and, consequently, not feasible for daily tasks. To solve this problem, we are using a wristband capable of recording physiological signals, thus making the process of collecting physiological data much easier.

Most of the studies in the field of affective computing use multiple physiological signals. Although this approach increases the accuracy of the results, it requires more processing and it is not always possible to analyze the data in real time. Our assumption in this study is that EDA signals have the essential parameters such as tonic and phasic responses that are sufficient for detecting highlights of the stimulus. Our focus is on stimulus that might arouse fear in order to reduce the number of independent variables, gain a better insight and provide consistency among all subjects.

To test our approach, we conducted a user study with two stimulus that might arouse fear. We selected a scene from the movie "Halloween" as our ground truth for our method. The result of the study by Philippot [27] shows that the selected section of this movie can arouse fear. Additionally, the selected scene has elements of surprise, anticipation, loud sound and music that can be considered as highlight of the video.

To test the accuracy of our model, we selected another scene from a video game "Evil Within" [1] that might arouse fear but with all elements that has been reported by Lynch et al. [23] that might cause fear. The model needed to be able to detect these elements as the highlights of the video content that might cause affective response by analyzing EDA signal. Our goal for selecting a video game was to select a different medium, unrelated to movie, while sharing the same highlights.

In this study, highlights are any event in the stimulus that might cause physiological changes. This includes any sudden change in sound volume, change of scene or any content that might surprise the audience.

4   Methods and Techniques

In our previews work [30] we explored a real-time system for processing physiological signals. We divided the system into two parts: collector and analyzer. The collector provides the infrastructure for gathering the data when conducting the user study. The purpose of the collector is to store streamed data and synchronize the input data with the video stimulus. Before sending the data to the processing unit, the physiological data and the information about stimulus needs to be transferred to a local machine to be synchronized using the same clock time of the local machine. The process of synchronization involves checking the quality of the recorded signal and syncing the input sensory data with the video stimulus. The synchronized data then will be send to the analyzer. The purpose of the "Analyzer" is to run the algorithm and report the highlight of the stimulus.

Figure 1 illustrates the system. The top section of the figure shows the process for collecting the data and the bottom section demonstrates how we process the signal for detecting highlights. Different sub units, such as a clustering unit, can be added in the processing output layer for later studies.

The biometric sensor that we are using for this study is E4 wristband by Empatica [13]. One of the main advantages of using the E4 compared to other devices is that Empatica E4 is easy to use. This makes it possible for people to use the device with ease during daily activities. Also, the study by Ragot et al. [29] compares Biopac MP150 to Empatica E4 in terms of emotion recognition accuracy using Support Vector Machine as their learning algorithm. The result from the study shows there is not significant differences in accuracy between two devices in recognising emotion. One of the capabilities of E4 device is to measure electrical conductance of the skin in the $[0.01, 100]\mu S$ (micro-Siemens) range with digital resolution of 1 digit per 900 pS (pico-Siemens) [13].

5   Experiment Design

The first step is to provide the stimulus that might arouse emotion. In the review article about how to measure emotion by Mauss [25], the author concludes "there is no gold standard measure of emotional responding. emotions are constituted by multiple, situationally and individually variable processes".

Each stimulus includes three parts (Fig. 2). The first part (30 s) named as "Baseline" is a black screen without any sound, to collect the baseline of the user. The second section (90 s) is called "Relaxed", and the purpose is to ease the user. The content for this section was selected from the video game named "Flower" (2009). Finally, the "Fear" section is the "Halloween" movie scene for movie stimulus and "Evil Within" for video game stimulus (210 s).

To be able to detect the highlights in both movie and video game, we removed any element of interaction between user and the content by asking participants to watch a prerecorded section of the video game, passively, instead of asking them to play the content of the video game.

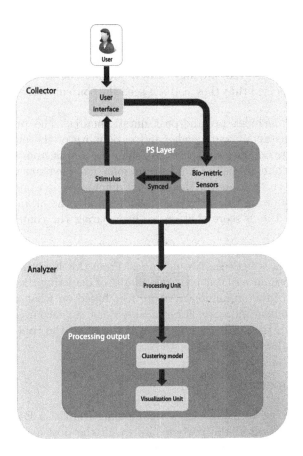

Fig. 1. The system is divided into two subsystems. The collector subsystem is capable of storing and streaming different biometric sensory data. After the data is synced with the video stimulus, the data will be send to analyzer subsystem. Different processing units can be added to analyze input signals.

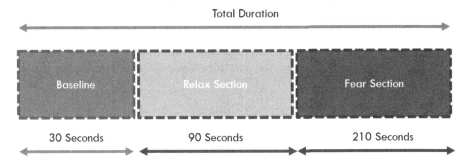

Fig. 2. Three parts of the video stimulus.

5.1 Running the Experiment

A total of 20 users (female = 8, male = 12), with ages between 18 to 40, ($\mu = 27.15$, $\sigma = 6.62$) participated in the study. All the participants were college students; 7 were undergraduate and 13 were graduate students. All the participants but one reported that they had not seen the content of the stimulus before the study.

Each section includes pre-and-post questionnaires. The pre-questionnaire includes questions about age, gender and nationality of the participants. The post-questionnaire includes six questions asking for a rank from 1 to 5. The goal of the post-questionnaires is to be able to compare two mediums and find out the differences between them and if there is any differences, does physiological signals capable of showing this differences. Additionally, the mean of the answers can be considered as a score that shows how strong the content is to arouse emotion.

Knowing that both stimulus might cause fear, our hypothesis is there is no significant differences between two mediums. From this hypothesis we can then explore the performance of our proposed model of detecting the highlights.

The content of the stimulus can cause fear based on what is considered as scary in entertainment industry. For ethical reasons, we encouraged participants to withdraw from the study at any stage if they find the content too strong. There was no withdrawal from the study.

6 Data Processing

During the study we measured EDA signal using Empatica E4 wristband and after the study we asked the participants to fill the post-questionnaires. The recorded data has the frequency of 4 Hz with total duration of 330 s for each section. The required steps for processing the raw data follow.

6.1 Standardizing the Data

One problem with quantifying EDA signal is the existence of large variability because of individual differences. For example, the amplitude of 0.5 μS EDR might be high for one person while it may be the baseline for another person. To correct these differences, the process of standardization is required.

There is no universal approach on methods to standardize EDA signals. For our system, we use *transforming raw data into Z-scores* [4] to standardize a raw data (Eq. 1).

$$X_n = \sum_{n=1}^{N} \frac{x_n - \bar{\mu}}{\bar{\sigma}} \tag{1}$$

where x_n is the value of raw signal at time n, $\bar{\mu}$ is the mean of the raw signal, and $\bar{\sigma}$ is the standard deviation of the raw signal.

After standardizing raw EDA data, we decompose it into phasic and tonic responses using the continuous decomposition analysis (CDA) method [2].

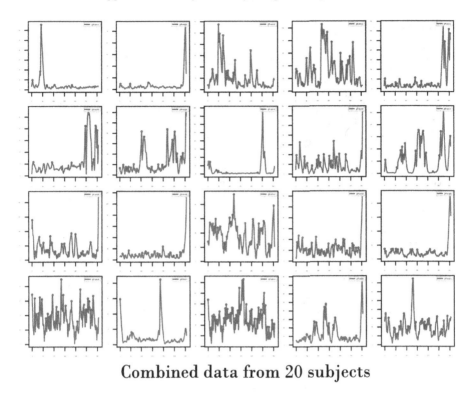

Combined data from 20 subjects

Fig. 3. Detected peaks from Z-score of the phasic response for 20 subjects. The x axis is the duration of the stimulus while y axis is the Z-score of the phasic response.

6.2   Detecting Highlights

We considered *Area Under the Curve* and *Sum of Squares*, with the window size of three seconds [4] and moving window of one second, as possible features for detecting highlights. After exploring and analyzing user responses of each, we decided to use *Area Under the Curve* for phasic responses as our main feature for detecting highlights.

After calculating this feature for all users, we detect and locate the peaks of the feature for all users. Figure 3 shows the detected peaks for 20 users. The x axis is the total duration of stimulus, while the y axis is the Z-score calculated from phasic response.

The histogram of the calculated peaks can be used to locate the time of the stimulus (Fig. 4). Specifically, bins with higher values show a larger group of people having higher phasic responses during bin's duration. By adjusting the threshold for the number of users in the bins, we have a selection of bins that can be analyzed further for detecting highlights.

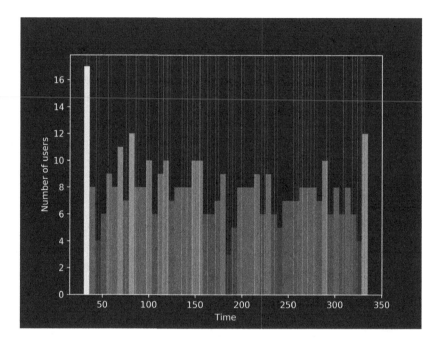

Fig. 4. Histogram from the calculated peaks.

To analyze the bins, we calculate the *Jaccard similarity* between bins within the same level of users. **Jaccard similarity coefficient** [15] is a method for measuring similarity of a sample set. It is defined as the size of the intersection over the size of the union of the set (Eq. 2). The result from Jaccard dissimilarity is between zero and one, and the value closer to one represents higher similarity. Jaccard distance was used because it is a good indicator to measure commonality between users.

$$J(A,B) = \frac{|A \bigcap B|}{|A \bigcup B|} \tag{2}$$

By defining the threshold for Jaccard dissimilarity, we can select bins on the same level of the histogram that have similarities to each other. We define a graph to connect similar members on the same level together. For every similar bin, we find the intersections between two bins. Using stack data structure, we push the intersections onto the stack, then we pop one member and connect that member to the remaining items in the intersection and add the connected edge to the graph. We repeat the same process for all the bins in different levels.

The graph with the highest number of edges has highest probability to locate the time that might be considered as highlight. By defining a threshold for the number of edges in the graph, we can use bins that might include some highlights from the stimulus. Algorithm 1 shows the steps taken to report the highlight.

Figure 5 shows the result as a karate graph [32], from the histogram of size 30 bins. In this example, bins with a size bigger than four were considered as bins

---

Algorithm 1. Reporting highlights.

---

input : Bins at the same level of the histogram, Jaccard Dissimilarity
          Threshold, Edge density Threshold
output: Possible time stamp of the highlights

for *bin* ∈ *InputBins* do
   for *bin* ∈ *InputBins* do
      | Calculate Jaccard Dissimilarity between bins
   end
end
graph ← new Graph()
while *not at the end of bin* ∈ *InputBins* do
   CurrentBin ← bin
   for *bin* ∈ *InputBins* do
      if *jaccardDissimilarity(CurrentBin, bin)* ≥ *JaccardThreshold* then
      intersection ← *Intersection(CurrentBin, bin)*
      while *length(intersection)* ≥ 1 do
         CurrentPerson ← intersection.pop()
         for *members* ∈ *intersection* do
            | graph.addEdge(CurrentPerson, members)
         end
      end

   end
end
if *graph.EdgeNumber* ≥ *EdgeDensityThreshold* then Report timestamp of
the bins in the level.

---

with potential highlights in them. The density of the edges in each graph, shows the similarity between bins in that level. Bins with higher number of edges have higher probability to be considered as highlight of the stimulus.

The three threshold that we use in this approach are as follow:

- Number of bins in the histogram
- Jaccard dissimilarity threshold
- Edge density threshold for karate graph

Different threshold levels can provides different level of certainty. For example, with low number of bins, low Jaccard value and low edge density threshold, the timestamp of highlights may point to the whole duration of the stimulus. Figure 5 shows the output with total number of 30 bins, with 0.45 Jaccard dissimilarity threshold and edge density of 40.

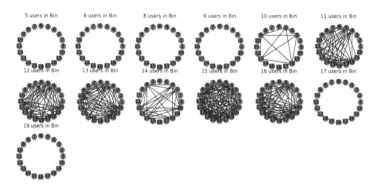

Fig. 5. Karate graph shows the timestamp of the highlights based on the number of the edge in each bin.

7   Result and Discussion

To implement our method, we assumed EDA signal by itself is sufficient for detecting highlights of the stimulus without using other physiological signals. Further, the phasic component of EDA signal played an important role in detecting the highlights.

We selected two different medium, "Halloween" movie as our ground truth and "Evil Within" as our testing stimulus. To explore the differences between the two mediums, due to the small sample size and, therefore, uncertain underlying distribution of the data, we considered both parametric and non-parametric approaches for analyzing the data.

We used paired t-test for parametric and Wilcoxon test for non-parametric approach. The result for both approaches shows that participants are more engaged with the video game content compare to the movie (p-value < 0.05). Other than this, as we expected, there are no significant differences between two contents.

Table 1 shows specific means and standard deviations for each questions posed to participants after the study. The questions were ranked between one to five, where a value of 1 represented negative feedback to the question and a value of five represented positive feedback.

Table 2 shows the overall mean and standard deviation for all questions. The overall mean for the movie and video game can also be considered as the rank for how strong the content was. A value closer to 5 indicates the content might have higher emotion arousal on the users.

We can conclude, overall, the two stimulus are very similar to each other. The unique characteristics in the video game, for example using camera in first person perspective, caused the users to become more engaged to the content. Regardless, the mean and standard deviation for "Being in Control" shows that the level of interaction for both stimulus are identical.

Table 1. Mean and standard deviation between movie and video game.

	Movie		Video Game	
	Mean	Std	Mean	Std
Being engaged and involved	3.40	0.99	4.00	0.79
Negative or positive feeling	2.80	0.69	2.75	1.07
Being passive or active	2.75	1.02	2.95	1.14
Being relaxed or tensed	3.50	0.94	3.10	0.23
Dislike or like	3.15	0.18	3.15	0.26
Being in control	3.2	0.28	3.2	0.26

Table 2. Overall mean and standard deviation between movie and video game.

Movie		Video game	
Mean	Std	Mean	Std
3.13	0.30	3.19	0.42

Table 3. Highlight detection including all signals for movie.

Number of bins	Movie					
	Jaccard threshold = 0.0			Jaccard threshold = 0.4		
	Precision score	Recall score	F1 score	Precision score	Recall score	F1 score
100	0.93	0.84	0.88	0.93	0.84	0.88
90	0.89	0.80	0.84	0.90	0.93	0.92
80	0.93	0.87	0.90	0.96	0.83	0.89
70	1.0	0.74	0.85	0.95	0.74	0.83
60	0.93	0.90	0.92	0.96	0.93	0.95
50	1.0	0.87	0.93	1.0	0.87	0.93
40	1.0	0.84	0.91	1.0	0.83	0.91
30	1.0	0.64	0.78	1.0	0.74	0.85

The result for detecting the highlights based on the commonalities among bins is displayed in Fig. 6 using a karate graph. For each bin, we selected the top three graphs with the highest number of edges. From the selected graphs, we extracted the time stamp of the bins in that graph. Finally, we compared the extracted time stamps to our pre-defined time stamps for highlights.

The result show, for both movie and video game stimulus, the reported highlights point to the locations that can be considered as highlights. These highlights include sudden change of scene, starting of loud sound and element of surprise, that was common in both stimulus.

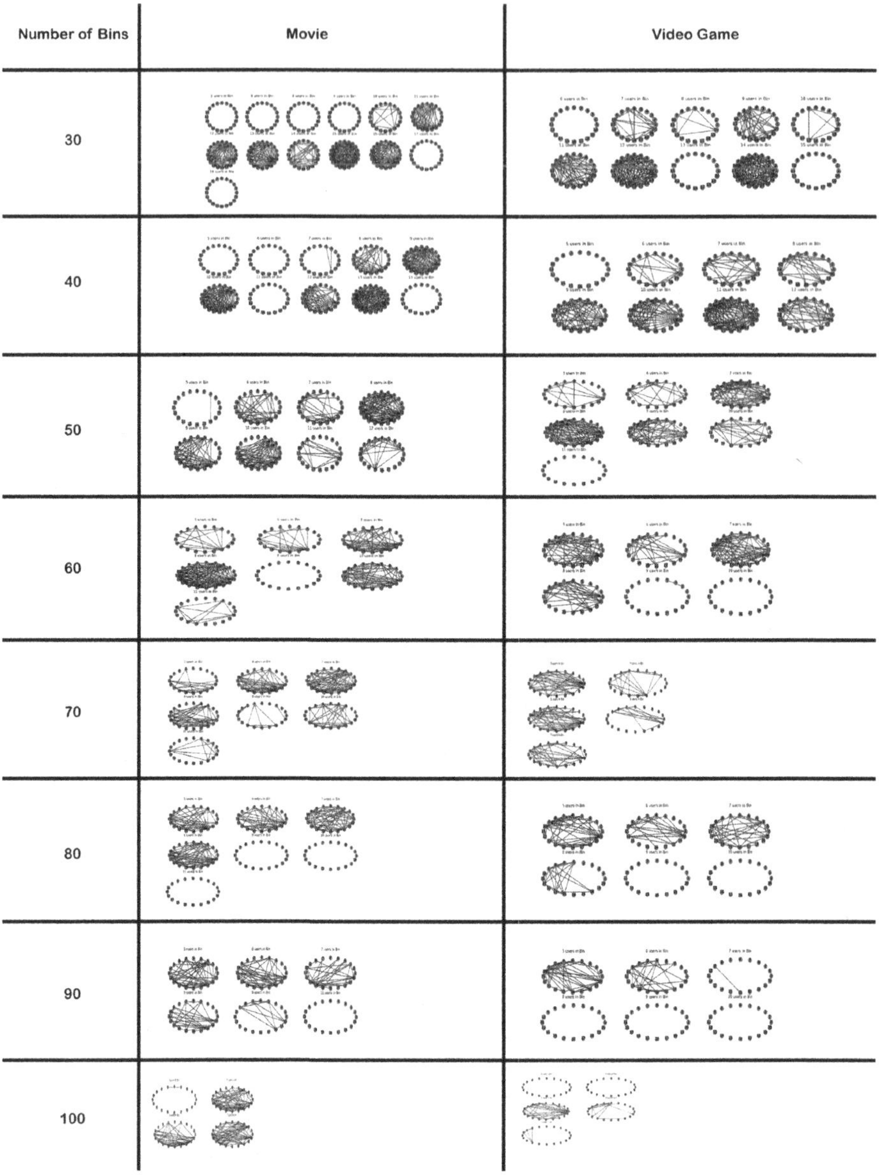

Number of Bins	Movie	Video Game
30		
40		
50		
60		
70		
80		
90		
100		

Fig. 6. Karate graph for measuring commonalities among size of bins for different number of bins.

Tables 3 and 4 show the precision, recall and F1 score for each bins, with and without including Jaccard threshold. Looking at the result, the two bins, number 60 for movie and number 50 for video game, show the Jaccard threshold caused improvement in F1 score. The selected threshold for Jaccard dissimilarity shows some improvement but overall, it is not significant.

Table 4. Highlight detection including all signals for video game.

Number of bins	Video game					
	Jaccard threshold = 0.0			Jaccard threshold = 0.4		
	Precision score	Recall score	F1 score	Precision score	Recall score	F1 score
100	0.96	0.67	0.79	0.92	0.7	0.8
90	0.93	0.75	0.83	0.9	0.78	0.84
80	0.96	0.78	0.86	0.96	0.81	0.88
70	0.92	0.83	0.87	0.96	0.78	0.86
60	0.91	0.86	0.89	0.89	0.95	0.92
50	0.96	0.75	0.85	0.97	1.0	0.98
40	0.96	0.67	0.79	1.0	0.62	0.76
30	1.0	0.73	0.84	1.0	0.7	0.84

Table 5. Highlight detection per individual.

Movie			Video game		
Average precision	Average recall	Average F1 score	Average precision	Average recall	Average F1 score
0.43	0.27	0.31	0.47	0.21	0.28

To further test our method, we ran the method for per-individual signals instead of including all the signals. Table 5 shows the average precision and F1 score among all participants.

The result from our study show our method has high accuracy when including EDA signals among all users and low accuracy when using per individual. The precision of this methods depends on the size of the bins and number of edges in karate graph.

By analyzing the time interval between each pre-defined highlights, the mean of 9.85 with a standard deviation of 4.51 for movie stimulus and mean of 8.65 with standard deviation of 5.70 for video game stimulus provides the best time interval in detecting highlights.

7.1 Combined Physiological Responses

WE are in a process of conducting a user study with several sensory devices, using IAPS [20] data set as our stimulus. The goal is to categorize users based on their affective responses to stimulus.

There are available data set that can be used for this purpose [19]. However, to the best of author knowledge, in these studies users are 'wired' to connect different sensory devices. Such a setup can reduce users' emotional response.

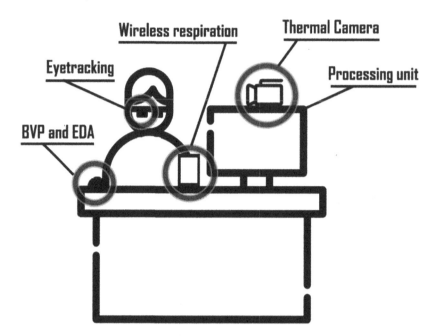

Fig. 7. The processing unit synchronizes the data and stores combined physiological signals. The system can provide real-time data analysis.

Also, the process of collecting these data sets does not consider the effect of precedence that might cause by strong contexts in the stimulus. For example, a physiological response caused by an unpleasant image followed by a pleasant image might not fully descend. This will cause to record the effect of viewing an unpleasant image when viewing a pleasant image.

We limit the use of wearable devices to a wristband and an eye-tracking device. The rest of the sensory devices are stationary.

The devices used in include:

- Empatica E4 [13] wristband: records a user's blood volume pressure and electrodermal activities.
- Jenoptik stationary thermal camera: records the users' facial skin temperature.
- Pupil [17] eye tracking headset device: records users' eye movement.
- Walabot [28], an RF sensory device: records user respiration.

Fig. 7 shows the setup and different devices that being used in the study.

Our stimulus is a collection of 120 images (60 neutral, 30 unpleasant, 30 pleasant) selected from IAPS. To reduce the effect of precedence caused by stimulus, we are using the proposed method of detecting highlights for selecting a sequence of images.

With this approach, the likelihood of affective response and the duration of physiological response for each image is known before hand. This gives us an approximation of a time interval that is needed to reduce the effect caused by unpleasant or pleasant images. During this time a sequence of neutral images will be shown. With this approach each image with pleasant or unpleasant context will have its own physiological responses.

Finally to reduce the cognitive load from affective response during our study, we divide the study into two sections. The purpose of the first section is to focus on physiological response cause by the stimulus. During this section, users' physiological responses are recorded without asking any self-report questionnaires. During the second section, we ask the users to only rate each image using an affective slider [3] rather than using the self-assessment Manakin (SAM) [5]. Using affective slider is easier for users to understand, compared to SAM.

We hope that this approach for collecting data can gives us a representative and more reliable data that can be used to explore causation and correlation between stimulus and users' emotion. The data set can be used to create a model capable of clustering users based on their response to the images and predict users' behavior.

8   Conclusions

Affective computing is growing and the idea that one day an application can make decisions for us without our cognitive front is not out of reach. Today, biometric sensors are becoming smaller with better accuracy that can easily be used in daily tasks.

These advancements require the need to explore new methods and approaches in affective computing that can help us to explore new ways of interaction between human and computers. The results from our study show it is possible to detect the highlight of the stimulus using only the EDA signal of the group of people. This opens a new door for creating a system capable of recommending the stimulus based on the current physiological changes of the users.

Although the result of the study shows that by only using EDA signal it is possible to detect the highlights of the stimulus, a symmetric histogram may occur by increasing the number of participants. This might lead to the case that the algorithm include the whole duration of the stimulus as highlight, which is meaningless. Studies with larger sample sizes are needed to explore the result in more detail.

We mainly focused on video stimulus that can cause fear. However, it would be useful to run the same study with other basic emotions to find the physiological differences between emotions.

Overall the result from this study, demonstrate the potential of EDA signals, independently, in affective computing. We were able to gain a better understanding of physiological signals and their correlation and causation to stimulus. Although it is always possible to provide self-report in study, but the results might not fully represent our affective response.

In studies with several sensory devices, having method such as this can be beneficial to validate the effect of stimulus before hand. This can be helpful for models to know the time intervals of the stimulus with higher likelihood of users' affective response. This information can be used to categeorize users based on their response or predict future responses based on the current ones. Further study needs to be done to explore if adding more sensory devices can narrows down the time interval for detecting highlights.

References

1. The evil within (2014). https://theevilwithin.bethesda.net
2. Benedek, M., Kaernbach, C.: A continuous measure of phasic electrodermal activity. J. Neurosci. Methods **190**(1), 80–91 (2010)
3. Betella, A., Verschure, P.F.M.J.: The affective slider: a digital self-assessment scale for the measurement of human emotions. PLOS One **11**(2), 1–11 (2016)
4. Boucsein, W.: Electrodermal Activity. The Springer Series in Behavioral Psychophysiology and Medicine. Springer, New York (2012). https://doi.org/10.1007/978-1-4614-1126-0
5. Bradley, M.M., Lang, P.J.: Measuring emotion: the self-assessment manikin and the semantic differential. J. Behav. Ther. Exp. Psychiatry **25**(1), 49–59 (1994)
6. Chênes, C., Chanel, G., Soleymani, M., Pun, T.: Highlight detection in movie scenes through inter-users, physiological linkage. In: Ramzan, N., van Zwol, R., Lee, J.S., Clüver, K., Hua, X.S. (eds.) Social Media Retrieval, pp. 217–237. Springer, London (2013). https://doi.org/10.1007/978-1-4471-4555-4_10
7. Cowie, R., Cornelius, R.R.: Describing the emotional states that are expressed in speech. Speech Commun. **40**(1), 5–32 (2003)
8. Dawson, M., Schell, A., Filion, D.: The electrodermal system. In: Cacioppo, J.T., Tassinary, L.G., Berntson, G.G. (eds.) Handbook of Psychophysiology, 2nd edn, pp. 200–223. Cambridge University Press, New York (2000)
9. Dhall, A., Asthana, A., Goecke, R., Gedeon, T.: Emotion recognition using PHOG and LPQ features. In: Face and Gesture 2011, pp. 878–883. IEEE, Piscataway (2011)
10. Ekman, P.: Facial expression and emotion. Am. Psychol. **48**(4), 384–392 (1993)
11. Feldman, L.A.: Variations in the circumplex structure of mood. Pers. Soc. Psychol. Bull. **21**(8), 806–817 (1995)
12. Gaebel, W., Wölwer, W.: Facial expression and emotional face recognition in schizophrenia and depression. Eur. Arch. Psychiatry Clin. Neurosci. **242**(1), 46–52 (1992)
13. Garbarino, M., Lai, M., Bender, D., Picard, R.W., Tognetti, S.: Empatica E3: a wearable wireless multi-sensor device for real-time computerized biofeedback and data acquisition. In: 2014 4th International Conference on Wireless Mobile Communication and Healthcare - Transforming Healthcare Through Innovations in Mobile and Wireless Technologies (MOBIHEALTH), pp. 39–42. IEEE, Piscataway (2014)
14. Haag, A., Goronzy, S., Schaich, P., Williams, J.: Emotion recognition using biosensors: first steps towards an automatic system. In: André, E., Dybkjær, L., Minker, W., Heisterkamp, P. (eds.) ADS 2004. LNCS (LNAI), vol. 3068, pp. 36–48. Springer, Heidelberg (2004). https://doi.org/10.1007/978-3-540-24842-2_4
15. Jaccard, P.: The distribution of the flora in the alpine zone.1. New Phytol. **11**(2), 37–50 (1912)
16. Joho, H., Staiano, J., Sebe, N., Jose, J.M.: Looking at the viewer: analysing facial activity to detect personal highlights of multimedia contents. Multimed. Tools Appl. **51**(2), 505–523 (2011)

17. Kassner, M., Patera, W., Bulling, A.: Pupil: an open source platform for pervasive eye tracking and mobile gaze-based interaction. In: ACM International Joint Conference on Pervasive and Ubiquitous Computing: Adjunct Publication (2014)
18. Kim, K.H., Bang, S.W., Kim, S.R.: Emotion recognition system using short-term monitoring of physiological signals. Med. Biol. Eng. Comput. **42**(3), 419–427 (2004)
19. Koelstra, S., et al.: DEAP: a database for emotion analysis; using physiological signals. IEEE Trans. Affect. Comput. **3**(1), 18–31 (2012)
20. Lang, P.J., Bradley, M.M., Cuthbert, B.N.: International affective picture system (IAPS): affective ratings of pictures and instruction manual. University of Florida, Gainesville, FL, Technical report (2008)
21. Levenson, R.W.: Autonomic nervous system differences among emotions. Psychol. Sci. **3**(1), 23–27 (1992)
22. Levenson, R.W., Ekman, P., Friesen, W.V.: Voluntary facial action generates emotion-specific autonomic nervous system activity. Psychophysiology **27**(4), 363–384 (1990)
23. Lynch, T., Martins, N.: Nothing to fear? An analysis of college students' fear experiences with video games. J. Broadcast. Electron. Media **59**(2), 298–317 (2015)
24. Marsh, A.A., Blair, R.J.R.: Deficits in facial affect recognition among antisocial populations: a meta-analysis. Neurosci. Biobehav. Rev. **32**(3), 454–465 (2008)
25. Mauss, I.B., Robinson, M.D.: Measures of emotion: a review. Cogn. Emot. **23**(2), 209–237 (2009)
26. Murugappan, M., Ramachandran, N., Sazali, Y.: Classification of human emotion from EEG using discrete wavelet transform. J. Biomed. Sci. Eng. **03**(04), 390–396 (2010)
27. Philippot, P.: Inducing and assessing differentiated emotion-feeling states in the laboratory. Cogn. Emot. **7**(2), 171–193 (1993). pMID: 27102736
28. Pierce, A.: Walabot diy can see into walls. Tech Direct. **76**(5), 8–9 (2017). Copyright - Copyright Prakken Publications, Inc., Jan 2017; Document feature - Photographs; Last updated - 2017-11-23
29. Ragot, M., Martin, N., Em, S., Pallamin, N., Diverrez, J.-M.: Emotion recognition using physiological signals: laboratory vs. wearable sensors. In: Ahram, T., Falcão, C. (eds.) AHFE 2017. AISC, vol. 608, pp. 15–22. Springer, Cham (2018). https://doi.org/10.1007/978-3-319-60639-2_2
30. Tasooji, R.: Determining correlation between video stimuli and electrodermal activity. Master's thesis, Virginia Polytechnic Institute and State University, Blacksburg, VA (2018)
31. Trubanova, A., et al.: The role of perspective-taking on ability to recognize fear. Curr. Res. Psychol. **6**(2), 22–30 (2016)
32. Zachary, W.W.: An information flow model for conflict and fission in small groups. J. Anthropol. Res. **33**(4), 452–473 (1977)

Affective Computational Interfaces

Suzete Venturelli[1](✉), Artur Cabral Reis[2], Gabriela Mutti[2],
Nycacia Delmondes Florindo[2], Prahlada Hargreaves[2],
Rodolfo Ward[2], and Tainá Luize Martins[3]

[1] Anhembi Morumbi University, São Paulo, Brazil
suzeteventurelli@gmail.com
[2] Medialab/UnB, University of Brasília, Brasilia, Brazil
arturcabralreis@gmail.com, muttigabriela@gmail.com,
nycadelmondes@gmail.com, prahladdasa@gmail.com,
rodolfoward@gmail.com
[3] Federal Institute of Brasília, Brasilia, Brazil
tainaluize@gmail.com

Abstract. The following text describes the development of affective computer interfaces that seek to provoke visual, tactile, gustatory and olfactory interactions, a process by which an external or internal stimulus causes a specific reaction that produce a perception, considering that in the *deleuzian* and *guattarian* sense (1992), an idea can thoroughly cross creative activities. For the authors, an idea arises in three distinct forms: (1) at one moment arises; (2) in the philosophical context; (3) in the form of concepts; in another moment, it appears in the artistic production of visual artists, in which artist invents perceptions, and it also occurs with musicians because according to the authors, the musician creates affections. Considering this and artistic and design computational production, we describe below the results of collaborative research that has in common the poetics of interactivity, provided by computational processes and methods that approach different ideas involving affective cartography, body, art, nature and artificial life, wearable computers and emergency.

Keywords: Interfaces · Poetics · Affectivity · Emergency

1 Introduction

Computational art has been a fundamental element in the development of research projects at University of Brasília's technological art laboratory Media Lab/UnB, and since 2018, it also has had Anhembi Morumbi University as a collaborator. According to Venturelli (2017), computational art even if it is occasioned by concepts that arise from aesthetic ideas, is now minimally written based on computing. An informed writing that the author defines as n-dimensional. The drivers were designed for the series of artists of the 1980s, that is: on an axis is an invisible construction elaborated by logistic formalisms in a network of codes; and on a second axis, is a form of social expression in the evolutionary memories of the binary code (in the Darwinian sense).

© Springer Nature Switzerland AG 2019
A. Marcus and W. Wang (Eds.): HCII 2019, LNCS 11583, pp. 510–520, 2019.
https://doi.org/10.1007/978-3-030-23570-3_38

The translation makes readable and interpretable a social memory, that is layered in scriptures of knowledge. Computational art seeks to bring from tradition the questions of science to the context of art. For the author, two postulates derive from computational art: programming, as an internal organization, and interactivity, as a condition of circulation and modification of data. In order to complete the possibilities worked by the artists, it is necessary to integrate in these perspectives: cybernetics, artificial intelligence and softwares that present the possibility of creativity and learning on their own. Consequently, computational art goes through a path where all disciplines mingle.

Computational art means creation by associating different media with computational processes. To discourse on computational art means to penetrate a complex mutant logic of discoveries and applications. Interactivity is not only a possibility offered by computational art, but it is, in fact, the foundation of the system in the treatment of information emanating from the user.

Systems are user centric. Public from computational art is effectively different from the public from traditional art works. The second one likes to interpret stories, images and music, but the first one want to do something more: they appreciate works that can be manipulated in its presentation, preferring artistic works that require others participation to make operation possible.

Users are able to generate and display a work. The role of the artist is to create some items of possibilities, through variables that are often part of a code executed by the computational process step by step. The artist uses his or hers knowledge to generate a work whose performance is specific to the user. The computer automates a generation of work so that users can get to know the work and explore their own views. Both the user and the artist are part of the work. The interactor is an artist and appreciates the work for the interactivity it contains; according to some art critics, this interactivity is the reason for a computational computer to have merit or not. The object for the computational artist is software.

The generation of artists that the author is part faced the need to learn formalism for the elaboration of codes, to also be able to "break" them in the production. The study did not belong to the field of arts because university education in Brazil was quite fragmented. Allied to the chaos, confusion, lack of technology and cultural access delineated in the art teaching implementation of arts education in Brazilian schools in the 1970s, the university education was cloistered in the reactionary universe that valued only the "artistic genius". Education, in general, is not an incentive to approximate the areas of knowledge or an art as a field of knowledge. The model in Brazil today has changed and is more focused on the transdisciplinary ones that are practitioners of smaller companies, in team or in group. From the moment that the graduate programs in art emerged, art research consolidated in the institutions and approaching with other areas became necessary, as we shall see later, in the reports of computational art works, performed and developed since 2017.

2 It Is All Sensation

For Deleuze and Guattari (1992), a work of art is a being of sensation and nothing else, since it exists in itself. In the context of computational work, sensation goes through the involvement in manipulation of different materials, as means of producing a compound of perceptions and affections. Often, in contact with people, perceptions are no longer perceptions; they seem independent of those people who experience them. Just as the effects they provoke, they are no longer feelings or affections, they go beyond the strength of those whom submit to them.

The authors remind us that sensations, perceptions and affections are beings, whose validity is within themselves and does not exceed any time lived beyond a work. It could be said that they exist in the absence of human, because is a composite of perceptions and affections itself. From this perspective, we bring transdisciplinary contributions on issues related to the materiality of emotional manifestations in the context of our research. They question the tangible and sensorial dimension of works of art, which awakens our imagination about how aesthetic images and narratives can be formed by emotions. The aim is to study sets of flows, circulations and affective intensities in the computational context for both the art and the field of design. It also seeks to build relationships with emotions using different artistic media. On this axis we discuss next, how emotional manifestations arise in the imaginary, how they are elaborated and produced.

Works of art involving hybrid features of art and computer design, overflow in the strictly computational environment, whether digital or not. But they consider an integral part of the work, the relation of interactivity between machines and living beings, or between machines only. They find their roots in the Dadaist movement of the 1920s, and more specifically in the work of Marcel Duchamp and Man Ray. Combinatory processes that follow combinatorial rules of Dadaist poetry were adopted by members of concrete poetry in Brazil, for example, through execution of their combinatorial sequences, and many authors of computational environments are still inspired by this type of creation. In the 1960s, the movement of contemporary art fluxus in Brazil, we have linked kinship with the Rex Group (1966–1967)[1], that was created in São Paulo, also influenced by Dadaism, because it touched mainly the visual arts, but also music and literature, and aimed with a devastating sense of humor, to break boundaries between the arts and the world, to build a link between art and life.

3 Affective Materiality

Emotion encompasses a semantic spectrum related to states of mind that allow us to touch on very concrete aspects of fluids, forms, and roughness of affectivity. In this perspective, our reflection brings contributions on issues related to materiality in the creation of works that intend to provoke some kind of emotional involvement through its poetics. In the scope of artistic cartography, the feeling of affection, which in the

---

[1] http://enciclopedia.itaucultural.org.br/grupo434025/grupo-rex.

work #prece_, was treated as a memory of the emotions, whereas the work deals with the poetic mapping inserted and concerns people who disappeared from Brasilia, the capital city of Brazil. In this work, interaction takes place through the social network twitter, where an interactor is able to add names of people from their family that are missing and thus, the cartography appears through postings. This work raises the following question: how to historicize and archive affective, fugitive, snapshot and variable phenomena? (see Fig. 1).

Fig. 1. Artwork #prece_ exhibited at *Museu Nacional*, Brasília-Brazil.

4 Ipêfeito

The work *Ipêfeito* (see Fig. 2) analyzes a computational arte_design relation through a research project that has developed a computational device emerging, since it presents itself as an unconventional visualization of data of environments. It functions as an artistic work by proposing reflections about our relationship with the environment and nature.

The work in question interweaves concepts of art, technology and design, to result in a wearable device, which aims to measure the quality of the air in which it is exposed through the MQ-7 gas sensor, detecting the carbon monoxide gas (CO), released into the environment naturally or by human action by burning fossil fuels, thermoelectric plants, heating systems and others. The visualization of the presence of the CO gas is possible through the leds present in the dress, which switches off when this gas is detected by the sensor, and all this action is controlled through the Lilypad arduino board, designed to be sewn into clothes and accessories.

The work involves natural and biological issues because it proposes to visually expose the action of a highly toxic gas found in our environment, but which has its emitting sources in greater quantity anthropic, that is, by human causes. Technology plays a fundamental role in enabling this visualization, where from electronic devices coupled in a dress, the interactor observes the assiduity of the CO gas, having the dress as a visual artifice where, due to the contribution of technology, it also becomes a device, a wearable.

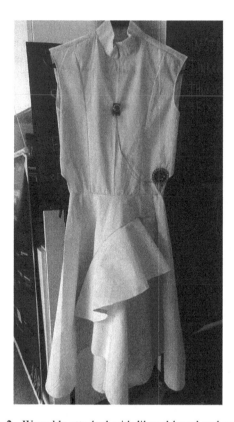

Fig. 2. Wearable attached with lilypad board and sensor

5   Unveiled Body

The "Unveiled Body" project seeks a dialogue between interfaces, the body and the digital medium with cameras, computers and projectors. Together, these interfaces allow a moment to explore the visual and plastic potentials of the unveiled body and the surrounding nature, it also gives opportunity to be placed next to other textures, expanding a powerful dialogue that comes from this observation. The images are captured by digital cameras and later the collages are produced by editing photos of plants with various textures, combined with photos of regions of the body, with the intention of approaching it as visual and plastic power, as well as enlarging the context of aesthetic experiences from the textures present in these forms.

Subsequently, these images are processed inside a code within the processing program, which together with the camera of the computer, interprets the color change of the pixels of the captured image and, in this unstable area of color change, projects the collage, causing the printing from the motion, unveiling a "hidden" image behind that disturbance in the pixels (see Fig. 3). As the person moves in front of the camera, the projected image is transformed, so that the motion captured by the color change its pixels through the software processing, identifies the area and replaces it with the collage image. This replaced area changes cyclically over a period of time.

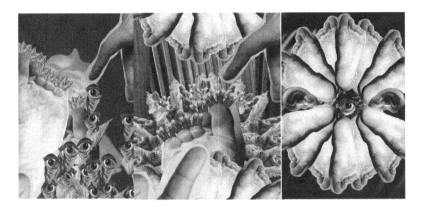

Fig. 3. Collages made from photographs of body parts and plant textures.

The experience of the work takes place in an environment with music, where the purpose is to stimulate the movement and consequently the interaction and revelation of the collage. The act of unveiling an image, a region, is related to the act of unveiling the body, to discover its limits and sensations, in the case of the work "Body Unveiled", it moves to observe. This observation has the potential to open dialogue with new textures and collages by mixing different textures. The viewer's gaze is guided by curiosity and strangeness stimuli to keep moving and observing, to extend the aesthetic experience with the veiled image, taking that look into a space of imagination.

6   Emotional Politics: Orchis Food Truck Project

In the genesis of our artistic process, at the center of the system and the device of artistic work, affectivity can be studied under the angle of individual and collective sensibility, as in an informational relational process. In this sense, our research is interested in several aspects related to art and nature, its sharing and its collective work with teams and other laboratories. In addition, we study the effects of human relationships with their environment, to understand current political issues and individual feelings, as proposed in the work Orchis Food Truck (see Fig. 4).

The term Orchis, which means testicles, was first used by Theophrastus (c.372: 287 BC), Greek philosopher, disciple of Aristotle. Theophrastus compared the tuberous roots of some Mediterranean orchids with the human testicles. For this reason, since the Middle Ages, aphrodisiac properties are attributed to orchids. The relation of art and nature is not recent, but the relation artificial_natural gave rise to a type of art that became known as bioarte (1997), or art and artificial life (2004). In the Computational Art Research Laboratory of the Universidade de Brasília (Media Lab/UnB), we developed an artistic project, in which a beautiful Orchid controls a 3D chocolate printer that symbolically controls the artificial nature, currently referred as technology, to enter into communication with humans.

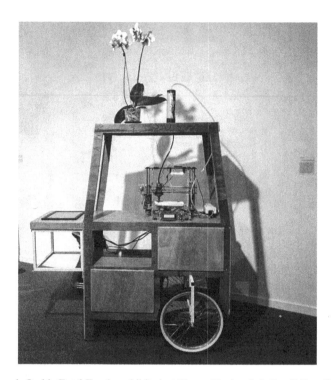

Fig. 4. Artwork Orchis Food Truck, exhibited at Museu Nacional da República, Brasília-Brazil

The first prototype of the Orchid as an aphrodisiac cyber flower, converted the flower's vital signs like moisture and heat from the environment, to the 3D printer that printed real-time random shapes from genetic algorithms. It was thought about the possibility of generating mutating forms to approximate the context of artificial life in relation to natural life, with generative forms as environment for the print.

7   Morphogenesis

In the artistic context, we think of its origin in the primitive geometric cube as morphogenesis of the design, which, when subdivided by random parameters, generates a complex pattern by repeating itself within the form. The repetition of the pattern gives rise to a form known as fractal. The modeling of the final form is given from the logic of self-similarity.

For Mandelbrot (2016), fractals are graphic representations of chaos and the logic of self-similarity refers to the forms of nature. The research considers that the origin of its form, is its DNA, that arises from algorithms structured from the concept of art and artificial life, meaning that no two equal impressions will ever occur. Another characteristic, which according to Varela and Maturana, the living being is defined according to its capacity to self-organize. After the artificially generated form, artificial life, establishes contact with the natural environment, receiving signals that will cause its mutation and new adaptation of its morphogenesis. The Food Truck, in this proposal aims to bring to the community of Brasília-Brazil located in risky areas, moments of socialization, considering the relation of art and gastronomy.

From the morphogenic (see Fig. 5) point of view, Media Lab/UnB research works with the primitive form of the cube as a original element. It is considered that, when subdivided by random parameters, it generates a complex pattern that repeats itself inside the form. The repetition of the pattern gives rise to a form known as fractal[2], as shown in the figure below.

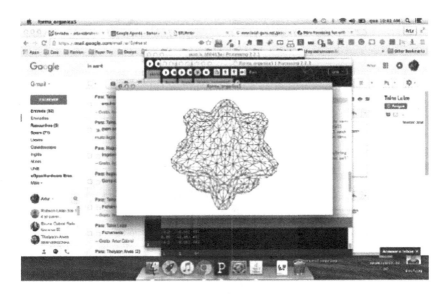

Fig. 5. Form created from pattern repetition

8   Art and Artificial Life

The initial genes in this generative way function as parameters stored in an array of variables that constitute the genetic matrix of the form to be printed. The sensors that monitor the plant, as well as the plant itself, acting as a natural sensor, sends data to the system, producing a new matrix and altering the generation of the form, synthesized as a new genetic coding. From a process known as "crossing over", the original form exchanges information between the matrices of different genetic codes for a mutation to occur (see Fig. 6). The final form gives rise to a genetically modified organism. As feedback to the plant, the system returns process data in the sound form, which functions as stimuli for the monitored plant. The prints resulting from this process are sequences in which the primitive forms intertwine with poetic results, unexpected, and therefore emergent forms.

---

[2] Theory developed by Benoit Mandelbrot (2016).

Fig. 6. Printed forms made by the orchid

In another experience we proposed a telematic version of the process, through which an orchid was monitored in an environment located at Museu do Amanhã - Rio de Janeiro, Brazil, where the *Hyperorganic* event (coordinated by professor Guto Nóbrega) was held in 2018. A setup was tested in which the two laboratories remained connected via video conferencing through Google Hangout platform (see Fig. 7).

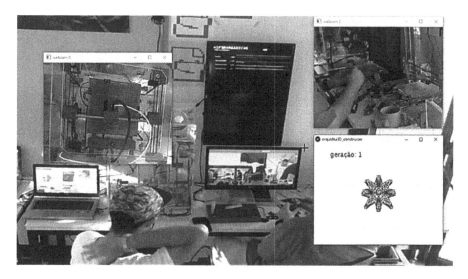

Fig. 7. Remote vision of the Media Lab during the *Hyperorganics* event

Data exchanges between the two environments (Media Lab/UnB and Museu do Amanhã) were facilitated using the OSC protocol, which interconnected the two laboratories through the NANO server, located in the laboratory at UFRJ in Rio de Janeiro, Brazil. The ambient signals (temperature, humidity and lighting) were captured immediately from the sensors connected to the Arduino and consequently sent to the network. But the galvanic response of the plant requires very specific and variable adjustments because it is a living organism. Two electrodes are connected to the plant leaf so that, a small current transits from one point to the other through the leaf.

Variations of this potential depends on the conductivity of the plant, which varies according to its biological characteristics and its interaction with the environment. After setting up the system at the Museu do Amanhã, we began the experiments. A 40 in. TV screen was used as a monitor for the plant signals sent to the server, as well as for receiving images of the Media Lab/UnB in Brasilia. After a series of adjustments that practically took place in the first and second days of the experiment, we finally got a good response of the system to the given stimulus in the orchid. The data traveled from a setup at the Museu do Amanhã to a server at UFRJ and could be viewed in the form of graphs in our interface, created in the programming language JavaScript for this purpose.

9   Orchid Prints Its Aphrodisiac Information

In the new version of the proposal, the orchid prints its aphrodisiac information in chocolate, as an art form in a Food Truck. Aphrodisiac type of foods such as chocolate, pepper or cinnamon have nutrients with stimulating properties and therefore increase the production of sex hormones and activate libido.

The first version of the proposal shows how its signals are transmitted, and in a process of visualization, the viewer realizes that there is a correlation with the printer. The new version aims to mount a 3D printer to print specifically chocolate. For its formal fulfillment, was necessary structure from the current open source technology of 3D printing, an adaptation to make printing of information in the form of chocolate possible. For the first version, with the team and support of teachers specialized engineers, it was possible to implement the current system. The new proposal is based on our own experience on setting-up a 3D printer created from the philosophy of free hardware and software (see Figs. 8 and 9).

Fig. 8. First version of the work exhibited (2017).

Fig. 9. New version with chocolate print (2018)

10 Conclusion

How to study emotions in the context of computer art? To do so, it is necessary to advance studies on computational and cybernetic art to create interactive systems with artificial life components involving nature and programmable machines. According to Venturelli (2017), computational art is an art form, which is structured from four basic references: a definition, an ontology, aesthetic characteristics and recognition of its status as art. For the author, computational art shows that creation in this field involves more general common issues, in *statu nascendi*, to the artistic, technoscientific and social domains, which provide the modes of structuring, methodology and programming techniques introduced in the process.

Computational poetic does not always refer to the computer or to logical-mathematical operations; sometimes it is based on intuition only, in which art works as mathematics without logic and truth. In the development of the work, artistic references were analyzed by renowned Brazilian artists such as Guto Nóbrega, Gilbertto Prado and Eduardo Kac, who in the field of art and technology approach issues that will be studied as the machinic relation and nature, when they complement themselves and raise the possibility of coexistence.

References

Deleuze, G., Guattari, F.: O que é a filosofia? vol. 34. Editora, Rio de Janeiro (1992)

Mandelbrot, B.: The Fractal Geometry of Nature. Freeman and Company, New York (1977). http://ordinatous.com/pdf/The_Fractal_Geometry_of_Nature.pdf. Accessed 15 Juin 2016

Venturelli, S.: Arte Computacional. Edunb, Brasília (2017)

EMOINEC: Exploring the Application of the EMOINAD Guide to an E-commerce Context

Angela Villareal-Freire[1(✉)], Andrés F. Aguirre[1(✉)], Jaime Diaz[2(✉)], and César A. Collazos[1(✉)]

[1] Universidad del Cauca, Popayán, Colombia
{avillarreal,afaguirre,ccollazo}@unicauca.edu.co
[2] Universidad de la Frontera, Temuco, Chile
jaimeignacio.diaz@ufrontera.cl

Abstract. This article presents an adaptation of the process of construction of the EMOINAD guide to the context of electronic commerce, with which it is expected to obtain a set of guidelines that support interface designers in their work to build pleasant and usable sites that consider the emotions of the clients. To do this, an exploration is made of the studies related to interface design guidelines and user experience guidelines for e-commerce, then the methodology of the EMOINAD guide is presented to finally make the adaptation in the last section. The validation of the resulting EMOINEC guide is left for future work. Through the development of the work presented in this article, it is concluded that the methodology of the EMOINAD guide is versatile and can be applied to different contexts.

Keywords: Design · Interface · E-commerce · Guidelines

1 Introduction

One of the most important problems that companies face today is to maximize their profits through a website; However, the definition of a "good website" is not easy as it depends on the services to be offered, general purpose, and final clients [1].

The interface appearance and navigation of a website can affect the client in different ways, because if it is inefficient, people will have difficulties in carrying out their daily activities and more mistakes will be made [2]. This fact leads to increased levels of frustration and stress; without forgetting that a poor interface design has a huge impact on the financial cost of organizations and in some cases, it can even compromise the security of its users or the public in general. On the other hand, the benefits of having a good interface design are countless as the reduction of training costs, and most importantly, the user satisfaction is increased [3].

© Springer Nature Switzerland AG 2019
A. Marcus and W. Wang (Eds.): HCII 2019, LNCS 11583, pp. 521–532, 2019.
https://doi.org/10.1007/978-3-030-23570-3_39

Due to the above, several researchers have focused on providing guidelines, principles and heuristics to facilitate the task of designing interfaces and guaranteeing a better response from the customer. These studies could be enough if what is sought is to have a starting point for the design of an e-commerce; However, if they are analyzed in depth, it can be perceived that they are not recent investigations and that the emotional perspective is not addressed in a deeper way. Bidin and Lokman [4] mention that the emotions of users have been what has made many products successful in the market, and that if a product such as a website can not attract visitors at first sight, it will go out of business even if it is useful and convenient to use. Also authors such as Pengnate [5] and Cyr [6] mention that less attention has been paid to affective aspects although the affective dimension has been explored during the last years [7]. Furthermore, emotional engagement has been found to impact and influence decision making, perception, attention, performance, users memories of product and cognition [8].

At this point, it is very important that the guidelines that are proposed for the design of e-commerce interfaces, not only incorporate aspects of Human-Computer Interaction (HCI) and User Experience (UX), but also consider how to design to evoke positive emotions.

It is for this reason that the EMOINAD (Emotive Interfaces for Attention Deficit) and EMOVLE (Emotive Interfaces for Virtual Learning Environments) guides have been created, each of which tries to contribute to the design of emotive interfaces for attention deficit disorder and for virtual learning environments, respectively [9, 10]. These guides are a compilation of the best practices in the field of user experience seeking to incorporate the emotional factor within the design in order to obtain not only functional but also attractive interfaces to the user. The guidelines, principles, and patterns that make up these guidelines, despite having been applied to specific environments, are transverse in nature and could be applied in different contexts. These guides with the studies analyzed, turn out to be a good starting point to gather the best practices in the context of e-commerce.

The purpose of this article is to make a proposal to adapt the construction methodology of the EMOINAD guide to an e-commerce environment. To do this, an exploration of the construction methodology is carried out and a detailed analysis is made of each element that makes it up to establish if it could be adapted or applied in the established context. Once this process is completed, a set of guidelines is made, forming a new guide called the EMOINEC guide (Emotive Interfaces for E-Commerce) which also incorporates some principles and guidelines focused on electronic commerce to give to the guide a greater depth.

The organization of this article is as follows: Sect. 2 explores the studies related to the design of interfaces for electronic commerce. Later, in Sect. 3, the methodology used for the construction of the EMOINAD guide is described and in Sect. 4 the proposal is made to adapt the methodology for the creation of the EMOINEC guide. Finally some conclusions of the work are presented.

As a result of this article, it will be obtained a preliminary set of guidelines that can be put into practice in the interface design of an e-commerce site and one example of one of the heuristic that is part of the EMOINEC guide. This is expected to contribute to the lack of specific guidelines for this context that consider the emotional aspect of the customer.

2   Guidelines for E-commerce Interface Design

Among the research related to the design of e-commerce interfaces are the Huang & Benyoucef's studies who have compiled a set of design principles grouped into five categories: usability, information quality, system quality, service quality, and playfulness [3]; For its part Stefani [11], considers that in the design process of the e-commerce should be considered the characteristics and sub-characteristics proposed by the ISO 25000 such as accuracy, consistency, functionality, understandability, and learning.

Fang and Salvendy [12] are more specific and list the 19 most important customer-centered design rules; Bonastre and Granollers [13] carry out a compilation of heuristics in e-commerce sites grouped according to the stage of the purchase decision process, and, finally, and among the latest research, there are those of Diaz et.al [14] and Rusu et.al [15, 16] who propose 12 usability heuristics for e-commerce that consider the cultural aspect, and a comparative study of user perception in three sets of usability heuristics, respectively.

Wang and Emurian [17], in turn, propose a conceptual framework of the characteristics that induce confidence, which belong to three dimensions: visual design, content design and social-cue design.

Barnes and Vidgen [18], relate the quality aspects of e-commerce to the evaluation criteria of the WebQual method, an instrument that establishes the categories of usability, information and service interaction. Nah and Davis [19] establish the concept of web usability as the ability to find one's own way through the web to locate the desired information, to know what to do next and most importantly, to do it with minimum effort. This is how they link the usability of e-commerce with the concepts of ease of navigation and search.

Lokman and Noor [8] present the concept of Kansei engineering applied to e-commerce websites and also establish the importance of affection and emotion. They declare the notion of the Perceived Affecive Quality (PAQ) as a primary affective reaction that the user obtains as the first impression of a website. Dorman [20] relates color and emotion in e-commerce systems and presents the importance of seducing consumers and evaluating emotions. Cyr [6] shows the relationship between navigation design, visual design and information design with trust, satisfaction and fidelity. It also establishes the characteristics of trust in a website, which are: reputation of the seller, quality of service, social presence, accuracy of online information and reputation of the firm. Basso [21] makes a model of trust in e-commerce contexts where it describes activities related to the formation of trust. Sheng [22] introduces the Stimulus-Organism-Response paradigm (S-O-R) which proposes that stimulus of the environment affects the internal states of the users which in turn influence their behavior and response.

Chandler and Hyatt [23], also perform a compilation of case studies and rules for a successful website and finally Beyer and Hotltzblatt [24] speak of contextual design as the process centered on the client that tries to understand how people work and that includes techniques that allow working in interdisciplinary teams providing explicit steps and deliverables.

All the studies described above serve as a starting point when building interfaces that take into account the user experience and that consider general design aspects; However, a structure and methodology is necessary to migrate all this information into an easy-to-use guide. Below is each of the steps of the EMOINAD methodology in which it is expected to migrate all the information gathered from the studies carried out.

3   The EMOINAD Guide Construction Process

Before adapting the methodology of creating the EMOINAD guide to the e-commerce context, it is necessary to explore each of the activities that comprise it. Figure 1 shows the different processes and activities that comprise it, which are described below.

1. **Bibliographic review of the context**
   - *To define the key areas of the context:* It is necessary to delimit the study in terms of its key areas. In the case of the EMOINAD guide, the key areas are design for emotion, child-centered design and attention deficit disorder.
   - *To explore the bibliography for each area:* After delimiting the key areas it is necessary to carry out a bibliographic exploration of each of them in order to know the most up-to-date studies.
2. **Information Selection process**
   - *To define the selection criteria:* After obtaining the most current and relevant studies in the areas in which the guide is framed, it is necessary to establish criteria that allow filtering the information and to guarantee the adaptation of the information to the context.
   - *To apply the criteria to the information:* Once the criteria are established, the information is classified according to the criteria to obtain the principles, heuristics and guidelines that should be considered in the design of interfaces.
3. **Guide construction**
   - *To define the categories according to the context:* It is important to classify the resulting information into sections that allow not only a possible extension of the guide but also facilitate its use. In the case of the EMOINAD guide, four categories were established: layout, navigation and interaction, content and performance. These categories will depend on the context.
   - *To define the template:* With the established sections and the information relevant to each section, an efficient and effective mechanism is chosen to

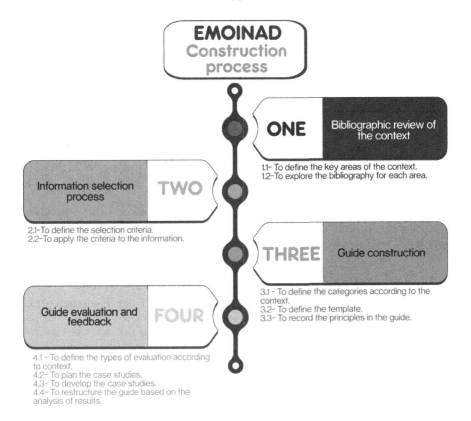

Fig. 1. EMOINAD guide construction process.

record this information. In the case of the EMOINAD guide, the template of the word wide web consortium (W3C) was chosen and then the application of the guide to cards for a more interactive application was explored.

– *To record the principles in the guide:* The information is organized in the template or in the chosen mechanism to socialize the guide.

4. Guide Evaluation and feedback

– *To define the types of evaluation according to context:* Depending on the impact and the users that will use the guide, the experts that support the guide should be defined and the type of evaluation that will be carried out with each of them. In the case of the EMOINAD guide, 3 experts were defined: experts in creation of guidelines, experts in the treatment of attention deficit disorder and interface designers. A survey was conducted with the first experts to obtain feedback on whether the guide was complete and understandable. With experts in the treatment of attention deficit it was decided to hold a meeting in which the guide were exposed to validate that it did not contain inaccurate information regarding the attention deficit. Finally, with the last group of experts, the interface designers, a workshop was held for the construction of a prototype where they had to apply the guidelines of the guide and evaluate if the guide had been useful or not.

- *To plan the case studies:* It refers to the detailed planning of each evaluation, logistics, communication with the experts and definition of spaces and times as well as the construction of the corresponding tests.
- *To develop the case studies:* To execute the plan that was defined in the planning.
- *To restructure the guide based on the analysis of results:* With the results obtained, generate a new version of the guide and repeat the validation if necessary.

After reviewing each of the steps in detail, we proceed to the next phase, which consists of applying each of the processes in the context of electronic commerce. This process is done in the next section.

4 The EMOINEC Guide: The Application of the EMOINAD Guide Creation Process to an E-commerce Context

In order to adapt the EMOINAD guide to the context of e-commerce, it is necessary to start with the methodological construction process described in the previous section. In this way we proceed to retake each of the activities and apply the process in the e-commerce context. Given that the intention and scope of this article is to make a first approximation of the EMOINEC guide, only the adaptation of the process in the first three phases of the methodology will be presented. Validation will be left for future work.

The following describes each of the phases and how they could be adapted to create the EMOINEC guide.

1. **Bibliographic review of the context**
   - *To define the key areas of the context:* The key areas are: design for emotion and design for e-commerce.
   - *To explore the bibliography for each area:* The theories for design for emotion for interfaces defined for the EMOINAD guide are also valid for e-commerce, so they will be taken into account together with the bibliographic review presented in the Sect. 2.
2. **Information Selection process**
   - *To define the selection criteria:* The criteria chosen for the selection of information will be:
     - Updated information (published during the last 10 years).
     - Information without ambiguities.
     - Applicable to an e-commerce environment.
   - *To apply the criteria to the information:* When applying the criteria described in the previous section, a series of principles and heuristics are obtained. These are summarized below:

- **Key area 1: Design for emotion**
  * Take into account aspects such as typography and color theory considering contexts and cultures. This directly affects the intrinsic motivation.
  * Show personality, that is, that the page is friendly, friendly, or humorous. This encourages creativity.
  * Include delighters (surprises, rewards, etc).
  * Beware of attention grabbers that are unnecessary and distracting.
  * If multimedia are used as videos, take into account the segmentation, that is, that they are not too long but can be visualized quickly.
  * Use visual narratives to encourage flow and engagement.
  * Use multimedia elements to provide context, show relevance and encourage curiosity. Support self-expression through personalization to subscribe, follow the page and share content.
  * Show and reward progress
  * Consider connectivity since it is the third pillar of the theory of motivation.
- **Key area 2: Design for e-commerce**
  * Show obvious navigation and logical hierarchy.
  * Allow filters by categories.
  * Have a search box for products and information and allow advanced search, as well as the refinement of the search.
  * Present relevant results in the search of information.
  * Show guidance elements, progress indicators and site maps.
  * Present elements that direct attention and offers and products correctly announced.
  * Show the number of visitors of the page.
  * Categorize products in a way that is meaningful to regular customers and the depth of the categories should be no more than 3.
  * Present the information of the products in an appropriate format, in a precise, informative, convincing, updated, easy to remember and with added value. Also use images in good resolution and complete where you can estimate the size. Take care that there are no broken links.
  * Do not eliminate products that are out of stock.
  * It must have maximum 3 clicks to find a product.
  * Show product availability indicator.
  * Include reviews and scores for each product, as well as allow comments on the reviews of other customers. To do this, participants must be encouraged to comment and share the content of the page, generating a spirit of community.
  * To encourage participants to express their experiences, knowledge and interests, such as the Twitter "Like" button.
  * People who give their opinions should present their information along with a photo of their social networks to provide more credibility.

* Include tools for product comparison.
* Submit order charges, taxes, shipping costs and shipping dates
* Show recommended products and products related to the selected product.
* Offer monetary and non-monetary rewards based on the client's performance.
* The shopping cart must always be accessible.
* Show a wish list option.
* Provide assistance information in the purchase process.
* Divide and show logical steps for the purchase process.
* Carry out a short and simple registration process.
* Present different delivery alternatives as well as different payment options and different ways to complete the order. Likewise, the costs and discounts applied before the approval of the purchase must be shown.
* Show security logos.
* Inform the level of security when paying by credit card.
* Send a confirmation e-mail after the order.
* Allow to track the status of an order from the client's account and manage the orders from the website.
* Allow the return of an item from the website.
* Reasonable response time as well as short waiting time in searches.
* Provide an exciting and consistent interface style with an innovative and attractive image
* Allow the personalization of the information addressed to the client.
* Possibility to be a VIP client or to have a loyalty program.
* The website should be simple and easy to use.
* Allow the client to leave the site at the time he/she requires it.
* Prevent the user from making mistakes and help in the recovery of errors.
* Allow the accessibility of all users.
* Keep the conventions of the real world.
* Avoid the horizontal scroll and the width of the page should be less than the browser.
* The texts in the links and buttons should be descriptive and clear.
* In the shopping cart page, provide a link that directs the customer back to the page he/she left for continuing the shopping.
* There must be coherence between systems and cultural aspects.
* Application of page design techniques (e.g., white space and margin, strict grouping, visual density, etc.)
* Use of synchronous communication media (instant messaging, chat lines, video telephony, etc.).
* Provide the customer with the privacy policy, as well as the return policy, shipping, etc.
* Provide a security certificate from an external company.

* Present visible contact information during the purchase process, as well as provide different forms of contact depending on the customer's need.
* Submit a section of frequently asked questions.
* Answer comments and concerns.
* Provide a safe and reliable appearance.

3. **Guide construction**

  – *To define the categories according to the context:* Given that there are numerous classifications related to the elements that make up the e-commerce experience, the one of Bonastre and Granollers [13] (based on the stages of the Buying Decision Process described by Engel et al. [25]) was chosen for considering the user experience in their studies. This classification is presented in Table 1.

  – *To define the template:* The template to be used will be an adaptation of the W3C, which contains the following sections:

    (a) Number and name: The heuristic is assigned a name that is clear and concise and an identification number.
    (b) Intention: The purpose of the heuristic is exposed.
    (c) Examples: Practical cases of the application of the heuristic.
    (d) Related resources: In case there are templates or complementary material.
    (e) Key terms: Explanation of specialized terms, if necessary.

  – *To record the principles in the guide:* After grouping the principles according to the categories presented in the step *to define the categories according to the context*, a series of heuristics are obtained which are recorded in the defined template. One of the resulting heuristics of this process is "Product Visualization", which belongs to the stage "Information Search". This heuristic compiles all the information related to how the information of the products promoted on the e-commerce website should be presented and is shown in Table 2.

Table 1. Clasification proposed by Engel et al. [25]

STAGE	SUBSTAGE
Need Recognition and Problem Awareness	Search and Navigation tools
	Stimulating the desire to purchase
Information Search	
Purchase decision making	Alternative Evaluation
	Choice
Transaction	
Post-sales behavior	
Factors that affect the UX during the whole purchase process	General
	Trust building

Table 2. Heuristic: Product Visualization

Number and name	3. Product Visualization
Intention	Present the information of the products in an appropriate format, in a precise, informative, convincing, updated, easy to remember way and with added value. Also use complete images in good resolution where can be estimated the real size. Take care that there are no broken links. Do not neglect the typography, color and personality of the site when promoting a product The description must include specifications and characteristics with non-technical and persuasive language. Include lists of the best selling products and trends and base the content on the needs of the product rather than its own characteristics. Finally, if a product is not available, it must be notified when it will be available
Examples	On the Modus Nutrition page (Fig. 2) you can see the use of complete images of the product in good resolution, with a good balance between the colors and with consistency between the brand and the presentation of the product. Also in the presentation of the product the characteristics are mentioned and it presents a photo with the supplement facts On the page of Rebecca Atwood (Fig. 3) it is possible to visualize different perspectives of the same product where the actual size and width can be estimated, as well as the texture

Fig. 2. modusnutrition.com screenshot

Fig. 3. rebeccaatwood.com screenshot

(*continued*)

Table 2. (*continued*)

Number and name	3. Product Visualization
Related resources	No related resources
Key terms	*Good resolution for web images:* It is recommended 72 pixels per inch and make use of vector images so that they can be adjusted depending on the characteristics of the screen

5 Conclusions

- Many of the authors who compile interface design guidelines do not take into account the emotions of the users and most of their studies are not updated, so it is necessary to group the latest research in one place to facilitate the work to the interface developers.
- Emotions are decisive when making decisions so to consider the emotional aspect in the process of buying electronic commerce is an important and innovative work.
- The methodology for creating the EMOINAD guide is transversal enough to be applicable to other contexts. This article showed an example of application of this guide in an e-commerce environment.
- It is important to perform the validations of the EMOINEC guide to verify if the guidelines they contain are useful, meaningful and if they facilitate the work to the developers.

References

1. Lee, S., Koubek, R.: The effects of usability and web design attributes on user preference for e-commerce web sites. Comput. Ind. **61**(4), 329–341 (2010)
2. Galitz, W.: The Essential Guide to User Interface Design: An Introduction to GUI Design Principles and Techniques. Wiley, Indianapolis (2007)
3. Huang, Z., Benyoucef, M.: From e-commerce to social commerce: a close look at design features. Electron. Commer. Res. Appl. **12**(4), 246–259 (2013)
4. Bidin, S.A.H., Lokman, A.M.: Enriching the comfortability emotion on website interface design using kansei engineering approach. Proceedings of the 7th International Conference on Kansei Engineering and Emotion Research 2018. AISC, vol. 739, pp. 792–800. Springer, Singapore (2018). https://doi.org/10.1007/978-981-10-8612-0_82
5. Pengnate, S., Sarathy, R.: An experimental investigation of the influence of website emotional design features on trust in unfamiliar online vendors. Comput. Hum. Behav. **67**, 49–60 (2017)
6. Cyr, D.: Modeling web site design across cultures: relationships to trust, satisfaction, and e-loyalty. J. Manage. Inf. Syst. **24**, 47–72 (2008)
7. Lokman, A.M., Noor, N.M.: Kansei Engineering Concept in E-Commerce Website, pp. 117–124 (2006)
8. Lokman, A.M., Noor, N.L.M., Nagamachi, M.: ExpertKanseiWeb: a tool to design kansei website. In: Filipe, J., Cordeiro, J. (eds.) ICEIS 2009. LNBIP, vol. 24, pp. 894–905. Springer, Heidelberg (2009). https://doi.org/10.1007/978-3-642-01347-8_74

9. Villareal-Freire, A., Aguirre, A.F., Collazos, C.A.: EMOVLE: an interface design guide. In: Marcus, A., Wang, W. (eds.) DUXU 2017. LNCS, vol. 10289, pp. 142–161. Springer, Cham (2017). https://doi.org/10.1007/978-3-319-58637-3_11

10. Villareal, A., Collazos, C.: The EMOINAD guide construction proposal: an emotive interface design guide for attention deficit disorder in children. Rom. J. Hum. - Comput. Interact. **9**(4), 347–361 (2016)

11. Stefani, A.: On the design of effective e-commerce applications: an ISO-based life-cycle model. J. Comput. Commun. **6**(5), 15 (2018)

12. Fang, X., Salvendy, G.: Customer-centered rules for design of e-commerce web sites. Commun. ACM **46**(12), 332–336 (2003)

13. Bonastre, L., Granollers, T.: A Set of Heuristics for User Experience Evaluation in E- commerce Websites (2014)

14. Diaz, J., Rusu, C., Collazos, C.: Experimental validation of a set of cultural-oriented usability heuristics: e-commerce websites evaluation. Comput. Stand. Interfaces **50**, 160–178 (2017)

15. Rusu, C., Rusu, V., Quiñones, D., Roncagliolo, S., Rusu, V.Z.: Evaluating online travel agencies' usability: what heuristics should we use? In: Meiselwitz, G. (ed.) SCSM 2018. LNCS, vol. 10913, pp. 121–130. Springer, Cham (2018). https://doi.org/10.1007/978-3-319-91521-0_10

16. Quinones, D., Rusu, C., Roncagliolo, S.: Redefining usability heuristics for trans-actional web applications. In: 2014 11th International Conference on Information Technology: New Generations, pp. 260–265 (2014)

17. Wang, Y.D., Emurian, H.H.: Trust in e-commerce: consideration of interface design factors. J. Electron. Commer. Organ. **3**(4), 42 (2005)

18. Barnes, S.J., Vidgen, R.T.: An integrative approach to the assessment of e-commerce quality. J. Electron. Commer. Res. **3**(3), 114–127 (2002)

19. Nah, F.F.-H., Davis, S.: HCI research issues in e-commerce. J. Electron. Commer. Res. **3**(3), 98–113 (2002)

20. Dorman, C.: Seducing consumers, evaluating emotions (2001)

21. Basso, A., Goldberg, D., Greenspan, S., Weimer, D.: First impressions: emotional and cognitive factors underlying judgments of trust e-commerce. In: Proceedings of the 3rd ACM Conference on Electronic Commerce - EC 2001, pp. 137–143. ACM Press (2001)

22. Sheng, H., Joginapelly, T.: Effects of web atmospheric cues on user's emotional responses in e-commerce. AIS Trans. Hum. -Comput. Interact. **4**(1), 1–24 (2012)

23. Chandler, K., Hyatt, K.: Customer-Centered Design: A New Approach to Web Usability. Prentice Hall PTR, Upper Saddle River (2003)

24. Beyer, H., Holtzblatt, K.: Contextual Design: Defining Customer-Centered Systems. Morgan Kaufmann, Burlington (1998)

25. Engel, J.F., Blackwell, R.D., Kollat, D.T.: Consumer Behavior, 3rd edn. Dryden Press, Hinsdale (1978)

Research on Production Form Attractiveness Factors Based on Users' Emotional Needs

Tianxiong Wang[✉] and Meiyu Zhou[✉]

School of Art Design and Media,
East China University of Science and Technology,
NO. 130 Meilong Road, Xuhui District, Shanghai 200237, China
wangtx_2018@163.com, zhoutc_2003@163.com

Abstract. The consumer market of products has gradually changed from enterprise-oriented to users-oriented. Research on products from the perspective of users emotional needs is also on the rise. This study extracts the attractive factors of the product through the evaluation grid method (EGM) to improve product form attraction. Then, in order to explore the users' satisfaction of product appeal factors and users' feelings and preferences are more complex and changeable, so it is difficult to grasp and extract. The fuzzy Kano model is introduced to capture the emotional factors of the human. This is because the index values under the fuzzy Kano model contain more information above the index value under the traditional Kano model, so that they can accurately capture their emotions and the quality of the users' key needs, and then judge the quality attributes of each image semantics. Furthermore, the quality attributes of each image semantics are judged, and the image semantics expressed as excitable requirements are selected to improve users satisfaction. Therefore, this research uses the research method of evaluation grid method (EGM) and the fuzzy Kano model to explore the users preference factors of electric bicycle, and then enhance the product's form attractiveness for electric bicycle, this research provides a new way for the optimal design of electric bicycle. Thus actively guiding the designer to carry out the innovative design of the electric bicycle.

Keywords: Fuzzy Kano model · Users' preferences · Users' demands · Quantitative I theory · Product development · Electric bicycle

1 Introduction

Environmental protection is an important survival issue that people have to face. The rapid development of economy not only brings about the improvement of people's living quality, but also result in the greenhouse effect, serious haze and other environmental pollution problems. The number of days of serious air pollution reaches up to 60 days per year in Beijing, Tianjin and Hebei province. The environmental pollution is mainly caused by the increasing number of motor vehicles, traffic congestion and exhaust emissions. Taking Beijing as an example, according to the research results of National School of Development at Peking University in 2014, the annual losses caused by traffic congestion in Beijing is about 70 billion yuan including increased fuel costs due to congestion time, and the resulting pollution costs are also rising year by year.

© Springer Nature Switzerland AG 2019
A. Marcus and W. Wang (Eds.): HCII 2019, LNCS 11583, pp. 533–546, 2019.
https://doi.org/10.1007/978-3-030-23570-3_40

With the development and perfection of new energy technology represented by battery technology, more and more electric-driven vehicles appear in the lives of urban residents. As a convenient means of transportation, electric bicycle is popular with users. However, currently a large number of electric bicycles are becoming larger, heavier and faster with poor safety performance and big traffic safety risks, which result in a large number of casualty accidents. In May 2018, the Ministry of Industry and Information Technology organized the revision of the compulsory national standard of *Electric bicycles–General technical requirements*, which tends to solve the development problems of the electric bicycle industry in a guided way.

According to the new national standard, electric bicycles belong to non-motor vehicles, which cannot be rode in the motor lane. The maximum speed and the weight of the whole vehicle are strictly limited. The speed cannot exceed 25 km/h and the weight of the whole vehicle cannot exceed 55 kg. The motor power is 400 W and they must be equipped with pedal. According to the definition of the new national standard, electric motorcycles belong to motor vehicles, which requires driving qualification, vehicle number plate and compulsory insurance (Table 1).

Table 1. Detailed comparisons between electric bicycles and electric motorcycles

General name	Electric two-wheeler	
Classification of vehicles	Non-motor vehicle	Motor vehicle
Product name	Electric bicycle	Electric motorcycle
Speed requirement	Speed $\leq$ 25 km/h	Speed > 25 km/h
Vehicle weight	Total weight $\leq$ 55 kg	/
Driving license	No need	Need
Insurance	No need for compulsory insurance	Need compulsory insurance
Driving lane	Non-motorized Lane	Motor vehicle lane
Speed warning	Warning sound will appear when the speed reaches 15/h	None
Battery voltage	$\leq$48 V	/
Rated power of motor	$\leq$400 W	/

Compared with electric motorcycles, electric bicycles have two advantages: 1. Electric motorcycles and automobiles need relatively high price of and cumbersome registration procedures, while electric bicycles are cost-effective without requirement for license and related documents, which is more preferred by consumers. 2. Electric motorcycles is dangerous due to the high speed, while electric bicycles conform the user' requirements of safe driving due to their limited speed and weight. Therefore, as a green and convenient means of transportation, electric bicycle has become one of the irreplaceable short-distance travel modes for urban residents. Internet and industrial 4.0 era drive the transformation of product design paradigm, promote the process of manufacturing informatization, digitalization and intellectualization, which makes the design of electric bicycle evolve to intellectualization and servitization. After the data of electric bicycle is acquired by terminal, it will be analyzed and processed by the technology of cloud and big data, so as to diagnose and alarm the faults of the vehicle. The classical ones on the market are MI electric bicycle and Bywin electric bicycle, as shown in Fig. 1 below.

Fig. 1. Electric bicycle

According to the changes of national standard of the electric bicycle industry, the model of the electric bicycle should be redesigned and the psychological preferences of consumers should be deeply dug. More and more consumers require the electric bicycle not only to meet the most basic functional needs, but also to meet their emotional needs. How to design an intelligent electric bicycle that meets the users' psychological preferences has become a new issue. In order to help enterprises better understand the emotional needs of users, and feedback them to product design, so as to put forward the best product development solutions, Kansei Engineering [1] was adopted by some scholars to explore the users' emotions in recent years, Nagamachi, a Japanese scholar, has developed the new product technology of Kansei Engineering for consumers, which is defined as a transformation technology that transforms consumers' feelings and imaginations about products into design elements and integrates them into the development of new products. However, although KE can identify customers' emotional attributes and associate them with design elements, it cannot provide information related to various emotional attributes on consumer satisfaction [2]. Therefore, some scholars study the emotional attributes of products with the help of KANO Model [3], which is a theory based on Herzberg's Motivation Theory developed in 1959, also known as the Attractive Quality Theory. The influence of customers on the products and services can be understood through the Kano model questionnaire survey, which can be regarded as a reference to improve customer satisfaction [4]. However, in the process of categorizing consumers' needs, Kano Model neglects the uncertainty of the tester's feeling. In order to improve the accuracy of the emotions captured, this the method of fuzzy Kano model is used to explore the users, which can more accurately acquire the customers' needs in questionnaire design so as to improve the users' satisfaction with the products. At the same time, some scholars put forward that the attractive factors can be dug out with the help of the Evaluation Grid Method (EGM) [5], which acts as an expert evaluation method of Miryoku Engineering, aiming at understand the evaluation items and the various factors that constitute the grid through extracting consumer language. By investigating and utilizing the hierarchical structure with semantic visualization, the original items of upper and lower levels are evaluated from abstraction to representativeness [6]. In this research, with the help of the Evaluation Grid Method, the key reasons for attracting users are analyzed (mid-level), followed by the specific performance factor characteristics of the mid-level (lower level). Finally, the emotional characteristics (upper level) of the users are captured, so as to analyze the relationship between the upper perceptual image of the electric bicycle and the specific morphological characteristics of the lower level. Afterwards, the user's quality requirements for the electric bicycle is analyzed through Fuzzy Kano, so as to complete the research on the shape design of electric bicycle.

2 Review

2.1 Miryoku Engineering

The attractive factors of products are called "miryoku" or "miryokuyinsi" in Japanese and translated into "attraction" or "attractive factors" in English. Miryoku Engineering is a technical system or preference-based design for creating attractive objects. As an expert evaluation method of Miryoku engineering, the goal of EGM is to understand various factors of evaluation items through extracting consumer language, which is also a method to understand how consumers evaluate product value through in-depth investigation. By investigating the hierarchical relationship between the image semantics of the upper level and the specific attractant features of the lower level, the original items of the upper and lower levels are evaluated from abstract to concrete, so as to visualize and immobilize the consumer value structure [6]. Therefore, the Evaluation Grid Method (EGM) is an effective method for qualitative analysis. Miryoku Engineering is used by some scholars to study the shape attraction of products. For example, Shen and Changyu [7] chose Miryoku Engineering method in order to find out the attractive factors of heavy motorcycle and used EGM (evaluation grid method) in order to find out the structure of attraction. Shen [5] aim to explore the social and cultural attractiveness of SNS game from the perspective of human emotions caused by the interaction between players and games. After interviewing knowledgeable game players with the help of the Evaluation Gird Method (EGM), it was analyzed using the I-type quantification theory. On this basis, this paper explores the relationship between the perceptual image (upper level) and the specific morphological characteristics (lower level) of electric bicycle through the Evaluation Gird Method of Miryoku engineering, and analyses the attractive factors of users to electric bicycle products, so as to explore the Attractive.

2.2 Fuzzy Kano Model

In recent years, some scholars have begun to find ways to reach human satisfaction with products. Kano et al. [8] proposed a two-dimensional quality model map, as shown in Fig. 2 below. Kano model is used to analyze user needs and develop questionnaires. The questionnaires acquire the usefulness of user needs through both positive and negative questions, that is, whether the user is satisfied if the demand is provided, whether the user is not satisfied if it is not provided. By analyzing whether there is a linear relationship between the two, the category of user needs can be identified. The results can be divided into five categories: Attractive (A), One-dimensional (O), Indifferent (I), Reverse (R) and Must-be (M), which are described as follows:

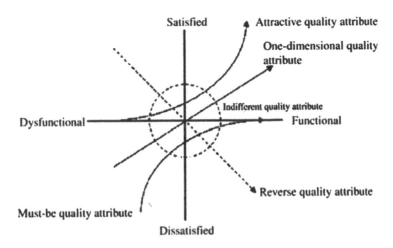

Fig. 2. Kano model

1. Attractive Quality Element: Attractive Quality means that when products or services are available, customers will feel satisfied, but when products or services are not available, customers will also not be dissatisfied.
2. One-dimensional Quality Element: One-dimensional Quality means that when a product or service is available, the customer will be satisfied, but when the product or service is not available, the customer will be dissatisfied.
3. Must-be Quality Element: Must-be Quality means that when products or services are available, customers will take it for granted, but when products or services are not available, customers will be dissatisfied.
4. Indifferent Quality Element: Indifferent Quality refers to whether products or services are available or not, it will not affect customer satisfaction.
5. Reverse Quality Element: Reverse Quality means that when the product or service is available, the customer will not be satisfied, but when the product or service is not available, the customer will be more satisfied.

Kano model illustrates the relationship between customer satisfaction and product or service performance, as shown in Table 2 Kano's evaluation table [9].

Table 2. Kano's evaluation table

Customer needs	Dysfunctional				
	Like	Must-be	Neutral	Live-with	Dislike
Functional					
Like	Q	A	A	A	O
Must-be	R	I	I	I	M
Neutral	R	I	I	I	M
Live-with	R	I	I	I	M
Dislike	R	R	R	R	Q

However, the results obtained by traditional Kano model are not accurate, because it ignores the uncertainty caused by customers' complex and changeable psychology, therefore, it requires the introduction of fuzzy theory to solve the fuzzy problem in reality. In 1965, L. A. Zadeh, a professor of automation from the University of California, Berkeley, first proposed Fuzzy Sets Theory. He used mathematical methods to express the uncertainty in real life [4]. In order to deal with the fuzziness of human thought, Zadeh first introduced the theory of fuzzy sets, which rationally determines the uncertainties under fuzzy or unknown conditions. The characteristics of such sets are that the distribution range of each element is between 0 and 1 [10]. Therefore, the Fuzzy Kano Model [11] has become a more valuable research subject, whose results will be more accurate. Improved and developed on the basis of traditional Kano model, Fuzzy Kano Model is introduced to capture people's emotional factors mainly based on the consumers' fuzzy demand for products, so as to accurately capture people's emotions and their key quality. The relevant cases are applied in some feelings of industrial design: For example, Wang and Wang et al. [12] proposed a hybrid framework, which combines fuzzy AHP, fuzzy Kano model and zero-one integer programming (ZOIP), and integrates customer preference and customer perception into the decision-making process of product configuration. Finally, the best smart camera products in different markets were determined with the help of ZOIP by maximizing the overall customer utility (OCU) and considering the company's pricing policy. Lee et al. [4] used the method of fuzzy questionnaires to modify Kano two-dimensional questionnaires and develop mathematical computing performance according to the quality classification of Kano two-dimensional fuzzy model. Finally, the service quality of theme park will be taken as an example. Shafia and Abdollahzadeh [13] put forward a new solution with the help of fuzzy TOPSIS and fuzzy KANO technology in their research. By prioritizing FR to improve beneficiary satisfaction, investment will be more efficient. In order to solve the uncertainties in product development process, Chen and Ko et al. [14] introduced Kano model into the fuzzy theory to improve user satisfaction. finally, the effectiveness of the method is verified in practice. On this basis, this research explores the satisfaction factors of product perceptual image through the fuzzy Kano model, so as to develop the user demand products theory that meets consumer preferences, and then enhance the shape attraction of products.

3   Method

3.1   Analysis of Shape Factors of Products

Firstly, the classical samples of electric bicycles on the market were select and in-depth interview of users were carried out through EMG method, whose research process includes the following steps: 1. Print out all the sample product pictures in A4 printing paper and display them in front of users, so that users can select the sample pictures whichever they like; 2. Ask the specific reasons why users like the sample pictures, and determine the key reason for attracting users, that is the mid-level item of attractive factors of the products; 3. Further inquiring about the specific shape characteristics of products liked by users, whose result is the lower-level characteristics of the product's attractive factor; 4. Further inquiring about user's psychological feelings caused by the specific attractive features of the product, and the result is the upper perceptual image of the product's attractive factor; 5. Merge the same or similar upper (perceptual image) and lower (specific modeling features) by kJ method, and the number of times after merging is equal to the sum of times mentioned by all users before merging, and then integrate and rank by KJ method, so as to construct the evaluation grid map of the product attractive element. According to the evaluation grid map, the hierarchical relationship between the image semantics of the upper level of product attractive factors and the specific attracting features of the lower level is constructed.

3.2   Quantification Theory I

Quantification Theory is a branch of multivariate statistic put forward by Professor Lin Zhijifu of Japan. Quantification theory I mainly deals with the prediction of quantitative variables of qualitative variables. The application of this theory can quantify the problems that are difficult to study in detail and quantitatively, so as to study and discover the relations and laws between things more comprehensively [15]. Therefore, the Quantification Theory is to study the linear relationship between a set of qualitative variables X (independent variables) and a set of quantitative variables y (dependent variables), and to establish the mathematical model between them through multiple regression analysis. This research intends to use the Quantification Theory I as a tool to analyze the attractive factors of electric bicycle. Through the Quantification Theory I, the quantitative relationship between the upper perceptual image and the lower specific shape features is analyzed, and the most critical shape features affecting the upper perceptual image are explored.

According to Quantification Theory I [16], the shape design item is regarded as an item, represented by X, and the design elements in shape design item is regraded as Category, expressed as C. Suppose the M item XM has RM categories, then the xm item has cmrm categories including cm1, cm2, cm3... and suppose δ_i (j, k) (i = 1,......,n; j = 1,2,......,m; k = 1,2,......rj) is the value of the K category in the j item in the i sample.

3.3 Fuzzy Kano Model

Based on the fact that the traditional Kano model forces people to choose an answer, which ignores the uncertainty of human thinking, a Fuzzy Kano Questionnaire (FKQ) and a Fuzzy Kano Model (FKM) are proposed to capture users' emotional needs. The image semantic level of attractive factors is introduced into the fuzzy Kano model to classify the quality. The user's reactions to the situations when each image semantic expression is sufficient or inadequate are investigated through the positive and negative questionnaires, and the quality attribute of product image semantics is judged. The relationship between the attractive factors of electric bicycle and customer satisfaction is further analyzed.

The FKQ questionnaire enables the respondents to present their usual ideas and solutions more comprehensively and to match them with the human thinking model. Even if there is a little bit of feeling or thinking, the service providers will also understand through the questionnaire survey. Therefore, model and quality attribute classification of Kano are more real [4]. Hereby, the FKQ questionnaire assigns the corresponding proportion according to the user's fuzzy emotional thinking, as shown in Table 3.

Table 3. Fuzzy Kano questionnaire

Product Function	Like	Must-be	Indifferent	Can tolerate	Dislike
Can be realized	0.1	0.8	0.1		
Cannot be realized		0.2	0.8		

The basic steps of the Fuzzy Kano algorithm are three steps: First, assuming that a function can include functional and dysfunctional, the matrix that can be implemented fun = [0.1 0.8 0.1 0 0], and the matrix that cannot be implemented dys = [0 0.2 0.8 0 0], and the fuzzy relation interaction matrix Z is generated by fun $\otimes$ dys;

$$Z = \begin{bmatrix} 0 & 0.02 & 0.08 & 0 & 0 \\ 0 & 0.16 & 0.64 & 0 & 0 \\ 0 & 0.02 & 0.08 & 0 & 0 \\ 0 & 0 & 0 & 0 & 0 \\ 0 & 0 & 0 & 0 & 0 \end{bmatrix}$$

Secondly, after obtaining Z matrix, the value of matrix is corresponded with the attributes of requirement attribute classification table proposed by Matzler and Hinterhuber [9] according to previous literature or experience, and the membership vector T of requirement category is obtained.

$$T = \left\{ \frac{0}{M}, \frac{0}{O}, \frac{0.1}{A}, \frac{0.9}{I}, \frac{0}{R}, \frac{0}{Q} \right\}$$

Finally, the value of confidence level α is introduced for further screening. If an element in the membership vector is greater than or equal to α, the corresponding quality attribute of the element is represented by 1; otherwise, it will be represented by 0. According to the relevant scholar's argument, a = 0.4. Therefore, the customer requirement attribute vector is transformed into T = [0, 0, 0, 1, 0, 0] through the value of a, and the quality attribute is known as indifferent quality requirement. At the same time, according to this requirement, the steps mentioned above are repeated on all users in this survey and the tendency of each customer to this requirement is counted, and the classification of customer's demand tendency with highest frequency to this product is calculated, that is, the category of demand items corresponding to the product characteristics.

4   Discuss the Case Example

4.1   Analysis of the Attractive Factors of the Product

Firstly, the electric bicycle products that sell well on the market are collected for the research on the attractive factors of the products. 18 kinds of users' favorite electric bicycle products were collected from the online shopping platform, magazines and related book channels as test samples. Then, the sample photos were processed through Photoshop software to make the samples into A4 size with uniform resolution format. Figure 3 below is sample example. At the beginning of the experiment, a team consisting of 20 experienced designers and users of electric bicycles needs to participate in the research of attractive factors of products, including 12 males and 8 females. The age of the research group is from 19 to 38. The original evaluation items (mid-level) and the performance characteristics (lower-level) of specific attractive factor and the affective factors (upper-level) were inquired by EGM method. The results showed that there were 23 mid-level evaluation items, 92 lower-level evaluation items and 135 upper-level evaluation items. Then similar vocabulary and specific shape features were further merged by KJ method and the results showed that there were three mid-level evaluation items, 14 lower-level evaluation items and 11 upper-level evaluation items and thus constructing the attraction level of electric bicycles. In this paper, only the design of front structure shape and saddle are discussed in the original evaluation item

Fig. 3. Sample example of electric bicycle

of the mid-level. Due to the limited research energy, the wheel hub of is not researched here. The concrete hierarchical framework of saddle and front structure shape are shown in Fig. 4.

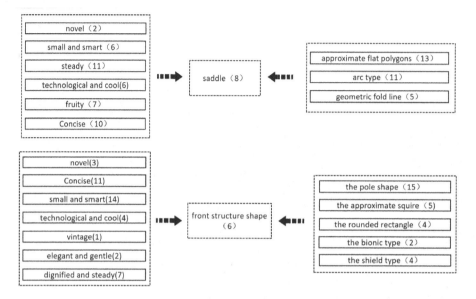

Fig. 4. Product framework hierarchy diagram

4.2   Fuzzy Kano Model

The relationship between product attractive morphological characteristics and product emotional imagery is found out through the above theoretical qualitative analysis. But in order to explore the customer satisfaction of product attractive factors, it is necessary to introduce the Fuzzy Kano model, classify the types of customer satisfaction according to customer demand, and define the demand into five categories: attractive demand, one-dimensional demand, indifferent demand, reverse demand and Must-be demand, so as to explore the real demand of users. In this paper, seven key evaluation items are selected from 11 perceptual images of electric bicycle according to the number of times mentioned by users. User satisfaction is discussed through Kano model and the final statistical calculation results are shown in Table 4: concise and small smart style is attractive demand, which can greatly affect user satisfaction when these two factors are outstanding. The perceptual images of dignified and stable, novelty and personality, roundness and fullness, elegance and gentleness are indifferent demands, which have no great relationship with the satisfaction of users. Technological and cool performance is one-dimensional demand, which will affect user satisfaction, but when such factors are not enough, it will reduce customer satisfaction.

Table 4. Statistical result of Fuzzy Kano

Evaluation index	M	A	I	O	R	Q	类别
Concise	4	15	9	2	0	0	A
Dignified and stable	6	3	17	2	2	0	I
Cool and technology	1	6	4	19	0	0	O
Novelty and personality	2	8	16	1	3	0	I
Roundness and fullness	3	4	14	7	2	0	I
Small and smart	3	14	9	3	1	0	A
Elegance and gentleness	1	13	14	2	0	0	I

In the design process of electric bicycle, the concise and small smart shape style need to be highlighted to improve customer satisfaction. Through the hierarchical relationship diagram of the above-mentioned evaluation grid method, the corresponding specific morphological characteristics of the style image of electric bicycle can be further qualitatively explored.

4.3 Quantification Theory

In order to accurately analyze the relationship between the specific shape and the upper-level perceptual image, the design features of the attractive factors of the electric bicycle shape are categorized to explore the contribution value of the design elements to the style image. According to Fig. 4, the shape of saddle can be divided into three design types, while the front structure shape of electric bicycle can be divided into five design types. Table 5 below is the specific shape classification table of product design.

Table 5. Classification of design elements

Design items	Specific morphological features	Named
Saddle (X_1)	Approximate flat polygons	X_{11}
	Arc type	X_{12}
	Geometric fold line	X_{13}
Front structure shape (S_2)	The pole shape	S_{21}
	The approximate squire	S_{22}
	The rounded rectangle	S_{23}
	The bionic type	S_{24}
	The shield type	S_{25}

Fuzzy Kano-based results of attractive demands only contains two styles of concise and small smart, so it is necessary to investigate the two image semantics of all samples with the help of SD method. Finally, the image semantics scores of all samples are obtained, and then the results of the questionnaire are sorted out, and the average number of image vocabulary is calculated. Afterwards, the multivariate regression

Table 6. Perceptual evaluation matrix

Sample	X_1	X_2	Concise	Small and smart
1	X_{11}	X_{21}	4.18	4.20
2	X_{12}	X_{21}	4.51	4.70
3	X_{12}	X_{21}	4.63	4.75
⋮	⋮	⋮	⋮	⋮
18	X_{12}	X_{24}	4.65	4.50

analysis is carried out with the perceptual image vocabulary as dependent variables and product modeling feature categories as independent variables, so as to obtain the corresponding category score of type elements. Each category score is the contribution value of each sample type element to perceptual image. Then statistical analysis of Partial Correlation coefficient is carried out to obtain the score of Partial Correlation coefficient. Accordingly, the product perceptual evaluation matrix is shown in Table 6, and the final numerical results of the relationship between product morphological characteristics and perceptual intention are shown in Tables 7 and 8.

Table 7. Analysis results of the relationship between design elements and perceptual vocabulary (concise)

Design item	Design characteristics	Category score	Partial correlation coefficient	Perceptual image
Saddle	X_{11}	− 0.197	0.858	Concise
	X_{12}	0.334		
	X_{13}	0.237		
Front structure shape	S_{21}	0.129	0.863	
	S_{22}	− 0.263		
	S_{23}	− 0.313		
	S_{24}	0.367		
	S_{25}	− 0.563		
Constant term: 4.26			$R^2 = 0.74$	

In Table 7, it can be seen that the front structure shape has greater effect on the design items that affect the perceptual image of concise design style, and the partial correlation coefficient score is 0.863. In the specific shape design of the front structure of electric bicycle, S24 and S21 are positive values, among which the bionic design of S24 reaches 0.367, which is most inclined to the concise style. In the saddle design of electric bicycle, the arc shape is 0.334, which can most affect the concise style. At the same time, according to Table 8, in the design item of small and smart style image, the partial correlation coefficient of saddle is 0.852, among which the X_{12} curved saddle can most affect the perceptual style characteristics of small and smart products, while the bionic design of the front structure can be up to 0.551. Accordingly, a bionic style design of the front structure can trigger small and smart style image.

Table 8. Analysis results of the relationship between design elements and perceptual vocabulary (small and smart)

Design item	Design characteristics	Category score	Partial correlation coefficient	Perceptual image
Saddle	X_{11}	− 0.239	0.852	Small and smart
	X_{12}	0.428		
	X_{13}	0.201		
Front structure shape	S_{21}	0.120	0.837	
	S_{22}	− 0.454		
	S_{23}	0.001		
	S_{24}	0.551		
	S_{25}	− 0.599		
Constant term: 4.20			$R^2 = 0.70$	

5 Conclusion

With electric bicycle as an application case, this research extracts its shape attractive factors with the evaluation grid method, and merges similar items into three mid-level evaluation items, 14 lower-level evaluation items and 11 upper-level evaluation items, thus forming the hierarchical relationship between the shape and emotional image of electric bicycle. Then the quantitative relationship between perceptual image and specific design features is explored through the quantitative theory I, and then by introducing it into the fuzzy Kano model, the attractive demand is analyzed. This research method can aid product developers in accurately analyzing consumers' perceptual demands, so as to actively guide designers for innovative design of electric bicycles.

References

1. Nagamachi, M.: Kansei engineering: a new ergonomic consumer-oriented technology for product development. Int. J. Ind. Ergon. **15**, 3–11 (1995)
2. Shahin, A., Javadi, M.H.M., Shahrestani, H.V.: Integrating Kansei engineering and revised Kano model with a case study in the automobile industry. Prod. Qual. Manag. **13**(2), 201–218 (2014)
3. Lee, Y.-C., Lin, S.-B., Wang, Y.-L.: A new Kano's evaluation sheet. TQM J. **23**(2), 179–195 (2011)
4. Lee, Y.-C., Huang, S.-Y.: A new fuzzy concept approach for Kano's model. Expert Syst. Appl. **36**(3), 4479–4484 (2009)
5. Shen, K.-S.: Measuring the sociocultural appeal of SNS games in Taiwan. Internet Res. **23**(3), 372–392 (2013)
6. Shen, K.-S., Chen, K.-H., Liang, C.-C., Pu, W.-P., Ma, M.-Y.: Measuring the functional and usable appeal of crossover B-Car interiors. Hum. Factors Ergon. Manuf. Serv. Ind. **25**(1), 106–122 (2012)

7. Shen, K., Changyu, P., Lu, Y., Liu, Z., Chuang, C., Ma, M.: A study on the attractiveness of heavy duty motorcycle. World Acad. Sci. Eng. Technol. Int. J. Humanit. Soc. Sci. **3**(6), 1050–1054 (2009)
8. Kano, N.: Attractive quality and must-be quality. J. Jpn. Soc. Qual. Control **14**(2), 39–48 (1984)
9. Matzler, K., Hinterhuber, H.H.: How to make product development projects more successful by integrating Kano's model of customer satisfaction. Technovation **18**(1), 25–38 (1998)
10. Zadeh, L.A.: Fuzzy sets. Inf. Control **8**, 338–353 (1965)
11. Yadav, H.C., Jain, R., Shukla, S.: Prioritization of aesthetic attributes of car profile. Int. J. Ind. Ergon. **43**(4), 296–303 (2013)
12. Wang, C.-H., Wang, J.: Combining fuzzy AHP and fuzzy Kano to optimize product varieties for smart cameras: a zero-one integer programming perspective. Appl. Soft Comput. **22**, 410–416 (2014)
13. Shafia, M.A., Abdollahzadeh, S.: Integrating fuzzy Kano and fuzzy TOPSIS for classification of functional requirements in national standardization system. Arab. J. Sci. Eng. **39**(8), 6555–6565 (2014)
14. Chen, L.-H., Ko, W.-C.: Fuzzy approaches to quality function deployment for new product design. Fuzzy Sets Syst. **160**(18), 2620–2639 (2014)
15. Li, Y.-F.: Research on product image form design based on quantification theory type I. J. Mach. Des. **27**(4), 40–45 (2010)
16. Huang, C., Tang, W., Shao, J.: Research on the consumer psychology and Kansei engineering on form design of smart watch. Mach. Des. Manuf. Eng. **43**(11), 32–37 (2014)

The Application of "Emotion Retrospection" in the Design of Museum Cultural Creative Products

Liu Yang[1], Wei Yu[2(✉)], Sijia Jiang[2], and Siyu Jia[1]

[1] College of Communication and Art Design,
University of Shanghai for Science and Technology, Shanghai, China
[2] School of Art Design and Media,
East China University of Science and Technology, Shanghai, China
weiyu@ecust.edu.cn

Abstract. As the Internet evolves from the times of network to the times of internationalization, a latest cultural phenomenon and economic phenomenon, "experience-based cultural assumption", keeps gaining attention society-wide, with a wide variety of cultural creative products having popped up. Museum is a palace of humanity and spiritual civilization, maintaining encyclopaedical culture resources, and thus, museum may have innate advantages in developing and designing cultural creative products with the philosophy of emotion retrospection. Besides, museum is of great publicity, so it should possess multiple functions, such as to serve and guide the public, to release cultural creativity, to satisfy contemporary individual demands and so on. In the past few years, driven by policy, technology and capital, the development of museum cultural creative products has gradually accelerated, but the design of many products has over focused on a mono-directional aesthetic perspective, which leads to that the functional worth of the products have not yet completely fulfilled. Therefore, a urgently problem currently to be worked out is how to design a popular product with both epochal features and function of carrying forward Chinese traditional culture and regional civilization. The perspective of "Emotion Retrospection" is innovationally introduced in this essay. In terms of the cultural emotion connotation of museum cultural creative products, this essay creatively discusses the worth and application of the philosophy of Emotion Retrospection in design process of museum cultural creative products, so as to supplement the topics of researches on how to design museum cultural creative products and to offer some inspiration of designing.

Keywords: Museum cultural creative products · Product design · Mode of emotion retrospection

1 The Cultural Emotion Connotation of Museum Cultural Creative Products

1.1 Status Quo of Museum Cultural Creative Products in China

Museum cultural creative products, including tangible products and intangible products, refer to those products that are creatively designed and developed based on the

© Springer Nature Switzerland AG 2019
A. Marcus and W. Wang (Eds.): HCII 2019, LNCS 11583, pp. 547–556, 2019.
https://doi.org/10.1007/978-3-030-23570-3_41

museum collections. Tangible products are those museum souvenirs and derivative products, which are designed and developed according to museum collections with typical museum style, while intangible products mean those cultural activities and events held by various museums [1]. Hereby in this essay, the main research object is the tangible museum cultural creative products.

Since 1980s, museum stores have been gradually built up in the western world. These stores have expanded the space of the consumption of museum service as well as broaden the space of the communication of museum culture. The curtain of developing museum cultural creative products rose in May 2016, when a notification named "Some opinions on promoting the development of cultural and creative products of cultural relics units" was issued by several government departments, including National Development and Reform Commission, Ministry of Finance of the People's Republic of China, and State Administration of Cultural Heritage etc. The development and popularization of Mobile Internet technology have promoted the marketization of museum cultural creative products and thus the consumption of museum cultural creative products becomes a fashionable culture consumption. In such a circumstance, Social media and E-commerce platform become the major path of purchasing museum cultural creative products. For instance, in T-Mall (a famous online shopping platform belonging to Alibaba), there are two cultural creative product shops with different market positioning, which both belonging to Beijing Palace Museum. They have altogether over five hundred kinds of products and nearly 40,000,000 followers in total. It is obvious that museum cultural creative products in China owns a huge potential market, which is drawing international attention more and more. In 1st, July, 2018, the first flagship store of British Museum opened up in T-Mall, selling museum cultural creative products, and only within one month, the followers are up to 1,600,000, most items sold out soon.

1.2 Relationship Between the Cultural Emotion and the Design of Museum Cultural Creative Products

For a city, museum bears an important responsibility on producing and recreating culture. Museum, via space design, becomes a culture place to meet people's visual needs, providing a public space for interpersonal communication and dialogue, through which people's sense of identity will be strengthened. As products of museum, an institution that cares for (conserves) a collection of objects with artistic, cultural, historical, or scientific importance and the cultural diffusion and generation, the museum cultural creative product is not only a vital element carrying historical culture, but also an indispensable component of museum. Culture's semiotically has hence become the primary property of the museum cultural creative products, quite different from other usual industrial products, in their design process, in which the designers need to make full use of various creative elements to construct a significance space that is able to reappear and reconstruct history culture.

Fundamentally, the designing of museum cultural creative products is a designing of a substantial culture designing [2], which means that it is the fruit of combining cultural tradition and innovative design. So far, many researchers have explored and studied the cultural significance and the application of cultural elements, for example:

to enhance the quality of product design of museum cultural creative products by excavating digital heritage [3]; exploration on the model of consumers' regional cultural image and designing method of product [4]; to establish a design-semiotics-based recreating process, techniques and methods of cultural elements [5]. All these researches have offered inspirations for this research. "Emotion" serving as a point of penetration, this essay mainly explores the designing philosophy and creative application of museum cultural creative products. The philosophical essence of "emotion" is human's subjective reflection of objective things' value-relationship and value-characteristics [6]. Meanwhile, emotion is a kind of social phenomenon closely related to the unique social culture. It is shaped by the social culture and in turn exerts influence on social culture and its progress [7]. All in all, the perception and inheritance of culture is a process of emotion's flow and diffusion.

2 The Worth of Emotion-Retrospection-Based Experience Mode in Product Design for Museum Cultural Creative Products

2.1 Experience Mode of Emotion Retrospection

In the era of Experience Economy, service product providers supply consumers with memorable experiences, considering service as the core and using products as materials. Consumers' behavior thus becomes an activity that pursues sensibility and scene moulding and so the interaction between consumers, and products is playing an essential role in this process. This Emotion retrospection experience mode rightly roots in such a big-time background. In detail, this mode hails from the concept of "Emotion retrospection". Here "Emotion" can be understood as a reflection of experiences in brain. The essence of such experience is feelings and emotional memories caused by people, things or events appearing in daily life [8]. "Emotion retrospection" experience mode intends to construct consumers' familiar cognitive scenes and projective scenes, and to seek consumers' emotional triggering point or pain spot in the process of product design, and the purpose is to ultimately build up a emotional link between consumer and product. Product design and consumers' emotion have mutual effects on each other, which is to say their emotion will affect their comprehension over the cultural connotation conveyed by cultural creative products and various design elements will simultaneously bring about feelings fluctuation and emotion varieties to the users.

2.2 The Worth of Emotion-Retrospection-Based Experience Mode in Product Design for Museum Cultural Creative Products

Museum is a special space that is able to reappear and reconstruct cultural significance and to visit a museum is a personal experience. Since consumption of the museum cultural creative products is a crucial part of it, "Emotion retrospection" experience mode shows its momentous sense and worth in product design for museum cultural creative products. "Emotion retrospection" experience mode owns great significance and mechanism. In terms of product itself, its cultural semitropical function can be better fulfilled if the philosophy of "Emotion retrospection" can be applied in designing museum cultural creative products, because the museum cultural creative products should not only meet the needs of contemporary individuals, but also take the function of directing the public aesthetic and civic literacy into consideration. No matter in which form the cultural creative product is, its spirit always relates to the city that the museum represents and its life is endowed by the historical and cultural charm of the city and the knowledge information together with the artistic appeals of the collections in that museum. In terms of consumption, the perceived value of consumers can be better realized if the philosophy of "Emotion retrospection" can be applied in designing museum cultural creative products. Here, "perceived value", commonly including function value, emotion value and price value, refers to consumers' overall evaluation, on product utility according to their own deliberation about products advantages and disadvantages. As mentioned previously, the perception and inheritance of culture is a process of emotion's flow and diffusion and according to Meini Guo (2018), there is a positive correlation between consumers' perception of the cultural connotation in cultural creative products and their satisfaction about products. Consumers sentiment trend and attitude towards the products significantly influence their perception on products' cultural connotation. So, in the process of developing museum cultural creative products, designers can try to waken and activate consumers' emotional memories, so as to reinforce consumers' perception of the cultural connotation in cultural creative products, which will lead to their purchase intention and increase their satisfaction.

3 The Application of Emotion-Retrospection-Based Experience Mode in Product Design for Museum Cultural Creative Products

The process of Cultural creative products' loading and storing culture includes two periods: in the first period, consumers merely have a superficial perception of the products; in the second period, consumers may have a deeper recognition and understanding of the product's inner mechanism. These two periods are namely "modal level" and "intensional level". "Modal level" refers to the form and appearance of the product, which can present the cultural elements and be directly perceived, such as typical historic figures, scenery, architectures and so on. "Intensional level" means those various cultural connotation and value orientation contained within the product, which are not tangible but need consumers to sense, experience and comprehend [9]. In terms of consumers, their learning about and then purchasing the museum cultural creative products is actually a process of feelings transition: from perception to acceptance. They obtain the information about products in "modal level", while they gain resonance in "intensional level" by experiencing and comprehending the cultural connotation and value orientation inside products. When the philosophy of emotion retrospection is introduced into product design of the museum cultural creative products, the culture is likely to be better conveyed and spread in both periods (modal level and intensional level), so as to enhance consumers' satisfaction of experience, boost consumption decisions and fulfill the conveyance and direction of cultural meaning and value. There are three different application modes in product design of the museum cultural creative products:

3.1 Scene Principle: To Arouse the Existing Emotion Experience

"Scene" is originally a terminology of film ology, and when used in design, it means the description about interactive behaviors between people and environment or system. Many scenes possess emotional triggering point, which is a key factor to help expand the cultural connotation of a product from modal level to intensional level. Therefore, before developing new museum cultural creative products, the designer needs to firstly identify an item that carries the target cultural connotation and then redesign it with a proper emotional triggering point that can arouse the existing emotion experience of consumers.

The "Wen-ZhengMing Chinese wisteria seeds gift box" (see Fig. 1), a cultural creative product from Suzhou Museum, is a case that has successfully applied "scene principle" to provide consumers an emotion-retrospection-based Experience. The inspiration of such a brilliant product comes from a 480-year-old ancient Chinese wisteria (see Fig. 2), which was planted by a painting master ZhengMing Wen himself, a Suzhou local, in the Palace of Prince Zhong located in Suzhou Museum, in Ming Dynasty. From 2013 on, there will be 3000 seeds selected out of 5000 after the florescence of that Chinese wisteria every year. These carefully selected seeds are packed into small delicate boxes, 3 in each, and then sold as limited edition gift box. Once rolled out, the "Wen-ZhengMing Chinese wisteria seeds gift box" have gained a lot of peculiarities among consumers. Its limited edition makes it even not easy to get one. The reason of this success is that the cultural connotation of this product has aroused consumers' emotional memories about the famous ancient city Suzhou. The Chinese wisteria is a symbol of Suzhou's cultural heritage, as well as a representation of a connotation with dignified sense of culture passed from one generation to the next. When consumers plant these Chinese wisteria seeds on their own, observing the seed sprouting and coming in leaf, they will experience what their ancestors experienced.

3.2 Exploration Principle: To Establish a Brand New Experience Based on Intrinsical Emotion Experience

Museum cultural creative products are mainly based on a series of collections of a certain museum, and under such a premise, other derivative products with various functions and meanings are developed. Let's take the Rosetta Stone of British Museum as an instance. In the official store of British Museum, there are 55 kinds of products based on it, including mouse pads, USB flash disks and mugs. However, what must be paid attention is that nowadays most design of museum cultural creative products are mugs, key rings and other types of accessories, leading to a convergence in the categories of museum cultural creative products. In order to design distinguished products, designers need to think about new patterns and forms of the museum cultural creative products, which are yet familiar to consumers and able to arouse their old experience

Fig. 1. Wen-ZhengMing Chinese wisteria seeds gift box

Fig. 2. Wisteria

and emotional memories. Designed in this way, the products may drive consumers to explore new reception based on intrinsical emotion experience and finally bring them a brand new experience.

The most faddish museum cultural creative products "Food Weapon–sword-shaped ice-cube maker" (see Fig. 3) of Taipei Palace Museum is an excellent example of emotion-retrospection-based product designed with exploration principle. Ice-lolly mould will recall many people's memories about their golden childhood. In those good old days, when material life was not so abundant as it is today, to DIY some cold drinks or ice-lollies must be one of the happiest things in summer and for children, to fight like a sword knight a millennium ago is always what they longed to. Therefore, nowadays when people use these sword-shaped ice-cube makers to repeat what they loved to do when they were young, such objects looking like Yue Goujian Sword, Qi Zi Sword or Wu Shou Sword and with strong sense of history and tableaux may, again, trigger their yearning for Robinhood-style life. What an impressive scene: in broiling summer, one pulls out an "ice sword" from the sword-shaped ice mould, just as the dream of childhood comes true. It is the sword-shaped ice-cube maker, this special product, that fulfills the "emotion retrospection" about their childhood for consumers, enabling them to retrospect that happiest memory of summer.

Fig. 3. Food Weapon–sword-shaped ice-cube maker

3.3   Prototype Principle: To Utilize Symbolic Significance to Conduct Emotion Retrospection

"Prototype" here refers to "collective unconscious", a psychological terminology, which means a combination of the basic ideas and images that all people are believed to share because they have inherited them. Due to the existence prototype, human's emotions and behavioral patterns have regional universality and ethnic universality, so that people can react similarly in some psychological processes such as perceiving, comprehending and imaging etc. One of the key characteristics of museum cultural creative product is its strong symbolism. Because of the symbolic meaning in the same traditional culture, people will associate specific words, characters, letters, names or images with corresponding meanings. For example, in China, people will think of best wishes when seeing the word "Fu Lu Shou (福禄寿)", or have a sense of calmness and noble and unsullied characters when seeing the images of pine trees, bamboos and plum blossom. People's emotional imagery is affected by percipience and consciousness, and that is to say when people are observing a category of object, the relevant images will reappear in their brains and relevant emotional comprehension will be activated. So, if the concept of "prototype" is applied in designing museum cultural creative products, the design ideas can be both improved an enriched vastly. Furthermore, the emotional functions and practical functions will be better accomplished.

"3D Deer Night Lamp" (see Fig. 4) of Chinese National Museum is a delicate example of emotion-retrospection-based product designed with prototype principle. The lamp is equipped with a tapping switch and a USB interface. The configuration of it is derived from eight Chinese cultural relics, full of semioticalness and symbolic meaning. Its appearance looks like a procumbent little deer, 9.8 cm high, stemming from the famous "Deer-shaped bronze paperweight decorated by shells", which was excavated in Hou Chuan Han Dynasty Tombs in Xia Xian, Henan Province, in 1957. On deer's back is a grand cowrie shells as a decoration, which makes the lamp beautiful as well as practical. In Chinese, a procumbent deer has the same pronunciation with "Fu Lu(福禄) ", meaning happiness and fortune, and the shell is a symbol of treasures and all these will bring the users of this lamp a wonderful feeling.

Fig. 4. 3D Deer Night Lamp

4   Expectation of the Philosophy of Emotion Retrospection Applied in Development of Product Design for Museum Cultural Creative Products in the Future

As the Internet and the Internet of Things rapidly develop, the society gradually enters the era of interconnected intelligence with the background of big data and artificial intelligence. Development of technologies have induced the change of thought. In the fields of design, the philosophy has evolved from the conventional design of agrarian age and the modern design of industry time into the creative design, which is suitable to the current knowledge network time [10]. Nowadays, experience-based museum cultural creative products tend to become the mainstream products in the coming years because of the technique innovation and increasing demands in cultural consumption. Therefore, the emotion-retrospection-based experience mode will be bound to present a new look in the near future.

4.1   User-Involvement-Based Design

In the era of intelligence, as users' statuses are getting higher and higher, users' engagement and the establishment of users' community becomes a kernel part in product design. At the same time, besides the needs of product function, users will focus more on their aesthetic needs and value orientation conveyed the products they plan to purchase. "Emotion retrospection" experience mode is based on the interaction of users and products, and as a result, the degree of users' involvement and their acceptance of products will greatly affect their using experience. At the moment, society-wide media marketing is the major marketing approach and social media such as Weibo and WeChat Official Account of museums have become the front battlefields of product promotion. Some museums have tried to take users' suggestions, implementing their ideas in designing the museum cultural creative products, and gains amazing success. A famous example is that Beijing Palace Museum once rolled out "Cold Palace" and "Royal Kitchen" fridge magnets, which was originally proposed its fans, and with the products, there laid introduction cards telling people the secrets of the royal palace. The moment this series of fridge magnet was released, it has got onto the Weibo's Top Hot Topics and soon becomes a most-sought product. Allowing users to participate in product designing may cultivate their autonomy and motivation, building an innate emotional link between products and users, so that when they use the products, they will obtain more emotional resonance. In addition, "User-involvement-based design" assists consumers with different consumption demands to form a unified cognition about the products, which may provide them common topics on values, triggering points and demands about the products, and consequently consumers' behaviors will bring new inspiration to product development and more energy to spread product's reputation.

4.2   Expansion of Products' Connection Properties

The greatest highlight of product design in the era of intelligence is to develop and realize product's connection-property, the function of which will highly expand the range and possibility of products application and enhance the interaction between users and products. Currently, the functions and usages of the museum cultural creative products are still so limited that they are usually used in the fields of crafts and home decoration. But in the long future, once the technologies such as AI, VR or AR can better meet consumers' emotional needs, for example: the chronologies can supply people with more refined scenery details and underlying psychological experience, consumers will be likely to have more imaginary and cognitive spaces for their emotional memories. Moreover, as the product optimizing become more and more consummate, the boundary to limit product's application range will gradually vanish, and finally the cultural connotation of the museum cultural creative products can be better conveyed.

5 Ending

Museum is a spiritual homeland of human culture, and emergence of the museum cultural creative products have significantly widen the paths and approaches to promoting the culture of museums. The museum cultural creative products with the philosophy of "emotion retrospection" can better fulfill the inheritance and promotion of the cultural connotation and also enable the user to deeply sense the practical functions of the products. The application of "emotion retrospection" in the design of museum cultural creative products brings about a whole new orientation to carry forward Chinese traditional and can be consider as an exploration and a trial on Chinese-style design.

References

1. Zhang, L., Zhao, S.: Research on prototype-principle-based design of museum cultural creative products. Sichuan Drama **7**, 173 (2017)
2. Xu, X.: On the nature of design. J. Zhejiang Univ. Layout Humanit. Soc. Sci.
3. Ruotsalo, K., Aroyo, L., Schreiber, G.: Knowledge based linguistic annotation of digital cultural heritage collections. IEEE Intell. Syst. **24**(2), 64–75 (2009)
4. Zhu, S.: Research on regional cultural image of modern product design. Packag. Eng. **5**, 209–210 (2009)
5. Zhu, S., Luo, S.: Recreation of relic elements in product design based on design-semiotics. J. Zhejiang Univ. Layout Eng. **11**, 2065 (2013)
6. Shuai, Q.: Research on the emotional consumption of urban women based on the concept of new advance. **9**, 211–213 (2016)
7. Santangelo, P.: Emotional Culture in Chinese History: Interdisciplinary Text Study on Literature of Ming Dynasty and Qing Dynasty. Trans. Lin, S. Commercial Press, Beijing (2009)
8. Gui, C., Li, S.: Research on "emotion retrospection" experience mode applied in design of interactive style products. Pack. Eng. **12**, 58–60 (2012)
9. Zhang, Z., Sun, Y., Zhu, Y.: Research on culture conveying model in the design of cultural creative product. Pack. Eng. **4**, 95–98 (2018)
10. Lu, Y.: The evolution of design and creative design in the future China. Globalization **6**, 5–13 (2014)

Analysis of One-Person Households Who Is Young's Characteristics in Combination with Social Experience from the Perspectives of Interaction Process in Product Use, Social Situation and Public Space

Tongtong Zhao and Zhen Liu[✉]

School of Design, South China University of Technology, Guangzhou 510006,
People's Republic of China
liuzjames@scut.edu.cn

Abstract. There is a special group as a product of the times constantly expanding: OPHY. One-person Households who is Young (OPHY), aging between 20 and 35 years old. Combined with the characteristics of the OPHY group, this paper introduces a concept based on multi-dimensional user experience: social experience. This paper will focus on the OPHY, through three methods of design research, with the concept of "social experience", analyze the deeper characteristics and needs of this group, seeking design directions and concepts that can help these strugglers enhance their interaction with society and improve their social experience. Through research, this paper finds that the living status of OPHY have a great correlation with their salary level, social status, personal mentality and gender. However, no matter what kind of typical participants, the status of living alone would indeed reduce their social interaction, even if they have a strong social tendency. On the one hand, designers should combine the OPHY's characteristics to make change, through product design and interior design. On the other hand, designers should insist on enhancing the attractiveness of the outside world to help OPHY get out of their house, through service design, architecture design and environmental design. Based on the existing research, this paper has carried out a more detailed subdivision of the OPHY group. At the same time, this paper improves the user research methods in design, and innovatively applies them on sociological problems.

Keywords: One-person households who is young · User experience ·
Social experience · Emotional experience · Product use · Social situation ·
Social sustainability · Space interaction

1 Introduction

With the development of economy and modern network, coupled with the change of some traditional concepts, such as the change of marriage and love concepts and the enhancement of self-concept, there is a special group that is expanding as a product of the Times: OPHY. They struggle alone in the big city for self-realization, enjoying the

© Springer Nature Switzerland AG 2019
A. Marcus and W. Wang (Eds.): HCII 2019, LNCS 11583, pp. 557–576, 2019.
https://doi.org/10.1007/978-3-030-23570-3_42

satisfaction of pursuing ideal, but also experiencing the emotional loneliness and the awkward predicament in life. This paper will focus on OPHY, use three design research methods and analyze the characteristics and requirements of this group, with the concept of "social experience", in products, users and environment three directions. With the combination of product design, service design, architectural design and other related professional knowledge in the field of design, from the perspective of the designer, seek to help the foreign land striver increase social interaction and improve their social experience.

2 Literature Review

2.1 One-Person Household Who Is Young (OPHY)

According to the census bureau, only 7.6% of U.S. households chose to live alone in 1967, but today, more than 35 million Americans live alone, accounting for 14.5% of U.S. households, nearly double the number from 50 years ago [1]. Living alone has become the second largest household registration in the United States, far beyond nuclear family, trunk family, roommate cohabitation and other forms [2]. The number of one-person households has also almost doubled in the Seoul metropolitan region of Korea between 2000 and 2010 [3, 4]. Almost 30 years ago, the one-person household was identified as the fastest growing group throughout most of the developed world [5]. These changes were experienced by the developed countries previously through the so-called second demographic transition [6].

This growth is also evident in some developing countries which promote social culture. Podhisita and Xenos studied the phenomenon of living alone in south and southeast Asia. The research shows that the average level of living alone in Asia, while the lowest in the world, has been on the rise in recent years and young people are most likely to live alone [7]. According to the latest population sampling survey data from National Bureau of Statistics of China, the number of one-person households accounted for 13.15% of total households in 2015, compared with 9.14% a decade ago in 2006 [1].

The situation of living alone is closely related to social environment, wealth, age and other factors. This paper concentrates on the One-person Households who is Young (OPHY), aging between 20 and 35 years old.

In China and some other developing countries, which have a strong family concept and where the project group has only begun to grow substantially in recent years, scholars' researches in the field of the youth who live alone mainly focuses on the following five aspects: Firstly, the cause of this particular group: 1. Frequent social mobility [8, 9, 19, 29] 2. The change of the concept of marriage and childbirth [20–22] 3. Non-traditional lifestyle [8, 20]; Secondly, the group's definition: 1. Age: 20–35 [8, 10, 11] 2. Leave their parents and live alone in big cities [9, 10, 12] 3. Work hard for their dreams [12–14, 21]; Thirdly, the group's characteristics: 1. High level of education [15, 16, 19] 2. Strong sense of independence [23, 24] 3. Strong sense of self-esteem and self-confidence [11, 15, 16]; Fourthly, macro solutions: from the aspect of psychology [14, 25, 26], policy [13, 27, 28] and so forth; Finally, disagreements in the academic community about this group: some argue that the group contains lots of problems and should be treated with caution [16, 28, 29]. However, other researchers believe that this is a social progress and we should be optimistic [9, 17, 18].

In the developed countries, such as the U.S. and Japan, single solitary living has become a relatively common social phenomenon. In the interview process of the recording of "Nothing to Society", the recording team of the NHK special program in Japan put forward the concept that "it is now the time to take living alone for granted [30]". Although the famous American sociologist Eric Klinenberg wrote the book "Going solo" presenting us with a "single society" with richer levels through a survey [2], most researchers only focused on the health [31–33] and diet [34–36] of solitary people and did not subdivide young solitary people for analysis.

However, there are few researches aimed at the OPHY phenomenon, and most of the existing literatures remain at the direct description level of media reports, and many reports lack empirical materials' support. Only a few researches that have reached conclusions through actual research via interview. And there is a lack of in-depth knowledge and group segmentation.

2.2   Extension of User Experience: Social Experience

User experience: The user's responses and perceptions that arise from the anticipated use or use of a product, service or system [37]. And the aim of User Experience Design (UXD) is enabling joy and fun, eliciting emotions and satisfying psychological needs, which means creating experiences [38]. And Simon also proposed that incorporation and shaping atmosphere are possible triggers for experience. Human beings are social creatures. Decades of research on human happiness shows that engaging in positive social interactions is critical for well-being [39–41]. Dourish identified the development of social computing through three distinctive "waves": the first wave concentrated on virtual communities, such as online environment, chat rooms and MUDs; the second wave concentrated on large-scale collaborative actions, such as micro-blogging, virtual worlds, online games and social networking platforms; and the third wave concentrated on the integration of everyday life and social and collaborative digital [42]. The need for designing the interaction experience between individuals and the society is increasing and unstoppable.

Hence, it is natural that the concept of user experience needs to be expanded to encompass not only the individual side of experience, but also to take the social side into account. This paper will concentrate on the interaction of the special group OPHY with society, searching for the way to help them to engage into the society better and improve their sense of social belongings.

Here, this paper introduces another concept: the social experience (SX).

The term social is *"multi-faceted and used with different viewpoints. It means inter-personal, ceremonial, informal, public, non-profit, or humanity on a massive-scale. It involves emotion, trust, ties, and norms"* [43].

This paper assumes the social experience to be identical to the experience which generates from the interaction between people and the interaction between people and the society, such as the public utilities and the public open spaces, such as parks and public architectures.

Table 1. Summary of related studies on social experience.

Topics	Content	Studies	Aim	Research Method: Literature Review	Questionnaire	Interviews	Case Studies	Experiment	Other	Outcome
		Express Yourself: Designing Interactive Products with Implicitness to Improve Social Interaction [51]	The aim of this paper is to simplify the interaction between users within the system and encourage users to have more physical social interaction in their daily life.		√		√	√		1. Identify the possibility of designing interactive products that let users to express themselves with daily behaviors to make their own special experiences., which also encourage them to interact with each other in their daily life. 2. users would be much expressive when interacting with physical objects. Therefore, we suggest designers to utilize physical form while designing computational products with this concept.
	Product design	Based on the Experience of Product Interaction Design [52]	To discuss the interaction design's objective, principle and design process, as product interaction design is the development direction of the future products. In view of interaction design of contents and category is very wide.	√						To establish the user experience of product interaction design goal is to grasp the interaction design positioning. At the same time, in the product interaction design it should follow the next several design principles.1. pleasure principle 2. differentiation principle 3. personalized principle 4. continuity principle 5. innovative principles; flow chart of product interaction design
Commerce		An Empirical Framework for Designing Social Products [53]	To provide designers with a framework and a particular methodology for designing products with social behaviors.	√				√		designers of social products should ascertain in advance that the interaction style of the product fits the social context of use as well as individual attributes of the users.
		Shop-i: Gaze based Interaction in the Physical World for In-Store Social Shopping Experience [54]	To find how should we design the visual attentive interface in physical world.	√				√		Most people particularly thought the product comparison feature was useful. Also, users felt that using the physical environment as a display was more natural than using an additional wearable device, such as Google Glass, to accomplish the same goal.
	Service design	The influence of user interaction and participation in social media on the consumption intention of niche products [55]	To consider the context of social media platforms for promoting niche cultural products to investigate how user interaction patterns could promote overall user participation levels in content generation to allow commercial value to be better derived in this context.	√				√	Social network analy-sis(SNA)with UCINET v.6.212	provide support for the hypothesis that user participation in such a platform (e.g., in generating content such as product reviews) can indeed lead to favorable commercial benefits. Given the importance of attaining a high level of user participation in content generation, it makes sense for the hosting firm to encourage greater interactions among users, with the hope that they can stimulate one another to contribute more content to the social media platform. However, not all types of interaction could lead to higher participation in content generation. Our findings indicated that in the context of discussions on niche cultural products, although inclusiveness and betweenness centralization can promote overall participation, out-degree centralization and core-periphery structures have a detrimental effect.
		Experience Design of Social Interaction for Generation Y Based on Tangible Interaction [56]	To explore the experience design based on tangible computing in the hope of better communication and interaction of Generation Y	√	√			√		The design principle of their chameleon installation is appropriate. Provide a framework of ideas and methods for them to determine design principles for specific groups of people.
	Experience design	Culture and Co-experience: Cultural Variation of User Experience in Social Interaction and Its Implications for Interaction Design [57]	Aim at exploring relationship between culture and a social aspect of user experience.	√			√	√		1. The paper brings important implications for interaction design in two aspects: "cultural aspect of co-experience" as a sensitizing concept for new design and an evaluation tool for cultural fitness. 2.Designed a novel interactive technology called "Visual-talk table," inspired by the concept of role-taking, which make convincing contributions in studies on cultural aspects in tangible and ubiquitous interaction.
		Co-experience: The Social User Experience [58]	To presents a critical view of existing models of user experience.				√			The definition of co-experience: social, multi-modal, creative, for fun.
		Exploring Social Interaction in Co-located Multiplayer Games [59]	The aim of our experimental study is to identify and analyze the interplay of contextual conditions in MagicDuel, a co-located multi-player game				√			1. The key opportunity of this MagicDuel game is to establish, understand and evaluate the symbiotic relationship between the players who are immersed in the game and the audience engagement. 2.The socio-spatial inter dynamics between player-game system-audience engagement contexts are areas that influence gameplay experiences. 3.the study of social interaction aspects of the younger demographic, defined by social experience (SX) is a domain that could lead to creation of digital games affording the enhancement of human lifestyle, creation of memorable and motivated human experiences for any specific demographic in public spheres.
Applications	Game design	Design Implications of Social Interaction in Online Games [60]	To gain a better understanding of the patterns of player interaction and their implications for game design, we analyze how players interact from packet traces.				√		Develop an algorithm for data analysis	Game designers could increase the "stickiness" of games by supporting, or even forcing, team playing.
		The Impact of Game Patterns on Player Experience and Social Interaction in Co-Located Multiplayer Games [61]	To establish a research model for social player interaction highlighting the impact of the game design, the player group, and the gaming sitting	√	√		√	√		Results indicate that high player interdependence implies more communication and less frustration, whereas shared control results in less perceived competence and autonomy. Moreover, individual player characteristics also impact the social interaction.
		Design for Social Interaction in Public Spaces [62]	To look into the challenges brought up by social computing, in de- signing for social interaction in public spaces, in particular in cities and professional environments.				√			Presented eight design cases of interactive installations for social interaction in public spaces. The targeted spaces and user groups, design concepts and implementing technologies vary, aiming at different social experiences.
	Interaction design	Designing for Social Interaction: An Experimental Design Research Project [63]	To develop a conceptual framework that will make designers able to better discuss design projects in the developmental phase, and subsequently design systems that are more likely to be successful social systems.				√	√		The outcome of the project is one or more conceptual frameworks that will enable designers to better describe and design technologies supporting social interaction.
		Interactive Experience [64]	while playing, exploring, and being creative alongside a typically developed companion.	√				√		The slow introduction of richer interactions has proven to be positive for helping children get comfortable with the system and gently encouraging socialization and collaboration behaviors.
		Typologies of Architectural Interaction: A Social Dimension [65]	To explore interactive architecture's potential role as catalyst for social activity.				√	√		Proposes a new way of thinking "socially" about interactive systems, expanding on a crucial ongoing discussion about the relationship between interactive buildings, humans, and the environment.
	Architectural design	Social Theatres: A Web-Based Regulated Social Interaction Environment [66]	To propose a model for interaction regulation and control for virtual, social interaction spaces, called Social Theatres.				√			This paper discusses the advantages of regulated interaction, addresses the Social Theatre metaphor and presents the software architecture for the implementation of these regulated social interaction spaces.
		Social Interaction Design Patterns for Urban Media Architecture [67]	To offer an overview and analysis of social interaction in media architecture	√			√			Firstly, a framework outlining six different modes of social interaction in relation to media architecture: appreciation, self-expression, playfulness, collective narratives, triangulation, and negotiation of space; secondly, a set of seven social interaction design patterns for media architecture, which represent different strategies for designing media architecture to achieve specific types of social interaction: shadow playing, remote control, smooth operator, soapbox, amusement park, swarm, and automatic gate.
Physical		Design for Social Interaction in Public Spaces [62]	To look into the challenges brought up by social computing, in de- signing for social interaction in public spaces, in particular in cities and professional environments.				√			Presented eight design cases of interactive installations for social interaction in public spaces. The targeted spaces and user groups, design concepts and implementing technologies vary, aiming at different social experiences.
		Designing urban furniture through user's appropriation experience: Teaching social interaction design [68]	Analyze needs of persons in their role of users with the objective of making their experience more enjoyable and unique.	√			√			The result of combining technical tools and interpreting emotions is attractive and leads to significantly improved designs, can be used to capture information for other design tools (QFD, Concept Evaluation and Selection Matrix, etc.), as well as submitting these designs to real users' experience.
	Environmental design	Social interaction and cohesion tool: A dynamic design approach for Barcelona's superilles [69]	The purpose of the methodology is to use a Grasshopper-based platform to collect social data from scratch, 'codify' it, develop respective scales and modes of visualization, and iteratively design a language of visualization.	√					√ the new methodology	This paper outlines a methodology to use new parametric workflows closely orchestrated with sociological 'coding' protocols, measuring indicators of social interaction and cohesion at various points along sidewalks for new walkable urban units in Barcelona.
		Influence of Interactivity on Social Connectedness A Study on User Experience in an Interactive Public Installation [70]	To find out how interaction with public installations affects its users by evaluating the experience of social connectedness	√	√			√		The experiment was successful in providing evidence that if a public installation is interactive, having the users interact simultaneously increases the level of social connectedness significantly compared to a single user interaction. However, there was no significant difference in the level of social connectedness between having a non-interactive installation and having an interactive installation. Therefore, no conclusions can be drawn from this experiment and this would be a topic for further investigation.

Yamakami used the metaphor of user experience design in social contexts and proposed the concept of social experience design [44]. He assumed the social experience to be identical to multi-user experience. He concentrated on the interaction between people and ignored the influence of the social objective material environment. However, living in the society, the social environment and social equipment play a significant role in our interaction experience. This paper focuses SX on the following two aspects: firstly, the relationship of social experience design and user experience design [45–47]; secondly, the application of social experience design in virtual network world [48–50]. Combined with the definition of SX in this paper, literature in relevant fields has been screened, as shown in Table 1.

The above-mentioned studies contribute to our understanding of social experience. However, they also have limitations. First, the definition of social experience is too narrow. The social experience should be extended to the experience of personal involvement in a society, the interaction with the society. The society can be considered as a system or an environment, which contains not only human beings but also the material facility and cultural conditions. The spatial arrangement of residential area has been found to enhance social interaction among residents and influence their activity patterns. To achieve the social interaction must provide physical space, such as parks. Second, as this is still a new emerging field of research, it focused on the introduction of concepts and models about SX, being lack of research data.

Therefore, based on the existing literature, this paper will use the relevant methods of design research to describe the social experience of this special group in depth. From the perspective of the group's daily social habits, living habits and emotional changes to define the following questions:

What problems exist in social construction make the number of solitary people increase?

How can we help them to improve their social experience and their sense of social belongings?

3   Methods

In order to better understand the OPHY group's interaction experience status quo, this paper, from the aspects of their product use, social interaction and interaction with public spaces, such as public buildings and city parks, chooses three specific design methods combining with the special group's feature: "Personal Belongings", "A Day In The Life" and "Map". In-depth research is carried out from the perspectives of user with products, user with user and users with environment to explore the status and potential design points of OPHY in these three dimensions.

3.1   Personal Belongings

Purpose. By recording the items that participants carry under different scenarios (weekday and weekend), the product usage habits and internal demands of OPHY group are analyzed. From the perspective of interaction between user and products, this paper explores the phenomena and potential design points existing in the use of products by this group.

Materials. Sticky paper for personal belongings (2 sheets), camera.

Executive Routine. *Step 1-Record.* Take out all the items in bag in the morning and evening and put them in order for a group photo. *Record Twice.* on the weekday (blue sticky paper) and weekend (red sticky paper). *Step 2-Return Visit.*

3.2   A Day in the Life

Purpose. By recording social situations in different scenarios (weekday and weekend), the social habits and psychological state of OPHY group are analyzed. From the perspective of interpersonal interaction, this paper explores the phenomena and potential design points in the social interaction of this group.

Materials. Booklets (2 copies, as shown in Fig. 1), Emoji stickers (1 copy), Pens.

Fig. 1. The digital demo given by the researcher about how to complete the booklet (left). The inside pages of the booklet which need to be filled in according to the listed items (middle). The booklet: blue for weekday, pink for weekend (right). (Color figure online)

Executive Routine. *Step 1-Record.* Make detailed records of effective social contact during the day by combining with the demo given. Effective social contact is defined here as "effective social contact with others regardless of online or offline contact and communication. Items to be recorded: time, place, interlocuter, method, trigger point, content and feelings (transcript and emoji graphical expression). *Record Twice.* on the weekday (blue booklet) and weekend (red booklet). *Step 2-Return Visit.* Open questions.

3.3   Map

Purpose. By recording the locations of different scenarios (weekday and weekend) to work and live, the living habits and living conditions of OPHY group are analyzed. From the perspective of interaction between users and environment, this paper explores the phenomena and potential design points existing in the interaction with public space, such as public architectures and urban parks.

Materials. Map of different provinces, Markers (2, red/blue).

Executive Routine. *Step 1-Record.* Mark the locations on the map and mark the names of the locations. *Record Twice.* on the weekday (blue marker) and weekend (red marker). *Step 2-Return Visit.*

3.4   Additional Materials

Commitment (2 sheets), Personal information form, Task Table (2 sheets), Demos.

4   Conduct

4.1   Participants

Basis for Selection. *Basic Requirements.* Age: 20 to 35 years old; Residence: China's first and second tiered cities; Living alone.
Additional Requirements. At the same time, in order to ensure the sociality and typicality of the survey, this paper selected a total of 5 survey subjects for analysis based on the two important factors affecting the living state of OPHY group: gender and characteristics (extravert/introvert).

Participants' Information (as shown in Table 2).

Table 2. Participants' information.

Participant	Age	Residence	Gender	Characteristics (extraverted/introverted)	Conduct time
M1	27	Shijiazhuang, Hebei	Male	Introverted	June 18 2018 (June 16 2018)
M2	30	Shijiazhuang, Hebei	Male	Extraverted	June 14 2018 (June 16 2018)
F1	21	Shanghai	Female	Extraverted	June 12 2018 (June 16 2018)
F2	25	Changsha, Hunan	Female	Introverted	June 12 2018 (June 16 2018)
F3	32	Beijing	Female	Introverted	August 15 2018 (August 12 2018)

Note: The determination of extroverted or introverted is derived from the self-statement in the personal information form.

4.2   Timetable

The following (as shown in Fig. 2) is the specific execution time of each task of the participants (24-h system):

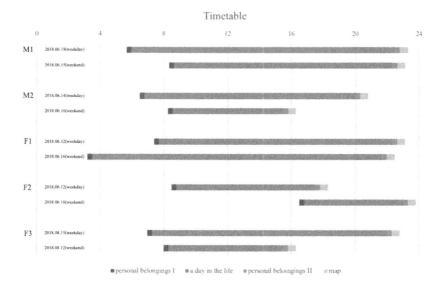

Fig. 2. Timetable about when the participants completed the tasks (in 24-h system).

5   Consequence

5.1   Personal Belongings

(1) Carry-on items: keys, mobile phones (as shown in Figs. 3 and 4).
(2) Items with gender differences: bags, lipsticks, tissues (as shown in Figs. 3 and 4).
(3) Items with age differences: earphones (as shown in Figs. 3 and 4). (Participants under 30 years old tend to carry earphones)
(4) Items with different personality differences: wallet, cash, bank card (as shown in Figs. 3 and 4).
(5) Items on weekdays and weekends are different from: lipstick and earphones. It can be obtained from the later interview of F2 that don't carry earphones on weekends is a kind of performance that is more relaxing and tends to communicate with friends (as shown in Figs. 3 and 4).
(6) Many items with more individualized features are not listed in the chart because they are not universal. In general, the number of items that women need to carry is: 10+, while that of men is: 5−, the gap is large. According to the later interviews M1, F1, F3: women will carry what they might use when they leave home (even though they admitted that these things in the bag were never used), such as emergency medicine; on the contrary, men pursue a "simple" lifestyle.

Belongings (weekday)

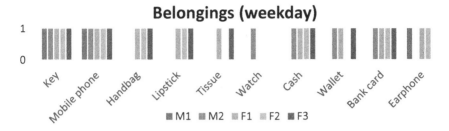

Fig. 3. On the weekday, items which the participants carry.

Belongings (weekend)

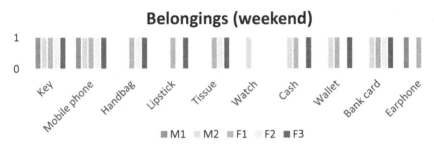

Fig. 4. On the weekend, items which the participants carry.

5.2   A Day in the Life

(1) **Quantity:** The number of social interactions happened on weekdays is much higher than on weekends. The number of social interactions is not necessarily related to their personality and gender, but has a great relationship with the nature of work (as shown in Fig. 5).

(2) **Location:** Social places are concentrated in companies and consumer places, and some exist in home which are acquaintances and required passive social interaction. Extroverted personality has more active social interactions in public places. For the younger participants, weekend time would also be occupied by work (as shown in Fig. 6).

(3) **Interlocutor (as shown in** Fig. 10)**:** Weekday socializing focus on communications with colleagues (most of the contents are about work and some are entertainment), and weekend socializing is concentrated with friends. On weekends, the number of interactions with strangers is zero. There is less communication with parents, even less than the number of interactions with practitioners of service industry. Extroverted personality loves to communicate with parents. The number of friends the five participants keeping communicating with is maintained at 1 or 2. In addition, the older the age, the greater the correlation between the source of friends and work (as shown in Fig. 7).

(4) **Media:** On weekdays, men tend to socialize face to face, women tend to socialize online (related to the nature of work); on weekends, they all tend to socialize face to face. On weekends, both social medias would be reduced to a certain extent (as shown in Fig. 8).

(5) **Emotional changes:** The mood changes on weekdays are more abundant. On workdays, men have more positive emotions and women have more negative emotions: on weekends, positive emotions dominate for both men and women. Among them, positive emotions mainly arise from interactions with colleagues and friends. Negative emotions mainly come from difficulties in work (female negative emotions also come from interactions with friends: such as they do not get positive feedback or they do not receive friends' full attention). Introverted personality is more likely to produce negative emotions than extroverted personality, whether it is workday or weekend (as shown in Fig. 9).

(6) **Content:** From the conversations of private socially interactions other than work interactions, it can be seen that people with introverted personality are more eager to be recognized and willing to give and women prefer sharing more than men.

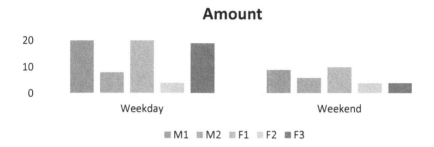

Fig. 5. The amount of social intercourse in a day.

Fig. 6. The places where social intercourse took place.

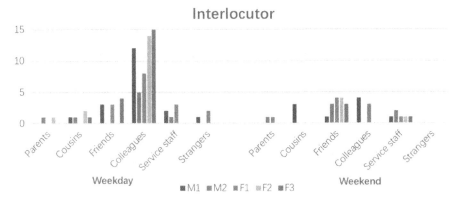

Fig. 7. The people who the participants talked with.

Fig. 8. The medium used to have social intercourse.

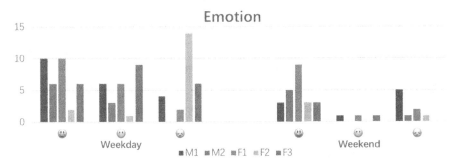

Fig. 9. Participants' feelings when they were socializing.

Social intimacy

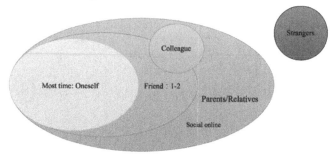

Fig. 10. Social intimacy model.

5.3   Map

(1) In addition to the company, OPHY stay at home most of time (as shown in Figs. 11 and 12).
(2) Eating out is not their only choice. In most cases, they will choose to cook, order take out or take the dishes home. The specific situation is affected by the income level.
(3) Men have the habit of exercise, but women do not (as shown in Figs. 11 and 12).
(4) Women are more inclined to stay at home, whether it is after work or on weekends (as shown in Figs. 11 and 12).
(5) On weekends, work would deprive men's holiday time (as shown in Fig. 12).
(6) The idle time mode that OPHY spends tends to stay at home, go hiking, and rarely appear in cultural venues such as cinemas, museum and libraries (as shown in Figs. 11 and 12).
(7) Urban public spaces such as parks and plazas do not appear in their lives (as shown in Figs. 11 and 12).

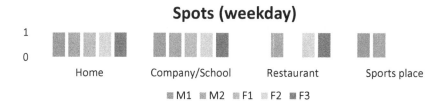

Fig. 11. On the weekday, places that have been visited.

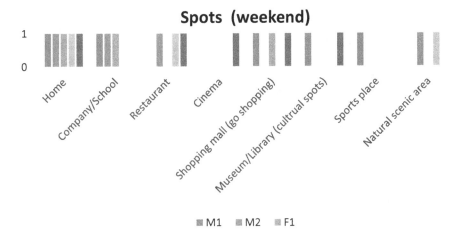

Fig. 12. On the weekend, places that have been visited.

6 Discussion

Through investigation and research, this paper finds that the phenomenon and the survival status of the OPHY group are closely related to their personality characteristics and income levels, and the individual differences are very large. It is not possible to view the survival status of this group only through the overall trend and changes of the society. The literature [8, 15–17, 27, 28] did not pay enough attention to independent individuals in the process of examining this group.

6.1 Product Use

Chang and Liang [51] pointed out in the study that users should be encouraged to express their emotions by designing some physical interaction products to enable users to create experiences in their daily lives. However, this paper did not find products with interactive feature from the user's personal belongings. There may be two situations: First, the research case of Chang and Liang is in a larger private space, such as bedroom, and this paper focuses on the items that are carried around, with a smaller scope, more functional purposes, and less interactive scenarios. Second, the current interactive products (especially physical products) do not combine portability, functionality and emotional interactivity, and the emotional interactivity of portable products (such as headphones) is almost zero. In combination with the product user experience proposed in Hu and Huang [52], in addition to the usability, the product should be interesting, creative, personalized. We can draw a conclusion that the existing portable products have problems in this aspect of design. At the same time, because users will inject a lot of personal emotions and experience memories on such products, how to design the life cycle of such products more effectively, to make the products from the purchase, use to discard or collection become more elegant need to be carefully considered by the designers. For some daily necessities, the product life cycle is generally very short. While optimizing the user experience, it is necessary to pay attention to the sustainability and green environmental protection of the product.

This paper shows that the OPHY group has a willingness to talk and communicate, and most of the positive emotions in their lives come from the communication experience with others, such as share gets positive responds). Lee [57] and Battarbee [58] proposed a new concept: co-experience, which emphasizes that different individuals create experiences together when using a certain product to gain happiness. This paper shows that this concept is established, and the experience created by people in the process of using mobile phones (or social software) far exceeds the value brought by the product's own functional value. However, OPHY is limited by its own environment (often alone), their co-experience is mainly generated by mobile phones (virtual social networks). How to help them create more and more diverse co-experience need more products to enhance user engagement and self-motivated, not just mobile phones.

6.2   Social Situation

Kim et al. [54] pointed out that user interaction on the social platform, such as product reviews, can indeed bring good social benefits, but the research in this paper shows that young female users (F1, F2) are willing to interact on the platforms. The male research users and the older female users (M1, M2, F3) rarely interact on the public network platform. How to mobilize their social interaction (social experience) online should be concerned in service design field and information design field.

Among the five respondents, only the young male M1 has the habit of playing games. Game is the way he spends his free time, and it is also a medium for him to maintain friendship. But he is only limited to playing games with old friends. At the same time, he will gain a sense of accomplishment in the game (M1 became much more excited about the topic of the game in the interview). Chen and Lei [60] emphasized the importance of teamwork for game viscosity, but how to improve the viscosity between users, increase their communication and personal relationship development to maintain the stability and continuity of teamwork, which game designers need continue thinking about. In addition, the OPHY group's private time is actually quite long and boring, at the same time, they are eager to be recognized (playing games can quickly achieve a sense of accomplishment to meet their needs), so how to make female users and older male users involve in games and fulfill their social needs in the game (the lower threshold for communicating with strangers in games) is also the possible direction of game design.

6.3   Public Space Interaction

Oh et al. [65] indicated that the experience and participation of buildings that users can participate in is far greater than that of ornamental buildings with a sense of mystery. Although ornamental buildings create subtle social connections between designers and users, they rarely trigger social activities and people are less curious about them. In contrast, by creating surprises, happiness, and communication with people, a building that is interactive is a temporary re-adjustment of the social atmosphere. This paper finds that the buildings mentioned by OPHY are all related to functions (such as cinemas). There is no conflict between the functionality of the interior of the building and the entertainment on the exterior wall. Enhancing the interactive design of the architecture is a good way to increase social experience and promote social interaction between strangers. However, in this process, the construction of interactive facilities is an additional function and is easy to produce burnout, high cost, and fast update speed, so how to effectively use the easy-to-assemble, easy-to-move sustainable materials and modules for flow assembly between different buildings' display is a problem that the designers should pay attention to.

This paper shows that public space (such as parks and squares) has a small chance of appearing in the daily life of the participants. On weekdays, most of them went home directly after work (only M2 went to the park for a walk in the evening), there is not much interaction with the outside world; on weekends, they were more inclined to stay at home or go to nature with two or three friends, such as mountains, but not the public spaces in the city. These reflect some of the problems that may exist in the design of public environment: First, public spaces in urban areas such as parks generally have special areas for children to have fun and sports venues for the elderly. Only some of the larger amusement facilities are set up for young people. However, when OPHY has time, specifically after work, these facilities have been closed, and the public spaces lack a relaxing entertainment program and atmosphere that meets the needs of the crowd; second, the public space are never showed up in female participants' lives and at the same time they do not have the habit of exercising. In return visit, the reason for this phenomenon is not only the participants' laziness but their concerns about safety issues. Therefore, how to strengthen the attractiveness and security of the public space in the evening, that is, to better combine the characteristics of the work-in-the-jobs to make the public space of the night rejuvenate is an issue that environmental designers could consider. Van and Hu [70] gave some good examples and methods for enhancing the social function and fun of public spaces through user collaboration.

7 Conclusion

This paper aims to explore the characteristics and needs of the OPHY group, and combines the characteristics of this group (basing on literature review) to select three design research methods: Personal Belongings, A Day In The Life and Map. Five typical users from four cities were selected for in-depth research based on gender and personality characteristics. Through research, this paper finds that the living status of this group has a great correlation with their income level, social status, personal mentality and gender. But no matter what kind of typical users, the status of living alone would indeed reduce their social interaction, even though they have a strong social tendency. Therefore, from the designer's point of view, how to expand their communication range, help them maintain stable communication and improve their social communication experience is the direction should be worked hard. On the one hand, designers should combine the special group's own characteristics, such as more time at home, from their living environment or from the game they love to play, find the direction of improvement to help them experience social and interactive pleasure at home. On the other hand, designers should continue to enhancing the attractiveness of the world outside the house to help them get out of the house by improving the services they receive, the buildings they pass by and the public spaces they have been neglecting to. Make integrating more actively and simply to help them make more new friends and create more interesting experience in society.

Based on the existing research, this paper has carried out a more detailed subdivision of the OPHY group, and a broader survey on the three dimensions of user with products, user with user, users and environment, and found out more specific needs and survival of this group in some specific scenarios. At the same time, this paper flexibly applies the user research methods in design, and applies them in solving sociological problems innovatively. The typical users replace the big data statistics to conduct more in-depth user research, which makes the user image more vivid, the research level more diverse, and to some extent, it expands a new idea of user research.

In addition to more specific research on enhancing the interaction of the external environment, future research can also explore the concept of "home" from the existing living habits of OPHY. How to better help OPHY integrate into the society through the design of interior design, product design or virtual product design. And how to integrate the relationship of "being at home" and "entity social" which are seemingly contradictory.

OPHY is a growing population and is a social phenomenon that cannot be ignored. Researchers can't simply define the good or bad of their lives, but the designers can use the power of design to enhance their social experience to help the young people who are struggling between dream and reality gain a stronger sense of social integration and cultural belonging.

Acknowledgements. The authors wish to thank all the people who provided their time and efforts for the investigation. This research is supported by South China University of Technology (SCUT) project funding x2sj-K5180600.

References

1. A solitary person in a foreign land. http://kreader.cnki.net/Kreader/CatalogViewPage.aspx? dbCode=cdmd&filename=1017096171.nh&tablename=CMFD201702&compose=&first= 1&uid=. Accessed 10 May 2017
2. Eric, K.: Going Solo. Penguin Press HC, London (2012)
3. Chae, J., Park, S., Byu, B.: An analysis of spatial concentrated areas of single person households and concentrating factors in Seoul. Seoul Stud. 1–16 (2014)
4. Yi, C., Lee, S.: An empirical analysis of the characteristics of residential location choice in the rapidly changing Korean housing market. Cities **39**, 156–163 (2014)
5. Sorrentino, C.: The changing family in international perspective. Mon. Labor Rev. **113**(3), 41–58 (1990)
6. Yi, C.: Relationship between the formation conditions and durations of one-person households in the Seoul Metropolitan Region. Demography **53**(3), 675–697 (2016)
7. Chai, P., Peter, X.: Living alone in South and Southeast Asia: an analysis of census data. Demogr. Res. **32**(41), 1113–1146 (2015)

8. Yu, A.: Phenomenon of empty nesters: expression, cause and cognitive attitude. Forw. Pos. **7**, 78–82 (2017). (in Chinese)

9. Li, C., Ma, F.: "Empty nest youth": a group that walks between "survival" and "dream". Thoughts Public Opini. **4**, 118–119 (2017). (in Chinese)

10. Guo, L., Zhu, L.: "Empty nest youth": "nest space" does not mean "heart empty". Dec. Explor. **3**, 12–13 (2018). (in Chinese)

11. Dou, X.: Psychosocial diagnosis and support of the "empty nest youth" group image. Gansu Soc. Sci. **1**, 179–185 (2018). (in Chinese)

12. Wu, G., Yang, X.: "Empty nest youth"—dream catcher of rootless duckweed. Reform Open. Up **4**, 101–102 (2018). (in Chinese)

13. Xia, C.: Perspective and guiding strategy of "empty nest youth" phenomenon. J. Shanxi Youth Vocat. Coll. **30**(2), 8–10 (2017). (in Chinese)

14. Chang, J.: What makes empty nest youth's nest empty—an interpretation of time and space sociology. Chin. Youth Res. **5**, 79–83 (2017). (in Chinese)

15. He, S.: Multidimensional interpretation of the "empty nest youth" group. Chin. Youth Res. **3**, 40–45 (2017). (in Chinese)

16. Dou, X.: The psychosocial problems of "the empty nest youth" and the counter measures. Chin. Youth Res. **2**, 89–95 (2018). (in Chinese)

17. Yang, H.: "Empty nest youth" is a false proposition. New Compos. Coll. Entr. Exam. Online **1**, 108 (2017). (in Chinese)

18. Ling, B.: "Empty Nest Youth" becomes stronger in loneliness. China Labor Secur. News **9**(2), 1 (2016). (in Chinese)

19. Hu, Y., Qi, B., Zhu, X.: From the "empty nest" mentality to the "cluster" behavior: "empty nest youth" phenomenon perspective and network mapping. Chin. Youth Res. **8**, 36–43 (2017). (in Chinese)

20. Li, R.: Incomplete reversal of group: the social connection of "empty nest youth". Contemp. Youth Res **1**, 85–91 (2018). (in Chinese)

21. Zhu, Y., Wang, F.: An isolated island in the city: a study on the relationship network construction of "empty nest youth. Res. Trans. Competence **10**, 217–218 (2017). (in Chinese)

22. Huang, S., Li, Q.: Study on the life and mentality of young people living alone in big cities. Youth Explor. **4**, 75–87 (2018). (in Chinese)

23. Lin, J., Xian, Y.: Research on the construction of social network model of "empty nest youth" under the "micro age". Educ. Fine Arts **2**, 16–17 (2018). (in Chinese)

24. Zhang, Y.: Freedom or risk: the dual face of "empty nest youth" from the perspective of individualization. Soc. Sci. Ningxia **7**(4), 141–146 (2018). (in Chinese)

25. Nie, W., Feng, X.: Empty nest is "hollow"?—Analysis and countermeasures of the living state of "empty nest youth. Chin. Youth Res. **8**, 57–63 (2017). (in Chinese)

26. Wang, J.: How to make "empty nest youth" not "hollow". Thoughts Public Opini. **4**, 124–125 (2018). (in Chinese)

27. Bao, H.: From "nest space" to "heart reality": re-discussing the problem of "empty nest youth" in china in the new era. Chin. Youth Res. **4**, 40–46 (2018). (in Chinese)

28. Xie, L.: Talking about the phenomenon of empty nest youth and its guiding method. Law Soc. **5**, 142–143 (2018). (in Chinese)

29. Yang, L., Ji, H.: Exploring the problem of solving the problem of empty nest youth. Res. Trans. Competence **6**, 230–231 (2017). (in Chinese)

30. NHK Special Program Recording Group: Missing Society (2010) (in Japanese)

31. Stahl, S.T., et al.: Living alone and depression: the modifying role of the perceived neighborhood environment. Aging Mental Health 1–7 (2016)

32. Haw, C., Hawton, K.: Living alone and deliberate self-harm: a case–control study of characteristics and risk factors. Soc. Psychiatry Psychiatr. Epidemiol. **46**(11), 1115–1125 (2011)

33. Aoun, S., Breen, L., Skett, K.: Supporting palliative care clients who live alone: nurses' perspectives on improving quality of care. Collegian **23**(1), 13–18 (2016)

34. Yukako, T., et al.: Combined effects of eating alone and living alone on unhealthy dietary behaviors, obesity and underweight in older Japanese adults: results of the JAGES. Appetite **95**, 1–8 (2015)

35. Wakako, T., Melissa, K.M.: Spatial, temporal, and health associations of eating alone: a cross-cultural analysis of young adults in urban Australia and Japan. Appetite **118**, 149–160 (2017)

36. Sellaeg, K., Chapman, G.E.: Masculinity and food ideals of men who live alone. Appetite (APPET) **51**(1), 120–128 (2008)

37. Mashapa, J., Chelule, E., Van Greunen, D., Veldsman, A.: Managing user experience – managing change. In: Kotzé, P., Marsden, G., Lindgaard, G., Wesson, J., Winckler, M. (eds.) INTERACT 2013. LNCS, vol. 8118, pp. 660–677. Springer, Heidelberg (2013). https://doi.org/10.1007/978-3-642-40480-1_46

38. Kremer, S., Lindemann, U.: Extracting insights from experience designers to enhance user experience design. In: Marcus, A. (ed.) DUXU 2016. LNCS, vol. 9746, pp. 304–313. Springer, Cham (2016). https://doi.org/10.1007/978-3-319-40409-7_29

39. Baumeister, R.F., Leary, M.R.: The need to belong: desire for interpersonal attachments as a fundamental human motivation. Psychol. Bull. **117**(3), 497–529 (1995)

40. Epley, N., Schroeder, J.: Mistakenly seeking solitude. J. Exp. Psychol. Gen. **143**(5), 1980–1999 (2014)

41. Sandstrom, G.M., Dunn, E.W.: Social interactions and well-being: the surprising power of weak ties. Pers. Soc. Psychol. Bull. **40**(7), 910–922 (2014)

42. Giaccardi, E., et al.: Explorations in social interaction design. In: 31st Annual CHI Conference on Human Factors in Computing Systems, pp. 3259–3262. Association for Computing Machinery, Paris (2013)

43. Yamakami, T.: Relationship models of social experience design and user experience design. In: IEEE International Conference on Computing, Management and Telecommunications, pp. 36–40. IEEE Computer Society, Shenzhen (2014)

44. Yamakami, T.: From user experience to social experience: a new perspective for mobile social game design. In: IEEE International Conference on Ubiquitous Intelligence and Computing, UIC 2012 and 9th IEEE International Conference on Autonomic and Trusted Computing, ATC 2012, pp. 792–796. IEEE Computer Society, Brussels (2012)

45. Yamakami, T.: Exploratory analysis of difference between social experience design and user experience design. In: 16th International Conference on Advanced Communication Technology: Content Centric Network Innovation!, pp. 769–773. Institute of Electrical and Electronics Engineers Inc., PyeongChang (2014)

46. Yamakami, T.: An evolutionary path-based analysis of social experience design. In: Park, J., Ng, J.K.-Y., Jeong, H.Y., Waluyo, B. (eds.) Multimedia and Ubiquitous Engineering. LNEE, vol. 240, pp. 69–76. Springer, Dordrecht (2013). https://doi.org/10.1007/978-94-007-6738-6_9

47. Yamakami, T.: A layered view model of social experience design: beyond single-user user experience. In: Jeong, H.Y., SO, M., Yen, N.Y., Park, J.J. (eds.) Advances in Computer Science and its Applications. LNEE, vol. 279, pp. 35–41. Springer, Heidelberg (2014). https://doi.org/10.1007/978-3-642-41674-3_6

48. Lei, T., Zhang, S.: Research on the social experience of mobile internet products. In: Meiselwitz, G. (ed.) SCSM 2017. LNCS, vol. 10282, pp. 84–93. Springer, Cham (2017). https://doi.org/10.1007/978-3-319-58559-8_8
49. Crenshaw, N.: Social experience in world of warcraft: technological and ideological mediations. In: 3rd ACM SIGCHI Annual Symposium on Computer–Human Interaction in Play, pp. 1–4. Association for Computing Machinery, Inc., Texas (2016)
50. Qin, H., Rau, P.-L.P., Gao, S.-F.: The influence of social experience in online games. In: Jacko, Julie A. (ed.) HCI 2011. LNCS, vol. 6764, pp. 688–693. Springer, Heidelberg (2011). https://doi.org/10.1007/978-3-642-21619-0_81
51. Chang, H.-M., Liang, R.-H.: Express yourself: designing interactive products with implicitness to improve social interaction. In: Jacko, Julie A. (ed.) HCI 2011. LNCS, vol. 6763, pp. 175–184. Springer, Heidelberg (2011). https://doi.org/10.1007/978-3-642-21616-9_20
52. Hu, J., Huang, X.: Based on the Experience of Product Interaction Design. In: 2nd International Conference on Intelligent Systems Design and Engineering Applications, pp. 175–180. IEEE Computer Society, Taiwan (2012)
53. Mutlu, B.: An empirical framework for designing social products. In: 6th ACM Conference on Designing Interactive Systems, pp. 341–342. Association for Computing Machinery, PA (2006)
54. Kim, M., Lee, M., Dabbish, L.: Shop-i: gaze based interaction in the physical world for in-store social shopping experience. In: 33rd Annual CHI Conference on Human Factors in Computing Systems, pp. 1253–1258. Association for Computing Machinery, Yonsei University, South Korea (2015)
55. Phang, C., Zhang, C., Sutanto, J.: The influence of user interaction and participation in social media on the consumption intention of niche products. Inf. Manag. **50**(8), 661–672 (2013)
56. Shi, Y., Guo, Y., Gong, Z., Yang, B., Zhou, L.: Experience design of social interaction for generation y based on tangible interaction. In: Streitz, N., Markopoulos, P. (eds.) DAPI 2017. LNCS, vol. 10291, pp. 192–202. Springer, Cham (2017). https://doi.org/10.1007/978-3-319-58697-7_14
57. Lee, J.-J.: Culture and co-experience: cultural variation of user experience in social interaction and its implications for interaction design. In: Aykin, N. (ed.) IDGD 2009. LNCS, vol. 5623, pp. 39–48. Springer, Heidelberg (2009). https://doi.org/10.1007/978-3-642-02767-3_5
58. Battarbee, K.: Co-experience: the social user experience. In: Conference on Human Factors in Computing Systems—Proceedings, pp. 730–731. Association for Computing Machinery, Fort Lauderdale (2003)
59. Kappen, D.L., et al.: Exploring social interaction in co-located multiplayer games. In: Conference on Human Factors in Computing Systems—Proceedings, pp. 1119–1124. Association for Computing Machinery, Paris (2013)
60. Chen, K.-T., Lei, C.-L.: Design implications of social interaction in online games. In: Harper, R., Rauterberg, M., Combetto, M. (eds.) ICEC 2006. LNCS, vol. 4161, pp. 318–321. Springer, Heidelberg (2006). https://doi.org/10.1007/11872320_41
61. Emmerich, K., Masuch, M.: The impact of game patterns on player experience and social interaction in co-located multiplayer games. In: CHI PLAY 2017—Proceedings of the Annual Symposium on Computer–Human Interaction in Play, pp. 411–422. Association for Computing Machinery, Inc., Amsterdam (2017)
62. Hu, J., Frens, J., Funk, M., Wang, F., Zhang, Yu.: Design for social interaction in public spaces. In: Rau, P.L.P. (ed.) CCD 2014. LNCS, vol. 8528, pp. 287–298. Springer, Cham (2014). https://doi.org/10.1007/978-3-319-07308-8_28

63. Ludvigsen, M.: Designing for social interaction: an experimental design research project. In: Proceedings of the Conference on Designing Interactive, pp. 348–349. Association for Computing Machinery, Tsukuba (2006)
64. Mora-Guiard, J., et al.: Lands of fog: helping children with autism in social interaction through a full-body interactive experience. In: Proceedings of IDC 2016—The 15th International Conference on Interaction Design and Children, pp. 262–274. Association for Computing Machinery, Inc, Manchester (2016)
65. Oh, S., et al.: Typologies of architectural interaction: a social dimension. In: 2014 Symposium on Simulation for Architecture and Urban Design, SimAUD 2014, Part of the 2014 Summer Simulation Multiconference, pp. 49–56. The Society for Modeling and Simulation International, CA, USA (2014)
66. Paredes, H., Martins, F.M.: Social theatres: a web-based regulated social interaction environment. In: Haake, J.M., Ochoa, S.F., Cechich, A. (eds.) CRIWG 2007. LNCS, vol. 4715, pp. 87–94. Springer, Heidelberg (2007). https://doi.org/10.1007/978-3-540-74812-0_7
67. Hespanhol, L., Dalsgaard, P.: Social interaction design patterns for urban media architecture. In: Abascal, J., Barbosa, S., Fetter, M., Gross, T., Palanque, P., Winckler, M. (eds.) INTERACT 2015. LNCS, vol. 9298, pp. 596–613. Springer, Cham (2015). https://doi.org/10.1007/978-3-319-22698-9_41
68. Del, R.W., et al.: Designing urban furniture through user's appropriation experience: teaching social interaction design. In: Proceedings of E and DPE 2006, the 8th International Conference on Engineering and Product Design Education, pp. 39–44. The Design Society, Lund (2006)
69. Speranza, P., Keisler, R., Mai, J.V.: Social interaction and cohesion tool: a dynamic design approach for Barcelona's superilles. In: Proceeding of the 35th Annual Conference of the Association for Computer Aided Design in Architecture, pp. 468–481. ACADIA, Ohio (2015)
70. van Boheemen, T., Hu, J.: Influence of Interactivity on Social Connectedness. In: Meiselwitz, G. (ed.) SCSM 2014. LNCS, vol. 8531, pp. 59–66. Springer, Cham (2014). https://doi.org/10.1007/978-3-319-07632-4_6

A Study of Emotional Communication of Emoticon Based on Russell's Circumplex Model of Affect

Ke Zhong[1], Tianwei Qiao[2], and Liqun Zhang[1(✉)]

[1] School of Design, Shanghai Jiao Tong University, Shanghai, China
zhanglliqun@gmail.com
[2] School of Electronic Information and Electrical Engineering,
Shanghai Jiao Tong University, Shanghai, China

Abstract. With the rapid spread of the Internet, there are more and more people being fond of using emoticons to convey emotions on the Internet. However, due to the high abstraction of real things and expressions and the arbitrariness in the production of emoticons, many misunderstandings have happened. At the same time, more and more emoticons emerge in endlessly, people even do not know how to choose and use appropriate emoticons, which seriously affects the efficiency and the experience. This research tried to purpose an approach to verify and optimize the effectiveness of emoticons in emotional communication based on Russell's Circumplex Model of Affect. This research used emoticons in Wechat, which is the most widely used application in China, as an example to construct a quantitative coordinates of emotional cognition system based on Russell's Circumplex Model of Affect, through variable control, perceptual map, cluster analysis and statistical data analysis to verify and improve the present emoticons. The results of verification experiment indicated that it is practical and effective for emoticons classify and use. On the basis of these results, then we can tag the emoticons more effectively and apply it to the recommendation system to further improve the experience and efficiency in the process of using the emoticons. It is foreseeable that the theory of this research can be applied to other things related to emotional communication. Meanwhile, the research methods and results not only provide a new way of thinking for the application of Russell's Circumplex Model of Affect in the Internet era, but also can be applied to psychology, sociology re-search and other specific areas, playing a guiding and testing role.

Keywords: Emoticon · Emotional communication ·
Russell's Circumplex Model of Affect · Emotional cognitive

1 Introduction

With the increasing popularity and rapid development of computers and the Internet, network communication has become one of the main ways of communication in modern society. This new way of communication also promotes the development and wide application of network symbolic language, especially the emoticon. However, in

© Springer Nature Switzerland AG 2019
A. Marcus and W. Wang (Eds.): HCII 2019, LNCS 11583, pp. 577–596, 2019.
https://doi.org/10.1007/978-3-030-23570-3_43

the context of the Internet era has gradually changed from the information technology age to the current data technology age, the use of emoticon has highlighted the inconsistency of user perception and the cumbersome use of traditional methods.

Therefore, this paper took the emotional communication of emoticon as the entry point, after deeply studying the emotional theory and personalized recommendation system, based on Russell's Circumplex Model of Affect, the effectiveness and completeness of emotional communication of emoticon were studied by means of user perception positioning experiment and user perception experiment. Based on the results of the research, the optimized design were put forward, and the optimized design was verified better by a series of experiments.

After research and verification, the emoticon optimization design ideas and schemes obtained by the research can greatly improve the user's cognitive efficiency and the production efficiency of the emoticon, and improve the effectiveness and completeness of emotional communication in the process of using emoticon. Research ideas and results can also be applied to personalized recommendation systems to further improve user efficiency and optimize user experience.

The innovative design and verification scheme based on Russell's Circumplex Model of Affect proposed in this study has the following advantages:

- The emoticon (or even images) can be studied in a quantitative way on emotional communication to arrive at quantitative data results.
- Quantitative analysis and verification of the effectiveness and completeness of online expressions in emotional communication, and the experimental method is highly feasible, which can be used to optimize the design of network expressions.
- Design ideas and methods have high scalability and follow-up research space. For example, "emotion" can be used as an intermediate connection point to implement personalized recommendations for web expressions.

The rest of the paper is organized as follows. In the second part, a general description and desktop study of Russell's Circumplex Model of Affect, personalized recommendation system, and emotions will be made. The third part will conduct a series of quantitative experiments on the most used emoticon in China, the emoticon of the application software WeChat. The fourth part will produce the optimal design ideas and schemes of the emoticon based on the experimental results, and verify its effectiveness and completeness in emotional communication through experiments. The fifth part will give an example of applying the optimized design ideas and schemes obtained in this study and applying it to the personalized recommendation system. The sixth part is the summary and expectations.

2   Desktop Research

Emotion. Emotion refers to the subjective feelings or experiences of the individual [1]. Emotional experience refers to the individual subjective experience of emotion [2]. Emotion is a part of attitude. It is in harmony with the introverted feelings and intentions in attitude. It is a more complex and stable physiological evaluation and experience of physiology [3, 4]. And for the same thing, each person always has a different emotional feedback and experience [5].

Russell's Circumplex Model of Affect. Early psychologists believe that basic emotions should be discrete and have a fixed expression of nerves and bodily functions to correspond to corresponding emotional expressions and feelings [6–9]. However, later scholars found that emotions and emotions are not simple and simply in a discrete state. There is actually a certain relationship between emotions and emotions, and dimension classification can be performed. In such a situation and background, the theory of emotional dimension has emerged [10] (Fig. 1).

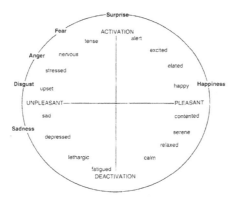

Fig. 1. Russell's Circumplex Model of Affect

Russell's Circumplex Model of Affect is a classic theoretical model in the theory of emotional dimension. He believes that there is a certain correlation or opposition between emotions. Therefore, eight emotional words are extracted from the previous literature: happy and excited, amazement, disappointment, misery, depression, fatigue, satisfaction, in the case of these eight emotional keywords as a benchmark, through a certain experimental approach he proposed two dimensions to classify emotions: pleasant and activation [11] (Fig. 2).

Fig. 2. Russell's Circumplex Model of Affect in Chinese

Recommendation System. Recommendation system is a subclass of information filtering system that seeks to predict the "rating" or "preference" that a user would give to an item [12, 13]. In the era of big data in the Internet, users can label resources in the form of tags [14]. Users may be contributing resources, or they may be collecting resources for subsequent use, or they may be personally commenting on them [15]. However, no matter what kind of interaction behavior, the user exposes his preference for some of the items through the form of labels, which can be used as a clue to realize the personalized recommendation of the project [15] (Fig. 3).

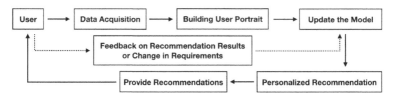

Fig. 3. Recommendation system

Emoticon. The emoticon is different from the language symbol in origin. It is a non-verbal symbol, which is the result of non-verbal rework design such as expressions or shapes used in daily life. It fuses emotions (emotion) with small icons (icon), and is responsible for non-verbal communication, which is a graphical symbol in network non-verbal communication. It is a new graphical language used by users on the Internet to communicate and interact. Its function is to create, enhance or attenuate, adjust and supplement the semantic information and emotional emotions that users want to express [16] (Fig. 4).

Fig. 4. The first emoticon: ASCII Code :-)

The emergence of online expressions simplifies the process of understanding and interpreting language in communication and interaction, and improves the efficiency of communication and expression of information between people on the Internet. Therefore, it is favored especially by the younger generation [17]. In the process of using a large number of online expressions, the following two problems are highlighted:

- Different users have cognitive biases in the interpretation of online expressions [18, 19].
- Excessive emoticon and reduced user productivity [20].

Therefore, this paper selected the most used emoticon in China - the application WeChat's own emoticon as the research and optimization design object, based on the model to conduct a series of quantitative experiments, proposed optimized design and solutions to solve the two problems mentioned above, and provide guidance and ideas for future emoticon design.

3 Exploratory Research

This part of the research firstly designed a user perceptual positioning experiment based on the Russell's Circumplex Model of Affect in the form of the Likert 5-point scale [21] to explore the validity and completeness of the research object in emotional communication. And then through user cognition, experiments were conducted to explore the clustering and correlation of research objects.

3.1 Data Collection

This paper selected the most used emoticon as the sample of research objects: the application software: WeChat's own emoticon, the version number of the application is the latest version of October 2018 - version 6.7.3, extracted all the emoticons that come with this version, a total of 99. And the 99 emoticons are numbered in the order of natural arrangement: 1–99. As shown below (Fig. 5).

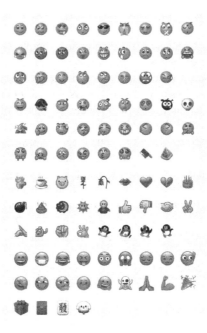

Fig. 5. All emoticon in WeChat 6.7.3

3.2   User Perception Positioning Experiment

A total of 20 volunteers were recruited for the experiment. All of them were citizens of the People's Republic of China and their first language was Chinese.

The experiment firstly took the form of Likert 5-point scale [21] and asked the subjects to score the above 99 emoticon samples on the two dimensions of pleasant degree and activation degree respectively. In order to avoid the basic cognitive difference between the two dimensions of scoring, the user was trained to establish the basic cognitive consensus of the two dimensions through a simple Russell's Circumplex Model of Affect diagram before the specific experiment starts (Fig. 6).

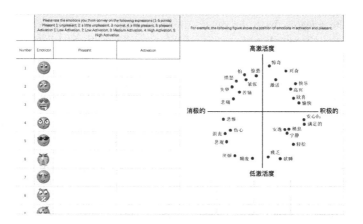

Fig. 6. A screenshot of the experiment for 99 initial emoticon

According to the scoring result, the expression samples with different cognitive differences between different users are first removed.

At this stage, the study used quadratic variance to measure the results of the questionnaire. In the specific study, 20 volunteers scored 99 emoticon samples in the two dimensions of pleasant and activation. Then, 20 results of 99 emoticons in each dimension can be obtained. If the number of times the same emoticon sample is hit at the same time on all the scores of the two dimensions is lower than a specified value, it will be regarded as a emoticon with large cognitive differences and will be washed away. This stipulation here we took 12 (i.e. $p < 5\%$, using a significant level of sampling commonly used in biology). With such a standard value, it can be guaranteed that the error in the experiment could be accepted by most people (95%) [22].

Some of the results of the experiment are shown in Fig. 7. Among them, especially the 32nd emoticon in the figure, although the scores of the pleasant 3 (normal) and the activation 3 (medium activation) are more than 12 times (all 13 times), but according to the Russell Circumplex Model of Affect, which says that such emotions are meaningless [11], because emotions need to be biased, so such emoticons need to be washed away.

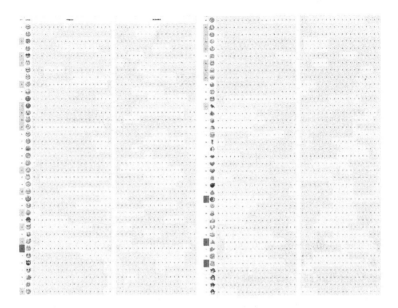

Fig. 7. Part of the experiment results

After cleaning, 29 emoticons conforming to the user's cognitive consistency were finally obtained. Form a new sample of emoticons, as shown below (Fig. 8):

Fig. 8. 29 emoticons after cleaning

At this time, 29 emoticons were positioned into the model coordinates in combination with the Russell's Circumplex Model of Affect. We got the following intuitive graph (Fig. 9):

According to the research of user perception positioning experiment, we could find the sample of emoticon selected: on the one hand, there are a lot of ambiguities in user perception, on the other hand, the emoticons composed of these more consistent expressions are conveyed in the emotion. There is also a large incompleteness in the reception and reception.

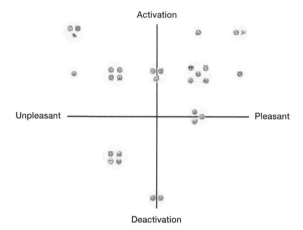

Fig. 9. The position map of 29 emoticons in Russell's Circumplex Model of Affect

3.3 User Cognition Experiment

Subsequently, professional researchers used the 29 expressions obtained above as stimulus, the distance between the 29 expressions was defined by the Euclidean distance (1) using the user cognitive experiment. Based on the relevance coefficient in the matrix to build N-dimensional space, the Euclidean distance formula (1) can be used to calculate the spatial distance of two samples. The closer, the more similar samples can be considered.

$$Euclid(1,2) = \sqrt[2]{(x_1 - x_2)^2 + (y_1 - y_2)^2 + (z_1 - z_2)^2} \tag{1}$$

After this step, the distance matrix between the emoticons could be obtained. By SPSS analysis software the data results obtained can be further observe the problems in emotional transmission and reception of these 29 emoticons by the multidimensional scaling analysis and the clustering method after the data sample reliability verification (Fig. 10).

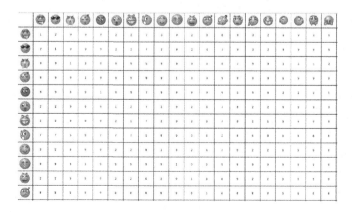

Fig. 10. Partial screenshots of distance matrix of 29 emoticon samples

Firstly, the reliability of the obtained data was verified. According to the analysis of the results, the AIPha value of the obtained sample distance matrix data was 0.937, and the sample reliability was relatively high, which can be used as a follow-up multidimensional scaling analysis and clustering analysis for 29 emoticon samples.

A multidimensional scaling analysis of the experimental data of the sample could be obtained as shown in Fig. 11. Through the multidimensional scaling analysis of the location map, we could visually see the two-dimensional plan with the distance correlation between the emoticon samples as the analysis standard, which could intuitively display the distance and cluster relationship between the emoticon samples from another dimension, which helped the researchers to intuitively the spatial distribution of these 29 emoticon samples was observed.

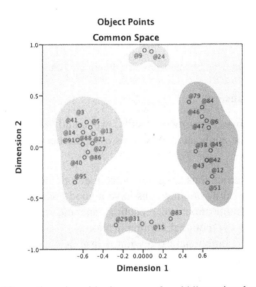

Fig. 11. The 29 emoticons' positioning map of multidimensional scaling analysis

The clustering analysis was performed on the sample data to obtain a cluster analysis tree. The cluster analysis tree could clearly and intuitively show the results of clustering induction of these 29 emoticon samples. As shown in Fig. 12, 29 emoticons were clustered into 4 groups of expressions, meaning that in 4 groups, there was little difference in emotion communication between emoticons and emoticons.

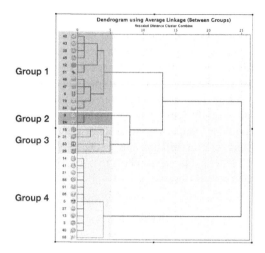

Fig. 12. The 29 emoticons' dendrogram of cluster analysis

3.4   Research Conclusion

According to the above experiment results, we could get current the most used emoticon in China - the application WeChat's own emoticon with the following three basic conditions:

1. A large number of emoticons are ambiguous in emotional expression. Only a small amount (about one-third) of emoticons have a good consistency in user perception of emotional communication and reception, and the rest of the emoticons have certain ambiguities in emotional communication;
2. The completeness of emotional expression is insufficient. Based on the positioning of Russell's Circumplex Model of Affect, these emoticons that can achieve higher user cognition consistency still have large deficiencies in the completeness of emotional expression and reception.
3. The clustering is too concentrated, and the gap between emoticons is not obvious. According to clustering and correlation analysis, it was found that there was a high correlation between some emoticons, there is not much cognitive difference between some emoticons and emoticons in emotional transmission and reception, which will cause certain damage to the efficiency of emoticons use and production.

4   Optimized Design and Experimental Verification

4.1   Design Thinking

According to the research and analysis results of the original emoticon described above, the core ideas of the optimized design are as follows:

1. Add text elements as part of the icon to solve the problem of inconsistent user perception of the emoticon.

2. Orienting new and optimized emoticons based on the Russell's Circumplex Model of Affect.
3. In the specific design of the expression, use appropriate exaggeration and other micro-improvement techniques to widen the difference between the icons.
4. Simplify the design of the icon to improve the efficiency of the transmission of emotions and key information.
5. Extract and retain the excellent design points in the original emoticon, such as the yellow color that is more in line with the Chinese cognition.

4.2   Design Scheme

Under the five core optimized design ideas mentioned above, and after some experimental feedback and design iteration, the emoticon scheme of the final optimized design of the output is shown in Fig. 13. The final optimized design consists of 42 emoticons.

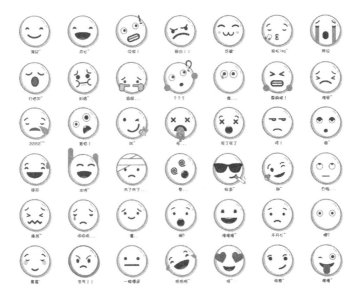

Fig. 13.   Optimized design of the emoticons

From the perspective of visual expression, the optimized design not only retains the excellent design points in the original emoticon, but also adopts a flat design style, which simplifies the design content, thereby improving the communication efficiency of emotions and key information. And each emoticon has a corresponding Chinese text as part of the pattern to improve the accuracy of the user's cognition.

In addition, the optimized design scheme also adopts exaggerated design methods to open the gap between emoticons and emoticons, and hopes to cover the Russell's Circumplex Model of Affect more, so as to improve its emotional expression completeness.

4.3   Experimental Verification

The researchers designed and performed a user-perceived positioning experiment based on the Russell's Circumplex Model of Affect, the emoticon sample cleaning, and certain cluster analysis and correlation analysis.

First, the 42 emoticons of the optimized design were numbered as sample objects. Also taking the form of the Likert 5-point scale [21], 20 volunteers scored 42 samples in both the pleasant and activation dimensions (Fig. 14).

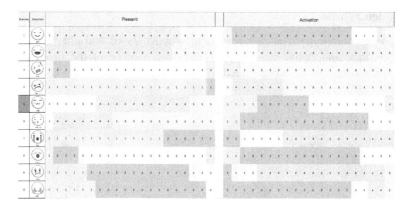

Fig. 14. Partial screenshots of the experimental statistics

According to the experimental statistical results, the emoticon samples with inconsistent emotional cognition were cleaned by the sampling level of the commonly used biology, and 35 emoticon samples with high user cognition in emotional expression are obtained. The agreement rate is 83.3%, which is much higher than the original emoticon of 34.3%.

Finally, 35 emoticon samples to be analyzed and verified in the next experiment are shown in Fig. 15 The results of these 35 emoticon samples positioned in the Russell's Circumplex Model of Affect are shown in Fig. 16.

Next, we used the user cognition experiment again to define the distance relationship between the 35 emoticon samples by Euclidean distance, and used the SPSS analysis software to score the data results. Firstly, the reliability of the obtained data matrix was verified. It was found that the AIPha value of the obtained sample distance matrix data is 0.911, and the sample reliability is high. It could be used as a follow-up multidimensional scaling analysis and cluster analysis for 35 emoticon samples. The specific results are shown in Figs. 17 and 18.

Therefore, from the above verification experimental data, the optimized design of the emoticon scheme based on the Russell's Circumplex Model of Affect has a significant improvement in user perception consistency, completeness and effectiveness in emotional expression, achieving the intended purpose.

The logic of the optimized design idea and verification scheme of the final specific output of this study is shown in Fig. 19.

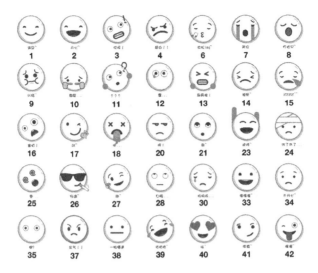

Fig. 15. 35 emoticons after cleaning

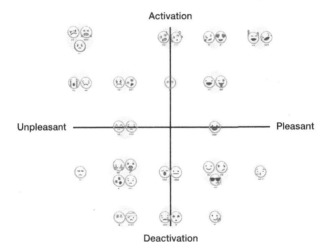

Fig. 16. The position map of 35 emoticons in Russell's Circumplex Model of Affect

It can be foreseen that the emoticon optimized design ideas and verification methods based on the Russell's Circumplex Model of Affect proposed in this study can be applied to more design scenarios and verification of design results, so as to improve the user experience and efficiency. And this paper would give an example in the next chapter.

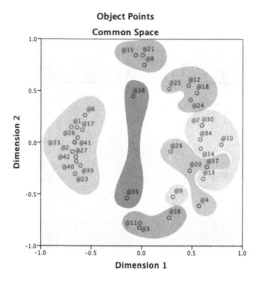

Fig. 17. The 35 emoticons' positioning map of multidimensional scaling analysis

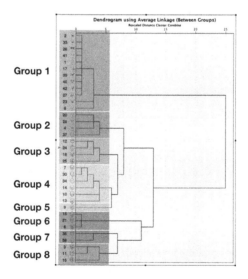

Fig. 18. The 35 emoticons' dendrogram of cluster analysis

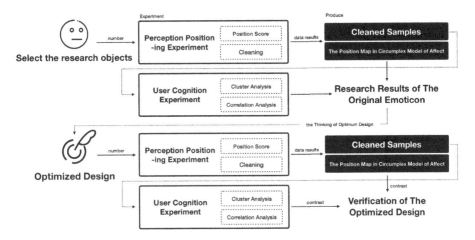

Fig. 19. The thinking of the research and design

5 Application Example: Recommendation System of Emoticon

Based on the above research, we could get the relationship between "emoticons" and "user emotions", so combined with the relationship between "user emotions" and "emotional words" in existing research, relying on neural network and other technologies. We could build a personalized recommendation system for emoticons [23, 24]. The specific logical framework is shown in Fig. 20.

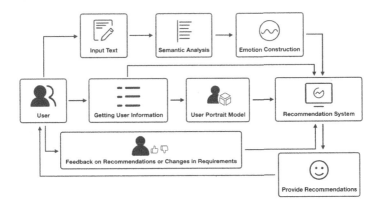

Fig. 20. Recommendation system of emoticon

The Jieba word segmentation algorithm can realize the word segmentation calculation of the user input text, and then realize the word frequency and weight calculation of the word segmentation result of the user input text through the TF-IDF technical principle, and realize the word vectorization. The corresponding semantic analysis of the text input by the user is completed. At this time, through the neural network algorithm and the collaborative filtering method, the logical correspondence between the "emotional words" - "user emotions" - "emoticons" can be realized.

The core of these is neural network computing, neural network is a processing system with strong self-learning, self-organization and self-adaptation capabilities. The basic neural network has three levels of input layer, hidden layer and output layer, as shown in Fig. 21.

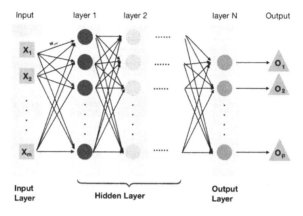

Fig. 21. Basic neural network hierarchy

In the neural network operation, firstly we input the words matrix to the neural network input layer, and the formula is shown in (2).

$$I_m = \begin{bmatrix} x_1 \\ x_2 \\ \ldots \\ x_m \end{bmatrix} \tag{2}$$

Where I_m represents the input system words matrix, and m represents the number of words.

Then, the weight matrices (3) and (4) from the input layer to the hidden layer and from the hidden layer to the output layer are respectively obtained through hidden layer operation.

$$w_{ih} = \begin{bmatrix} w_{i1h1} & \cdots & w_{imh1} \\ \cdots & \cdots & \cdots \\ w_{i1hn} & \cdots & w_{imhn} \end{bmatrix} \tag{3}$$

w_{ih} represents the weight matrix of the trained input layer to the hidden layer.

$$w_{h0} = \begin{bmatrix} w_{h1o1} & \cdots & w_{hno1} \\ \cdots & \cdots & \cdots \\ w_{h1op} & \cdots & w_{hnop} \end{bmatrix} \qquad (4)$$

w_{ho} represents the weight matrix of the trained hidden layer to the output layer.

The new emotional words are input into the trained neural network system, and the emoticons probability matrix of the output category can be obtained. The formula is shown in (5).

$$O_p = \begin{bmatrix} o_1 \\ o_2 \\ \cdots \\ o_p \end{bmatrix} \qquad (5)$$

O_p represents a probability matrix that outputs emoticons, and p represents the number of emoticons.

To sum up, the output matrix of the hidden layer is calculated by $H = f(w_{ih} * I_m)$, that is the output layer of the input layer, and then the probability matrix of each emoticon is obtained by $O_p = f(w_{h0} * H)$. Finally, combined with some weights of other dimensions, the final recommended emoticon and its corresponding front-and-back order can be obtained through the collaborative filtering algorithm.

The initial data and preliminary correlation and weight relationship will be established based on the Russell's Circumplex Model of Affect, which come from the researchers' collation, and then continuously optimized and adjusted along with the data generated by the user's interaction.

In this paper, the researchers first sorted out 435 almost all Chinese emotional words related to emotional state, and then used the user perception positioning experiment to locate the emotional words into the Russell's Circumplex Model of Affect, and at the same time, the word meaning blur could be eliminated in the process of localization. That was the user's cognitive inconsistency and uncommon words, eventually got 201. At the same time, the Russell's Circumplex Model of Affect was divided into 8 regions during the experiment, and 201 emotional words are located in these 8 regions to obtain the number of emotional words contained in each partition [22], as shown in Fig. 22. The correspondence between these words and emotions, together with the relationship between emotions and emoticons, could be used as data for preliminary training of neural networks.

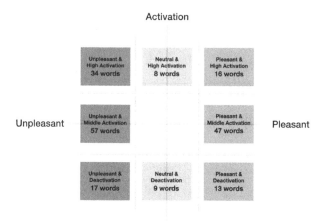

Fig. 22. Russell's Circumplex Model of Affect after partition

6 Conclusion

This paper initially envisaged a emoticon optimization design ideas and verification schemes based on Russell's Circumplex Model of Affect and a series of quantitative user perception positioning experiment and user cognitive experiments. Its core idea is to integrate the factors of user's emotional expression and cognition to the original design of emoticon to optimize the design flow of emoticon.

At the same time, based on Russell's Circumplex Model of Affect, we can get a lot of data feedback on the emotional communication of emoticons. An application example in the fifth section of this paper can also be seen that the emoticon optimized design and verification ideas obtained in this paper can be applied to more practical scenarios. Relying on Russell's Circumplex Model of Affect to better quantify "user emotion" to optimize the design of emoticon, even the design of icons and patterns.

However, the emoticon optimized design and its verification scheme proposed in this paper still have great limitations. For example, in the user perception positioning experiment, because the use of the Likert 5-point scale type of scoring, the subdivsion of the granularity is not enough, it is difficult to achieve a more rigorous level of quantification. Therefore, we actually need more samples of users and more subdivided quantitative indicators to get a more rigorous level of quantification.

It is foreseeable that the theory of this research can be applied to other things related to emotional communication. Meanwhile, the research methods and results not only provide a new way of thinking for the application of Russell's Circumplex Model of Affect in the Internet era, but also can be applied to psychology, sociology research and other specific areas, playing a guiding and testing role.

References

1. Fox, E.: Emotion Science Cognitive and Neuroscientific Approaches To Understanding Human Emotions. Palgrave Macmillan, Basingstoke (2008)
2. Carstensen, L.L., Pasupathi, M., Mayr, U., Nesselroade, J.R.: Emotional experience in everyday life across the adult life span. J. Pers. Soc. Psychol. **79**(4), 644 (2000)
3. Scherer, K.R.: What are emotions? And how can they be measured? Soc. Sci. Inf. **44**(4), 695–729 (2005)
4. Norman, D.A.: Emotional Design: Why We Love (Or Hate) Everyday Things. Basic Books, New York (2004)
5. Carstensen, L.L., Pasupathi, M., Mayr, U., Nesselroade, J.R.: Emotional experience in everyday life across the adult life span. J. Pers. Soc. Psychol. **79**(4), 644 (2000)
6. Ekamn, P., Cordaro, D.: What is meant by calling emotions basic. Emot. Rev. **3**(4), 364–370 (2011)
7. Izard, C.E.: Forms and functions of emotions: matters of emotion-cognition interactions. Emot. Rev. **3**(4), 371–378 (2011)
8. Levenson, R.W.: Basic emotion questions. Emot. Rev. **3**(3), 379–386 (2011)
9. Panksepp, J., Watt, D.: What is basic about basic emotions? Lasting lessons from affective neuroscience. Emot. Rev. **3**(4), 387–396 (2011)
10. Bradley, M.M., Codispoti, M., Cuthbert, B.N., et al.: Emotion and motivation I: defensive and appetitive reactions in picture processing. Emotion **1**(3), 276–298 (2001)
11. Russell, J.A.: A circumplex model of affect. J. Pers. Soc. Psychol. **39**(6), 1161–1178 (1980)
12. Ricci, F., Rokach, L., Shapira, B.: Introduction to recommender systems handbook. In: Ricci, F., Rokach, L., Shapira, B., Kantor, Paul B. (eds.) Recommender Systems Handbook, pp. 1–35. Springer, Boston, MA (2011). https://doi.org/10.1007/978-0-387-85820-3_1
13. Weaver, A.: Facebook and other Pandora's boxes. Access **24**(4), 24 (2010)
14. 毛进, 易明, 操玉杰,等. 一种基于用户标签网络的个性化推荐方法. 情报学报, **31**(1), 23–30 (2012).(Mao Jin, Yi Ming, Cao Yujie, et al. A personalized recommendation method based on user label network. Journal of Information Science, 2012, 31 (1): 23-30. in Chinese)
15. Arabi, H., Balakrishnan, V.: Social tagging in recommender systems. In: International Conference on Computational Science & Technology (2015)
16. 赵爽英, 尧望. 表情·情绪·情节:网络表情符号的发展与演变. 新闻界, **2013**(20), 29–33. (Zhao Shuangying, Yao Wang. Expressions, Emotions and Circumstances: Development and Evolution of Network Emotional Symbols. Press, 2013 (20): 29-33. in Chinese)
17. 滕雪梅, 华乐功. 网络表情符号初探——以当代青少年网络文化为基点. 北京联合大学学报 (人文社会科学版), **7**(3), 79–82 (2009). (Teng Xuemei, Hua Legong. A Preliminary Study of Network Emotional Symbols - Based on Contemporary Youth Network Culture. Journal of Beijing Union University (Humanities and Social Sciences Edition), 2009, 7 (3): 79-82. in Chinese)
18. 谭文芳. 网络表情符号的影响力分析. 求索, **2011**(10), 202–204. (Tan Wenfang. Impact Analysis of Network Emotional Symbols. Seeking, 2011 (10): 202-204. in Chinese)
19. 宫瑛. 网络表情包的传播价值及问题应对. 北京印刷学院学报, **2017**(8), 144–146. (Gong Ji. Communication Value and Problem Response of Network Expression Packet. Journal of Beijing Printing University, 2017 (8): 144-146. in Chinese)
20. 李树青, 崔北亮. 基于个性化信息推荐服务的Web搜索引擎技术综述. 情报杂志, **26**(8), 98–101, (2007). (Li Shuqing, Cui Beiliang. Overview of Web Search Engine Technology Based on Personalized Information Recommendation Service. Intelligence Journal, 2007, 26 (8): 98-101. in Chinese)

21. Wuensch, K.L.: What is a Likert scale? and how do you pronounce 'Likert?. East Carolina University, 4 October 2005. Accessed 30 April, 2009
22. 温思玮. 基于情绪词汇的产品外观研究. 清华大学, 2007. (Wen Siwei. Product Appearance Research Based on Emotional Vocabulary. Tsinghua University, 2007. in Chinese)
23. Zhong, K., Zhang, L., Guan, X.: Research on information recommendation optimization mechanism based on emotional expression and cognition. In: Marcus, A., Wang, W. (eds.) DUXU 2018. LNCS, vol. 10920, pp. 133–146. Springer, Cham (2018). https://doi.org/10.1007/978-3-319-91806-8_11
24. Liang, T., Zhang, L., Xie, M.: Research on image emotional semantic retrieval mechanism based on cognitive quantification model. In: Marcus, A., Wang, W. (eds.) DUXU 2017. LNCS, vol. 10290, pp. 115–128. Springer, Cham (2017). https://doi.org/10.1007/978-3-319-58640-3_10

Research on Design Style of Cartoon Medical Science Interface Based on Kansei Engineering

Li Zhu, Chunxiao Li, and Zhijuan Zhu$^{(\boxtimes)}$

School of Mechanical Science and Engineering,
Huazhong University of Science and Technology,
Wuhan 430074, People's Republic of China
zhuzhijuan@hust.edu.cn

Abstract. In this study, we analyzed the relationship between user's liking for medical science comics and their design elements and design styles based on Kansei Engineering method, and explored what styles were more popular, what style was more relevant to medical treatment and popular science. This study aim to inspire the design of medical science comics. Focus group method was used at the start stage. A survey based on questionnaire was utilized in the research and quantitative analysis was conducted. Results indicate that, (1) in the style of comics, the correlation between the style of exquisite and rough and the degree of user's affection is the highest; (2) the highest correlation with medical treatment is the style of complex and simple, and the highest correlation with science is the style of simple and gorgeous, complex and simple, and serious and lively; (3) the correlation between medical, popular science, and favorite degree is relatively low. The findings will have a certain reference role in the design of future medical science comics.

Keywords: Design style · Cartoon medical science interface ·
Kansei Engineering

1 Introduction

Nowadays, with people's improved health awareness and the developed Internet, more and more people are hoping to contact, understand and learn general knowledge of medical science via the Internet [1]. Meanwhile, as the general knowledge of medical science needs to be realized through user interface, different styles of interfaces will make users experience differently, and have an influence on their liking. However, the users' needs are usually seldom considered in the design of medical science interactive interface at present, therefore, it has been more and more urgent to discuss the design style of general medical science interface, and improve its user experience. Many users choose products through their perceptual judgement, while perceptivity is difficult to be explained. Nevertheless, in recent years, Kansei Engineering, an analytical method quantitatively studying the perceptual factors in a rational way of engineering, makes design more humanized [2], which can measure perceptual elements. Bai [3] has developed his idea and designed through Kansei Engineering by taking an air purifier as a practical case, and achieved good results. In this paper, we aimed to sum up the

© Springer Nature Switzerland AG 2019
A. Marcus and W. Wang (Eds.): HCII 2019, LNCS 11583, pp. 597–606, 2019.
https://doi.org/10.1007/978-3-030-23570-3_44

comic styles of general medical science interface with better user experience which are favored by people through Kansei Engineering.

Currently, many scholars have done relative research on animated medical science interface design. Xu [4] started from the aspects of creativity, styling and expression techniques of medical science comics, and analyzed his creation. Yang, Chen, etc. [5] stimulated the interest of young people in scientific knowledge by integrating the emotional concept into the innovative design of the interactive interface of popular science exhibits, and achieved the goal of emotional education. Guo [6] explained the design of popular science interface, including interactive mode, art style setting and page layout elements. Combined with the current domestic and international popular science design, the interactive interface design of network science was discussed.

However, the existing literatures are focusing on the related creative approaches such as expression mode and interactive mode of designing medical science interactive interface, as well as cartoons of popular medical science, lacking relevant targeted research on the interactive interface style of animated medical science which has a great effect on the cognition and experience of users, influencing their cognition and acceptance of relevant knowledge. Therefore, we aimed to sum up the comic styles of general medical science interface with better user experience which are popular among people through Kansei Engineering.

2 Relative Definitions

2.1 Kansei Engineering

The term of Kansei Engineering" was first proposed by Kenichi Yamamoto, the former master of MAZDA Automobile Group, in his lecture with the title of "Theory of Automobile Culture" in University of Michigan, USA in 1986 [7]. Kansei Engineering, as a research method, mainly converts the feeling and affection need that are difficult to be measured by users, into visual design elements for combining "human" sensibility with the design features of "objects", to satisfy the emotional needs of consumers. Its core idea is emotion quantification and image analysis [8].

In terms of Kansei Engineering research, Zhang and Huang [9] proposed an innovative design framework for furniture modeling based on the inferential Kansei Engineering of forward quantification via their analysis on the necessity of Kansei Engineering applied to the innovative design of furniture; and they also provided a quite good guidance for the furniture design later on by combination with the innovative design of new Chinese-style sofa modeling.

In this paper, the research objective is mainly about the styles of cartoon medical science interface, and it is also a quantitative study on users' abstract and vague feeling of different-style medical science comics through Kansei Engineering, which can be converted into visual design elements, so as to get the styles that are favored by users and most consistent with the interface of animated medical science.

2.2   Degree of Liking

Liking can be viewed as an attitude, and this attitude will influence purchase decision direction and behavior, making consumers the behavioral tendency to buy specific products or not to buy other products [10]. Degree of liking means users' preference for product forms or functions in their subjective feeling, which may be dependent on many factors such as user's personal experience, characteristics of a product itself, and the environment of using product. It is a perceptual judgement.

In this research, degree of liking refers to users' judgement of preference for the design style of cartoon science interface according to their personal subjective factors. Through degree of liking, the popularity and acceptability of various cartoon styles among users can be evaluated.

3   Research Process

3.1   Method

"Focus Group", as a research method, refers to material collection for the specific topic prepared by researchers through communicative dialogue among team members [11]. At present, this method is widely applied in multiple research fields including user experience (UE).

In this research, the approach of focus group was used to collect cartoon pictures and adjectives, and initially classify them according to their characteristics. All members of the focus group screened samples together to identify samples of cartoon features and the appropriate samples of adjective pairs for discussing in group, drafting and revising the questionnaire. Later, a survey based on questionnaire was utilized in the research and quantitative analysis was conducted.

3.2   Research Process

The research process includes several stages. First, picture samples and adjective-pair Kansei words were collected to screen and classify, and representative samples for deconstructing the cartoon samples were determined. Then, a survey based on questionnaires was conducted to investigate the degree of liking and adjective-pair matching degree of sample cartoons. Later, the data quantitative was analyzed questionnaire results, while an experiment was conducted to verify the relationship between questionnaire results, degree of liking and cartoon design elements. (As shown in Fig. 1)

3.3   Selection of Experimental Samples

As the factor determining the design style of cartoon medical science interface is mainly the style of cartoon itself, more than 130 cartoon pictures were collected as the initial samples by random and relative personal subjective factors were collected via the internet. A focus group composed by designers and medical students were set up to classify all cartoon samples according to their overall styles. These cartoon samples

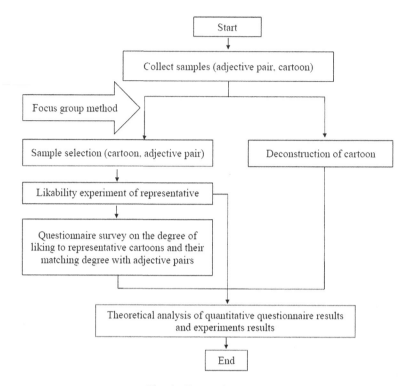

Fig. 1. Research process

were divided into 5 kinds of styles, including 3d style (4 samples, 2%), flat style (30 samples, 22%), linear style (23 samples, 17%), linear combined with flat style(30 samples, 22%), and painting style (52 samples, 37%).

Then samples were determined according to the number of samples represented in each category based on its percentage [12], and the number of featured samples should cover the classification of each sample. Thus 10 featured samples was taken into research in the next survey. According to results of collected cartoon classification, the featured samples include 1 piece of 3d style, 2 pieces of flat style and linear style each, 2 pieces of linear combined with flat style, and 3 pieces of painting style, which are shown in Table 1.

One hundred adjective pairs were randomly collected without difference. The focus group was also used to eliminate those adjective pairs irrelevant to the mental feelings arisen from cartoon styles, and then these adjective pairs suitable for this research were selected. In addition, the adjective pairs 'medical-non medical' and 'popular science-non popular science' which are targeted at popular medical science were added on purpose. Later, the adjective pairs were screened according to the possible mental feelings of users, in order to deprive these adjectives of commendatory or derogatory tendency for reducing interference. Thus the following adjective pairs are determined into next survey research: plain-gorgeous, cold-warm, exquisite-rude, beautiful-ugly

Table 1. Cartoon representatives

Picture 1 (S1)	Picture 2 (S2)	Picture 3 (S3)	Picture 4 (S4)	Picture 5 (S5)
Picture 6 (S6)	Picture 7 (S7)	Picture 8 (S8)	Picture 9 (S9)	Picture 10 (S10)

cute, solemn-lively, classical-modern, round-rigid, complex-simple. At last, the adjective pair "like-dislike" was intentionally added to evaluate the users' attitudes.

3.4 Questionnaire Survey of Cartoon Preference

Ten pictures selected by the focus group in the early stage with ten pairs of adjectives were combined together in a questionnaire to analyze them by five-section scale of Likert scale with a score of -2 to 2 to investigate users' feelings and degrees of liking to different pictures. In total, one hundred and six copies of the questionnaire were actually collected and analyzed. Judging from the reliability analysis of the questionnaire, the Cronbach coefficient is over 0.7 ($p < 0.05$), which shows the questionnaire is reliable (Table 2).

Table 2. Reliability statistics

Cronbach coefficient	Cronbach coefficient based on standardized project	Items
0.700	0.798	106

Results of questionnaire survey showed that those people between 18 and 25 accounted for 88.57%, and undergraduates accounted for 90.48%. It can be basically thought that the majority of respondents to the questionnaire are college students, which is of great reference significance to investigate the popularity of different styles of comic medical science interface among college students.

3.5 Deconstruction of Design Elements in Cartoon Styles and Test of Experimental Results

First, the cartoon styles are deconstructed as start. Cartoon styles can be divided into thick-line, thin-line, and non-linear ones according to the types of their lines. They can be divided into multiple-color and single-color ones in terms of how many colors are adopted. They can be divided into flat and stereoscopic ones on their stereoscope. Results of deconstruction are showed below in Table 3.

Table 3. Deconstruction of cartoons

Picture I (S1)	Picture II (S2)	Picture III (S3)	Picture IV (S4)	Picture V (S5)
Thin lines, stereo-scope, and multiple colors	Thick lines, flat, and single color	Non-linear, stereoscope, and multiple colors	Thin lines, flat, and single color	Thick lines, flat, and single color

Picture VI (S6)	Picture VII (S7)	Picture VIII (S8)	Picture IX (S9)	Picture X (S10)
Non-linear, flat, and multiple colors	Non-linear, stereoscope, and multiple colors	Thin lines, stereoscope, and multiple colors	Non-linear, flat, and single color	Thin lines, stereo-scope, and multiple colors

Considering the results of survey may be inaccurate due to too long questionnaires, too many questions, and other possible subjective reasons, these pictures were printed and numbered from 1 to 10 in order to verify results of questionnaire survey. Then, ten interviewees were asked to order these pictures according to how they like and dislike these pictures to show how much they like different style cartoons.

4 Quantitative Theoretic Analysis and Results

4.1 Analysis on Correlation of Questionnaire Results

Analysis on correlation of questionnaire results can figure out the pair of adjectives tightly related to how much the users like cartoons. Pearson correlation coefficient and P value of confidence are compared in the analysis on correlation. Correlation is significant when the confidence stands at 0.05 (double test).

The correlation coefficient in Table 4 indicates that the "elegant - rough" embraces the strongest correlation with how much people like cartoons, and the "beautiful–ugly" was the second. The "medical - non-medical", the "simple - gorgeous", and "popular science - non-popular-science" have weak correlation with how much they like cartoons. Users like elegant/warm/beautiful/modern/simple cartoons with the topic of medical popular science. Meanwhile it can be seen that how much the users like different cartoon styles impacts little on medicine and popular science.

Table 4. Correlation with how much the users like cartoons

Pairs of adjectives	Pearson correlation coefficient	P value of confidence
Popular science - non-popular-science	0.008	0.982
Medical - Non-medical	− 0.254	0.480
Simple - Gorgeous	0.022	0.952
Cold - Warm	0.694*	0.026
Elegant - Rough	− 0.751*	0.012
Beautiful - Ugly	− 0.715*	0.020
Serious - Lively	0.462	0.179
Classic - Modern	0.626	0.053
Round - Pointed	− 0.538	0.109
Complex - Simple	0.057	0.876

* $p < 0.05$

In addition, analysis on the relationship between other pairs of adjectives and popular science and medicine shows that users think that those with simplicity and popular science possess more features of cartoons involving medicine. They think that simple and serious style possesses more characteristics of cartoons with the theme of popular science.

4.2 Analysis on Correlation Between How Users like Cartoons and Deconstructed Elements

How much users like cartoons in different styles was calculated as from 1 point to 10 points according to results or survey. The average of points for each picture was calculated to reflect how much the users like it (Table 5).

Table 5. Evaluation of how much users like cartoons in different styles

Orders of pictures	S5	S1	S2	S4	S8	S10	S7	S3	S6	S9
Points	4.3	6.8	7.6	6.4	2.7	5.6	6.3	2.6	5.6	8.0

Results showed that users like picture 10 the most. Meanwhile, how much the users like other pictures is corresponding to results of questionnaires, which proves the confidence of questionnaire results.

Then, experiment results on how much the users love these cartoons are basically corresponding to those in the questionnaires, which proved high confidence of questionnaires.

How much the users like the deconstructed elements was ordered as follows in Table 6.

Table 6. Points of how much users like deconstructed elements

Orders	1	2	3	4	5	6	7
Sort	Pictures with single color	Picture with thick lines	Pictures in flat styles	Pictures with thin lines	Pictures with multiple colors	Pictures with stereoscopic style	Pictures with non-linear style
Average value	6.6	6.6	6.4	5.4	4.9	4.8	4.8

Results of research indicate that users like the pictures with thick lines, flat styles, and single color the most.

5   Design Application

A series of cartoons interfaces involving medical popular science were designed according to principles based on research and analysis as mentioned above (As shown in Fig. 2). In terms of style, thick lines and flat image form a contemporary style which gives people warmth, comfort, and freshness and caters to people's tastes on cartoon styles at present was applied in design. Warm colors can relieve people's discomfort brought by medicine, therefore warm colors were apply in design for the purpose. To make people feel comfort. In terms of lines design, thick lines make people feel secure and stable. Therefore, more curves are adopted by designers to express their emotions, which make them feel cordial.

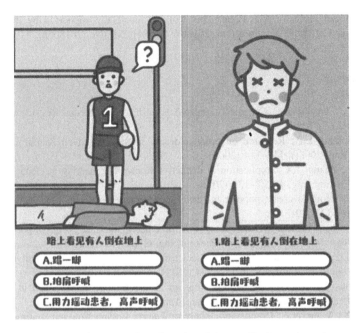

Fig. 2. Part of cartoons interfaces involving medical popular science

6   Conclusions

With the development of the economic level, people pay more and more attention to health and medical knowledge. Comic Medicine Popularization Programs and APPs have attracted more and more attention as media that can be widely disseminated, but they are relevant because of their own professionalism. There is a lack of research in this area, which has led to the current comic medical APP interface design can not meet people's needs. In this paper, Kansei Engineering methods were utilized to explore people's perceptions of medical comics. First, focus group method were adopted to select representative carton images and adjective pairs from a more professional per-spective to ensure professionalism of the results. Then, by quantitative analysis, the user's favorite medical science comic styles were explored. Results indicate that, (1) In the style of comics, the correlation between the style of exquisite and rough and the degree of user's affection is the highest; (2) The highest correlation with medical treatment is the style of complex and simple, and the highest correlation with science is the style of simple and gorgeous, complex and simple, and serious and lively; (3) The correlation between medical, popular science, and favorite degree is relatively low. Therefore, it is recommended to use these styles in cartoons involving medicine APP, which will be more popular. The findings will have a certain reference role in the design of future medical science comics.

Acknowledgement. We would like to thank professors who taught the course of *Social Design and Creative Practice* in 2018 spring at Huazhong University of Science and Technology

(HUST), especial professor Ren Long. This work is financially supported by the Teaching Research Project of Hubei Province (No. 2016075) and HUST (No. 2018056).

References

1. Shan, B.C.: Exploration of medical science data-push by new media. Res. Commun. Force **2**(11), 102 (2018)
2. Li, Y.F., Zhu, L.P.: Research on product design method based on Kansei Engineering. Packag. Eng. **29**(11), 112–114 (2008)
3. Bai, R.F., Zhang, J.X.: Application of deductive Kansei Engineering in electronic product design. Packag. Eng. **4**, 128–132 (2015)
4. Xu, Y.H.: How to create popular medical science cartoons. Chin. Med. Educ. Technol. **27**(3), 369–371 (2013)
5. Yang, J., Chen, Y., Wang, D.D., Zhong, F.X.: Interactive interface design of popular science exhibits based on emotion concept. Packag. Eng. **6**, 109–113 (2016)
6. Guo, S.D.: Design and analysis of interactive interface for network involving popular science. Southeast Commun. **9**, 122–124 (2011)
7. Yamamoto, K.: Kansei Engineering - the art of automotive development at Mazda. In: Special Lecture at University of Michigan, Ann Arbor, pp. 1–24 (1986)
8. Zhang, Y., Yang, N.F.: Comparative study on Kansei Engineering and sentimental design methods. J. Nanjing Arts Inst. (Fine Arts Des.) **5**, 178–181 (2017)
9. Zhang, Z.F., Huang, K.: Innovative design of furniture modeling based on Kansei Engineering. J. Central South Univ. For. Technol. **32**(11), 195–199 (2012)
10. Howard, J.: The Theory of Buyer Behavior. Wiley Publishing, New York (1969)
11. Fang, Z.Z., Cheng, J.K.: Significance of research method in comparative education for "Focus Group Interview". Foreign Educ. Res. **6**, 19–25 (2016)
12. Zhu, Z., Cao, H., Li, B.: Research on logo design and evaluation of youth education brands based on visual representation. J. Prod. Brand Manage. **26**(7), 722–733 (2017)

Author Index

Printed in the United States
By Bookmasters